Appeasing Hitler

Chamberlain, Churchill and the Road to War

Appeasing Hitler

Chamberlain, Churchill and the Road to War

TIM BOUVERIE

THE BODLEY HEAD
LONDON

1 3 5 7 9 10 8 6 4 2

The Bodley Head, an imprint of Vintage,
20 Vauxhall Bridge Road,
London SW1V 2SA

The Bodley Head is part of the Penguin Random House group of companies
whose addresses can be found at global.penguinrandomhouse.com

First published by The Bodley Head in 2019

www.penguin.co.uk/vintage

A CIP catalogue record for this book is available from the British Library

ISBN 9781847924407 (hardback)
ISBN 9781847924414 (trade paperback)

Typeset in 11.5/14 pt Dante MT Std
by Integra Software Services Pvt. Ltd, Pondicherry

Maps by Bill Donohoe

Printed and bound in Great Britain by Clays Ltd, Elcograf S.p.A.

To my parents,
with love and gratitude

Germany:
Territorial Acquisitions
and Frontier Changes,
March 1935–March 1939
DENMARK
SWEDEN
Kiel Canal
Lübeck
Hamburg
R. Elbe
Stettin
Bremen
NETHERLANDS
Hanover
Berlin
R. Oder
Münster
Magdeburg
Frankfurt a.d.O.
Essen
Dortmund
Düsseldorf
BELGIUM
Leipzig
Cologne
R. Weser
Aachen
Erfurt
Dresden
R. Meuse
GERMANY
R. Rhine
Frankfurt a.M.
LUX
Prague
Saarbrücken
Mannheim
Nuremberg
Karlsruhe
Strasbourg
Stuttgart
Augsburg
Munich
R. Danube
FRANCE
Basle
AUSTRIA
SWITZERLAND
ITALY
YU

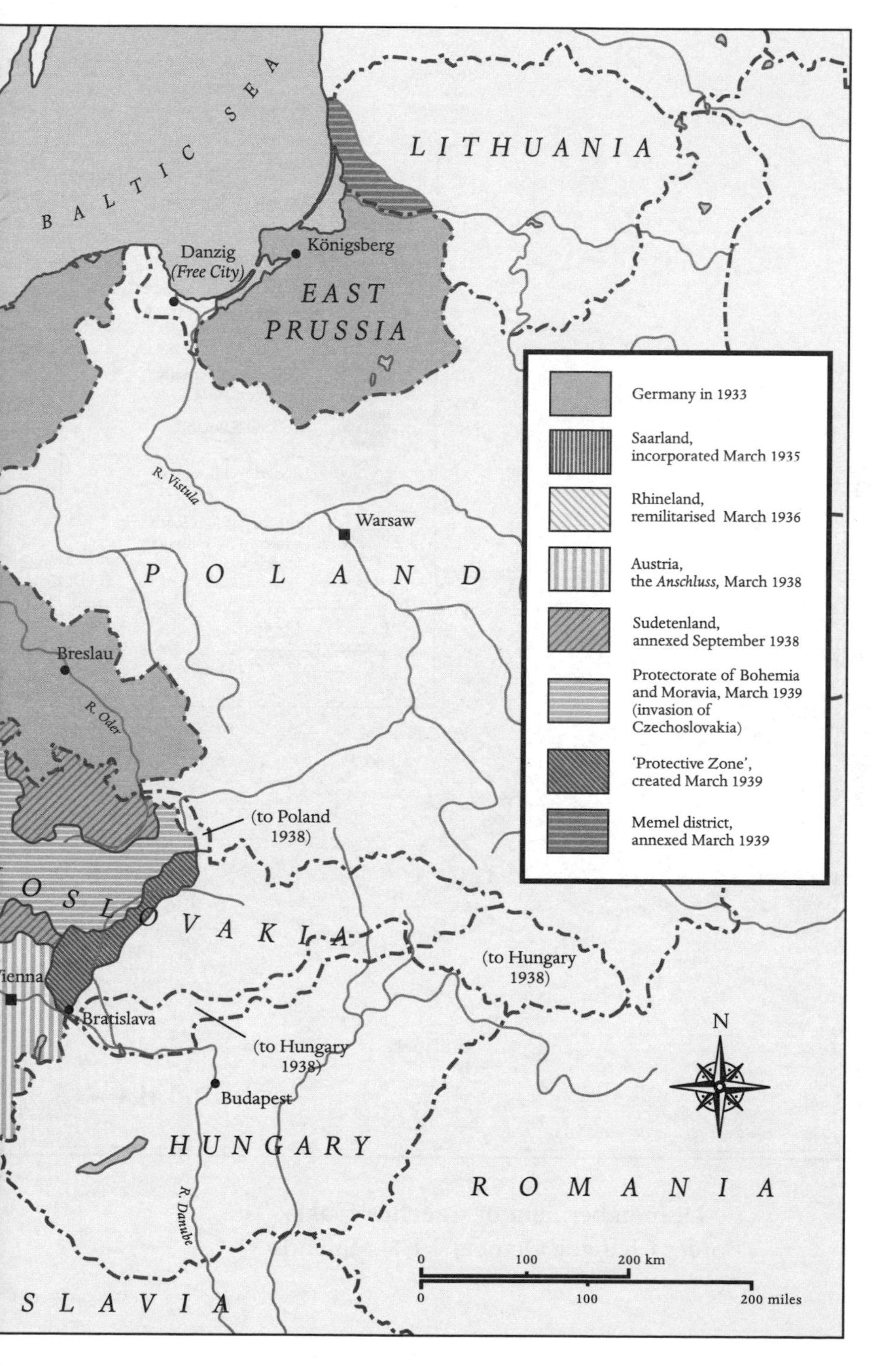
BALTIC SEA
LITHUANIA
Danzig
(Free City)
Königsberg
EAST
PRUSSIA
R. Vistula
Warsaw
POLAND
Breslau
R. Oder
(to Poland
1938)
OSLOVAKIA
Vienna
Bratislava
(to Hungary
1938)
(to Hungary
1938)
Budapest
HUNGARY
R. Danube
ROMANIA
SLAVIA
N
0
100
200 km
0
100
200 miles
Germany in 1933
Saarland,
incorporated March 1935
Rhineland,
remilitarised March 1936
Austria,
the *Anschluss*, March 1938
Sudetenland,
annexed September 1938
Protectorate of Bohemia
and Moravia, March 1939
(invasion of
Czechoslovakia)
'Protective Zone',
created March 1939
Memel district,
annexed March 1939

Dismemberment of Czechoslovakia:
Border Changes, October 1938–March 1939

Contents

Preface

'Never Again!'

The desire to avoid a second world war was perhaps the most understandable and universal wish in history. More than 16.5 million people died during the First World War. The British lost 723,000; the French 1.7 million; the Russians 1.8 million; the British Empire 230,000; the Germans over 2 million. Twenty thousand British soldiers died on the first day of the Battle of the Somme, while the ossuary at Douaumont contains the bones of some 130,000 French and German soldiers – a mere sixth of those killed during the 302-day Battle of Verdun. Among the survivors there was scarcely a soul that was not affected. Almost everyone had a father, husband, son, brother, cousin, fiancé or friend killed or maimed. When it was over, not even the victors could feel victorious. The Cenotaph, unveiled on Whitehall on 19 June 1919, was no Arc de Triomphe but a symbol of loss. Every Armistice Day, thousands of Britons shuffled past it in mournful silence, while, on both sides of the Channel, schools, villages, towns and railway stations commemorated friends and colleagues with their own memorials. In the years that followed the mantra was as consistent as it was determined: 'Never again!'

But it did happen again. Despite the best of intentions and efforts aimed at both conciliation and deterrence, the British and French found themselves at war with the same adversary a mere twenty-one years after the 'war to end all wars'. The purpose of this book is to contribute to our understanding of how this happened.

The debate over appeasement – the attempt by Britain and France to avoid war by making 'reasonable' concessions to German and Italian grievances during the 1930s – is as enduring as it is contentious. Condemned, on the one hand, as a 'moral and material disaster', responsible for the deadliest conflict in history, it has also been described as 'a noble idea, rooted in Christianity, courage and common-sense'.[1] Between these two polarities lies a mass of nuance, sub-arguments and historical skirmishes. History is rarely clear-cut, and yet the so-called lessons of the period have been invoked by politicians and pundits, particularly in Britain and the United States, to justify a range of foreign interventions – in Korea, Suez, Cuba, Vietnam, the Falklands, Kosovo and Iraq (twice) – while, conversely, any attempt to reach an accord with a former antagonist is invariably compared with the infamous 1938 Munich Agreement. When I began researching this book, in the spring of 2016, the spectre of Neville Chamberlain was being invoked by American conservatives as part of their campaign against President Obama's nuclear deal with Iran, while today the concept of appeasement is gaining new currency as the West struggles to respond to Russian revanchism and aggression. A fresh consideration of this policy as it was originally conceived and executed feels, therefore, timely as well as justified.

There is, of course, already a considerable body of literature on this subject – though neither as extensive nor as up to date as is sometimes assumed. Indeed, while books on the Second World War have multiplied over the last twenty years, the build-up and causes of that catastrophe have been relatively neglected. Furthermore, while there have been many excellent books on appeasement, most of them have tended to focus on a particular event, such as Munich, or a particular person, such as Neville Chamberlain. What I wanted to do, by contrast, was to write a book which covered the entire period – from Hitler's appointment as German Chancellor to the end of the 'Phoney War' – to see how the policy developed and attitudes changed. I also wanted to consider a broader canvas than that merely encompassing the principal protagonists. The desire to avoid war by reaching a modus vivendi with the dictator states extended well beyond the confines of government and, therefore, while the characters of Chamberlain, Halifax, Churchill, Daladier and Roosevelt are central to this story, I have also examined the actions of lesser-known figures, in particular the amateur diplomats. Finally, I wanted to write a narrative history which captured the uncertainty, drama and dilemmas of the period. Thus, while there is commentary and analysis throughout, my main purpose was to construct a chronological narrative, based on diaries, letters, newspaper articles and diplomatic despatches, which guides the reader through these turbulent years. In pursuit of this, I have been fortunate to have had access to over forty collections of private papers – several of which yielded exciting new material. Not wishing to disrupt my narrative, I have not highlighted these finds in the text but, where possible, have favoured unpublished over published sources in respect of both length and frequency.

A book on international relations naturally has an international scope. Yet this is primarily a book about British politics, British society, British diplomacy. Strange as it may now seem, Britain was still nominally the most powerful country in the world in the 1930s – the proud centre of an empire covering a quarter of the globe. That America was the coming power was obvious. But the United States had retreated into isolationism in the aftermath of the First World War, while France – the only other power capable of curtailing German ambitions – chose to surrender the diplomatic and military initiative in favour of British leadership. Thus, while the British would have preferred not to become entangled in the problems of the Continent, they realised that they were, and were perceived as, the only power capable of providing the diplomatic, moral and military leadership necessary to halt Hitler and his bid for European hegemony.

Within Britain, the choices that would affect not only that country but potentially the entire world were made by a remarkably small number of people. As such, the following pages may seem like the ultimate vindication of the 'high-politics' school of history. Yet these men (and they were almost exclusively men) were not acting in a vacuum. Acutely conscious of political, financial, military and diplomatic constraints – both real and imagined – Britain's political leaders were no less considerate of public opinion. In an age when opinion polls were in their infancy this was a naturally amorphous concept. Yet exist it did – divined from letters to newspapers, constituency correspondence and conversations – and was treated with the utmost seriousness. For the majority of the 1930s the democratically elected leaders of Britain and France were convinced that their populations would not support a policy which risked war, and acted accordingly. But what if war was unavoidable? What if Hitler proved insatiable? And what if the very desire to avoid it made war more likely?

Prologue

The Storm Breaks

On the evening of Friday 1 September 1939, the former First Lord of the Admiralty, Alfred Duff Cooper, changed as usual into his dinner jacket before joining his wife, Diana, and three fellow Conservatives at the Savoy Grill. A day of brilliant sunshine had given way to a balmy evening and there was nothing within the splendid art deco dining room to denote a crisis. Emerging later, however, the Coopers were bewildered to find themselves in complete darkness – a result of the hastily imposed blackout. Taxis were nowhere to be found and the couple were beginning to wonder how they were going to get home when 'Bendor' Grosvenor, 2nd Duke of Westminster, appeared in his Rolls-Royce and offered them a lift. Gladly, the Coopers accepted, only to regret their decision when the Duke began to inveigh against the Jews, whom he held responsible for the coming war. Reminding himself that he and his wife were guests in the Duke's car, Cooper, who had a volcanic temper, held his tongue. When, however, the Duke expressed his joy that Britain was not yet at war with Germany, since we were really Hitler's 'best friends', the former First Lord could restrain himself no longer. Before making a swift exit at Victoria, he erupted, telling His Grace that he hoped Hitler would 'soon find out that we were his most implacable and remorseless enemies'. The next day, Cooper was amused to hear that Westminster was going around saying that if Britain did end up going to war then it was all the fault of 'the Jews and Duff Cooper'.[1]

Twelve hours earlier, 1.5 million German soldiers, 2,000 aeroplanes and over 2,500 tanks had invaded Poland from the north, south and west. Luftwaffe bombers were currently laying waste to airfields and cities, while the Panzer divisions were well into their lightning dash across the Polish countryside. In London, politicians and public alike felt sure that they were on the brink of war. Under the terms of the Anglo-Polish Agreement, signed just six days earlier, Britain was committed to coming to Poland's aid immediately following an attack. 'We are in the same boat now', the Chancellor of the Exchequer, Sir John Simon, assured the Polish Ambassador, Count Edward Raczyński, that morning. 'England never breaks her word to her friends.'[2]

Later that day, the Prime Minister, Neville Chamberlain, raised cheers in the House of Commons when, banging his fist on the despatch box, he declared that 'the responsibility for this terrible catastrophe lies on the shoulders of one man – the German Chancellor, who has not hesitated to plunge the world into misery in order to serve his own senseless ambitions'. Hearing these words, the Conservative MP Edward 'Louis' Spears could not help recalling Chamberlain's boast, of only a year previously, to have secured 'peace for our time' at the Munich Conference. Now, however, the Prime Minister appeared firm, even bellicose. The Cabinet had authorised full mobilisation that morning, while the British Ambassador to Berlin had told the German Foreign Minister that if the German Government was not prepared to cease hostilities and withdraw its forces then 'His Majesty's Government' would 'without hesitation fulfil their obligations to Poland'. The British Government had, however, conspicuously failed to set a time limit on this semi-ultimatum.[3]

The next day, Saturday 2 September, the heat became heavy and oppressive. As MPs, unaccustomed to being in town over the weekend, struggled to entertain themselves, dark clouds began to marshal on the horizon; it was clear a storm was brewing. Meanwhile, precautions against the bombing onslaught which it was expected would follow Britain's declaration of war were continuing. Women were being evacuated to the country, following their children (most of whom had left the previous day) and most of the Old Masters from the National Gallery. Sandbags were piled in front of Government buildings while, overhead, an armada of barrage balloons floated listlessly. In a gesture of delusional futility the Duke of Windsor, the former Edward VIII, sent Hitler a telegram urging him to 'do his best for peace'.[4]

In the afternoon, crowds began to form in Whitehall as Cabinet Ministers arrived at Downing Street and MPs scurried to Parliament. The atmosphere, noted Rear-Admiral Tufton Beamish, Conservative

MP for Lewes, was markedly different to that of twenty-five years previously, when Britain had entered the First World War. 'Whitehall was then full of cheering crowds, with no thought of the millions to be killed, the conscription to come, the squalor and misery and chaos … Now I see heavy hearts, clear minds and grim determination.'[5]

Members of Parliament were less calm. Disconcerted by the lack of precision in Chamberlain's statement the previous evening, they gathered in the Commons chamber at 2.45 p.m. expecting to hear that Britain was at war. Instead, Sir John Simon rose and explained that the Prime Minister had been delayed and would be making a statement later in the evening. Troubling rumours began to spread: the Italian dictator, Benito Mussolini, had proposed an international conference which the Cabinet were considering; the Labour Party had refused to join a coalition; the French were preparing to rat.

In order to kill time and calm their nerves, MPs indulged heavily in the Commons smoking room. 'The amount of alcohol being consumed was incredible!' recorded the former Cabinet Secretary Lord Hankey.[6] 'There was a torrent of talk', recalled one Conservative MP. 'In every breast there was a gnawing anxiety about our guarantee to Poland.'[7] 'We felt the honour of Britain vanishing before our eyes', noted another witness.[8] Eventually, the bells rang out and MPs, filled with 'Dutch courage', piled back into the Chamber to hear what they assumed would be the belated declaration of war.[9] The atmosphere was 'like a court awaiting the verdict of the jury'.[10]

At 7.42 p.m. Chamberlain entered and was cheered by his supporters. Two minutes later he was on his feet. Members leaned forward. 'One and all were keyed up for the announcement that war had been declared', wrote Louis Spears.[11] But it did not come. After speaking wearily of the Government's recent exchanges with Germany, the Prime Minister confirmed the rumours about an Italian proposal for a five-power conference to resolve the German–Polish dispute. Of course, he explained, it would be impossible to contemplate this while Poland was 'being subjected to invasion'. If, however, the German Government would 'agree to withdraw their forces, then His Majesty's Government would be willing to regard the position as being the same as it was before the German forces crossed the Polish frontier'. Indeed, they would be prepared to associate themselves with any negotiations which then ensued.[12]

The House was aghast. The Poles had suffered the most appalling bombardment for over thirty-six hours and the British Government was still prevaricating. Worse, many MPs concluded that the Prime Minister was actively seeking a shabby compromise – a second Munich. 'Members sat as if turned to stone', recalled Spears. 'The shock was such that for a moment there was no more movement than there was sound when the Prime Minister sat down.'[13] Not one single 'Hear, hear' greeted the close of Chamberlain's statement.

When the acting Labour leader, Arthur Greenwood, rose to reply he was hit by a wall of sound. His own MPs cheered him, as was normal, but what was extraordinary was the roar of encouragement which came from the Conservative side of the House. 'Speak for England!' cried the former Colonial Secretary Leo Amery.[14] Taken aback, Greenwood almost staggered with surprise. He rose to the occasion, however, declaring that 'every minute's delay' meant 'imperilling our national interests … the very foundations of our national honour'. There might be good reasons for the Prime Minister's hesitation (he was aware of the difficulty the Government was having in getting the French to commit to a time frame for the ultimatum) but this could not continue.

> The moment we look like weakening, at that moment dictatorship knows we are beaten. We are not beaten. We shall not be beaten. We cannot be beaten; but delay is dangerous, and I hope the Prime Minister … will be able to tell us when the House meets at noon tomorrow what the final decision is.[15]

When Greenwood sat down there was uproar. Waving their order papers, the normally servile Tory backbenchers cheered the Labour leader until they were hoarse. 'All those who want to die abused Caesar', recorded the junior Foreign Office Minister Henry 'Chips' Channon. It was 'the old Munich rage all over again'.[16] A pacifist Labour MP tried to punch one of his more bellicose colleagues. Chamberlain went white. Well he might, thought the National Labour MP Harold Nicolson: 'Here were the PM's most ardent supporters cheering his opponent with all their lungs. The front bench looked as if they had been struck in the face.'[17]

In his seat below the gangway, one man remained silent.

No one had been more vindicated over the danger posed by Nazi Germany than Winston Churchill. In the longest and most desperate political battle of his life, he had campaigned noisily for rearmament and a firm stand against German aggression since 1932. Now, in this most critical moment, he was quiet. His dilemma lay in the fact that he had agreed, the previous day, to join the War Cabinet and, in one sense, considered himself already a member of the Government. On the other hand, he had heard nothing from Chamberlain since and it now appeared that Britain was vacillating over her commitment to Poland. Racked with emotion, he summoned like-minded parliamentarians for a meeting at his flat for 10.30 that evening. There, Anthony Eden, Bob Boothby, Brendan Bracken, Duff Cooper and Duncan Sandys contemplated full-blown insurrection. To Boothby's mind, Chamberlain had lost the Conservative Party for ever and it was Churchill's duty to go down to the House of Commons the next day and seize power for himself.

By this time, the storm had truly broken. As thunder cracked like cannon and the rain lashed its Gothic windows, twelve members of the Cabinet staged a mutiny in Sir John Simon's room in the Palace of Westminster. Earlier that afternoon, the Cabinet had agreed that the Italian proposal for a conference should be rejected and that an ultimatum, to expire no later than midnight, should be issued to Germany, regardless of the decision of the French. Now, the twelve Ministers – over half the Cabinet – felt that the Prime Minister had gone back on this decision and refused to leave the Chancellor's room until Chamberlain agreed to hold another Cabinet. It was unprecedented, recalled the Minister for Agriculture, Sir Reginald Dorman-Smith: 'We were on strike.'[18]

Eventually, after much telephoning to Paris and a meeting with the French Ambassador, Chamberlain called another meeting for 11.30 p.m. Tired and grubby, the dissenting Ministers made their way through the deluge to 10 Downing Street, where they were disconcerted to discover that the Foreign Secretary, Lord Halifax, had found time to dress for dinner. Coldly, Chamberlain apologised to the Cabinet for the misunderstanding and explained the problems he had been having with the French, who refused to contemplate an ultimatum before they had completed their mobilisation and evacuated their women and children. He was, however, prepared to accept his colleagues' view that a British ultimatum should be issued and have expired before MPs reconvened at noon the next day. His Majesty's Ambassador to Berlin would be instructed to call upon the German Foreign Minister at nine o'clock the following morning and deliver an ultimatum to expire at 11 a.m. British Summer Time. Did anyone object to this? No answer. 'Right, gentlemen,' Chamberlain summarised, 'this means war.' 'Hardly had he said it', recalled Dorman-Smith, than 'there was a most enormous clap of thunder and the whole Cabinet Room was lit up by a blinding flash of lightning. It was the most deafening thunder-clap I've ever heard in my life. It really shook the building.'[19]

Eleven hours later, Chamberlain broadcast to the nation.

I

The Hitler Experiment

> I have the impression that the persons directing the policy of the Hitler Government are not normal. Many of us, indeed, have a feeling that we are living in a country where fanatics, hooligans and eccentrics have got the upper hand.
>
> British Ambassador to Berlin to the Foreign Secretary, 30 June 1933[1]

The ice on the Thames was causing difficulties for Oxford's rowers. In Yorkshire, the East Holderness Foxhounds had braved the frost but struggled with poor scent. There was a new polo committee of the Hurlingham Club and the popularity of professional football was having unfortunate effects on the amateur game. In 'Home News', behind *The Times*'s sports pages, a 'Special Correspondent' reported on the urgent need for a muniment room for the Buckinghamshire county archives; and there was a warming story about some cases of 'serum and bacteria', previously stolen from the back of a doctor's car, now reunited with their owner. The lead item at the top of the 'Imperial and Foreign' section dealt with the exchange rate in New Zealand. Only on page ten, next to a column on the latest French Cabinet crisis, was the news that the President of the German Republic, the 85-year-old Field Marshal Paul von Hindenburg, had received the leader of the National Socialist German Workers' Party, Adolf Hitler, and asked him to become Chancellor of Germany.[2]

The appointment of Hitler on 30 January 1933 was more exciting than the anachronistic layout of *The Times* implied, but not much. Since the war, German Chancellors had lasted, on average, just under a year and the economy was in the midst of the Great Depression – with 24 per cent of the workforce unemployed. The Nazis had caused mild consternation with their electoral breakthrough in 1930 and their amazing gains in July 1932, but they had lost votes later that year and many assumed that their popularity had peaked. As if proof of this, Hitler had been forced to accept a coalition Government, with the former Chancellor, the Catholic-conservative Franz von Papen, as Vice-Chancellor. Just as the conservatives, who outnumbered Nazis in the Cabinet, believed that they could control Hitler, so their presence blunted foreign anxiety. 'Hitler has become Chancellor in Germany', recorded the British Conservative MP Cuthbert Headlam, 'but not on his own – he has von Papen as Vice-Chancellor and a good many of the National Party in his Cabinet – I don't fancy that he will be allowed to do much.'*[3]

Nor did the figure of Hitler necessarily strike terror into the hearts of peace-loving democrats. The *Daily Telegraph* wondered how a man who looked so uninspiring, 'with that ridiculous little moustache', could prove 'so attractive and impressive' to the German people.[4] The Liberal-supporting *News Chronicle* mocked the triumph of 'the Austrian house decorator', while the Labour *Daily Herald* scoffed at the 'stubby little Austrian with a flabby handshake, shifty brown eyes, and a Charlie Chaplin moustache'. Nothing, continued the *Herald*, 'in the public career of little Adolf Hitler, highly strung as a girl and vain as a matinee idol, indicates that he can escape the fate of his immediate predecessors'.[5]

The previous day, following the collapse of General Kurt von Schleicher's 55-day-old Chancellorship, *The Times* noted that a Hitler Government 'was held to be the least dangerous solution of a problem bristling with dangers'.[6] The Nazi leader's commitment to eradicate the Treaty of Versailles would cause 'some anxiety in foreign countries' but, the paper continued the following day, 'in fairness to the Nazis it must be admitted that they have in fact said little more on the subject of German disabilities ... than the most constitutional German parties'.[7] *The Economist* and the *Spectator* agreed, while the Labour-supporting *New Statesman* was even more sanguine: 'We shall not expect to see the Jews' extermination, or the power of big finance overthrown',

---

* In fact, Alfred Hugenberg (Minister of Economics) and Franz Gürtner (Minister of Justice) were the only members of the German National People's Party (DNVP), while five posts were occupied by Ministers without formal party affiliations.

commented the magazine on 3 February 1933. 'There will doubtless be an onslaught on the Communists; but if it is pressed to extremes it will provoke a powerful resistance, and may even result in a "united Marxist front" which will give the Nazis and their allies more than they bargained for.'[8] As it turned out, the imperialist *Morning Post* was nearer the mark when it argued that the latest turn in German politics did not augur well for internal peace and predicted that the new Government was likely to 'seek a solution of difficulties at home in adventures abroad'.[9]

In France, as was so often to happen during the next six years, major events in Germany coincided with a domestic political crisis. On 28 January, the day that Schleicher resigned, the Socialists withdrew their support from Prime Minister Joseph Paul-Boncour over his plan to 'save' French finances with a 5 per cent increase in all direct taxes.* Paul-Boncour resigned and the Radical-Socialist War Minister, Edouard Daladier, became Prime Minister for the first time.† Despite this, the arrival of Hitler did not go unnoticed. 'Germany now shows her true face', commented *Le Journal des débats*, while the influential *Paris-soir* thought that Germany had moved one step nearer to the restoration of the monarchy and 'a more uncompromising foreign policy'.[10] Yet while some French newspapers (particularly those on the left) were alarmed, others offered more ambiguous responses. As in Britain, there were those disposed to underestimate a 'common demagogue' and 'house painter', while the French right were torn between their traditional anti-Prussianism and admiration for Hitler's anti-communist policies. Thus, while *L'Ami du peuple* – owned by the super-rich perfumer and founder of the French fascist league, François Coty – recognised Hitler's 'implacable hatred of France', it also believed that the Nazis were performing a great service for 'civilisation' by stamping out 'the frightful experience of Bolshevism'.[11] Similar sentiments, though less extremely expressed, appeared in *L'Echo de Paris*, *Le Petit Journal* and *La Croix*.

---

* The French deficit stood at £100 million, at the then exchange rate, and was increasing at £250,000 pounds a day. The country, commented *The Times* on 30 January 1933, was 'living from hand to mouth'.

† Founded in 1901, the Radical-Socialist Party sprang from the radical republican tradition. Originally a left-wing party, it moved to the centre after the founding of the Socialist Party in 1905. Four out of the eight Prime Ministers of France between 1933 and 1939 were Radical-Socialists.

The French Ambassador to Berlin, André François-Poncet, and his British counterpart, Sir Horace Rumbold, had written off Hitler at the end of 1932. Now, they were phlegmatic in the face of their predictions being confounded. 'The Hitler experiment had to be made sometime or other', Rumbold wrote to his son, 'and we shall now see what it will bring forth.'[12] François-Poncet agreed. 'France has no reason to lose her calm', he reassured Paris on 1 February 1933, but 'must wait the actions of the new masters of the Reich'.[13] They did not have to wait long.

Hitler hardly paused a week before showing the world that the persecution and violence which had characterised his route to power were to become the hallmarks of his rule. Without a majority in the Reichstag, he persuaded Hindenburg to call fresh elections and the Nazis, now with the power of the state behind them, launched a campaign of violence and terror. Brown-shirted storm troopers broke up political meetings, smashed Communist and Social Democrat headquarters and beat up opponents. The German press was muzzled but foreign correspondents reported, with growing horror, on the daily toll of murders, beatings and suppressions. On 27 February 1933, six days before polling day, the Reichstag was set on fire. A Dutch Communist was arrested at the scene and the Nazis declared the arson the start of an attempted Bolshevik revolution. This provided Hitler with the excuse to establish his dictatorship. Civil liberties were suspended, Communists and other political opponents were arrested en masse and, on 23 March, the newly elected Reichstag voted itself into oblivion with the passage of the Enabling Act, granting Hitler the power to rule by decree. That same month, a derelict explosives factory, just north of the medieval town of Dachau in Bavaria, was converted into a camp for the 'protective custody' of political prisoners.

And then there were the Jews.

Neither Germans nor really human, according to Hitler, the Jews were to blame for the majority of Germany's ills. From the beginning of the Nazi takeover, they were fair game for the SA, who vandalised their property and committed both assaults and murder with impunity. On 1 April 1933, the first nationwide act of persecution took place when the Nazis enacted a boycott of Jewish shops and businesses. International opinion was outraged. Forty thousand people protested in Hyde Park and there were other demonstrations in Manchester,

Leeds and Glasgow, as well as New York. The *Scotsman* called it the 'High Watermark of Hate' and Lord Reading, the former Foreign Secretary and only the second nominally practising Jew to be a member of the Cabinet,* resigned as President of the Anglo-German Association.[14] After a day, Joseph Goebbels, the Nazis' diminutive Propaganda Minister, lifted the boycott, but this did not halt the wholesale removal of Jews and other 'undesirables' from all areas of German public life. For the vast majority it was impossible to find alternative work and thousands were forced into exile. Nor, the British Ambassador noted, did the purge exclude Jews of international repute, such as the composer Arnold Schoenberg, the conductors Bruno Walter and Otto Klemperer and the physicist Albert Einstein. Even Mendelssohn, who had died in 1847, could not escape the Nazi revolution and had his portrait removed from the hall of the Berlin Philharmonic.

Of course, there were those who chose not to believe the tales of atrocities which appeared both in the newspapers and in books such as *The Brown Book of the Hitler Terror and the Burning of the Reichstag*, published in August 1933. Lord Beaverbrook, owner of the mass-market *Daily Express* and *Evening Standard*, for one, visited Berlin in March 1933 and came back convinced that 'the stories of Jewish persecution are exaggerated'.[15] This, predictably, was the line fed to all enquiring visitors by the German Government and its supporters – though most did not bother, or were not brave enough, to enquire. 'All the reports abroad are humbug and lies', wrote the ardent Nazi Colonel Ernst Heyne to the British First World War General Sir Ian Hamilton on 1 April 1933. 'No country, I am certain, would have been so tolerant towards that crowd [the Jews] as we have been.' Heyne went on to ask Hamilton to 'do your utmost among your circle of friends to prevent the atmosphere from being intensified by the broadcasting of the Press [*sic*] of such an anti-German campaign'.[16] Hamilton did not reply until October but when he did he was encouraging, complimenting Heyne on his 'new Nazi uniform with extremely neat

* The first was Herbert Samuel (Chancellor of the Duchy of Lancaster in 1909–10 and later Postmaster General and Home Secretary), who, though nominally practising, was known for his personal atheism.

breeches and gaiters'. 'Everyone is excited now about all of you over in Germany and wonders what you are going to do next. As for me, you know I am a true friend of your country and I am quite confident that in the long run you will get where you want.'[17] A few weeks later he was more emphatic, declaring in a letter to another German correspondent, 'I am an admirer of the great Adolf Hitler and have done my best to support him through some difficult times.'[18]

Hamilton was neither a fascist nor a habitual anti-Semite. Although he refused to sign a letter condemning the persecution of the German Jews, on the weak grounds that he was already involved in too many public causes, he assured the journalist and author Rebecca West that he had no 'anti-Jewish prejudice' and had twice been chosen to lead Jewish World War veterans towards the Cenotaph on Armistice Day.[19] When Hitler came to power, Hamilton was eighty and, as one of the leading figures of the British Legion, had spent the last fifteen years unveiling war memorials and trying to help ex-servicemen. He believed passionately in the need to reconcile former enemies – not least through ex-servicemen's associations – and in 1928, along with Lord Reading, had been a founder member of the Anglo-German Association. Last but not least, he had long considered the potential collapse of Germany to Bolshevism 'the most deadly misfortune to Europe'.[20] For all these reasons, he was not prepared to condemn the Nazi treatment of the Jews and, on the contrary, became a notable apologist for the regime.

Hamilton's attitude was fairly typical of his class. Although most members of Britain's socio-political elite found Nazi Jew baiting distasteful, abhorrent even, there was a tendency among some to find excuses for it. 'We all condemn the folly and violence of those attacks upon the Jews in Germany', wrote the Bishop of Gloucester in his diocesan magazine in mid-1933, but it was nevertheless important to recall that 'many Jews were responsible, particularly at the beginning, for the violence of the Russian Communists; many Jews have helped to inspire the violence of the Socialist communities; [and that] they are not altogether a pleasant element in German, and in particular in Berlin life'.[21]

Still, the overwhelming reaction to the Nazi pogroms was disgust and, as the Foreign Secretary, Sir John Simon, told the Nazi emissary Alfred Rosenberg, 'in two months Germany had lost the sympathy which she had gained here in ten years'.[22] Simon instructed Sir Horace

Rumbold to repeat this point to Hitler but beyond this the British Government was powerless: forced to agree with the character of the 'Prince of Wales' who, in the film version of *The Scarlet Pimpernel*, released the following year, laments that 'If a country goes mad it has the right to commit every horror within its own walls.'[23] Besides, there was the more pressing question of what policy the new Germany intended to pursue beyond her walls.

*

Long before Hitler came to power, any idea that the Treaty of Versailles guaranteed European peace had been abandoned. Indeed, major players had warned that it would lead to disaster even before the document was signed. 'You may strip Germany of her colonies, reduce her armaments to a mere police force and her navy to that of a fifth-rate power', wrote the British Prime Minister, David Lloyd George, in the so-called Fontainebleau Memorandum of March 1919, but 'if she feels that she has been unjustly treated in the peace of 1919 she will find means of exacting retribution from her conquerors'.[24] Unfortunately, neither Lloyd George nor the American President, Woodrow Wilson (who advocated the greatest leniency), were able to dissuade the French Premier, Georges Clemenceau, who was determined to hobble Germany. The Twenties were, consequently, spent searching for ways to correct the defects of Versailles.

In 1925, the Treaty of Locarno reaffirmed Germany's western frontier – this time with the Germans as willing signatories – and the following year Germany was admitted to the League of Nations. The Kellogg–Briand Pact of 1928 outlawed war as a means of settling international disputes, while the Dawes and Young plans readjusted and reduced German reparations until they were effectively abolished by the Lausanne Conference in 1932. None of this, despite the spray of Nobel Peace Prizes awarded to the various architects, was enough. Only the abolition of the weapons of war itself, it was felt, could guarantee peace. A World Disarmament Conference was therefore opened, with much fanfare, in Geneva on 2 February 1932. 'If all nations will agree wholly to eliminate from possession and use the weapons which make possible a successful attack,' wrote President Franklin D. Roosevelt in a message to his fellow heads of state, 'defences automatically will become impregnable and the frontiers and independence of every nation will become secure.'[25] Unfortunately, by the time of Roosevelt's message, the Disarmament Conference was already bogged down. No one could agree what constituted 'defensive' as opposed to 'offensive' weapons, while, more fundamentally, the Germans were demanding equality of armaments with their neighbours – something which the French were never going to allow.

As she was apt to point out, France had experienced two German invasions in the last sixty years, the second of which had 'bled her white'. Her overwhelming determination at Versailles, therefore, had been to make Germany pay for what she had done and to weaken her to such an extent that she might never again be in a position to threaten French security. For this reason, the French, in contrast with other belligerents, had remained heavily armed throughout the Twenties and in 1933 possessed the most powerful army in the world. This was no mere paranoia. Even with chunks of her territory hacked off and distributed to other nations, Germany still had a population of some sixty-five million compared to France's forty. The Deuxième Bureau (French military intelligence), even prior to Hitler's advent, was providing substantial evidence of illegal German rearmament and, as the Chiefs of Staff continually reminded their political masters, France was shortly to go through the 'lean years', whereby the number of conscripts for the army would halve as a result of the low birth rate during the First World War.

The task of reconciling the French and German positions fell to the British, who, for the most part, sympathised with the Germans and grew increasingly exasperated with the French. In part this was a reversion to traditional national prejudices. Prior to 1914 many Britons felt that they had more in common with the Germans than the French, a feeling not entirely dissipated by the First World War. As Robert Graves wrote in *Goodbye to All That*, 'anti-French feeling among most ex-soldiers amounted almost to an obsession', while the poet Edmund Blunden (who had fought at both the Somme and Passchendaele) vowed that he would never take part in another war 'except against the French. If there's ever a war with them, I'll go like a shot.'[26] In official circles, anti-French feeling was spurred by the desire to tie Germany to an armaments convention before it was too late and the British Government was forced to consider the alternative: massive rearmament. Thus the Prime Minister, Ramsay MacDonald, described France as the 'peace problem of Europe' in February 1930; J. L. Garvin, the pro-Mussolini Editor of the *Observer*, criticised Britain's former ally for wanting to preserve her 'artificial dominance'; and even the Francophile Permanent Under-Secretary of the Foreign Office, Sir Robert Vansittart, thought the French 'unduly vindictive' in their relations with the Germans.[27] Nor did the arrival of Hitler initially change this. 'I don't think Hitlerism has made our people pro-French,' wrote the former Deputy Secretary to the Cabinet, Thomas Jones, 'but it has made them pause and question the wisdom of confidence in Germany which had been steadily growing since the War.'[28]

One man whose confidence was severely shaken was the British Ambassador, Sir Horace Rumbold. With droopy eyes, a neat little moustache and a stolidly impassive expression, Rumbold appeared the ultimate Old Etonian and as 'English as eggs and bacon'.[29] The former Foreign Secretary Lord Curzon had thought him 'not alert enough for Berlin', but beneath the slightly inane exterior was a penetrating mind and, as Vansittart was to reflect, 'his warnings were clearer than anything that we got later'.[30] Shocked by the ruthlessness with which Hitler had established his dictatorship, the Ambassador saw, right from the start, how the ideology which underpinned Nazi domestic policy could be transferred to the international sphere. Yet it was in analysing *Mein Kampf*, Hitler's autobiography-cum-manifesto, that Rumbold perceived the true nature of a future Hitlerian foreign policy. In a masterly 5,000-word despatch, written in April 1933 – just three months after Hitler's accession to power – Rumbold laid bare Hitler's social Darwinism:

> He starts with the assertions that man is a fighting animal; therefore the nation is, he concludes, a fighting unit, being a community of fighters. Any living organism which ceases to fight for existence is, he asserts, doomed to extinction. A country or a race which ceases to fight is equally doomed. The fighting capacity of a race depends on its purity. Hence the necessity for ridding it of foreign impurities. The Jewish race, owing to its universality, is of necessity pacifist and internationalist. Pacifism is the deadliest sin, for pacifism means the surrender of the race in the fight for its existence ... The German race, had it been united in time, would now be master of the globe today. The

> new Reich must gather within its fold all the scattered German elements in Europe. A race which has suffered defeat can be rescued by restoring its self-confidence. Above all things, the army must be taught to believe in its own invincibility. To restore the German nation again 'it is only necessary to convince the people that the recovery of freedom by force of arms is a possibility'.

Rumbold went on to highlight the importance Hitler placed on building a mighty military – since 'Germany's lost provinces cannot be gained by solemn appeals to Heaven ... but only by force of arms' – as well as his assertion that Germany must not repeat her mistake in the last war of fighting all her enemies at once but must pick them off one by one. It was, of course, uncertain how far Hitler intended to implement these ideas but Rumbold warned against pinning hopes on a radical change of philosophy. Hitler might throw out protestations of peaceful intent from time to time but this was merely to 'lull the outer world into a sense of security'. Ultimately, Rumbold was convinced that 'a deliberate policy' was now being pursued, the aim of which was 'to bring Germany to a point of preparation, a jumping-off point from which she can reach solid ground before her adversaries can interfere'.[31] Germany's neighbours, he warned, must be vigilant.

The '*Mein Kampf* despatch', as it became known, caused a stir in the Foreign Office, which showed it to MacDonald, who, in turn, had it circulated to the Cabinet. Nor was this the only warning to reach the top. On 10 May 1933, Brigadier A. C. Temperley, one of the British delegates at the Disarmament Conference, sent the Foreign Office a memorandum urging the Government to abandon disarmament and call Germany out on her illegal military. It would be madness, Temperley argued, for the former Allies to consider further disarmament at a time when Germany was in a 'delirium of reawakened nationalism and of the most blatant and dangerous militarism'. The whole of the German nation was being infused with the spirit of war, and alleged programmes for the inculcation of discipline, such as 'Defence Sport', were merely 'camouflage for intensive military training'. The Germans, Temperley wrote, already possessed 125 fighter aeroplanes – in contravention of the Treaty of Versailles, which prohibited a German Air Force – while secret information revealed that an order had been made to Dornier for 36 twin-engined night bombers.

What then was to be the attitude of His Majesty's Government? Was it prepared to proceed as if nothing had happened? Could it afford to ignore what was going on in Germany? To Temperley's mind there was only one solution. Britain and France, together with the United States, should tell Germany that there would be no relaxation of Versailles and no moves towards equality of status unless a complete reversion of her present military preparations and tendencies took place. Admittedly this ran the risk of starting a war but, as Temperley pointed out, it was a small risk since there was no way that Germany could confront the combined might of the French Army and the Royal Navy. Germany's bluff should thus be called and Hitler, for all his bombast, must give way. The only alternative, concluded the Brigadier, was to allow things to drift for five years, by which time there would either be a new regime in Germany or war. 'There is a mad dog abroad once more', he concluded his paper, 'and we must resolutely combine either to ensure its destruction or at least its confinement until the disease has run its course.'[32]

At the Foreign Office, Sir Robert Vansittart was in complete agreement and circulated Temperley's paper to the Cabinet. He had already written his own memorandum warning that the present German regime would, 'on past and present form, loose off another European war just so soon as it feels strong enough'. This, he acknowledged, might appear a crude analysis but then 'we are considering very crude people, who have very few ideas in their noddles but brute force and militarism'.[33] The Cabinet agreed that the international situation was 'definitely disquieting' but otherwise these warnings had little effect.[34] The Government was committed to the Disarmament Conference, while the idea of a 'preventive war' to halt German rearmament was – thanks to the pacific nature of public opinion – beyond the realms even of discussion.

*

In maintaining their hope of reaching some form of agreement with Germany, the British, as Rumbold had predicted, were encouraged by Hitler, who lost no opportunity to present himself as a man of peace. On 17 May 1933, in a much-publicised speech to the Reichstag, he proclaimed his pacifism to the world. We have 'no use for the idea of

Germanisation', the new Chancellor declared. 'The mentality of the past century which made people believe that they could make Germans out of Poles and Frenchmen is completely foreign to us.'[35] Even more encouragingly, he stated his willingness to accept the latest British proposals for international disarmament.

This was good news for London but less welcome in Paris. The French military were implacably opposed either to a reduction of their own arsenal or to an increase in German capabilities. German demands for equality, warned General Maxime Weygand, Commander-in-Chief of the French Army, were a trap: 'In reality there will be no equality, but a very pronounced superiority for Germany given the military culture of this nation and the intensive efforts already undertaken to prepare the German armaments industry for rearmament.'[36] On the other hand, was there any alternative to trying to come to an arrangement with Hitler before German illegal rearmament got completely out of hand? Goebbels would later claim that the only sensible course open to a French Prime Minister was to stamp on Hitler as soon as he came to power, citing *Mein Kampf* as evidence of the Führer's aggressive intentions.[37] But this analysis was based on a number of assumptions: that the French had read *Mein Kampf*; that they took it at its word; and that they were prepared, if necessary, to prevent German rearmament by force. As it was, few of these assumptions held any basis in reality.

The first French edition of *Mein Kampf* did not appear until 1934 and then for only a few months before Hitler won a legal case and had it withdrawn. An English version had been published in the United States the previous year but had been purged of the most incendiary passages, including Hitler's call for the 'destruction' of France as the necessary precondition for German expansion in the east.[38] French intelligence had read the original and was warning, even in 1932, that Hitler's goal was the annihilation of France and the domination of Europe. But the French Ambassador to Berlin was ambivalent. Although François-Poncet, who had read the book and spoke German fluently, recognised that 'the pacifism of Hitler is relative, temporary and conditional', he was torn between considering *Mein Kampf* a blueprint for Hitler's rule and the moribund rantings of a young firebrand.[39] On the whole, he tended towards the latter.

For French statesmen, this debate was largely academic. Few had read the book, while even fewer were prepared to contemplate a military solution. Notoriously, this had already been tried in 1923 when, responding to the latest German default on her reparations payments, Prime Minister Raymond Poincaré had ordered French troops to occupy the Ruhr. In doing so he brought widespread condemnation on France and did much to stimulate sympathy for Germany. Ten years later, Germany was no longer an emaciated republic and Poincaré was gone. His successor, Edouard Daladier, had to work within the confines of a colossal budget deficit and the need to retain the support of the Socialist Party. Neither allowed him to consider a preventive war or an arms race. In March 1933, therefore, with reluctance, the French accepted the British plan to standardise Continental armies at 200,000 men. The Germans would be allowed to double the size of the Reichswehr, while the French would be forced to take an axe to their own battalions. But this was as far as the 'MacDonald Plan' got. Hitler never had any intention of limiting himself to an arms convention and the French insistence on controls and inspections provided him with the excuse he needed to break off negotiations. On Saturday 14 October 1933 – the first of his weekend coups – Hitler announced that Germany was withdrawing not merely from the Disarmament Conference but from the League of Nations as well.

Foreign opinion was stunned and incensed. The French considered their distrust justified, while the British felt that their good faith had been hurled back in their face. Despite the German tantrum, however, there was no change in British policy. In July, Horace Rumbold had retired as Britain's Ambassador to Berlin. He was sixty-four – retirement age – but it still seemed odd that the British Government should change horses midstream, or mid-tidal wave in this case. The new man, Sir Eric Phipps, was perceptive and quick-witted. When Hermann Göring, Reichsminister for Aviation and second in the Nazi hierarchy, arrived late for a dinner shortly after the 'Night of the Long Knives' (during which a number of senior Nazis had been murdered) he excused himself by explaining that he had been shooting. 'Animals, I hope', replied Phipps.[40] Yet despite his distaste for the Nazis, Phipps echoed the Government's view that there was no alternative but to try to bring Hitler back to the negotiating table. 'We cannot regard him solely as the author of *Mein Kampf*', he wrote in November 1933, 'for in such case we should logically be bound to adopt the policy of a "preventive" war, nor can we afford to ignore him. Would it not, therefore, be advisable soon to try to bind that damnably dynamic man?'[41]

What was happening in Germany was certainly dynamic and it was not just the Foreign Office that made efforts to understand it. Throughout 1933 a number of politicians, journalists, civil servants and private individuals travelled to Germany to experience the revolution for themselves. One of these was the journalist Vernon Bartlett, who bought himself a collapsible canoe and paddled his way down the Rhine, the Moselle and the Isar. The product of these splashings was a book, *Nazi Germany Explained*, published in the autumn of 1933. A liberal and committed pacifist, Bartlett was under no illusions about the nature of the new order in Germany, predicting that the anti-Jewish campaign would continue, since belief in the 'Aryan' race was among the most profoundly held by the Nazi leaders. He was, however, dismissive of *Mein Kampf* and felt, on balance, that Hitler did not want war. 'If I have properly understood the National Socialist idea', Bartlett wrote, 'the conquest of territory has ceased to be important.'[42]

Another visitor was the Cabinet Secretary, Sir Maurice Hankey. An exceptionally hard-working and talented administrator, Hankey was not known for his imagination. (The most human thing Major Henry Pownall, Assistant Secretary of the Committee of Imperial Defence, heard him say was: 'The [World Economic] Conference and the Cabinet don't matter a bloody damn, I want a cup of tea, quick.'[43]) In August 1933, therefore, he decided to take himself and his wife to Germany on what was, at least in part, a busman's holiday. There, having spent a few days walking through the Black Forest, they witnessed an immense torchlight parade of 'thousands of Nazis, nearly all in uniform, with brass bands, drum and fife bands, bugle bands, singing, and the like'. Hankey was impressed, particularly by the German youth movement, which 'appears to be enlisted, encadred and under some kind of discipline in the Nazi Forces'. 'If Germany intends to rearm,' he continued in a paper for the Cabinet, 'she could not take a more effective first step.'[44]

The same thought did not fail to occur to a young Scottish Conservative MP. Bob Boothby was handsome, talented and cocky. He had become MP for Aberdeen at the age of twenty-four and, although he knew nothing about farming and even less about fishing, took up the issues of his constituency with gusto. One day when

Stanley Baldwin entered the chamber to find Boothby holding forth with his customary zeal, he paused before muttering 'Herrings, *again*!', and turned on his heels.[45] Boothby was a great traveller and visited Germany every year between 1925 and 1933, often making the pilgrimage to Bayreuth to hear the music dramas of Richard Wagner. In January 1932, he was in Berlin delivering some lectures on the economic crisis when Hitler, not yet Chancellor, asked to see him. Boothby was taken to a room in the Esplanade Hotel where 'a short, dark, spare figure with a small moustache and limpid blue eyes' jumped up, clicked his heels together, raised his arm and shouted 'Hitler!' The mischievous MP hardly paused before he clicked his own heels, saluted and yelled 'Boothby!'[46] In the conversation which followed, Boothby asked Hitler about the Jews and received the tart assurance that 'there will be no pogroms'. When he returned to Germany the following year, however, he was disturbed to find signs outside villages reading 'Jews forbidden here', swastikas everywhere and Bayreuth 'turned, or distorted, into a Nazi shrine'.[47] He left convinced that Germany was preparing for war and, in October 1933, delivered the first of a series of warnings to his Aberdeenshire constituents. Germany was in 'the grip of something very like war fever', he declared. Soon she would be rearmed and in a position to menace the peace of Europe. In these circumstances, it was essential that Britain provide herself, immediately, 'with the armed forces necessary to protect our own country, and to carry out our foreign policy'.[48]

Boothby was not alone in reaching this conclusion. Although he had not been to Germany since the Nazi takeover, there was another politician, far more famous and with an unrivalled eloquence, who had become convinced that Nazi Germany spelt danger and that Britain was inadequately prepared to meet this new threat. But while Boothby was on the rise, this man's career appeared to have entered its twilight.

II

'I Sing of Arms and the Man'

> The right hon. Gentleman is one of those brilliant and erratic geniuses who, when he sees clearly, sees very, very clearly; and sometimes he does not.
>
> Clement Attlee, House of Commons, 8 March 1934

Winston Churchill had seen and done it all. As a supernumerary Lieutenant serving with the 21st Lancers in the Sudan, he had taken part in one of the last major British cavalry charges, against the 'Dervishes' at the Battle of Omdurman in 1898. During the Boer War he escaped from a prisoner of war camp and became a national hero. A journalist and well-known author, in 1900 he entered Parliament and embarked on what was to become a dazzling, if volatile, political career. Over the next thirty-four years he served as President of the Board of Trade, Home Secretary, First Lord of the Admiralty, Secretary of State for War, Secretary of State for Air, Secretary of State for the Colonies and Chancellor of the Exchequer. The only two senior posts he had not held were Foreign Secretary and Prime Minister. At times both appeared within his reach – his talents obvious even to his opponents – but by 1934 he had quarrelled with his party and his political career seemed in terminal decline.

Churchill was never a traditional Tory. In 1904, he had abandoned the Conservatives for the Liberals and went on to work closely with both Asquith and Lloyd George. Many Conservatives never forgot this ratting, while many others never forgave him for his role in the disastrous Dardanelles campaign of 1915.* Stanley Baldwin redeemed

* Widely blamed for the Royal Navy's ill-fated attempt to capture Constantinople by forcing the Dardanelles straits between February and March 1915 and the

him by making him Chancellor of the Exchequer in 1924 – when Churchill also rejoined the Conservative Party – but in 1930 the two men fell out over Baldwin's support for limited powers of self-government for India. Churchill resigned from the Shadow Cabinet and when, in 1931, Ramsay MacDonald formed a National Government to deal with the crisis caused by the Great Depression, he was not invited to join. Alienated from the Conservative leadership, Churchill and his new allies on the Tory right spent the next four years waging a noisy campaign against the Government's India Bill as well as that 'seditious Middle Temple lawyer', the leader of the Indian National Congress, Mahatma Gandhi.[1]

India, however, was not Churchill's only cause. Even before Hitler came to power, he was warning of the danger of a rearmed Germany. He opposed the Disarmament Conference and challenged those who argued for parity of arms between France and Germany by provocatively asking if they wished for war. On 23 November 1932, in a speech to the House of Commons, he cautioned the Government against believing that all Germany desired was equality of status with the other European powers:

> That is not what Germany is seeking. All these bands of sturdy Teutonic youths, marching along the streets and roads of Germany, with the light in their eyes of desire to suffer for their Fatherland, are not looking for status. They are looking for weapons and, when they have the weapons, believe me, they will then ask for the return, the restoration of lost territories and lost colonies.[2]

The Nazi takeover only increased Churchill's apprehension. Initially he adopted an isolationist attitude, hoping to keep Britain from being sucked into Europe's troubles. But neutrality could only be maintained by superior strength. In March 1933, therefore, he publicly thanked

---

subsequent invasion of the Gallipoli peninsula – resulting in 187,000 Allied casualties – Churchill continued to be haunted by the debacle well into the 1930s. Indeed, as V. W. Germains wrote in a book entitled *The Tragedy of Mr Churchill*, published in 1931: 'The true tragedy of Mr Churchill is that whilst he has in reality nothing to *offer* the genuine Labour man, or Liberal, he fails to command the confidence of the genuine Conservative. For the ghosts of the Gallipoli dead will always rise up to damn him anew in times of national emergency.'

God for the existence of the French Army and demanded a strengthening of British arms in the air and upon the seas.[3] The following month he attacked the entire Nazi edifice – composed of 'grim dictatorship', the persecution of the Jews and 'appeals to every form of fighting spirit' – while calling on the Government to abandon the chimera of disarmament in favour of urgent repairs to Britain's defences.[4]

The problem Churchill faced was that there was probably a stronger spirit of pacifism in Britain between 1933 and the end of 1934 than at any other time since the end of the war. The late Twenties and early Thirties saw a spate of books, plays and films about the war released and consumed voraciously. Robert Sherriff's *Journey's End*, Robert Graves' *Goodbye to All That*, Vera Brittain's *Testament of Youth*, Siegfried Sassoon's *Memoirs of an Infantry Officer* and Erich Maria Remarque's *All Quiet on the Western Front* brought home the horrors of the trenches to those lucky enough not to have experienced them, while the publication of a number of high-profile political memoirs suggested that the catastrophe had been one tremendous bungle. 'The nations', wrote Lloyd George in his best-selling *War Memoirs*, 'slithered over the brink into the boiling cauldron of war without any trace of apprehension or dismay.'[5] The statesmen had failed in 1914 and the younger generation was not going to allow them to fail again. On 9 February 1933, students at the Oxford Union approved by 275 votes to 153 the motion that 'This House will in no circumstances fight for its King and Country'.

The 'King and Country' debate caused a furore. Although the *Daily Express* tried to dismiss the vote as the action of 'woozy-minded Communists', 'practical jokers' and 'sexual indeterminates', many people were deeply shocked.[6] Churchill called it a 'disquieting and disgusting symptom' of the times, the *Daily Telegraph* attacked 'disloyalty at Oxford' and a box containing 275 white feathers was delivered to the Union buildings.[7] Nor were the waves of excitement confined to Britain's shores. Speaking in the Commons the following year, the Liberal MP Robert Bernays recalled a recent visit he had made to Germany during which he had been asked about the vote: 'The fact is that you English are soft', remarked a Nazi youth leader, with an 'ugly gleam in his eye'.[8] The same predatory interest was evident to the eighteen-year-old Patrick Leigh Fermor during his 1933–4 walk across Germany, while Mussolini, who cited the motion during the Abyssinian crisis, claimed it as evidence of British degeneracy.[9]

In reality, the Oxford debate was seriously overplayed. As attendees later explained, the majority of members were not pacifists and had simply been swayed by the oratory of the guest speaker, the popular philosopher C. E. M. Joad. The proposer of the motion, Kenelm Digby, admitted that the result was representative of neither the University nor the youth of the country, while the former German spy Captain von Rintelen predicted, in an interview with the *Daily Sketch*, that if war were to break out tomorrow 'those young fellows would be the first to join the Colours'.[10] Yet there was more than a whiff of rebellion in the air and copycat motions were soon passed by both Manchester and Glasgow universities; while Cambridge, which had the temerity to threaten to pull out of the 1933 Boat Race on account of the vote, endorsed pacifist motions in 1927, 1930, 1932 *and* 1933.

Nor was pacifism the preserve of dewy-eyed undergraduates. The belief that the arms race had caused the last war was widespread and the campaign against arms manufacturers – the so-called 'merchants of death' – was continued by the left well into the decade. The Liberals were wholly committed to disarmament; while the Labour leader, the Christian socialist George Lansbury, wanted to disband the Army, dismiss the Air Force and dare the world to 'Do your worst!'[11] At the party conference in October 1933, Labour delegates voted in favour of total disarmament and a general strike in the event of war, to cripple the economy and bring down the Government. That same month, the National Government suffered a severe shock when a Conservative majority of nearly 15,000 was turned into a Labour majority of nearly 5,000 at the Fulham East by-election. A number of domestic and political factors contributed to the result but the fact that the victorious candidate, John Wilmot, had campaigned on the twin issues of disarmament and pacifism seemed to many contemporaries to have been decisive.

Three years later, Stanley Baldwin would cite the Fulham by-election in his explanation to MPs as to why the Government had been unwilling to initiate a significant rearmament programme in 1933:

> My position as the leader of a great party was not altogether a comfortable one. I asked myself what chance was there – when that feeling that was given expression to in Fulham was common throughout the country – what chance was there within the next year or two of that feeling being so changed that the country would give a mandate for rearmament? Supposing I had gone to the country and said that Germany was rearming and that we must rearm, does anybody think that this pacific democracy would have rallied to that cry at that moment? I cannot think of anything that would have made the loss of the [General] Election from my point of view more certain.[12]

The 'appalling frankness' of this confession was mercilessly exploited by Churchill in his war memoirs, where he called it a statement 'without parallel in our Parliamentary history' and referenced it in the index under 'confesses putting party before country'.[13] But this was not the whole picture.

Stanley Baldwin was not easily rattled. The son of a rich Worcestershire ironmaster, he had been in Parliament since 1908 and twice been Prime Minister. A shrewd political operator with an unrivalled intuition for public opinion, he nevertheless hid these attributes behind a detached languor which at times bordered on self-parody. One day when Robert Bernays was reading a news item headed 'Lords', Baldwin came up behind him and said, 'I thought you were reading about cricket. I always forget that Lords may mean the House of Lords.'[14] On another occasion, while on a train journey to Edinburgh, the Conservative leader simply watched as Bob Boothby absent-mindedly picked up the Prime Ministerial sandwiches and proceeded to wolf them down.[15]

Yet Baldwin was also a romantic who, despite his industrial ancestry, liked to invoke an image of England as a pastoral idyll. In 1919, he had given practical demonstration of his patriotism when he anonymously donated £120,000 (one fifth of his fortune) to the Treasury, to help pay off the national debt. Deeply conscious of the sacrifices which had been made during the war, he was determined to preserve the thin crust of civilisation and reduce class tension at a time when left-wing revolution was haunting the Continent. He therefore handled the 1926 General Strike with tact and magnanimity and was arguably more responsible than any other politician for making Britain 'safe for democracy'.* In 1931 he accepted the need for a National Government to save the British economy and generously agreed to serve under the Labour leader, Ramsay MacDonald. Baldwin became Lord President of the Council but, with the Conservatives by far the largest party in the Commons,† was de facto co-Prime Minister for the next four years.

Baldwin was no card-carrying pacifist. Yet his horror of war was extreme and he subscribed to the popular view that 'great armaments lead inevitably to war'.[16] In particular, he had developed a profound fear of war from the air. 'Any town which is within reach of an aerodrome can be bombed within the first five minutes of war', he told MPs in a much-publicised speech of November 1932. What was even more alarming, according to the Lord President, was that there was no practical defence against this new weapon. 'I think it is well also for the man in the street to realise', he continued, 'that there is no power on earth that can protect him from being bombed. Whatever people may tell him, the bomber will always get through.'[17]

This terrifying statement was far from unique. Although Britain had suffered only a small number of casualties from air bombardment during the First World War, advances in aircraft and their war potential – demonstrated by the Japanese bombing of Shanghai in January 1932 and later, to an even greater extent, by the Spanish Civil War – convinced many that the next conflict would see the complete and near-instant destruction of whole cities. 'Picture, if you can', the result of a modern air raid, invited the military theorist, future fascist and yoga enthusiast J. F. C. Fuller:

> London for several days will be one vast raving Bedlam, the hospitals will be stormed, traffic will cease, the homeless will shriek for help, the city will be in pandemonium. What of the government at

* This phrase was used by President Wilson in his address to the joint session of Congress on 2 April 1917, in which he sought approval for the declaration of war on Germany. In 1928 Baldwin noted: 'Democracy has arrived at a gallop in England and I feel all the time that it is a race for life; can we educate them before the crash comes?'

† The 1931 General Election was a triumph for the Conservatives, who won 473 seats in a landslide victory for the National Government. The National Labour Party, under Ramsay MacDonald, won 13 seats, while the Liberal Nationals, under Sir John Simon, won 35. The Labour Party was reduced to a rump with only 52 seats.

> Westminster? It will be swept away by an avalanche of terror. Then will the enemy dictate his terms, which will be grasped at like a straw by a drowning man.[18]

London was an obvious and succulent target – Churchill likened it to a 'tremendous fat cow ... tied up to attract the beasts of prey' – but the terror of the air spread beyond the metropolis.[19] During a garden party in July 1933, the progressive Conservative MP Vyvyan Adams startled his constituents when he warned that Leeds was just as vulnerable as London and that foreign bombers, using gas and incendiary bombs, could render the city uninhabitable 'within fifteen minutes'.[20] Adams was strongly in favour of disarmament and campaigned vociferously for a ban on military aircraft. But while Baldwin had been one of the earliest enthusiasts of disarmament in general, and a ban on bombers in particular, he became increasingly torn as the spectre of a rearmed Germany loomed while Britain's own defences remained in arrears.

*

To the untrained eye, Great Britain appeared at the height of her powers. The Treaty of Versailles had divided Germany's colonial possessions among the victors and the British Empire had grown by almost one million square miles and thirteen million new subjects. South-West Africa, Tanganyika, Iraq, Transjordan and Palestine were now shaded pink on the map. But while the Union Jack fluttered over more foreign lands than ever before, this expansion had coincided with an economic slump and the British were soon to face civil war in Ireland, an independence movement in India, a revolt in Palestine and the greatest economic depression of the century. Like Rome 1,500 years earlier, the British Empire was overextended and by the mid-1930s in existential danger.

The First World War had bequeathed Britain a national debt of £6 billion (135 per cent of national income) and, after a brief boom, an economy sloping into depression. To try to balance the books the post-war Government inaugurated a period of swingeing cuts that reduced defence spending from £604 million per annum in 1920 to £111 million by 1922 – the rough level at which it would stay throughout the decade. The justification for this was found in the 1919 'Ten Year

Rule', whereby the Government assumed that the British Empire would 'not be engaged in any great war during the next ten years'.[21] The rule was renewed in 1929 and 1930 but by 1932 the Chiefs of Staff were worried. On 18 September 1931, a junior Japanese officer deliberately blew up a small part of a railway line owned by Japan's South Manchuria Railway near Mukden. The damage was minimal and a train passed along the track moments later but the 'sabotage' was used as an excuse by the Japanese to launch an invasion of the Chinese province of Manchuria. The League of Nations, which had been created to resolve such international disputes, was put to the test and found wanting. But the outbreak of fighting in the Far East concentrated minds in Whitehall.

Imagining what would happen 'if Japan showed an inclination to press matters to extremes', a 'Most Secret' Naval Staff report in January 1932 revealed that British possessions in the Far East were appallingly vulnerable and concluded that even if British forces were able to escape destruction in the opening battles there was nothing which could prevent the capture of Hong Kong and Singapore before the arrival of the main fleet.[22] The Chiefs of Staff endorsed this judgement, noting that 'our vast territorial and trade interests in the Far East, and our communications with the Dominions and India', were horribly exposed.[23] The Ten Year Rule was, consequently, scrapped but the effects of the Great Depression, coupled with the opening of the Disarmament Conference, meant that little was done to repair Britain's dilapidated defences between 1932 and 1935, by which time a new threat had outstripped the danger of Imperial Japan.

The British were determined to ignore Germany's illegal rearmament while the Disarmament Conference lumbered on. This was made increasingly difficult, however, by the insouciance with which the Germans pursued their programme. In June 1933, Britain's Air Attaché in Berlin, Group Captain J. H. Herring, attended a civil air display at Berlin's Tempelhof airport. There, while talking to the wife of an important German aeronautical official, he pointed out the new Heinkel and Junkers postal aircraft. 'Oh,' the lady replied casually, 'those will be two of the new single-seater fighters, I suppose.'[24] The following month, Göring showed considerable chutzpah by asking the British Government to sell him twenty-five English aircraft for 'police purposes'; July also saw German planes scattering pro-Nazi leaflets over Austria; and on 24 October, Hitler unveiled his own 'disarmament' proposals, which would allow for a German peacetime army of 300,000 men – three times that allowed by Versailles. The British Government turned this down but the civil servants were worried things were getting out of hand.

In October 1933, Sir Robert Vansittart, the Permanent Head of the Foreign Office, Sir Warren Fisher, the Permanent Head of the Treasury, and Sir Maurice Hankey, Cabinet Secretary and Secretary to the Committee for Imperial Defence, asked the Cabinet if they were prepared to consider any sort of warning to Germany over her rearmament programme and, if not, whether they were prepared to contemplate it at some later stage, for example in relation to 'German aggression against Poland or Austria, or a German aggression in the West'.[25] The answer was no. The British Government was not prepared to do anything to try to stop Germany from violating Versailles at this time. Nor was it prepared to publicise German rearmament lest it appeared to condone Germany's behaviour tacitly or, worse, provoke the French into demanding remedial action.

Churchill had no such qualms. In November 1933, he drew attention to the large quantities of scrap iron, nickel and other war metals pouring into Germany and pointed to the 'philosophy of blood lust' which was being inculcated in the German youth.[26] In February 1934, in the debate on the Government's White Paper on disarmament, he claimed that Britain was more vulnerable than at any time in her history and urged the Government to put its house in order before the people were forced to hear the crash of bombs exploding in London and witness 'cataracts of masonry and fire and smoke'.[27] The claim about vulnerability was an exaggeration but the speech marked the start of Churchill's dogged campaign to protect Britain from German air attack.

The Government had been aware of the Nazi intention to build a military air force since the summer of 1933. In the same despatch in which he recalled the Tempelhof air display, Captain Herring reported a conversation with a senior official at the German Air Ministry who admitted that it was useless to deny that Germany was arming in the air since Arado, one of the leading German aircraft manufacturers, never built 'anything other than high-powered military types of single-seaters'.[28] Two months later and Vansittart circulated a memorandum summarising the 'mass of secret information' on the nascent German Air Force.[29] The Air Ministry, however, did not seem worried. It would not be until the end of 1935 at the earliest, it reassured the Cabinet, that Germany would possess any military aircraft.[30] Were this to be the case, it would have been fortunate since the 1923 plan to equip the RAF with fifty-two squadrons – the minimum considered necessary for home and imperial defence – was still incomplete and the Under-Secretary of State for Air had just announced a further cut in the Air Estimates. In 1934, Britain was only the fifth largest air power in the world.

Ministers soon realised that they had underestimated both the speed and the extent of German air rearmament. Indeed, they contributed to this feat by bizarrely agreeing, in February 1934, to the sale of 118 Armstrong Siddeley aero engines to the Germans, with a potential order for a further 260. Originally, the Cabinet had considered a boycott of air materiel to Germany provided other countries followed suit. But their requests had been ignored and when it was discovered that both the French and the Americans were selling aero engines to the Germans, the Cabinet agreed to approve the deal. Indeed, as the former conscientious objector and architect of the most recent disarmament plan, Ramsay MacDonald, told the Cabinet, having made the decision, it was in Britain's interest to try to secure 'as large a proportion of the [German] order as possible'.[31]

As if to compensate for this, the Cabinet were then informed of the Chancellor's decision to approve four new squadrons for the Royal Air Force. In the Commons, Sir Philip Sassoon, the flamboyant Under-Secretary of State for Air, described this as a 'modest upward trend'.[32] It was certainly modest. As a result of the cuts imposed since 1930, the air budget was still approximately £1 million lower than it had been in 1931, while the 'new' programme was, in fact, nothing more than the resumption of the lapsed 1923 plan. Yet even this token increase was too much for the Opposition. Echoing Baldwin's assertion that the bomber would always get through, Clement Attlee, leading the debate for the Labour Party, denied that there was such a thing as defence against air attack and reaffirmed his party's commitment to 'total disarmament' and the pooling of national air forces into one international police force.

Attlee was followed by the Conservative MP for Plymouth Drake, Captain Freddie Guest. A decorated soldier and Olympian, Guest was an aviation enthusiast who had served briefly as Secretary of State for Air between 1921 and 1922. He therefore spoke with authority when he criticised the Air Ministry's estimates as both inadequate and misleading. The Government was trying to get a larger air force with less money, while Germany was arming as quickly as she could. The Government had no clear policy and was drifting towards momentous dangers. 'If I am wrong,' Guest concluded, 'so much the better. If I am right, then God help the Prime Minister of this day.'[33]

Churchill picked up where Guest left off. In pursuing disarmament, the Government had taken the country 'to the very edge of risk'. He did not possess the exact details of Germany's air programme but he did not doubt that those gifted people, with their factories, sense of discipline and capacity for science, were capable of creating a most powerful air force within a very short time. 'I dread the day when the means of threatening the heart of the British Empire should pass into the hands of the present rulers of Germany', he declared. 'I dread that day, but it is not, perhaps, far distant. It is, perhaps, only a year, or perhaps eighteen months, distant.'[34] There was still time, Churchill asserted, for Britain to repair her defences but she was not going to do it with these Air Estimates, with their meagre £135,000 net increase. What Britain needed, he continued, to growing cheers from Tory MPs, was parity in the air and he exhorted Baldwin to provide this.

But Baldwin was not yet for turning. Government policy, the Lord President explained, was for an air convention which would restrict the size of national air forces. Parity was the aim but it was parity by levelling down rather than levelling up. He ended his speech, however, with the concession that 'if all our efforts fail and if it is not possible to obtain this equality', then the Government 'will see to it that in air strength and air power this country shall no longer be in a position of inferiority to any country within striking distance of our shores'.[35] It was not long before this promise returned to haunt its author.

*

In pressing for an expanded Air Force, Churchill, although he did not know it, had an ally in the Chancellor of the Exchequer, Neville

Chamberlain. In the aftermath of Germany's withdrawal from the Disarmament Conference, the Government had set up a committee to enquire into the state of Britain's defences. Comprising Hankey, Vansittart and Warren Fisher, along with the Chiefs of Staff, the Defence Requirements Committee (DRC) decided that Germany, rather than Japan, was Britain's ultimate potential enemy and should, therefore, provide the focus for all 'long range' defence planning. Having identified the danger, the DRC recommended that every effort should be made to get back on friendly terms with Japan, while proposing a £76 million package to rebuild Britain's defences.[36]

As Chancellor, Chamberlain had been at the forefront of recent cuts to the armed services. By the autumn of 1933, however, he had decided that the dangers arising from deficiencies in defence were now at least equal to the economic hazards. Nevertheless, he considered £76 million an 'impossible' amount and reminded the Cabinet that 'we must cut our coat according to our cloth'.[37] Baldwin suggested raising a defence loan but Chamberlain vetoed this as 'the broad road that leads to destruction'.[38] This was a predictable response from a Conservative Chancellor, committed to balancing the budget and mindful of a public overwhelmingly opposed to increased spending on armaments. What was extraordinary was how Chamberlain – a civilian who had never worn uniform – then succeeded in reversing the recommendations of the Chiefs of Staff.

With Germany identified as Britain's principal enemy, the DRC wanted to apportion the majority of the money to the Army, specifically for the creation of an Expeditionary Force which could be despatched to the Continent to aid the French and defend the Low Countries. Conversely, its recommendation for the Air Force went no further than the completion of the fifty-two squadrons approved in 1923. Chamberlain considered this all wrong. The horrors of the Somme and Passchendaele had rendered expeditionary forces politically unacceptable – Ramsay MacDonald was later to ban the term from all official papers – while, as Baldwin commented, something had to be done to 'satisfy the semi-panic conditions which existed now about the air'.[39] Setting aside the fact that it was the Lord President who had done much to stoke these fears, Chamberlain took away the DRC report, returning it, in June 1934, only after he had reversed the committee's recommendations. While the military and civil servants proposed a significant expansion of the Army and only a modest increase in the Air Force, Chamberlain wanted a significantly larger Air Force and was only prepared to spend modestly on the Army. 'Our best defence', the Chancellor declared, 'would be the existence of a deterrent force so powerful as to render success in attack too doubtful to be worthwhile. I submit that this is most likely to be attained by the establishment of an Air Force based in this country of a size and efficiency calculated to inspire respect in the mind of a possible enemy.'[40]

The concept of an air deterrent flowed naturally from the apocalyptic conception of aerial warfare. In his 'terror from the air' speech, Baldwin had declared that the only defence against bombing was offence, 'which means that you have to kill more women and children more quickly than the enemy if you want to save yourselves'.[41] Yet, while this strategy had a certain logic, the Chiefs of Staff were appalled by the Chancellor's proposals, which derived, they believed, from political rather than strategic considerations. Chamberlain's 'ideas on strategy would disgrace a board school', fulminated Lieutenant-Colonel Henry Pownall, Hankey's deputy on the secretariat for the Committee of Imperial Defence. It was extremely dangerous to assume that the Air Force could substitute for the other two services, he argued, particularly when the Army was currently only good for 'Tattoos' and the Navy for reviews in 'Navy Weeks'.[42]

The Admiralty was similarly perturbed. Seizing on the DRC's conclusion that Germany constituted the primary danger, Chamberlain wanted to cut the proposed expenditure on the Navy and even went as far as to argue that in the event of war with Japan it would be impossible to send the Fleet to the Far East. 'Bad enough to have to fight the world at the forthcoming Naval Conference', complained the First Lord of the Admiralty, Sir Bolton Eyres-Monsell, 'but disheartening to be stabbed in the back by the Chancellor at the same moment.'[43] Yet Chamberlain got his way. He defeated Eyres-Monsell and he defeated the Secretary of State for War, Lord Hailsham, who was fighting to prevent the Army from becoming 'the Cinderella of the Services'.[44] The proposed expenditure on the Army was halved from £40 million to £20 million; the Navy was denied the long-term rebuilding programme it had requested; while, on the upside, the Air Force was to have thirty-eight new squadrons.

This was Chamberlain's 'limited liability' strategy.* Britain would rearm but the priority would be deterring Germany with a mighty air force rather than preparing troops to fight on the Continent. Were it to come to war, Britain would provide air support and a naval blockade, while the French held the Germans on land. In many ways this was simply a reversion to traditional British defence policy. Britain, after all, was an island and maritime power, while France possessed the second largest army in the world and what Chamberlain described as 'impregnable' land defences.† As events in 1934 were to show, however, reliance on French strength was an increasingly precarious assumption.

*

The Great Depression had hit France, belatedly, in 1931. Prices tumbled, industrial production slumped and unemployment rose. Between 1930 and 1933 French national income fell by nearly 30 per cent and in February 1933 the Finance Minister, Georges Bonnet, was forced to go cap in hand to the Dutch for a loan just to keep French finances afloat. Among the most prominent casualties of the crisis were the defence budgets, which between 1931 and 1934 were slashed by 25 per cent. This was despite reports from the Deuxième Bureau, which predicted that Germany would be capable of waging a war of aggression within two years, as well as providing detailed breakdowns of Germany's air building programme.[45] In 1934, the French still possessed the second largest air force in the world but this included dozens of wooden biplanes, while French aircraft production was a shambles.

In 1930, the French Parliament had approved funds for a massive chain of fortifications along the German frontier. Named after War Minister André Maginot, the Maginot Line – which became operational in 1936 – appeared the apogee of modernity. Sixty feet below the

---

* The concept had been conceived and popularised by the military theorist Basil Liddell Hart, who argued that in a future war Britain should avoid sending large armies to the Continent and focus on reducing the enemy's core strength through bombing and a naval blockade.

† The Soviet Union had the largest army as well as the largest air force.

surface, heavy guns, bunkers, command posts and barracks were connected by electric trains. There were subterranean hospitals, a concrete-protected telephone network and cinemas. The line was impervious to aerial or artillery bombardment, while its guns were capable of firing four tons of shells a minute. Yet however much the Maginot Line might have appeared like something out of the imagination of H. G. Wells, its entire conception was the opposite of modern. Haunted by the scar of trenches, which had stretched from Switzerland to the Channel, and most particularly by the carnage of Verdun, the French were preparing for another static war of defence. For imaginative soldiers, like Lieutenant-Colonel Charles de Gaulle, this was an appalling error. The future of war, de Gaulle believed, lay in mobility and tanks. The Maginot Line was a *folie de grandeur*: an 'army of concrete', incapable of reacting to circumstances, devouring money which could have been spent mechanising the Army and a block to strategic thinking.[46]

At least the Maginot Line appeared solid. The same could not be said for French politics. In order to guard against another Napoleon, the constitution of the Third Republic had apportioned power to the legislature at the expense of the executive. The result was a merry-go-round of ministries, with no fewer than ten administrations between January 1930 and November 1933. Then, in December 1933, a swindling, if enterprising, financier named Serge Alexandre Stavisky absconded after selling hundreds of millions of francs' worth of false bonds. The uproar caused by the Stavisky affair stemmed from his close association with several prominent Third Republic politicians and his Jewish parentage. The French right smelt conspiracy and when Stavisky committed suicide, claimed that he had been murdered in order to protect France's corrupt politicians. The Government of Camille Chautemps fell and Edouard Daladier was recalled to try and resolve the crisis. On 6 February 1934, as the new Prime Minister struggled to achieve a vote of confidence in the Chamber of Deputies, a bloody battle broke out in the Place de la Concorde between royalists, communists and the police. Railings were hurled as spears, the Ministère de la Marine was torched and the former Prime Minister Edouard Herriot narrowly escaped being thrown in the Seine. The morning after France's worst night of violence since the Paris Commune, fifteen people lay dead and two thousand injured.

Having been Prime Minister for only ten days, Daladier resigned with such haste that he failed to inform his Cabinet.

*

The turmoil in France was noted in England but it was events in Germany which were the greater cause for anxiety. In March 1934, the Government was shocked to discover that the Germans already possessed some 350 military aircraft and that their output had risen to 60 machines a month. This information helped bolster support for Chamberlain's proposals for an enlarged Air Force and on 18 July the Cabinet accepted 'Scheme A', whereby forty new squadrons would be added to the RAF over the next four years. According to the Colonial Secretary, Sir Philip Cunliffe-Lister, the new programme 'would be a great deterrent to war and would discourage Germany in time of peace'.[47] As the Chief of the Air Staff, Sir Edward Ellington, pointed out, however, the Chancellor's plan flattered to deceive.

Ellington had been seriously awry in assessing Germany's aircraft programme. Having initially pronounced that she was unlikely to possess any military aircraft before the end of 1935, he was now confidently predicting that the Germans would have no more than 500 first-line machines by the same date. He was, however, alarmed by Chamberlain's proposal to save money by doing without war reserves for the new squadrons. As things currently stood, only five RAF squadrons (barely sixty planes) had reserves and without these the Air Force 'would not be capable of operating on a war footing for more than a week or two'.[48] Scheme A was, therefore, largely window dressing, designed to reassure the public and deter Germany. It was not a practical defence against attack.

When Baldwin rose to defend the new squadrons in the Commons on 30 July 1934 he made the dramatic declaration that the frontiers of Britain were no longer 'the chalk cliffs of Dover' but the Rhine. This failed to sway the Opposition, however, who moved a motion of censure against the Government. 'We deny the proposition that an increased British Air Force will make for the peace of the world', reprimanded Clement Attlee, 'and we reject altogether the claim to parity.'[49] Churchill defended the Government, describing it as the most 'pacifist-minded' in history, before going on to lay a number of assertions before MPs. Where the Government had tiptoed gingerly around the subject of German rearmament, Churchill stated, baldly, that the Nazis were well advanced in building a military air force in contravention of the Treaty of Versailles. This force, he claimed, would be equal to the RAF by the end of 1935 and, at the current rate of expansion, would overtake it sometime in 1936. Finally, he argued that there was a danger that once Germany had obtained a lead in the air it would be impossible for Britain to catch up.[50]

Churchill's warnings – which were sounded, with increasing volume, throughout the summer and autumn of 1934 – drew mixed responses from MPs. While many Tories, particularly on the right of the party, supported his campaign, there were those, like his old foe the Secretary of State for India, Sir Samuel Hoare, who considered his agitations a self-interested attempt to resurrect his flagging career. The Labour Party branded him a warmonger, while the former Liberal leader Sir Herbert Samuel accused him of stirring up 'blind and causeless panic'.[51] Fortunately, such attacks had little effect on Churchill, who, in his bid to frighten the Government into greater action, was aided by the surreptitious help of two senior civil servants.

Major Desmond Morton had been shot through the lung in 1917 at the Battle of Arras. Amazingly, he survived and went on to serve as aide-de-camp to Field Marshal Haig, with the bullet still inside him. In 1924, having spent the early Twenties studying the Soviet Union for the Secret Intelligence Service, he became head of the Industrial Intelligence Centre of the Committee of Imperial Defence. Morton had known Churchill since their days spent together on the Western Front and, with his home in Kent only a fifteen-minute walk from Chartwell, Churchill's country house, the two men had become close friends. Now, as Churchill strove to shake the Government out of its torpor, Morton was in an ideal place to help him – even if this did mean breaking the Official Secrets Act.

Churchill's other senior Government source was Ralph Wigram. One of the best brains in the Foreign Office, Wigram was perceptive, personable and brave. At the age of thirty-six, this fit man, who loved tennis, was struck down by polio. The doctors thought he was unlikely to survive but by sheer determination, or so it seemed, he not only survived but went on to be become head of the Foreign Office's Central Department, covering Germany. Wigram shared Vansittart's assessment of Nazi Germany. That she was rearming was beyond doubt and it was only with strength and an active foreign policy that Britain stood a chance of containing her. Through Morton, Wigram got to know Churchill and together the pair became the former Chancellor's chief sources of information during the early years of his fight for rearmament.

Meanwhile, the information the Government was receiving – not least from Morton and Wigram – was cause for serious concern. The Air Staff had been confident that the German Air Force would be no larger than 500 first-line aircraft by the end of 1935 and 1,000 by 1939. In October 1934, however, secret information revealed German plans for a first-line strength of 1,296 planes, with full reserves, by the autumn of 1936. Faced with this fresh intelligence, the Secretary of State for Air, Lord Londonderry, tried to persuade the Cabinet to bring forward the date for the completion of Scheme A from March 1939 to the end of 1936. But Chamberlain was against this, arguing that there was 'nothing in our information in regard to German preparations to justify the proposed acceleration'. In the end, the Cabinet considered the situation sufficiently grave to expedite the building of half the new squadrons, yet it was no longer merely the development of the German Air Force which was becoming too blatant to ignore.[52]

On 20 November, the Committee of Imperial Defence informed the Cabinet that the Germans now possessed a regular army of 300,000 men, with plans for further expansion and mass mechanisation. A week later and Sir Eric Phipps pointed to an increase in German Government spending of £17.5 million. The Germans have been 'feverishly re-arming on land and in the air', the Ambassador reported, and have done so 'without hindrance or even protest':

> The impression left by the summer and autumn is one of incessant marching and drilling. It is evident to any foreign observer that the German people, with their innate love of discipline and military training, are revelling in their new freedom. Even the demonstrations of the labour front and the peasant rallies seem to the outsider to be mainly military parades. We have to face the fact that, while other countries enjoy playing football or sipping coffee at little tables under trees, German youth is happiest playing at soldiers, and German manhood is happiest on the barrack square.[53]

Ministers were alarmed but their initial concern was political rather than strategic. 'We may be attacked', wrote the Foreign Secretary, Sir John Simon, 'that since Germany left the Disarmament Conference in October 1933 we have done nothing but twiddle our thumbs and rush about to Geneva and back.'[54] In particular, the Cabinet were disturbed by the news that Churchill intended to put down an amendment to the Loyal Address, accusing the Government of failing to provide for the safety of its citizens. The root of ministerial apprehension lay in the justice of the charge. As one unnamed Minister stated during the Cabinet discussion of 21 November, it now appeared that Germany would, within a year, possess as large 'an air force as the United Kingdom'.[55] Yet to admit this publicly was politically unconscionable. The decision was therefore taken that while it was impossible to hold off acknowledging that Germany was rearming, it would nevertheless be made clear that 'Mr Churchill's charges are exaggerated'. Above all, as Sir Samuel Hoare told the Cabinet, it was vital 'to show the world that the Government has just as much and more information than Mr Churchill'.[56]

Churchill's speech of 28 November 1934 marked the high point of his early campaign for rearmament. Delivered to a packed House, he restated the undeniable fact that Germany – that 'mighty power which only a few years ago … fought almost the entire world, and almost conquered' – was rearming. The threat from the air was real and terrible. Ten days of intensive bombing on London would result in 30,000 or 40,000 people 'killed or maimed'.[57] Considering that only a few thousand more were killed during the course of the entire Blitz, this was a wildly inaccurate forecast. Yet neither Churchill nor other MPs were to know this. The film version of H. G. Wells' *The Shape of Things to Come*, released in 1936, imagined the complete destruction of London following a surprise air raid and, as Harold Macmillan later wrote, 'we thought of air warfare [in the 1930s] … rather as people think of nuclear warfare today'.[58]

To protect Britain from this apocalypse, Churchill demanded that the Government maintain for the next ten years an air force substantially stronger than that of Germany – which he claimed would reach parity with Britain sometime in the next year – and argued that 'it should be considered a high crime against the state … if that force is allowed to fall substantially below, even for a month, the potential force which may be possessed by that country abroad'.[59] When he sat down, he received a 'low and persistent ripple of cheering' from Conservative MPs, the majority of whom appeared deeply impressed.[60] Baldwin rose and proceeded to administer what the *Daily Mail* called 'soothing syrup'.[61] Germany, he admitted, was spending vast sums on rearmament and did indeed possess a military air force. There was, however, no ground for undue alarm since it was not the case that the RAF was in danger of being overtaken. The figures that Churchill had just quoted were total, not first-line figures. On this comparison, Germany's strength was only 50 per cent of the RAF's and would remain so for at least a year. Baldwin, whose figures had been supplied by the Air Ministry, said that it was impossible to look beyond this date. Yet the Air Ministry was itself forecasting a German superiority of 100 to 200 first-line aircraft by November 1937. Thus, while Churchill's projections were indeed inflationary, Baldwin's statement was deliberately misleading. His speech, however, did the trick. 'His Majesty's Government', the Lord President affirmed, 'are determined in no conditions to accept any position of inferiority with regard to what air force may be raised in Germany in the future' and Churchill withdrew his amendment.[62]

The debate surrounding Churchill's amendment to the Address added to those voices arguing in favour of legalising German rearmament. Germany could not be stopped from developing her military, asserted Lord Londonderry, and, as such, the logical course was to offer to cancel the armaments clauses of the Treaty of Versailles in exchange for her return to the League of Nations. The Foreign Secretary, Sir John Simon, agreed, while, speaking in the same debate, Britain's former war leader, David Lloyd George, warned against turning Germany into a 'pariah'. The Germans had been driven into revolution by the refusal of the Powers to redress their grievances, asserted the 'Welsh Wizard'. Now was the time to right past wrongs; to engage, not condemn, and bring Germany into the community of nations. Given that the alternative was an arms race and possibly another war, it is unsurprising that many, both within and outside Government, agreed and now set off on various missions to tame Hitler.

III

Tea with Hitler

Rightly or wrongly, all sorts of people who have met Hitler are convinced that he is a factor for peace.

Thomas Jones, Diary, 1 March 1934[1]

Dressed in his immaculately tailored morning coat, the Lord Privy Seal was led along a succession of guard-lined passages to a room of vast proportions. There he was received by a man, smaller than expected, yet smart and, despite his 'incongruous' uniform, 'almost dapper'.[2] This was high praise coming from Anthony Eden, widely considered the best-dressed man in London, and whose matinée idol looks put the gilt on a reputation for integrity. In sending him to sound out Hitler in February 1934, the British Government had made a prudent choice.

Only thirty-six and already number two at the Foreign Office, Eden was a rising star in a firmament of dullish men. At Eton he had won the Divinity Prize and later took a First in Oriental languages at Christ Church, Oxford. This linguistic flair, which included fluency in both French and German, was a diplomatic asset which Eden was able to put to good use when he was sent to Geneva as Britain's representative to the Disarmament Conference. There he won plaudits for his unstinting efforts and established himself as a leading supporter of the League of Nations.

Eden's 'peace credentials', as well as his general prestige, were reinforced by his war record. The First World War had broken out when the young Anthony was still at school, yet he left Eton as soon as he could and in 1915 joined the King's Royal Rifle Corps. Although the war was a universal tragedy, the years 1914–18 in the life of Anthony

Eden stand out as particularly poignant. His eldest brother, John, was killed in France in October 1914. His second brother, Timothy, who had been in Germany at the outbreak of hostilities, was interned in a prison camp outside Berlin. In February 1915, his father died and the following year his sixteen-year-old brother, William, drowned at the Battle of Jutland. Eden's uncle, who commanded a squadron in the Royal Flying Corps, was shot down and captured and his brother-in-law was seriously wounded at the Battle of the Somme. Thus, as he was later to write, in a matter of two years, 'every single male member of the family, with whom I had spent my life before the war, was dead, wounded or captured'.[3]

Despite this battalion of sorrows, Eden did not flinch and endured some of the worst fighting on the Western Front. In 1917, he was awarded the Military Cross and in March 1918 became the youngest Brigade Major in the British Army. This shining record, coupled with his efforts at Geneva, established Eden as the embodiment of the aspirations of the war generation – acutely conscious of the sacrifices that had been made and determined to build a better, more idealistic, world.

It also helped with Hitler, who loved to reminisce about the war. During lunch at the British Embassy on the second day of Eden's visit, Hitler, who seemed uninterested in the vegetarian dish which had been prepared for him, only warmed up when Eden mentioned their shared experience in the trenches. The Chancellor visibly thawed and the pair spent an agreeable time recollecting the various sectors on which they had served.

Eden was charmed by Hitler, whom he considered 'much more than a demagogue' and who even possessed a 'suspicion of humour'.[4] He had been warned by Sir Eric Phipps against being seduced by the Chancellor's honeyed words about peace but the Lord Privy Seal nevertheless concluded that Hitler was sincere. 'I find it very hard to believe that the man himself wants war', he reported to Baldwin.[5] He had been sent to Berlin to test Hitler's reaction to the Government's latest disarmament proposals and was relieved by the Führer's response. Hitler said that he would honour the Treaty of Locarno, promised to guarantee the 'non-military' nature of the SA and the SS, and did not rule out Germany's return to the League of Nations. His main demand was that Germany should be allowed an air force. Eden, who knew that Germany was already building an illegal air force, thought this not unreasonable and relayed Hitler's demands to London with the comment that 'the Chancellor's proposals were much better than expected'.[6] His enthusiasm, however, ran into the brick wall of the Permanent Under-Secretary of the Foreign Office, Sir Robert Vansittart.

In many ways, 'Van' and Eden were similar characters. Well dressed and suave, Vansittart was also a gifted linguist, who won both the French and German prizes at Eton and later wrote several plays in French. In 1903 he passed out top of the Foreign Office exams and in 1930 was appointed Permanent Under-Secretary, in charge of the department. While the Weimar Republic lasted, Vansittart had sought to redress or 'appease' German grievances over Versailles. With the advent of Hitler, however, he soon changed his attitude and became the most notorious Cassandra within Whitehall. In this context, Vansittart felt that 'young Eden, straight from charm-school', had taken too rosy a view of Hitler and his promises.[7] The Foreign Secretary, Sir John Simon, agreed. His Majesty's Government could never consider a proposal which would be so objectionable to France and must inevitably lead to an arms race, he wrote to Phipps on 23 February.[8]

Eden was furious at this rebuke, fuming that Simon was 'not only a national but an international calamity'.[9] Only a few weeks later, however, Hermann Göring provided what Phipps called a 'resounding negative' to those who, like Eden, were inclined to believe in German pacifism.[10] Speaking at Potsdam on 10 March 1934, the larger-than-life former air ace, Minister of Aviation, Minister President of Prussia and Reich Master of Forestry and Hunting delivered a eulogy on Prussian militarism, which had defied the 'whole world' and would do so again.[11] This was to reawaken an old fear. Although it was the Prussians who had come to the Duke of Wellington's aid in 1815 and tipped the balance at Waterloo, Prussianism, in Britain and France, was synonymous with pre-eminent military might, iron discipline and two invasions of France. Eden had been pleased to find that there was 'nothing of the Prussian' in Hitler: the Chancellor was a 'typical Austrian' or, as Eden's Parliamentary Private Secretary, Lord Cranborne, thought, an 'inspired peasant'.[12] Yet to many observers the Nazi regime appeared a totalitarian enhancement of Prussianism.

'The whole place is military mad', exclaimed the former diplomat Harold Nicolson, on a visit to Munich in February 1934. 'The passion for uniforms is greater even than in 1912', while the suspended wreaths in the Feldherrnhalle, representing Germany's lost provinces, were definitely a bad omen. Nicolson went to bed thoroughly depressed. 'Germany is again the Germany of before the war', he wrote in his diary, but 'with a new fanatical look in its eye'.[13] The former Foreign Secretary Sir Austen Chamberlain concurred. The Nazi revolution, he told the Commons on 13 April 1933 – just two and a half months after Hitler's accession to power – was 'the worst of the all-Prussian Imperialism, with an added savagery, a racial pride, an exclusiveness which cannot allow to any fellow subject not of "pure Nordic birth" equality of rights and citizenship'.[14] It would be madness, Chamberlain argued, to contemplate a revision of the peace treaties with Germany in such a state. This judgement was shared by some. But there was an alternative, more popular, view which held that Germany would only settle down once the shackles of Versailles had been removed.

*

By the early Thirties, the Treaty of Versailles had few defenders. A peace which, from the German perspective, had been 'dictated' by the victorious allies had 'humiliated' Germany by assigning her sole responsibility for starting the war, gutted her armed forces, imposed 'ruinous' reparations, seized her colonies and amputated parts of her territory for the benefit of new nations, like Czechoslovakia and the reconstructed Poland. During the Twenties, the Germans mounted a sizeable and effective propaganda campaign against the Treaty in general and the so-called war guilt clause in particular. There were, however, plenty of people in Britain who were prepared to condemn the document of their own volition. 'The Treaty of Versailles compelled them [the Germans] to subscribe to the most ruthless and sweeping moral condemnation in history, and riveted on the German people for another generation the fetters of their old inferiority complex', wrote the future historian E. H. Carr in January 1933.[15]

Carr published his article in the *Fortnightly Review* under a pseudonym, since he was a Foreign Office civil servant who, indeed, had been part of the British contingent at the Peace Conference. Two other members of the delegation were the Cambridge economist John Maynard Keynes and the young Harold Nicolson. Like Carr, both men were profoundly disillusioned by what was being done and Keynes resigned from the Treasury in protest at the level of reparations being imposed on the defeated powers. Five months later, in December 1919, he published *The Economic Consequences of the Peace*, in which he castigated the 'Peace Makers' and their 'Carthaginian Peace'. 'The policy of reducing Germany to servitude for a generation', wrote Keynes, was not merely 'abhorrent and detestable' but sowed 'the decay of the whole civilised life of Europe'.[16] The book became an international best-seller and set the tone for the series of critiques, including Nicolson's, which followed.*

By 1933, therefore, there was a strong feeling of *mea culpa* in Britain. Hardly anyone of influence believed that Germany had been solely responsible for the war and there was a widespread sense of guilt about Versailles. Writing at the time of the Peace Conference, the Minister for Education, H. A. L. Fisher, had comforted himself with the idea that the Treaty would be followed by 'an appeasement, and by degrees readjustments and modifications can be introduced which will give Europe a prospect of stability'.[17] Yet despite Germany's admittance to the League of Nations and the reduction and then cancellation of reparations, there was still a belief that the Allies, in particular the French, had not done enough either to ease Germany's burden or restore her much-damaged self-respect.

Germany had done its best to 'carry the Treaty through', claimed David Lloyd George to an audience of 8,000 people, squashed into Ashford cattle market on 11 March 1933. She had fulfilled the 'disarmament clauses honourably' but the Allies had failed to keep their side of the bargain and reduce their own arsenals. As a result, Germany had been driven into 'an aggressive military dictatorship'.[18] This, as Lloyd George knew, was not an accurate version of events. British military spending had been massively reduced since the war, while the Germans had been breaking the disarmament clauses even before

---

* Keynes was later criticised by anti-appeasers for helping to establish the legend of the Versailles 'diktat'. Bob Boothby accused the economist of having produced 'the bible of the Nazi movement', while the American Pulitzer Prize-winning journalist Edgar Mowrer (Paris correspondent for the *Chicago Daily News*) thought it one of the 'most harmful' books ever written. These views have been endorsed by recent scholarship which makes clear that the Treaty of Versailles was neither as punitive as the Germans claimed nor, in itself, responsible for the outbreak of the Second World War. Few contemporaries, however, shared this judgement.

the Nazi takeover. Yet the former Prime Minister was far from alone in blaming Britain and France for the rise of Hitler. At the 1933 Labour and Socialist International Conference in Paris, the Labour leader, George Lansbury, found himself the odd man out for not joining in the attacks on the German Government and left early, insisting that the Allies were '100 per cent to blame for Hitler'.[19] The journalist Robert Bruce Lockhart thought the Francophile Vansittart 'must be held largely responsible' for events in Germany, while *The Times* never missed an opportunity to lash a Treaty that 'provided every grievance the heart of a German nationalist could desire'.[20]

The sense that the Allies were to blame for the Nazis was critical to the mentality from which appeasement developed. If Britain and France had 'created' national socialism then, logically, they could 'appease' it by redressing the grievances on which it had prospered. As Eden told Parliament in March 1933, the Government's aim at the Disarmament Conference was to 'secure for Europe that period of appeasement which it needs'.[21] Since then, however, the Germans had walked out of the negotiations and British attempts to coax Hitler back were floundering. By April 1934, the French had run out of patience. In March, published figures showed that German military spending had risen by 356 million reichsmarks on the previous year's estimates, with air expenditure alone going up by 121 million. Hitler's words may be 'of peace', the French Foreign Minister, Louis Barthou, told the Nazi envoy, Joachim von Ribbentrop, 'but the actions are of war'.[22] The French, therefore, broke off disarmament negotiations, telling London that France's desire for peace could not come at the abdication of her own defence.

The French '*non*' was received with anger by the British, who came to believe that France had squandered a unique opportunity to bind the German leviathan. Yet while the French action effectively ended the chances of a multilateral agreement it opened the door for that curious phenomenon of the appeasement years: the amateur diplomats.

*

The initial prospects for friendship between Great Britain and Nazi Germany were not good. The British were shocked by the destruction of German democracy, alarmed by the revival of militarism and disgusted by the treatment of the Jews. The visit of the Nazi ideologist Dr Alfred Rosenberg to London in May 1933 had been a disaster. Rosenberg made a dreadful impression at the Foreign Office and caused public outcry when he laid a large swastika wreath at the Cenotaph. A retired Army officer threw the wreath in the Thames before giving himself up to an approaching police constable with the cheery salutation, 'I was just going to look for one of you chaps.'[23]

By 1934, however, it was clear that the Nazi revolution was entrenched and even those on the moderate left agreed that some effort should be made to build bridges with the regime. One maverick idea, floated by no less a person than the Prime Minister, was that Hitler should be invited to visit London. As Ramsay MacDonald emphasised to the German Ambassador, this was a purely personal idea, of which the Cabinet knew nothing, but 'he was sure that the Reich Chancellor would receive a most friendly reception in England from the people and the Government'. The German Foreign Minister, Konstantin von Neurath, rightly considered this notion 'absurd'.[24] Yet while the unpopularity of the Nazis restricted the Government from overt acts of courtship, there were no such restraints on individuals, a number of whom now set out on missions to improve Anglo-German relations.

The British amateur diplomats came from across the political spectrum and acted from a variety of motives. They were, however, united by a number of beliefs, the most important of which was that Nazism, whatever their personal view of it, should not preclude friendly relations between Britain and Germany. On the contrary, the majority saw Nazism as the natural, if violent, reaction to legitimate grievances stemming from Versailles. From both a moral and political point of view, it was, therefore, imperative that the Treaty should be altered and Germany allowed to regain that place and status to which her size and history entitled her.

Foremost among holders of this opinion was the Liberal politician the Marquess of Lothian. A Christian Scientist, with an ostentatious sense of morality, Lothian, then known as Philip Kerr, had worked in colonial administration in South Africa between 1905 and 1910, before going on to edit the imperial journal *Round Table*. His editorship exempted him from war service but in 1916 he became Private Secretary to Lloyd George, later accompanying him to Paris, where he had played a role in drafting the peace treaties. Distinguished-looking, if a little portly, his sense of mission could be irritating. Baldwin thought him a 'queer bird', even a 'rum cove'.[25] Yet as their mutual friend Thomas Jones explained, Lothian possessed both intelligence and ability. His fault was lack of judgement.

Like most Liberals, Lothian detested Nazism. He was, however, convinced that its 'brutal aspects' derived, in considerable measure, from Versailles and the failure of the Allies to alter it while they had the chance.[26] The first condition to reforming the regime, therefore, was that the Allies should 'be willing to do justice to Germany'.[27] This meant cancelling Part V of the Treaty of Versailles – thereby allowing Germany to rearm up to the level of her neighbours – and revising, or reversing, a number of the territorial clauses. As Vernon Bartlett wrote in *Nazi Germany Explained*, 'It is a paradox, but I believe it to be true, that Germany will be less of a danger to peace when her neighbours are less obviously stronger than she is.'[28]

In January 1935, Lothian travelled to Berlin, where he was scheduled to attend a meeting of the Rhodes Scholarship Committee, to test this theory on Hitler in person. The visit had been arranged by the wildly pro-German T. P. Conwell-Evans, a Welsh academic and friend of Ribbentrop, who had spent the last two years lecturing on Anglo-German diplomatic history at Königsberg University. Like Lothian, Conwell-Evans was convinced that Nazi Germany had a case and had taken it upon himself to act as a go-between for the regime and leading members of the British elite.

The Germans were excited by Lothian's visit. He was 'without doubt the most important non-official Englishman who has so far asked to be received by the Chancellor', communicated Ambassador Leopold von Hoesch, adding that Lothian was 'favourably inclined towards Germany and wishes to contribute to promoting better understanding between Germany and England'.[29] Lothian was accordingly granted an audience with Hitler, lasting over two hours, during which he was treated to a lecture on the dangers of Russia, the lack of French goodwill and the importance of Anglo-German friendship. Lothian was impressed by Hitler's sincerity. He considered the Führer 'a prophet' and eagerly sent a typescript of his conversations to Baldwin, Simon and MacDonald, with the covering comment that there was 'quite clearly a political foundation for a settlement which will keep the peace of Europe for ten years on the basis of equality if we take the opportunity'.[30] Two days later, in an article for *The Times*, he declared that the central fact in Europe today was 'that Germany does not want war and is prepared to renounce it absolutely as a method of settling her disputes with her neighbours, provided she is given real equality'.[31]

Lothian was not the only non-Tory to be gulled by Hitler. A few days before Lothian's meeting, Hitler had received the National Labour peer Lord Allen of Hurtwood. Clifford Allen was a political crusader who, as a conscientious objector, had been imprisoned three times during the First World War and in November 1914 had published a speech under the provocative title 'Is Germany Right and Britain Wrong?' He supported MacDonald over the formation of the National Government and in 1932 was rewarded with a peerage: 'Lord Conchie of Maidstone', suggested one wag.[32] Allen was horrified by the Nazis but he was equally opposed to the 'wicked' Treaty and the 'evil policies of France', which he believed were a danger to peace.[33] In late 1933, he helped establish the Anglo-German Group – a body chiefly comprising men from the centre-left – and, in January 1935, he travelled to Germany to meet leading figures in the regime.

The ever-alert German Foreign Ministry saw in Allen the potential to influence prominent National Labour figures, including the Prime Minister, and arranged an interview with Hitler – who was clearly on his best behaviour. 'What a contrast he is to the picture British people have formed of him', exclaimed Allen. There was no speech making, no sudden bursts of passion, no hint of the demagogue. Hitler was 'quiet, restrained, but nonetheless ruthless'. His fanaticism, Allen imagined, resembled that of Oliver Cromwell and he had no doubt that, like Old Ironsides, he was prepared to 'persecute for his religion, kill for it and die for it'.[34] Despite these insights, Allen accepted Hitler's claims of peaceful intent – evidenced by his recent non-aggression pact with Poland and his renunciation of the French province of Alsace-Lorraine – and left his audience confident in the belief that he had found a future partner for British diplomacy. 'I watched him with the utmost vigilance', he wrote in the *Daily Telegraph* on his return, 'and I am convinced he genuinely desires peace.'[35]

*

Lothian and Allen were men of the centre and centre-left who believed that it was both morally right and politically necessary to reach some form of agreement with Nazi Germany based on a revision of Versailles. This view, which had a considerable following among liberals, also made significant inroads into conservative thought. There it melded with that other great spur to Anglo-German friendship: a profound fear of communism.

Although the Communist Party of Great Britain had only 6,000 members in 1931, the spectre of communism loomed large in the mind of the British ruling class. The Russian Revolution of 1917 was a recent memory which had produced a horrifying impression, most vividly encapsulated by the murder of the Tsar and his family. This had been followed by a wave of communist and socialist uprisings which destroyed much of the old European order and, in 1927, led to the outbreak of civil war in China. In 1924, Joseph Stalin limited the aims of the Bolsheviks to 'Socialism in One Country' (i.e. the USSR) but the principle of 'world revolution' was considered by many as intrinsic to the movement and kept the fear of communist contagion alive. In 1919, riots on 'Red Clydeside' in Scotland caused the British Government to despatch 10,000 English soldiers to restore order (their Glaswegian comrades not being trusted to remain loyal). The General Strike of 1926 produced a similar scare, while in the meantime the British had witnessed and even participated in the bloody struggle between the Reds and the Whites in the former Russian Empire. These events and the ideology that inspired them – based on the abolition of private property and social hierarchy – conferred on communism the status of the Antichrist. The British upper classes, for obvious reasons, were at the forefront of this view but their fears readily seeped into the minds of their conservative-minded 'inferiors'. 'Can you do anything to destroy the evil of communism in this town?' asked one constituent of her Essex MP, in November 1932, after her local vicar had begun to preach Marxist ideas from the pulpit, while the under-butler at Cliveden – the Italianate mansion on the banks of the Thames belonging to Lord and Lady Astor – was wont to reply to his mistress's admonitions that he had failed, yet again, to provide rugs for the car with the rejoinder: 'Well, we shan't have any rugs at all when Moscow is in control.'[36]

Against the malevolent force of communism stood fascism. Fascism had 'saved' Italy from the Bolsheviks in 1922, while the more aggressive Teutonic strain was widely credited with the same feat in Germany. In both doctrines, though particularly the latter, there were aspects which the British elite found offensive. Yet when faced with the choice, in the 'Age of Extremes', fascism appeared the lesser evil and was, indeed, considered a barrier against the communist tide.[37] In this vein, Winston Churchill assured Mussolini in 1927 that, had he been an Italian, he would have supported him in his 'triumphant struggle against the bestial appetites and passions of Leninism'; the imperialist *Morning Post* gave thanks for those 'trim handsome black-shirted [Italian] lads'; while the Governor of the Bank of England, Montagu Norman, described Hitler and Hjalmar Schacht, the German Minister of Economics, as 'bulwarks of civilisation' engaged in a war for 'our system of society'.[38]

In the vanguard of the fight against communism stood the press baron Lord Rothermere. The joint creator of 'popular journalism', along with his brother Alfred (later Lord Northcliffe), Harold Harmsworth had founded the mass-market *Daily Mail* in 1896, before going on to launch the *Daily Mirror* in 1903 and acquire the *Glasgow Record and Mail* and *Sunday Pictorial*. By 1929, Harold – who had been created Viscount Rothermere in 1919 – owned fourteen newspapers and was one of the richest men in the country. The First World War had brought Rothermere into politics, when he served briefly as Britain's first Air Minister, yet it had also brought tragedy. Rothermere's second son, Vere, was killed at the Battle of Ancre in November 1916, followed by the death of his eldest son, Vyvyan, in February 1918. Remembering an occasion when the press baron had taken him into Vyvyan's bedroom while the young man was home on leave, Churchill attested that Rothermere was 'eaten up with love of this boy' and this double tragedy left an indelible mark.[39]

By the start of the 1930s Rothermere had established himself on the far right of conservative opinion. This wing, which comprised a number of prominent individuals, saw the British Empire in decline and democracy undermined by decadence and the Great Depression. In contrast, fascism in Italy and national socialism in Germany shone for having rejuvenated national pride and defeated communism. Eminent British Conservatives, including Sir Austen Chamberlain, issued paeans to Mussolini, while in April 1933 students at St Andrews

University endorsed the motion that 'This House approves of the Nazi Party, and congratulates it on its splendid work in the reformation of Germany'.[40]

Rothermere's anti-Red paranoia was extreme. On a personal level he transferred part of his wealth to Hungary as an insurance against a Bolshevik takeover of Britain, while politically he came out first in support of Mussolini, then Sir Oswald Mosley (leader of the British Union of Fascists) and finally Hitler. 'I urge all British young men and women to study closely the progress of the Nazi regime in Germany', he wrote in a *Daily Mail* editorial of July 1933. The press had greatly exaggerated the atrocities, which consisted of only a few isolated incidents, while ignoring the achievements of the Nazi revolution, which included an expansion of national spirit 'like that which took place in England under Queen Elizabeth'.[41] In November 1933, he was even more explicit, declaring that the 'sturdy young Nazis' were 'Europe's guardians against the communist danger'.[42]

Rothermere first visited Hitler in December 1934, accompanied by his only surviving son, Esmond, and the foreign correspondent of the *Daily Mail*, George Ward Price. The visit had been arranged by the mysterious Stephanie von Hohenlohe, an Austrian Princess by marriage who had wormed her way into both Hitler's inner circle and London society. The security services were convinced that she was a German spy and yet failed to warn Rothermere, who had already been converted to the cause of revising Hungary's post-war borders thanks to the Princess's influence.

Well aware of Rothermere's power to mould British public opinion, Hitler honoured him with the first dinner party he threw for a foreign visitor. Nazi bigwigs, including Göring, Goebbels and Ribbentrop, joined twenty-three other guests in the Reich Chancellery. A few evenings later, Rothermere returned the favour by hosting his own dinner at the Adlon Hotel. Hitler came, as did the Foreign Minister, Konstantin von Neurath, Göring (accompanied by the actress Emmy Sonnemann, soon to be the second Frau Göring), Joseph and Magda Goebbels, and Ribbentrop. Princess Stephanie acted as translator and Hitler orated on the benefits of Anglo-German friendship. Unfortunately for Rothermere, the evening ended in farce when someone accidentally knocked into a large vase, sending it crashing to the floor. SS men, fearing an assassination attempt, rushed into the room brandishing revolvers and Hitler was whisked away before the final course had been served.

Despite this debacle, Rothermere left Germany a confirmed friend of the regime. 'We have no ground to quarrel with these people', he assured the *Daily Mail*'s nearly two million readers on his return, while an Anglo-German alliance would prove one of the greatest boons to mankind.[43] Unlike other fellow travellers, however, he was under few illusions as to the direction of Nazi foreign policy. 'I do not trust Hitler as a statesman', he confided in a letter to Churchill in May 1935. 'I am quite sure that his group harbour the most ambitious designs. They have the full intention of making Germany *the* world Power.'[44] It was under the sway of this conviction that Rothermere had launched, through his newspapers, a frantic campaign for British rearmament. In November 1933, the *Daily Mail* had demanded 5,000 new warplanes, later increasing this to 'at least 20,000', in view of the expansion of the Luftwaffe.[45] The paradoxical nature of the press baron's position was not lost on contemporaries. Rothermere 'wants us to be very strongly armed and frightfully obsequious at the same time', noted Churchill in a letter to his wife, criticising the *Daily Mail* for its 'boosting of Hitler'. The best that could be said for this, he continued, was that it was a more practical attitude than that adopted by most Labour politicians: 'They wish us to remain disarmed and exceedingly abusive.'[46]

Rothermere, Allen and Lothian were not the only English politicians to be dazzled by their Nazi reception. In September 1933, the far-right Conservative MP Thomas Moore declared that 'peace and justice' were the watchwords of the Führer's policy, after a meeting with Hitler, while another Tory MP, Sir Arnold Wilson, claimed that the Nazi leader was 'at heart, like the best Socialists in all countries, profoundly Conservative in that he desires to conserve what is best'.[47]

Unsurprisingly, these amateur diplomats were an unwelcome complication to the life of Sir Eric Phipps, who struggled in vain to correct false impressions on both sides. Goebbels describes the Ambassador 'almost fainting' during a lunch hosted by Ribbentrop for Rothermere in which the latter attacked Versailles and the Propaganda Minister thanked him for advocating the return of Germany's lost colonies.[48] A spluttering Phipps interjected (in both English and

German) to say that His Majesty's Government had no such intention. But there were plenty of other occasions when English visitors were able to muddy the waters of official diplomacy unimpeded.[49] 'The fact is', the Ambassador complained following Lord Lothian's visit, 'British missionaries of peace of varying shades of political thought seem to come here in growing numbers, and, after conversations with various personages, return to England with some plan of their own whereby peace is to be ensured for a given number of years.'[50] Sir Robert Vansittart deeply sympathised and assured Phipps that he was doing all he could to 'prevent these foolish and offensive busybodies from having any credentials or encouragement'.[51] Yet in this, as in so much else, the Permanent Under-Secretary was fighting a losing battle.

The fact was that many British visitors found much to admire in the new Germany. During his 1933 tour, Sir Maurice Hankey had been struck by the disappearance of beggars and other 'down-and-outs', which were such a 'disagreeable' feature of many British streets.[52] More amazing still was the 'miracle' Hitler seemed to have performed in curing unemployment. Sir Arnold Wilson, who despaired of his own Government's indifference to the unemployed, applauded German 'interventionist' policies which had put so many people back to work and produced such energy and enthusiasm among the youth of the country. 'There are things in the new Germany which we should do well to study, adapt and adopt', he declared in a speech in Hamburg in May 1934.[53]

Almost all British visitors noted the zeal with which the partisans of the New Order tried to ingratiate themselves with English tourists. 'The "G.B." on my car was a talisman with officials, Nazi, and public alike', wrote Hankey. 'No-one knew who I was and yet everyone seemed anxious to help and to be friendly, almost to an embarrassing degree.'[54] The young Oxford historian Hugh Trevor-Roper was certainly embarrassed when, during a 1935 trip to Germany, he was accosted by a father and son on the banks of the Rhine who then proceeded to proselytise on the wonders of the new Germany and the Führer's sincere desire for friendship with England.[55] Trevor-Roper's travels turned him into an uncompromising opponent of the regime but there were plenty of others who, as Phipps complained to London, really did see a 'Wonderland' filled with 'smiling townships, well-dressed inhabitants, no sign of poverty or unemployment, hotels and beer gardens filled to capacity, money being spent as freely as at a Blackpool wake'.[56]

Phipps was not the only person to worry that the British were getting the wrong impression. In February 1935, no less a person than Mussolini confronted the British Ambassador to Rome over the gulf between the Nazi reality and British comprehension. 'Was it possible', the Duce asked, that there could ever exist a 'Legion of Death' in England such as that which 'now existed in Germany, which was devoted to killing people dangerous to the regime'?[57] Coming from the murderer of Matteotti* this was pretty rich, but the Italian dictator had a point. The evils of the regime were plain to see and yet many within the British elite chose to embrace Nazi Germany on account of its achievements and its opposition to communism. In so doing they were wont to indulge in moral relativism or make invidious parallels, such as Lloyd George's comment that Hitler had not shown half the ferocity towards the Jews as Cromwell had towards the Irish Catholics.[58]

To understand Hitler and his dark ideology, enquirers might have studied *Mein Kampf*. Yet in Britain, as in France, that declaration of intent was little read and even less understood. To begin with, the first English translation did not appear until 1933 and had been so heavily pruned of incriminating material that it was a third shorter than the original. Some enterprising individuals, such as the imperialist Tory MPs Brigadier Sir Henry Page Croft and the Duchess of Atholl, had it translated or read it in the original. Alarmed by what they found, they did their best to disseminate their discoveries among their colleagues. Another who read the full text was the former Colonial Secretary Leopold Amery, who took advantage of a wet Berlin afternoon, in May 1934, to purchase a copy and retreat to his hotel room. Amery found the book stimulating, yet he also realised that Hitler was 'quite insane about Jews and Socialists' and that his 'success all round may be a great danger'.[59] The historian and German expert John Wheeler-Bennett came to a similar view after he had read the book

* Giacomo Matteotti was an Italian Socialist politician who, on 30 May 1924, accused the Fascists of electoral fraud and denounced the violence they had used to gain votes during the recent election. Eleven days later he was kidnapped and murdered by the Fascists. Mussolini's precise involvement in the murder remains a matter of dispute but his moral responsibility is not in doubt.

and repudiated his earlier belief that Hitler was a moderate who only desired self-respect for his country. These, however, were the exceptions. Most people had not read the book and of those who did there were a considerable number who, like General Sir Ian Hamilton, were inclined to dismiss it as mere juvenilia.[60] When in September 1934 Prince Otto von Bismarck, the German Chargé d'Affaires in London and grandson of the Iron Chancellor, asked A. L. Kennedy, the pro-German diplomatic correspondent of *The Times*, what people in England really thought of the Germans, the journalist replied that most people would say that 'you were not quite civilized and not quite normal'. 'Not quite normal,' exclaimed the amused Prince, 'is that all!' Well, explained Kennedy, 'all that "Heil Hitler" struck us as quite eccentric'.[61]

Some things, however, went beyond eccentricity. On 30 June 1934, Hitler moved against the leadership of the SA, as well as a number of other rivals. During the 'Night of the Long Knives' (it actually lasted forty-eight hours), at least eighty-five people were murdered, including Hitler's former comrade the storm troop leader Ernst Röhm, the former Chancellor General Schleicher and his wife, and the leader of Catholic Action. The British were stunned. Shocked at the ruthlessness, there was also confusion over what had happened. A number of papers, most notably the *Daily Mail*, swallowed and even applauded Hitler's claim to have quashed a plot. Others interpreted it as a victory for the Army and a blow to Hitler's power. The Liberal *Manchester Guardian* was perturbed by the terrifying nature of events yet welcomed the fact that 'the criminal lunatics, or some of them, have been destroyed'. 'Germany may become an easier country for the Catholic or Protestant or Jew to breathe in', the paper speculated.[62]

For some, the thought of swastika-crazed thugs bumping each other off was cause for mirth. On the evening of 2 July 1934, the young Liberal MP Robert Bernays was at an 'ultra grand' dinner given by Lord and Lady Astor and attended by the American Ambassador, Lord Lothian and Anthony Eden. Events in Germany dominated the conversation and just before dinner, Lady Astor took Bernays off to hear the latest news from the wireless. When they returned to the party, the young MP reported that Röhm had been executed after declining to commit suicide. Guffaws of laughter rang around the dining room, as Bernays read Goebbels' statement saying that events had 'passed off without a hitch'. 'Well, that was a hitch,' came the cry, 'he refused to commit suicide!' The young Tory MP Harold Macmillan joked that it was like the Chief Whip telling MPs that, instead of topping himself, the Prime Minister had decided to take a holiday to New Zealand. 'How callous this generation is getting about human life', thought Bernays. 'There was no other expression but delight that Röhm was dead.'[63] As the idea of a plot against the Führer crumbled, however, reaction became increasingly disgusted. The *Daily Telegraph* spoke of 'Frightfulness in Germany' and accused Hitler of following the 'manual of ruthless and Oriental dictatorship'.[64] The Chancellor of the Exchequer, Neville Chamberlain, correctly thought the purge would 'increase dislike of dictatorships' and it was from this point that comparisons between the Nazis and American gangsters became common.[65]

A few weeks later another shock was administered when, on 25 July 1934, Austrian Nazis assassinated the Austrian Chancellor, Engelbert Dollfuss, at the start of an attempted coup. Hitler, who had spent the evening attending a performance of *Das Rheingold* at Bayreuth, tried to retain deniability by going out to dinner with the Wagners. But when German-sponsored terrorism and propaganda had been so overt it was impossible to stop the blood from spattering the regime. 'What an ominous tragedy', wrote Neville Chamberlain to his sister, 'with Austria once again at the centre of the picture, with another murder almost on the anniversary of that of the Archduke [Franz Ferdinand] and with Germany once more behind instigating, suggesting, encouraging bloodshed and assassination for her own selfish aggrandisement and pride.' Although the Austrian Chancellor was an authoritarian and dictator – the founder of 'Austrofascism' – Chamberlain had admired 'poor little Dollfuss' and felt his death keenly. 'That those beasts should have got him at last and that they should have treated him with such callous brutality makes me hate Nazi-ism and all its works with a greater loathing than ever.'*[66]

Equally upset, though more for strategic than personal reasons, was Mussolini. The independence of Austria was a major Italian interest and the Duce moved troops to the Brenner Pass as a warning to Germany that Italy was not going to stand by and allow the union

* Having been shot in the throat, Dollfuss was denied medical treatment and slowly bled to death.

of Germany with Austria, the so-called *Anschluss*. This had a lasting effect on Chamberlain, who would continue to view Mussolini as a check on Hitler right up to the outbreak of war.

Negative impressions also came from a number of visitors who returned from Nazi Germany less than enamoured with the regime. Lord Astor came away from a September 1933 visit 'more conscious of the terror in Germany than I was two years ago in Russia'.[67] People he met begged him not to quote them in England as reports had a way of 'getting back' and 'they know that the concentration camps are very real and the rulers ruthless'. Astor had met Hitler and told him that there was no chance of friendship between Britain and Germany so long as the latter continued to persecute the Jews. For others the plight of the Jews mattered less than Hitler's attacks on the churches. When Lord Beaverbrook met Prince Louis Ferdinand, the Kaiser's grandson, in July 1933, he explained that despite being naturally 'pro-German', he disliked Hitler since he was 'a persecutor'. The Prince, no standard bearer for Nazism, replied nervously that he thought there had been 'some exaggeration about the Jewish affair'. 'To hell with the Jews!' barked Beaverbrook. 'He's persecuting the Lutheran Church.'[68]

As this anecdote suggests, the British attitude towards the Jews was complicated. On the one hand there was a strain of anti-Semitism among the British. Jews were the butt of frequent jokes, prey to stereotypes, and generally disparaged. John Maynard Keynes defined an anti-Semite as someone who disliked Jews 'unreasonably', while even someone as eminent as the Secretary of State for Transport, Leslie Hore-Belisha, suffered on account of 'his face, his manner, and his name'.[69] 'Sapper's' Bulldog Drummond stories are filled with anti-Semitic descriptions, while a number of John Buchan's hugely popular Richard Hannay novels play on the fantasy of an international Jewish conspiracy. This idea was given its greatest boost by the fraudulent *Protocols of the Elders of Zion*,* published in English

* *The Protocols* were supposed to reveal instructions from the 'Elders' – a secret committee first appointed by King Solomon – to the Jewish people for a revolution which would destroy Christian civilisation before creating a new world-state to be run by Jews and Freemasons. They were exposed as a forgery in 1921, but many chose to interpret the Russian Revolution along these lines and conspiracy theories continued to circulate well into the Thirties.

in 1920. *The Times* exposed *The Protocols* as a forgery but this did not stop the proliferation of conspiracy theories which, paradoxically, accused the Jews of seeking power through both international finance and communism.

Against this stands the fact that Hore-Belisha had reached the Cabinet (he would be promoted to Secretary of State for War in 1937), while Sir Philip Sassoon, the Jewish Under-Secretary of State for Air, was one of the most popular figures in Conservative social circles. There were, of course, some serious British anti-Semites who naturally gravitated towards the British Union of Fascists and other racist organisations, but these were a small minority. The fact was that British anti-Semitism, though shocking and offensive today, was broadly social and snobbish, rather than racial and extremist – a clear contrast with Nazism.

The difference is exemplified by that paragon of Englishness Sir Horace Rumbold. When Rumbold arrived in Berlin in 1928 he was shocked 'by the number of Jews in this place' and joked, in a letter to the then Permanent Under-Secretary, that he was thinking of having a ham-bone amulet made 'to keep off the evil nose'.[70] Yet Rumbold was appalled by the Nazi persecution and reported on the dismissals, crimes and atrocities in great detail. Even Lord Londonderry, who admitted to having 'no great affection for the Jews' and was to become one of the leading apologists for the Nazi regime, was baffled by the German obsession. 'The continued effort to exterminate the Jews', he wrote to General Sir Ian Hamilton in August 1938 – four years before the Wannsee Conference at which the 'Final Solution' was agreed – 'is the part of their policy which I cannot understand and this is turning world opinion against them with all its dangerous repercussions ... I have spoken with Göring about it [and] with Ribbentrop and Himmler and their replies are not convincing at all.'[71]

One man who attempted to understand the Nazi persecution first-hand was Robert Bernays who, as special correspondent for the Liberal *News Chronicle*, in addition to being MP for Bristol North, made several trips to Germany in 1933 and 1934. Bernays, whose paternal grandfather was Jewish (his father was a Church of England clergyman), tried to shield his reports from charges of distortion by attempting to see things from the Nazi perspective. In *Special Correspondent*, the book he published in 1934, he therefore conceded that there 'is something in the contention that the German Jews have made little attempt to understand the German national psychology' and that it was 'unfortunate that, since the war, the best seats at the theatre, the most expensive restaurants, the most luxurious cars, have been in the possession of the Jews'.[72] He was, nevertheless, horrified by the climate of fear he found. 'I cannot get out of my mind, even now,' he wrote, 'the expression of terror on the faces of so many with whom we talked.' Whole Jewish families had been thrown out of employment, random beatings – though less common than in the early days of the Nazi revolution – still occurred and there were tales of multiple suicides. The Nazi treatment of the Jews was 'inhuman', their plight 'impossible to get away from'. 'I cannot exaggerate my horror', wrote the MP, 'and detestation of what has occurred.'[73]

At the start of his visit, Bernays had done his best to get an interview with Hitler. Accordingly, he went to see Ernst 'Putzi' Hanfstaengl, the head of the Foreign Press Bureau, who was said to send the Führer to sleep with his piano playing.[74] After a rather violent argument about the treatment of the Jews, in which Hanfstaengl claimed that British law, finance, politics and the press were all under Jewish control, Bernays asked if he might see Hitler. 'Why, of course,' replied the press agent with enthusiasm. 'But let me tell him something about you.' 'I am a Nationalist MP', explained Bernays, carefully omitting the prefix 'Liberal'. 'Who is your leader?' enquired Hanfstaengl. For a moment Bernays thought of saying 'Lloyd George' but truth overcame journalistic ambition and he replied, 'Sir Herbert Samuel.' That finished it. When one of Bernays's friends chased up the interview a few days later the Bureau chief spat, 'Do you think that I am going to get an interview for a sow of a Jew?'[75]

Despite such treatment, Bernays thought it 'a real tragedy that there is so little contact between the Nazis and the British'.[76] Lord Lothian agreed and on his return from Germany, in February 1935, urged the Foreign Secretary, Sir John Simon, to visit Hitler himself. In many ways, the timing was propitious. In January, the inhabitants of the Saar region – an Anglo-French-administered protectorate since the end of the war – voted by a margin of just under 91 per cent to rejoin Germany. The result was not surprising and the British hoped that it might herald a new era of co-operation between Germany and the former Allies. As if proof of this, Hitler announced that he had 'no further territorial demands to make of France' and told the *Daily Mail*'s sympathetic foreign correspondent, George Ward Price, that 'Germany will of its own accord never break the peace'.[77]

Complementing this new wind from Berlin were changes in Paris. On 9 October 1934, the formidable French Foreign Minister, Louis Barthou – an indefatigable upholder of treaties and architect of the developing Franco-Soviet alliance – bled to death, having been caught up in the assassination of King Alexander I of Yugoslavia by Bulgarian and Croatian separatists. Barthou was replaced by Pierre Laval, the highly ambitious and intelligent former Prime Minister, whose trademark white ties could not dispel a well-deserved reputation for deviousness. Laval favoured rapprochement with Germany and was more than willing to co-operate with the British in search of a settlement.

In February 1935, French and British Ministers met in London and decided that the defunct armaments clauses of the Treaty of Versailles should be abolished. They would be replaced by a new agreement on arms – in particular an air pact – as well as an 'Eastern Locarno', in which Germany would 'accept' her eastern frontiers. In return, Hitler would be asked to join a multilateral pledge to uphold Austrian independence and to return Germany to the League of Nations. Sir Eric Phipps, who had been instructed to keep the Führer abreast of the discussions, was not optimistic. The Saar plebiscite, he told his political masters, had strengthened Hitler's hand and the Führer had already stated his refusal to join either an Austrian guarantee or an eastern pact. Furthermore, the Ambassador sensed that Hitler was already eyeing his next target. After the presentation of the Anglo-French communiqué on 3 February, Hitler had brought up the subject of the demilitarised Rhineland. His tone became 'threatening' and, as Phipps reported to London, it seemed clear that 'German acquiescence in existence of that zone would only last as long as the German army was in the process of expansion and not a day longer'. All in all, Hitler's attitude 'resembled rather that of a victor than of a defeated party'.[78]

Yet there was nothing to be gained by rejecting the Anglo-French proposals out of hand. Hitler, therefore, said that he would welcome talks and invited the British, though not the French, to visit Berlin. As both the British and French realised, this was a crude attempt to drive a wedge between them. To the latter's pique, however, the

British decided to accept the invitation. Determined that an opportunity should not be lost – as it was believed the French had done the year before – it was agreed that Simon and Anthony Eden should travel to Berlin and that Eden would then continue to Moscow, Warsaw and Prague.

The idea of a visit to Moscow, which had been concocted between Sir Robert Vansittart and the wily Soviet Ambassador, Ivan Maisky, was no less controversial than the visit to Berlin. No government minister had visited Russia since the Revolution and the Soviet Union was regarded by many with even greater distaste than Nazi Germany. Nevertheless, there were those, even on the right, who were prepared to come to terms with the USSR in light of the German menace. 'I hate Eden's visit to Russia, but the great importance of keeping Russia and Germany apart at this juncture does, I conceive, justify an otherwise extremely doubtful step', wrote the die-hard imperialist Lord Lloyd.[79] Indeed, the alarming possibility of a détente between Germany and the Soviet Union was raised by the Foreign Office at the very time the Russian invitation was received.[80]

Juggling these multiple invitations was a nightmare. Apart from the excluded French, the Germans were concerned that a visit to Moscow would reduce the lustre of their own talks, while the Russians were no less anxious not to be snubbed. The whole business was made inordinately more complicated by the incessant dithering of the Foreign Secretary.

Sir John Simon was a tall, slim, upright lawyer who, according to one journalist, looked 'dangerously like his own butler'.[81] As this snobbish comment suggests, he was from a relatively humble background (his father was a Congregational minister) and had managed to get where he had owing to his exceptional brain. Scholarships to Fettes and Wadham were followed by the Presidency of the Oxford Union, a First in Classics and a fellowship at All Souls. To these prizes he was to add the offices of Foreign Secretary, Home Secretary and Chancellor of the Exchequer – making him one of only three twentieth-century politicians to hold all three of the great offices of state, outside the Premiership.* He longed for the top job but, being both nominally a Liberal and personally unpopular, this ultimate prize was denied him.

* The others were Rab Butler and James Callaghan.

Variously described as 'cold-blooded', 'unimaginative' and 'supercilious', his efforts at courting popularity – such as asking Cabinet colleagues to call him 'Jack' and buying backbenchers champagne for breakfast – fell flat.[82] A telling anecdote from the 1940s has the socialist intellectual G. D. H. Cole trying to escape the then Lord Chancellor by retreating to the third-class carriage of a train from Oxford. To Cole's horror Simon followed, only for both men to produce first-class tickets for the inspector.[83]

At the Foreign Office he was not only unpopular but the despair of both colleagues and observers. The *Times* journalist Colin Coote believed the only foreigners he understood were the ancient Greeks, while almost everyone who knew him commented on his chronic inability to make up his mind.[84] The Foreign Secretary had 'sat on the fence so long', quipped Lloyd George, 'that the iron had entered into his soul'.[85] But it was no laughing matter. The speech he made to the League of Nations Assembly in December 1932, in which he failed to deliver an unequivocal denunciation of Japan's conduct in Manchuria, became notorious, while, more generally, he could never decide whether to reproach or cajole Germany over her illegal rearmament.

Simon's indecision over the various foreign visits was finally resolved when Ramsay MacDonald and Stanley Baldwin stepped in and ruled that both Simon and Eden should go to Berlin but only Eden would travel on to Russia, Poland and Czechoslovakia. This compromise succeeded in annoying the Germans and insulting the Russians but, other than by going nowhere at all, it is hard to see how both regimes could have been kept happy. The visit to Germany was thus fixed for 7 March 1935, but before the Foreign Secretary and the Lord Privy Seal could board their aeroplane a new diplomatic storm broke.

On 4 March, the Government published a long-planned White Paper which announced a spending increase of £10 million to meet 'serious deficiencies' in Britain's defences. This was no great sum and, as Simon noted in his diary, 'we are not increasing armaments at all (except in the air) but are repairing what is outworn'.[86] Yet even this produced the familiar outcry from the Opposition, with Clement Attlee arguing that the Government was fostering an arms race which would 'ultimately lead to war'.[87] This, in turn, provoked a furious denunciation from Sir Austen Chamberlain, who asked the Labour spokesman if he would dare hold such talk if he were in Government and London was being bombed. 'If he does,' the former Tory leader continued, 'he will be one of the first victims of the war, for he will be strung up by an angry, and a justifiably angry, populace to the nearest lamp-post.'[88]

But it was in Germany that the backlash was strongest. To justify the new defence estimates, the White Paper explicitly pointed to German rearmament and the cultivation of a war spirit among the youth of that country as the primary dangers to European peace. At Goebbels' command, the German press exploded with indignation and Hitler developed a diplomatic 'cold', thereby postponing Simon's visit. A few days later, Göring officially informed the foreign air attachés of the existence of the Luftwaffe. This was not news but it was the first time the Germans had admitted to breaking the Treaty of Versailles and indicative of their growing confidence.

Then, on 16 March, one day after French deputies approved the re-establishment of two-year military service – the necessary offset for the 'lean years' – Hitler detonated his own bombshell. Summoning first the French and then the British Ambassadors to the Reich Chancellery, he informed them that he was reintroducing conscription and creating a peacetime army of thirty-six divisions – some 500,000 men. This brazen repudiation of Versailles and restoration of German military pride produced a wave of euphoria in Germany which contrasted with consternation across the rest of the Continent as well as in Washington. The French were particularly alarmed and drew attention to the 'paean of joy with which the announcement was greeted by the German public'.[89] The Italians were no less concerned and joined the French in demanding urgent consultations between the British, French and Italian Governments. Above all, as the British Embassy in Paris reported, the French no longer believed that Hitler had any desire to conclude an arms convention and regarded any effort to reach a settlement along the German terms as 'equivalent to payment of blackmail and as calculated to incite her to fresh excesses among first of which would be violation … of clauses relating to the demilitarized [Rhine] zone'.[90]

The French and Italians were therefore furious when the British, without consulting either Paris or Rome, delivered a solitary protest to the German Foreign Ministry, entirely undermined by the final sentences, which meekly enquired if the Foreign Secretary's visit could still proceed. The Germans were astonished. 'We never expected that the English would, after this indignant protest, politely ask in the same breath whether they could come to Berlin', wrote the Foreign Ministry translator Paul Schmidt.[91] The German press was cock-a-hoop and talked gloatingly of having successfully split the British from the French. The French newspapers bitterly agreed, accusing the British of breaking the united front and of condoning the German action. 'There is no doubt', wrote Lord Cranborne a few days later from Berlin, 'that the French and Italians were very very angry with us for what they regarded as our treachery.'[92] Yet the majority of opinion in Britain remained in favour of negotiation. That model of mainstream Conservatism, Cuthbert Headlam, could see 'no earthly use' in giving up the trip simply because the Germans had 'come out into the open', and even sceptics, like Sir Horace Rumbold, thought there could be benefits in Simon, 'a congenital pacifist', seeing Hitler with his own eyes and being 'brought to a sense of realities'.[93]

Initially, it seemed that this might be the outcome. Startled by a fusillade of sharp-worded barks of command and an SS officer wielding a sword, as he descended from his aircraft, the civilian-minded Foreign Secretary arrived at the British Embassy muttering about 'the bottomless pit of hell' that 'had opened before him'.[94] This was not the impression the Germans wished to convey. As Cranborne recorded, the welcome for the British party was embarrassingly over the top, with a crowd of thousands lining the street 'as for an Emperor'.[95] 'It seems that the Govt have quite made up their mind that we could be detached from France', wrote the Foreign Office Minister, before going on to blame both Ribbentrop and Lothian for this misapprehension.

The next day, Hitler welcomed Simon, Eden and Phipps with effusion. Well he might, thought Paul Schmidt, the Führer's newly appointed interpreter, 'the presence of the English guests was a triumph for him'. Hitler launched into a long monologue about his messianic purpose, to which Simon listened with 'paternal benevolence'.[96] It was his life's work to revive the German people but his English guests must understand that 'National Socialism had no expansive character'.[97] Germany had been accused of violating the

Treaty of Versailles yet this was a document that he, Hitler, would have rather died than sign. Nor was it the first time that Germany had had to break an agreement. In 1806 Napoleon had imposed a treaty on Prussia but he did not think the Duke of Wellington had complained when Marshal Blücher had ridden to his aid at Waterloo. Eden thought this 'a good thrust' and the 'nearest to humour Hitler ever approached' during the meeting. But it was delivered 'without a flicker of a smile'.[98]

Simon pressed Hitler to accept an eastern pact which would guarantee Europe's eastern borders but Hitler was intractable. He disliked multilateral agreements and flew into a rage at the suggestion that Lithuania, which he said was abusing the German minority in Memel, could participate in any such treaty. Besides, the great threat to European peace was Communist Russia. At this, Eden, whose quizzical expression betrayed his scepticism, challenged Hitler. 'Russia was not able, nor did she wish, to wage a war', posited the Lord Privy Seal. Hitler begged Eden not to underestimate the threat from the Soviet Union, already the strongest power on land as well as in the air. He did, however, assure his guests that he would never contemplate war against either Russia or Czechoslovakia.

In the afternoon, Hitler disclaimed any intention of violating Austrian independence, before linking the restitution of Germany as a major power, including the return of her colonies, with Britain's own place in the world. Germany desired an agreement with both France and Britain, the Chancellor explained, but while an understanding with the former was riddled with complexities, an understanding with the latter could be mutually beneficial. It was a fact, Hitler continued, that Great Britain could not defend all of her colonial possessions and so it might be that the British Empire would 'one day be glad to have Germany's help and Germany's forces at her disposal'. If, therefore, the two Governments could find a solution which would give 'satisfaction to Germany's most urgent and primitive demands' then it would be easy to bring Germany back into full 'co-operation and friendly relations with Great Britain'. Simon reacted coolly. Britain was desirous of good relations with Germany but these could not come at the expense of her relations with France. The British did not wish to substitute one friend for another but 'to be loyal friends to all', explained the Foreign Secretary.[99]

'Results bad', wrote a despondent Eden in his diary that evening. The whole temper of discussions was very different from the previous year and 'the old Prussian spirit' was very much in evidence.[100] Despite this, the Nazis were eager to please and had organised a lavish banquet in a magnificent rococo room, with damask walls and hordes of flunkeys in splendid liveries and powdered hair. The entire hierarchy of the Third Reich was in attendance. Göring made a particularly striking spectacle in a sky-blue uniform with masses of gold braid. To Cranborne he seemed jovial but also ruthless – 'a real gangster type'. By sartorial contrast, Hitler arrived wearing 'rather a badly cut evening suit', which gave Cranborne the impression of a 'comic waiter on the films'. Cranborne, whose grandfather, Lord Salisbury, had been Prime Minister at the end of Queen Victoria's reign, sat next to the wife of the Mayor of Berlin, who shocked him by asking if he had come 'to bring us war'. Cranborne strongly denied this, only for the lady to declare, unprompted, that there was no contradiction between the Germans' desire for a large army and their naturally pacific character. 'Soldiering was their national sport', she explained, to which Cranborne retorted that it was not Britain's.[101]

In the centre of the table, Eden and Hitler were getting on rather better. Hitler had picked up on a remark by the younger man about the last German offensive of the First World War and the two men were once again discussing the positions of the opposing forces. By an amazing coincidence it transpired that Hitler and Eden had been entrenched almost opposite one another at the time, near La Fère on the River Oise. Together they drew a map of the front line on the back of a menu which they then both signed. After dinner, the French Ambassador hurried over to the Lord Privy Seal to ask if it was true that he had been opposite Hitler in March 1918. Eden replied that it appeared so. 'And you missed him?' exclaimed the Frenchman. 'You ought to be shot!'[102]

The next day's talks were no more fruitful than the first's. Eden and Hitler wrangled over the expansion of the German Army, including the Führer's extraordinary claim that Britain, unlike Germany, had her own paramilitary organisations which trained youths with rifles, vide Eton. Eden laughed at this absurd comparison and explained that the Officer Training Corps, far from being a rigorous military incubator, was more an occasion for boys to smoke on field days. Nor did things improve when discussion moved on to the subject of air forces. Hitler said that he was in favour of a prohibition on indiscriminate bombing but insisted on attaining air parity with France or Britain, whichever was the greater. At this, Simon casually enquired how large the German Air Force was at present. Hitler paused before replying, solemnly and untruthfully, that Germany had already reached parity with Great Britain.

This put the gilt on the German gingerbread. While conceding nothing, Hitler had gained de facto sanction for his wholesale repudiation of Versailles and was now taunting the British over their impotence. Eden and Cranborne were thoroughly depressed. 'I am afraid that there is no doubt that the German Govt is pursuing a policy which they know very well may lead to war, and that they would not shrink from it', wrote Cranborne to his Conservative colleague Billy Ormsby-Gore. 'The Saar has gone completely to their head – they think that they are the greatest nation in the world, and their idea of equality is rapidly becoming undistinguishable from world domination ... Blast them!'[103] Writing in his diary of the trip, the Foreign Office Minister acknowledged that 'sooner or later' it would be necessary to 'call a halt' to Germany's activities and that this would have to be done through the threat of force. 'The idea of Philip Lothian and *The Times* that by beaming seductively on the present German Government we shall persuade them to moderate their attitude is to my mind pure bunkum.'[104]

Eden was of the same view. On board the train from Berlin to Moscow the next day, he wrote a report of the British visit in which he expressed grave doubts as to whether Germany would ever be prepared to come to an agreement unless her colonies were returned and a host of other demands also met. In such circumstances, he argued, there was only one option: to rally and reaffirm the purpose of the League of Nations in order to provide a united front against future German provocation. Ostensibly, Simon agreed. Organising his thoughts in a note shortly after his return from Berlin, the Foreign Secretary stated, 'If Germany will not co-operate for confirming the solidarity of Europe, the rest of Europe will co-operate to preserve it in spite of Germany.' This might lead, he continued, to the 'curious spectacle of British Tories collaborating with Russian communists, while the League of Nations Union thunders applause'.[105]

Yet Simon had not entirely lost hope of rapprochement. While in Berlin he had toyed with the idea of letting Hitler expand eastwards, only for Eden to stamp on this, pointing out that, apart from the innate dishonesty of the proposal, 'it would be our turn next'.[106] Nevertheless, the Foreign Secretary was prepared to seize on Hitler's suggestion for an Anglo-German naval agreement. In June 1935, therefore, the increasingly prominent Ribbentrop, now Hitler's Ambassador at Large, arrived in London for talks and, despite acting like a 'bull in a china shop', found the British prepared to accept Hitler's demand for a fleet 35 per cent the size of the Royal Navy.[107]

To understand this astonishing step, it is necessary to remember the wider context of British defence policy. As has already been noted, the British Empire faced a plethora of defensive challenges in the mid-1930s, not all of which could be met. In December 1934, the Japanese had given notice that they would not be renewing the Washington Naval Treaty, which gave Britain and the United States each a 5:3 ratio of naval superiority over Japan. This betokened a naval race with Japan, which Britain had already decided it could not afford. To face a German challenge at the same time was unthinkable. Haunted by the memory of Admiral Tirpitz's attempt to outbuild the Royal Navy in the lead up to the First World War and aware of Admiral Raeder's ambitions for a new German Battle Fleet, the Admiralty advised the Cabinet to grab Hitler's offer with both hands. France's refusal to negotiate the previous year had only increased German demands and the British were not going to repeat the same mistake. Limiting German capacity to 35 per cent of the Royal Navy was compatible with Admiral Chatfield's plans for a new two-power standard and the Admiralty correctly estimated that the Germans would not reach that limit until 1942. Yet if the military arguments were sound, diplomatically the Anglo-German Agreement was a disaster.

Only two months earlier, between 11 and 14 April 1935, the British and French Prime Ministers had met Mussolini near the northern Italian town of Stresa to try and form a united front against German aggrandisement. The French had wanted a League of Nations resolution promising to respond to future treaty violations with sanctions but this had been vetoed by the British.* Nevertheless, the conference ended with a semblance of unity and resolution. The delegates reaffirmed their commitment to Locarno – which included the maintenance of the demilitarised Rhineland – and declared their determination to oppose, 'by all practicable means, any unilateral repudiation of treaties which may endanger the peace of Europe, and [to] act in close and cordial collaboration for this purpose'.[108] The French and Italians were, therefore, justifiably furious when the British themselves unilaterally repudiated Versailles by signing the Anglo-German Naval Treaty ten weeks later on 18 June. The so-called Stresa Front was exposed as a sham and Hitler's momentary bout of nerves at the thought of three major European powers combining against him was allayed. In the Commons, Churchill attacked the agreement, which 'nullified and stultified' the League of Nations' condemnation of treaty breaking, while also drawing attention to the threat from German U-boats, formally proscribed but now permitted.[109] Even more calamitous was the effect the successful negotiations were to have on the career of Ribbentrop, who, by providing Hitler with 'the happiest day of his life', was launched on a trajectory which was to see him become Ambassador to London and later Foreign Minister.[110]

But this was an unpredictable consequence. What was predictable was the fallout which would occur between the erstwhile Stresa partners. Though outwardly calm, Laval, who had become Prime Minister of France on 7 June while remaining Foreign Minister, was incandescent at the British betrayal.[111] French security had been sacrificed on the altar of British self-interest and the master of realpolitik had been outplayed at his own game. Anglo-French *solidarité* existed only when it was expedient and the French Premier took note. In Rome, Mussolini, similarly annoyed, drew two important conclusions: Britain was no friend of collective security and would bend when confronted by strength. The stage was set for the Duce's own adventure in East Africa.

---

* The incompetence of the British delegation amazed Lord Cranborne, who was attending in Eden's absence. On the first day he, MacDonald, Simon and Vansittart met, only for the two junior members of the team to discover that 'neither the P.M. nor the Secretary of State seemed to have the smallest idea what our policy should be'. (Salisbury Papers, Cranborne to Eden, April 1935, box 62.)

IV
The Abyssinian Imbroglio

The time is over when Mussolini's ambition can be satisfied by a few palm trees in Libya.

Senator Henry de Jouvenel, 3 March 1933[1]

The haze had lifted and the sun was dancing on the water as a fitful breeze ruffled the vast panoply of flags. Flashes of light bouncing off brass and portholes were answered by the winks of the telescopes and binoculars belonging to some of the 250,000 spectators who lined the twelve-mile Portsmouth waterfront. From eight o'clock that morning an armada of steamers, paddle-boats, yachts, launches and tugs had been ferrying patriotic punters to the great men-o'-war. Gaily dressed ladies with parasols were greeted by officers in cocked hats while gentlemen, watching from the shore, tried to identify the various vessels from the programme. Just after two o'clock, the Royal Yacht, with its stately black hull, cream-coloured funnels and gold-leaf scroll, emerged from harbour, followed by the Admiralty Yacht, *Enchantress*. A twenty-one-gun salute wreathed the Fleet in thick smoke and the massed bands crashed into the national anthem. One hundred and fifty-seven warships, the bulk of the Mediterranean and Home Fleets, lay ready for His Majesty's inspection. There were eight battleships – including HMS *Nelson*, *Rodney* and *Queen Elizabeth* – cruisers, destroyers, minelayers, two aircraft carriers and a hospital ship. As the Royal Yacht glided down each of the seven rows, there was a flurry of caps and succession of hearty cheers. The King, standing on the bridge, in the full uniform of an Admiral of the Fleet, acknowledged each of his ships with a salute. It was a stunning spectacle.

The Fleet Review of 16 July 1935, to mark George V's Silver Jubilee, was one of the last great sights of Empire. The *Daily Telegraph* called it 'a Royal pageant of surpassing grandeur', while *The Times* rhapsodised on a Navy which had 'charted the seas of the world, rid them of pirates, established trade routes for all lands, and preserved Britain from invasion for eight hundred years'.[2] As both papers conceded, however, the Fleet was not as impressive as at first it might seem. As Hector C. Bywater, the *Telegraph*'s appropriately named naval correspondent noted, the Fleet was 'sadly deficient in the heavier elements of fighting power typified by big guns and armour' and, furthermore, 'contains an unduly large proportion of antique material which is no longer really effective'. The Conservative MP Cuthbert Headlam, a guest on one of the warships, noticed that the majority of the ships pre-dated the last war, while Robert Bernays thought that he had witnessed the 'ghost of the Grand Fleet'.[3] He was not wrong. In 1910, Britain had thirty-six battleships and twenty-three armoured cruisers. Now, thanks to the Washington Naval Treaty, she possessed only fifteen capital ships, almost all of which were in serious need of modernisation. The Royal Navy was thus ill equipped to take part in any major action and yet, in the summer of 1935, this was exactly what Mussolini was threatening.

*

The Italian–Abyssinian dispute dated back to 1896, when the Abyssinians – or Ethiopians as they were less frequently called – routed an Italian army at the Battle of Adowa. Italian nationalists longed for revenge and, to fulfil his imperial pretensions, Mussolini determined to conquer the East African country. A border dispute at Wal-Wal in December 1934 provided the pretext and soon large quantities of Italian troops were being shipped through the Suez Canal to Eritrea and Italian Somaliland. None of this went unnoticed and, by the spring of 1935, the British Minister in Addis Ababa was forecasting that war would break out 'quite definitely' once the rains had ended in October.[4] Despite this, neither Ramsay MacDonald nor Sir John Simon warned Mussolini that Britain might object to his plans when they met at Stresa in April. Indeed, with full cognisance of its implications, they allowed the Duce to insert the phrase 'in Europe' into the communiqué pledging the three countries to the maintenance of international peace.[5] Germany was their principal concern and Italy was a valuable ally against German expansion. By simply ignoring Mussolini's African ambitions, however, the British Ministers were courting a diplomatic and political fiasco.

A few decades earlier and the Italian conquest of Abyssinia would not have caused an international crisis. Italy had already successfully penetrated the country economically and was in possession of three other North and East African colonies – Libya, Eritrea and Italian Somaliland – two of which shared borders with Abyssinia. Out of the ashes of the First World War, however, rose a new set of international principles, enshrined by the League of Nations. The days of brazen imperialism and gunboat diplomacy were meant to be over and the age of international law had supposedly dawned. The Covenant of the League was revered as the guarantor of peace and from this the League developed, in some quarters, an almost religious significance. That this was so demonstrably the case in Britain was in large part thanks to the evangelism of Lord Robert Cecil and the influential League of Nations Union.

The third son of the Victorian Prime Minister Lord Salisbury, 'Bob' Cecil had been a crusader ever since he had tried to stop the older boys from overworking their fags at Eton. A devout High Anglican, he had little interest in worldly comforts. 'If you cannot dress like a gentleman, I think you ought at least to try and dress like a Conservative', the future Archbishop of Canterbury, Cosmo Lang, had remonstrated with him when they had both been undergraduates at Oxford.[6] During the First World War, Cecil had served in the Cabinet as Minister for Blockade and it was here that he adopted his greatest cause: a League of Nations which would consult together to resolve international disputes. In 1918, the League of Nations Union (LNU) was founded and was soon transformed, thanks in large part to Cecil, into a potent political pressure group. In October 1934, the LNU began by far its most ambitious project. Convinced that public opinion was firmly behind the League and as a counter to isolationism, Cecil decided to conduct a national survey of public opinion. Half a million volunteers, many of them women, set out on a mass canvass and returned with 11.6 million responses – 38 per cent of the adult population.

The questions were not subtle. 'Are you in favour of an all-round abolition of national military and naval aircraft by international agreement?' (*Yes*, 9,600,274; *No*, 1,699,989.) Nor was the execution impartial. Nevertheless, the results showed an overwhelming support for the League and for collective security. Nearly 96 per cent of respondents supported Britain's membership of the League, while over ten million Britons (86.6 per cent) were in favour of economic sanctions against aggressor nations. Crucially, six and a half million (58.7 per cent) responded 'Yes' when asked if they supported collective military measures under the same circumstances.[7]

Many Conservatives resented the so-called Peace Ballot as tendentious and interfering. The supreme isolationist, Lord Beaverbrook, dubbed it the 'Ballot of Blood' and warned his many readers that 'the plebiscite will drag you and your children into war on behalf of the League of Nations'.[8] Yet it could not be ignored. Following the result, Austen Chamberlain predicted that any government which sought to abandon collective security would be swept from power and, as chance would have it, there was a General Election in the offing.[9]

On 7 June 1935, Ramsay MacDonald had retired as Prime Minister. He had not been well for some time and his failing faculties invited the derision of his colleagues. In May of the previous year, Robert Bernays had been shocked when Sir Stafford Cripps had called MacDonald a 'nincompoop' across the despatch box. Neither the Speaker nor MPs protested. 'It must be unprecedented for the Prime Minister to be called a nincompoop', thought Bernays, 'but then … it is unprecedented for the Prime Minister to be a nincompoop.'[10] MacDonald was succeeded by Stanley Baldwin, who inaugurated his third term as Prime Minister with a shuffling of the chairs. To the delight of almost everyone, Simon was moved from the Foreign Office to become Home Secretary. He was replaced, to rather less enthusiasm, by the Secretary of State for India, Sir Samuel Hoare – 'the last in a long line of maiden aunts', according to the late Lord Birkenhead.[11]

Neither Baldwin nor Hoare was going to allow Britain to become embroiled in a war over Abyssinia. Apart from the head waters of the Nile, which gathered in Lake Tana, a Government report concluded that Britain had no vital interests in the country. Mussolini seized on this conclusion – having managed to procure a copy of the report thanks to a spy in the British Embassy in Rome – as further evidence that Britain would not interfere. But both he and the British were ignoring the issue of the League of Nations. In 1923, Abyssinia had joined the League, ironically at Mussolini's insistence, and thus fell under the jurisdiction of Article 16 – which stipulated that an attack on any one member constituted an attack on the entire League. In December 1934, the diminutive but impressive Abyssinian Emperor, Haile Selassie, had appealed to the League for arbitration over the border conflict with Italy and in June 1935 the new British Prime Minister had declared the League 'the sheet anchor of British policy'.[12] Baldwin was in a bind.

In order to try and break free, Anthony Eden was despatched to Rome with an offer. 'Italy will have to be bought off', noted Sir Robert Vansittart, 'or Abyssinia will eventually perish ... That might in itself matter less if it did not mean that the League would also perish (and that Italy would simultaneously perform *another* volte-face into the arms of Germany).'[13] Eden, therefore, proposed that the Abyssinians cede large tracts of territory to Mussolini in return for a thin slice of British Somaliland. Mussolini was contemptuous. He could not understand why Britain was interested in the fate of a degenerate African backwater and petulantly pointed out that Laval, the French Foreign Minister, had promised him a 'free hand' in Abyssinia when the pair concluded the Franco-Italian Agreement in January. This was news to Eden, who interjected to say that he was sure his French colleague had only meant 'economically' – the claim Laval later made himself.[14] Yet even if the Machiavellian Frenchman had avoided giving Mussolini a direct assurance, it seems likely that he did intimate his assent, or at least indifference, to the Duce's plans. Indeed, as the French diplomat Armand Berard told the American Ambassador to Berlin in May 1935, 'we had to promise him [Mussolini] the annexation of Abyssinia', in order to create an alliance against German aggression. 'I hope Mussolini has sense enough to annex a little of the country at a time, as we did in Morocco. We have urged that upon the Italians.'[15]

Without a solution in sight and with the continual amassing of Italian forces on the Abyssinian border, the prospect of war loomed over the British public. Newspapers spoke of the worst crisis since 1914 and the Opposition leaders were invited to Downing Street for consultations. From the start, opinion was divided between intervention and isolationism. Leading the charge for the latter, the *Daily Mail* attacked the League enthusiasts, while proclaiming that British sympathy was 'wholly with the cause of the white races, which Italy is so firmly upholding'.[16] This was far from being universally true, yet there were plenty who agreed with Evelyn Waugh in dismissing Abyssinia as a 'barbarous country', which still practised the slave trade; or with the Conservative MP Henry 'Chips' Channon, who asked why Britain should be plunged into war over Abyssinia 'when most of our far flung Empire has been won by conquest'.[17] Others, regardless of moral considerations, simply refused to contemplate the prospect of conflict. 'I will not have another war. *I will not*', shouted a clearly distressed King George V to Lloyd George. 'The last one was none of my doing and if there is another one and we are threatened with being brought into it, I will go to Trafalgar Square and wave a red flag myself sooner than allow this country to be brought in.'[18] On another occasion, the King threatened to abdicate if Britain went to war with Italy. 'I'll sign a piece of paper', yelled the agitated sovereign. 'I don't know what sort of bit of paper but I'll find it.'[19]

On the other side, liberal opinion was outraged by Mussolini's proposed action. Assessing its correspondence over the summer of 1935, *The Times* observed that there was no division of opinion over the 'reckless immorality of the Italian preparations for war', while the *Daily Herald* condemned Mussolini's desire to 'murder Abyssinians in order to steal their land'.[20] The dilemma was what to do about it. For the majority of 'small L' liberals – which included a great many Conservatives – the answer was clear: Britain must stand by the Covenant of the League and support sanctions against Italy. If she failed to do so then the authority of the League, already undermined by the Japanese invasion of Manchuria, would collapse and the world would lose an instrument with which to restrain aggressors, in particular Germany. This was Churchill's argument, although he also had considerable sympathy with the view that firm action against Italy would merely break the Stresa Front and send Mussolini scuttling into Hitler's arms. Acutely conscious of these dangers, the Government would have preferred to restrict its actions to an ostentatious display of hand wringing. But with public opinion being what it was and a General Election planned for November, this was not an option.

On 11 September 1935, the Foreign Secretary, Sir Samuel Hoare, nailed his colours to the mast. Addressing the League General

Assembly in his clear, precise tones, he stated that 'the League stands, and my country stands with it, for the collective maintenance of the Covenant in its entirety, and particularly for steady and collective resistance to all acts of unprovoked aggression'.[21] The reception was rapturous. British newspapers, with the exception of the Beaverbrook and Rothermere titles, lauded the principled declaration, while other League members, including France, fell into line behind the British lead. In fact, Hoare had not intended to give a British lead. This, though, was the inescapable impression, reinforced the following day when the battle cruisers *Hood* and *Renown*, accompanied by several destroyers, were sent to Gibraltar to bolster the Mediterranean Fleet. Writing from Geneva, Lord Cranborne described the terrific effect this display of strength had made: 'All the small countries are ecstatic. The Italians here, who were arrogant, have become affable to a degree.'[22]

Mussolini was neither affable nor perturbed. Reassured by Laval that France would not support military sanctions, he launched his invasion of Abyssinia on 3 October 1935. Italian planes bombed Adowa (including the hospital), while General Emilio de Bono, in charge of some 500,000 Italian troops, crossed the border from Eritrea. The League found Italy in breach of the Covenant and started the process of imposing sanctions. Britain and France went along with this but the discrepancies of the embargo list – which banned foie gras but not coal, iron, steel or, most crucially, oil – revealed their extreme reluctance to antagonise the Duce. The British Chiefs of Staff, in particular, were worried that strong action might induce Mussolini into some 'mad dog' attack on either the Royal Navy or British bases in the Mediterranean. This would obviously start a war and Laval was being ambivalent, at best, as to whether France was prepared to support Britain.

In the midst of all of this, Baldwin called the General Election. Neville Chamberlain had wanted to fight the Conservative campaign on a pro-rearmament ticket but Baldwin, with his fine ear for public opinion, was more subtle. Faced with a Labour Party standing on a platform of international disarmament, Baldwin assured voters on 31 October that there would be 'no great armaments', while continually stressing the need to bring Britain's defences up to date.[23] This, he explained, was the natural corollary of support for the League, to which the Conservative Party was wholly committed. The Prime Minister had been an elusive figure during the recent crisis. 'Stanley would think about nothing but his holiday and the necessity of keeping out of the whole business almost at any cost', complained Hoare to Chamberlain.[24] Yet when the time came Baldwin was shown to have correctly judged the mood of the nation and the National Government – now really a Conservative Government – was returned to power on 14 November with another massive, though slightly reduced, majority.*

*

The election over, the Abyssinian crisis now threatened to escalate. Having successfully imposed some not very punitive sanctions on 18 November 1935, the next step under League consideration was whether these should be extended to include oil. Italy was highly dependent on oil imports and there was little doubt that an embargo would have a serious effect on her ability to wage war.† Mussolini responded by making it known that he would regard such a step as tantamount to a declaration of war. This alarmed the British Chiefs of Staff, who warned the Cabinet strongly against risking war in the Mediterranean. This is not to say that there was any real doubt about the outcome of such a conflict: the Italians were not renowned for their fighting prowess and the Commander-in-Chief in the Mediterranean, Admiral Sir William Wordsworth Fisher, was entirely confident of his ability to beat the Italian Navy. There was, however, concern about the potential for Italian bombers to inflict serious damage on the Fleet, which, at a time of both deficiency and widespread international danger, was not something the Admiralty thought it could sustain. Added to this was the fear that Japan might seize the initiative and launch an attack in the Far East, the less than committed attitude of France, and the growing threat from Germany. Indeed, as Sir Eric Phipps wrote to Hoare on 13 November, 'the present Ethiopian embroglio [*sic*] is mere child's play compared to the problem that

---

* The Labour Party made some gains at the 1935 General Election, ending up with 154 seats to the Conservatives' 386 and the National Liberals' 33.

† Hitler's interpreter, Paul Schmidt, later claimed that Mussolini had admitted to Hitler that he would have had to end the war in Abyssinia if oil sanctions had been applied.

will in some not very distant future confront His Majesty's Government'.[25] A way out had to be found.

At the end of November 1935, Laval asked Hoare to Paris for talks. United in their desire to find a peaceful resolution, if on little else, the British and French had been conferring on a potential carve-up of Abyssinia. 'We intend to go all out for bringing the conflict to an end', explained a confident Hoare to the King's Private Secretary.[26] The 'we' included Sir Robert Vansittart, who, despite his later reputation as the most implacable of anti-appeasers, had become so panicked by the prospect of war with Italy – which he believed would only result in giving Hitler a free hand to do as he wished – that he was almost as desperate for a deal as Laval. Eden, who was not going to Paris, cautioned Hoare against both Laval and Vansittart, but the Foreign Secretary was relaxed: 'Don't worry,' he assured his junior just before his departure, 'I shall not commit you to anything.'[27]

The atmosphere in Paris was not relaxing. A mob of reporters laid siege to the Quai d'Orsay, while inside a chain-smoking Laval played Mussolini's hand for him. After twenty-four hours of intense wrangling the two sides reached a deal. Abyssinia would cede roughly two-thirds of her territory to Italy, to be compensated with a thin strip of Eritrea, providing access to the sea. A satisfied Hoare urged his colleagues in London to accept the proposals, which were duly agreed at a special meeting of the Cabinet on 9 December 1935. On the same day, however, details of the plan – almost certainly leaked by enemies of Laval in the Quai d'Orsay – appeared in *L'Echo de Paris* and *L'Œuvre*. British public opinion erupted in a lava of moral indignation. Having wrapped itself in the mantle of the League, the Government was now revealed to be involved in a shady deal which would see Mussolini rewarded for his aggression. MPs were bombarded with letters from their constituents and even the normally servile *Times* came out against the proposals, derided as a 'corridor for camels'.[28] In Geneva, the other members of the League cried betrayal, while American newspapers spoke of 'an international disgrace' and a 'staggering defeat for the League of Nations'.[29] 'Our whole prestige in foreign affairs at home and abroad has tumbled to pieces like a house of cards', wailed Neville Chamberlain in a letter to his sister. 'If we had to fight the election over again we should probably be beaten and certainly would not have more than a bare majority.'[30]

Hoare was in Switzerland when the storm broke. Completely exhausted, he had recently suffered a series of fainting fits and was now trying to regain his health by means of an ice-skating holiday. Not the most sensible recreation for a man prone to blackouts, he fainted during his first session on the ice and broke his nose in two places. The Foreign Secretary was thus out of action while Baldwin struggled to defend his Government not only from public opinion but from his own MPs. According to Harold Nicolson, the House was 'seething' over the affair.[31] 'Everyone goes about with sunken head', recorded the Conservative MP Victor Cazalet. 'Shame. Betrayal. What were we elected for three weeks ago?'[32] In the end it was too much. On 17 December, fifty-seven Tory MPs signed an Early Day Motion criticising the Government and a heated meeting of the Conservative backbench Foreign Affairs Committee decided that the Foreign Secretary should resign. At the Cabinet meeting the next day, at least five Ministers expressed the same view. Neville Chamberlain was deputed to break the news to a miserable Hoare, who resigned that evening. The following day, his nose still covered in plasters, he saw the King, who tried to cheer him up with the happy thought that he would now have more time for woodcock shooting. 'You know what they're all saying,' joshed the frail monarch, 'no more coals to Newcastle, no more Hoares to Paris.' Understandably, the late Foreign Secretary found this less amusing. 'The fellow didn't even laugh', complained the King.[33]

*

The Hoare–Laval debacle was a squalid affair, the implications of which extended far beyond the immediate political crisis. British and French prestige suffered a severe blow, while relations between the two countries, already strained, reached their nadir. The wound to the League of Nations was mortal. Created to forestall international crises, the supreme, idealistic invention of the post-war settlement had been undermined by the two great European democracies. There was, it is true, precious little evidence that other nations were prepared to go to war in defence of Abyssinia, and American posturing over the League was especially hypocritical. But this did not change the result. Collective security was dead, as was the belief that the League could protect small nations from aggressors. In Abyssinia, Mussolini continued his conquest unabated. The Abyssinian 'Christmas Offensive' was halted when the Italians broke the Geneva Protocol and deployed mustard gas in a 'deadly rain', alongside a shower of conventional bombs. Later, one of Mussolini's sons, a pilot serving in Abyssinia, would recall the 'diverting' spectacle of watching groups of tribesmen 'burst out like a rose after [he] had landed a bomb in the middle of them'.[34] On 5 May 1936, Italian troops entered Addis Ababa and four days later Mussolini proclaimed the annexation of Abyssinia and establishment of the Fascist Empire. Haile Selassie fled to London but at the end of June travelled to Geneva to oppose the lifting of sanctions against Italy. In a moving and dignified speech, which was to become a rallying cry for anti-fascists across the world, the Abyssinian Emperor, clad in a simple black cloak, laid bare what was at stake:

> It is the confidence that each state is to place in international treaties. It is the value of promises made to small states that their integrity and their independence shall be respected and ensured. It is the principle of the equality of states on the one hand, or otherwise the obligation laid upon small powers to accept the bonds of vassalship. In a word, it is international morality that is at stake.[35]

Five days later the League Assembly voted to lift sanctions against Italy.

Even more than Mussolini, the victor of the Italian–Abyssinian war was Hitler. Schadenfreude over the Duce's initial discomfort was replaced with delight at the destruction of the Stresa Front and the opprobrium heaped on Britain and France. The authority of the League, which could have been used as a tool to rally opposition to German expansion, had been destroyed and the diplomatic isolation of the regime was at an end. On 7 January 1936, Mussolini told the German Ambassador, Ulrich von Hassell, that he did not object to Austria becoming a de facto German satellite, the latest in a series of moves towards Italo-German rapprochement. Mussolini had shown what could be achieved by naked aggression, just as the Western Powers had demonstrated their failure to stop it. Hitler took note and accelerated his plans.

V

Across the Rhine

> On each successive international issue the Government has had persuasive arguments for dishonouring our obligations – but the fact remains that each surrender has led to a worse one, and to a worsening of our situation as well as that of civilization.
>
> Basil Liddell Hart, military correspondent for *The Times*, September 1936[1]

At 12.50 p.m., on Saturday 7 March 1936, members of the 6th German Army Corps goose-stepped past the bronze equestrian statues of Friedrich IV and Kaiser Wilhelm I and across the Hohenzollern Bridge straddling the Rhine at Cologne. There they were greeted by the Mayor before marching on to the city's great Gothic cathedral and a rapturous reception. In all, 22,000 troops, previously concealed in schools, parish halls and customs houses, had crossed into the Rhineland – that area of north-west Germany along the French, Belgian and Dutch border, first occupied and then demilitarised by the Allies at Versailles. The move had begun at dawn and was well advanced by the time Hitler arrived at the Kroll Opera House in Berlin to address a specially convened session of the Reichstag at noon. Looking down on the uniform-clad deputies – none of whom knew why they had been summoned – Hitler delivered a ferocious attack on Bolshevism before claiming that the Franco-Soviet Pact ratified by the French Chamber of Deputies nine days earlier, on 27 February, had broken the Treaty of Locarno.* This point was crucial, for while

* Agreed on 2 May 1935, the Franco-Soviet Pact committed the two nations to lending each other immediate 'aid and assistance' in the event of unprovoked aggression.

the demilitarised zone had been created by the 'diktat' of Versailles – as a guarantee of French and Belgian security – it had been confirmed by Locarno, to which the Germans had been willing signatories.

Hitler then quoted from the memorandum which, an hour earlier, had been handed to the French, British, Italian and Belgian Ambassadors. Germany, he stated, no longer considered itself bound by Locarno and 'in the interest of the primitive rights of a people to the security of its borders' had decided from today to restore 'the full and unrestricted sovereignty of the Reich in the demilitarized zone of the Rhineland'.[2] At this the 600 deputies – 'little men with big bodies and bulging necks and cropped hair and pouched bellies and brown uniforms and heavy boots, little men of clay in his fine hands', as the American journalist William Shirer described them – jumped to their feet in an ecstasy of '*Heils*'. When Hitler revealed that German soldiers were at that very moment making their way to garrisons in the prohibited zone, the eruption of emotion was such that he was unable to continue. 'They spring, yelling and crying, to their feet', continued Shirer: 'their hands are raised in slavish salute, their faces now contorted with hysteria, their mouths wide open, shouting, shouting, their eyes burning with fanaticism, glued on the new god, the Messiah.'[3]

*

For the Western Powers, the remilitarisation of the Rhineland was both long anticipated and a complete surprise. Sir Eric Phipps had predicted in December 1935 that Hitler would reoccupy the zone whenever a favourable opportunity presented itself, although he thought that this would not occur before a further effort had been made to 'square' Great Britain.[4] The Foreign Office, in turmoil over the Hoare–Laval debacle, was slow to respond to this warning but by February 1936 almost everyone, including the new Foreign Secretary, Anthony Eden – promoted by Baldwin to replace Sam Hoare – was convinced that the Rhineland was the next item on Hitler's agenda.

This conviction added urgency to the Government's desire to restart negotiations with Germany. Above all, the Foreign Office had been anxious to avoid a fait accompli. Under the terms of the Treaty of Locarno, Britain was pledged to defend the demilitarised zone. If, therefore, the Germans reoccupied the Rhineland and the French requested help in expelling them, the Government would be faced with the unpalatable choice of dishonouring Britain's treaty obligations or a potential war. The question was, what could Britain offer Hitler?

For E. H. Carr, working in the Southern Department of the Foreign Office, the answer was to allow Germany a free hand in central and south-eastern Europe.[5] This notion was vehemently opposed by Sir Robert Vansittart, whose preferred option ran along the lines of offering Germany some form of colonial restitution. 'I believe that Germany will expand somehow and sometime ... [and] if it can't be in Africa, it will be in Europe', he wrote.[6] This, however, was anathema to the imperialist wing of the Tory Party – ambivalent or even supportive of German expansion in eastern Europe but die-hard in its defence of British possessions in Africa – as well as the Cabinet Secretary, Sir Maurice Hankey, who feared that the Germans would merely regard such concessions as weakness.[7]

Eden was torn. With his natural distrust of dictators, the new Foreign Secretary began his tenure by circulating a compilation of past warnings from the British Embassy in Berlin entitled 'The German Danger'. Hitler, Eden commented, was determined to make Germany 'the dominant Power in Europe' and yet, while hastening rearmament at home, he argued that Britain should try to reach a 'modus vivendi' with Germany.[8] In pursuit of this goal, Eden was prepared to put the status of the Rhineland on the table. Indeed, faced with the prospect of an imminent German coup, the Foreign Secretary was in a hurry to use the demilitarised zone as a bargaining chip while it still had value. Hitler, however, was too fast.

*

The Wehrmacht's entry into the Rhineland was as much anticipated in Paris as it was in London. French military intelligence had been forecasting the move for over a year and recent reports even identified the ratification of the Franco-Soviet alliance as the likely pretext. There were, however, no military plans to eject the German troops. Depressed by further large cuts to military spending in 1935, the French General Staff were convinced that they were in no position to risk war with Germany. The Deuxième Bureau, though prescient in its assessment of German intentions, had significantly overestimated the size of the

German armed forces, while Germany's industrial potential was correctly recognised as being considerably greater than that of France.

For the defensive-minded General Maurice Gamelin, Chief of the French General Staff, French military action to push the Germans out of the Rhineland was just the sort of 'madcap' scheme he believed it was his duty to oppose.[9] He therefore warned his political masters that any military initiative would require at least partial mobilisation – at a cost of thirty million francs a day – and would inevitably lead to a bloody war of attrition. To bolster his case, Gamelin distorted the already inflated tally of German troops believed to have entered the zone, adding an extra 295,000 men – comprising the German Labour Corps, the military police, the SS and the SA – to the total of trained, combat-ready soldiers.[10] This defeatism was complemented by an angry pacifism which swept France in the aftermath of the coup. The left attacked the right-wing warmongers, while the right, not to be outdone and dismayed by the alliance with communist Russia, attacked the socialist sabre rattlers. Almost every French newspaper came out against war, as did the trade unions and veterans' associations.

The French Government was disoriented and divided. Having made himself unpopular with his deflationary policies and horse-trading with Italy, Laval had been forced from office in January 1936. He had been replaced by the Radical Albert Sarraut, who was leading a caretaker administration before fresh elections could be held at the end of April. Though personally brave – a veteran of several duels as well as of the Battle of Verdun – Sarraut was not the man for a crisis. On the evening of Sunday 8 March 1936, the day following the German reoccupation, he broadcast a message of defiance, declaring that the French Government was 'not disposed to allow Strasbourg to come under the fire of German guns'.[11] Yet in the Cabinet of the same day, his support for an immediate military response – as advocated by the Minister of Posts, Georges Mandel – had not been enough to overcome the multitude of military, financial and diplomatic objections. On the contrary, the Cabinet agreed that France could not engage in '*action isolée*' and decided that the only immediate response for the moment – beyond the purely defensive manning of the Maginot Line – was to appeal to the League of Nations and consult with the other Locarno signatories. 'Splendid', commented Goebbels.[12]

*

In London the mood was no more bellicose than in Paris. 'Great excitement about Hitler's coup', recorded Harold Nicolson, recently elected National Labour MP for Leicester West, on 9 March. 'Eden makes his statement at 3.40 ... Very calm. Promises to help if France attacked, otherwise negotiation. General mood of the House is one of fear. Anything to keep out of war.'[13] The City was 'overwhelmingly pro-German', while *The Times* produced an optimistic leader entitled 'A Chance to Rebuild'.[14] This was a reference to the peace offer with which Hitler had accompanied his coup and which included non-aggression treaties with Germany's neighbours, an air pact in the west and the tantalising suggestion of Germany's return to the League of Nations.

Determined to avoid war, many influential Britons fastened on these proposals. 'Welcome Hitler's declaration wholeheartedly', the former Deputy Secretary to the Cabinet, Thomas Jones, urged Baldwin over the telephone the day after the reoccupation. 'Treat this as relatively *de minimis*: and not to be taken tragically in view of the peace proposals which accompany it ... Accept Hitler's declaration as made in good faith and put his bona fides to the test by trying it out.'[15] These, as Jones explained, were the views of the majority of the house party staying at Blickling – Lord Lothian's Norfolk seat – who, on hearing the news, had taken it upon themselves to form a 'shadow cabinet' to thrash out the situation. Apart from Jones and Lothian, the other guests included Lord and Lady Astor; the Attorney General, Sir Thomas Inskip; the US diplomat Norman Davis; the Chairman of *The Economist*, Sir Walter Layton, and his wife; the Canadian High Commissioner and his wife; and the historian Arnold Toynbee, freshly returned from visiting Hitler.

Although he had not been able to get to Blickling as planned, Eden was of much the same view. Despite stating in a memorandum to the Cabinet on 8 March – the day after the invasion – that Hitler could no longer be trusted to abide by treaties even when they had been freely entered into, he nevertheless, and contradictorily, argued that the Government should use this opportunity to conclude 'as far-reaching and enduring a settlement as possible whilst Herr Hitler is still in the mood to do so'. Above all, Eden concluded, 'we must discourage any military action by France against Germany'.[16]

As we have already seen, there was no danger of this. Yet while the French Government had ruled out unilateral military action, it was equally anxious to prevent a complete German victory, which would destroy Locarno and expose the full extent of French weakness. At a meeting of the Locarno representatives in Paris, therefore, the French Foreign Minister, Pierre-Etienne Flandin, talked tough. France would ask the League Council to confirm that Germany had broken the Treaty of Versailles, after which she would place all her resources, both economic and military, at the disposal of the League. This, Flandin argued, was the moment to accept the German challenge. Germany would be stronger next year but was currently isolated. If the League applied or even threatened sanctions – at first economic but later military – Hitler would surely yield. The Belgian Prime Minister, Paul Van Zeeland, agreed. The risk of war 'was one chance in ten' if the Locarno powers acted together, while war in the future seemed inevitable if the democracies allowed Hitler to get away with it.[17]

Alarmed by this apparent resolution, Eden returned to London to report to the Cabinet. There he found consternation at the French proposals and universal opposition to sanctions. Above all, the British did not believe that Hitler would bow to threats and as such did not consider it wise to 'threaten in the hope of having not to perform'.[18] This attitude was supported by the Chiefs of Staff – rapidly gaining a reputation as the worst defeatists in the country – who stated that Britain's armed forces were in no condition to fight Germany, and by public opinion, which came out overwhelmingly against war and in support of the German action. 'To Stratford on Avon for L. of N. Meeting', recorded Victor Cazalet, a couple of days after the reoccupation. '200 present – really breathless excitement. 197 to 3 in favour of negotiating with Hitler.'[19] Startled by the contrast with the Italian invasion of Abyssinia – in which the same collective security enthusiasts were clamouring for a robust international response – Cazalet concluded that the country would never accept military action to eject the Germans from their own territory. This view was echoed by Robert Bernays's findings in Bristol and by Leo Amery's experience in Leicester, where, to his amazement, a group of ex-servicemen revealed themselves to be entirely on the side of the Germans.

Some took this attitude to extremes. The Dean of Chichester believed that 'the ordinary man almost breathed a sigh of relief when he heard that Hitler had entered the Zone', while a canon of Liverpool Cathedral was so outraged at the suggestion that the Rhineland should be occupied by an international police force that he banned prayers from being offered to the Government during services.[20] The fact was, as the Secretary of State for War, Duff Cooper, told the German Ambassador, most Englishmen 'did not care "two hoots" about the Germans reoccupying their own territory'.[21] This fact was brought home to Eden directly when, on the morning of 9 March, he asked his taxi driver what he thought of the news. 'I suppose Jerry can do what he likes in his own back garden', came the reply.[22]

*

In this climate, the French insistence on action provoked a wave of Francophobia. Scores of MPs remarked on the anti-French feeling of their constituents and there was a concomitant surge in support for Germany. 'The general view seems to be that France has been the stumbling block in the path of peace for the last fifteen years', wrote one Liverpool Conservative, who noted that 'everybody I meet just now seems to be pro-German or at any rate anti-French'.[23] In Parliament, the Conservative backbench Foreign Affairs Committee was overwhelmingly against sanctions and in favour of negotiation. Harold Nicolson made an impassioned appeal against Britain dishonouring her obligations but, as he revealed in a letter to his wife, the writer Vita Sackville-West, even he was in two minds over the best course to follow:

> The French are not letting us off one jot or tittle of the bond ... We are thus faced either with repudiation of our pledged word or the risk of war. The worst of it is that in a way the French are right. We know that Hitler gambled on this coup. We know that Schacht told him it would lead to financial disaster, that Neurath told him it would create a dangerous diplomatic situation, and that the General Staff told him that if France and Great Britain acted together there would be no chance of resistance. Thus if we send an ultimatum to Germany, she ought in all reason to climb down. But then she will not climb down and we shall have war. Naturally we shall win and enter Berlin. But what is the good of that? It would only mean communism in Germany

> and France, and that is why the Russians are so keen on it. Moreover, the people of this country absolutely refuse to have a war. We should be faced by a general strike if we even suggested such a thing. We shall therefore have to climb down ignominiously and Hitler will have scored ... But it does mean the final end of the League and that I do mind dreadfully. Quite dreadfully.[24]

Though less concerned over the fate of the League, both Baldwin and Neville Chamberlain were similarly convinced that war with Germany could have no positive outcome. France 'might succeed in crushing Germany with the aid of Russia', mused the Prime Minister, 'but it would probably only result in Germany going Bolshevik'.[25] When the Council of the League met in London on 12 March 1936, therefore, the priority was to restrain the French while avoiding the accusation that Britain was trying to wriggle out of Locarno. 'Peace with as little dishonour as possible', as Oliver Stanley, President of the Board of Education, put it.[26]

Flandin, on the other hand, did his best to persuade the British to join France in demanding Germany withdraw her troops from the zone. 'We know that Hitler is bluffing and that if you remain faithful to your engagements we shall be able to obtain satisfaction', he told a dinner of twenty National Government MPs. 'But if you break your word, then indeed the world will be shown that violence is the only political factor which counts, and Germany, as the most powerful single force on the Continent, will become the mistress of Europe.'[27] The MPs were impressed but when the French Foreign Minister put the same argument to Chamberlain – emphasising his belief that Hitler would back down in the face of Anglo-French resolution – the Chancellor replied that the Government could not 'accept this as a reliable estimate of a mad dictator's reactions'.[28]

In the end, Flandin had to accept that the British were determined not to act. On 17 March, the Russian Foreign Minister, Maxim Litvinov, made a strong speech at Geneva in favour of collective action but this – with the implication of Anglo-Soviet solidarity – only served to increase British obduracy. Two days later, the League Council declared Germany in violation of both Versailles and Locarno but did not recommend sanctions or demand a German withdrawal from the zone. The Locarno powers proposed the creation of a new demilitarised zone and requested that Hitler refrain from reinforcing his troops or from constructing fortifications within the Rhineland. If Hitler was prepared to accept these conditions then Britain, France, Italy and Belgium were prepared to enter into negotiations on the status of the zone and on new mutual-assistance pacts. In the meantime, the Locarno guarantee, protecting Belgium and France against 'unprovoked aggression', was reaffirmed and, in the most significant concession to French apprehension, staff talks would be held between the British, French and Belgians.

Even this was too much for some in Britain. 'I am simply in despair about the European situation', wrote the social reformer Violet Markham to Thomas Jones on 22 March 1936. 'Germany was, of course (as always), utterly wrong in method though right in fact. But she has flung us into the arms of France in a deplorable way ... Does this new agreement mean that if France gets embroiled with Germany we have to go and fight with Italy and Russia?'[29] This view was not unique. Many believed that secret military alliances had been responsible for dragging Britain into the First World War and there was widespread opposition to Continental entanglements. In the Cabinet, Sir John Simon led the charge against staff talks and, in particular, a commitment to send an expeditionary force to the Continent in the event of war. 'I cannot believe that if London was being heavily bombed we should be despatching regiments of soldiers to the Low Countries', he wrote to Baldwin on 26 March.[30]

Baldwin reassured Simon but in the Commons – which, as Harold Nicolson noted, was 'terribly "pro-German", which means afraid of war' – there was even greater concern.[31] 'The boys won't have it', Kingsley Wood, the Minister for Health, informed the Prime Minister.[32] Baldwin conveyed this warning to Eden, who was inspired to make one of the most admired speeches of his career. Staff talks were the necessary compensation for the loss of what had been a central plank of Franco-Belgian security, he told MPs. Moreover, Britain was bound to maintain this security by the Treaty of Locarno. 'I am not prepared to be the first British Foreign Secretary to go back on a British signature', Eden solemnly, if hypocritically, declared.[33]

In fact, the staff talks were nothing for British MPs or the German Government – which reacted with fury – to get agitated about. Taking the technical nature of the conversations to extremes, the Chiefs of

Staff were permitted to tell their French and Belgian counterparts what was in the British cupboard – 'bare enough', noted Lieutenant-Colonel Henry Pownall – but under no circumstances to agree what forces could or could not be used in the event of war.[34] Joint planning was strictly forbidden and, as a Foreign Office official confessed, the whole exercise was merely 'eye wash' to placate the French.[35]

Meanwhile, Hitler had rejected the London proposals. On 29 March 1936, he savoured his triumph when 98.8 per cent of the German electorate voted in favour of reoccupying the Rhineland in a referendum. He then renewed his earlier peace proposals, demanding that the democracies accept his offer by 1 August 1936. The British response was typical. Sceptical of the Führer's sincerity, yet desperate to reach an agreement, they sent Hitler a questionnaire asking which treaties he was prepared to respect. Six months later, the Foreign Office was still waiting for a response.

*

In retrospect, the remilitarisation of the Rhineland was seen as a watershed in the inter-war years: the last chance of stopping Hitler without a major war. This interpretation, propounded by Churchill in *The Gathering Storm*, was based on the knowledge that Hitler's bold stroke had been a massive gamble and that even limited action by the French Army would have been enough to drive the Germans out of the zone. Indeed, contrary to the hundreds of thousands of soldiers reported by General Gamelin, only three thousand German troops had crossed onto the western bank of the Rhine. There they were under orders to resist advancing French forces, though this could never have been more than a token effort before a full-scale retreat. 'Considering the situation we were in, the French covering army could have blown us to pieces', admitted General Alfred Jodl, the former Chief of the Operations Staff of the German Armed Forces, at his Nuremberg trial in 1946.[36]

Broadly, however, this was clear only in hindsight. Although some appreciated the true state of affairs at the time, a majority of the decision makers, in France and especially Britain, were convinced that military action would lead to war. This outcome was strongly deprecated by the Chiefs of Staff, while the domestic situations on both sides of the Channel made a military response all but impossible. France was in the run-up to the most divisive elections of the decade and the franc, already on the verge of collapse, would not have survived mobilisation. In Britain, widespread pacifism was complemented by a lack of *casus belli*. The reoccupation of the Rhineland was considered both justified and inevitable, while virtually no one was prepared to argue that it posed a direct threat to British security. For Paul Emrys-Evans, Chairman of the Conservative Foreign Policy Committee, this represented a dereliction of duty by the Government. 'The events of this year have been little short of disastrous', he remonstrated to the Chief Whip on 13 July 1936. 'Everyone in Europe anticipated the reoccupation of the Rhineland, and yet it is clear that the Government had not thought out what action should be taken. They certainly never prepared the country for any crisis and, when one came, instead of giving a lead to public opinion they sheltered behind it.'[37]

Despite the above qualifiers, it is hard to disagree with this view. Though few in Britain appreciated or cared about it at the time, the remilitarisation of the Rhineland greatly restricted France's ability to come to the aid of her allies in eastern Europe – Czechoslovakia, Poland, Romania and Yugoslavia, not to mention Austria – by launching an invasion of Germany through the undefended zone. The door to Germany had been closed and the French had been humiliated in the process. Conversely, Germany had grown considerably stronger and Hitler had scored a triumph in the face of scepticism from his own Generals. His belief in his own star increased, while the ability of the more cautious military to restrain him from other outlandish ventures declined. The League of Nations, effectively destroyed over Abyssinia, was quietly buried. The machinery of Geneva would rumble on until the outbreak of war but there was never again a serious attempt to use the League as a means by which to coerce aggressors. It was, indeed, a turning point.

VI

The Defence of the Realm

> The terror of the Roman arms added weight and dignity to the moderation of the emperors. They preserved peace by a constant preparation for war; and while justice regulated their conduct, they announced to the nations on their confines, that they were as little disposed to endure, as to offer an injury.
>
> Edward Gibbon, *The Decline and Fall of the Roman Empire*

The Abyssinian crisis brought to the fore concerns over the state of Britain's defences. In January 1936, the *Morning Post* ran a series of articles exposing grave deficiencies across all three services. These included a shortage of ammunition for the Navy, a lack of reserves for the Army, the absence of modern tanks and guns, the minuscule provision for anti-aircraft defences and the size of the Royal Air Force compared to the Luftwaffe. In all, the *Post* concluded, 'we have sunk far below the limits of safety and of prudence'.[1] Many in Parliament agreed. On 14 February, the former Foreign Secretary Sir Austen Chamberlain shocked the parliamentary press gallery by delivering a stinging attack on the Government's handling of defence, adding his voice to the growing chorus in favour of a new minister to oversee a far more vigorous stage of British rearmament. 'I did rather flutter the journalistic dovecotes', Chamberlain told his half-sister, 'and I think rather surprised S[tanley] B[aldwin].' But 'to tell the truth I thought that the time was overdue for trying to shake him out of his self-complacency. Of course it is true that no man can do all the work which in these days the Prime Minister is supposed to do, but what angers me is that the present Prime Minister does none of it.' As to who the new minister should be, Chamberlain was in no doubt. There was only one man who, owing to his 'studies and special abilities', would fit the bill and 'that man is Winston Churchill'.[2]

Churchill was desperate for a return to power. On 13 February 1936, Victor Cazalet found him 'furious at not being "in" [government] – contemptuous of [the] present regime, and overwhelmed with German danger – v unbalanced I thought'.[3] Churchill had hoped that Baldwin might bring him back after the 1935 election. Many thought he would and the anticipation spread to Berlin, where Hitler was heard to express anxiety at the idea. But Baldwin was determined to exclude him. 'I feel we should not give him a post at this stage', the Prime Minister explained to J. C. C. Davidson, Chancellor of the Duchy of Lancaster. 'Anything he undertakes he puts his heart and soul into. If there is going to be a war – and no one can say that there is not – we must keep him fresh to be our war Prime Minister.'[4]

Despite these patronising if prophetic words, Churchill's claim to office generally improved in the four months leading to the Rhineland crisis. The international situation deteriorated and the Government suffered as a result of the Hoare–Laval affair. Other events, however, served as a reminder of past disloyalties. In January 1936, Randolph Churchill, Churchill's wayward son, accepted the invitation of the Unionist Association of Ross and Cromarty, in northern Scotland, to stand as its candidate in the forthcoming by-election. Randolph, whose candidature had already caused a Labour victory at Liverpool Wavertree the previous year, was standing against the official National Government candidate, Malcolm MacDonald – son of Ramsay and Secretary of State for the Dominions, despite having lost his seat at the recent General Election.* The situation was fraught with embarrassment. Churchill, still hoping to be offered either the Admiralty or the new defence job, was horrified by his son's actions, which he feared would be interpreted as a declaration of war by him on Baldwin. To make matters worse, Lord Rothermere, who had encouraged Randolph in his exploits, decided to send Oliver Baldwin, the Prime Minister's

* Having lost their seats at the 1935 General Election, both Ramsay and Malcolm MacDonald had been promised fresh seats by Stanley Baldwin. These were to be found among vacated Conservative constituencies but Unionist Associations were independent and, in this case, resented the idea of having a couple of lapsed socialists foisted upon them.

son, to Scotland to write up Randolph and write down MacDonald for the *Daily Mail*. 'So we shall have Ramsay's son, Baldwin's son and my son – all mauling each other in this remote constituency', wrote a despairing Churchill to his wife.[5]

Fortunately for all three fathers, Randolph's prospects were not good. As the Tory MP and Churchill confidant Brendan Bracken cabled in mid-January, 'Socialist win probable. More stags than Tories in Cromarty.'[6] This was almost certainly true. When the ballots were counted, Randolph had secured fewer than 2,500 votes, compared to nearly 6,000 for the Labour candidate, and just under 9,000 for MacDonald. The *Edinburgh Evening News* described the result as another 'nail into the political coffin of Mr Winston Churchill, either as a candidate for the Admiralty or Cabinet Minister charged with the co-ordination of Defence Services'.[7] Many people, however, continued to believe that Churchill's talents were too considerable for Baldwin to ignore. Churchill certainly hoped so and pulled punches he had intended to throw during the defence debate on 10 March 1936, while his reaction to the reoccupation of the Rhineland was notably muted.

All this was in vain. On 13 March, six days after the Rhineland invasion, Baldwin shocked Westminster when he revealed that the new Minister for the Co-ordination of Defence was not Churchill but the Attorney General, Sir Thomas Inskip. 'London rocks with the latest example of Baldwin's futility – or his cynicism', noted the Harmsworth journalist Collin Brooks in his diary.

> After weeks of suspense as to who would be the new Co-ordinating Minister of Defence, what strong man, what experienced departmentalist or tough man of business, it is announced that the lot has fallen upon Sir Thomas Inskip, a second-rate Attorney General whose chief claim to fame is that he was a stalwart of the Protestant cause in the prayer-book debates.[8]

Churchill's friends were incandescent. 'It is the most cynical thing that has been done since Caligula appointed his horse a consul!' fumed the Oxford scientist Professor Frederick Lindemann.[9] The man was no less surprised. 'I may say, with all sincerity, that it never occurred to me that I was likely to be asked to accept these responsibilities', Inskip humbly admitted. 'Nor did it ever occur to me – I can say this in all seriousness – that I would ever be able to discharge these duties even if they were offered to me ... I do not claim to be a superman.'[10]

In fact, Inskip performed his duties with greater skill than either he or his contemporaries expected. In particular, his influence on the decision, in December 1937, to reorder the RAF's priorities in favour of fighter rather than bomber production, even if motivated by cost, was to prove crucial to Britain's survival during the Battle of Britain. The new Minister, however, owed his post not to who he was but to who he was not – namely Churchill. As Baldwin told Victor Cazalet, he would rather exclude Churchill and 'have a row for four months' than include him and have a row 'for four years'.[11] Eight weeks later, he elaborated this view to Thomas Jones:

> One of these days I'll make a few casual remarks about Winston. Not a speech – no oratory – just a few words in passing. I've got it all ready. I am going to say that when Winston was born lots of fairies swooped down on his cradle with gifts – imagination, eloquence, industry, ability, and then came a fairy who said 'No one person has a right to so many gifts', picked him up and gave him such a shake and twist that with all these gifts he was denied judgement and wisdom. And that is why while we delight to listen to him in this House we do not take his advice.[12]

Many Conservatives shared this judgement. Writing to Baldwin in November 1935, Nancy Astor, Conservative MP for Plymouth Sutton and the first woman to take her seat in the Commons, begged the Prime Minister not to include Churchill in his Government. 'It will mean war at home and abroad', she claimed, adding, 'I know the depths of Winston's disloyalty – and you can't think how he is distrusted by all the electors of the country.'[13] Neville Chamberlain was certainly relieved not to have Churchill as a colleague when the Rhineland crisis blew up. 'We should be spending all our time in holding him down instead of getting on with our businesses', he stated in a letter to his sister. It was, however, as Baldwin's heir presumptive that Chamberlain was most relieved to find the Prime Minister in accordance with his views. According to Sam Hoare, Baldwin refused to countenance the possibility of Churchill, chiefly owing to 'the risk that would be involved by having him in the Cabinet when the question of his (SB's) successor became imminent'.[14]

*

Churchill was disappointed but stoical. Within a few weeks he had renewed his warnings about the German danger along with his criticism of the Government's lethargy over defence. On 1 May 1936, he pointed to further vast increases in German imports of raw materials necessary for arms manufacturing. 'All the signals are set for danger', he wrote in the *Evening Standard*. 'The red lights flash through the gloom. Let peaceful folk beware. It is time to pay attention and to be well prepared.'[15]

In fact, the Government was already taking significant, if belated, steps to increase Britain's preparedness. In March, it announced a new five-year programme which would see two new battleships and one aircraft carrier built, the modernisation of existing capital ships, an increase in cruiser strength from fifty to seventy vessels and four new infantry battalions for the Army. Most significant of all, the front-line strength of the Air Force was to increase from 1,500 to 1,750 planes, with 225 per cent reserves, by March 1939. The scheme was another victory for the Chancellor of the Exchequer and his strategy of 'limited liability'. Responding to the Third Report of the Defence Requirements Committee, Chamberlain had once again succeeded in diverting resources away from a proposed expeditionary force and towards an expanded Air Force. This caused dismay among some senior military figures. 'They cannot or will not realize that if war with Germany comes again (whether by Collective Security, Locarno or any other way) we shall again be *fighting for our lives*', complained Lieutenant-Colonel Pownall, Military Assistant Secretary to the Committee of Imperial Defence. 'The idea of the "half-hearted" war is the most pernicious and dangerous in the world. It will be 100 per cent – and even then we may well lose it … The Chancellor's cold hard calculating semi-detached attitude was terrible to listen to.'[16]

This was overly harsh. Having pressed Baldwin to fight the 1935 General Election on a rearmament ticket, Chamberlain was clear that rebuilding Britain's defences was *the* priority for the re-elected Government. As Chancellor, however, he was determined to do nothing which might upset the economy, only recently free from the clutches of the Great Depression. In these circumstances, Chamberlain grew increasingly frustrated with those, such as Churchill, who seemed to assure the public that they could have all the armaments they wished without having to pay for them. Defence spending had to be carefully targeted and Chamberlain, convinced that the next war would be decided in the air rather than through the clash of great armies, saw the Air Force as the most worthy, as well as the most efficient, recipient of funds. What Chamberlain and the Treasury failed to appreciate was that spending on rearmament could help revive the economy as it had in Germany after 1933 and would in the United States after 1941. Indeed, when Britain did begin to spend serious amounts on arms between 1936 and 1939, the benefits for both employment and productivity were plain to see.

If the Government appeared short-sighted in this regard, the same could be said for the Opposition, who, reflecting a substantial body of public opinion, continued to oppose any increase in armaments spending whatsoever. Things had looked as if they might change when, in October 1935, Clement Attlee replaced George Lansbury as Labour leader.* But even Major Attlee – who had faced Turks as well as Germans during the First World War – was unwilling at this stage to support rearmament. 'The safety of this country and the peace of the world', declared the Labour amendment to the Government's 1936 White Paper on defence, would not come from weapons but from 'adherence to the Covenant of the League of Nations, general disarmament ... and economic co-operation so as to remove the causes of war'.[17]

Many Conservatives, keen to build a consensus around national defence, regretted the Labour stance. For those high-profile Tories who had been campaigning for rearmament from the start, however, the principal enemy remained the Government itself. Towards the end of April 1936, Churchill chastised Ministers for their failure to meet trade union officials to negotiate a programme for increased arms

* This followed the overwhelming vote at the Labour Party Conference at Brighton in favour of economic sanctions against Italy. Lansbury, who opposed sanctions, was subject to a devastating attack by the General Secretary of the Transport and General Workers' Union, Ernest Bevin, who told him to stop 'hawking your conscience around from body to body asking to be told what to do with it'.

production and called for a Ministry of Supply to oversee the crucial relationship between industry and the services. Unwilling to upset the normal course of trade, Baldwin and Chamberlain rejected the idea. Yet there were those within Government, such as Lord Weir, an adviser on industrial matters, and Sir Maurice Hankey, who thought the economy would have to be put on some sort of war footing if large-scale rearmament was actually to be achieved.

*

Throughout 1935 and 1936 Churchill continued to receive classified information relating to Germany's growing military strength. Desmond Morton provided figures on German armaments, while Ralph Wigram kept him up to date with the latest information from the Foreign Office. Churchill was also approached, secretly, by a growing number of serving officers who, distressed at the state of their respective services, turned to him for help. One of the most important of these was Squadron Leader Torr Anderson, who telephoned Churchill's secretary on 20 May 1936. 'As a Service officer you would appreciate his position', wrote Violet Pearman to Churchill. 'He did not wish to write, but … he would confidently say you would be much interested in what he had to say.'[18] Anderson, who was Director of the RAF's Training School, was concerned that educational standards were falling and that too few observer-navigators were being trained. On 25 May, he articulated these concerns to Churchill and presented him with a seventeen-page memorandum which argued that not enough was being done to prepare the RAF for war.

Already convinced that this was the case, Churchill spent much of the summer harrying Ministers with his own memoranda and letters. In particular, he was able to make a thorough nuisance of himself as a member of the Government's Air Defence Research Committee. This body – a sub-committee of the Committee of Imperial Defence – had been set up to look at ways of improving Britain's air defences through scientific experiments. To the intense irritation of his colleagues, Churchill used his position to range across and criticise the entire breadth of the Government's air policy, while also lobbying in favour of some of the more eccentric ideas of his friend Professor Lindemann, such as the development of aerial mines.

In fact, the Air Ministry, under the leadership of Lord Swinton (previously Philip Cunliffe-Lister), was undergoing a transformation. In February 1936, the Cabinet had approved the latest and most long-lasting expansion scheme of the inter-war period – 'Scheme F'. This considerably increased Britain's air strike capability – replacing light with medium bombers – while also re-equipping the majority of the Air Force with the latest models. Hampdens, Wellingtons, Wellesleys, Blenheims, Hurricanes and Spitfires were ordered in bulk before the prototypes had even been tested. This was to speed up the process considerably and provide the RAF, in theory, with a total of 8,000 new planes by the spring of 1939. In addition, Swinton implemented the 'shadow factory' scheme, whereby the Government built, or provided grants for motor-car companies to expand, factories in which employees would be trained in the making of aircraft parts. This would allow aircraft production to swell, quickly and seamlessly, if war were to break out. Finally, the Air Ministry was providing virtually unlimited funding for the experiments of Robert Watson-Watt, whose work on radio waves would lead to the invention of radio detection finding (RDF), better known by its American acronym, RADAR.

There were, of course, still serious problems. The information now regularly being provided to Churchill by Torr Anderson constituted a litany of deficiencies, while even Watson-Watt was forced to complain that Air Ministry red tape was causing intolerable delays to his work. Scheme F, for all its ambition, came up short. By the spring of 1938 – the year in which war almost broke out – only 4,500 out of the 8,000 aircraft had been delivered and scarcely one Spitfire, Wellington, Hampden, Beaufort or Lysander was ready for use. The best that can be said for the Air Ministry in 1936 is that it had moved away from the window-dressing schemes of previous years and was now heading, slowly, in the right direction. It was certainly in a better state than the War Office, which revealed its anachronistic mindset with the 1935–6 Army Estimates, which increased spending on forage for horses by £44,000 but only provided an extra £12,000 for motor fuel.[19]

*

As the summer parliamentary session for 1936 neared its end, Churchill joined Austen Chamberlain in calling for a secret session of the House of Commons. This would allow members to debate the real status of Britain's defences without advertising deficiencies to foreign powers. Baldwin, reluctant to duel with Churchill even when spared the onlookers from the parliamentary press gallery, refused. He did, however, agree to receive a deputation of MPs and peers to discuss their concerns and on 28 July, eighteen Conservative grandees – thirteen MPs and five peers – trooped through the door of 10 Downing Street to be received by the rather underwhelming triumvirate of Baldwin, Lord Halifax and Inskip.

Churchill dominated proceedings. Well prepared by Morton and Anderson, he challenged the Government on almost every aspect of air defence, while stating his belief that the French estimate of a total of 2,000 German first-line planes by the end of the year was considerably short of the mark. At the second meeting, on 29 July, he expressed concern at the extraordinarily slow rate of munitions, tank and machine-gun production and ended with a plea that all decisions now taken be treated as in an emergency.

Baldwin's reply was striking. Without engaging with any of the specifics that had been put to him, he explained, with startling honesty, the thinking which had guided him over the last few years:

> Most of you sit for safe seats. You do not represent industrial constituencies; at least, not many of you. There was a very strong, I do not know about pacifist, but pacific feeling in the country after the war. They all wanted to have nothing more to do with it, and the League of Nations Union have done a great deal of their propaganda in making people believe they could rely upon collective security, and it was a question in 1934 whether if you tried to do much you might not have imperilled and more than imperilled, you might have lost the General Election when it came. I personally felt that very strongly, and the one thing in my mind was the necessity of winning an election as soon as you could and getting a perfectly free hand with arms.

Baldwin explained that the rearmament programme had been slow because it had had to start from scratch. (Owing to the decline in Government orders, many of the armaments factories had shut down in the 1920s.) Yet both he and Chamberlain were against turning the economy over to even semi-war conditions, since this might damage the ordinary trade of the country. Of course, if there *were* an emergency then he, as Prime Minister, would be fully prepared to contemplate emergency powers. Here lay the main difference. Churchill believed that Nazi Germany posed an immediate threat to the security of Europe and thus the British Empire, while Baldwin, as he made clear, did not consider war with Germany inevitable:

> The worst of it is we none of us know what goes on in that strange man's mind; I am referring to Hitler. We all know the German desire, and he has come out with it in his book, to move east, and if he should move east I should not break my heart, but that is another thing. I do not believe she [Germany] wants to move west because west would be a difficult programme for her, and if she does it before we are ready I quite agree the picture is perfectly awful.

Finally, the Prime Minister assured his colleagues that he had no intention of plunging the country into war – not for the League of Nations or anyone else. There was one danger he could foresee, yet even then he believed it would be both possible and sensible to keep Britain out of it:

> Supposing the Russians and Germans got fighting and the French went in as the allies of Russia owing to that appalling pact they made, you would not feel you were obliged to go and help France, would you? If there is any fighting in Europe to be done, I should like to see the Bolshies and the Nazis doing it.[20]

Churchill was not satisfied. Baldwin had promised air parity and yet by Churchill's pretty accurate calculations, the RAF was still significantly behind the Luftwaffe and would remain so for some time. On 12 November 1936, during the debate on the King's speech, he unleashed a 'sledge-hammer' attack on the Government.[21] It had been two years, Churchill declared, since he had first moved an amendment to the Loyal Address, stating that the country's defences were no longer adequate for her safety. Two years on and here he was offering the same amendment. During the intervening period Germany had grown exponentially stronger. She had built a vast air force, reintroduced conscription, begun to construct a submarine fleet and remilitarised the Rhineland. What had Britain done in the same period? She had lost air superiority and then parity; she had failed to develop new tanks and other weapons; she had deprived the Territorials of basic equipment; and she had granted Germany the right to build up to 35 per cent of the Royal Navy. Well might Sir Thomas Inskip, who had deployed the biblical quotation by way of mitigation, describe the years 1933–5 as 'the years that the locust hath eaten'.[22]

For Churchill, the remedy was obvious and urgent. The Government must establish a Ministry of Supply to expedite rearmament and regulate industry to prioritise this effort. This would, inevitably, involve some interference with trade but it was better than the absurdities of the situation as it currently stood, with firms allowed to prioritise more lucrative contracts from abroad – including Germany – over the needs of the British Government. Inskip was sympathetic to this idea. He had, however, been forced to oppose it in Parliament, while at the same time assuring Members that the decision was not final. Churchill ridiculed this shilly-shallying:

> The Government simply cannot make up their mind, or they cannot get the Prime Minister to make up his mind. So they go on in strange paradox, decided only to be undecided, resolved to be irresolute, adamant for drift, solid for fluidity, all powerful to be impotent. So we go on preparing more months and years – precious, perhaps vital to the greatness of Britain – for the locusts to eat.[23]

Responding to this onslaught, Baldwin made his statement of 'appalling frankness', in which he confessed his belief that it would have been electorally impossible to initiate large-scale rearmament before the 1935 General Election. The feelings of the people had been too pacific and, for this reason, 'democracy is always two years behind the dictator'. Now, however, the Government had a mandate for rearmament and there was a deep conviction among the British people that 'there must be no going back on our resolution for such rearmament as we deem necessary to meet any possible peril'.[24]

That this was now the case owed much to Churchill's campaign which, during 1936, had broadened to embrace a significant section of liberal and even left-wing opinion. This developed as Churchill sought to harness support for the League of Nations and collective security to his own policy of rearmament. His speeches took on the liberal shibboleths of the age and soon he was being invited to collaborate with such cross-party organisations as the League of Nations Union, the Anti-Nazi Council and the New Commonwealth Society.

At the same time, the left was moving, slowly, towards Churchill's position. In July 1936, a group of Spanish Generals took up arms against the centre-left republican Government of Santiago Casares Quiroga. The ensuing Civil War, which saw Spanish towns destroyed by German planes, shattered the chimera of disarmament. The world was a dangerous place and fascism – responsible for atrocities in Abyssinia, Germany and now Spain – required the democracies to defend themselves and their values. Yet there was an alternative narrative to the year 1936: one which saw admiration for Nazi Germany reach its zenith and a new wave of tourists and right-wing fellow travellers set out to experience what one journalist described as 'Hitler's Wonderland'.[25]

VII

Hitler's Wonderland

> I have rather come to the conclusion that the average Englishman – whilst full of common sense as regards internal affairs – is often muddle-headed, sloppy and gullible when he considers foreign affairs.
>
> Sir Horace Rumbold to Geoffrey Dawson, 10 June 1936[1]

Ernest Tennant and his wife rose early. Leaving Nuremberg's Grand Hotel at seven o'clock on the morning of Sunday 15 September 1935, they drove south-east, out of the town, towards the vast rally grounds. There, as the sun rose, the sight of 120,000 uniformed storm troopers, already lined up in perfect ranks, hit spectators like a 'gigantic tulip field' bursting into bloom. Tennant was mesmerised. 'If anyone in any country still lacks conviction of the might of Nazi Germany, the cyclopean spectacle of this steel-discipline party parade would supply it', he wrote.

> None of the great war kings of the past, from Xerxes to the Kaiser, ever dreamt of such pomp and pageantry as Hitler's organisers at Nuremberg have made a matter of annual routine … What I saw in Nuremberg has altered none of my opinions about the steady progress of Germany and the vital importance of Anglo-German friendship … Possibly, if the present regime survives, we are witnessing the birth of a super race.[2]

The Nuremberg Rally of 1935 was not Tennant's first experience of Nazi Germany. A well-connected merchant banker, he knew Germany from previous business trips and was an early enthusiast for the regime. In 1932, he had been befriended by Joachim von Ribbentrop and together the pair set out to create contacts between the Nazis and leading politicians in Britain. Initially, these efforts had limited success. Stanley Baldwin was so wary of being caught talking to Tennant in Downing Street that, when he remembered that the Foreign Secretary was due, he abruptly ended their conversation, told Tennant that they must not be seen together and ordered him out of the room. 'I thought for one moment that Mr Baldwin was going to ask me to hide in a cupboard', recalled the banker.[3]

By 1936, however, circumstances had changed. The Nazi revolution, so shocking and turbulent in 1933 and 1934, appeared to have calmed. The Treaty of Versailles had been eviscerated, the Stresa Front destroyed. Hitler had restored German self-respect and appeared to have found a miracle cure for unemployment. German strength, German unity and German achievement were wonders to behold. At the same time, British disillusionment with France had reached new heights. Failure to support Britain over Abyssinia and perceived attempts to drag her into war over the Rhineland were compounded by the election of the Popular Front – an alliance of left-wing parties, including the Communists – in May 1936, just two months after the ratification of the highly suspect Franco-Soviet Pact. Traditional Francophobia melded with a renewed fear of communism, while the outbreak of the Spanish Civil War suggested that Europe was dividing into rival ideological camps. Under these circumstances, a noticeable swing towards Germany occurred. This change was, of course, far from universal. Many Britons still considered Nazism abhorrent, while the majority of the population were more concerned with the economy and living standards than events abroad. Nonetheless, there was a perceptible shift which saw admiration for Nazi Germany increase and a fresh wave of enthusiasts set out to experience the new Reich for themselves. The Anglo-German moment had come.

*

As has already been noted, there were a number of reasons why members of the British ruling class felt sympathetic towards fascism, the most important of which was fear of communism. 'Nearly *all* my relations are ... tender to Mussolini (not so much lately) and to the Nazis and idiotic about "communism"', recorded Lady Nelly Cecil, wife of Lord Robert and daughter of the Earl of Durham, in November 1936. Later she would create a file of correspondence under the label 'An attempt – unsuccessful – to persuade leading Conservatives in Society to show German visitors that political and religious persecution, imprisonment without trial, murder and torture are not social recommendations in this country'.[4] Douglas Reed, central European correspondent for *The Times*, observed that 'class-prejudice and property obsession' had turned 'the snobs ... Fascist', while in May 1938 Harold Nicolson came across three young peers in Pratt's club who admitted that 'they would prefer to see Hitler in London than a Socialist administration'.[5] 'People of the governing classes think only of their own fortunes, which means hatred of the Reds', lamented the Government MP a few weeks later. 'This creates a perfectly artificial but at present most effective secret bond between ourselves and Hitler. Our class interests, on both sides, cut across our national interests.'[6]

At the same time, the Third Reich possessed a noxious glamour which, from its inception, attracted some of the more frivolous members of English society. Maggie Greville, one of London's leading hostesses, attended the 1934 Nuremberg Rally and returned 'full of enthusiasm for Hitler'; Lady 'Emerald' Cunard, another society hostess, travelled to Munich in August 1933, having proclaimed herself 'pro-Hitler'; while Lord Redesdale's fourth daughter, the appropriately named Unity Valkyrie Mitford, liked to astonish those she met – including her village postmistress – by greeting them with raised arm and 'Heil Hitler!'*[7]

This trend was encouraged by the well-known sympathies of the Prince of Wales, or King Edward VIII as he became on 20 January 1936. Lacking both intelligence and a sense of constitutional propriety, the Prince made his views clear when he told Prince Louis Ferdinand of Prussia, in July 1933, that it 'was no business of ours to interfere in

* Unity would later become notorious for her friendship with Hitler, who described her and her sister Diana (who in September 1936 married the leader of the British Union of Fascists, Sir Oswald Mosley) as 'the perfect specimens of Aryan womanhood'. When war broke out in 1939 she attempted suicide by shooting herself in the English Garden in Munich but failed to kill herself. Invalided back to England on Hitler's orders, she died in 1948.

Germany's internal affairs either *re* Jews or *re* anything else' and that 'dictators were very popular these days and that we might want one in England before long'.[8] Four months later, he told the former Austrian Ambassador Count Mensdorff that national socialism was 'the only thing to do', while, in June 1935, the diarist and Tory MP Chips Channon noted 'much gossip about the Prince of Wales' alleged Nazi leanings'.[9]

The reason tongues had been set wagging was the speech the Prince had given to members of the British Legion on 11 June 1935, in which he praised the forthcoming visit to Germany of a delegation of ex-servicemen. This took place the following month and was, as Anthony Eden had warned, a propaganda gift for the regime. A two-hour audience with Hitler was followed by a visit to the British War Prisoners' Cemetery, a sanitised tour of Dachau concentration camp – in which guards disguised as prisoners succeeded in deceiving the tourists – and a 'quiet family supper with Herr Himmler'.[10] At public functions, the delegation declared the First World War a 'colossal blunder', received the Hitler salute, and laid wreaths at various memorials – though not, as their hosts requested, one commemorating the 'martyrs' of the Nazis' 1923 'Beer Hall Putsch'.[11]

Another visit to cause controversy was that of Charles Vane-Tempest-Stewart, 7th Marquess of Londonderry. Described by the former Conservative MP Cuthbert Headlam as 'stupid' and 'conceited' – 'the proud nobleman in an old-fashioned novel' – Londonderry had been Secretary of State for Air (1931–5) and Lord Privy Seal (1935) in the National Government.[12] That such a 'half-wit', as Churchill called him, was able to retain his place in the Cabinet for so long was due to his wife's influence over Ramsay MacDonald and the fact that Britain's first working-class Prime Minister 'greatly enjoyed standing at the top of the grand staircase in Londonderry House as the first Minister of the Crown in full evening dress'.[13] But MacDonald's susceptibilities could not sustain Londonderry for ever and, in November 1935, Stanley Baldwin dropped him from the Cabinet, having sacked him from the Air Ministry four months earlier. As his biographer has observed, it was Londonderry's resentment at his treatment which prompted him to search for new causes in fresh pastures. He craved 'external esteem' and, having long been a critic of the Government's foreign policy, decided to visit Germany in order to gather the opinions of her leaders.[14]

The visit, which he undertook with his wife and fourteen-year-old daughter, occurred between the end of January and the second week of February 1936. Escorted by Göring's minions, they viewed a torch-light procession from the Reich Chancellery, visited Luftwaffe installations and listened to a Wagner recital. On the second day of their visit, they were entertained by Göring at his country estate and, on 2 February, enjoyed a lunch given by Ribbentrop for twenty-five people, including Hitler's party deputy, Rudolf Hess. The highlight was the two-hour audience Londonderry had with Hitler at the Reich Chancellery on the afternoon of 4 February. As the interpreter, Paul Schmidt, recalled, 'It was almost like a wooing by Hitler of the coy Britannia.' Hitler expounded on the dangers of Bolshevism, expressed his desire for an understanding with England (as he invariably referred to Britain) and emphasised the need for German expansion. The success of this courtship was revealed when Londonderry issued a press statement on his return, declaring that he had encountered 'a very friendly feeling towards this country [in Germany], and a very strong desire for the friendship of Great Britain and France'. A few days later, he described Hitler as a 'kindly man with a receding chin and an impressive face' to an audience in Durham and repeated the Führer's assertion that he was building a strong Germany in order to prevent communist expansion in the west.[15]

Predictably, this parroting of German propaganda by a former Cabinet Minister provoked criticism. The *Manchester Guardian* mocked the Marquess's gullibility, while Harold Nicolson gave his verdict on the former Air Minister's behaviour in his diary:

> My new pal Maureen Stanley [wife of Oliver Stanley, President of the Board of Education, and Londonderry's eldest daughter] asked me to come round and meet her father who is just back from hob-nobbing with Hitler. Now I admire Londonderry in a way, since it is fine to remain 1760 in 1936; besides, he is a real gent. But I do deeply disapprove of ex-Cabinet Ministers trotting across to Germany at this moment. It gives the impression of secret negotiations and upsets the French. But we are incorrigibly irresponsible in such things.[16]

Londonderry's visit, which he repeated several times over the next two years, established him as the most prominent advocate of

Anglo-German friendship and leading British apologist for the regime. In April 1938, he published *Ourselves and Germany*: a plea for co-operation, in which he emphasised the 'racial connection' between the two nations and ridiculed the notion that Germany was 'impatiently waiting until her rearmament has reached a further stage so as to fall upon her neighbours'.[17] He was, though, by no means the only non-fascist to be duped. Apart from Lord Lothian, who had a second audience with Hitler in May 1937, and Ernest Tennant, there was the historian Arnold Toynbee – who left his 1936 meeting with Hitler 'convinced of his sincerity in desiring peace' – the former Deputy Secretary to the Cabinet, Thomas Jones, and even the former Labour leader, George Lansbury.[18]

Lansbury's meeting with Hitler in April 1937 and subsequent endorsement – he 'will *not* go to war unless pushed into it by others' – is only the most glaring evidence that the right did not possess the monopoly for gullibility during this period.[19] Indeed, as the Oxford don and Labour candidate A. L. Rowse later noted, 'not one of the Left intellectuals could republish what they wrote in the Thirties without revealing what idiotic judgements they made about events'. Apart from the pro-appeasement Editor of the *New Statesman*, Kingsley Martin – who desired a policy not merely of isolation but of 'Little Englandism' – Rowse was thinking of his fellow don and future Labour Cabinet Minister Richard Crossman, who for a considerable part of the decade believed that Hitler intended to introduce socialism in Germany.[20] 'I remember walking him around the quad at All Souls,' recalled Rowse, 'shouting at the blond brute: couldn't he see that Hitler meant not socialism, but fascism? Dick would defend Hitler with, "At least you must admit that he is *sincere*!"'[21]

*

For those who perceived the true nature of Nazism, the growing procession of amateur diplomats and Third Reich tourists during 1936 and 1937 was a source of irritation and even despair. 'I realise that in our free country the Government cannot always prevent Mayfair from heading Hitlerwards', wrote the long-suffering Sir Eric Phipps on 10 November 1936. 'But if some of the visitors could be choked off I think it would be a good thing. So far as I can see they only raise false hopes here and will eventually arouse more resentment in the German breast than even that curmudgeon – the British Ambassador – who has always obstinately declined to give Göbbels, Schacht and Co. the slightest hope of obtaining the smallest colony.'[22] Viscount Cecil agreed. 'These people who go to Berlin are really rather a nuisance', he complained to his fellow League enthusiast, the Oxford classicist Gilbert Murray. 'They seem to me to be entirely taken in by the Germans. What is the use of Allen [Lord Allen of Hurtwood] assuring us that they mean peace, when Germany never loses an opportunity of arrogant and anti-international action? … My friends on the right wing seem to me to be insane in their fear of communism.'[23]

The most damning analysis, however, came from Phipps' predecessor in Berlin, the unfailingly perceptive Sir Horace Rumbold, who, in June 1936, wrote to the doggedly pro-appeasement Editor of *The Times*, Geoffrey Dawson:

> I have rather come to the conclusion that the average Englishman – whilst full of common-sense as regards internal affairs – is often muddle-headed, sloppy and gullible when he considers foreign affairs. One often hears such phrases as 'the Germans are so like us'. Nothing is more untrue … I could quote many points of difference. For one thing Germans have a streak of brutality which is quite absent in the ordinary Englishman and Germans like to put up with things that are repugnant to the average man in this country. My point is, therefore, that we should know the people with whom we propose to deal.
>
> Now Hitler has quite consistently applied the principles of 'Mein Kampf' in Germany herself – he has now got to apply them in his foreign policy and that's where the trouble is coming. The value to us of an understanding with Germany is not only that it may bring peace and stability in western Europe but that it may act as a drag on Hitler's adventures in central and eastern Europe. Once he embarks on any adventure in those regions war is, to my mind, a dead certainty. The ordinary Englishman does not realise that the German is an invariable Oliver Twist. Give him something and it is jumping off ground for asking for something else.
>
> I thought that after Hitler had reoccupied the Rhineland he had admitted that Germany had achieved '*Gleichberechtigung*' [equal rights] – but I now read that she still has not got it. Perhaps she will admit that

> she has it if and when Hitler's dream comes true and Europe is inhabited by a block of 250 million Teutons.[24]

Yet the tide, for the moment, was with the Germanophiles. In October 1935, the Anglo-German Fellowship had been formed, following the closure of its predecessor, the Anglo-German Association, over a row about its Jewish members.* By the summer of 1936, this self-consciously elite organisation could boast twenty-four lords and seventeen MPs among its members, as well as numerous bankers, businessmen, generals and admirals. Corporate subscribers included such well-known names as Thomas Cook, Dunlop Rubber, Lazard Brothers, Price Waterhouse and Unilever.[25] By no means all of these people or companies were Nazi sympathisers. Many simply wanted to use the Fellowship to further their business interests. Yet while the organisation claimed to be apolitical, it was, in reality, a vehicle for German propaganda: facilitating contacts and trips for those members of the British elite interested in visiting the Third Reich. Its Chairman was Lord Mount Temple – who, as Wilfrid Ashley, had been Conservative Minister of Transport between 1924 and 1929 – and its secretaries were those unofficial travel agents for the regime, Ernest Tennant and T. P. Conwell-Evans. On the German side, the most important figure was Ribbentrop.

Vain, arrogant and shallow, Joachim von Ribbentrop had been trying to foster ties between the British and the Nazis since 1933. Born into the officer class of the old Wilhelmine Germany – though without the 'von', which he later bought – he had made his fortune by marrying the daughter of the largest German producer of sparkling wine, before going on to become the agent for such well-known brands as Green and Yellow Chartreuse, Johnnie Walker whisky and Pommery champagne. Having played a minor role in Hitler's accession to power, the highly ambitious and, by now, devoted Ribbentrop managed to carve

* In the autumn of 1934, the German equivalent of the Anglo-German Association was dissolved and replaced by a 'Fellowship', exclusive to those of 'pure Aryan' descent. After some internal debate, its British version followed suit in April 1935. Writing at the time of its dissolution, the President of the Association, General Sir Ian Hamilton, claimed that he was sympathetic to the plight of the German Jews but that he did not consider it patriotic or right that 'the whole question of internationalism be clouded over by this one aspect of Germany's present condition'.

a niche for himself, in the early years of the Third Reich, as the Führer's unofficial emissary and propagandist abroad.

Initially, his political efforts were unsuccessful. Sir John Simon responded coolly to his advances, while other Government figures, such as Ramsay MacDonald and Neville Chamberlain, regarded him as an interfering parvenu. He was, however, favoured by a number of leading hostesses, including Lady Londonderry and 'Emerald' Cunard, and in 1935 successfully negotiated the Anglo-German Naval Agreement. On 24 July 1936, Hitler rewarded him by appointing him Ambassador to the Court of St James, though not, as Ribbentrop had hoped, State Secretary. According to Frau von Ribbentrop, the Führer's parting words to her husband were: 'Ribbentrop, bring me the English alliance.'[26]

This was not to be. Although the newspapers put a brave face on it, Ribbentrop's tenure in London was, as many predicted, a disaster. Arriving at Victoria station on 26 October 1936, he shocked political opinion by breaking with protocol and making a bombastic speech on the platform. He astounded the congregation in Durham Cathedral by giving the Nazi salute during the hymn 'Glorious things of Thee are spoken' – which can employ the same Haydn melody as 'Deutschland über Alles' – while the repetition of this gesture to King George VI, in February 1937, became infamous. Soon the object of ridicule, he was christened 'Ambassador Brickendrop' and even the pro-appeasement Nancy Astor accused him, to his face, of being a 'damned bad Ambassador'.[27] Before this reputation was cemented, however, Ribbentrop enjoyed a certain amount of social if not political success, while, at the same time, the Nazis benefited from a series of propaganda coups.

*

On 1 August 1936, the eleventh modern Olympiad opened in spectacular style in Berlin. Over 100,000 people watched the ceremony in the new stadium in the west of the city, while an estimated half a million gathered to cheer the processions along Unter den Linden. Twenty miles of garlands and 40,000 square yards of flags gave the capital the appearance of a gigantic 'battle tent of some great emperor'.[28] Having driven in triumph from the Reich Chancellery,

Hitler opened the Games at 5.30 p.m. Twenty thousand carrier pigeons were released into the sky, while Germany's greatest living composer, Richard Strauss, conducted his own Olympic Hymn. As the music died away, the final torch-bearer, Fritz Schilgen – the seeming epitome of Aryan athleticism-appeared, completed a lap of the stadium and ignited the Olympic cauldron. High above, the world's largest airship, the 800-foot-long *Hindenburg*, loomed menacingly: a symbol of German might and, ultimately, tragedy.

The Berlin Olympics were a propaganda gift which the Nazis exploited to the full. Having originally decried the Games as the 'invention of Jews and Freemasons ... a play inspired by Judaism which cannot possibly be put on in a Reich ruled by National Socialists', Hitler soon realised, once in power, that he had been presented with a unique opportunity to play host to the world and dazzle it with his creation. With this in mind, the year 1936 – the remilitarisation of the Rhineland aside – saw a self-conscious effort on the part of the regime to become 'respectable'. No fresh steps along the bloody road to a racial utopia were taken – the Nuremberg laws, which turned Jews into second-class citizens, had been promulgated in September 1935 – and when a leading Swiss Nazi was murdered by a Jewish student in February, there was no pogrom as would occur after a similar assassination in November 1938. As the Games approached, signs forbidding Jews disappeared from the streets, as did Julius Streicher's semi-pornographic and virulently anti-Semitic newspaper, *Der Stürmer*. Books which had been proscribed reappeared in shops and jazz was once again played in nightclubs. In the days before the opening ceremony, 7,000 prostitutes were bussed into the capital from the provinces to compensate for the clear-out which had occurred since the Nazi takeover.

One hundred and fifty thousand foreign visitors travelled to Berlin for the Nazi sports jamboree. The British contingent was particularly large: Ribbentrop described it as a 'friendly invasion'.[29] It included the press barons Lords Rothermere, Beaverbrook, Kemsley and Camrose, as well as Lord Monsell (until June First Lord of the Admiralty), Sir Robert and Lady Vansittart (there to dispel the notion that the Permanent Head of the Foreign Office was irredeemably anti-German), Lord and Lady Aberdare, Lord Barnby, the Marquess of Clydesdale MP, Lord Hollenden, Lord Rennell of Rodd, Lord Castlereagh, Lord

Jellicoe, Kenneth Lindsay MP (Civil Lord of the Admiralty), Harold Balfour MP and Unity and Diana Mitford.*

Competing to impress their distinguished guests, the leading figures of the regime threw a series of ludicrously lavish parties. Ribbentrop turned his garden at Dahlem into a 'fairyland' for 600 people; Goebbels entertained 3,000 guests on an island on the River Havel; while Göring outshone both of his rivals by creating a miniature eighteenth-century village – complete with post office, inn, bakery, donkeys, merry-go-round and dancing peasants – on the lawns of the Air Ministry.[30] The American-born Conservative MP and socialite Chips Channon – who, as Harold Nicolson observed, had 'fallen much under the champagne-like influence of Ribbentrop' – was enraptured. 'There has never been anything like this since the days of Louis Quatorze', someone remarked. 'Not since Nero', exulted Channon, who left the Games convinced that Britain 'should let gallant little Germany glut her fill of the reds in the East'.[31] Even André François-Poncet, the sceptical French Ambassador, confessed that it was hard to remember that these men, 'so obviously pleased with this fashionable and exquisite entertainment', were also 'the persecutors of Jews and the torturers of the concentration camps'.[32]

The Olympics were a triumph for the Nazis. No sooner had they ended, however, than Hitler was presented with another propaganda coup. On 4 September 1936, the man who had led Britain to victory in the Great War, David Lloyd George, arrived at the Berghof to have tea with the German dictator. The visit, which had been arranged by Ribbentrop in collaboration with T. P. Conwell-Evans, yielded everything the Nazis could have hoped for. Delighted to find himself once again conferring with world leaders, the 73-year-old former Premier lapped up the Führer's compliments and returned them, proclaiming Hitler 'the greatest German of the age'.[33] When he returned, he was no less fulsome, describing the Führer as 'the George Washington of Germany'. 'German hegemony in Europe which was the aim and

* A small number of prominent Englishmen made a point of not attending the Games. Harold Nicolson, en route to Austria, decided not to drive through Germany, while Sir Austen Chamberlain, who had accompanied the Kemsleys on their yacht, refused to leave it and set foot on German soil.

dream of the old pre-war militarism is not even on the horizon of Nazism', he reassured the readers of the *Daily Express*.[34]

Five days after the Lloyd George visit, the annual party rally opened at Nuremberg. The increase in the number of British attendees compared to the previous year was noticeable. Lord Mount Temple, Chairman of the Anglo-German Fellowship, was there, as was the former Deputy Secretary to the Cabinet, Thomas Jones; the royal physician, Lord Dawson of Penn; Conservative MPs Lord Apsley, Frank Sanderson, Arnold Wilson, Thomas Moore and Admiral Sir Murray Sueter; and Lady Ravensdale, Lord Curzon's daughter and sister-in-law to Sir Oswald Mosley.

The calibre was certainly higher than the following year when, according to an undercover British Secret Service officer, the English contingent consisted chiefly of 'nonentities, race-purity maniacs, and undeveloped mental cases, with one or two really dangerous individuals'. Foremost among the latter was Captain George Pitt-Rivers – anthropologist, eugenicist, anti-Bolshevik, racist and Dorset landowner – who 'expressed at great length rabid anti-British sentiments, preferably to a German audience, talked anti-Semitism unceasingly, and though despised by the Germans is obviously being used by them'. Pitt-Rivers was accompanied by his secretary-cum-mistress, Catherine Sharpe, who proclaimed her sympathies by sporting a gold swastika badge, in addition to a gold bangle decorated with fasces and swastikas. The SIS agent – who had struggled to get information from their companion, a Major Watts, since 'he was seldom sober for periods of any length' – recommended that the couple be prevented from doing further harm by having their passports confiscated.[35]

*

While an increasing number of the British socio-political elite enjoyed the splendour of Hitler's new Reich, the British Government remained in limbo. Baldwin expressed his desire for better relations with Germany but when his Foreign Secretary, Anthony Eden, asked 'How?' retorted, 'I have no idea, that is your job.'[36] Hitler had failed to reply to the widely ridiculed 'questionnaire' enquiring which treaties he intended to honour, and, over the summer, had renewed his campaign for the restoration of Germany's lost colonies. The British still hoped to find a permanent agreement but struggled to see how this could be achieved. Their suggestion for a five-power conference to replace the now defunct Treaty of Locarno was ignored, while the outbreak of the Spanish Civil War in July reduced the chances of a general European settlement still further. In June, the Secretary of State for War, Duff Cooper, caused a row by emphasising the importance of Anglo-French co-operation in the face of German aggression – an indication of the residual fear of alliances, not least with the French – and in November Eden declared, at Leamington, that Britain would only take up arms to defend her own vital interests. Four days earlier, on 16 November 1936, King Edward VIII told Stanley Baldwin that he intended to marry an American divorcée named Wallis Simpson.

The importance of the Abdication to our story is twofold. First, it removed a monarch who exhibited a worrying admiration for dictatorships in general and Nazi Germany in particular. Describing the crisis on 22 November, Chips Channon noted that the King, who 'is insane about Wallis, insane', was also 'going the dictator way', being 'pro-German, against Russia and against too much slip-shod democracy'. 'I shouldn't be surprised', continued the Conservative MP, 'if he aimed at making himself a mild dictator.'*[37] This was unlikely. Yet it is possible to imagine a situation in which the King's sympathies, combined with his lack of respect for the constitution, could have triggered a worse crisis than that which occurred in December 1936. Then the monarchy was able to survive since it was essentially a personal affair and the King went quietly. A political rupture would have been a very different matter.

Second, the Abdication was wilfully misinterpreted by Ribbentrop, who persuaded Hitler that it constituted a plot by the British Government to rid itself of a pro-German monarch. 'Don't you know what expectations the Führer has based on the King's support in the coming negotiations? He's our greatest hope!' expostulated the Ambassador when the Embassy's Press Attaché, Fritz Hesse, tried to warn him about the crisis. 'Don't you think the whole affair is an

* The supreme demonstration of Edward's lack of judgement and troublemaking came in October 1937 when, as Duke of Windsor, he and his new wife paid a highly publicised visit to Germany, posed with Hitler and gave the Nazi salute on at least two occasions.

intrigue of our enemies to rob us of one of the last big positions we hold in this country? ... You'll see, the King will marry Wally and the two will tell Baldwin and his whole gang to go to the devil.'[38] When this turned out not to be the case, Hitler's confidence in the English and the possibility of an Anglo-German alliance was severely shaken. According to Hesse, he told Ribbentrop to pack his bags and return to Germany. There was, he said, 'no other person in England who is ready to play with us' now 'that the King has been dethroned'. He asked his Ambassador to report on what he had been able to achieve since his arrival but if it amounted to nothing he would not blame him.[39] The high noon of Anglo-German friendship was over.

VIII

Enter Chamberlain

> As Ch[ancellor] of Ex[chequer] I could hardly have moved a pebble; now I have only to raise a finger and the whole face of Europe is changed!
>
> Neville Chamberlain, August 1937[1]

On 30 January 1937, Hitler declared himself sated. Addressing the Reichstag on the fourth anniversary of his accession to power, he proclaimed that national honour had been restored and the battle for German equality among the Great Powers won. 'The time of so-called surprises has been ended', he announced.[2] Remarkably, Hitler kept this pledge (more or less) for an entire year. Although the Luftwaffe was to wreak carnage in the Spanish Civil War, provoking worldwide condemnation, 1937 was to see no fresh German challenge to European security or move to expand the borders of the Reich. Yet if 1937 appears a hiatus in Hitler's drive towards European hegemony, it could scarcely be described as a year of calm continuity. The open wound which was the Spanish Civil War grew deeper and became infected as German and Italian planes, ships, submarines and troops masquerading as 'volunteers' joined General Franco in his battle against the Republicans and the International Brigades, backed by arms supplied by the Soviet Union. No one could be sure that the fighting would not lead to a full-blown European war, while for millions of people Spain became the 'heart of the heartless world': a microcosm of the Thirties in which fascism and communism, totalitarianism and democracy, clashed in a battle for civilisation.[3] At the same time, war broke out between Japan and China, while, in Russia, Stalin presided over the 'Great Purge', responsible for the deaths of some three million people.[4] In

May, President Roosevelt was forced to sign a third Neutrality Act into US law, while, in June, the Government of Léon Blum fell, ushering in a new period of political turmoil in France. Against this backdrop, an orderly transition at the top of British politics took place.

Stanley Baldwin's retirement had been anticipated for some time. In January 1936, Churchill's friend the civil servant P. J. Grigg was wondering about the chances of that 'whited sepulchre Baldwin clearing out and allowing the country to be run by somebody with the normal number of faculties'.[5] In the aftermath of the Hoare–Laval fiasco this did not seem unlikely. Churchill thought him fatally undermined and in May was forecasting that the Prime Minister's long run, amazing 'considering his mediocre intellect', was drawing to a close.[6] This was neither fair nor accurate. Despite appearing like a half-awake tortoise or benevolent parson, Baldwin had an acute political sense and an extraordinary ability to weather crises. Having handled the Abdication as no one else could – certainly better than Churchill would have done – he had, however, finally drained his last reserves of energy. In February, Thomas Jones found him counting the hours 'like a schoolboy within sight of the holidays' and on 28 May 1937, two weeks after the coronation of King George VI, Baldwin finally surrendered the seals of office.[7] His advice to the new King was to send for the Chancellor of the Exchequer, Neville Chamberlain.

The accession of Neville Chamberlain to the Premiership was greeted with a flurry of newspaper profiles. *The Times* praised his 'Roman virtues' – austerity, realism, devotion to the *res publica* – while the *Sunday Times* noted his directness and determination.[8] The *Daily Telegraph* provided a more personal portrait. 'Despite his stiff and somewhat forbidding exterior', the new Prime Minister was in fact 'very human', the paper revealed. He was 'as devoted to his briar pipe as Mr Baldwin to his cherry' and was, reputedly, a 'good judge of claret'. A passionate fisherman, for whom 'the next best thing to fishing is to talk about fishing', he suffered from gout but was, happily, a sound sleeper who 'when he casts off his clothes … casts off his cares'.[9]

These were, no doubt, interesting insights. Yet the inescapable impression of the newspaper portraits is that there was more that was unknown than known about the new Prime Minister. As Chancellor of the Exchequer for over six years, Chamberlain was, of course, a prominent and recognisable public figure. Yet he was also something of an enigma: a formal and aloof politician; a technocrat, who concealed his personality behind a Victorian sense of propriety and public duty. Who then was Neville Chamberlain?

The most widely known fact about the new Prime Minister was his provenance. The son of the former Colonial Secretary Joseph Chamberlain, and half-brother to the former Foreign Secretary and Conservative leader Austen, Arthur Neville Chamberlain was the third member of what was, and would remain, the greatest political dynasty of the twentieth century. In many ways this was a daunting and difficult inheritance. 'Joe' Chamberlain had been a colossus: a man who, having begun adult life as the manager of a screw manufacturing business in Birmingham, became the statesman who, in Churchill's phrase, made the political weather.[10] A radical and socially reforming Lord Mayor of Birmingham, between 1873 and 1876, he transformed the city so that in three years it was 'parked, paved, assized, marketed, gas-and-watered and *improved*'.[11] He then entered national politics, where he carried out the unique feat of splitting both the Liberal and Conservative parties – first through his opposition to Home Rule for Ireland and then through his energetic campaign to introduce a system of imperial preference in trade and tariffs. As Colonial Secretary he was the foremost champion of Empire and, not insignificantly considering his son's career, made several unsuccessful attempts to forge an Anglo-German alliance in the late 1890s.

According to Neville's sister Hilda, 'father never made favourites among his children'.[12] Yet, while this may have been true, there is no doubt that 'Pushful Joe' conceived of very different roles for his two sons. The elder boy, Austen – the product of Chamberlain's first marriage – was destined to continue his father's political work. Born into a red despatch box, as his father put it, Austen was sent to Trinity College, Cambridge, where he read history, and then to the Continent to continue his training as a future statesman. In 1892, aged twenty-nine, he joined his father in the Commons and within three years he had received his first Government post as Civil Lord of the Admiralty.

Neville Chamberlain, by contrast, was not meant to have a political career. Six years younger than Austen – the son of Chamberlain's second wife – Neville, his father determined, was to be the businessman of the family. Thus, while Austen was set on a manicured path to Cambridge and Westminster, Neville was made to study mathematics, metallurgy and engineering in Birmingham, before joining a local firm of chartered accountants.

This may not have been wildly exciting but it was certainly more sociable than the next venture which Joe imposed on his younger son. Having lost substantial amounts of money in the South American securities crash of the late 1880s, as well as by general extravagance, Chamberlain senior was looking to Chamberlain junior to repair the family fortunes. A conversation with the Governor of the Bahamas, Sir Ambrose Shea, convinced him that vast sums were waiting to be made farming sisal – an agave vaguely resembling a giant pineapple, whose large, sword-shaped leaves can be used to make a hemp-like fibre – within the archipelago and in 1891 he despatched the 22-year-old Neville to Andros Island, where he would first buy and then tend a 20,000-acre estate.

Years later, Alec Douglas-Home – who was Chamberlain's Parliamentary Private Secretary throughout his Premiership – drew a direct link between Chamberlain's famous reserve and the ghastly experience he had on Andros.[13] Hot, humid and mosquito-ridden, Andros was almost unbearably spartan. The ultimate backwater of Empire, there were virtually no other European settlers, which meant that under the accepted conditions of racial segregation, Chamberlain had practically no one to talk to. To make matters worse, the wretched plants would not grow. Shea's hot tip had turned out merely to be hot and after six hard, arid years – during which Chamberlain had to endure such trials as a fire destroying much of his first harvest and the irritation of being sent an American ensign instead of the Union Jack to display outside his office – the Chamberlains were forced to admit that the scheme had been a colossal failure, involving a loss of some £50,000.

Chamberlain was devastated. Although he had hated life in the Bahamas, he was desperate to succeed for the sake of his father and reproached himself bitterly for the failure of the scheme. 'I cannot blame myself too much for my want of judgement', the 27-year-old wrote, pitifully, to his father. 'I have been here all the time and no doubt a sharper man would have seen long ago what the ultimate result was likely to be.'[14] On a happier note, he was now free of the tropics and could begin to develop a richer life in England. Through the influence of an uncle he became the director of a metal company in Birmingham and also took on responsibility for the family-owned business, manufacturing cabin berths for ships. At the same time he began to discover those interests which would sustain him throughout his life. These included a love of fishing and shooting, a dedication to gardening, a passion for natural history, and a strong, if specific, enthusiasm for literature and music, his great loves being Shakespeare and Beethoven.

As his biographer has noted, Chamberlain was a progressive and benevolent employer. As Manager of Elliott's Metal Company he introduced both a welfare officer and a full-time surgery, and in June 1914 he created a profit-sharing bonus scheme for employees of the family firm.[15] At the same time, he was increasingly involved in the civic life of Birmingham: first as an active enthusiast for the development of Birmingham University – whose forerunner, Mason College, he had attended – and then as a no less dedicated member of the management board of Birmingham General Hospital. In 1911, he was elected to the city council and three years later he was invited to take up the post which his father had held with such distinction: Lord Mayor of Birmingham.

As this appointment suggests, Chamberlain was too old to fight in the war – he was forty-five in 1914.* Thanks to his position as Lord Mayor, however, he was able make a serious contribution to the war effort. In early 1916, he persuaded the Home Office to adopt his own plan for a co-ordinated warning system against Zeppelin raids, and in September of the same year he launched the Birmingham Municipal Bank, which allowed depositors to lend money to the state in support of the war. By contrast, Chamberlain's first foray into national administration, as Director General of National Service, was not a success. Tasked by Lloyd George, on Austen's recommendation, to come up with a plan for the implementation of conscription, while protecting essential war industries and at the same time forming a new government department, Chamberlain foundered. In his defence, it was a

* Though spared the horrors of the trenches, the tragedy of war was brought home to Chamberlain when his cousin Norman was killed at the Battle of Cambrai in 1917. Having always regarded Norman as a brother and 'one of the most intimate' friends he ever had, Chamberlain was devastated and wrote a short book commemorating his cousin.

Herculean task, made all the harder by Whitehall rivalries and a distinct lack of support from the Prime Minister. A politician with greater national administrative experience and more allies might have survived but Chamberlain had neither and in August 1917, after only eight months in the job, he resigned.

For Chamberlain, the failure of National Service was a public humiliation and personal setback which ranked alongside the disaster of the Andros sisal scheme. Writing to his sister Hilda one month before his resignation, he confessed to the same feelings of despair which had overcome him twenty years earlier in the Bahamas 'when the plants didn't grow'.[16] Fortunately he now had financial security to fall back on as well as the comfort of a family of his own. In the spring of 1910, at the comparatively late age of forty-one, he had fallen in love with the 29-year-old Anne Vere Cole, a vivacious and affectionate young woman from an Irish sporting family, and in January of the following year the pair were married.

'Annie' Chamberlain was a very different character to Neville. While he was shy, earnest and insecure, she was warm, sociable and confident. It was, however, an extremely happy marriage, complemented by the arrival of two adored children – Dorothy in 1911 and Frank two years later. Annie provided Neville with the love and unwavering support he needed and, in May 1937, he generously and sincerely attributed his success to her:

> I should never have been P.M. if I hadn't had Annie to help me. It isn't only that she charms everyone into good humour and makes them think that a man can't be so bad who has a wife like that … But besides all this she has softened and smoothed my natural impatience and dislike of anything with a whiff of humbug about it and I know she has saved me from making an impression of hardness that was not intended.[17]

With Annie's help, Chamberlain soon overcame the indignity of his failure at the National Service Department – though he never forgave Lloyd George, for whom he preserved a lifelong hatred. Realising that his political future lay in the House of Commons, he sought a seat and in the General Election of December 1918 was returned as Member of Parliament for Birmingham Ladywood. Like his marriage and entry into local politics, Chamberlain's arrival at Westminster, at the age of forty-nine, occurred comparatively late in life. He was, however, determined to make up for lost time and soon made his mark as an advocate of radical social reform. In 1922, following the break-up of the Lloyd George coalition – which ended Austen Chamberlain's chances of becoming Prime Minister – he was appointed Postmaster General and the following year joined the Cabinet as Minister for Health.

Chamberlain's six years at the Ministry of Health, responsible for housing, local government and social policy, made him. Displaying his Radical Liberal pedigree to the full, he piloted onto the statute book such progressive and improving bills as the Rating and Valuation Act (1925), the National Health Insurance Act (1928), the Local Government Act (1929) and, with Churchill, the Orphans and Old Age Pensions Act (1925). Rightly praised for this impressive record of social reform, by the end of the Twenties Chamberlain was widely talked of as a future Conservative leader and in 1931, two months into the National Government, he succeeded Philip Snowden at the Exchequer, charged with dragging the country out of the Great Depression.

Chamberlain's tenure at the Treasury has been much criticised. Lambasted at the time by both the Opposition and radical Tories, such as Harold Macmillan, it then became the subject of near-overwhelming censure for a whole generation of historians and economists writing in the Keynesian heyday. According to these critics, Chamberlain was a rigid, unimaginative, deflationary Chancellor – purely concerned with balancing the books – who waited passively for the economy to recover while doing next to nothing to reduce the appallingly high levels of unemployment that continued well into the decade. Indeed, if the first image of Britain in the 1930s is of a man with an Edwardian collar waving a piece of paper, the second is of the dole queues and soup kitchens, so vividly portrayed in George Orwell's *The Road to Wigan Pier* (1937). Chamberlain has not come out well from either of these images. Yet recent historians have been far kinder in their assessment of his handling of the economy, pointing to – in contradiction to the myth that Chamberlain was an advocate of laissez-faire – such initiatives as the protection and cartelisation of the iron and steel industries, the creation of the London Passenger Transport Board and the designation of four 'special areas', covering some of the country's worst-affected regions, in which experiments to induce economic growth were carried out. These ventures were not particularly bold and their impact on unemployment was negligible. Yet the fact remains that by the mid-1930s, growth had returned, sterling had recovered, exports were up and unemployment had been cut from a high of well over 3.4 million in 1932 to 1.8 million by 1937.[18]

Nor was the economy Chamberlain's only concern. With Baldwin lethargic and MacDonald increasingly senile, it was left to Chamberlain to provide the driving force for the entire Government. In many ways this was a role he relished. As he wrote to his sister Ida in May 1934, 'Unhappily it is part of my nature that I cannot contemplate any problem without trying to find a solution for it. And so I have practically taken charge now of the defence requirements of the country.'[19] As time wore on, however, he began to champ at the purely de facto nature of his status. 'As you will see I have become a sort of Acting P.M.,' he wrote to his other sister, Hilda, in March 1935, 'only without the actual power of the P.M. I have to say "Have you thought" or "What would you say" when it would be quicker to say "This is what you must do".'[20]

As this statement reveals, Chamberlain was not lacking in self-confidence and by the mid-1930s had already developed that conceit, some would say arrogance, which many were to identify as a weakness and cause for frustration during his Premiership. The most overt manifestation of this was in his treatment of the Opposition. While Baldwin was generous and emollient – believing it his duty to 'educate' Labour for government – Chamberlain had a complete intolerance for what he regarded as the muddle-headed, self-righteous and ineffective Labour Opposition. This came across in the House of Commons, where, even according to the most sympathetic of observers such as Alec Douglas-Home, he was a 'cruel debater' who seemed to delight in taking the Opposition to bits 'almost like a vivisectionist'.[21] Indeed, as Chamberlain himself relayed to Ida in the summer of 1927, 'Stanley [Baldwin] begged me to remember that I was addressing a meeting of gentlemen. I always gave him the impression, he said, when I spoke in the H. of C. that I looked on the Labour Party as dirt. The fact is that intellectually, with a few exceptions, they *are* dirt.'[22]

This impression was not lost on Labour MPs, the vast majority of whom detested Chamberlain. This was to have important, even historic, consequences when, in the autumn of 1939 and then again in the spring of 1940, Chamberlain tried to form a coalition but found that neither the Labour Party nor the Liberals were prepared to serve under him. By this time, of course, he was the man of Munich and the embodiment of a policy that had clearly failed, yet it would be wrong to underestimate the extent to which personal animosity played a part in the Opposition's rejection of Chamberlain.

Within Government, Chamberlain's intellectual self-assurance was no less apparent. As Douglas-Home recalled, 'He was never afraid to take a decision on his own, and would never just accept another's findings on any subject. He would listen to all the arguments, assimilate them very quickly, and then take his decision. Once his mind was made up he was full of confidence in his own decision.'[23] As the leading member of a Government whose other senior figures were often dilatory this was, in many ways, a virtue. Yet it was also a fault which led Chamberlain increasingly to disregard the views of others and ignore facts which did not suit his conclusions. 'His mind, once made up, was ringed round by a barrier so hard and so unimaginative that no argument could penetrate it', recalled the social reformer Violet Markham, who had worked with Chamberlain at the National Service Department, while Lord Swinton was one of a number of colleagues to observe a tendency to regard any views which deviated from his own as 'disloyal and personally hostile'.[24]

This prickly strain of intellectual arrogance was one of several factors which made Chamberlain a difficult man for colleagues to warm to. Appearing both in dress and manner like a 'provincial undertaker' – he was soon nicknamed 'the Coroner' – or a censorious bird of prey, he was the opposite of clubbable and frequently described as 'cold' and 'aloof'.[25] Arthur Balfour thought he had 'a heart like a stone', while Harold Macmillan, who recalled a 'sardonic, not to say contemptuous, look', likened a meeting with him to 'an interview with the headmaster'.[26] His voice possessed a harsh quality, 'without music or seductive charm', though, as the Independent MP Arthur Salter conceded, it was a 'serviceable instrument for his purpose' and reflected the 'orderly mind' behind it.[27] Humour was not his strong suit. Douglas-Home had to conspire to remove any jokes he might have attempted in his speeches – since 'they were terrible' – and he avoided the Commons' smoking room as much as possible.[28] It would, however, be unfair to write Chamberlain off as a cold fish with an ascetic's disdain for his fellow human beings. An acutely shy man – a reality which few of his detractors perceived – he could, as Douglas-Home and other intimates attested, be warm, even witty, in the right company. He and Annie laughed at Charlie Chaplin until they 'ached at his absurdities', while his rapture at seeing a new bird on his bird table or the first crocus of spring betrays a romantic side at odds with his austere image.[29]

*

When Ramsay MacDonald became Prime Minister for the second time, in 1929, he solemnly announced, 'We intend to do some thinking.' Later he added, 'There must be no monkeying.' As Malcolm Muggeridge observed, this was followed by little thinking and much monkeying.[30] Neville Chamberlain, by contrast, did not need more time to think and monkeying was out of the question. Although he realised that it was quite late in the day to become Prime Minister at the age of sixty-eight, he was 'glad to have the opportunity of getting some things done that ought to be done' and was determined to 'leave my mark behind me as PM'.[31] In an ideal world he would have liked his legacy to have been in social reform. By 1937, however, the world was far from ideal and it was almost inevitable that the new Prime Minister would be forced to spend the majority of his time on foreign affairs. Characteristically, Chamberlain already had a strong sense of what he needed to do.

In an oft-quoted remark, recorded by Anthony Eden after a dinner in the spring of 1936, Austen Chamberlain exhorted his half-brother, 'Neville, you must remember you don't know anything about foreign affairs.'[32] Unsurprisingly, given the subsequent course of events, this typical, and doubtless infuriating, elder-brotherly put-down has been repeated ever since.* It was not, however, entirely fair. Although Neville Chamberlain was no expert in this field – no barrier to a number of British Foreign Secretaries – he had taken a keen interest and played an active role in the formulation of foreign policy throughout the life of the National Government. Indeed he was twice asked if he would consider becoming Foreign Secretary, in December 1933 and again the following year.

---

* According to Eden, Neville, who was hosting the dinner, merely 'smiled wryly and remarked that this was rather hard on a man at his own dinner table'.

Pre-eminent among Chamberlain's already established beliefs was the very reasonable conviction that Britain must try to reduce the number of her potential enemies. As the Chiefs of Staff liked to remind the Cabinet at frequent intervals, Britain could not defend herself and her Empire against the combined might of Germany, Italy and Japan; and, as Chamberlain liked to remind his colleagues, the country could not afford to spend inordinate amounts trying. In 1934, therefore, Chamberlain attempted to persuade the Cabinet to open negotiations with Japan for a ten-year non-aggression pact. The desirability of such an agreement was reinforced by Chamberlain's complete lack of faith in the United States as an ally in the region. As he wrote perceptively to his sister Hilda in July 1934:

> We ought to know by this time that USA will give us no undertaking to resist by force any action by Japan short of an attack on Hawaii or Honolulu. She will give us plenty of assurances of goodwill especially if we will promise to do all the fighting but the moment she is asked to contribute something she invariably takes refuge behind Congress.[33]

'We have the misfortune to be dealing with a nation of cads', he had lamented on another occasion.[34]

Chamberlain's proposal for a pact with Japan came to nothing. The Cabinet were not prepared to forfeit American goodwill, however amorphous, in favour of a potentially illusory agreement with Tokyo, and when, in December 1934, the Japanese announced their intention not to renew the Washington Naval Treaty their scepticism appeared to have been vindicated. Chamberlain, reluctantly, dropped the scheme but the idea of improving relations with Britain's would-be adversaries, even following acts of naked aggression, remained. In June 1936, he decided to bounce Eden into dropping sanctions against Italy, just one month after Mussolini had annexed Abyssinia, by describing the continuation of the policy as 'the very midsummer of madness' in a speech to the 1900 Club.[35] Chamberlain's justification for this 'blazing indiscretion' – a clear breach of Cabinet collective responsibility – was that 'if those who should give a lead won't, someone else must'. Fortunately for him, most of his colleagues welcomed the move – the end of sanctions was announced eight days later – and Eden, who had not been consulted because 'he was bound to beg me not to say it!', graciously accepted the Chancellor's insincere apology.[36] It was, however, an early example of Chamberlain's tendency to act unilaterally as well as his determination to force through his own policy even if it meant employing underhand tactics. Within less than two years, this combination was to play a decisive part in the breach between Chamberlain and Eden.

*

Neville Chamberlain did not invent the policy of appeasement. A strategy which some historians have detected in British diplomacy as far back as the mid-nineteenth century, it had become the guiding principle in British foreign policy by the early 1920s. Anthony Eden told the House of Commons on several occasions that Britain's aim was 'the appeasement of Europe', while the various Government missions to Hitler and Mussolini were all attempts to try and put this policy into some sort of action.[37] The problem was that by 1937 very little had been achieved. Despite endless offers of pacts and conventions, the only actual agreement to have been struck in the four years since the Nazis came to power was the 1935 Anglo-German Naval Treaty. In the meantime, Hitler had succeeded in dividing his opponents while pursuing his own policy of aggressive treaty revision. Chamberlain hoped to change this. Determined from the outset to be his own Foreign Secretary, he sought to end the haphazard and lackadaisical nature of British foreign policy – which seemed merely to drift from one crisis to another – and establish friendlier relations with the dictator states. As he made clear in a letter to a distant relation in January 1938, the approach he intended was a highly personal one:

> The dictators are too often regarded as though they were entirely inhuman. I believe this idea to be quite erroneous. It is indeed the human side of the dictators which makes them dangerous, but on the other hand, it is the side on which they can be approached with the greatest hope of successful issue.[38]

In coming to this determination, Chamberlain was in no way motivated by admiration for Nazi Germany. No Rothermere or Londonderry, his letters to his sisters, though broadly silent on the persecution of the Jews and German domestic policy, demonstrate a clear aversion to the regime and its gangster tactics. He was, however, always an optimist. 'Hitler's Germany is the bully of Europe', he wrote after Hitler reintroduced conscription in March 1935. 'Yet I don't despair.'[39] A year later he explained his unwillingness to commit a greater proportion of Britain's financial resources to the arms race with Germany thus:

> If the menace of attack from Germany is as imminent as Winston [Churchill] would have us believe, there is nothing we could do which would make us ready to meet it. But I do not believe that it *is* imminent. By careful diplomacy I believe we can stave it off, perhaps indefinitely, but if we were now to follow Winston's advice and sacrifice our commerce to the manufacture of arms we should inflict a certain injury upon our trade from which it would take generations to recover.[40]

The first stage of this 'careful diplomacy' was to identify what the Germans actually wanted. As Chamberlain told the Soviet Ambassador two months after he became Prime Minister:

> I consider it very important to make the Germans move from general phrases about the 'haves' and 'have nots', the true meaning of which nobody understands, to a practical and business-like discussion of their wishes. If we could bring the Germans to the negotiating table and, with pencil in hand, run through all their complaints, claims and wishes, this would greatly help clear the air or at least clarify the current situation.[41]

This approach had, in fact, been suggested ten months earlier by the new Deputy Under-Secretary for Foreign Affairs, Sir Alexander Cadogan. Convinced that 'our so-called "policy" has been a complete disaster since 1919', Cadogan strongly deprecated the Foreign Office's preferred course of 'keeping Germany guessing' since 'all the guessing that's been done for the past three years has been done by *us*. That's the whole point: we've left the *whole* initiative to G[ermany] and therefore we're submitted time and again to *faits accomplis*.'[42]

Cadogan and Chamberlain wanted to 'call Germany out' on her demands. Once these were stated it would be possible to see whether they could be satisfied and, if so, attempt to lock Hitler into an agreement. The problem with this was that while Germany's immediate ambitions were actually well known, the majority did not lie within the gift of the British Government. As Lord Lothian reported following meetings with Hitler, Göring and Schacht in May 1937, Germany sought 'adjustments in eastern Europe about Austria and in favour of the German minorities in Danzig, Memel, Czecho-Slovakia and Poland and economic and colonial arrangements which will assure to Germany a steadily rising standard of living for her people'. Lothian did not think these demands 'in themselves unreasonable' and urged the Government to reach an agreement quickly along these lines since the 'temper in Germany is changing'.[43] Yet of the above list only the repatriation of Germany's lost colonies constituted a concession which Britain, with the co-operation of other powers, was in a position to make.* Furthermore, this was considered so divisive, both within the Conservative Party and the Dominions, that the Colonial Secretary, William Ormsby-Gore, did not believe that the Government could survive such a move.[44]

Chamberlain was undaunted. Though he did not believe that the surrender of Tanganyika on its own could purchase a lasting peace, he retained the hope that some form of colonial restitution could be used to coax Germany into a larger European settlement. The fact was, as Chamberlain realised, Britain had very few cards to play with and if the colonial card had some value – the 'ace of spades' according to Sir Robert Vansittart – then there was no way that he was going to discard it.[45] He therefore warned the participants of the 1937 Imperial Conference not to 'close their minds to the possibility' of colonial adjustments and then began to work on a scheme which would see the creation of a new German colony in central Africa at the expense of existing colonial suzerains, not to mention the native populations.[46]

*

In his mission to improve relations with the dictators, Chamberlain was driven by no small sense of urgency. This was fuelled, firstly, by

---

* The majority of the former German colonies were actually held by other countries – South Africa, Australia, New Zealand, Japan and France. Those granted to Britain after the First World War were Tanganyika, a third of pre-1914 Togoland and a sliver of the pre-1914 Cameroons.

the knowledge that, as far as Germany was concerned, Britain was dealing with a 'rising market' and, secondly, by the deterioration of the broader international situation.[47]

On 26 April 1937 the German Condor Legion bombed the Basque town of Guernica in northern Spain, causing a global scandal. This atrocity – which most brutally exposed the fiction of 'non-intervention' – was followed in May by an attack by Republican aircraft on the German pocket battleship *Deutschland*, in turn answered by the German shelling of the port of Almería. At the same time and despite the so-called Gentlemen's Agreement signed between Britain and Italy in January 1937, in which each party committed to respecting the other's rights in the Mediterranean, Italian submarines were conducting an unofficial blockade of all vessels heading to Spain. This was principally aimed at the Russians, who were supplying the Republicans, but by no means exclusively, as the British soon discovered. On the night of 31 August, the Italian submarine *Iride* fired torpedoes at the British destroyer HMS *Havock*. Fortunately they missed but a couple of days later a British merchant ship was sunk by the Italian submarine *Diaspro* near Valencia. British parliamentary and press reaction was outraged and on 3 September Churchill wrote to Eden with a plan designed to deter Italian piracy:

> Why not arrange with Mustapha Kemal [Atatürk] to slip a few parties of R[oyal] N[avy] personnel and a modern 4-inch gun on to tankers or other merchantmen coming from the Black Sea, with a trapdoor, etc. and let these vessels offer themselves to the pirate submarines, and get a few?[48]

Unsurprisingly, Eden was not enthusiastic about this scheme – an 'admirable' one 'if it were our policy to expedite the outbreak of war', commented Duff Cooper.[49] Having already announced that the Royal Navy would retaliate against attacks on British ships, the Foreign Secretary sought a diplomatic solution. A conference at the Swiss village of Nyon from 10 to 14 September 1937 established a system of international naval patrols in the Mediterranean to reduce what were laughably referred to as acts of 'unidentified' piracy. More ridiculous still, the British desire to appease Mussolini (who had boycotted the conference) was so great that the Italians were then invited to participate in the patrols. 'From suspected pirates to policemen of the Mediterranean – and the Russians, whose ships we were sinking, excluded!' gloated the Italian Foreign Minister, Count Galeazzo Ciano.[50] The Nyon Conference was, however, judged a major success. The submarine attacks ceased, and Eden won plaudits for his tough diplomacy. What the Foreign Secretary did not reveal was that the British knew that the Italians had decided to halt the submarine attacks on 6 September, before the conference opened.

No sooner had trouble died down in one part of the world than it ignited elsewhere. On 7–8 July 1937, Chinese and Japanese troops clashed at Lugouqiao (the Marco Polo Bridge), just west of Peking. By August the fighting had spread to Shanghai, threatening the considerable British interests in the region. On 26 August, the Union Jack-flying car of the British Ambassador to China, Sir Hughe Knatchbull-Hugessen, was attacked by a Japanese aeroplane, leaving the Ambassador seriously wounded. Not wishing to provoke a war, the Japanese quickly expressed their 'regret'. This was, however, followed by two more serious incidents on the Yangtze River in December, when a Japanese field battery shelled the British gunboat HMS *Ladybird*, and an American gunboat, the USS *Panay*, was sunk by Japanese aircraft. Chamberlain was furious but when even this outrageous act failed to produce the necessary co-operation from the United States the British Government reluctantly concluded that there was nothing that could be done. As the Prime Minister had told the Cabinet on 6 October, he 'could not imagine anything more suicidal than to pick a quarrel with Japan at the present moment when the European situation had become so serious. If this country were to become involved in the Far East the temptation to the dictator states to take action, whether in Eastern Europe or in Spain, might be irresistible.'[51]

Confronted with so many dangers and difficulties, other men might have despaired. Chamberlain, however, was not prone to pessimism. As he revealed to his sister Ida at the end of October 1937, he already had in mind 'far reaching plans ... for the appeasement of Europe and Asia and for the ultimate check to the mad armament race, which if allowed to continue must involve us all in ruin'.[52] The key to the situation was Germany. 'If only we could get on terms with the Germans I would not care a rap for Musso', he admitted in July.[53]

Unfortunately, the previous month had seen the cancellation of the planned visit to London by the German Foreign Minister, Konstantin von Neurath, thus denying Chamberlain the chance of testing his new diplomatic strategy. Then, seemingly from out of the blue, came what appeared the perfect opportunity. Lord Halifax, the Lord President of the Council and deputy to Eden at the Foreign Office, received an invitation to attend an international hunting exhibition in Berlin.

IX

Hunting for Peace

> It must have been strange, Hitler thinks he is God, and my father thinks God sent him to see Hitler.
>
> Lord Halifax's son on his father's meeting with Hitler[1]

Edward Wood, 3rd Viscount Halifax, was one of the most respected figures in British politics. Impeccably aristocratic – one of the largest landowners in the north of England – he was famous for having entered into direct negotiations with Gandhi to end the civil disobedience campaign when Viceroy of India between 1926 and 1931. Six feet five inches tall, with a slight stoop, a magnificent head, 'sympathetic kindly eyes' but no left hand (a deformity from birth), he gave, according to Robert Bernays, 'more the impression of a Prince of the Church than a politician'.[2] Indeed, religion was one of two constant passions in Halifax's life – the other being fox hunting. This distinctive, though by no means incongruous, combination caused a certain amount of teasing. Churchill came up with the pun 'Holy Fox', while Lord Beaverbrook described him as a 'sort of Jesus in long boots'.[3] It was, however, as a fox-hunting man that Halifax gained the opportunity, or rather the cover, to travel to Germany in the late autumn of 1937 and begin the process of trying to appease Hitler.

According to Halifax's memoirs, the origins of his visit to Germany were entirely innocent. A master of the Middleton Foxhounds, he happened one day, in early October 1937, to receive an invitation, via the Editor of the *Field* magazine, to attend a hunting exhibition in Berlin and then spend a few days fox shooting in Pomerania. This was not, however, the whole picture. As Eden recorded in his own memoirs, the idea of a visit by Halifax had been raised by the Nazis earlier in the year, while in June 1936 Ribbentrop had told Thomas Jones that if a Baldwin–Hitler meeting were not possible then 'the sooner Halifax met the Führer the better'.[4] Either way there can be no doubt that the invitation, which offered an ideal opportunity for establishing contact with the Nazi leadership on an unofficial basis, was warmly welcomed by both Halifax and Chamberlain. Indeed, as his biographer has noted, Halifax had already confessed to his ambition of 'squaring Hitler', having apparently convinced himself that the same techniques that had worked with Gandhi could be applied to this no less eccentric troublemaker.[5]

The Foreign Office was doubtful. While Eden was sceptical and huffy, Vansittart was so opposed to the venture that when details of the proposed visit were leaked to the *Evening Standard* it was widely assumed that the Permanent Under-Secretary had been the source. There was, however, Foreign Office support from one quarter. Britain's new Ambassador to Berlin was full of hopes for the visit.

In April 1937, Sir Eric Phipps had been transferred from Berlin to Paris. Considered too 'anti-Nazi' by his London masters to be able to make progress with the regime, the urbane Phipps was more than happy to swap Nazi Germany for what he had always regarded as his 'spiritual home' but not before he had warned, in his valedictory despatch, that Germany was planning to incorporate both Austria and the Sudeten Germans of Czechoslovakia and that, even then, there was no guarantee that Hitler would be contented.[6] His replacement was the little-known Ambassador to Argentina, Sir Nevile Henderson.

At first sight Henderson did not appear that different from his predecessor. Quintessentially English, his uniform for a train journey consisted of 'an old coat, a pair of flannel trousers, and that much abused and maligned article an old school tie, generally the old Etonian cricket colours'.[7] When not on a train he was considered dapper: a tall, elegantly dressed ladies' man, with a neat moustache and a red carnation in his buttonhole. His favourite pursuit was shooting and it was through this shared hobby that he developed a close friendship with King Alexander I of Yugoslavia during his time as Ambassador to Belgrade. He continued to shoot in Germany – not least with Göring – while at other times he enjoyed bamboozling his hosts by responding to their '*Heil Hitlers!*' with his own 'Rule Britannia!' salute.

Apart from a shared sprinkling of eccentricity, however, Eric Phipps and Nevile Henderson were very different men. While the former, like Horace Rumbold before him, quickly came to regard the Nazi regime as repulsive, inherently sinister and fundamentally dangerous, the latter possessed no a priori dislike of authoritarian regimes. Indeed, it was principally owing to his proven ability to 'get on' with dictators, such as King Alexander, that Henderson had been given the post. Moreover, the new Ambassador had a fatalistic streak which led him to believe that he had been plucked from obscurity (or Buenos Aires) 'by Providence for the definite mission of, as I trusted, helping to preserve the peace of the world'.[8]

This messianic zeal soon got Henderson into trouble. Having alarmed Eden by talking a lot of 'nonsense' about 'what he was going to do in Germany' at a dinner at Windsor Castle, one of his first acts in post was to write a memorandum on 'British policy towards Germany' in which he argued that Britain should seek German friendship by acquiescing to her union with Austria, recognising her right to colonies and allowing her 'economic and even political predominance in eastern Europe'.[9] To say this represented 'a very considerable departure from the policy hitherto followed by His Majesty's Government', as Orme Sargent, the head of the Central Department, wrote in a covering note for Lord Halifax (who had requested to read the memorandum for his journey to Berlin), was a major understatement. Vansittart was dismayed, yet he was soon distracted by two far more public controversies. The first occurred after Henderson had unilaterally made it known that he intended to break the unofficial boycott of his predecessor, as well as of the French and American Ambassadors, and attend the Nuremberg Rally. The second resulted from a conversation the Ambassador had with the Austrian Minister in which he intimated his support for the *Anschluss*. These gaffes were crowned in June 1937 when, in a much-publicised speech to the Deutsch-Englische Gesellschaft (the German equivalent of the Anglo-German Fellowship), Henderson chastised those in England who had 'an entirely erroneous conception of what the National Socialist regime really stands for', arguing that less attention should be paid to the Nazi dictatorship and far more to the great social experiment Germany was undertaking.[10]

Completely appalled, Vansittart and much of the Foreign Office soon came to regard the Ambassador's appointment as 'an international misfortune'.[11] Yet Henderson did not consider that his authority emanated from the Foreign Office. Apart from Providence, he correctly believed that he was faithfully carrying out the policy of the Prime Minister, who had set out his views in two separate interviews with the Ambassador in April and October 1937. 'I may honestly say that to the last and bitter end I followed the general line which he [Chamberlain] set me', Henderson later wrote, adding that this was all the easier 'since it corresponded so closely with my private conception of the service which I could best render in Germany'.[12] The two Nevil(l)es were thus in lockstep and with Halifax also marching to the same tune the scruples of the Foreign Office over the latter's visit were easily overcome. The Lord President would travel to Germany under the pretext of visiting the International Hunting Exhibition. The real purpose of the trip, however, would be a meeting with Hitler at Berchtesgaden.*

The object of this meeting was hotly disputed. While Eden and Vansittart wanted Halifax merely to 'listen and confine himself to [a] warning comment on Austria and Czecho-slovakia' – adding that they must do 'all we can to *discourage* German initiative in these two states' – Chamberlain, Henderson and Halifax himself had far greater ambitions.[13] 'I do really believe that the PM's idea, as outlined to me, opens a new door on to a road along which progress is really possible', Henderson wrote to the Lord President after his October meeting with the Prime Minister.[14] A few weeks later, he explained how this might be achieved. 'If Germany will undertake to be "satiated" by the concessions we make her, we should be generous. Whatever pessimists may say to the contrary, I believe that, if we are not too niggardly, Germany will keep her word, at any rate for a foreseeable period.' Ten days later he added: 'We must drop all fears and suspicions ... The main point is that we are an *island* people and Germany a *continental* one. On that basis we can be

* As with Chamberlain a year later, Hitler showed no willingness to meet Halifax somewhere more convenient like Berlin. Indeed, the choice of Berchtesgaden both in 1937 and in 1938 – forcing first Halifax and then Chamberlain to travel the length of Germany – was a vivid illustration of where the power lay.

friends and both can go along the road to its own destiny without the clash of vital interests.'[15]

This rationale, which effectively conceded Germany a free hand in eastern and central Europe, was shared by Halifax. Sending Chamberlain some notes on the line he intended to take in Germany, he explained that he was 'not happy over the FO attitude over Czecho S. or Austria' and hoped that 'we should not feel bound (in Henderson's words) to oppose "peaceful Evolution" – rather liberally interpreted, perhaps'.[16] This 'light-hearted cynicism' might seem odd coming from a man of such high moral principles as Halifax but, as he had confessed in a recent letter to Baldwin, he could not bring himself to condemn nationalism or even racialism as either 'unnatural or immoral'.[17] 'I cannot myself doubt that these fellows are genuine haters of communism, etc.!' he wrote on the eve of his departure. 'And I daresay if we were in their position we might feel the same!'[18]

*

Halifax arrived in Berlin early on the morning of 17 November 1937. Greeted by Henderson, as well as a crowd of photographers, he spent the morning at the British Embassy before attending a 'lighthearted' family lunch with the Neuraths and then making his way over to the hunting exhibition.[19] There he discovered a considerable crowd already mingling among the exhibits, which included a pack of French foxhounds, a stuffed giant panda, various trophies shot by members of the British royal family and an 'Imitation Forest and Wild Animal section', in which the roar of a stag was conveyed by means of a gramophone. More ominously, the Germans had created a pre-war colonial section in which a large map was prominently displayed showing the 'lost territories'.

To his surprise, especially given all this competition, Halifax found himself one of the principal points of interest. Christened 'Lord Halalifax' by the Berliners (a pun on *Halali!*, the German equivalent of 'Tally ho!'), he was followed round the galleries by a large throng, politely doffing his bowler to all the raised arms. 'It is good for Lord Halifax to see the exhibition, and it's a very good thing for all these people to see Lord Halifax', a clearly pleased German official told Henderson. That evening, he was entertained by staff at the British

Embassy – during which the First Secretary, Ivone Kirkpatrick, gave him a thorough briefing on the Nazi persecution of the Churches – before, the next day, revisiting the exhibition, paying his respects at the Tomb of the Dead, and inspecting the vast, newly constructed Döberitz barracks in Brandenburg. It 'is the same all over Germany', Kirkpatrick explained.[20]

Suitably warned, Halifax was then taken to the station where he and Kirkpatrick boarded Hitler's special train for the overnight journey to Berchtesgaden. This was a comfortable experience. Their German hosts were eager to please, though they were apparently under the impression that Englishmen lived on whisky since a waiter appeared, at half-hourly intervals, bearing a tray of whisky and soda. According to Kirkpatrick, the two Englishmen were 'disappointing customers'.[21] Had they been less abstemious, however, it might have explained Halifax's extraordinary behaviour at the other end, when, having arrived at the Berghof, he failed to recognise Hitler. Worse, in a scene which might have come from the pages of P. G. Wodehouse, he assumed that the man in black trousers, silk socks and patent leather shoes, waiting to lead him up the snow-covered steps to the house, was a footman. Fortunately Neurath was on hand and managed to hiss '*Der Führer, der Führer*' in the Lord President's ear before Halifax could hand Hitler his hat and coat.[22]

Disaster averted, Hitler and Halifax then settled down for three hours of talks.[23] These did not start promisingly. Despite Halifax's opening statement, in which he praised Hitler's 'achievements' – in particular the stemming of communism – Hitler was in a 'peevish mood' and showed no inclination to try and establish common ground.[24] Indeed, he launched into an angry denunciation of the democratic system, which prevented good Anglo-German relations by allowing scurrilous criticism of Germany in both Parliament and the British press. Taken aback, Halifax responded, coolly, that he had neither the power nor the inclination to alter the British constitution and that if Hitler was waiting for this event before allowing relations between their two countries to improve then he, Halifax, was clearly wasting his time. This brought a halt to Hitler's tirade and allowed Halifax to move on to more constructive ground. He had, however, fleetingly stumbled on the right conclusion: in trying to satisfy Hitler through peaceful concessions, the British Government was, indeed, wasting its time.

Two weeks before Halifax boarded his plane, Hitler had summoned the heads of the armed forces, as well as the War Minister, Werner von Blomberg, and Neurath for a conference at the Reich Chancellery. There he informed them that in order to survive economically Germany must wage a war for 'living space' (*Lebensraum*) by 1943–5 at the latest. Austria and Czechoslovakia must be brought into the Reich. For this he was prepared to launch a surprise attack as early as 1938, since every year that passed merely allowed Germany's enemies to close the gap in the armaments race. As to who these enemies were, Hitler left no doubt: 'German policy had to reckon with two hate-inspired antagonists, Britain and France, to whom a German colossus in the centre of Europe was a thorn in the flesh, and both countries were opposed to any further strengthening of Germany's position either in Europe or overseas.' Fortunately for Germany, Britain was in decline – vide her crumbling position in the Far East, India and the Mediterranean – while France was so riddled with division that civil war might break out at any moment. Blomberg and the head of the Army, Werner von Fritsch, were not convinced. Time and again they stated that if Germany was to succeed in a future war then Britain and France must not be counted among her enemies. Hitler responded that Britain and probably France too 'had already tacitly written off the Czechs'.[25] Yet he could not be certain. Western intervention remained a dangerous possibility and, for his Generals, the chief plank of their opposition. Then, just as Hitler was struggling to convince his leading subordinates of the merits of his argument, the Lord President of the Council – 'the most important statesman and politician England had at the present time', according to the brief given by Downing Street to the German Embassy in London – came along and went a considerable way towards confirming his assumptions.[26]

'I said that there were no doubt other questions arising out of the Versailles settlement which seemed to us capable of causing trouble if they were unwisely handled e.g. Danzig,* Austria and Czechoslovakia', Halifax wrote in his diary of the visit. 'On all these matters we were not necessarily concerned to stand for the status quo as today, but we

---

* Formerly part of western Prussia, Danzig, on the Baltic coast, was created a Free City by Article 100 of the Treaty of Versailles, although Poland gained considerable rights over it.

were concerned to avoid such treatment of them as would be likely to cause trouble. If reasonable settlements could be reached with the free assent and goodwill of those primarily concerned we certainly had no desire to block.'[27] This was the exact opposite of the warning which Eden and Vansittart had wished Halifax to impart – though there can be little doubt that both Chamberlain and Henderson approved. Indeed, so intent was Halifax in conveying this message – which amounted to an acquiescence to German ambitions in eastern and central Europe – that he repeated it several times. 'Halifax observed that England was ready to consider any solution, provided that it was not based on force', recalled the interpreter, Paul Schmidt, adding that this also applied to Austria.[28]

Despite receiving this remarkable news – which constituted a revolution in British foreign policy – Hitler's mood did not improve. During a 'rather indifferent meat lunch' (Hitler had vegetable soup) in a 'hideous dining room', the Führer behaved like 'a spoilt, sulky child', refusing to be drawn on any topic of conversation. Flying, the hunting exhibition, even that English stalwart the weather, failed to tempt him and it was with some relief when lunch ended and Hitler led his guests down to a garish sitting room where he drank a large cup of hot chocolate with a 'floating iceberg of whipped cream'. This delight seemed to revive him for he became talkative on the subject of India. There was an easy solution to Britain's troubles on the Subcontinent, he told the former Viceroy: 'shoot Gandhi'. Then, 'if that does not suffice to reduce them to submission, shoot 200 and so on until order is established'. According to Kirkpatrick, Halifax, who had developed a respect for Gandhi during their negotiations, listened to this incitement to murder with 'a mixture of astonishment, repugnance and compassion'.[29] It did not stop him, however, from repeating the line that Britain would be prepared to offer Germany a colony of her own if this could form part of a wider European settlement.

Summing up his impressions of Hitler and the meeting, Halifax wrote:

> I can quite see why he is a popular speaker. The play of emotion – sardonic humour, scorn, something almost wistful – is very rapid. But he struck me as very sincere, and as believing everything he said. As

> to the political value of the talk, I am not disposed to rate this very high. I should think it was all to the good making contact – but I definitely got the impression that apart from colonies there was little or nothing he wanted from us and that he felt time to be on his side as regards European problems … in short [he] feels himself to be in a strong position and is not going to run after us. He did not give me the impression of being at all likely to want to go to war with us over colonies; but no doubt if he cannot be met on this issue, good relations, under which I suppose we might exert a good deal of influence, and without which the present strain continues, would remain impossible.[30]

For his part, Hitler spoke contemptuously of the man he would later refer to as the 'English Parson'.[31]

Halifax's next stop was a visit to Göring at his Carinhall estate in the Schorfheide Forest in northern Brandenburg. This was the setting of a famous piece of Foreign Office literature: the so-called Bison despatch, composed by Eric Phipps after his tour of the estate in June 1934. As Phipps had recounted:

> The whole proceedings were so strange as at times to convey a feeling of unreality; but they opened, as it were, a window on the Nazi mentality, and as such were not, perhaps, quite useless. The chief impression was that of the most pathetic naïveté of General Göring, who showed us his toys like a big, fat, spoilt child: his primeval woods, his bison and birds, his shooting-box and lake and bathing beach, his blonde 'private secretary', his wife's mausoleum and swans and sarsen stones, all mere toys to satisfy his varying moods, and all, or so nearly all, as he was careful to explain, Germanic. And then I remembered there were other toys, less innocent, though winged, and these might some day be launched on their murderous mission in the same child-like spirit with the same childlike glee.[32]

Three years on and Göring's ostentation, like his figure, had only grown. Dressed in brown boots and breeches, a green jerkin – valiantly held together by a green leather belt from which hung a dagger in a red sheath – and a green hat with a large chamois tuft, Göring drove the bowler-hatted Halifax around the forest 'in a kind of shooting phaeton with two Hanoverian chestnut horses', proudly showing off his bison and elk. Arriving at the house – a gargantuan construction situated between two lakes – Halifax noticed the Union Jack flying between the swastika and a hunting flag. He was then conducted along an immense series of rooms stuffed, as he correctly deduced, with treasures looted from Germany's finest museums. There was then a lunch of some of the rawest beef Halifax had ever encountered, before the Master of the Middleton Foxhounds and the Reich's Master of Forestry and Hunting repaired for a tête-à-tête on the international situation.[33]

This was a much more friendly conversation than Halifax had had with Hitler. The Lord President repeated his line that Great Britain was amenable to changes in the European status quo and Göring stated that the colonial question was the only issue between them. He was a great admirer of the British Empire, which he considered a 'stabilising influence', and thought that Great Britain should have 'no difficulty in recognising that Germany [too] was entitled to have special spheres of influence'. Halifax agreed. The British Government 'had no desire to intrude into matters that were not primarily our concern' – in other words, eastern Europe – though he urged that change occur peacefully and that 'nothing should be done in any quarter that might involve dangerous reactions for us all'. To this, despite his presence at the Hossbach Conference at the Reich Chancellery (so named after the record of the discussion made by Colonel Friedrich Hossbach) two weeks earlier, Göring solemnly assured Halifax that the Nazis would never shed 'one drop of German blood' unless it was forced upon them.

In his diary of the trip, later sent to Chamberlain and the Foreign Office, Halifax admitted that he had been 'immensely entertained' by Göring. Although he remembered the General's part in the Night of the Long Knives and could not help wondering 'how many people he had been, for good cause or bad, responsible for having killed', he found his personality 'frankly attractive'. Göring was 'like a great schoolboy, full of life and pride in all he was doing', a 'film star, great landowner interested in his estate, Prime Minister, party-manager, head gamekeeper at Chatsworth'. Moreover, Halifax found their conversation 'not discouraging', noting that the General was evidently in favour of Anglo-German friendship and would 'not, I should guess, be too difficult about

Hitler at Nuremberg, May 1933. Like many British observers, the *Daily Telegraph* wondered how a man who looked so uninspiring 'with that ridiculous little moustache' could prove 'so attractive and impressive' to the German people.

Anti-Semitism in action: the Nazis announce a boycott of Jewish businesses two months after coming to power.

As English as 'eggs and bacon', but the British Ambassador to Berlin, Sir Horace Rumbold, was one of the few to understand the expansionist nature of the regime from the beginning.

A voice crying in the wilderness: Winston Churchill walks along Whitehall, September 1938.

The unassuming Prime Minister: Stanley Baldwin crosses Parliament Square, 7 June 1935.

The 'best dressed man in London': Anthony Eden at a reception at the Polish Embassy, November 1936.

The 'Holy Fox': Lord Halifax in the Foreign Office.

The most influential of the early amateur diplomats: Lord Lothian was convinced Hitler desired peace despite his reading of *Mein Kampf*, c.1935.

Wooing the coy Britannia: Anthony Eden and Foreign Secretary Sir John Simon are courted by Hitler in the Reich Chancellery, 25 March 1935.

The power of public opinion: Viscount Cecil gathers three million signatures in support of the International Disarmament Conference, January 1932.

The death of collective security: the Abyssinian Emperor, Haile Selassie, appeals to the League of Nations following the Italian invasion of his country, 30 June 1936.

A year of German triumphs: (*top*) German troops enter the demilitarised Rhineland, 7 March 1936; (*centre*) the Olympics open in Berlin, 1 August 1936; (*left*) Britain's former war leader, David Lloyd George, is greeted by the man he would go on to describe as 'the George Washington of Germany', 4 September 1936.

'An international misfortune': (*above*) Britain's last ambassador to Nazi Germany, Sir Neville Henderson, with Hermann Göring at the Nuremberg Rally; (*below*) Lord Halifax with Hitler and German Foreign Minister Konstantin von Neurath at the Berghof, 19 November 1937.

The fishing Prime Minister: Neville Chamberlain cast several flies over Hitler between May 1937 and October 1938.

The Premier and the Duce, September 1938: Chamberlain was convinced that Mussolini could be separated from the Axis.

colonies; but does definitely look forward to readjustments in central Europe'.[34]

Back in Berlin, Henderson hosted a dinner in Halifax's honour, attended by, among others, Blomberg, Schacht and Göring's deputy, General Erhard Milch. After dinner, Halifax had a frank talk with Blomberg, who candidly explained that the colonial issue was really secondary: 'The vital questions for Germany, with her expanding population and set as she was in the middle of Europe, were those which concerned her central and eastern European position.' As an attendee of the Hossbach Conference, Blomberg knew whereof he spoke, adding that 'if everybody tried to sit on every safety valve, there was bound some time to be an explosion'.[35] This clear message was, however, distorted by Schacht (who had not been at the conference), who emphasised the importance of colonies and suggested that Britain might return Togoland and the Cameroons.

The next day, 21 November 1937, Goebbels and his wife came to tea. Halifax had expected to dislike the Propaganda Minister intensely but, perhaps owing 'to some moral defect in me', did not. Goebbels asked the Lord President to try to stop the attacks on Hitler in the British press, claiming that 'nothing caused more bitter resentment in Germany'. In particular, he complained about cartoons lampooning Hitler and seemed to have singled out for special criticism the *Evening Standard*'s David Low, whose depictions of the Führer were already famous.*[36] To this, Halifax gave the standard reply about the freedom of the press in Britain. He was, however, sympathetic and promised that 'His Majesty's Government would do everything in their power to influence our press to avoid unnecessary offence'.[37]

Travelling back on the train to Calais, Halifax set out his immediate conclusions in a memorandum for Chamberlain and the Foreign Office. 'Unless I am wholly deceived', he wrote, the Germans, 'from Hitler to the man in the street, do want friendly relations with Great Britain'. Furthermore, he felt 'sure Hitler was sincere when he said

* Appropriately enough, Low had produced a brilliant cartoon of Halifax at the Hunting Exhibition, in which Hitler indicated to the Lord President such trophies as 'Weimar', 'Versailles' and 'Locarno'. More portentously, there were a number of blank slots marked 'Reserved', the largest of which had drawn the attention of a distinctly worried-looking British lion.

he did not want war: Göring too'. There was, however, the colonial issue as well as Germany's obvious ambitions in central and eastern Europe. In considering both of these problems Halifax came down in favour of offering Germany a colonial settlement in exchange for some 'assurance, however given and supported, *that she is not out for war*'. Of course, he conceded, this was a vague proposition and promises, unlike colonies, could easily be taken back. Yet the alternative was even less enticing. Halifax, therefore, laid out three logical assumptions: '(a) we want an understanding with Germany; (b) we shall have to pay for it in (c) the only coin we have, which is colonial rendition of some sort'. Finally, considering the sort of assurances Germany might be asked to give in return, Halifax repeated his belief that Britain should not demand the retention of the status quo but should seek promises from Germany that she would undertake to fulfil her well-known ambitions peacefully. 'The whole thing comes back to this', he concluded: 'However much we may dislike the idea of Nazi beaver-like propaganda, etc. in central Europe, neither we nor the French are going to be able to stop it, and it would therefore seem short-sighted to forgo the chance of a German settlement by holding out for something which we are almost certainly going to find ourselves in the last resort powerless to secure.'[38]

For Chamberlain the trip had been a 'great success'. As Henderson confirmed in a series of enthusiastic letters, it had achieved its objective, which was to create a positive atmosphere from which it would be possible to 'discuss with Germany the practical questions involved in a European settlement'. Halifax had convinced Hitler of 'our sincerity', while both Hitler and Göring had disavowed the use of war – a judgement endorsed by Halifax when he told the Cabinet that the Germans were currently focussed on 'building up their country' and so had 'no policy of immediate adventure'.[39] 'Of course', as Chamberlain acknowledged breezily in a letter to his sister Ida, 'they want to dominate eastern Europe; they want as close a union with Austria as they can get without incorporating her in the Reich and they want much the same things for the Sudetendeutsche' in Czechoslovakia. Yet these things were not necessarily incompatible either with the peace of Europe or with British policy. 'I don't see why we shouldn't say to Germany give us satisfactory assurances that you won't use force to deal with the Austrians and Czecho-Slovakians and we will give you similar assurances that we won't use force to prevent the changes you want if you can get them by peaceful means.'[40]

For his part, Halifax wasted little time in fulfilling his promise to Goebbels and applying pressure to Britain's 'free' press. In fact, the most important and influential British titles were already on side. 'I do my utmost, night after night, to keep out of the paper anything that might hurt their [the Germans'] susceptibilities' and drop in 'little things which are intended to soothe them', confessed the Lord President's close friend, the Editor of *The Times*, Geoffrey Dawson, in a letter from May 1937.[41] There were, however, papers on the liberal left which were consistently critical of Nazi Germany. Accordingly, Halifax arranged to see the Chairman of the Liberal *News Chronicle*, Sir Walter Layton, and the proprietor of the Labour-supporting *Daily Herald*, Lord Southwood. His talk with the latter did not appear to have an immediate effect since, only a couple of days later, the paper published a cartoon depicting a woman, personifying Europe, offering her baby, representing colonies, to an aggressive Hitler. 'Take my child but spare, oh spare me!' read the caption.[42] This wholly accurate portrayal of British foreign policy (except for the fact that Chamberlain and Halifax were also prepared to sacrifice countries in eastern and central Europe) provoked an angry and pompous letter from Halifax to Southwood, complaining of an 'unjustly cruel cartoon' which made the business of Anglo-German friendship all the harder. Chastised, Southwood assured the Lord President that it would not happen again.[43]

The *Evening Standard*'s David Low was not so easily fixed. Widely regarded as the greatest cartoonist of the age, Low's freedom of action was such that he was even allowed to parody his proprietor, Lord Beaverbrook. Indeed, with clairvoyant timing, his cartoon of 28 November 1937 showed the Editors of *The Times* (Dawson) and the *Observer* (J. L. Garvin), together with Lord Lothian and Nancy Astor, dancing to a tune conducted by Maestro Goebbels. Halifax, however, was determined to curb him and, following the suggestion of his close friend Lady Alexandra 'Baba' Metcalfe, arranged to have lunch with the *Standard*'s Chairman, Michael Wardell. Wardell, a 'fascist sympathiser' according to the Beaverbrook journalist Michael Foot, was understanding but said there was nothing that he could do since Low's contract guaranteed him editorial freedom. If, however, Halifax were to make a personal appeal then Low might be prepared to listen to reason. This was a pretty unorthodox suggestion – rarely, if ever, can a senior British Cabinet Minister have had to personally censor a newspaper cartoonist – yet this, like his attendance at an extremely boring Anglo-German Fellowship dinner later that month, Halifax was prepared to do 'in the interests of the good cause'.[44] Meeting in Wardell's Bayswater flat, Halifax asked Low to tone down his cartoons since they were having a detrimental effect on the Government's quest to secure a lasting peace. Put like this, Low could hardly refuse. 'Very well, I don't want to be responsible for a world war', the cartoonist replied, but 'it's my duty as a journalist to report matters faithfully … And I think this man is awful. But I'll slow down a bit.'*[45]

Henderson was delighted with these efforts. Although he claimed in his memoirs to have a great respect for that 'chartered libertine' the British press, he was, in reality, hardly less keen on stifling newspaper criticism of Germany than Dr Goebbels.[46] Writing to Eden on 29 November 1937, shortly after Halifax's return, he begged that 'nothing should be left undone which might prevent gratuitous and unnecessary, as well as ill-informed, irritation to Germany in the British press', adding that 'if the door which Lord Halifax has opened is to be kept ajar, something must be done to prevent the press from slamming it to again'.[47] It was with considerable anger, therefore, that Henderson reacted to two reports in the *Daily Telegraph*, on 2 and 3 December 1937, which claimed that the German Government had lobbied Halifax on the colonial question but that the British Government was determined to refuse Schacht's request that Germany should be awarded territory in central Africa currently held by Belgium and Portugal. Setting aside the fact that this was almost the exact scheme which Chamberlain was currently concocting, Henderson was apoplectic, citing the articles as prime examples of the 'immense harm which can be done' by the British press. 'I should like to wring the neck of Mr Victor Gordon-Lennox', the *Daily Telegraph*'s diplomatic correspondent, he raged to Halifax. Halifax replied that he had written

---

* Following this meeting Low made his cartoons less personal, though no less critical, through the invention of the character Muzzler – 'a composite character featuring well-known features of both dictators'. After Hitler had marched into Austria, however, the cartoonist felt free to resume his old ways.

in strong terms to Eden and 'exhorted him to come as near to wringing Gordon-Lennox's neck as he can'.[48]

Thus the new, or rather the evangelical, appeasers began their mission. The doctrine was not original but the fervour, the conviction, the ruthless determination were. What was previously a reactive and desultory policy, tempered by scepticism, was now an active, positive policy, which would carry all before it. Above all, the evangelical appeasers were optimists who placed an extraordinary amount of faith in a combination of goodwill and reasonable discussion. As Halifax had written just before his visit (in a statement which might just as easily have come from Chamberlain), 'I feel that if we could once convince them [the Germans] that we wanted to be friends we might find many questions less intractable than they now appear.'[49]

Unfortunately, this was the precise moment when the Germans were reaching the opposite conclusion. After waiting so long for the elusive Anglo-German alliance, Hitler had come to view Britain less as a potential friend and more as a probable enemy. Not unconnected with this state of mind was the transformation of Ribbentrop from chief Anglophile to leading Anglophobe. Embittered by his lack of success, both diplomatic and social, the German Ambassador spent December 1937 hidden away in his study, writing a monster report for Hitler explaining that his mission had failed and that Germany must henceforth count England among her most implacable enemies. The British would never abandon their commitment to the balance of power, nor their friendship with France. German policy, therefore, should be directed to cementing that series of alliances which could counter 'our most dangerous enemy' and, if necessary, dismember her Empire.[50] As the year 1937 drew to a close, British and German policies were therefore moving in opposite directions: an increasing polarity which would set the tone for the following year and take Europe to the very brink of war.

X

'Bowlers Are Back!'

I fear that fundamentally the difficulty is that N. [Chamberlain] believes that he is a man with a mission to come to terms with the dictators.

Anthony Eden, Diary, 18 January 1938[1]

As darkness fell on 11 January 1938, a tall, well-dressed figure slipped unobtrusively into the British Embassy in Washington. The late hour had been chosen to try and ensure the secrecy of the meeting and the British Ambassador duly saw his visitor alone in his private study. There, the American Under-Secretary of State, Sumner Welles, sat while Sir Ronald Lindsay, a gigantic Scot little given to effusion, read the small file of typewritten papers he had just been handed. At last he looked up from his reading stand and declared with profound emotion: 'This is the first hope I have had in more than a year that a new world war can be prevented.'[2]

The news which Lindsay had received and which, within an hour, was making its way to London under the strictest levels of secrecy, was that President Roosevelt, anxious at the deteriorating world situation and 'more than ever impressed by the danger of general conflagration', had decided to try and arrest this downward spiral by initiating the only course which, due to the strongly isolationist state of American public opinion, was open to him.[3] This amounted to a plan whereby the President would appeal to the nations of the world to come together to consider ways of harmonising international relations. Essentially a quid pro quo, the President's idea was effectively to purchase a disarmament agreement (conceded by the dictator states) in return for a new system for the equal distribution of the world's raw materials (conceded by other nations). He planned to make his appeal on 22 January and now asked the British Government for its support. If he did not receive its approval within five days he would abandon the scheme.[4] The chances of what became known as the Roosevelt Initiative succeeding were one in a hundred. It was, however, the first time the United States had proposed to assume a leading role in international affairs since the end of the Great War and its mere rejection by the dictators was likely have a powerful effect on American public opinion. For all these reasons, Lindsay was enthusiastic and urged London to 'give reply to this invaluable initiative with a very quick and very cordial acceptance'.[5]

This was not to be. Although Eden had told the Commons on 1 November 1937 that in order to obtain the co-operation of the United States he would happily travel 'not only from Geneva to Brussels, but from Melbourne to Alaska', the Foreign Secretary was currently in the south of France, playing tennis and hobnobbing with Churchill and Lloyd George.[6] In his absence, Chamberlain had taken charge of the Foreign Office and, as one leading official recorded, 'hated R's idea' and was determined to kill it.[7] He consequently wrote to the President, thanking him for his interesting and 'courageous' suggestion but nevertheless asking him to 'hold his hand'.[8]

In administering this 'douche of cold water', Chamberlain was not motivated merely by anti-Americanism.[9] Although he considered Roosevelt's idea a 'preposterous effusion' – just the sort of pious, woolly-minded conception he had come to expect from that quarter – he was far more concerned with the effect the initiative would have on his own plans.[10] As he explained in his reply to the President, the British Government was already engaged in projects designed to facilitate the 'appeasement' of Europe and believed that it might even 'be permissible to look forward to some improvement in the immediate future'. The Prime Minister was working on a colonial scheme to satisfy Germany, while the Italian Government had recently signalled its desire to open conversations, which should result in bringing 'appeasement to the Mediterranean region at least'.[11]

*

The move towards rapprochement with Italy had begun in the summer of 1937. Deflated by the cancellation of Neurath's visit,

Chamberlain was gratified when the Italian Ambassador, the bearded and beguiling Count Dino Grandi, came to see him on 27 July, apparently bearing a letter from the Duce. In this letter (actually an invention of the Ambassador's designed to kick-start negotiations), 'Mussolini' declared himself most anxious for the restoration of good relations between Britain and Italy and proposed that the two countries should begin conversations aimed at a complete resolution of their differences.[12] In particular, Grandi continued, Mussolini was eager that the British should recognise the Italian annexation of Abyssinia *de jure*. To this, Chamberlain had replied that such a step, which would provoke a great deal of criticism in Britain, could only be taken if it were part of a 'great scheme of reconciliation, which should remove suspicions and anxieties and lead to the restoration of confidence'.[13] He was, however, encouraged and promptly wrote Mussolini a letter – which he did not show Eden since he 'had the feeling he would object to it' – in which he assured him that the British Government was 'actuated only by the most friendly feelings towards Italy and will be ready at any time to enter upon conversations with a view to clarifying the whole situation and removing all causes of suspicion or misunderstanding'.[14]

This yielded a friendly (and this time genuine) letter from Mussolini, welcoming the prospect of talks, and soon Chamberlain was congratulating himself on the 'extraordinary relaxation of tension in Europe' which he had achieved. 'It gives one a sense of the wonderful power that the Premiership gives you', he wrote to his sister Ida from the Duke of Westminster's Highland estate on 8 August 1937. 'As Ch[ancellor] of Ex[chequer] I could hardly have moved a pebble; now I have only to raise a finger and the whole face of Europe is changed!'[15]

Eden was not convinced. Regarding Mussolini, even more than Hitler, as the 'anti-Christ', the Foreign Secretary was reluctant to add to the dictator's prestige at a time when the Italian military was pouring petrol on the Spanish inferno and while anti-British propaganda – which the Italians were skilfully directing towards the insurrectionist Arabs in Palestine – remained rife.[16] Above all, Eden, unlike Chamberlain, had no confidence in the Duce's goodwill. 'I have so often been promised that such and such action on our part would improve Anglo-Italian relations, and so often been disappointed', he wrote in a Foreign Office minute in the summer of 1937, 'that I do not share these optimistic views of *de jure* recognition … I fear that the cause is that Italy is determined to revive the Roman Empire and we are in the way.'[17]

At first, this major difference of opinion between Prime Minister and Foreign Secretary was masked owing to Chamberlain's assumption that Eden was merely the conduit for the Foreign Office's natural caution and prejudices. Convinced, like Sir Samuel Hoare, that the 'FO is much biased against Germany (and Italy and Japan)', Chamberlain grew increasingly frustrated with its inhabitants, who, he complained, 'seem to me to have no imagination and no courage'. Admittedly, Eden was 'awfully good in accepting my suggestions without grumbling, but it is wearing always to have to begin at the beginning again' and sometimes even rewrite Foreign Office despatches. 'I am terribly afraid', he continued in a letter to his sister Hilda, 'lest we should let the Anglo-Italian situation slip back to where it was before I intervened. The FO persist in seeing Musso only as a sort of Machiavelli putting on a false mask of friendship in order to further nefarious ambitions. If we treat him like that we shall get nowhere with him and we shall have to pay for our mistrust by appallingly costly defences in the Mediterranean.'[18]

As it turned out, it was the 'nefarious Machiavelli' rather than the Foreign Office who was responsible for the retrogression of Anglo-Italian relations during the late summer and autumn of 1937. Talks were impossible while Italian submarines sharked the Mediterranean, and a bombastic speech by the Duce, lauding Franco's capture of Santander, went down extremely badly. In September, Mussolini paid a much-publicised visit to Berlin and in November 1937, the Italians joined the German–Japanese Anti-Comintern Pact. In December Italy left the League of Nations.

During this time visible cracks began to appear in the Chamberlain–Eden relationship. Although the younger man – Eden was Chamberlain's junior by almost thirty years – had assured the elder that he did not mind his taking a greater interest in foreign affairs than Baldwin had done (he could hardly have taken less), the Foreign Secretary soon became resistant to the Prime Minister's determination to get on terms with the dictators, almost regardless of the circumstances. In particular, he was annoyed by Chamberlain's increasingly underhand methods. These included a clumsy attempt to recruit Eden's Parliamentary Private Secretary, Jim Thomas, as a Number 10 spy and press briefings designed to force both the pace and direction of foreign policy. Such briefings occurred in August 1937, when a number of newspapers eagerly began reporting on the imminence of Anglo-Italian talks, and then again in November when, contrary to Eden's wishes, Downing Street raised expectations over the Halifax visit. Indignant, a feverish Eden raised himself from his sickbed to remonstrate with Chamberlain. This led to a blazing row, culminating in the Prime Minister's famous dismissal of his Foreign Secretary to 'go back to bed and take an aspirin!'[19] The next day, Sir Horace Wilson – officially the Government's expert on industrial affairs but in reality Chamberlain's closest adviser on all matters – attempted to mend fences by assuring Jim Thomas that the 'PM was devoted to A.E. and regarded him as the first man in his Cabinet'. Chamberlain was, however, convinced that 'his own policy of using every opportunity of getting together with the dictators was right', that 'A.E. was wrong', and consequently the Prime Minister was 'saving A.E. from himself'.[20]

Nor was this the only point of difference between the two men. As Eden told Chamberlain in a letter of 3 November 1937, he was 'profoundly worried about the state of our rearmament'.[21] An Air Ministry memorandum showed that the RAF was still two years behind the Luftwaffe and the situation regarding anti-aircraft guns and searchlights was dire. Could Britain, Eden wondered, not make up some of the difference by purchasing equipment from abroad? Chamberlain did not think so. Although he accepted the need for rearmament until his policy of appeasement began to yield results, he refused to allow defence spending to rise above the level he considered financially prudent. To this Eden retorted sharply that 'a good financial position would be small consolation to us if London were laid flat because our Air Force had been insufficient'. But Chamberlain thought this 'too alarmist' a view, adding that 'he did not think anybody was going to attack us for the next two years'.[22]

Fortunately, one area where Eden was able to call on Chamberlain's support was in overruling the Chiefs of Staff, who, in an extraordinarily defeatist paper of February 1938, categorically opposed an extension of staff talks with the French and Belgians, chiefly on the political grounds that this would provoke the 'irreconcilable suspicion and hostility of Germany'.[23] They were also at one over Vansittart. Long piqued by his headmasterly manner, his emotional memoranda and his willingness to negotiate with Mussolini, Eden had tried and failed to get rid of 'Van' in 1936 by offering him the Paris Embassy. Chamberlain's motives were different. Regarding him as an alarmist who was continually trying to hamper his attempts to make friendly contact with the dictators, the Prime Minister believed that Vansittart had the unfortunate effect of multiplying 'Anthony's natural vibrations'.[24] Either way, his time was up. Forced to accept the grand-sounding but meaningless new post of Chief Diplomatic Adviser to the Government, Vansittart was promoted out of trouble and that 'sane slow man' Alexander Cadogan – previously head of the League of Nations section at the Foreign Office and British Minister in Peking – became the new Permanent Under-Secretary.[25] It was first blood to the appeasers.

*

The Roosevelt Initiative marked the beginning of the end of the Chamberlain–Eden relationship. Dismayed that the Prime Minister should have snubbed the President in his absence, Eden threw himself into trying to reverse the decision as soon as he arrived back in England on 15 January 1938. Visiting Chequers the next day, he told Chamberlain that he deeply regretted his actions, which had disappointed the President, and must inevitably prove a setback to the cause of ending American isolationism. Chamberlain retorted that the President's initiative would have confused 'our own efforts' with Italy and Germany, which, he believed, were on the brink of yielding results. This Eden could not accept. Although he was prepared to continue the negotiations with Germany, he was convinced that recognition of the Italian position in Abyssinia would be a mistake since it would increase Mussolini's prestige and 'therefore make him more attractive to Hitler'.[26] That night, Oliver Harvey, Eden's devoted Private Secretary, raised the prospect of resignation in his diary:

> I'm afraid the PM may have committed a colossal blunder which it is too late to retrieve. A.E. will have to consider his position very carefully, for he obviously cannot remain responsible for foreign policy if the PM persists in such a line. He cannot accept responsibility for a policy which will antagonise America.

> The PM is being advised in this folly by Horace Wilson who knows nothing about foreign affairs. He, the PM, is temperamentally anti-American, but he is also, I'm afraid, moved by some vanity over his own ventures with Hitler and Muss.[27]

Two days later and the arrival of Roosevelt's formal reply to Chamberlain's telegram confirmed Eden's fears. Although the President had agreed to postpone his initiative for a short period he was, as Welles relayed, seriously disappointed with the British response. Moreover, he was clearly horrified by the idea that Britain might be about to grant *de jure* recognition to Italy's conquest of Abyssinia, as set out in Chamberlain's initial communication. This, the President explained, would have the most unfortunate consequences – both in the Far East, where neither America nor Britain recognised the Japanese annexation of Manchuria, and with American public opinion. 'At a moment when respect for treaty obligations would seem to be of such vital importance in international relations as proclaimed by our two Governments', Roosevelt wrote, 'I cannot help but feel all repercussions of the step contemplated by His Majesty's Government should be most carefully considered ... Public opinion in the United States will only support the Government in measures of pacific co-operation with other peace loving nations of the world provided these measures of co-operation are destined to re-establish and maintain principles of international law and morality.'[28]

Seizing on this communication, Eden crossed the road to Downing Street to see the Prime Minister. But Chamberlain had his own ammunition: a letter from Ivy Chamberlain (Austen's widow),* who had spent the winter in Rome, flattering the Duce and reading him extracts from the Prime Minister's letters. As Chamberlain explained, Count Ciano, Mussolini's son-in-law and Foreign Minister, had told Ivy that the Duce was anxious to reach a settlement and that this was a 'psychological' moment that should not to be missed.[29] With this prospect before him, Eden found the Prime Minister impossible to budge, either on the Roosevelt Initiative or the recognition of Abyssinia. 'I fear that fundamentally the difficulty is that N. believes

---

* Austen Chamberlain had died in March of the previous year, aged seventy-three.

that he is a man with a mission to come to terms with the dictators', the Foreign Secretary recorded, dejectedly, in his diary.[30]

No less depressing for Eden was the fact that the Prime Minister seemed to have the support of their colleagues. Waiting for the start of a meeting of the Cabinet's Foreign Policy Committee on the afternoon of 19 January, the Foreign Secretary noticed a hand-scrawled line at the top of Thomas Inskip's papers which read, 'Eden's policy to line up the USA, Great Britain and France, result war.'[31] Eden tried to assure the Minister for the Co-ordination of Defence to the contrary but when the meeting started he discovered that the rest of the Committee were of the same opinion. Chamberlain read long extracts from Ivy's letters, full of Mussolini's expressions of goodwill, and then produced a draft telegram to Roosevelt explaining the benefits of recognising Italy's absorption of Abyssinia.

Isolated within the Cabinet, Eden was now openly contemplating resignation. The difficulty, as his friends in the Foreign Office pointed out, was that the Roosevelt plan was top secret and could not, therefore, be cited in explanation for his actions. This issue was raised by Jim Thomas in a stormy interview with Sir Horace Wilson on the morning of 20 January, at which the former warned the latter that if Eden did resign there was the chance that the whole story might leak out at the American end and 'that the country would then know that the PM preferred to turn down the help of a democracy in order that he might pursue his flirtations with the dictators untrammelled'. At this Wilson flew into a rage, telling Thomas that if 'America produced the facts he would use the full power of the Government machine in an attack upon A.E.'s past record with regard to the dictators and the shameful obstruction by the FO of the PM's attempts to save the peace of the world'.[32]

As it was, neither threat was carried out.* Finding Chamberlain less sure of himself on the afternoon of 20 January 1938, Eden managed to persuade him to rescind his request to Roosevelt to defer the launch

* If Thomas was trying to threaten Wilson then he did so almost certainly without Eden's blessing. Indeed, throughout his battles with Chamberlain, Eden behaved with punctilious honour: refusing to advance his cause by press leaks or even by lobbying his Cabinet colleagues. As Duff Cooper (who supported Chamberlain at the Cabinet meeting on 20 February) later wrote, if Eden had 'made an effort to win my support at the time he would probably have succeeded'.

of his plan. This seemed like a major victory. Having got Chamberlain to approve a telegram, in his name, warmly welcoming the President's proposal, Eden followed this up with his own message to Sir Ronald Lindsay, stating that 'in all circumstances we want the President to take his initiative'.[33] It was, however, too late. Roosevelt was having doubts and, after repeatedly postponing the scheme during the first half of February, finally decided that Chamberlain's initiative – the Italian agreement, including *de jure* recognition of Abyssinia – was 'entirely right' and he was, therefore, placing his idea in abeyance. 'This is excellent', commented Chamberlain.[34]

*

In order to open talks with Italy, Chamberlain had been vigorously pursuing his own unofficial diplomacy with Mussolini. For this there were two channels. There was Ivy Chamberlain – of whose flirtations with the Duce Eden was broadly aware and, increasingly, annoyed at – and then there were the shadowy activities of Sir Joseph Ball – of which the Foreign Secretary was almost entirely unaware.

Described by the former Chairman of the Conservative Party as 'undoubtedly tough', 'steeped in the Service tradition' and possessing 'as much experience as anyone I know in the seamy side of life and the handling of crooks', Major Joseph Ball had been an MI5 officer who in 1927 had left the service to work for the Conservative Party.[35] There, as head of publicity and then Director of the newly founded Conservative Research Department, he established a political intelligence service which, by the early 1930s, had not only managed to infiltrate the Labour and Liberal parties but had extended its tentacles across most of the competencies of Government. He had also developed a close friendship with the department's Chairman, Neville Chamberlain, with whom he would spend many hours over the coming decade stalking trout in the chalk streams of Hampshire.

In mid-1937, Ball was approached by Adrian Dingli, a British barrister of Maltese-Italian-British heritage and legal counsellor at the Italian Embassy. According to Ball, Dingli offered to supply him with 'information' about Italian diplomatic moves; in Dingli's version, the two men discussed ways in which Anglo-Italian relations could be 'improved'. Either way, the meeting led to the creation of an unofficial diplomatic channel which allowed Chamberlain to communicate with the Italian Government behind the backs of the Foreign Office and vice versa. This development, as events were to prove, was almost entirely to the Italians' advantage. Although Dingli claimed that a founding principle of his work with Ball was that British interests would always supersede Italian ones, the fact was that it was the British and not the Italian Foreign Office which the pair, along with Chamberlain, were conspiring to undermine. This point was immediately realised by the Italian Ambassador, Count Grandi, who saw in the Ball–Dingli relationship not only a heaven-sent means to catechise those close to the Prime Minister, but also an opportunity to 'drive a wedge into the incipient split between Eden and Chamberlain and to enlarge it more if possible'.[36]

To this obvious danger Chamberlain was oblivious. On 10 January 1938, taking advantage of Eden's absence in the south of France, he asked Ball to get in touch with Grandi to find out whether he could 'obtain permission from Rome to start "talks" in London with the PM', then in sole charge of the Foreign Office.[37] This scheme was wrecked when the Roosevelt Initiative ended Eden's holiday and placed him, once more, in nominal charge of foreign affairs. Chamberlain was not deterred. On 17 January, he took the extraordinary and surely unprecedented step of drafting, together with Ball, a letter for Grandi to send to Eden, requesting a meeting with himself and the Foreign Secretary. Initially, Dingli had his doubts about this ruse, which, he feared, placed the Italians in the role of suppliants. Yet when Ball appeared with the letter, in his own hand and on Downing Street writing paper, this ridiculous misconception of the situation soon evaporated. After imposing only minor changes, Grandi had the letter typed and signed it.

Two events then occurred which threatened to scupper the entire scheme. On Friday 21 January 1938, the British merchant ship *Endymion* was sunk by a Nationalist submarine off the coast of Spain and, in the evening, the BBC's news bulletin announced that 'no efforts to improve Anglo-Italian relations were at all contemplated' by the Government.[38] Immediately, Ball swung into action. By the Saturday he had got the BBC to repudiate its story – almost certainly inspired by Eden's supporters in the Foreign Office – and then launched his own press campaign, designed to garner public support for an agreement with Italy. Meanwhile, Ivy Chamberlain, having been chided by Ciano about Britain's unwillingness to start talks, decided to show him a letter she had recently received from her brother-in-law in which he expressed his belief that conversations would start before the end of February. 'The effect', as Neville Chamberlain recorded in his diary, 'was magical.'[39] Summoned for an audience with the Duce, Ivy was asked if she would mind reading the letter to him. This, of course, was pure charade. Thanks to the Italian Secret Service, Mussolini was well acquainted with the contents. He was, however, able to make a good show of spontaneous delight and asked Lady Chamberlain to convey to her brother-in-law the fact that he fully shared the Prime Minister's wishes and hoped that conversations would soon begin to cover all points 'including propaganda, the Mediterranean, colonies and economics'.[40]

Eden was furious. Learning of this latest bout of unofficial diplomacy after the weekend of 5–6 February, he wrote to Chamberlain complaining that it 'recreates in Mussolini's mind the impression that he can divide us and he will be the less ready to pay attention to what I have to say to Grandi'. Moreover, Rome was already 'giving out the impression from that interview that we are courting her, with the purpose, no doubt, of showing Berlin how worth courting she is'. This, he continued, was 'exactly the hand which Mussolini always likes to play and plays with so much skill when he gets a chance. I do not think we should let him.'[41] Chamberlain, though privately delighted, replied apologetically. He was 'distressed' that his sister-in-law's 'unorthodox procedure' should have caused Eden apprehension and assured him that he would tell Ivy 'very definitely' that his letters, in future, were to remain strictly private. He could not help adding, however, that he did not really believe she had 'done any harm'.[42]

The final showdown between Prime Minister and Foreign Secretary over the Italian conversations was precipitated by two events. On 12 February, Hitler summoned the Austrian Chancellor, Kurt von Schuschnigg, to Berchtesgaden. There he subjected him to a diatribe on Austrian iniquities before forcing him, under threat of immediate invasion, to lift the ban on Austrian National Socialists and accept two Austrian Nazis, Arthur Seyss-Inquart and Edmund Glaise-Horstenau, into his Government. The threat of *Anschluss* was clear and with it the Italians gained the necessary leverage to force the British hand.

On 17 February the Earl of Perth, Britain's Ambassador to Rome, reported that Ciano was urging an immediate start to conversations 'in view of [the] possibility of certain future happenings'.[43] The same day, the Italian Foreign Minister lunched with Lady Chamberlain where he begged her to understand that time was of the essence: 'Today an agreement will be easy but things are happening in Europe which will make it impossible tomorrow', he said cryptically.[44]

To Chamberlain, the meaning of these messages was obvious:

> Hitler had made his coup and M[ussolini] was furious about it. He wanted to know where he stood with us for if he had to regard us as a potential enemy he would have to make the best terms he could with Hitler and the closer he was tied to him the more difficult it would be to make an agreement with us.[45]

Remembering when Mussolini had despatched troops to the Brenner Pass after the failed Nazi takeover of Austria in July 1934, Chamberlain thought that an Anglo-Italian agreement would embolden Mussolini to resist the *Anschluss* while, conversely, the failure of the British to initiate talks would simply force the Duce to acquiesce to Hitler's plans. The Foreign Office interpretation was the exact opposite. Not believing that Mussolini – bogged down in both Spain and Abyssinia – had the power to resist a German invasion of Austria even if he wanted to, Eden was convinced by the information provided by the intelligence services that Mussolini had in fact struck a deal with Hitler in which he had agreed to allow the union of Germany and Austria in return for certain German pledges regarding Italy's interests in Spain.

Of these two interpretations, it was the latter which was closer to the truth. The Italians were, however, anxious to cover their backs and Ciano instructed Grandi 'to give a touch of the accelerator to the London negotiations'.[46] This Grandi was more than happy to do. No enthusiast for a German alliance, the Ambassador, who was hoping to 'play the part of the man who made peace with England', had decided of his own accord to force the elusive joint meeting with Chamberlain and Eden.[47] On 15 February, he warned Dingli – and in effect Ball and Chamberlain – that if this meeting did not occur within the next few days then he planned to abandon his efforts towards improving Anglo-Italian relations and leave London indefinitely. Worse, he threatened that if 'his' letter to Eden requesting the joint meeting were ever to be made public then he would, in the interests of Italian honour, be forced to reveal Chamberlain as its true author.[48]

Confronted with this blackmail, as well as the German threat to Austria, Chamberlain moved quickly to bring about the meeting with Grandi. Determined to open conversations with Italy even if it 'meant losing my Foreign Secretary', he refused Eden's request to see the Ambassador on his own and insisted on hosting the meeting himself. After considerable shenanigans involving the secret channel, it was finally scheduled for 11.30 on the morning of Friday 18 February in the Cabinet Room.[49] There, Grandi set about confirming Chamberlain's preconceptions. He strongly denied that there was any agreement between Italy and Germany regarding Austria before embarking on a long history of Anglo-Italian relations, in which Italy was cast in the role of the injured party. Reflecting on this extraordinary interview, fifteen years later Eden recalled:

> N.C. asked Grandi to speak to us of Anglo-Italian relations and Grandi, who was a very skilful diplomat, did his stuff admirably. Whenever he paused, N.C. encouraged him. He sat there nodding his head approvingly, while Grandi detailed one grievance after another. The more N.C. nodded the more outrageous became Grandi's account until in the end it would almost seem that we had invaded Abyssinia.[50]

A highly skilled diplomat indeed, Grandi had quickly realised what Chamberlain's game was. 'In addressing his questions directly to me', the Ambassador wrote in a now famous despatch, the Prime Minister wanted

> nothing more nor less than those details and definite answers which were useful to him as ammunition against Eden. This I at once realised and naturally tried to supply Chamberlain with all the ammunition which I considered might be useful to him to this end. There is no doubt that in this connection the contacts previously established between myself and Chamberlain through his confidential agent proved to be very valuable.[51]

Thus, the Ambassador explained that Mussolini's attitude with regard to recent events in Austria would have been very different if conversations with Britain had already been in progress. As it was, 'how could he [Mussolini] move troops to the Brenner as he did before, if he felt Great Britain was a potential enemy and that the Mediterranean at his back was not secure?'[52] To this, Chamberlain asked what Mussolini's attitude would be vis-à-vis Austria if conversations were to start now. Grandi replied that it would encourage Mussolini to take a stronger and more independent line. On the other hand, he emphasised that his denial as to the existence of a German–Italian deal over Austria referred to the present but not necessarily 'to the future'. Italy's future stance regarding the peace of Europe and the balance of power, he continued, depended 'exclusively' on the attitude of Great Britain. Chamberlain, who had listened to this barely disguised blackmail with rapt attention, leant forward. Was he to understand, he asked the Ambassador, that if Anglo-Italian relations were not immediately restored to a basis of friendship then Italy would feel herself forced to assume a position and give undertakings 'which may turn out to be hostile to the great Western Powers'? Grandi replied that the Prime Minister had understood the situation 'perfectly'.[53]

Sold, Chamberlain cut short Eden's few attempts to cross-examine the Ambassador and asked Grandi to return to Downing Street at three o'clock, by which time he would be ready to give him an answer. As soon as the Ambassador had left, Chamberlain told Eden that he was in no doubt as to what they should say upon his return: they should tell him that they were willing to open conversations immediately and were recalling the British Ambassador to receive instructions. When Eden objected, Chamberlain lost his temper. 'Anthony, you have missed chance after chance', he shouted, striding up and down the Cabinet Room. Eden retorted that Chamberlain's methods were only right 'if you have faith in the man you are negotiating with'. 'I have', snapped the Prime Minister.[54]

Eventually, the two men – who in Grandi's memorable description no longer resembled colleagues but 'two cocks in true fighting posture' – agreed that the only way out of the impasse was to lay the matter before the Cabinet.[55] Grandi was therefore asked to return after the weekend and Ministers were informed that, most unusually, there would be a Cabinet meeting the following afternoon, Saturday 19 February 1938.

By this time, the newspapers had got wind that there was a serious rift at the heart of Government. On the Saturday morning, most titles included some reference to the differences between the Prime Minister and the Foreign Secretary, and when Eden crossed the road to Downing Street he was cheered by a large crowd. Chamberlain opened the meeting with an hour-long recital of Britain's dealings with Italy over the last two years. Lord Halifax, who, strangely, was far from alone in being almost entirely unaware of the impending crisis, passed a note to Sam Hoare asking 'what was the purpose of this rather boring lecture on history'.[56] Only gradually did it emerge that there was a difference between the Prime Minister and the Foreign Secretary over opening talks with Italy. These conversations, Chamberlain declared, were essential, before cleverly portraying the difference with Eden not as one of principle but 'rather of method' and whether the present moment was opportune or not.[57]

Eden's presentation was not impressive. As Duff Cooper noted, 'Anyone who had not already made up his mind must have been convinced by the Prime Minister.'[58] This, as it soon transpired, was indeed the case. Calling on each Minister in turn, Chamberlain found that of the eighteen Ministers present, fourteen agreed with him entirely, while only four appeared ambivalent. What the Cabinet had not grasped, however, was that this was an issue on which Eden intended to resign if he could not carry his colleagues. When this became apparent there was a 'gasp of horror' and several Ministers began saying that this changed the situation. In order to head off a mass about-turn, Chamberlain intervened to say that he could not accept 'any decision in the opposite sense'.[59] The Cabinet were, thus, faced with the choice of either the Prime Minister's or the Foreign Secretary's resignation.

Although efforts were made to find a formula which would allow Eden to remain, it soon became clear that compromise was impossible. Eden was determined to resign and Chamberlain was not prepared to make any effort to stop him. On the contrary, his main concern was to secure public support for his policy, which was now responsible for the resignation of the most popular member of the Government. On the evening of 19 February – just after Eden had told the Cabinet that he intended to resign – Ball contacted Dingli and explained that, in order to bring his policy to fruition, Chamberlain needed to be able to announce that the Italians had agreed to the British demand – in fact Eden's demand – for a withdrawal of Italian 'volunteers' from Spain. To this Ciano readily agreed. Fearful lest Eden's resignation precipitate Chamberlain's downfall, he instructed Grandi to give the Prime Minister this assurance – duly conveyed by Dingli to Ball in the back of a London taxi. The Italian Foreign Minister's diary captures the drama from the Italian perspective:

> In London the crisis is on. The Duce has been telephoning from Terminillo for information every half-hour. The situation is fluid. Eden resigned at 1 p.m. and appeared at the Cabinet after his resignation ... Eden was cheered by the crowd when he left, surly and alone, with shouts of 'Eden Prime Minister'. Labour, Liberals, and left-wing Conservatives have already tabled a motion in favour of Eden. The crisis is perhaps one of the most important which has ever taken place. It may mean peace or war. I have authorized Grandi to take any step which may add an arrow to Chamberlain's quiver. An Eden Cabinet would have as its aim the fight against the dictatorships – Mussolini's first.[60]

This was an overestimation of the man. Eden had never been an advocate of pre-emptive action against Italy and was a supporter, albeit half-hearted, of Chamberlain's attempts to appease Germany. Furthermore, as Chamberlain and his supporters pointed out, he was a notably indecisive politician who had flip-flopped more than once over the question of negotiations with Italy. By resigning at this time, however, Eden ensured his later reputation as one of the leading 'anti-appeasers', an image reinforced by Churchill's highly romantic – even Gothic – account of his reaction to the news in his war memoirs, in which he lay awake from midnight to dawn, consumed by 'sorrow and fear', grieving that the one 'strong young figure, standing up against long, dismal, drawling tides of drift and surrender', was no longer in the Government. 'I watched the daylight slowly creep in through the windows, and saw before me in mental gaze the vision of Death.'[61]

At the time, however, depression at Eden's resignation was by no means universal. Apart from the inevitable rejoicing in Berlin and especially Rome, there was considerable celebration among the

Government's pro-appeasement supporters. 'I could scarcely contain my excitement', wrote Chips Channon when he heard. 'The doctrinaire "Leftist" policy of the Foreign Office has received a check, and there is jubilation in the House.'[62] Harold Nicolson, who had accused Chamberlain of butchering Eden 'to make an Italian holiday', expressed his revulsion at this attitude, common to much of the British right, in a bitingly sarcastic letter to the papers:

> Not that I mind the calm jubilation of Lord Londonderry or Sir Arnold Wilson. After all, they have for years waved the swastika aloft and have the right to shout aloud in joy. Nor do I mind the wild-west cries of Lady Astor. She also has fought bravely for Hitler and Mussolini and is entitled, during her fleeting visits to the House of Commons, to indulge in her whoopee. What I mind is the glow of unctuous relief which illumines the features of the average Tory. That, again, is hard to bear.[63]

There were, of course, many middle-of-the-road people and foreign policy experts who thought that Eden's attitude was wrong. Maurice Hankey, Alexander Cadogan, Robert Vansittart, even Robert Bernays, all concluded that Chamberlain's policy of trying to reach an agreement with Mussolini was right. The country, however, appeared to be on Eden's side. In early March, one of the first national opinion polls ever held in Britain found that 71 per cent of voters thought Eden right to resign, with 58 per cent opposed to Chamberlain's foreign policy.[64] Left-wing and liberal opinion was particularly outraged. One hundred and sixty-three university dons signed a petition attacking the Government and there were protests from the League of Nations Union, Welsh miners, the National Peace Council, the Trades Union Congress, the New Commonwealth Society and the Youth Peace Assembly. Though it is unclear how hard he looked, Lord Auckland told Eden that he could not find 'one person who does not regret your resignation as much as I do', while the unfailingly shrewd Sir Horace Rumbold wrote to his son from a Nile cruise to complain about the new turn in British foreign policy which consisted of 'licking the boots of that snarling blackguard Mussolini'. 'I don't think Chamberlain knows the technique of dealing with dictators, who are necessarily bullies', the former Ambassador continued. 'The more you truckle to them the more arrogant they become.'[65]

If Eden's departure hurt Chamberlain and the Government, however, the damage was far from fatal. The whips began a rumour that the real reason for the resignation was that Eden was ill (on the verge of a nervous breakdown, no less), while Joseph Ball ensured that the Tory press came out strongly on Chamberlain's side in the dispute. Apart from his Foreign Office colleagues Lord Cranborne and Jim Thomas, no other Ministers resigned. Eden had hoped that his friend and ally Oliver Stanley might follow his lead but in the end the President of the Board of Trade decided to remain, provoking Lady Cranborne's acid observation that 'the Stanleys have been trimmers ever since Bosworth'.*[66]

Above all, Eden did not help his own cause. Ignoring Churchill's plea to state his case boldly and clearly, his resignation speech on 21 February was so underwhelming and cautious that many Members were at a loss as to understand what had prompted it. Fortunately, Cranborne spoke far better, accusing the Government of a 'surrender to blackmail' which was 'likely to discourage our friends and to encourage those who wish us ill'.[67] The next day Churchill spoke. Possibly encouraged by a telegram from a group of 'Leeds Patriots' who asked him to 'give it Neville hot', he declared that this had been 'a good week for dictators'.[68] The duel between the former Foreign Secretary and the Italian dictator had been long and arduous but there could be no doubt who had triumphed. Signor Mussolini had won and now all the small countries in Europe would take their cue and 'move to the side of power and resolution … I predict that the day will come when, at some point or other, on some issue or other, you will have to make a stand, and I pray to God, when that day comes, that we may not find, through an unwise policy, we are left to make that stand alone.'[69]

Despite this sombre warning, the domestic political storm passed quickly. Chamberlain defended his policy in what many considered the best speech they had ever heard from him and although he complained that he was 'being abused like a pickpocket by many bookish people … who would run like rabbits if we got into war', he

* Bosworth was the last battle of the Wars of the Roses (22 August 1485). In it the Stanleys, despite having received lands and titles from King Richard III, supported the cause of the invader and eventual victor, Henry Tudor.

was pleased to receive support from more serious quarters, including a number of former ambassadors.[70] The Conservative-dominated House of Commons remained loyal throughout and within a week had become enthusiastic about the new, clearly delineated, direction of British foreign policy. 'Chamberlain's stock soars', enthused Chips Channon. 'I think he is the shrewdest Prime Minister of modern times; and it is a pity he did not drop Anthony months ago.'[71]

Channon was a direct beneficiary of Eden's fall, becoming Parliamentary Private Secretary to the new Under-Secretary of State for Foreign Affairs, the 35-year-old 'Rab' Butler. 'I felt exhilarated … my life's dream … I, "Chips", PPS – how lovely – but to the Foreign Office, is beyond belief exciting', wrote the vain but candid diarist.[72] Less jubilant was the new Foreign Secretary, Lord Halifax. While considering whether to accept the role, he told Oliver Harvey (one assumes half-jokingly) that he 'was very lazy and disliked work' and (more seriously), 'Could he hunt on Saturdays?'[73] His acceptance was, however, crucial to Chamberlain's strategy of reaching terms with the dictators. While Eden had been a reluctant appeaser, fundamentally hostile to dictators, Halifax was committed to Chamberlain's policy and had no such prejudices. His appointment was, thus, seen for what it was: an unambiguous boost for the Prime Minister and his policy. Indeed, this defining moment was even marked in fashion. On his first day at the Foreign Office, the hugely excited Channon was taken aside by Butler and told that he must abandon his homburg hat since it was 'too Edenesque – and buy a bowler'. Still revelling in Eden's downfall, the dandyish Channon was tickled. Just think, he exulted, 'Bowlers are back!'[74]

XI

The Rape of Austria

> The independence of Austria is a key position. If Austria perishes, Czechoslovakia becomes indefensible. Then the whole of the Balkans will be submitted to a gigantic new influence. Then the old German dream of a central Europe ruled by and subject to Berlin will become a reality ... with incalculable consequences not only for our country, but for the whole Empire.
>
> Sir Austen Chamberlain, 1 April 1936[1]

The week of 7 March 1938 heralded the arrival of spring in London. The sun emerged from hiding and adventurous daffodils began to show themselves in the Royal Parks. Walking amidst the neatly planted primulas and flowering magnolia of St James's, opposite the Foreign Office, the former Conservative MP Cuthbert Headlam came across Lord Halifax.

> 'Edward, may I congratulate you?'
>
> 'No,' replied the new Foreign Secretary, 'you certainly may not!'
>
> 'May I condole with you?'
>
> 'Yes, you may.'
>
> 'How easy the job would have been 3 or 4 years ago!'
>
> 'Yes, indeed.'
>
> 'Can it be done now, I wonder?'
>
> 'I wonder too!' – and so we passed on.[2]

As this quintessence of English understatement and self-deprecation illustrates, the task facing British foreign policy makers in the spring of 1938 was a formidable one. Although Chamberlain believed he was on the cusp of removing Italy from the list of Britain's potential enemies, there remained the threat from Japan; the ongoing war in Spain; and, as almost everyone agreed, the greatest danger of all – the expansionist ambitions of Nazi Germany.

*

At the same time as the Italian drama was playing out, preparations were being made for the appeasement of Germany. Apart from the main thrust, which was to take the form of a colonial offer in central Africa, the Government was considering whether Göring should be invited to visit Britain as a gesture of goodwill. The difficulties attached to this idea were first raised in February 1937 when it was speculated that the General might be chosen to represent the German Government at the coronation of King George VI. Enthused, Lord Londonderry had invited the Görings to stay at Londonderry House. The Foreign Office, however, was less keen. 'If we resist we may incur Göring's undying hostility', wrote Sir Eric Phipps in November 1936 (then anticipating the coronation of Edward VIII), 'and if we let him come we run quite a good risk of his being shot in England. Neither of these alternatives would be likely permanently to improve Anglo-German relations.'*[3]

In January 1938, however, the Foreign Office gave serious consideration to a suggestion from the Earl of Derby – a former Cabinet Minister and racing enthusiast – that he might invite Göring to Knowsley Hall (the Derbys' Merseyside pile) to watch the Grand National. Writing a paper for Eden on the subject, the head of the Central Department, William Strang, believed that there was 'a good deal to be said' for the proposal. The Grand National was a popular event and it would be 'extremely churlish, and unlike our people, to take it amiss that General Göring should come for it. Indeed, it might be regarded rather as a point in his favour that he should choose such an occasion for a visit.'[4] Before the General could be sounded out, however, questions were asked in the Commons about the possibility of a German minister being invited to London to inspect air raid precautions, in return

* The dilemma was resolved when Hitler ruled that the War Minister, General Werner von Blomberg, was to be his representative at the ceremony.

for the recent visit to Berlin of the Under-Secretary for Air. Anticipating the likely recipient of such an invitation, Labour's Herbert Morrison informed Sir Samuel Hoare (now Home Secretary) that if Göring were to come to London there would be a row. Conservative Members shouted 'Why?' Whereupon William Gallacher, Britain's sole Communist MP, asked the Secretary of State if he was 'aware that General Göring is soaked in blood and is regarded as a butcher'.[5]

Offended not so much by these attacks as by the failure of Tory MPs to defend him, Göring was in no mood to receive invitations to British sporting events. The idea, however, persisted within Whitehall that a visit to Britain, accompanied by 'some flattery ... and a little country-house life', might work wonders with the General, who, despite his well-known role during the Night of the Long Knives, was regarded as a moderate within the Nazi hierarchy.[6] As Halifax explained to Harold Nicolson in May 1938, for all their bravado the Nazis were extremely sensitive. In particular, they hated the idea of being mocked abroad as a bunch of vulgarians and parvenus. 'You have three hundred years' tradition behind you', Goebbels had told the then Lord President in Berlin. 'We have only four.' 'That means', noted an understanding Nicolson, 'that they really do regard themselves as something quite new' and are 'thus enraged when we suggest that Hitler might go to a better tailor'. Nicolson was, nevertheless, appalled when Halifax mentioned that the Government was considering inviting Göring to shoot partridges with the royal family at Sandringham. 'Ronnie [Cartland, Conservative MP for Birmingham King's Norton] and I say that we would resent any such thing.' It would lower Britain's dignity and have a disastrous effect on American public opinion. 'No,' insisted the increasingly excited MP, 'ask Göring to Nepal as much as you like, but do not expect the Queen to shake hands with him.'[7]

*

The Göring controversy aside, the main diplomatic effort towards Germany in the first quarter of 1938 was the colonial offer. Although Chamberlain suffered a temporary wobble after reading Stephen Roberts's influential *The House That Hitler Built* – a searing analysis of Nazism which argued that 'Hitlerism cannot achieve its aims without war' – he had managed to regain confidence in his policy by deciding that Roberts was simply wrong.[8] 'If I accepted the author's conclusions I should despair', he told his sister Hilda, 'but I don't and won't.'[9] On 24 January 1938, therefore, Chamberlain unveiled to the Cabinet's Foreign Policy Committee his plan to offer Germany colonial territory in central Africa in the hope that this would satisfy her desire for expansion and, thus, pave the way towards a general settlement.

By no means all members of the Committee were taken with the scheme. Sam Hoare thought it extremely unlikely that Germany would be content with such an offer, while the Dominions Secretary, Malcolm MacDonald, pointed out that the 'whole of the coloured world' would be angered by the transfer of native populations from one power to another. Many of the inhabitants of these lands had been under British administration for twenty years and there was, MacDonald continued, a strong moral case against forcing them to repatriate. He had, however, always believed that Germany must be given some colonial territory somewhere and, as Lord Halifax argued, it was 'on balance' more important 'for the world at large that war should be avoided than that the natives in the territories to be transferred should remain permanently in the position they had been in during the last 20 years'.[10] Sir Nevile Henderson was therefore instructed to seek an interview with Hitler at the earliest possible date at which he would present the Prime Minister's plan. Before this meeting could take place, however, several events occurred which boded darkly for the future of European peace.

In late January 1938, the German Minister of War, Field Marshal Werner von Blomberg, was forced to resign after it was revealed that the woman he had recently married (in a ceremony at which Hitler had been a witness) had previously worked as a prostitute and was well known to the Berlin police. Shocked, Hitler – who now believed that 'If a German field marshal marries a whore, anything in the world is possible' – decided to re-examine an old claim relating to the head of the Army, General Werner von Fritsch, being blackmailed by a rent-boy in 1933.[11] Fritsch was confronted, deemed (unjustly) guilty, and also forced to resign. Faced with a first-class crisis, Hitler, prompted by Goebbels, decided that the only way to avoid public humiliation was to obscure the departure of the two Generals by initiating a complete reorganisation at the top of the Wehrmacht and the German Foreign Ministry. The War Ministry was, thus, dissolved and a new structure, the Supreme Command of the Armed Forces (Oberkommando der Wehrmacht), was created. Hitler made himself Supreme Commander and the hawkish Ribbentrop replaced the more cautious Neurath as Minister for Foreign Affairs.

Foreign opinion did not know what to make of these developments. Though most saw through the smokescreen to the political crisis, observers were divided over the implications of the reshuffle. Although no one could know that the departing Generals were the two men who had expressed the greatest scepticism towards Hitler's plans at the Hossbach Conference, it was obvious, in the words of the German radio announcement, that the changes had brought about the 'strongest concentration of all political, military and economic forces in the hand of the supreme leader'.[12] On the other hand, a number of British onlookers were able to take comfort from the belief that the reorganisation meant a certain amount of *dis*organisation (at least initially) within the German armed forces: Germany had become 'more menacing but less formidable', pronounced Anthony Eden at the Cabinet meeting on 9 February 1938.[13] As for the appointment of Ribbentrop, there was further ambivalence. Although almost everybody was pleased that the clodhopping Ambassador would be leaving London, it was hard to take much pleasure in the promotion of a man who, in Henderson's words, was 'as vain as he is stupid and as stupid as he is vain' and who, as most recognised, had developed into a bitter Anglophobe.[14]

One immediate effect of the changes was the decision to postpone Henderson's interview with Hitler. Within two weeks, however, the true details of the Hitler–Schuschnigg meeting were known and the threat of *Anschluss* was hanging over Europe like the blade of a guillotine. Eden wanted Henderson to warn Hitler that Britain had an interest in the independence of Austria and that the colonial offer was dependent on guarantees concerning the security and stability of central Europe. Henderson argued strongly that this would have no practical effect other than to infuriate Hitler and prejudice him against the British offer. The argument continued via telegram but was halted on 20 February when Eden resigned as Foreign Secretary. Henderson was relieved by the news. Although the Ambassador admitted that the rejoicing of the Germans was 'naturally a compliment to Eden', the fact of the matter was, he told his new master, Lord Halifax, that it was most 'unlikely that any understanding with Germany was possible so long as Eden was Secretary of State'. Now, however, there were grounds for hope. Recognising that 'even with the best will in the world' there was nothing that Britain could do to help Austria, Henderson urged Halifax not to make Austrian independence a precondition of an Anglo-German agreement, adding that if this line was adopted then the Germans might well 'co-operate in other matters'.[15] This optimism contrasted starkly with what Henderson regarded as the comic paranoia of the French Ambassador. As he relayed to Halifax a few weeks later, François-Poncet was so pessimistic about the future that he had taken the precaution of storing 30,000 francs' worth of gold bars in his safe. When the British Ambassador asked what these were for, the Frenchman explained that they were meant for purchasing the special train which was to return him to France after the declaration of war.* Amused, Henderson pointed out that he himself could not possibly raise 30,000 francs even if he wanted to, whereupon the earnest François-Poncet generously promised to try to save him a seat on his train.[16]

As should have already been clear to Henderson, François-Poncet's attitude, if too dramatic for English phlegm, was the more realistic of the two. On 3 March 1938, the British Ambassador had his long-awaited interview with Hitler and, as he was forced to report back, it could hardly have gone worse. Ironically, considering the frequent accusation that Henderson was too sympathetic towards the Nazis, both Hitler and Ribbentrop nursed a particular dislike for this typical English gent. As Reinhard Spitzy, Ribbentrop's aide, later recalled, the Foreign Minister was always denigrating the British Ambassador, while the Führer enjoyed being reminded of Henderson's friendship with the Rothschilds or the accusation that he had turned up improperly dressed for audiences at the Reich Chancellery. 'How on earth could anybody take seriously a man who wore a blue pin-stripe suit with a claret pullover and a red carnation?' demanded Ribbentrop.[17]

It was not, however, his attire but the British scheme and Henderson's exposition of it which caused Hitler to lose his temper on 3 March. As the Ambassador reported to Halifax, Hitler had sat 'glowering in his chair' while Henderson explained that the offer he had been tasked with communicating was conditional upon Germany being prepared

* François-Poncet was haunted by the fate of his predecessor Jules Cambon, who, in August 1914, had struggled to find the vast amount of cash which the Germans were demanding for the use of a train to deliver him and his staff across the frontier.

to play her part in the pacification of Europe. True to forecast, specific mention of Austria and Czechoslovakia only caused Hitler's scowl to deepen and by the time he got to the actual offer the Führer was too agitated to be able to concentrate.[18] As soon as Henderson had finished, Hitler burst into a disjointed diatribe. He complained about the British press, about busybody English bishops interfering in Germany's religious affairs, and about his spurned offers for Anglo-German friendship. He would brook no foreign interference in Germany's relations with kindred nations or with her efforts to find a settlement for those Germans currently excluded from the Reich. On the contrary, he would rather risk a general war than that justice should continue to be denied to those millions of Germans currently languishing in Austria and Czechoslovakia. As for the question of colonies, Hitler declared that this matter was not urgent and could wait for four, six, eight or even ten years. His priority was central and eastern Europe: the Austrians must be given the opportunity of joining with Germany, while the ethnic Germans living within Czechoslovakia must be granted full autonomy. The only moment of harmony came at the end of the interview when Henderson produced a crumpled drawing of the Führer, sent to him by a woman in New Zealand with the hope that he might get it autographed. Hitler agreed and the Ambassador observed that even if the interview could hardly be described as a success, it had at least 'given pleasure to one young woman'.[19]

Henderson left the Reich Chancellery thoroughly discouraged. Writing to Halifax, he lamented that Hitler's 'sense of values is so abnormal that argument seems powerless … His capacity for self-deception and his incapacity to see any point which does not meet his own case are fantastic, and no perversion of the truth seems too great for him to accept the gospel of Hitler and of Germany.' The idea of colonial appeasement was clearly a non-starter. As Göring had said to Henderson a few days earlier, Britain could offer Germany the whole of Africa and still she would not consider this a fair price for Austria. Yet, the Ambassador continued to refuse to believe that Hitler was 'thinking in terms of Anschluss or of annexation'. He trusted Hitler when he said that he would abide by the agreement he had recently made with the Austrian Chancellor but did warn that the Führer, although he 'hates war as much as anyone', would not shrink from it if he felt it necessary to secure the rights of Germans living outside the Reich.[20]

In London, both the Foreign Office and the Cabinet were suitably depressed. A settlement was clearly impossible while Hitler maintained his current attitude and Halifax decided to express his disappointment to Ribbentrop when the new Foreign Minister returned to London a few days later to present his letters of recall. Before this could happen, however, Chancellor Schuschnigg tried to steal a march on Hitler by announcing on 9 March that a plebiscite would be held on the question of Austrian independence within a matter of days – Sunday 13 March 1938. The move, which caught Hitler completely by surprise, forced him to act and ensured that Ribbentrop's London meetings were considerably more dramatic than either the British or the German Foreign Minister could have imagined.

*

Ribbentrop saw Halifax at eleven o'clock on 10 March. There was a crowd outside the Foreign Office and as the German Foreign Minister emerged from his car he was greeted with shouts of protest. Inside, Halifax was waiting to deliver a carefully prepared warning. Britain, he explained, desired friendship with Germany and had no wish to stand in the way of peaceful evolution. He would, however, be less than frank if he did not express his view that the current German attitude regarding Austria and Czechoslovakia was running grave risks with the maintenance of European peace. Of course, Britain did not wish to see war in Europe but the experience of 'all history went to show that the pressure of facts was sometimes more powerful than the wills of men: and if once war should start in central Europe, it was quite impossible to say where it might not end, or who might not become involved'.[21]

Not surprisingly, this sermon had no effect whatsoever. Having left the Foreign Office, past the demonstrators, now chanting 'Ribbentrop get out!', Ribbentrop returned to the German Embassy where he answered an urgent letter from Hitler, asking what Britain would do if Germany invaded Austria. 'I am convinced', replied the Foreign Minister, 'that England of her own accord will do nothing in regard to it at present, but that she would exert a moderating influence on the other powers.'[22] When Hitler read these words he was exultant. 'It's exactly as I thought', he told Reinhard Spitzy. 'We needn't fear any complications from over there.'[23]

That evening, Ribbentrop hosted a farewell party at the German Embassy, recently redecorated, at his behest, in the most lavish and vulgar style. Almost everyone he knew in England had been invited, including the entire British Government and the whole of the diplomatic corps. Aware of reports that the German Army was, at that very moment, massing on the Austrian border, one Foreign Office attendee was disgusted to see the German Foreign Minister walking up and down the large reception room with the Austrian Minister, talking in the 'most affectionate manner'.[24] Also at the party was the Director General of the British Broadcasting Corporation, John Reith. Described by one contemporary as 'a cross between a canny Scot and a medieval saint – but more of the fanatic in him than the academic', Reith was a puritanical crusader whose admiration for both the Nazis and Mussolini was reflected in his own, rather more benign, dictatorship at Portland Place.[25] One of the few people to seem genuinely sad that Ribbentrop was leaving, Reith asked the German Foreign Minister to assure Hitler that 'the BBC was not anti-Nazi' and that if they were to send his German opposite number over for a visit he would fly the swastika from the top of Broadcasting House.[26]

At 6.10 the following morning, Friday 11 March, the Foreign Office received a telegram from the British Ambassador in Vienna saying that the German–Austrian frontier had been closed and that there were reports of troop movements on the German side of the border.[27] At 10.20 the British Consul General in Munich reported general mobilisation in Bavaria and 'troops pouring towards the Austrian frontier'.[28] Receiving this information, Henderson immediately instructed the Military Attaché, Colonel Noel Mason-MacFarlane, to visit the new Wehrmacht supreme headquarters and find out what was going on. There, 'Mason-Mac', as he was known – an intelligent and dynamic soldier, who liked to contemplate shooting Hitler from his drawing room window* – received a flat denial of any troop movements,

* 'Easy rifle-shot', the Military Attaché had told Ewan Butler, *The Times*'s Berlin correspondent, pointing out of his window to Charlottenburger Chaussee below. 'I could pick the bastard off from here as easy as winking, and what's more I'm thinking of doing it.' When, in the spring of 1939, Butler feared he might be arrested, Mason-Mac's successor, Colonel Denis Daly, offered the journalist sanctuary. 'Come and stay with us … and if they try to run you in we'll shoot it out with them – I've got a couple of pistols at home.'

although by this time Henderson had received similar reports from Nuremberg and Dresden. Determined to learn the truth himself, Mason-Mac got in his car and headed south. No sooner had he left Berlin than he came across 'well over 3,000 armed police' as well as members of the SS moving towards Austria in a miscellany of vehicles, including motorbikes, radio cars, petrol tankers and Berlin buses.[29]

While this was unfolding, Ribbentrop – who had been kept deliberately uninformed by Hitler about the unfolding coup – was arriving at 10 Downing Street for a lunch given in his honour by the Prime Minister. The other guests included most senior members of the Cabinet as well as the Cadogans, Londonderrys and Churchills. About halfway through the meal a Foreign Office messenger entered the dining room and handed Cadogan an envelope. The Permanent Under-Secretary opened it, digested its contents and passed it to Halifax. The Foreign Secretary read it and passed it to Chamberlain. As Churchill recalled, Cadogan's demeanour was inscrutable but the Prime Minister was clearly perturbed by the information he had received: Hitler had issued Schuschnigg with an ultimatum, demanding the cancellation of the plebiscite.

Remarkably, the lunch continued as if nothing had happened. After the party had adjourned for coffee, however, it became obvious to the English guests that something was up and that their hosts wished to bring proceedings swiftly to an end. Only the German Foreign Minister and his wife appeared oblivious to the atmosphere and kept up what became increasingly strained small talk for a further half-hour. Eventually, Anna von Ribbentrop was induced to leave on her own, while the Prime Minister escorted her husband, along with Halifax, Cadogan and the German First Counsellor, Ernst Woermann, to his study. Chamberlain read Ribbentrop two telegrams, the second of which stated that Hitler was now demanding Schuschnigg's resignation and that the Austrian Chancellor had appealed to the British Government for advice. Though he remained 'calm and coolheaded' throughout the meeting, Chamberlain urged Ribbentrop to understand how serious this was, while Halifax, who had become uncharacteristically excited, spoke of an 'intolerable' threat of force and begged the Foreign Minister to persuade Hitler to stay his hand.[30] These entreaties, as Chamberlain expected, had zero effect. Genuinely ignorant of what had been occurring between Berlin and Vienna, though his British interlocutors did not believe it, Ribbentrop refused to accept the reports while at the same time justifying the 'non-existent' German action by pointing to Schuschnigg's 'breach of faith'. Chamberlain despaired. 'He is so stupid, so shallow, so self centred and self satisfied, so totally devoid of intellectual capacity', he complained to his sister Hilda, 'that he never seems to take in what is said to him.'[31]

Returning to the Foreign Office, Halifax learnt that if Schuschnigg had not resigned by 6 p.m. (Austrian time) then the German Army would invade. Outraged by these 'highwaymen's methods', he nevertheless recognised that there was nothing that Britain could possibly do to prevent them.[32] He therefore sent a cable to Vienna stating that the British Government was unable to offer Schuschnigg any advice and then left for a prearranged farewell cup of tea with Ribbentrop at the German Embassy. There, Halifax found the German Foreign Minister, who had just finished a telephone call with Berlin, still insisting that no such ultimatum had been issued. Almost as soon as he had said this, however, Woermann came in and announced that Schuschnigg had resigned and that the Austrian Nazi Arthur Seyss-Inquart was now Chancellor. Humiliated, Ribbentrop quickly began to argue that this was, undoubtedly, for the best. The solution of the Austrian problem would render Anglo-German relations more harmonious and, as to method, had not Britain had to behave similarly with regard to Ireland? Halifax was having none of this. What they were witnessing, he told the German Foreign Minister, was 'an exhibition of naked force, and the public opinion of Europe would inevitably ask … what there was to prevent the German Government from seeking to apply in similar fashion naked force to the solution of their problems in Czechoslovakia' or to any other part of the world. As for the comparison with Anglo-Irish history, the former imperial Viceroy, Christ Church man and fellow of All Souls could 'hardly imagine an analogy that had less substance'. Ireland had been as much a part of the United Kingdom as London or Yorkshire, whereas Austria was an independent sovereign state. A more apt analogy would be if Great Britain were to suddenly issue the Belgian Government with an ultimatum stating that if they did not dismiss their Prime Minister then 'we should bombard Antwerp'.[33]

To this reprimand were added two official protests from Henderson to the German Government. No one expected these to have any effect. On the contrary, Hitler merely took them as evidence of British degeneracy. They were, however, all that the British Government could realistically do at this late stage. The brutish facts of the matter were illustrated by a row between Cadogan and Vansittart over the wording of the telegrams. Having watched him behave 'like a cat on hot bricks' all day, Cadogan had finally rounded on his predecessor and demanded to know exactly what it was he proposed to *do.* 'It's easy to be brave in speech', but 'will you fight?' Vansittart replied that he would not. 'Then what's it all about?' asked the exasperated Cadogan. 'To me it seems a most cowardly thing to do to urge a small man to fight a big if you won't help the former.'[34]

*

The invasion of Austria began at 5.30 a.m. the next day, Saturday 12 March 1938. German troops crossed the frontier at Bregenz, Innsbruck, Braunau and Salzburg, while hundreds of Luftwaffe aircraft took off from Bavarian airfields, transporting officials and showering Austrian cities with propaganda leaflets. As it turned out, these were largely superfluous. Not only was there no resistance: the invaders were warmly welcomed. Cheering crowds lined the roads and flowers were offered to the German soldiers as they passed. Around 4 p.m. Hitler and his entourage crossed the border in a fleet of open-topped Mercedes. After a brief and emotional pause at the Führer's birthplace, Braunau am Inn, they headed east in the direction of Linz. Bells pealed, bands played and progress slowed as the jubilant crowds surged towards the convoy, waving, weeping, throwing flowers and holding their babies aloft. At Linz the reception was stupendous. The city's entire population seemed to have come out in welcome and the streets, rooftops, balconies, 'even the trees and street lamps were full of screaming, shouting people'.[35] With tears running down his cheeks, Hitler addressed the throng from the balcony of the town hall. It was Providence, he claimed, which had selected him to restore his homeland to the German Reich.[36]

Unfortunately, Providence seemed to have neglected some of the more basic facilities necessary for the surprise takeover of another country. Checking into the Hotel Weinzinger, Linz's largest hotel, the Führer's party discovered that there were neither enough rooms nor enough food for them all. The hotel had only one telephone and it took over nine hours to establish a connection with Berlin. Despite this and the queue of Nazi officials waiting to relay instructions or receive urgent news, it was decided that the valuable device should first be put at the disposal of the pro-Nazi George Ward Price, who had managed to secure a brief interview with Hitler for the *Daily Mail*. As Reinhard Spitzy recalled with complete sincerity, 'His need, we felt, was greater than ours, as it was of the utmost importance that at least one of the world's newspapers should report an accurate and unbiased version of events.'[37]

The next day, Hitler signed the Law for the Reunion of Austria with the German Reich – a euphemism since no such union had ever previously existed – and the following afternoon, Monday 14 March, he made his triumphal entry into Vienna. There, his reception exceeded the expectations even of those who had been with him in Linz. 'In a way it was quite frightening', recalled Spitzy. 'The streets and squares resounded with the most deafening cheers' and it was 'with some difficulty [that] we made our way through the Ringstrasse'.[38] Ward Price, who at Hitler's invitation had joined the cavalcade, remembered crowds, ten people deep, all along the route and brass bands playing but unable to be heard on account of the tumult.[39] Outside the Imperial Hotel a mass of swastika-waving Viennese chanted 'We want to see our Führer' until Hitler appeared. And on the following morning, an estimated quarter of a million people crammed into Heldenplatz ('Heroes' Square') to hear their new leader announce the greatest 'triumph' of his life: the incorporation of Austria into the Reich.[40] As the British Ambassador reported to London, it was impossible to deny the enthusiasm and it would appear that 'Herr Hitler is certainly justified in claiming that his action has been welcomed by the Austrian population'.[41]

*

British reaction to the annexation of Austria was ambivalent. Although there was general outrage at the methods used, this was tempered by the widespread view that the *Anschluss* was bound to have occurred at some stage and was neither immoral nor a threat to British interests. Indeed, as *The Times* proclaimed after Hitler had bullied Schuschnigg into signing the Berchtesgaden Agreement, 'One of the least rational, most brittle, and most provocative artificialities of the peace settlement was the ban on the incorporation of Austria into the Reich.'[42] Thus, while the paper, along with most others, was prepared to condemn the use of force – the so-called 'Rape of Austria'* – it also believed that 'there would have been no British protest if this process of attraction had developed naturally through growing confidence and mutual good will'.[43]

There were, of course, those who regarded the swallowing of Austria with horror. The Conservative MP Victor Cazalet recorded his feelings as 'Furious, raging, impotent ... The invasion of Austria – the country we all love, by those bloody Nazis.'[44] The former Colonial Secretary Leo Amery lamented the disappearance of the 'last home of German culture, the last citadel in which the true soul of the German race could still find a refuge',[45] while a letter from the Vienna correspondent of *The Times* to his Editor, Geoffrey Dawson, captures the agony of the man on the spot:

> In my wildest nightmares I had not foreseen anything so perfectly organised, so brutal, so ruthless, so strong. When this machine goes into action, it will blight everything it encounters like a swarm of locusts. The destruction and loss of life will make the World War look like the Boer War ... From what I have seen of England in my last visits we have no chance of withstanding this gigantic machine when it is turned against us, and the vital thing to remember is that the ultimate object is precisely the destruction of England. This is a thing which nobody can understand, apparently, who has not lived with the Germans. Their real hatred is for England.[46]

Thinking along similar lines, Sir Horace Rumbold fancied that our 'pro-Germans in London' must be feeling pretty foolish right now.[47]

---

* This headline, from *The Times* (15 March 1938), reached the ears of Hitler, who, as he descended the stairs of the Hofburg Palace after addressing the delirious crowds, turned to Ward Price and asked scornfully, 'Is that a "rape"?', gesturing with his hand in the direction of the multitude. Later, the *Daily Mail* correspondent commented that if the *Anschluss* had been a rape then 'never have I seen a more willing victim'.

But this was not the case. Lord Lothian welcomed the end of the 'disastrous period' when the League powers denied the Germans their national unity 'and so drove them to accept a totalitarian régime', while the Nazi-admiring Tory MP Thomas Moore celebrated a 'bloodless' coup which had removed 'a source of friction and discord from international relationships'.[48] On Good Friday 1938, Rumbold attended a dinner at which he found himself sitting next to Lord Peel's sister. 'She got my goat', he confessed to his son,

> by talking in the way I am afraid so many or quite a number of people in her class of society talk. Thus, the annexation of Austria was a good thing, it would be a bad day for England if Hitler got bumped off – the only thing that really mattered was our trade. I replied bluntly that a good many people over here were lamentably ignorant about Germany and the Nazis and talked a lot of foolishness. She saw I was roused and looked rather frightened.[49]

One man who could not claim to be ignorant of Germany or the Nazis was the amateur diplomat and Secretary of the Anglo-German Fellowship, Ernest Tennant. Yet Tennant saw no reason why the annexation of Austria, or the means by which it was achieved, should inhibit the Anglo-German understanding for which he had long been striving. Writing a summary of his views in the immediate aftermath of the *Anschluss* – sent to, among others, Rab Butler and Lord Mount Temple – he reaffirmed his conviction that 'the probability of war with Great Britain does not come into the calculations of the Germans'. He had seen Ribbentrop recently in Berlin and had told the German Foreign Minister, tongue in cheek, that what he most resented about the present situation was having to do ARP Drill on his Saturday afternoons at Saffron Walden, 'instead of playing tennis, and this was what most people resented in England'. Ribbentrop had laughed and assured Tennant that this fear was completely absurd. 'We never think of war with England', he had reassured his visitor. As to making progress towards an Anglo-German agreement, Tennant believed that the main difficulty lay in a lack of mutual comprehension:

> It is unfortunately very difficult for those members of the German Government (and they are over 90%) who have never been to England

> and those members of the British Government who have never visited the 3rd Reich to understand each other's points of view. England is still mainly governed by an aristocracy with ancient traditions basically unchanged for centuries. Germany is governed by one comparatively young man risen from low beginning with no personal experience of other countries and surrounded by advisers of similar type, all men of vital, dynamic energy who have gone through an incredibly hard school, who are tough, ruthless but immensely able ... [Nevertheless,] I still believe that it should not only be possible, but easy, to make friends with them. From 1933 to 1935 they looked upon Britain much as a new boy looks upon a house master – even today that feeling has by no means gone, but Germany is growing terribly fast – we must not wait much longer.[50]

Not coincidentally, the official reaction was almost identical to that of *The Times*. Although shocked by the methods used, the truth was that the British Government had written off Austria some time before. Austria was regarded as a legitimate German interest and the impossibility of preserving her independence, short of all-out war, was recognised by almost everybody. The chief British concern – as Halifax had more than intimated to Hitler at Berchtesgaden – was not, therefore, that the *Anschluss* should be prevented but that it should occur peacefully. Indeed, Halifax, along with some of the more notorious pro-Germans, believed that an Anglo-German settlement would be easier to accomplish after the 'inevitable' absorption of Austria by the Reich. As he wrote to the Duke of Buccleuch following the Berchtesgaden Agreement:

> I have always thought that the Germans would, in one form or another, continue to reach for the ripening plum in such a way as not to let anybody else have much occasion, or opportunity, for intervening, and that when they had got further with their plum business they and we should find it a good deal easier to come to an understanding. It rather looks as if it was working out that way.[51]

As for Sir Alexander Cadogan, the Permanent Head of the British Foreign Office had come 'almost [to] wish Germany would swallow Austria and get it over. She is probably going to anyhow – [and]

anyhow we can't stop her.'[52] This latter truth was recognised by Eden, who in February 1938 had refused to get himself into the 'false position' of advising the Austrians and then being 'saddled with the responsibility' if the situation got worse.[53] Nor was there the slightest expectation that the French would prove any more interventionist. Although Yvon Delbos, the French Foreign Minister, wanted to make a joint démarche in the wake of the Berchtesgaden Agreement, this was vetoed by the British on the grounds that protests unsupported by the threat of force were meaningless. 'Brave words butter no parsnips', as Cadogan was fond of saying.[54] Added to this was the chronic instability of French domestic politics, which, with impeccable timing, succumbed to yet another crisis. On 10 March, the Government of Camille Chautemps had resigned, thus depriving France of effective leadership while Hitler issued ultimata and ordered his troops into Austria. The French press and French deputies expressed consternation but action, like in Britain, was limited to a formal protest.

For Chamberlain the whole episode was 'disheartening and discouraging'. Writing to his sister Hilda the day after the invasion, he conceded that it was now 'perfectly evident' that 'force is the only argument Germany understands and that "collective security" cannot offer any prospect of preventing such events until it can show a visible force of overwhelming strength backed by determination to use it'. Furthermore, such force could never be marshalled from Geneva but must emanate from old-fashioned power politics. 'Heaven knows I don't want to get back to alliances, but if Germany continues to behave as she has done lately she may drive us to it.'[55]

This was not the crossing of the Rubicon. As Chamberlain made clear in his next paragraph, he still had considerable faith in his Italian policy and had by no means despaired of eventually reaching an agreement with Germany. Although Britain must show her determination 'not to be bullied', by announcing an acceleration in her rearmament programme, he thought that if a German coup in Czechoslovakia could be avoided – something 'which ought to be feasible' – then 'it may be possible for Europe to settle down again and some day for us to start peace talks again with the Germans'.[56] His speech to the Commons on 14 March was thus notably undramatic and signalled no significant change in British policy other than to emphasise that Britain had never and would never disinterest herself from eastern Europe.

For those who saw the annexation of Austria as a turning point, this was not enough. Already convinced that the Nazis were bent on widespread European conquest, the socially conscious Managing Director of Lewis's department stores, Sir Frederick Marquis (the future Lord Woolton), decided that he could not let this moment pass without making some form of protest. He therefore instructed the company's fourteen buyers in Germany to close their books and, on 23 March 1938, made a powerful speech in Leicester announcing a complete boycott of German goods. Taken aback by the considerable and largely positive reaction to this intervention, Marquis concluded that this was just the sort of firm, moral lead the country desired. But it was not all praise. Summoned to Downing Street by Sir Horace Wilson, the businessman was given a 'high-powered rocket' on behalf of the Prime Minister, who strongly disapproved of his action and reprimanded him for daring to interfere in the foreign policy of the country.[57]

Marquis's principled stand was strengthened by the reports of Nazi atrocities emanating from Vienna. Having been officially suppressed under the Schuschnigg regime, the Austrian Nazis used the proclamation of the *Anschluss* to indulge in what William Shirer described as an 'orgy of sadism', worse than anything he had seen in Germany.[58] Political opponents were arrested, tortured and even murdered but it was Austria's 200,000 Jews, most of whom lived in Vienna, who bore the brunt. Forced out of their homes and shops, their windows smashed and property looted, the Viennese Jews were dragged into the streets and made to scrub pro-Schuschnigg graffiti off the pavements, while laughing mobs hurled insults and blows. International journalists were horrified. John Segrue of the London *News Chronicle* came across a group of Jewish men and women press-ganged into washing cars, while their tormentors, a cohort of SS men, administered jeers and kicks, to the delight of a crowd. Noticing that Segrue was not joining in the merriment, one of these men collared him, thrust a dirty rag into his hand, and spat, 'There, you damned Jew; get to work and help your fellow swine.' For a while Segrue complied. After helping an elderly woman with her task, however, he strode over to the black-clad figure and produced his passport. 'I am not a Jew, but a subject of His Majesty the King of England', he explained. 'I could not believe that the stories about your brutality were true and wanted to see for myself. I have seen. Good day.'[59]

Segrue's despatches were both thorough and harrowing, a worthy accompaniment to the work of G. E. R. Gedye, the *Daily Telegraph* and *New York Times* correspondent whose fearless reporting led the coverage of the Austrian Terror. Not that this was enough to change Western policy. As Gedye lamented in *Fallen Bastions*, his chilling account of the Nazification of central Europe published in February 1939, the British and American public were too far removed, too comfortable and too ignorant to appreciate the true horror of what was happening on the Continent:

> It is no fault of yours, but your very good fortune, that you cannot believe that one after another families are being turned out of their houses and herded into a ghetto merely because they are not of undiluted Teutonic blood ... You cannot believe the stories you read in your newspapers of Jewish families, after living for generations in Burgenland villages, being taken out to an island breakwater – children, old men and women, cripples of eighty and more, and very sick persons – and abandoned in the midst of a raging storm in the Danube ... You will shrug your comfortable shoulders and say 'Bogey tales' when I tell you of women whose husbands had been arrested a week before without any charge, receiving a small parcel from the Viennese postman with the curt intimation – 'To pay, 150 marks, for the cremation of your husband – ashes enclosed from Dachau' ... You have never seen Nazis gloating over the daily suicide lists, you have not looked into the indescribably bestial pages of Julius Streicher's *Der Stürmer*, or seen the slavering mouth of this scarlet-faced, bald-headed vulture ... And so you do not need to feel the horror which I cannot escape as I remember that in all this we acquiesce, and soothe our consciences with a bottle of Evian water and a few more committees. I envy you – believe me, I envy you. But yesterday I was asked by an Englishman for the address of a cheap hotel in Vienna where he could spend his holidays – *holidays* in Austria, amidst all this! Him I did not envy.[60]

Though in tone an indictment, there was some truth and, therefore, mitigation in what Gedye wrote about Western ignorance. Some of these horrific details were not relayed in the press – though many, such as the mass suicides, were* – while a far greater impression was made by the extraordinary scenes of jubilation which greeted the *Anschluss*. This, at any rate, seems to be the most charitable explanation for the debate in the House of Lords on 29 March 1938, when no less a moral figure than the Archbishop of Canterbury welcomed the union of Germany and Austria on the grounds that a 'continuing sore' at the heart of European politics had been removed 'without any bloodshed whatever'. Lord Redesdale believed that Hitler deserved 'the gratitude of the whole world' for preventing a catastrophic civil war in Europe, while the Labour peer Lord Ponsonby called on the Government to abandon its armaments programme and engage the Germans in friendly negotiations since there was 'no obstacle that cannot be overcome by goodwill'.[61] Watching from the gallery on his virgin outing to the Upper House, the Soviet Ambassador, Ivan Maisky, could hardly believe what he had witnessed. 'Never in my life have I seen so reactionary a gathering as this House of Lords. The mould of the ages lies visibly upon it … The men sitting on these red benches are historically blind, like moles, and are ready to lick the Nazi dictator's boots like a beaten dog. They'll pay for this, and I'll see it happen!'[62]

The contrast with Churchill's speech in the Commons, five days earlier, could not have been greater. The 'rape of Austria', he stated, had significantly increased the might of Nazi Germany, whose appetite would now grow along with her stature. There could be no complacency, no relaxation while the 'boa constrictor' digested its latest victim. Britain must assemble the greatest range of deterrents against future acts of aggression. As such, he called for a full military alliance with France, a public commitment to defend Czechoslovakia and the most speedy acceleration of rearmament. The foreboding of his conclusion sent a shiver down the spines of many Members who were listening:

> For five years … I have watched this famous island descending incontinently, fecklessly, the stairway which leads to a dark gulf. It is a fine broad stairway at the beginning, but after a bit the carpet ends. A little further on there are only flagstones, and a little further on still these

* *The Times* reported that an estimated 7,000 Jews had committed suicide in the first four months of the *Anschluss* in Vienna alone.

> break beneath your feet ... Now the victors are the vanquished, and those who threw down their arms in the field and sued for an armistice are striding on to world mastery.[63]

'It was like our old drawing room clock emitting the strokes of doom', recorded one MP.[64]

XII

Last Train from Berlin

Dear Czechoslovakia
I don't think they'll attack yer
But I'm not going to back yer.

Hilaire Belloc, March 1938[1]

As soon as German troops crossed into Austria the fate of that country was settled. Austria is 'finished', noted Sir Alexander Cadogan in his diary. The question now was whether Britain and France could prevent a general conflagration from breaking out over Czechoslovakia. 'Must we have a death-struggle with Germany again?' wondered the Permanent Head of the British Foreign Office. 'Or can we stand aside?' The former did 'no one any good'. Would the latter 'be fatal?' Cadogan was inclined to think not. In a few short sentences, however, he had articulated the dilemma over which Western policy makers were to agonise for the next seven months.[2]

Created in 1918 out of the rubble of the former Habsburg Empire, the democratic state of Czechoslovakia was a hotchpotch of lands and nationalities. Centred around the old 'Bohemian Crown Lands' of Bohemia, Moravia and Silesia, the new nation also comprised Slovakia (formerly Upper Hungary), Teschen and Sub-Carpathian Ruthenia. The Czechs – roughly seven and a half million of them – formed the ruling majority but there were also significant minorities, including nearly two and a half million Slovaks, half a million Hungarians, half a million Ruthenians, eighty thousand Poles and, most significantly of all, three and a quarter million Germans. These ethnic Germans, who lived principally on the fringes of Bohemia and Moravia – the so-called Sudetenland – had (contrary to the assumption of some Western contemporaries) never formed part of modern Germany. Previously subjects of the Habsburgs, their forebears had nevertheless inhabited the region for at least eight hundred years. While the Austro-Hungarian Empire survived, the *Sudetendeutsche* (as they subsequently became known) were in the ascendant. Their position was reversed, however, after the First World War and the foundation of the Czechoslovak state. Although the Sudeten Germans enjoyed civil, political, religious and economic liberties, such as could only be dreamt of in Nazi Germany, and could, with justice, be described as the most 'privileged' minority 'in the whole of Europe', they resented Czech political, cultural and economic dominance – a feeling exacerbated both by the Great Depression (which hit the Sudeten areas disproportionately hard) and by the rise of national socialism across the border.[3]

For Hitler, Czechoslovakia was a prime target. As an Austrian he had an instinctive loathing for the Czechs – a prejudice shared by many of the German-speaking subjects of the former Habsburg Empire – while, as the ultimate pan-German nationalist, he saw it as his mission to unite all Germans within the boundaries of the Reich.* In addition to these personal and ideological motivations were strategic ones. As the Führer later complained to Chamberlain, Czechoslovakia thrust like a 'spearhead' into the side of Germany.[4] Her mountainous western border – one of the most natural defensive frontiers in Europe – and her million-strong army constituted a block to German ambitions in eastern Europe, while her defensive treaties with France and Russia were conceived as an attempt to 'encircle' the Reich. If Hitler wished to plunder the oil fields of Romania, acquire *Lebensraum* in eastern Europe, or forcibly repatriate the Polish Corridor that separated East Prussia from the rest of Germany, then he had first to deal with Czechoslovakia.

Fully aware of where the next trouble spot would be, the question of a British guarantee to defend Czechoslovakia began to be debated even as German soldiers made their way to Vienna. Thanks to the 1925 Franco-Czechoslovak Treaty, the French were already committed

* The exception was the ethnic German population of South Tyrol, which Hitler was, pragmatically, prepared to renounce in favour of Italian–German friendship.

and on 14 March 1938 restated their determination to come to Czechoslovakia's aid if she were the victim of unprovoked aggression. Was Britain prepared to do the same? For some, such as Leo Amery, the shock of Hitler's Austrian coup was enough to overcome the traditional British aversion to Continental commitments. German ruthlessness meant 'facing realities ... [and] I am inclined to think that the best hope of peace now lies in telling Germany that if she touches Czechoslovakia we are in it too'.[5] Other Conservative anti-appeasers such as Churchill, Bob Boothby, Vyvyan Adams and the Duchess of Atholl (the MP for Kinross and West Perthshire) agreed and, in the days following the *Anschluss*, called for a British guarantee. They were, however, a minority.

The idea of a commitment to defend Czechoslovakia was regarded by most Tory MPs with profound scepticism and even as anathema. Unlike Belgium or France, Czechoslovakia was not considered a vital British interest and, as Alan Lennox-Boyd told his Bedfordshire constituents, Germany 'could absorb Czechoslovakia, and Great Britain would remain secure'.[6] Since Lennox-Boyd was a member of the Government (albeit a junior one), this tactless expression of realpolitik caused a political storm. Boothby considered it 'an incitement to Germany to get on with the job'.[7] His views were, however, typical of many who sat on the Government benches. According to George Tryon, Postmaster General and Conservative MP for Brighton, it was ludicrous to 'guarantee the independence of a country which we can neither get at nor spell', while the full force of Tory isolationism and Czechophobia was conveyed in a letter from Michael Beaumont, the blimpish Conservative MP for Aylesbury, to the Under-Secretary of State for Foreign Affairs, Rab Butler:

> For God's sake do what you can to stop the country being stampeded by hysteria over this most unpleasant business [the *Anschluss*], into entering into any more foreign commitments, particularly with regard to Czecho-Slovakia. Quite apart from people like me who would sooner be tortured at the stake than fight for that beastly country (there are more of them than you might think), I am quite sure that while the bulk of the country now is so shocked over Austria that it is prepared to do anything, the old unwillingness to risk their lives for anything in which we are not directly concerned, will revive very

> quickly. Even now, there would I think be strong opposition to any further commitments, but later on, it would be difficult to get the people to honour them.[8]

Fortunately for Beaumont, the British Government was no more eager to guarantee Czechoslovakia than he was. On 18 March, five days after the *Anschluss*, the Cabinet's Foreign Policy Committee met to consider a memorandum by Lord Halifax entitled 'Possible Measures to Avert German Action in Czechoslovakia'. Based on the assumption that the German Government would 'by fair means or foul' work for the incorporation of the Sudetenland into the Reich, the paper outlined the three courses which, the Foreign Secretary believed, were now open to the British Government. There was the 'Grand Alliance' (as advocated by Churchill), in which Britain and France would weld a number of states together into a defensive bloc; a new commitment to France, whereby Britain would pledge to come to her assistance if she were attacked by Germany as a result of her honouring her obligations to Czechoslovakia; or the 'negative' option of undertaking no fresh commitments and advising the Czechs to seek the best possible terms with Germany.[9]

As his summation made clear, Halifax favoured this third course. The Grand Alliance was 'impractical', while any new commitments risked involving Britain in a war 'in which we might be defeated and lose all'. His colleagues did not dissent. Although Oliver Stanley (President of the Board of Trade) and Sir Samuel Hoare (Home Secretary) made noises in favour of a further commitment to France, this idea foundered when it was pointed out that there was nothing which either France or Britain could practically do to defend Czechoslovakia against invasion. The *Anschluss* had 'turned' the Czech defences on her western border and, as the Minister for the Co-ordination of Defence, Sir Thomas Inskip, explained, it 'seemed certain that Germany could overrun the whole of Czecho-Slovakia in less than a week'.[10] In addition to this, Ministers had been greatly influenced by a recent despatch from Basil Newton, the British Minister in Prague, which argued that owing to her 'geographical situation, her history and the racial divisions of her population, Czechoslovakia's present political position is not permanently tenable'.[11] If this was the case – and Ministers were apt to give weight to the 'man on the spot' – then why, the politicians asked, should Britain risk a fight to the death in order to preserve the status quo? Indeed, what grounds were there for objecting to the incorporation of the Sudeten territories into the Reich, provided that this was done peacefully? At this point the Cabinet Secretary, Sir Maurice Hankey, reminded the meeting that it had been recognised at Versailles that Czechoslovakia could only survive if the whole of her territory remained intact. Her manufacturing and industrial districts, the best agricultural land, her fortifications and defences, were all located within the Sudeten territories. If these were taken away then Czechoslovakia would become a vassal state, at the mercy of Nazi Germany.

Ministers listened but were not swayed. There was not 'a soul in this country' who would support a direct guarantee for the Czechs, believed Stanley, while the Secretary of State for the Dominions, Malcolm MacDonald, warned that war over Czechoslovakia risked the break-up of the British Commonwealth.[12] After some further discussion, in which the weakness of France and the isolationist stance of the United States were touched upon, the meeting concluded overwhelmingly in favour of the third option. 'F.P.C. unanimous that Czechoslovakia is not worth the bones of a single British Grenadier', noted Cadogan with approval.[13]

Chamberlain was pleased. As he explained in a letter to his sister Ida, he had already considered a number of potential courses, including the Grand Alliance, but had rejected them all on grounds of practicability:

> You have only to look at the map to see that nothing that France or we could do could possibly save Czecho-Slovakia from being over-run by the Germans if they wanted to do it. The Austrian frontier is practically open; the great Skoda munition works are within easy bombing distance of the German aerodromes, the railways all pass through German territory, Russia is 100 miles away. Therefore we could not help Czecho-Slovakia – she would simply be a pretext for going to war with Germany. That we could not think of unless we had a reasonable prospect of being able to beat her to her knees in a reasonable time and of that I see no sign. I have therefore abandoned any idea of giving

> guarantees to Czecho-Slovakia or to France in connection with her obligations to that country.[14]

Few contemporaries would have disagreed with this analysis. Although Chamberlain underestimated the potential for Russian assistance (in some ways a wise precaution), his contention that a guarantee for Czechoslovakia would be a bluff which, if called, would land the country in an extremely precarious position was shared by many. In March 1938, the British Army was almost non-existent. Two poorly equipped divisions and one mobile division were the most which could be sent to the Continent in the event of war. The Territorial Army was 20,000 men short of its target for manning an insufficient number of anti-aircraft batteries and there was a dearth of modern equipment. Reflecting on this mass of deficiencies, the head of Eastern Command, General Edmund Ironside, concluded that the country was 'in no state to go to war', while Cadogan believed that Britain would be 'smashed' if a conflict were to break out now.[15]

More open to doubt was the Prime Minister's and Foreign Secretary's assessment of Hitler and his aims. As Halifax told the Foreign Policy Committee on 18 March, he did not believe that they were dealing with a man possessed of a 'lust for conquest on a Napoleonic scale'.[16] The *Anschluss* had been a shock but, as he confessed in a letter to Sir Nevile Henderson, the thing he found hardest to forgive was the stupidity of the Germans in not realising 'the hullabaloo it would all make'.[17] As to the future, Halifax conceded that it would be foolish to discount the possibility of another display of German power politics, yet neither he nor the Prime Minister believed that Hitler's ambitions extended beyond the aim of bringing all Germans within the boundaries of the Reich. Indeed, as Chamberlain revealed to Ida in a letter of 20 March, his current plan was to approach Hitler directly and ask what he wanted for the Sudeten Germans. If the Führer's demands were reasonable then the British Government would urge the Czechs to accept them, while Hitler would be asked to provide assurances that he would leave the rest of Czechoslovakia alone.[18]

On Tuesday 22 March, the Cabinet ratified the decision of the Foreign Policy Committee. The discussion had centred on the report of the Chiefs of Staff into the military situation, a document which, as Inskip had predicted, made grim reading. Despite two years of rearmament, twenty out of twenty-seven fighter squadrons were reported to be operating with obsolete or obsolescent machines; there were no 3.7-inch or 4.5-inch anti-aircraft guns; while the Navy's ability to defend British home waters and maintain a deterrent in the Far East could only be achieved by abandoning the Mediterranean to the Italians. As for the defence of Czechoslovakia, the Chiefs of Staff confirmed the forecasts already made: 'No pressure which this country and its possible allies could exercise would suffice to prevent the defeat of Czecho-Slovakia.' Someone, probably Duff Cooper (the Cabinet minutes are unclear), pointed out that although the situation was undoubtedly bad there was nothing in the report to suggest that it would improve with time. The Chiefs of Staff had ignored the potential for Russian assistance and had taken little account of the weaknesses of the German military, exposed during the invasion of Austria when a large number of tanks broke down and had to be abandoned at the side of the road. Moreover, if Germany were allowed to continue her process of aggrandisement, then surely this would only make her more powerful in the future? Today, Czechoslovakia and the other small states in central and eastern Europe were potential allies but tomorrow they could be sources of still greater German strength. Not even Cooper, however, called for a direct guarantee and the meeting concurred with the Prime Minister who believed they were in no position to adopt a policy which entailed the risk of war.[19]

Despite this, Chamberlain's statement to Parliament two days later, on 24 March, managed to satisfy many who had been calling for a firmer policy. Although the Prime Minister said that he was disinclined to add to Britain's formal commitments, he made the crucial point that 'where peace and war are concerned, legal obligations are not alone involved, and, if war broke out, it would be unlikely to be confined to those who have assumed such obligations'. Indeed, 'the inexorable pressure of facts might well prove more powerful than formal pronouncements, and in that event it would be well within the bounds of probability that other countries, besides those which were parties to the original dispute, would almost immediately become involved'.[20]

The deliberate ambiguity of this statement – implying but not promising that Britain would intervene if a general war broke out over Czechoslovakia – won a wide range of plaudits. The anti-appeasers (including Cooper but excluding Churchill) were broadly satisfied, while the isolationists rejoiced that Britain was not going to risk her Empire over the 'nonesuch State' of Czechoslovakia.[21]

Not everyone was happy, however. On 17 March 1938 – four days after the *Anschluss* – the Soviet Foreign Minister, Maxim Litvinov, took the unusual step of addressing a gathering of foreign journalists in Moscow. Fully alive to the Nazi menace, Litvinov (who unlike his British counterpart had read *Mein Kampf*) had become a convert to the policy of collective security in the wake of Hitler's accession to power. As such and under his leadership, he had overseen a revolution in Soviet foreign policy, which saw the USSR join the League of Nations (1934), form a defensive alliance with France (1935), support sanctions against Italy (1935–6) and even offer to join in sanctions against Germany following the reoccupation of the Rhineland (1936). In May 1935, the Russians had made their own treaty with Czechoslovakia, promising to come to her assistance if she was attacked, providing that France fulfilled her obligations first. To Litvinov's distress, however, none of this had met with corresponding efforts by Britain or France. Blinded by their fear of communism, the Western Powers seemed to prefer to allow Hitler to fulfil his objectives piecemeal rather than form a joint deterrent with the USSR. Litvinov's policy was not yielding fruit and his enemies in the Politburo began to look forward to another revolution and the reorientation of Russian foreign policy towards a deal with Germany.

Before this could occur, however, Litvinov obtained Stalin's permission for a further and possibly final effort to form an alliance against German aggression. Addressing the foreign correspondents in the Ministry of Foreign Affairs, the Russian Foreign Minister therefore explained that the Soviet Union – profoundly disturbed by the invasion of Austria – was prepared to enter into discussions with any nations wishing to halt further acts of aggression and thus 'eliminate' the danger of a new world slaughter. 'Tomorrow it may be too late', he warned, but the time had not yet passed when the Great Powers could unite for the 'collective salvation of peace'.[22]

Having ignored it for a week, Chamberlain rejected this offer in his Commons statement. Profoundly distrustful of the Russians – who he believed were 'stealthily and cunningly pulling all the strings behind the scenes to get us involved in war with Germany' – he also had little faith in the USSR's military capability.[23] To a large extent this was understandable. In June 1937, Stalin had extended the 'Great Terror' to the Red Army and Soviet Navy. Three out of five marshals, thirteen out of fifteen army commanders, eight out of nine admirals, fifty-seven out of eighty-five corps commanders and all seventeen army commissars were purged. Sixty-five per cent of the higher ranks of the Soviet military were thought to have been removed in all and the advice from the British Military Attaché was that Russia was now incapable of waging anything other than a defensive war.*[24] These reports, which shocked and horrified the Western democracies, augmented Chamberlain's prejudices. Yet in spurning the Soviet Union the British were rejecting the possibility of threatening or confronting Germany with a protracted two-front war, while also bolstering those within the Soviet hierarchy who advocated either a policy of isolationism or rapprochement with Germany.

The other power which had reason to be disappointed with Chamberlain's statement was France. On 15 March, Joseph Paul-Boncour – who had been hastily appointed Foreign Minister in the midst of the *Anschluss* – requested that 'His Majesty's Government should declare publicly that, if Germany attacked Czechoslovakia and France went to [the] latter's assistance, Great Britain would stand by France'.[25] This request had also been rejected. Yet the damage to Anglo-French relations was limited for two reasons: first, because the French had no option but to keep in with the British, and second, because the Blum Government fell on 10 April, after only a month in power. The new Prime Minister, Edouard Daladier – who had been serving as Defence Minister since June 1936 and already been Prime Minister twice – was significantly closer to the British perspective of the situation. For a brief moment, however, it appeared that Daladier was going to ask the hawkish Paul-Boncour to remain at the Quai d'Orsay. Horrified, the British, who considered the silver-haired Frenchman 'a positive danger to the peace of Europe', took the extraordinary step of informing Daladier that such an appointment would be 'most unfortunate'.[26] Daladier – having probably reached

---

* French analysis was similar: the Red Army was 'no more than a decapitated corpse', stated the Deuxième Bureau in the summer of 1938.

the same conclusion on his own – agreed and appointed Georges Bonnet, a fellow Radical and known supporter of conciliation with the dictators.[27]

*

Chamberlain was full of confidence. He considered his speech of 24 March an 'éclatant success' and predicted that if there were a general election now 'we should romp in'.[28] On 4 April he routed the Opposition with a 'real fighting speech' in defence of the Government's foreign policy, and, a few days later, relayed to his sister Hilda a spate of accolades, including Lord Beaverbrook's judgement that he was 'the best PM we've had in half a century'.[29] During the following fortnight he was able to point to two notable achievements emanating from his policy of appeasing troublesome countries: on 16 April the Anglo-Italian Agreement was concluded in Rome and on 25 April a new Anglo-Irish Treaty was signed in Downing Street.

Neither was without controversy. As Anthony Eden observed, the rapprochement with Mussolini was based on a number of promises which the Duce had already broken (notably to withdraw Italian 'volunteers' from Spain), while the deal with the Irish leader, Eamon de Valera, relinquished Britain's rights to ports in the Republic. Churchill, who had guaranteed the use of the ports in the 1921 Irish Treaty, blasted this decision as 'an improvident example of appeasement' – a verdict that would be confirmed when de Valera upheld Irish neutrality at the start of the Second World War and refused Britain access.[30] Yet Churchill spoke for only a small minority. Most of the Government's supporters – and in the case of the Irish Treaty, the Labour and Liberal parties were no less supportive – welcomed the two agreements as diplomatic coups which reduced British liabilities in an all too dangerous world.

For Chamberlain, this double achievement served to reinforce his faith in his own diplomacy – the so-called 'Chamberlain touch'. As he boasted to his sisters in mid-March, any Anglo-Irish deal would be entirely due to 'the influence I have established over De Valera' – a perception the canny Irishman had confirmed on more than one occasion.[31] Owing to the *Anschluss* he realised that it was currently impossible for him to exercise these skills on Hitler, yet the Government were intending to press the Czechs to solve their minority problem and if this were achieved, he told Ida, 'then it might presently be possible to re-start again in Berlin'.[32]

Indeed, on 22 April, Ernst Woermann, the First Counsellor at the German Embassy, reported to Berlin the contents of a conversation he had had with Rab Butler in which the young Foreign Office Minister had apparently been at pains to emphasise that the *Anschluss* had in no way diminished the Prime Minister's desire for a 'real understanding' with Germany. 'The German and British peoples were of the same blood', Butler allegedly declared (echoing Nazi racial theories), and it was 'inconceivable that Germany and England should meet again on the battlefield'. As to Czechoslovakia, there were perhaps some things about which the two men could not speak frankly. Yet, in the next breath, Butler stated that 'England was aware that Germany would attain "her next goal"' and was only concerned about 'the manner in which this was done'.[33] If Ribbentrop harboured any doubts as to the possibility of British bellicosity over Czechoslovakia, then such conversations served to allay them.

*

On 27 April 1938, the new French Ministers arrived in London for talks. Three days earlier, Konrad Henlein, the leader of the Sudeten German Party (SdP), had issued a series of far-reaching demands at Karlsbad, including the recognition of the Sudeten areas as a distinct legal entity, full equality for the Sudeten Germans and freedom to disseminate Nazi ideology. These desiderata – which amounted to a demand for complete autonomy within the state – had been rejected by the Government in Prague. Now, the British sought to co-opt the French into supporting their policy of pressurising the Czechs into concessions.

To begin with, Daladier made a show of defiance. Henlein, he averred, was not after autonomy but the 'destruction' of the Czechoslovak state. More importantly, they were dealing with a Germany which aimed to gain a position of hegemony within Europe. In his opinion, 'the ambitions of Napoleon were far inferior to the present aims of the German Reich'. Of course, there were dangers attached to confronting Germany at this moment, yet it was important not to forget the strength of the Czech Army – 'well trained, well equipped, and animated by a public spirit' – the 5,000 aircraft of the Soviet Air Force and the weaknesses, as well as the strengths, of the German military. If Britain and France stated unequivocally that they would not permit the destruction of Czechoslovakia then, the French Prime Minister believed, 'the peace of Europe might be saved'.[34]

'Very beautiful, but awful rubbish' was Sir Alexander Cadogan's verdict on this speech.[35] Yet while history was not to vindicate this judgement, there was some truth in what the Permanent Under-Secretary said. Six weeks earlier, in the immediate aftermath of the *Anschluss*, the French Permanent Committee of National Defence had met to consider the question of aiding their eastern ally and, like the British, had come to the conclusion that there was nothing which could practically be done to prevent a German conquest. The most which France could offer, Daladier (then Defence Minister) had stated, was indirect aid – mobilising the French Army so as to pin down German forces along their western frontier – while General Gamelin, the French Commander-in-Chief, was sceptical of the potential for Russian assistance. Outwardly, France remained committed to 'defending' Czechoslovakia and the new Prime Minister – highly conscious of French honour – certainly hoped that the day would never come when he would be forced to break his pledge. Daladier's appointment of Bonnet to replace Paul-Boncour is, however, telling and, as the new German Ambassador to London reported to Berlin, it seems likely that the French were hoping that the British would make the case for pressurising the Czechs so that they might 'acquiesce without seeming to have taken the initiative in the matter'.[36]

This they duly did. After Chamberlain had softened Daladier with a good lunch, his execrable French and the small concession of naval staff talks, the 'Bull of Vaucluse', as the French Premier was colloquially known, withdrew his horns and fell into line behind the British policy.* Both the British and the French were to press the Czechs to reach a speedy understanding with the Sudetens, while the British were to ask Hitler what solution he would deem

* The nickname stemmed from the constituency Daladier had represented since 1919 and his bovine appearance. His horns, however, as his critics were apt to point out, were those of a snail.

acceptable. The rationale of the scheme rested on the British belief that German demands were reasonable and limited to the Sudetenland. Indeed, as Henderson wrote to Halifax on 6 May 1938, it was vital for the Czechs to grant the majority of Henlein's demands now since 'both Herr Hitler and Henlein are moderate compared to many of their followers and M. Beneš's [the Czechoslovak President] sole hope in my opinion and in the interests of his country is to make such a maximum offer that these two cannot well decline it'.[37]

Yet it was Daladier's analysis of German intentions which was to prove the more accurate. Four weeks earlier, on 28 March 1938, Hitler had received Henlein and his deputy, Karl Hermann Frank, in the Reich Chancellery. There, he had told his guests that he intended to solve the Sudeten question in the 'not-too-distant future' and that their job was to keep the situation boiling by making unacceptable demands of the Government in Prague. 'We must always demand so much that we can never be satisfied' was Henlein's neat summary of his instructions.[38] A few weeks later, Hitler summoned the Chief of the Armed Forces High Command, General Wilhelm Keitel, and instructed him to update 'Case Green' – the plan for the invasion of Czechoslovakia, initiated after the Hossbach Conference. There were at least three scenarios by which a crisis might be provoked, the Führer explained, but his favoured one was for some internal incident. Two months later, it appeared that this moment had come.

*

Early on the evening of Thursday 19 May 1938, Sir Nevile Henderson received a telegram from the Acting Consul at Dresden stating that German troops were concentrating along the southern border with Czechoslovakia and that Army leave had been suspended for that coming Sunday. The Ambassador thought little of it. There was no evidence of abnormal military activity in Berlin, he cabled London, and the cancelled leave was likely to do with the local elections due that weekend in the Sudeten districts. On the following morning, however, Basil Newton, the British Minister in Prague, received an alarmed call from the Czech Foreign Ministry, informing him of reports of German soldiers massing in Saxony and Bavaria. Henderson was asked to investigate and duly visited the Foreign Ministry, where the State Secretary, Ernst von Weizsäcker, rang up the Wehrmacht High Command, requesting information. Later, Weizsäcker telephoned Henderson to say that he had been assured by General Keitel that all talk of troop concentrations was 'absolutely nonsense'. No troops had been assembled in Saxony, only at Königsbrück, where routine exercises were taking place. Henderson was sceptical. He reminded Weizsäcker that he had received the same denials on 11 March, when the German Army was preparing to invade Austria, and warned the Foreign Office that if an 'incident' occurred during the elections, then Hitler would 'give orders for the German troops to cross the frontier immediately'.[39]

In London, the major players were packing up for what promised to be the first weekend of summer. Halifax was due to visit both his alma maters, first Oxford, then Eton, while Chamberlain was looking forward to a weekend's trout fishing. Unfortunately, neither man was to enjoy the tranquillity they had hoped for. 'Those d——d Germans have spoiled another weekend for me', raged Chamberlain after he had been fetched from the river to be informed of the cascade of telegrams which had arrived early that morning, Saturday 21 May.[40] These contained further accounts of German military build-up along the Czech border, including the claim that the 7th and 17th infantry divisions were advancing towards the Bavarian–Czechoslovak frontier and that German planes had been spotted flying over northern Bohemia. The Czech General Staff were extremely jumpy and late the previous evening had persuaded the Government to mobilise a section of the reserve – some 174,000 men.

The efficiency and enthusiasm with which this order was carried out gave the lie to those who sought to belittle the Czechoslovak military or believed that the Czechs would simply roll over, as the Austrians had done. The orders reached the Czech towns and villages by 10 p.m. on Friday 20 May and by 3 a.m. the next day around 70 per cent of the reservists were at their posts. By dawn, all but sixteen of the expected 174,000 soldiers had reported for duty, and the frontiers, as well as the entire Sudeten territory, had been manned by the military. It was 'miraculous', wrote the British journalist Shiela Grant Duff: 'Each garrison moved up, relieving the one ahead with clock-like precision.'[41] Her American colleague Virginia Cowles, who was covering the elections for the *Sunday Times*, first became aware of the impending crisis while travelling to an SdP rally with the party's chief press officer. 'I will tell you a secret', the official told her: 'Henlein is with Hitler this very moment at Berchtesgaden. The German Army may cross the frontier at any hour.' The young reporter was aghast. 'But that would mean a world war', she exclaimed. 'Not at all', the press officer replied. 'It will all be over in a few days.'[42]

Cowles was not reassured. She attended the rally – a 'nightmare of flags, swastikas … and ear splitting "Heils"' – but when she was woken at five o'clock on the Saturday morning and discovered Czech soldiers patrolling the streets, she decided to return to Prague. There, at the Hotel Ambassador, she found no signs of crisis. A charwoman was washing the floor, the desk clerk was sifting the post and the bell boy was reading the newspaper. Suddenly, Reynolds Packard, the flamboyant United Press reporter, came rushing through the lobby in a state of high excitement. There were rumours of a German invasion and the Government had started to mobilise, he explained. Cowles ran to the telephone and, after several attempts, managed to get through to the *Sunday Times*. The male voice at the end of the line seemed as if from another world:

> 'Good morning,' he said amicably. 'How are you?'
> 'Not very well. The Czech Army is mobilizing.'
> 'I say! Why are they doing that?'
> 'They think the German Army's coming across the frontier.'
> 'I say! Are you sure?'
> 'I'm sure the Czechs are mobilizing.'
> 'I say! Fancy that. That *is* news.'[43]

By this stage, the Foreign Office was no less excited. The Secret Intelligence Service (SIS) had warned of a possible German attack towards the end of May and it was now reported that two Sudeten Germans had been shot dead by the Czech police. 'Is it 1914 all over again?' wondered Chips Channon.[44] At 3 p.m., the Foreign Office received details of a violent interview which Henderson had had with Ribbentrop that morning. The German Foreign Minister, the Ambassador reported, was in a 'highly excitable and pugnacious frame of mind'. In particular, he was incensed that Henderson had informed Reuters of the denial he had received regarding German troop movements and was now refusing to provide the Ambassador with any military information – an attitude, Henderson retorted, that forced him to infer that military measures *were* taking place. The Foreign Minister then turned to the 'murder' of the two Sudetens and, using the most 'bloodthirsty language', assured the Ambassador that if such provocations continued then Czechoslovakia would be destroyed.[45]

Things seemed to be getting out of hand and Halifax, despite agreeing with Cadogan that 'we must not go to war!', decided that Hitler should be warned of the dangers he was courting.[46] That afternoon, Saturday 21 May, France had reconfirmed her pledge to Czechoslovakia and Henderson was instructed to call again at the Wilhelmstrasse and warn Ribbentrop that if France were to become involved in war then 'His Majesty's Government could not guarantee that they would not be forced by circumstances to become involved also'.[47] In contrast to his voluble irascibility that morning, Ribbentrop listened to the majority of this message in sullen silence. At the delivery of the British warning, however, he immediately flared up. If France were so crazy as to intervene, he shouted, it would lead to 'the greatest French defeat in world history and, if Britain were to join her, then once again we should have to fight to the death'.[48]

Nor were tensions lessened by the farcical incident of the 'special train'. As Henderson was forced to explain, repeatedly, it had long been planned that the Embassy's Naval Attaché would begin a period of leave with his family on Saturday 21 May. Unfortunately, there proved to be insufficient room on the train for both the Attaché's family and the children of another Embassy official. The solution offered by the railway company was for an extra coach to be added and, with room to spare, the Attaché persuaded another two Embassy families to join what looked like a mass exodus. The fact that these arrangements coincided with a diplomatic crisis was extremely bad luck. Returning from the Ministry of Foreign Affairs on the Sunday morning, Henderson was surprised to find the French Ambassador standing on his doorstep. Was it true, an alarmed François-Poncet enquired, that the Ambassador was evacuating the Embassy? Henderson assured him that it was not. He had hardly got through the front door, however, before he received an urgent call from London asking him what on earth was going on – they had heard that 'women and children' were leaving that night by 'special coach' – followed by a call from Weizsäcker, begging the Ambassador 'not to be an alarmist'.[49] In the end, the Attaché was allowed to proceed with his leave but Henderson forbade all other departures.

*

As it turned out, the drama over the fictional British evacuation was an appropriate episode in what was, essentially, an imaginary crisis. There was no German plan to invade Czechoslovakia on the weekend of 21–22 May 1938 nor, as the British Military Attaché reported after driving some 700 miles first towards and then along the German–Czech frontier, was there any evidence of unusual German military activity. What appears to have happened was that the Czechs, under intense pressure from aggressive German propaganda, overreacted to real and imagined Army manoeuvres, having previously received intelligence which claimed that the Germans were planning to use 'disturbances' during the elections as an excuse to invade.[50]

If the crisis had been imaginary, however, it had real consequences. The world believed that Czechoslovakia had been threatened and a German invasion only prevented by the actions of the Western democracies. In particular, the resolution of Great Britain was singled out for lavish praise in the international press: Hitler had intended to strike but had been deterred by a growl from the British lion. This, Henderson believed, was a disaster. Holed up in the Obersalzberg, Hitler was enraged at the suggestion that he had been forced to back down and began a 'brain storm' which, so the Ambassador claimed, pushed him 'over the border-line from peaceful negotiation to the use of force'.[51]

This was not an accurate interpretation of events. Hitler had never contemplated solving the Czechoslovak issue peacefully and, for the last few months, had been actively engaged in planning a military solution which would destroy the Czech state. What the May Crisis did was to harden his resolve and accelerate his plans. After brooding at Berchtesgaden for a week, Hitler returned to Berlin, where he summoned his leading Generals for a meeting in the Reich Chancellery. There, on 28 May, he proclaimed his 'iron will' that Czechoslovakia would shortly 'disappear from the map'.[52] Despite the events of the previous weekend, he did not believe that Britain or France would intervene. Nevertheless, he instructed Admiral Raeder to accelerate the battleship and submarine programme (an obvious deterrent to Great Britain) and now ordered work on the West Wall – the series of defensive fortifications along the French border – to be urgently stepped up. Though a number of Generals had serious doubts about the Führer's plan, for the moment they kept quiet. Case Green was redrafted and now opened with Hitler's declaration that it was his 'unalterable decision to smash Czechoslovakia by military action in the near future'.[53] The date by which the military preparations were to be complete was 1 October 1938, 'at the latest'.[54]

In London, most people were convinced that the threat to Czechoslovakia had been real. 'There is no doubt that Germany *were* [*sic*] up to some monkey tricks Friday–Sunday', recorded Major-General Henry Pownall, adding that 'C' – the head of SIS, Admiral Hugh 'Quex' Sinclair – had information that 'someone in Germany called it all off on Monday'.[55] Chamberlain believed that it had been 'a d—n close-run thing'. It was all very well the German press denying that anything untoward had been going on, but why, in that case, had Ribbentrop abused Henderson for sharing these denials with Reuters? In all, the Prime Minister could not doubt

> (1) that the German Government made all preparations for a coup (2) that in the end they decided after getting our warnings that the risks were too great (3) that the general view that this was just what had happened made them conscious that they had lost prestige and (4) that they are venting their spite on us because they feel that we have got the credit for having given them a check.

The whole episode served to illustrate 'how utterly untrustworthy and dishonest the German Government is'.[56]

Yet despite the (incorrect) conclusion that it was British firmness which had prevented a German attack, the May Crisis did not lead to a new policy of resistance. On the contrary, horrified at how close things had got, the Government became even more determined to force the Czechs to satisfy the Sudeten German demands before another crisis could occur. This attitude led to some odd discussions. As Duff Cooper recorded after the emergency Cabinet meeting on the evening of Sunday 29 May, 'The general feeling ... seemed to be that great, brutal Czechoslovakia was bullying poor, peaceful little Germany.'[57] A few days later, Halifax impressed on Jan Masaryk, the Czech Minister in London and son of the country's founding President, the urgency of Beneš reaching a generous agreement with Henlein, adding his own belief that the very most the Czechs would be able to get away with was autonomy for the Sudetens on 'the Swiss model'.[58] In Paris, Sir Eric Phipps – who, infected by French defeatism, had moved firmly into the appeasement camp – asked Bonnet to apply similar pressure. As the Ambassador reported to London, the French Foreign Minister was delighted to oblige. Desperate to avoid the dilemma of war or dishonouring France's signature, Bonnet promised to exert all possible pressure on Prague, including the threat that France would consider herself 'released from her bond' if the Czechs proved unreasonable.[59] At the same time, the British made it clear to the French that their actions over the crucial May weekend in no way implied a British commitment to Czechoslovakia.

While this was technically the case, however, the May Crisis did lead, de facto, to an increase in British commitments. Having been credited with snuffing German aggression in May, was it really possible for Britain to stand aside when the next crisis emerged? In order to avoid this dilemma the British took steps to force the Czechs to reach a deal, including the despatch of a British mediator. Yet this only served to draw the fates of the two countries closer together. If the Czechs followed the British advice and were nevertheless attacked, how could Britain abstain? At the heart of British policy was, therefore, a paradox: the British were resolved that they should not and could not commit to the defence of Czechoslovakia and yet, by their own actions, they became almost inextricably linked to the fate of that fragile country.

XIII

Hons and Rebels

This is not the time for fine party feelings, but to save your country.
Sir Timothy Eden to his brother, Anthony, 16 May 1938[1]

On the evening of Wednesday 16 March 1938, Winston Churchill dined with his son, Randolph, Harold Nicolson and Bob Boothby at Pratt's club. The *Anschluss* was three days old and the man who had been warning about the German threat for nearly six years was in bellicose mood. 'Never', he told his fellow diners, 'has any man inherited a more ghastly situation than Neville Chamberlain.' Thanks to the lethargy of the Baldwin years, Britain was now in a position whereby she stood to lose everything if she failed to take a stand and yet 'if we take strong action, London will be a shambles in half an hour'. The Conservative Party was filled with 'blind and obstinate men' and he, Churchill, was not going to put up with it much longer. If the Government did not produce a new, clear policy within the next few weeks, he would resign the whip and take some fifty Conservatives with him in a full-blown act of insurrection.[2]

Churchill must have known that this was wishful thinking. Eight months later (by which time his standing had considerably improved), he called for fifty Conservatives to follow him into the lobby to support a Liberal motion calling for a Ministry of Supply but only Harold Macmillan and Brendan Bracken answered the call.* Yet the takeover of Austria did lead to the early stages of an increasingly cohesive

* Considering that Churchill had been able to rely on the support of around sixty Conservative MPs during his campaign against Indian Home Rule, the extent of his isolation within his own party during this period becomes even more apparent.

opposition to appeasement within the Conservative Party. Late on the night of 7 April 1938, Ronald Cartland, the young and courageously independent MP for Birmingham King's Norton, confided to Labour's foreign affairs spokesman, Hugh Dalton, that around forty Tory MPs had been so stirred by the *Anschluss* that he believed they would have voted against the Government if there had been some alternative combination in waiting. On the other hand, the majority of his colleagues were 'still terrified of the communist bogy' and, therefore, blind to the danger from Nazi Germany. As for his leader, Cartland told Dalton that Chamberlain was getting increasingly dictatorial and that 'they had now a Führer in the Conservative Party'.[3]

The greatest problem facing Conservative would-be rebels was lack of leadership. In January 1938, Leo Amery had set up a 'study group' for some twenty like-minded Tory MPs who intended to meet regularly in the hope of developing a common line on foreign policy. Yet Amery, though respected as a former Cabinet Minister and Fellow of All Souls, was not the man to inspire a following. Small and wiry, with a dull voice and an even duller habit of speaking too long, it was joked that this extremely capable politician could have been Prime Minister if he had been half a head taller and his speeches half an hour shorter. If it was oratory that was needed, then Churchill was undoubtedly the man. Yet for most Conservatives, the former Liberal, architect of the Gallipoli disaster, opponent of Indian reform and champion of Edward VIII during the Abdication crisis remained an object of considerable distrust.

The leader the anti-appeasers craved was Anthony Eden. To their increasing frustration, however, this was a role the former Foreign Secretary seemed loath to assume. Having resigned on 20 February, an exhausted Eden had retreated to the south of France. One day, while listening to the wireless, he was startled by the demonic voice of Hitler proclaiming '*Ein Volk, ein Reich, ein Führer*', before a crowd of hysterical Austrians. His friends and supporters urged him to return to England immediately. 'The next few days, weeks and months – but particularly days and weeks – will surely be among the most vital in our history', wrote his elder brother, Sir Timothy. 'We must *pledge* ourselves with the French to protect the independence of Czecho-Slovakia ... This is not the time for fine party feelings, but to save your country.'[4] A week later he tried again: 'The danger is that we shall all go to sleep again and then, one Sunday morning we shall hear of Hitler in Prague. You must not let us go to sleep. Surely the Germans are the danger, not those useless Italians ... Now – old war-horse – let us hear you sniff the battle from afar and cry Ha ha among the trumpets!'[5]

Other letters came from Jim Thomas (Eden's former PPS), Ronald Tree (Conservative MP for Harborough) and Duncan Sandys (Conservative MP for Norwood and Churchill's son-in-law). The latter articulated the problem succinctly:

> What we want more than anything else is for someone like yourself to give us some cohesion. Most of us are heartily sick of fighting little independent guerrilla engagements all over the place ... You alone can provide the leadership which will make these elements in the party united and effective.[6]

But Eden refused to answer the call. He remained on the Riviera until 4 April and, when he did return, made it plain that he was not prepared to challenge Chamberlain or even be branded an 'irreconcilable opponent of the dictators'.[7]

In part, this was due to Eden's natural defects as a politician. As he later put it in his diary, 'I truly hate the "game" of politics, not because I am better than these [Churchill and Beaverbrook, with whom he was dining] ... but because I lack the "Spunk".'[8] This was an accurate self-assessment. Never as resolute an anti-appeaser as his supporters imagined, Eden looked too good to be true and was. Although photogenic, conscientious and hard-working, he was also indecisive, timid and vain. In the eighteen months he spent on the back benches, from February 1938 to September 1939, he vacillated continually over whether or not to make a political intervention and, when he did, failed to make an impact by openly attacking the Government. This was partly lack of 'spunk', yet it was also self-seeking calculation. Aware of his position as front-runner to succeed Chamberlain should the Prime Minister's policy be seen to fail, Eden considered that there was little to be gained by criticising the Government and engendering those accusations of disloyalty and ambition which had blighted Churchill. He therefore declined the role his supporters wished him to assume and, in the words of Nicolson, continued to miss 'every boat with exquisite elegance' right up to the outbreak of war.[9]

Nor was Eden's former deputy, Lord Cranborne, prepared to lead in his master's absence. 'I don't like the Prime Minister's policy', he wrote from his Dorset seat on 5 July 1938:

> The impression he gives of truckling to the dictators is, I believe, disastrous … It takes the heart out of our real friends and provides us, at best, with some very undependable new ones in exchange. It alienates American opinion too, which is of essential importance at the present time … But at any rate it must be given a fair trial, and that it is certainly having. In the meantime I am quite happy cultivating roses at Cranborne. The results are both quicker and more satisfying.[10]

As this letter indicates, the Edenites – or 'Glamour Boys' as Chamberlain's supporters derisively labelled them – were particularly concerned about the effect of the Prime Minister's policy on the United States. American support would be crucial in any future war and, although US public opinion was still overwhelmingly isolationist, there was a discernible trend of mounting outrage – particularly on the east coast – as each fascist coup was succeeded by another. In these circumstances, Chamberlain's policy of seeking common ground with the dictators was both questioned and increasingly criticised. As Thomas Jones's New York friend the educator Dr Abraham Flexner reported in March 1938, the most popular revue on Broadway was an 'excruciatingly amusing number entitled "Four Little Angels of Peace"', featuring Chamberlain, Hitler, Mussolini and a Japanese General, each of whom betrayed the others in turn.[11] At almost exactly the same time, Lord Astor was visiting his country of birth and observed that American political opinion was distinctly less isolationist than it had been the previous autumn. There were warm feelings towards England but incomprehension as to why she was seeking an agreement with Nazi Germany.[12]

Roosevelt's attitude was ambivalent. On 5 October 1937, he had made his apocalyptic 'Quarantine' speech in Chicago, in which he called on the peace-loving nations to join together to protect the world against 'the present reign of terror' from which there was 'no escape through mere isolation or neutrality'.[13] Yet he had also been toying with a grand scheme of economic appeasement – hence the Welles Plan, which would have seen a new system for the distribution of the world's natural resources in return for international disarmament. The British rejection of this scheme, followed by Eden's resignation, alarmed the President. Talking to the French Ambassador on 11 March 1938, he described Chamberlain as a 'City man' who had decided to abandon France in the hope of making a 'business deal' with the dictators. Three days earlier he had expanded on the dangers inherent in the Prime Minister's policy with a typically American analogy:

> If a chief of police makes a deal with the leading gangsters and the deal results in no more hold-ups, that chief of police will be called a great man, but if the gangsters do not live up to their word, the chief of police will go to jail. Some people are, I think, taking very long chances.[14]

The *Anschluss* stiffened the President further. American opinion was outraged at the Nazi takeover and, on 17 March 1938, Secretary of State Cordell Hull declared in a speech, approved by Roosevelt, that isolation was no route to security but a 'fruitful source of insecurity'.[15] The following evening, however, the bumptious new American Ambassador to the Court of St James's, Joseph P. Kennedy, spoke at a gathering of the prestigious Pilgrims Society at Claridge's Hotel. Kennedy, who did not believe that German ambitions in central Europe affected the United States one jot, wanted to use the occasion to curry favour with isolationists back home by assuring them that there was no danger of him 'going native' in London. He had already delivered a 'delightful piece of democratic demagoguery' by refusing to wear knee-breeches for his audience with the King and by announcing his intention to end the practice of presenting American débutantes at Court – although not before his own daughters had been presented.[16] Now he planned to use the white tie dinner to disabuse the British of the idea that they would be able to rely on the United States to 'pull their chestnuts out of the fire' in the event of war. The State Department was horrified and insisted on a rewrite. Yet the general tenor of the speech remained true to the Ambassador's original intention. Although Kennedy reassured his audience – which included Lord Halifax as well as the Duke of Kent – that it was wrong to assume that the United States 'would not fight under any circumstances short of actual invasion', he emphasised the fact that most Americans opposed 'entangling alliances' and stated that the US was determined to remain aloof from European squabbles.[17] As the Ambassador noted in his diary, these parts of his speech fell distinctly 'flat'.[18]

*

Despite Kennedy's cool reception at the Pilgrims Society, it was the appeasers who remained in the ascendant during the first half of 1938. Not only did the small band of anti-appeasement Tories lack leadership and cohesion, but the chances of any serious opposition to Chamberlain developing from within were rendered all the harder by the power of the Conservative Party machine.

The leading cog was the Chief Whip, Captain David Margesson. Over six feet tall, with high cheekbones, slicked-back hair and dark penetrating eyes, Margesson was a renowned martinet, described by various MPs as 'a rigid disciplinarian', 'a real dictator' and even 'David Himmler'.[19] To some he could be kind and charming. Harold Macmillan, who rebelled on almost every issue during this period, gave the balanced assessment that he was a 'typical Harrovian, tough, not very sensitive but very fair'.[20] Yet there seems little doubt that his ruthless management of the parliamentary party – relying, as one commentator put it, on the same methods as a public school – played a significant role in quelling potential dissent. Indeed, when the authors of *Guilty Men* – a merciless polemic on the appeasement years, published by three Beaverbrook journalists in July 1940 – asked themselves how it was that there was never 'a serious revolt among the massed legion of ... Tory backbenchers' during this period, their answer was simple: Captain David Margesson.[21]

Equally important, though considerably less visible, was Sir Joseph Ball. Already encountered as the British half of the 'secret channel' which operated between Chamberlain and Mussolini, Ball, though technically Director of the Conservative Research Department, was also Chamberlain's conduit to the media. Not that the most influential elements of that industry needed to be pressured into taking the Government line. The BBC's Director General, John Reith, believed that, 'assuming that the BBC is for the people, and the Government is for the people, it follows that the BBC must be for the Government' – a sophistry which also applied to a number of newspapers.[22] It was Ball's particular responsibility, however, to brief the press against the

Prime Minister's internal enemies. Thus we find him writing to Chamberlain after Eden's resignation speech to assure him that it had flopped and that he had 'taken certain steps privately, with a view to getting this point of view over to the whole country'.[23]

In June 1936, Ball had secretly acquired, on behalf of the Conservative Party, the old Radical publication *Truth*. Thereafter transformed into a Tory propaganda sheet, this weekly 'newspaper' offered a pro-German, isolationist defence of appeasement, specialising in vituperative attacks on the Prime Minister's Conservative critics. Ball's involvement was a closely guarded secret – not revealed until Sir Robert (by then Lord) Vansittart conducted a private inquiry into the editorship in 1941 – but there is no doubt that Chamberlain was both aware and approved of his friend's activities. Writing to his sister Ida in July 1939, he gloated that Churchill was 'distressed by a couple of witty articles making fun of the suggestion that he [Churchill] would help matters in the Cabinet which appeared in *Truth* (secretly controlled by Sir J. Ball!)'.[24]

The third man to wield considerable behind-the-scenes influence was Sir Horace Wilson. Slight of frame, though lithe, with long fingers and a face like a pike, Wilson was nominally the Government's Chief Industrial Adviser. Baldwin had brought him into 10 Downing Street but it was under Chamberlain that his role expanded yet further and it was not long before the softly spoken civil servant was recognised as the Prime Minister's closest confidant on all matters, including foreign policy. That Chamberlain trusted Wilson's judgement and relied on his counsel to an inordinate extent is clear. 'He is the most remarkable man in England. I couldn't live a day without him', he told the art historian Kenneth Clark, who admired the civil servant's 'supple ... Jesuitical turn of mind'.[25] Wilson's room adjoined the Prime Minister's and every day the two men would walk together in St James's Park.

In the portrait painted by Wilson's enemies (of which there were many), he is depicted as a somewhat sinister *éminence grise*. Yet while it is true that Wilson enjoyed considerable influence – more power than anyone 'since Cardinal Wolsey', according to one Labour critic – it would be wrong to suppose that he did more than enforce and reinforce the Prime Minister's own policy decisions.[26] He was, however, dangerously inexperienced in foreign affairs, while his background in industrial relations augmented Chamberlain's own natural inclination to view international disagreements as in some way akin to commercial or municipal disputes. The German Embassy considered him 'decidedly pro-German'.[27]

For all these reasons, Wilson soon became the bugbear of the anti-appeasers (particularly within the Foreign Office), some of whom drew an invidious link between his modest background and his dedication to appeasement. 'He came from Bournemouth and destroyed the British Empire and has now returned to Bournemouth', commented Orme Sargent, following Wilson's enforced retirement in 1942.[28] Indeed, the issue of class features prominently in the correspondence of anti-appeasers, typically cited as a denigrating 'explanation' of their opponents' views. The aristocrats were 'all for singeing Musso's beard', wrote Viscount Cecil, shortly after the Abyssinian crisis, but 'S[tanley] B[aldwin], Ramsay [MacDonald], Runciman, Simon and co. and the Chamberlains are terrified if he frowns at them. *Conspuez les Bourgeois!!*' Later, Cecil's sister Gwendolen would argue that Halifax's desire to conciliate Hitler deserved greater censure than Chamberlain's since 'a poor old middle-class monster could not be expected to know any better'.[29] Harold Macmillan thought Chamberlain 'very middle class … very narrow in view', while Harold Nicolson considered the Prime Minister 'no more than an ironmonger'.[30]

Conversely, left-wingers and critics in the United States saw appeasement as a plot by aristocrats and plutocrats, designed to maintain their privilege at the expense of European liberty. The centre of this supposed conspiracy was Cliveden, the Buckinghamshire home of Lord and Lady Astor where, according to the communist scandal sheet the *Week* (and, thereafter, most of the left-wing press), politicians, newspaper proprietors, civil servants and society figures would gather for weekend parties and intrigue in the interests of an Anglo-Fascist alliance. The Halifax visit to Hitler, the purging of Vansittart, the Italian Agreement, the 'knifing' of Eden: all these, claimed the *Week*, had been planned at Cliveden. 'Who are the men – and the women – behind the Cabinet crisis and Great Britain's surrender to Fascist blackmail?' asked *Reynolds News*, following Eden's resignation. 'The answer is the Cliveden Set, [a] group of aristocratic politicians, newspaper owners and financiers, now exercising, through Mr Chamberlain, a dominating influence in the British Cabinet.'[31]

In fact, the 'Cliveden Set', as the *Week*'s roguish editor, the Stalinist Claud Cockburn, later admitted, was largely his own invention. Although leading appeasers – such as Lord Lothian, Geoffrey Dawson, Thomas Jones, Nevile Henderson, Halifax and Chamberlain – stayed at Cliveden, they were not a cabal (most 'would not have known a plot if you handed it to them on a skewer', confessed Cockburn) and spent as much time playing childish games, such as musical chairs (won by Chamberlain), as discussing politics.[32] Furthermore, while it is true that the majority of the aristocracy supported appeasement, this was true of the rest of the country and not confined to any one class.

A more interesting potential divide is presented by one historian's observation that the 'senior anti-appeasers all had fine war records', while those in favour of conciliating the dictators within the National Government 'had not themselves seen action'.[33] Yet while it is indeed noteworthy that Duff Cooper, Harold Macmillan, Eden and Churchill had all displayed gallantry in the Great War, while Baldwin, MacDonald, Chamberlain, Halifax, Simon and Hoare were spared the horrors of battle (the latter three served but not in the front line), there are important counter-examples. Ten lesser members of the 1938 Chamberlain Cabinet supported appeasement (albeit often reluctantly) despite front-line experience (five of them won the Military Cross), while some of the most prominent aristocratic appeasers, such as the Duke of Buccleuch, the Duke of Westminster and Lord Londonderry, could also boast fine war records. Indeed, of the 387 Conservative MPs elected at the 1935 General Election – the overwhelming majority of whom gave unwavering support to Chamberlain's foreign policy – 171 had performed some form of uniformed service during the First World War.[34]

On the other hand, it is notable how many of the prominent anti-appeasers – Churchill, Eden, Cooper, Nicolson, Spears, Vansittart, Austen Chamberlain – were Francophiles with a strong sense of British history as linked to the Continent. The leading appeasers, by contrast, had little attachment to France and had, traditionally, understood foreign affairs from the perspective of the Empire and the English-speaking dominions. As Oliver Stanley put it, cruelly but with more than a grain of truth, 'to Baldwin, Europe was a bore, and to Chamberlain only a bigger Birmingham'.[35]

Fundamentally, however, support or opposition to appeasement was determined by judgement – specifically an assessment of Hitler and his aims. If these were considered reasonable and limited, as the Führer claimed, then concessions to German demands in order to avoid another war made sense. If, on the other hand, Hitler was set on a programme of conquest and domination, as the small band of anti-appeasers maintained, then the Prime Minister's policy was, in Lord Hugh Cecil's memorable phrase, akin to 'scratching a crocodile's head in the hope of making it purr'.[36]

XIV

A Faraway Country

> I cannot see that we are on good moral grounds – in this 20th Century with the principles of nationality and the light of self-determination – if we make war to compel 3¼ million Sudeten Germans to remain inferior subjects of a Slav state.
>
> Sir Nevile Henderson to Lord Halifax, 20 March 1938[1]

British knowledge of Czechoslovakia was not good. Shakespeare, in *The Winter's Tale*, described Bohemia as a 'desert country, near the sea' and, three hundred years later, one member of the House of Lords claimed (with probable justification) that there was not one Englishman in a hundred who knew where that country actually was.[2] For the amiable Czech Minister in London, Jan Masaryk, it had at first been something of a joke. 'I spend most of my official time in there explaining to the gentleman inside that Czechoslovakia is a country and not a contagious disease', he told a friend as they were passing 10 Downing Street.[3] Yet in the summer of 1938 the British found themselves having to play the role of experts, even mediators, in the affairs of that 'faraway country'.

The May Crisis had been a severe shock. Suddenly Ministers had found themselves on what they believed to be the brink of war. Now, as they stepped back and contemplated the abyss which had opened up before them, they determined to do everything they could to avoid falling into it. In practice, this meant compelling the Czechs to solve the Sudeten problem before Hitler solved it by force. That the Sudeten Germans had a case almost everyone agreed. As Sir Nevile Henderson was continually reminding his masters in London, the Sudetens had a 'moral right to self-administration and eventually to self-determination'. This, after all, had been the guiding principle of President Woodrow Wilson at the Peace Conference and, while there was no question of it being extended to the British Empire, it was, the Ambassador insisted, 'morally unjust to compel this solid Teuton minority to remain subjected to a Slav central government at Prague'.[4]

As this double standard implies, Henderson's primary motivation was not the liberation of repressed minorities. Although he continued to believe that Hitler would prefer a peaceful solution to the Czechoslovak question, the Ambassador was acutely aware that a fresh crisis could arise at any moment and was consequently desperate for the Sudeten issue to be resolved as soon as possible. At the same time, he believed that there was still the chance for Germany to 'become one of the satisfied angels' if only she was allowed to fulfil her ambition of incorporating all Germans within the boundaries of the Reich.[5] This, the Ambassador felt, was both reasonable and inevitable. Writing to Lord Halifax on April Fool's Day 1938, he argued that Hitler was only seeking the completion of the work 'which Frederick the Great and Bismarck left unfinished' and, as he had written to the Chairman of the Anglo-German Fellowship, Lord Mount Temple, a few weeks earlier, there was, in any case, 'nothing' which was going to 'prevent the unity of Germany during this century or the oneness of the *"Deutsches Volk"*'.[6] Finally, as might be expected considering this sympathetic view of Nazi foreign policy, Henderson had a contempt for the Czechs and noted with approval the sentiments of a former British official who had begun a despatch with the statement, 'There is no such state as Czechoslovakia'.[7]

By this stage, Sir Robert Vansittart, the Government's highly frustrated Chief Diplomatic Adviser, considered Henderson a 'complete Nazi' who had become 'almost hysterical in the Berlin atmosphere'.[8] Yet the Foreign Office was united over the need to apply pressure to the Czechs. Immediately following the May Crisis, the head of the Central Department, William Strang, had been sent to assess the situation from the 'front trenches' in Berlin and Prague and, when he returned, it was decided to use the 'big stick' on the Czech President, Edvard Beneš.[9] Accordingly, Basil Newton, the British Minister in Prague, was instructed to warn Beneš that he risked losing British sympathy if he prevaricated while, at the same time, Halifax asked Georges Bonnet to threaten the Czech Government with the cancellation of the Franco-Czech Treaty if they continued to be 'unreasonable'.[10]

Nor was British pressure on Czechoslovakia confined to the Foreign Office. On 3 June 1938, *The Times* published a leading article in which it suggested that the Sudeten Germans should be granted a plebiscite to decide their future, even if it meant 'their secession from Czechoslovakia to the Reich'.[11] The uproar this caused was entirely predictable. *The Times* was regarded abroad as the unofficial mouthpiece of the British Government, and Government policy remained to encourage a settlement of the Sudeten question 'within the framework of the Czechoslovak state'.[12] The Sudeten German leader, Konrad Henlein, could scarcely be expected to demand less than *The Times* deemed reasonable and, as even the paper's Manager complained to the Editor, Geoffrey Dawson, it was hardly moral to champion 'the cause of the Wolf against the Lamb'.[13] Of course, if Dawson had listened to his own diplomatic correspondent then he would have been fully aware of the dangers he was courting. Following the *Anschluss*, Leo Kennedy (previously a German sympathiser) had written to his Editor from Prague to express his profound conviction that 'Nazi Germany has a long-term programme which she is determined to carry out – however peaceful her declarations are between the bursts of action – and that she means both to break up this country [Czechoslovakia] and to challenge the British Empire.'[14] But Dawson, who had hardly set foot on the Continent, had no time for experts.

*

Throughout June and July, while Hitler tinkered with Case Green, the Foreign Office grappled with the Czech problem. Communications ricocheted between London and Prague but negotiations between the Czechs and the Sudeten Germans were grindingly slow and, as the British Ambassador reported, the chances of a deal appeared slim. Despite this, and the increasingly belligerent tone of the German press, Chamberlain was remarkably optimistic. 'I am disposed to think that they [the Germans] have missed the bus and may never again have such a favourable chance of asserting their domination over central and eastern Europe', he told Ida on 18 June 1938, reflecting on the May Crisis.[15] A few weeks later, he addressed a large National

Government rally in the grounds of Boughton House, seat of the Duke of Buccleuch, near Kettering. The previous weekend, Churchill had been among the guests at Boughton and had been consulted by the Duchess about where she should place the Prime Minister for his speech. Anywhere 'with the sun in his eyes and the wind in his teeth' was Churchill's mischievous reply.[16] But the speech was a success. Remembering the horrors of the Great War – the seven million men 'who were cut off in their prime … the thirteen million who were maimed and mutilated, the misery and suffering of the fathers and mothers' – Chamberlain repeated the pacifist mantra that in war there were no victors, only losers, before going on to proclaim his confidence that there was not a soul in the country who did not wish him to continue his efforts for peace.[17]

There were also moments when the drumbeat of war could be drowned out by the gentle patter of the London social scene. Chips Channon recorded in his diary on 22 June 1938:

> We dined with the indefatigable Laura Corrigan, a festival of 137 people, all the youth and fashion of London with the Kents [the Duke and Duchess] enjoying themselves wildly and leading the revels … There is a new dance called the Palais Glide which smacks of the servants' hall, and, lubricated with champagne, the company pranced about doing this absurd 'pas' till 4 a.m. Leslie Belisha [Secretary of State for War] was in the gayest of moods and 'cracked the dawn', as did half the Cabinet. In spite of the general frivolity of the evening, I gleaned some news – i.e. that the King is sound, and is very against Anthony Eden, who, in two years, has caused us more trouble than any Foreign Secretary since Palmerston.*[18]

A further source of optimism for Chamberlain was the secret visit, on 18 July, of Hitler's personal adjutant, Captain Fritz Wiedemann. Meeting Lord Halifax and Sir Alexander Cadogan at the Foreign Secretary's house in Eaton Square, the burly emissary explained that he had been sent with the full knowledge of the Führer to enquire

---

* Rather less enjoyable was the reception hosted by the new German Ambassador, Herbert von Dirksen, a few weeks earlier. As Sir Alexander Cadogan noted, 'Had to go to a musical party at German Embassy. Atmosphere like the inside of a cow.'

about the possibility of Göring coming to London to continue the talks begun by Halifax the previous November. The Foreign Secretary replied that he would be 'delighted, in principle' but it would be much better if the Czech question could be cleared up first.[19] At this, Wiedemann, who had been Hitler's commanding officer in the First World War, 'cooed softly as any dove' and gave Halifax the most 'binding assurance' that Hitler was planning 'no forcible action' in this area, provided that there were no major incidents, such as a massacre of Sudeten Germans.[20] The Foreign Secretary was encouraged, later commenting on the Captain's 'transparent honesty', and agreed to the possibility of a Göring visit.[21] Indeed, according to Wiedemann's report – which must be treated with some scepticism – Halifax not only asked to be remembered to Hitler but stated that he would like to see, as the culmination of his work, 'the Führer entering London, at the side of the English King, amid the acclamations of the English people'.*[22]

The hope generated by the Wiedemann visit soon faded. By the end of the second week of July, negotiations between the Czechoslovak Government and the Sudeten Germans had reached deadlock and rumours of a German coup in August began to swirl. Henderson remained convinced that Hitler would not risk war unless provoked but the Government was not willing to take that chance. A scheme which had been fermenting in the Foreign Office was put into action. Lord Runciman, the former Cabinet Minister and shipping magnate, would be sent to Czechoslovakia to mediate between the parties.

Announcing the Runciman mission to the Commons on 26 July 1938, Chamberlain treated MPs to a cocktail of rose-tinted forecasts, dissimulation and outright lies. He claimed that the despatch of a British mediator was 'in response to a request from the Government of Czechoslovakia' (Runciman had in fact been forced on Beneš); he denied that the Government was 'hustling' the Czechs (the opposite of the truth); he stated that the mission was independent of the British Government (a technicality which nobody believed); and he claimed that throughout the Continent there was a 'relaxation of … tension'

---

* Wiedemann, who was working with Göring to avoid war with Britain, had an interest in emphasising British friendliness. Cadogan, who was present, mentions no such remark in his diary, nor does Halifax in his own account. On the other hand, Wiedemann's pencil notes mention the remark (substituting 'Buckingham Palace' for 'London') and in almost every other way mirror Halifax's notes.

compared to six months earlier (a fantasy).[23] Finally, despite the fact that Mussolini was openly flouting the Anglo-Italian Agreement and British ships were once again being bombed in Spanish ports, he pointed to his deal with the Duce as vindication of his policy:

> If only we could find some peaceful solution of this Czechoslovakian question, I should myself feel that the way was open again for a further effort for a general appeasement – an appeasement which cannot be obtained until we can be satisfied that no major cause of difference or dispute remains unsettled. We have already demonstrated the possibility of a complete agreement between a democratic and a totalitarian state, and I do not myself see why that experience should not be repeated.[24]

Responding to this statement, the Labour MP Josiah Wedgwood – who had been severely wounded in the First World War – delivered one of the most impressive and passionate critiques of appeasement ever heard in the Commons:

> What is the excuse for enabling the Nazi rule to be extended all round the frontiers of Czechoslovakia? The excuse is, as ever, that it is to be done in the interests of peace. I tell this House it is in the interests of war, inevitable war, and a war that we shall not be able to win. Every time you sacrifice one of your potential allies to this pathetic desire to appease the tyrants you merely bring nearer and make more inevitable that war which you pretend you are trying to avoid. At present, Czechoslovakia has a natural rugged frontier on three sides of her, and that frontier is armed. Cut off all that Sudeten area from Czechoslovakia and you put Germany across the frontier up against a perfectly easy advance to Prague.[25]

Leo Amery did not know whether to consider Runciman's appointment 'comic or a stroke of genius'. 'It may well be that his bland, invincible ignorance and incapacity even to realise the emotions and aspirations on both sides may help to bring down the temperature and so contribute to a peaceful solution', he waspishly recorded.[26] Elsewhere, praise for Runciman and his mission was less sarcastic. *The Times* pointed to the peer's 'able and unbiased mind' (code for the fact that Runciman had no known sympathy for the Czechs), while

J. L. Garvin, the fanatically pro-appeasement and anti-Czech Editor of the *Observer*, proclaimed that the nation could pack up for the summer holidays with a 'free heart' owing to the despatch of this 'pilgrim of peace'.[27]

As it turned out, the Runciman mission was closer to Amery's first thought than his second. Described by one French diplomat as looking as if he had 'fallen from the pages of Dickens and resented the fall', Lord Runciman of Doxford, with his winged collars (an anachronism he shared with Chamberlain), morning coats and 'puzzling demeanour', appeared exactly as he was: an old-fashioned Liberal politician and Methodist teetotaller, with little imagination or emotional understanding.[28] He could 'make the temperature drop, even at a distance', according to Lloyd George.[29] On this basis, he was hardly the man (whatever the papers said) who was likely to bring resolution to a dispute dominated by the most visceral nationalism. Nor was his staff better suited to the task. Out of the four men originally selected to accompany him, not one of them had any detailed knowledge of Czechoslovakia, while Runciman's principal assistant, Frank Ashton-Gwatkin, was a known sympathiser of German economic expansion in central and eastern Europe.

Of course, Runciman had been given an impossible task. Henlein was under instructions to reject any potential settlement and, even without this knowledge, the mission had been likened by its leader to being cast 'adrift in a small boat in the mid-Atlantic'.[30] Within a week of arriving in Prague, Ashton-Gwatkin was reporting that the gulf between the two sides was wider than had existed between Britain and Ireland 'at its worst' and, on 10 August 1938, only six days after beginning his work, Runciman wrote to Halifax in the most depressing tones:

> It is a pathetic side of the present crisis that the common people here ... are looking to me and my mission as the only hope for an established peace. Alas, they do not realise how weak are our sanctions, and I dread the moment when they find that nothing can save them.[31]

Halifax replied encouragingly, stating that if Runciman were able to breach the divide then he would have done 'more for the world than is given to many to do, and I am not at all disposed to let go the hope of your finding a way through'.[32] Time, however, was not on Runciman's side.

On 6 July, the Foreign Office had learnt from secret sources that German company commanders would be confined to barracks from the middle of the month since 'a continued state of alarm was to be expected from that date'.[33] Luftwaffe reservists were apparently being called up and oil stockpiled. Soon the Foreign Office was in possession of 'at least half a dozen' Secret Intelligence Service reports pointing to a German attack on Czechoslovakia in the autumn, probably after the Nuremberg Rally in early September – a forecast supported by the news that leave for all members of the German armed forces had been cancelled from 1 August onwards.[34] 'The German military machine is working at top speed', reported Colonel Mason-MacFarlane, the British Military Attaché, 'and war with Czechoslovakia is surely the most probable eventuality.' On the other hand, there was substantial evidence that the Army High Command was opposed to such a venture and Mason-Mac remained 'unconvinced that the military evidence at our disposal definitely indicates a clear intention to march this autumn'.[35]

This was Henderson's belief. Although the Ambassador felt that he was playing a part in a Greek tragedy – 'watching events moving steadily and inexorably onwards towards the final inevitable tragic ending' – he still refused to believe that Hitler was set upon a military solution.[36] 'War would doubtless serve the purposes of all the Jews, communists and doctrinaires in the world for whom Nazism is anathema', he wrote to Halifax, 'but it would be a terrible risk today for Germany herself and particularly for the new Nazi Germany which Hitler has built up in the past five years.' The key to the situation lay in Prague. The Czechs were a 'pig-headed race and Beneš not the least pig-headed among them', but it was still possible to reach a peaceful settlement if only Britain put her foot down and forced the Czechs to concede 'Home Rule' for the Sudeten Germans.[37] 'Just as I was always convinced and years ago that Austria must inevitably come into Germany sooner or later, so I am convinced that the Sudeten must also do so in the end', wrote the Ambassador.[38]

Halifax was not sure what to make of the German moves. Although by the beginning of August he had learnt that the Wehrmacht were planning a 'test-mobilisation' of seven or eight divisions for mid-September, he suspected that this and other military preparations were chiefly bluffs, designed to terrify the Czechs into submission. 'I find it difficult to believe that, if they were convinced it meant a general war, they would think it worth while to try and insist by force on their full desiderata for Czechoslovakia', he wrote to Henderson from Yorkshire. Of course, the British were not prepared to threaten a general war. Determined to avoid bloodshed over Czechoslovakia, British policy remained the so-called guessing position, whereby they were 'perpetually telling Beneš of what we might not do in the event of trouble: and tactfully remind[ing] the Germans of what we might do'. In pursuit of the former, the Foreign Secretary was more than happy to turn the screws on Prague. Yet it was equally important, Halifax continued in his letter to Henderson, to 'get it into the very stupid heads of the Germans that if they insisted on stepping on the spring, the gun was awfully likely to go off'.[39]

Four days after this letter, on 9 August, news broke that the Prime Minister was returning early from his Scottish holiday – not because of the international situation but due to a severe case of sinusitis. This was fortunate since, as Chamberlain explained to Hilda, 'things have been very difficult in Central Europe'.[40] The previous day, Henderson had written that the 'omens of the storm are rolling up in Germany and we must expect the rumours, particularly military, to be crescendo'. He still clung to his belief that Hitler wanted a peaceful solution but warned that 'he will not wait indefinitely'.[41] The Ambassador then sent Halifax an account of a lunch which Mason-Mac had had with a recently retired Army officer and former supporter of Hitler. The good news, the Military Attaché relayed, was that the German Army was apparently '*vollkommen untauglich*' (entirely unfit) for war. The bad news was that 'Göring, Himmler and Ribbentrop are determined on war this autumn, and that General Keitel is 100 per cent on their side'.[42] The sands were running out, the Ambassador warned, and the time frame for Lord Runciman to find a solution must be reckoned to be six weeks at the most.

Eventually, it was decided to appeal to Hitler to halt the military build-up. On 11 August, Halifax sent Henderson a memorandum for Hitler, stating that the 'Prime Minister and I' felt compelled to remind the Führer that such measures could only have a detrimental effect on the efforts of the British Government to find a peaceful solution to the Sudeten question, which in turn threatened 'the peace of every one of the Great Powers of Europe'. In this light, was it 'really necessary to run such grave and incalculable risks, and, incidentally, to endanger and perhaps even destroy the prospect of a resumption before long of the conversations between our two Governments'?[43]

To this most unterrifying communication the German dictator did not deign to reply. The previous day he had given a furious dressing-down to General Gustav von Wietersheim for daring to pass on a warning from General Wilhelm Adam, commander of Germany's 2nd Army Group, that the West Wall could not hold the French Army for more than three weeks; and on 18 August he accepted the resignation of General Ludwig Beck, Chief of the General Staff, and leading opponent of the Führer's plans.

One week later, on 26 August, Hitler and his entourage visited the western frontier, where Adam had the unenviable task of showing the Führer the fortifications. In a display of bellicose bravado, Hitler walked to the midpoint of the bridge over the Rhine at Strasbourg, the border between Germany and France. He was not able to leave, however, before Adam, who had insisted on a meeting with the Supreme Commander alone, repeated his belief that the West Wall was entirely inadequate and that, in his view, the British and French 'would be at war as soon as the first German shot was fired against the Czechs, and the French would soon break through'. At this, Hitler exploded. 'We have no time to listen any longer to this stuff', he shouted. 'You don't understand … We produce in Germany twenty-three million tons of steel a year, the French only six millions and the English only sixteen millions. The English have no reserves and the French have the greatest internal difficulties. They'll beware of declaring war on us.'[44]

XV

The Crisis Breaks

As Priam to Achilles for his Son,
So you, into the night, divinely led,
To ask that young men's bodies, not yet dead,
Be given from the battle not begun.

John Masefield, Poet Laureate,
The Times, 16 September 1938

The weather at Balmoral had been dreadful. Strong winds swept the King's Highland estate and the river Dee swelled with fresh rainwater. When the royal party, which included the Prime Minister, braved the moor in search of grouse, they were attacked by a hailstorm. Chamberlain shot badly. He was piqued that fewer grouse flew over him than anyone else but mainly his mind was elsewhere. Throughout August, reports of the deteriorating situation in the Sudetenland and the steady build-up of German forces along the Czech frontier had continued to pour into the Foreign Office. On the 21st, the British Military Attaché in Berlin reported a secret meeting between Hitler and his Generals at which the Führer had apparently announced his intention of attacking Czechoslovakia before the end of September. 'Germany could expect no more favourable moment', Hitler had reportedly told the Wehrmacht top brass. She would collect a 'magnificent harvest' and would be acting with the 'practical certainty that France and England would not intervene'.[1]

Three days earlier, Sir Robert Vansittart had been visited by Ewald von Kleist-Schmenzin, a Prussian conservative and staunch opponent of Nazism, who had come to London at the behest of the anti-war head of German military intelligence (the Abwehr), Admiral Wilhelm

Canaris, and General Ludwig Beck to alert the Government to Hitler's plans as well as to dissent within the German military leadership. According to Kleist-Schmenzin, war was now 'a certainty unless we stopped it'. 'How?' demanded Vansittart. Kleist-Schmenzin explained that the Army High Command, the German people, even Göring, were against war and if only Britain would threaten to intervene then there was a serious chance of stopping, even overthrowing, Hitler.[2] If the former scenario was a possibility, the latter was dismissed by Chamberlain (probably correctly) as fantasy. 'He reminds me of the Jacobites at the court of France in King William's time', wrote the Prime Minister, 'and I think we must discount a good deal of what he says.'[3] Yet Chamberlain was uneasy and felt that the Government needed to do something. A gentle warning was, therefore, inserted into a speech which the Chancellor of the Exchequer, Sir John Simon, was due to make at Lanark. As one of the leading advocates of appeasement, Simon spent much of his talk deprecating the notion that Britain could not reach an equitable arrangement with Germany. But – and this was all that was remembered – he warned his audience that the 'beginning of a conflict is like the beginning of a fire in a high wind. It may be limited at the start, but who can say how far it would spread, or how much destruction it would do, or how many may be called upon to beat it out?'[4]

The question of whether Britain and France would come to Czechoslovakia's aid in the event of German aggression was the overwhelming preoccupation of all players during the crisis. For the Czechs, it was a matter of life and death. If they could count on the Western democracies, then they were prepared to resist Hitler's demands, even an invasion. For Hitler, it was the difference between a safe bet and a massive gamble. And for the British and French themselves, it was a dilemma between honour and the horrors of a war that they were by no means certain they could win. Nevertheless, the British Government could not stand by while Hitler called up reservists and prepared to invade a sovereign democracy. Sir Nevile Henderson was, therefore, recalled from Berlin and on 26 August the Prime Minister summoned the Cabinet for an emergency meeting in four days' time.

Being August, most Ministers and senior civil servants were away from London. Halifax was in Yorkshire, Cadogan was playing golf at Le Touquet and the First Lord of the Admiralty, Duff Cooper, was on an official cruise in the Baltic. The majority of the Cabinet made it back, however, and were brought up to speed by Halifax. If Hitler had decided on war, the Foreign Secretary said, then 'the only deterrent which would be likely to be effective would be an announcement that if Germany invaded Czechoslovakia we should declare war upon her'. On the other hand, it was important to bear a number of considerations in mind: public opinion, in Britain and the Empire, was not prepared for war and would be divided on the subject; Czechoslovakia could not, in fact, be defended and, at the end of a war, was unlikely to be reconstructed as it currently was; and, crucially, if it was a question of standing up to Hitler, was it 'justifiable to fight a certain war now in order to forestall a possible war later'?[5]

Henderson endorsed each of these objections. Having spent the past two months assuring the Foreign Office, against the evidence, that Hitler was only interested in a peaceable solution, he now argued that a threat would only make Hitler more difficult and war more likely. It would, he said, 'strengthen the position of the extremists rather than the moderates'.[6] Kleist-Schmenzin had tried to explode this notion of the moderate Führer egged on by a zealous war party when he told Vansittart that 'there is only one real extremist and that is Hitler himself'.[7] But Chamberlain had discounted his opinion and now endorsed Halifax and Henderson. He dismissed Duff Cooper's proposal for a semi-mobilisation of the Fleet as 'pinpricking' and, after two and a half hours of discussion, the Cabinet came down, unanimously, against issuing a threat. Chamberlain thanked his colleagues for their attendance and then, after visiting his doctor, caught the train up to Balmoral. The Government, the Soviet Ambassador noted acidly, had taken one really 'important decision' – to do nothing.[8]

*

The Cabinet meeting on 30 August was meant to have been secret, but news inevitably leaked, as did the fact of Henderson's recall. Most newspapers correctly interpreted these events as signs that the Czech quarrel had reached a dangerous new phase. The *Daily Express*, however, was able to reassure its readers. 'THERE WILL BE NO WAR', proclaimed the headline on 1 September 1938, above a front-page leader signed by Lord Beaverbrook himself. There was nothing to worry about, the press baron explained, 'because the decision of peace and war depends on one man, the German Führer. And he will not be responsible for making war at present. Hitler has shown himself throughout his career to be a man of exceptional astuteness.' This was curious logic, since it was Hitler's accurate perception of Anglo-French weakness which was allowing him to plot the destruction of Czechoslovakia. Indeed, as Halifax had said, if Hitler was convinced that Britain and France would become involved then he might well be deterred.

This was Churchill's view. Despite having spent most of August 'horribly entangled' with the ancient Britons, Romans, Angles and Saxons for his *History of the English-Speaking Peoples*, he had kept a close eye on the developing situation in Bohemia and, on 31 August, had written to Halifax urging a joint note from Britain, France and Russia stating that the invasion of Czechoslovakia would 'raise capital issues for all three powers'.[9] Two days later, he expressed the view that the veto of these countries would 'certainly prevent the disaster of war'.[10] In particular, Churchill was anxious to enlist the support of the Soviet Union. On 2 September, he received an urgent request from the Soviet Ambassador, Ivan Maisky, to see him. Churchill responded that he was at the Ambassador's disposal and Maisky motored down to Chartwell, Churchill's home in the Weald of Kent, that afternoon. There, he was visibly awed by the splendour of Churchill's property, equipped with swimming pool, tennis court and various goldfish ponds. 'It's not a bad life for the leaders of the British bourgeoisie!' the Ambassador mused.[11] The purpose of his visit was to convey the news that after recent conversations in Moscow between the French Ambassador and the Soviet Foreign Minister, Maxim Litvinov, Russia was unequivocally committed to defending Czechoslovakia, provided, as per the terms of the Soviet–Czechoslovak Treaty, that France intervened first. He then passed on Litvinov's suggestion that Britain, Russia and France should invoke Article II of the League of Nations, whereby members were obliged to consult together if war was thought to be imminent. Churchill passed on these proposals to Halifax but the Foreign Secretary – who was almost as sceptical of

Russia and her feline Ambassador as Chamberlain – was unmoved. He preferred, he told Churchill, to await developments in Germany before making any definite move.

*

Henderson had not made a good impression at the Cabinet meeting on 30 August. Sir Samuel Hoare thought him 'overwrought' and 'governed by his nerves'. 'So anxious was he that war should be averted', recorded the Home Secretary, that, 'as in the case of the Austrians, so in the case of the Czechs, he was undoubtedly convinced that, if international peace was to be maintained, their small countries must accept virtual absorption into the Reich'.[12] Nevertheless, the Ambassador saw Ribbentrop on his return to Berlin and warned that if he believed that France and Britain would never march for Czechoslovakia then he was making a grave mistake.

Hitler did not think so. Convinced that the democracies would stand aside, as they had over conscription, over the Rhineland and over Austria, he was equally sure that the time had come to gain Germany's objectives by force. Having once thought that the creation of a new German Empire would take several generations, he now wished to experience the 'Greater Germanic Reich' himself but feared that he did not have long to live. Added to this was the fact that the Western Powers were belatedly rearming. He saw Germany's lead in armaments receding over the coming years and, like the German High Command in 1914, decided that it was better to provoke a reckoning sooner rather than later. Finally, there was the dark, destructive megalomania which caused him to relish what others feared and loathed. 'Long live war – even if it lasts from two to eight years', the Führer toasted Konrad Henlein on 2 September.[13]

The British leaders wondered if, in courting war, Hitler had 'crossed the borderline of insanity'.[14] Yet they still hoped to avoid it by pressuring the Czechs into an agreement with Henlein. On 2 September, Beneš offered the Sudeten Germans 'cantonal self-government'. Henlein, who was at Berchtesgaden with Hitler, was instructed to reject the offer. The Czech President – who had been told by the British Ambassador to make 'great sacrifices' or face the prospect of invasion – then produced his 'Fourth Plan', which amounted to a virtual acceptance of the previously unacceptable Karlsbad demands.[15] The SdP leaders were stunned. 'My God, they have given us everything!' exclaimed Henlein's deputy.[16] But Hitler was not interested in a resolution.

This message was brought home to the British Government when, on the evening of 6 September, a mysterious visitor was smuggled into Downing Street via the garden gate. The caller – whom Cadogan would only refer to as Herr X, since 'the man's life is at stake' – was Theodor Kordt, Chargé d'Affaires at the German Embassy and the brother of Ribbentrop's Chief of Staff. As Kordt explained – first to Horace Wilson and then, the following morning, to Halifax and Cadogan – he had decided to 'put conscience before loyalty' and had come to tell them that Hitler intended to 'march in' to Czechoslovakia on either 19 or 20 September.[17] The British dismissed his suggestion of broadcasting a warning to Germany but the crisis was clearly moving towards its climax and, with Hitler due to address the Nuremberg Rally in less than a week, Halifax asked Wilson to get Chamberlain down from Scotland.

While the Prime Minister travelled south, *The Times* caused a furore by repeating its view that the Czechs should cede the Sudetenland to the Reich, this time without a plebiscite. The effect was seismic. Cession was the apogee of Nazi aspirations but had not in fact yet been demanded by either Henlein or Hitler. France was bound by treaty to defend the integrity of the Czechoslovak state and Lord Runciman was still in Prague trying to negotiate a settlement. In a game of diplomatic tennis, which the democracies were losing forty–love, *The Times* had just cut a massive hole in their rackets. Unsurprisingly, the Foreign Office 'went through the roof'.[18] With *The Times* taken to reflect the views of the British Government, it now appeared that the British were prepared to carve up Czechoslovakia in order to save their own skins.

Halifax issued a statement denying that the article represented Government policy, but the damage was done. The leader was broadcast across Germany, where it was interpreted as a trial balloon, foreshadowing the inevitable surrender of the democracies. The effect, Vansittart reported to Halifax, was 'disastrous'.[19] Maisky called it 'a stab in Czechoslovakia's back at the most critical moment in her history'; Oliver Harvey, Halifax's Private Secretary, railed against 'that little defeatist Geoffrey Dawson'; while in Prague, Runciman asked *The Times*'s correspondent to convey his dismay at an article which was not merely 'unhelpful and unnecessary' but 'highly dangerous in the present stage of the negotiations'.[20] Everyone seemed furious with *The Times*. Everyone, that is, except the Foreign Secretary, who on the day the article appeared lunched with Dawson at the Travellers Club. *The Times*'s Editor arrived expecting a ministerial rebuke but was pleasantly surprised when he found that his good friend, fellow Eton Governor and Yorkshire neighbour, 'did not seem to dissent from it [the leader] himself'.[21]

The *Times* article brought to the fore the conflict of opinions over the Czech crisis. As Robert Bernays, now a junior Minister, explained to his sister, 'Such a proposal [cession] is, of course, an impossibility: the territory where the Germans live in Czechoslovakia affords a highly defensible frontier, and to surrender it would be for the Czechs to place themselves at the mercy of the Germans who could then do what they liked there and in eastern Europe.'[22] On the other hand, the Sudetenland was home to some three million Germans, a large number of whom wanted to be part of the Reich. Was it fair to prevent them? Many thought not. Yet, as others pointed out, the issue went far beyond the aspiration – legitimate or not – of a minority. 'The conflict has really nothing to do with Czechoslovakia', explained Oliver Stanley, the President of the Board of Trade, over dinner with Harold Nicolson, 'but is the final struggle between the principle of law and the principle of violence.'[23] Nicolson wholeheartedly agreed but feared that Chamberlain, 'who has the mind and manner of a clothes-brush', was blind to this. 'He would like to give Germany all she wants at the moment', Nicolson wrote in his diary on 6 June 1938, 'and cannot see that if we make this surrender we shall be unable to resist other demands. If we assuage the German alligator with fish from other ponds, she will wax so fat that she will demand fish from our own ponds. And we shall not by then be powerful enough to resist.'[24]

Chamberlain rejected this view because he did not believe that Hitler's aims were boundless and war with Germany, therefore, inevitable. Indeed, for a man whose nickname was 'the Coroner' and whose trademark was an umbrella, Chamberlain was an incorrigible optimist, always searching for positive signs. This did not stop him from being gravely alarmed by the situation. With Hitler expected to declare his intent in his speech to the Nuremberg Rally on 12 September, the Prime Minister confessed that 'the thing hangs over me like a nightmare'.[25] 'Is it not positively horrible', he wrote to Ida from Balmoral, 'to think that the fate of hundreds of millions depends on one man and he is half mad.' But fatalism was not Chamberlain's style and in the same letter he explained that he had been racking his brains to devise some means of averting catastrophe. Indeed, he had already come up with an idea which might, if all else failed, save the situation. This was 'Plan Z', by which the Prime Minister, in a dramatic gesture, would himself fly out to see Hitler to try to save peace. The plan was so secret that Chamberlain kept it even from his normally fully informed sisters. Horace Wilson had been there at its inception and Henderson had approved it during his visit to London. Beyond these few, only Halifax shared the secret.

*

Meanwhile, the situation in the Sudetenland continued to deteriorate. On 7 September, the SdP staged a riot at Moravská Ostrava during the course of which a Sudeten deputy was allegedly struck by a Czech policeman. This gave Henlein, under strict orders from Berlin, an excuse to reject Beneš's Fourth Plan and suspend negotiations. Fearing that troops might be on the march, Halifax and Cadogan left a dinner party to draft a message to Hitler only to discover from the BBC that the situation seemed to be holding. Nevertheless, the unremitting German military build-up and continuing stream of intelligence – all of which pointed to the imminence of invasion – convinced Halifax that the 'guessing position' was not working and that the Government should now send Hitler a warning. He therefore instructed Henderson, now at the Nuremberg Rally, to inform Hitler that if France intervened, as she declared she would, then Britain would inevitably follow. To demonstrate the hardening of British opinion, the Foreign Secretary told Henderson to draw attention to the recent declaration of Labour's National Council, urging the Government to 'unite with the French and Soviet Governments to resist any attack upon Czechoslovakia'.[26] But Hitler never received the message. Responding to his instructions in what had become a familiar hysterical tone, Henderson argued strongly that such a warning would 'drive Herr Hitler straight off the deep end'. 'I have already made [the] British position as clear as daylight to people who count', he claimed, but a repetition of the warning of 21 May would be 'fatal'.*[27] The Government took the Ambassador's advice and the note was dropped.

The decision was taken by the not very imaginatively named Situation in Czechoslovakia Committee. Consisting of Chamberlain, Halifax, Simon and Hoare, this was the 'Inner Cabinet' responsible for handling the crisis. Having decided to accept Henderson's recommendations, they left the cabinet room to find Churchill waiting in the hall. He had come, recalled Hoare, 'to demand an immediate ultimatum to Hitler'.[28] Eden was of the same opinion and had visited the Foreign Office the previous day to press for a warning. Two days later, on 11 September, he tried again, while Churchill returned to Downing Street to argue 'that we should tell Germany that if she set foot in Czechoslovakia we should at once be at war with her'.[29] But the Government was determined to stick to the 'guessing position' and so, while Chamberlain briefed journalists that Germany should be 'under no illusions' about Britain's commitment to France, Halifax warned the French that they should not assume that Britain would automatically find itself at war with Germany simply 'because France might be involved'.[30] That evening, Churchill wrote to his friend Lord Moyne, a former Conservative Minister:

---

* Henderson was not having a happy time at Nuremberg. The hotels were reserved for Hitler's guests and the diplomatic corps were forced to stay in the sleeping compartments of a set-aside train. It was extremely cramped and, as the journalist Virginia Cowles recorded, the sight of 'the Ambassadors of the three great democracies – Great Britain, the United States and France – leaning out of the windows of a derailed restaurant car ... brought it home to you that affairs in Europe had taken a turn for the worse!' Not making life easier for himself, Henderson had forgotten to bring any paper with him and was forced to send his despatches on blank pages torn out of detective novels. He was also not well – suffering from the throat cancer which within four years would kill him. Yet even this does not excuse his behaviour, which gave the impression of funk. Far from projecting British strength, he took little care to hide his nerves and, according to one Nazi official, 'expressed his aversion to the Czechs in very strong terms'.

> Alas, a cloud of uncertainty overhangs all plans at the present time … [and] I cannot pretend to be at all hopeful of the outcome. Owing to the neglect of our defences and the mishandling of the German problem in the last five years, we seem to be very near the bleak choice between War and Shame. My feeling is that we shall choose Shame, and then have War thrown in a little later on even more adverse terms than at present.[31]

In refusing to commit or sabre-rattle, Chamberlain was fortified by reading 'a very interesting book' on the nineteenth-century Foreign Secretary George Canning. 'Again and again', he told Ida, 'Canning lays it down that you should never menace unless you are in a position to carry out your threats and although if we have to fight I should hope we should be able to give a good account of ourselves we are certainly not in a position in which our military advisers would feel happy in undertaking to begin hostilities if we were not forced to do so.' This may have been true but it did not ease the strain. 'It has been a pretty awful week,' the Prime Minister confessed, 'enough to send most people off their heads, if their heads were not as firmly screwed on as mine.'[32] He had now discussed 'Plan Z' with the Inner Cabinet and received broad support. Vansittart, however, was implacably opposed and fought the idea 'tooth and nail', likening it to the supplication of the Holy Roman Emperor Henry IV before Pope Gregory VII at Canossa.[33] Chamberlain listened to his Chief Diplomatic Adviser with his head in his hands. But Vansittart had long ceased to be an influence. 'Plan Z' was Chamberlain's 'bold move', his 'masterstroke', which, if it succeeded, would not only solve the Czechoslovak crisis but 'might prove the opportunity for bringing about a complete change in the international situation'.[34] For this prize, he was more than prepared to risk his reputation.

*

The full Cabinet met for the first time since its emergency session on 30 August on the morning of Monday 12 September. As before, Halifax summarised the situation: the Czechs had set out fresh proposals which had been rejected; Daladier had repeated France's obligation to Czechoslovakia; and the French had manned the Maginot Line.

Most critically, the Government had received intelligence that Hitler had decided to 'march into Czechoslovakia' on some date between 18 and 29 September. Halifax explained that the Government had considered a formal warning to Hitler but Henderson 'had urged with all the force at his command that he should not be instructed to make the official *démarche*' and the Government had agreed. Indeed, having initially proposed the threat, Halifax now appeared to believe the Government powerless. Hitler was 'possibly or even probably mad' and if he had 'made up his mind to attack, it was probable that nothing which we could do would stop him'.[35] While most Ministers concurred, Duff Cooper drew attention to the cross-section of opinion arguing that Britain should make it clear that she was prepared to fight for Czechoslovakia: 'This advice came from the press ... from the Opposition, from Winston, from the French Government, from the US Government and even from the Vatican.' Chamberlain, who hated being contradicted, replied tartly that Henderson was the man on the spot and 'must know more about it than the Vatican'.[36]

That afternoon, Hitler made his much-anticipated speech at Nuremberg. Despite the crisis, many prominent English men and women had travelled to the medieval city to witness the festivities. Apart from the usual suspects – which included Ernest Tennant and Sir Arnold Wilson (Conservative MP for Hitchin) – there was Lord Stamp (Chairman of the London, Midland and Scottish Railway) and his wife, Sir Frank Sanderson (Conservative MP for Ealing), Norman Hulbert (Conservative MP for Stockport), Viscount Clive, Lord Hollenden (President of the Wholesale Textile Association) and his wife, and Lord McGowan (Chairman of Imperial Chemical Industries).

Also attending were the parents of the Hitler-worshipping Unity Mitford, Lord and Lady Redesdale. Observing these eccentric aristocrats in the lobby of Nuremberg's Grand Hotel, the American reporter Virginia Cowles could not help but be amused:

> Lady Redesdale was a small retiring woman who spent most of her time (when she was not at one of the reviews with Unity) in the corner of the hotel lobby sewing, while Lord Redesdale, a tall, handsome man with a large white moustache, wandered about with a bewildered air as though he were at a rather awkward house-party where (curiously enough) no one could speak any English ... All week long Lord

> Redesdale was inundated with frantic letters begging him to use his influence to stop the war. One day he received a note from the Buchman Society which was holding a conference in Geneva. The note begged him to show the Führer a letter which had been published in the London *Times* ... declaring that it might 'change the Führer and alter the course of history'. His slightly petulant comment was: 'Dammit all, I haven't got a copy of *The Times*.'*[37]

Some who attended were not Nazi sympathisers. The Tory MP Thelma Cazalet (sister of fellow Conservative MP Victor) sat behind Hitler thinking, 'If only I had the weapon *and* the guts to put an end to this man.'[38] Another anti-Nazi was the travel writer and aesthete Robert Byron. A friend of Unity Mitford's, he had come to Nuremberg out of morbid curiosity. At first, he was inclined to see the comic side. 'These people are so grotesque', he commented, that 'if we go to war, it will be like fighting a gigantic zoo'. When, however, he joined a group of senior Nazis – including Hitler's press chief, Otto Dietrich – and the infamous *Times* leader was invoked as proof that England understood that Czechoslovakia was not her concern, he became serious. 'What happens on the Continent is always England's concern', he interjected, the colour rising in his cheeks. 'Every now and then we are unfortunate enough to be led by a Chamberlain – but that's only temporary. Don't be misguided. In the end we *always* rise up and oppose the tyrannies that threaten Europe. We have smashed them before, and I warn you we will smash them again.'[39]

It was unfortunate that Byron was not invited to the tea party organised by Ribbentrop for important foreigners on 11 September, the day before Hitler's speech. Instead, the German Foreign Minister had carefully arranged the *placement* so that Hitler was sitting next to

---

* In her novels *The Pursuit of Love* (1945) and *Love in a Cold Climate* (1949), Nancy Mitford immortalised her father as the blimpish but benign Uncle Matthew, who loathed the Germans and liked to reminisce about the time he had killed eight 'Huns' with his 'entrenching tool'. The real Lord Redesdale was, in fact, a member of the Anglo-German Fellowship and (as his intervention in the House of Lords debate following the *Anschluss* exemplifies) a prominent apologist for the regime. In January 1935, he paid the first of several visits to Nazi Germany, having been encouraged by his two fascist daughters: 'Farve [Father] is really one of nature's fascists. He'd simply love the Führer', they insisted.

Lord Brocket, a leading member of the Anglo-German Fellowship and enthusiast for the regime, who appears to have agreed with the Führer's denunciations of the Czechs and their President.[40] Now, on the afternoon of Monday 12 September, Hitler repeated these indictments to the world. Before a sea of brown party uniforms, he inveighed against Beneš and the Czechs, accusing them of desiring the 'annihilation' of the German minority. There could be only one solution: the Sudeten Germans must be afforded the right of self-determination.[41] Listening to the live broadcast, which had not been translated, Oliver Harvey thought it sounded like 'a madman or rather an African chieftain haranguing his tribe', while Leo Amery, who spoke good German, found 'the raving tone and the fierce cheers of the crowd ... terrifying'. 'The only thing for our Government now', continued the former Colonial Secretary, 'is to avoid Edward Grey's mistake and leave them [the Germans] in no doubt where we stand.'*[42]

By this stage, Chamberlain and Halifax had decided that the Sudetenland could not remain within Czechoslovakia. Chamberlain had held this view for at least a month, while Halifax had gradually become convinced that no settlement between the Czechs and the Sudeten Germans was tenable. Encouraging the Prime Minister and Foreign Secretary towards this conclusion was the French Foreign Minister, Georges Bonnet, who, thanks to exaggerated reports on the Luftwaffe and the execrable state of the French Air Force, had entirely lost his nerve and was bombarding the British with appeals to save France from war at any price. The French preferred a solution that allowed the Sudetenland to remain within the Czech state but, in the last resort, were prepared to agree to a plebiscite to determine the territory's future. This the Czechs had always refused to contemplate. Yet the collapse in French morale allowed the British to consider cession with a clear conscience and Halifax now stated his support for a plebiscite, followed by a four-power conference to oversee the transfer.

*

* Sir Edward Grey, British Foreign Secretary at the outbreak of the First World War, was accused of failing to make Britain's position clear during the 1914 July Crisis, thus allowing the Germans to conclude that Britain would remain neutral in an ensuing war.

Away from the principal decision makers, people fretted over the prospect of war or, less commonly, the abandonment of the Czechs. 'Several people ring me up during the day begging me "to do something"', recorded Harold Nicolson. 'They have no idea what they want me to do but they are getting hysterical and it is some relief to them to bother other people on the telephone.'[43] Returning from a League of Nations meeting in Geneva, Robert Bernays thought that London was 'like a nightmare in a film'. 'Laughter and even smiles have gone from it. We are like a people waiting for the day of judgement.' Sandwich boards were dotted about the capital explaining where gas masks could be collected and eerie blue lines had appeared on pavements directing Londoners towards the nearest air raid shelter. At a dinner party, Bernays tried to improve the mood with a joke, only for a woman to turn on him: 'Damn you! Can't you realise that we may be dead next week!'[44]

Among the anti-appeasers there was a desperate search for leadership. Eden remained the preferred candidate but, beyond publishing a letter in *The Times*, the former Foreign Secretary refused to take a public stand. This led people, even on the left, to turn to Churchill. 'There is a great longing for leadership', wrote the Independent MP Eleanor Rathbone, 'and even those who are far apart from you in general politics realize that you are the one man who has combined full realization of the dangers of our military position with belief in collective international action against aggression.'[45] A few days later the Labour MP Josiah Wedgwood also wrote:

> My dear Winston,
>
> Do our folk really mean business? They seem to have seen everyone but you, and it is inconceivable to me that they should actually be facing up to war if they have not actually called you in …
>
> Not one of these people had anything to do with the direction of the last war. They are babies, if not cowards. You, or God, will have to help if this country is now to be saved.[46]

Meanwhile, the Sudeten Germans had risen in armed revolt. Taking their cue from Hitler's speech, SdP storm troopers in the Asch-Eger region attacked police stations, post offices, railway stations and customs houses. The Czechs responded by imposing martial law and putting troops onto the streets. By the end of the following day, Tuesday 13 September, thirteen Czechs and ten Sudeten Germans had been killed. Events were spiralling fast and at an evening meeting of British Ministers Duff Cooper urged Chamberlain to mobilise the Fleet. Chamberlain refused. He still had 'Plan Z' in reserve and had been waiting, he told Ida, until 'things looked blackest'.[47] Now he decided that the moment had come. The trigger was not in fact the bloodshed in the Sudetenland but the complete disintegration of French resolve. According to Eric Phipps – who saw both Bonnet and Daladier on the afternoon of 13 September – the French Foreign Minister was in a state of 'collapse' following a report by the American aviator Charles Lindbergh on the condition of the Luftwaffe, and even Daladier seemed to have lost his spirit. 'I fear [the] French have been bluffing', the Ambassador wrote to Halifax, before passing on the French Premier's suggestion for a three-power conference between Britain, France and Germany.[48] This was the last straw. Chamberlain was not going to allow the French to deprive him of his coup. He refused to take Daladier's call and, after an evening meeting of the Inner Cabinet, sent a message to Hitler proposing, 'in view of [the] increasingly critical situation … to come over at once and see you with a view to trying to find a peaceful solution. I propose to come across by air and am ready to start tomorrow.'[49]

'I fell from Heaven!' was one account of Hitler's reaction to Chamberlain's telegram.[50] He was certainly pleased and even claimed to have toyed with the idea of flying to London himself to spare the 69-year-old Premier the journey. Realising that this might not be wise, however, he replied early the following afternoon, Wednesday 14 September, that he was at the Prime Minister's disposal, 'and would not Mrs Chamberlain come too?'[51] Earlier in the day, Chamberlain had told the Cabinet of his plan. It was, of course, a fait accompli, since the Cabinet could hardly rescind the Prime Minister's self-invitation. But the majority applauded the move enthusiastically. Although it came as a 'bombshell' it 'appealed to everyone as a stroke of genius', wrote the Secretary of State for India, Lord Zetland.[52] Some, however, expressed concern. Leslie Hore-Belisha, the Secretary of State for War, thought the enterprise 'not without risk' and warned that Hitler was acting out a 'relentless plan on the lines of *Mein Kampf*'; Oliver Stanley spoke out against a plebiscite (which Chamberlain had said he was prepared to accept), saying that this 'would give Herr Hitler everything which he was demanding by force and would be a complete surrender'; while Duff Cooper argued that the choice was 'not between war and a plebiscite, but between war now and war later'. In the absence of an alternative, however, Cooper was prepared to back the Prime Minister and when Sir John Simon asked the Cabinet for its unanimous approval it was duly given.

Outside the cabinet room, the relief and consequent enthusiasm were even greater. 'It is one of the finest, most inspiring acts of all history', rhapsodised Chips Channon, who was attending a banquet given by the British delegation at the League of Nation's conference at Geneva when he heard the news. The company 'rose to their feet electrified, as all the world must be, and drank his [Chamberlain's] health'.[53] 'Good Luck Chamberlain', proclaimed the front page of the Labour *Daily Herald*, while the Liberal *News Chronicle* called it 'one of the boldest and most dramatic strokes in modern diplomatic history'.[54] Government bonds rose by £250 million and Lloyd's of London decided to cancel proposals for the inclusion of 'war-risks' into insurances.[55] Seventy out of one hundred people questioned in a working-class street approved of Chamberlain's actions, according to a Mass-Observation survey, while even some of the Prime Minister's critics, such as Leo Amery, praised what was undoubtedly a 'bold move'.[56] Churchill, on the other hand, thought it 'the stupidest thing that has ever been done'.[57]

Abroad, the reaction was overwhelmingly positive. The Dominion Prime Ministers applauded the actions of the Mother Country, while in Berlin observers reported an easing of tension. In Paris, the relief was palpable. Earlier in the day, the Government had been in full flight, with Bonnet telling Phipps that they simply could not 'sacrifice ten million men in order to prevent three and a half million Sudetens joining the Reich'.*[58] They were now prepared to agree to any solution which avoided war, he told the Ambassador. The Czechs, on the other hand, were flabbergasted. Neither consulted

* Having proposed a meeting *à trois*, Daladier was rather disgruntled when he learnt that Chamberlain had, without consulting him, decided to invite himself to Germany. It had several times been suggested that he should meet with Hitler but he had always refused, he told Phipps, on the grounds that a 'representative of Great Britain should be present'.

nor warned about Chamberlain's mission, they had already gone to what they considered the limits of concession only to find themselves excluded from the negotiations which would determine their fate. American opinion, devoid of the relief factor, was sympathetic to their plight. Although Roosevelt had assured Chamberlain of his support, the British Ambassador, Sir Ronald Lindsay, had only days before reported that US opinion was in favour of 'His Majesty's Government making a strong stand against German aggression' and that any compromise 'may bring a certain let-down of American friendliness'.[59] But it was in Rome that the most perceptive comment was made. 'There will be no war', Mussolini told his son-in-law and Foreign Minister, Count Galeazzo Ciano, but 'it is the liquidation of British prestige'.[60]

*

Shortly after 8 a.m. on 15 September 1938, a smiling Chamberlain arrived at Heston airfield in west London. As he got out of the car a voice shouted, 'Stand by Czechoslovakia! No concessions to Hitler!' But this was a solitary protester, safely behind a barrier.[61] A small farewell party was gathered on the tarmac, including Lord and Lady Halifax, Sir Alexander Cadogan, Theodor Kordt (in top hat and morning coat), the Chairman and Managing Director of British Airways and Lord Brocket, just returned from Nuremberg. As Chamberlain exchanged pleasantries with the group, Lord Londonderry arrived in dramatic style, swooping out of the air in his own aeroplane, which he had flown down specially to bid the Prime Minister farewell. The sun shone – a good omen, suggested Halifax – and Chamberlain seemed in the best of spirits. Clad in a grey overcoat, his collar starched and umbrella grasped, he posed for the photographers on the steps of the aeroplane before making a short speech for the newsreels:

> I am going to meet the German Chancellor because the present situation seems to me to be one in which discussions between him and me may have useful consequences. My policy has always been to try to ensure peace, and the Führer's ready acceptance of my suggestion encourages me to hope that my visit to him will not be without results.

The crowd gave him three cheers and, with a wave of his felt homburg, he disappeared inside the glistening, twin-engine Lockheed Electra.*

As his biographer has pointed out, and contrary to popular belief, this was not Chamberlain's first flight. Like a character in *Those Magnificent Men and Their Flying Machines*, he had briefly been aloft, complete with top hat, in 1923, when showing the Duke of York (the future George VI) around an industrial fair in Birmingham.[62] Compared to the journey he was now undertaking, however, that hardly counted and the myth of the 69-year-old Premier taking his first flight to save Europe from war was a powerful one. As he took to the skies, Chamberlain was undoubtedly taking with him the hopes and prayers of the majority of the British people and many more besides. Though there were some, like Duff Cooper, who thought that the Prime Minister had about as much chance of squaring Hitler 'as Little Lord Fauntleroy would have of concluding a satisfactory deal with Al Capone', they were a minority and, for the moment, a largely silent one.[63]

The British people had not been prepared psychologically for war and Czechoslovakia seemed a long way away. Even if they were willing to go 'once more unto the breach' in the name of European freedom, the consequences, the experts warned, would be severe. Only the previous evening, Chamberlain had read a report by the Chiefs of Staff, reaffirming their opinion that there was nothing that Britain and France could do to prevent Germany from overrunning Czechoslovakia within a matter of weeks. If there was to be war, it would be long and 'unlimited' and Britain should be prepared to suffer 500–600 tons of bombs a day for the first two months.[†64] This assessment weighed heavily with Chamberlain, who, on his return journey, had visions of a German bomber following the same route. A man of peace to his core, he viewed a future conflict in apocalyptic terms and could only consider war a viable policy if the foundations of European security were put at risk and all other options exhausted. He was not prepared to contemplate it in order that three and a quarter million Germans

---

* There were in fact two aeroplanes: one for Chamberlain, Horace Wilson and William Strang from the Foreign Office, and one for two shorthand typists and the Prime Minister's two detectives.

† In fact, fewer than 75,000 tons of bombs were dropped on Britain during the course of the entire war.

should be prevented from joining the Reich. Peace was, therefore, paramount. But if it had to be peace, what was the price? The answer depended on an assessment of Hitler and his aims. If, as he claimed, Hitler was a man of peace and the Sudetenland constituted his last territorial demand, then Chamberlain's strategy held good. But there was another possibility – the one raised by Hore-Belisha at the Cabinet meeting the previous day – that Hitler was acting out a master-plan which would lead to German hegemony in Europe. It would be up to Chamberlain to make the judgement.

*

The flight across France had gone smoothly and the Prime Minister and Horace Wilson had picnicked happily on ham sandwiches and whisky.[65] As they approached Munich, however, they hit a storm and the light aircraft 'rocked and bumped like a ship in sea'.[66] Fortunately, after some nervous moments, they were guided down by a German plane and Chamberlain emerged smiling from the craft. Although the *Manchester Guardian* considered the Prime Minister 'positively debonair', an official from the British Embassy thought the Germans were rather taken aback by the sight of 'this funny little man with an umbrella' emerging from an aeroplane. 'They simply couldn't believe that someone looking like that could be the Prime Minister of Great Britain', he recalled.[67] If this was the case, they did not show it and, as Chamberlain told Ida, he was 'delighted with the enthusiastic welcome of the crowds who were waiting in the rain and who gave me the Nazi salute and shouted "*Heil*" at the tops of their voices'.[68] Indeed, according to Hitler's interpreter, Paul Schmidt, the euphoria was even greater than that which had greeted Mussolini the previous September.

The official welcoming party comprised Ribbentrop, State Secretary Weizsäcker, Ambassador Henderson and his German counterpart, Herbert von Dirksen. There was a guard of honour, which Chamberlain inspected and, as Wilson noted, a rather 'strident' band.[69] The British were then driven in a fleet of Mercedes past more cheering spectators to the station, where they boarded Hitler's special train for the three-hour journey to Berchtesgaden. Chamberlain regretted that the bad weather prevented him from seeing the view, 'as the scenery must be very beautiful'.[70] More dispiriting than the shrouded mountains were the endless succession of military transports, filled with 'soldiers in new uniforms and gun barrels pointing skywards', which trundled past the train.[71] This was no coincidence and an indication of how Hitler intended to play the British Prime Minister.

At Berchtesgaden there was more '*Heil*'-ing and Chamberlain continued to enjoy the sensation of being saluted as he drove up the mountain to the Berghof. The Führer met him on the wet steps and after shaking him warmly by the hand led him and the rest of the party inside. Chamberlain was unimpressed by Hitler's appearance. Having relayed such details as the fact that the Führer wore 'black trousers such as we wear in the evening', he described Hitler's expression as 'rather disagreeable, especially in repose'. 'He looks entirely undistinguished', he explained to Ida. 'You would never notice him in a crowd and would take him for the house painter he once was.'[72] In his report to the Cabinet, he was more outspoken, describing Hitler as 'the commonest little dog he had ever seen' – though it 'was impossible not to be impressed with the power of the man'.[73] Now the one-time Austrian corporal and the former Lord Mayor of Birmingham took tea in the great hall, with its vast panoramic window, currently filled with grey mist. On the walls hung various German and Italian old masters including, Chamberlain noted prudishly, 'a huge Italian nude!'[74]

The conversation did not flow. Chamberlain praised the room. Hitler replied that it was England that had the big rooms. Chamberlain said that Hitler must come and see them for himself one day. Hitler retorted that he would be met with demonstrations of disapproval. Chamberlain conceded that it would be wise to choose the moment carefully. And that was that.

When they got down to serious conversation, in Hitler's private study, they were alone save for the interpreter, Paul Schmidt.* Chamberlain began by suggesting that they devote the rest of the afternoon to a clarification of each other's point of view and leave the specifics of the Sudeten issue until the next day. But Hitler interjected to say that this was quite impossible. According to today's

---

* This was a deliberate strategy, concocted between Henderson and Weizsäcker, so as to prevent Ribbentrop from taking part in the discussions.

information (a fabrication which, as a tactic, was to be repeated throughout the crisis) 300 Sudeten Germans had been killed and a solution must be reached at once. Hitler then embarked on a long exposition of his vision for Germany. He explained that, from his youth, he had been obsessed with racial theory and was determined to bring all Germans, wherever possible, into the Reich. Chamberlain interrupted. Was the Chancellor saying that if these three million Sudetens were incorporated into the Reich then there was nothing more that he would want? 'I ask because there are many people who think that is not all, that you wish to dismember Czechoslovakia.' Hitler categorically denied this. He believed in racial unity and as such did not want a lot of Czechs in the Reich. Czechoslovakia, however, was a 'spearhead in his side' and he would not feel safe until the defensive treaties between Czechoslovakia and Russia were abolished. More portentously, he believed that once the Sudeten Germans had been granted self-determination then the Polish, Hungarian and Slovakian minorities would demand the same and Czechoslovakia would cease to exist.[75]

For the majority of this exchange Hitler spoke softly, in low tones. Now he became suddenly excited and declared 'in a torrent of words' that all of this was academic.[76] Three hundred of his countrymen had been killed the previous day and he was not prepared to allow this to continue. 'I am determined to settle it', he shouted. 'I do not care whether there is a world war or not. I am determined to settle it and to settle it soon and I am prepared to risk a world war rather than allow this to drag on.' Chamberlain became indignant. If Hitler had decided on war, why had he allowed him to come all this way? 'I have wasted my time.'[77] Hitler took this check and quietened down. Realising that 'rapid decisions must be taken if the situation was to be saved', Chamberlain then reassured the Führer that he was fully prepared to accept the principle of self-determination. 'My personal opinion', he confided to Ida, 'was that on principle I didn't care two hoots whether the Sudetens were in the Reich or out of it.'[78] The difficulty, he explained to Hitler, was the means, not the end. He was, however, prepared to discuss this with his colleagues and then return to resume their negotiations at a later date. Hitler said he was sorry that Chamberlain should have to make two journeys but promised that next time he would meet him near Cologne. Chamberlain asked

Hitler if the situation could be held in the interval and Hitler pledged that he would not give the order to march unless some outrageous incident forced his hand.

Chamberlain was pleased by the meeting. Although he detected a 'ruthlessness' about Hitler, he felt that he had 'established a certain confidence' and that this was 'a man who could be relied upon when he had given his word'.[79] He was even more delighted to learn from Horace Wilson of Hitler's supposedly favourable impression of him. 'I have had a conversation with a *man*', Hitler allegedly declared in the presence of Ribbentrop's head of personal staff, who passed it on to Wilson.[80] The State Secretary, Ernst von Weizsäcker, however, recorded a very different scene. According to Weizsäcker, no sooner had Chamberlain departed than Hitler clapped his hands in delight and boasted that he had 'manoeuvred this dried-up civilian into a corner'. That night Hitler's mistress, Eva Braun, joined in jokes about this peculiar Englishman who seemed so attached to his umbrella.[81]

Hitler's claim to have manoeuvred Chamberlain into a corner is unfair but only in the sense that it gives Hitler too much credit for the position the Prime Minister now found himself in. Having already decided that the Sudeten Germans should be granted the right of self-determination, it did not take great skill on the Führer's part to get Chamberlain to accede to this demand. Nevertheless, this was Hitler's demand and Chamberlain was acceding to it. Moreover, Chamberlain had now made himself responsible for delivering the Sudetenland in a way that would prove acceptable to the Czechs, as well as to French, British and international opinion. If he succeeded then Hitler had gained his stated demand. If he failed – as Hitler expected – then the Führer could have the little war he dreamt of. It was hardly a triumph of British diplomacy.

*

Back in London, on the evening of Friday 16 September, a self-satisfied Chamberlain told the Inner Cabinet that he thought he had 'held Hitler for the moment' but it was clear that nothing other than self-determination for the Sudeten Germans would satisfy him.[82] On this point the Prime Minister thought they should agree. It was unthinkable, he said, that Britain should go to war in defiance of this principle. Henlein had fled the previous day to Germany – demanding immediate cession – and Lord Runciman, who had returned from Prague and joined the meeting, thought it impossible that the Czechs and Sudetens would ever be able to 'settle down and live happily together'.[83]

The next morning, the full Cabinet assembled to hear the Prime Minister's report. He was disparaging about Hitler personally but was impressed by his power and earnestness. Crucially, Chamberlain believed that 'Herr Hitler's objectives were strictly limited' and that he was 'telling the truth' when he said that he did not want to bring Czechs into the Reich.[84] When the meeting resumed in the afternoon, Lord Maugham, the Lord Chancellor, opened with a donnish lecture on the foreign policy of Canning and Disraeli. According to their policy, 'two conditions had to be satisfied before we intervened. First, that British interests were seriously affected; secondly, that we should only intervene with overwhelming force.' Duff Cooper countered, saying that Britain's policy had always been to prevent any one power from obtaining undue predominance on the Continent. They were now faced with 'probably the most formidable power that had ever dominated Europe', and resistance was, quite obviously, a British interest. He doubted that the Sudetenland was Hitler's 'last aim' and pointed to the series of promises the Führer had already broken. Owing 'to the fearful responsibility of incurring war', he was, however, unwilling to set his face against a plebiscite, provided that it was carried out under fair conditions, with international supervision. He thought it extremely doubtful that this would 'end our troubles' but it was, perhaps, worth trying on the off-chance that 'some unforeseen event might upset the rule of the Nazi party', sometime before the next crisis.[85]

Lord De La Warr, the Lord Privy Seal, supported the first half of Cooper's contribution and declared that he was 'prepared to face war in order to free the world from the continual threat of ultimatums'. Lord Hailsham rallied to the Prime Minister. It was already a fact, the Lord President of the Council said, that one power dominated the Continent and Britain had, therefore, 'no alternative but to submit to what the Lord Privy Seal regarded as humiliation'. This bravura performance of defeatist realpolitik provoked Lord Winterton, Chancellor of the Duchy of Lancaster, who argued that on this basis the Government might as well acquiesce 'in the invasion of Kent or the surrender of the Isle of Wight'. Oliver Stanley agreed. 'This was not the last of Hitler's coups', he warned colleagues and if, as he believed, it was a choice between surrender and fighting, then 'we ought to fight'.

The big beasts, however, were for surrender. Halifax concurred with the Prime Minister that it would be impossible to lead the country into war in defiance of the principle of self-determination, while Sam Hoare – following Runciman's slanted exposition of the situation – thought that the Czechs had already lost the Sudetens and until 'that fact was recognised there would be no peace in Europe'.[86] Yet even among the loyalists there was some doubt over the results of Chamberlain's negotiations. 'The impression made by the PM's story was a little painful', noted Sir Thomas Inskip in his diary. 'H[itler] had made him listen to a boast that the German military machine was a terrible instrument ... [and] the PM said more than once to us he was just in time. It was plain that H[itler] had made all the running: he had in fact blackmailed the PM.'[87]

If Hitler had blackmailed Chamberlain, then Chamberlain needed the French to help blackmail the Czechs into agreeing the surrender of the Sudetenland. Amazingly, the French – much to their chagrin – had so far been entirely excluded from the Prime Minister's diplomacy. On Sunday 18 September, however, Daladier and Bonnet arrived in London to hear the results. The meeting began in dramatic fashion when Chamberlain read out a telegram he had just received from the Czech Government saying that they must proceed to a general mobilisation. He then recounted the details of his meeting at Berchtesgaden, concluding that refusal of Hitler's terms must inevitably lead to an immediate invasion. There then followed an extraordinary game of buck passing, as both sides tried to escape responsibility for coercing the Czechs. Chamberlain said that the question was simply whether the French were prepared to accept the principle of self-determination. Daladier disagreed. His 'voice trembling with carefully modulated emotion', the French Premier spoke of France's 'sacred duty' towards Czechoslovakia and repeated his conviction that 'Germany's real aim was the disintegration of Czechoslovakia and the realisation of pan-German ideals through a march to the East'. If they gave in now, the 'result would be that in a very short time Germany would be master of Europe'.[88]

This was true but it was also bluster. Privately and not so privately, Daladier and (with less angst) Bonnet had decided that desertion was the better part of valour and, after a good lunch, at which Chamberlain served his favourite claret (Château Margaux), as well as an 1865 cognac, they duly capitulated.* 'In international discussions the darkest hour is generally before lunch', commented Chamberlain cynically.[89] Having extracted from the British the promise of a guarantee for the truncated Czech state, Daladier then agreed to a joint note telling Beneš to surrender. What if he refused, enquired Chamberlain. Then, replied the 'Bull of Vaucluse', 'the strongest pressure would have to be brought to bear'. Chamberlain thanked him and the French Ministers departed. The two great European democracies were now committed to the dismemberment of the only democracy to the east of the Rhine.

*

While the Inner Cabinet – which consisted entirely of appeasers – cajoled and cudgelled the French, the doubters within the wider Cabinet considered their positions. 'Tell Walter [Elliot, the Minister for Health] that if he goes I will', De La Warr requested his friend and fellow National Labour member Blanche Dugdale. 'Baffy', as she was widely known, said that she would do no such thing, but did all she could to induce De La Warr to resign. 'For one thing (though I did not say this)', she confided to her diary, 'he will count for nothing if he stays' whereas 'if he resigns, he may help to make a nucleus'.[90] This was indeed a problem for the anti-appeasers. Of those whom Chamberlain, paradoxically, labelled 'the weaker brethren', only Duff Cooper controlled a major department while the rest, as Oliver Harvey lamented, were rather a poor lot: 'Oliver Stanley flabby, Elliot a windbag, De La Warr sound but a very light weight, Morrison now quite *dégonflé* [deflated], it seems.'[91] Outside the Government, Eden was still unwilling to take a public stand and Churchill was considered too self-serving and bellicose for most Conservatives to rally around.

---

* Indeed, Daladier already knew that, in the last resort, Beneš was prepared to agree to some cession of territory, although the area the Czech President proposed – the absolute maximum which could be lost without affecting the viability of the state – was significantly smaller than that which Hitler demanded.

It did not help that much of the press – certainly its more powerful and popular elements – was slavishly loyal to the Government. On the day Chamberlain flew to Munich, Lord Beaverbrook had written to Halifax to tell him that he and his fellow proprietors were anxious to help the Prime Minister and could not a Cabinet Minister be appointed to keep the press lords informed of the Government line? Sam Hoare, whose career Beaverbrook was secretly subsiding, was duly despatched and on 22 September the *Daily Express* was able to inform its readers of 'THE TRUTH' about Czechoslovakia. 'There is no duty of responsibility whatsoever on this country to defend that central European power', declared Beaverbrook on the front page. 'It is wicked and untrue to accuse Great Britain, your own country, of selling Czechoslovakia and of deserting France.' Some of the anti-appeasers with public profiles – such as Bob Boothby, Harold Nicolson and of course Churchill – published alternative views, mainly in the *Daily Telegraph*, but these had little impact when compared to the pro-appeasement efforts of *The Times*, the *Observer*, the *Daily Mail* and the *Express*.

The Anglo-French note was sent to Prague on the afternoon of Monday 19 September 1938. The previous day, the Czech Ambassador, Jan Masaryk, had written to Halifax to say that his Government took it for granted that it would be consulted before any decisions regarding the future of their country were taken. Now, the British and French told the Czechs that the entire Sudetenland must be handed over to the Reich. Unsurprisingly, Beneš took this extremely badly, accusing the democracies of abandoning Czechoslovakia. He was enough of a realist to have foreseen that some territory might have to be ceded but never expected his allies to insist on the acceptance of the most extreme German demands.

That night, the Czech Cabinet sat, in agony, only to emerge without a decision the following morning. After a second marathon session on 20 September, they sent the British and French a note imploring them to reconsider. But the democracies were resolved and Chamberlain drafted a reply 'driving the screw home on [the] poor Czechs'.[92] At two o'clock in the morning, Basil Newton and Victor de Lacroix, the British and French Ministers, arrived at the Hradčany Castle to present Beneš with what he correctly deduced was an ultimatum. Either the Czechs capitulated or the French and British could not be responsible for the assured fate which would engulf them. Despite large demonstrations in Prague in favour of resistance, the Czechs could not contemplate a solitary war against Germany and Beneš gave way. While thousands gathered in Wenceslas Square – their banners proclaiming 'We won't give the Republic to the German house painter' – the Czech Government drafted its surrender:

> Under pressure of urgent insistence culminating in British communications of September 21 [the] Czechoslovak Government sadly accept French and British proposals on [the] supposition that the two Governments will do everything in carrying them out to safeguard the vital interests of [the] Czechoslovak state.[93]

It was a pathetic document: pitiful in the immediate, tragic given the fate which remained in store.

XVI

To the Brink

We must go on being cowards up to our limit, but *not beyond*.

Sir Alexander Cadogan, 21 September 1938[1]

Armed with the Czech surrender, Chamberlain departed for his second meeting with Hitler, due to take place at the spa town of Bad Godesberg, near Bonn, at 10.45 on the morning of Thursday 22 September 1938. The atmosphere was notably different to what it had been a week before. Then, the general feeling had been one of relief and admiration; the Poet Laureate, John Masefield, had even been moved to write some purple verse. Now, doubts had begun to appear and there was a press campaign, on both sides of the Atlantic, against the 'Betrayal of Cz[echoslovakia]'.[2] This was spurred on by Churchill, who responded to the news of the Czech surrender, on the evening of 21 September, with an excoriating press release:

> The partition of Czechoslovakia under Anglo-French pressure amounts to a complete surrender by the Western democracies to the Nazi threat of force. Such a collapse will not bring peace or safety to Great Britain and France. On the contrary, it will bring both countries into a position of ever-increasing weakness and danger.
>
> The neutralisation of Czechoslovakia alone means the liberation of twenty-five German divisions to threaten the Western front. The path to the Black Sea will be laid wide open to triumphant Nazi-ism. Acceptance of Herr Hitler's terms involves the prostration of Europe before the Nazi power … The idea that safety can be purchased by throwing a small State to the wolves is a fatal delusion. The German

> war power will grow faster than the French and British can complete their preparations for defence.[3]

That same afternoon, the Cabinet had met to discuss the line which Chamberlain should take at Godesberg. The general sentiment was that they had gone to the limit of concession and that it was now time for Hitler to show some good faith. Duff Cooper urged the Prime Minister to speak to the German Chancellor in the most direct terms. He should say that he had done 'all and more than he had undertaken, that he was bringing him Czechoslovakia's head on a charger – that he had incurred in order to do this charges of surrender, betrayal and cowardice. Further he could not go. He would prefer, if it were necessary, to go to war.'[4] No one dissented and the Cabinet was unanimous in saying that Chamberlain should prevent Hitler from invoking the claims of the Hungarians and Poles who, with the Führer's encouragement, were circling, vulture-like, over the Czech carcass.

Chamberlain landed at Cologne at 12.36 p.m. on 22 September, where, 'grasping the symbol of peace, his umbrella', he inspected a section of the SS Leibstandarte Adolf Hitler, before driving the short distance to Godesberg.[5] The British party, which comprised Sir Nevile Henderson and Ivone Kirkpatrick (First Secretary of the British Embassy), as well as the ubiquitous Sir Horace Wilson, had been provided with lavish rooms in the Petersberg Hotel, on the right bank of the Rhine. On orders from the German Foreign Ministry, a suite of Louis XV furniture had been acquired, along with vast quantities of fruit, cigars, hydrangeas and eau de cologne. Hitler was stationed on the other side of the river, in one of his favourite haunts, the Hotel Dreesen. It was here that he had planned the murder of Ernst Röhm and his supporters – 'The Night of the Long Knives' – in June 1934 and it was here that his second meeting with Chamberlain was to take place.

The British crossed the Rhine on ferries, passing a luxury yacht on which Hitler had planned to take the Prime Minister on a trip down the Wagnerian river. Why Hitler should have thought Chamberlain would be in the mood for sightseeing is hard to fathom; he had certainly not come with the intention of accepting the Prime Minister's peace plan. Indeed, Chamberlain had scarcely finished explaining the deal he had struck with the Czechs when Hitler interrupted to say that he was sorry but this would not do. Chamberlain was thunderstruck. Snapping to attention in his chair, his face flushed, he enquired what could have possibly changed since their last meeting? Hitler replied coolly that they must consider the demands of other nationalities who sought freedom or autonomy from the Czechoslovak state. Furthermore, he refused to accept the timetable which Chamberlain was proposing. The situation had to be resolved in the next few days, by 1 October at the latest. Aghast, Chamberlain said that he was both disappointed and puzzled by Hitler's reply. He had managed to secure what Hitler wanted and 'without the expenditure of a single drop of German blood'. In so doing he had taken his political life into his hands and, at home, was accused of selling the Czechs and yielding to dictators. He had even been booed on his departure. There then followed a long period of 'ill-tempered floundering' while fabricated reports of Czech atrocities were brought in. Hitler demanded the immediate drawing of a language frontier and Chamberlain was shown the map which Hitler had prepared. But no cartography could bridge the gap which had emerged and after an exhausting couple of hours, the Prime Minister decided to adjourn the meeting and return to his hotel.

*

Back in London, Halifax was waiting anxiously for news. The Foreign Office was already in a state of consternation over reports that the Sudeten German Freikorps (paramilitary) – created at Hitler's instigation the day after the Berchtesgaden summit – had crossed the border from Germany and occupied the towns of Asch and Eger. Could the British continue to advise the Czechs not to mobilise under such circumstances? Halifax thought not and sent a message to Godesberg to that effect. From the Petersberg Hotel, he received the depressing news that Hitler, far from accepting the Anglo-French settlement, was demanding an immediate occupation. The fair-minded Halifax was appalled, though for the moment he accepted Chamberlain's request to hold off advising the Czechs to mobilise.

A group of leading anti-appeasers was, meanwhile, meeting at Churchill's flat. Harold Nicolson arrived at the same time as his host was getting out of a taxi. 'This … is hell', stated Nicolson. 'It is the end of the British Empire', responded Churchill. The two men were joined by five peers – Lloyd, Horne, Lytton, Wolmer and Robert Cecil – as well as the Liberal leader, Archie Sinclair, and Brendan Bracken. Churchill poured himself a whisky and soda and then relayed to the group the line which Chamberlain intended to take, having just learnt it from Downing Street. Someone asked what would happen if Hitler rejected the Anglo-French proposals. Then 'Chamberlain will return tonight and we shall have war', replied Churchill. In that case, someone else suggested, it might be inconvenient to have Chamberlain on German territory. 'Even the Germans would not be so stupid as to deprive us of our beloved Prime Minister', replied Churchill. Later, the telephone rang and the group learnt from Clement Attlee that the Labour Party was prepared to join with Tory rebels in opposing any further concessions. With this significant inflation of support, the meeting broke up, resolved to come out against Chamberlain if he tried to bring back 'peace with dishonour'.[6]

Churchill and his acolytes were not alone in feeling anger at the British policy. That evening, 10,000 people protested in Whitehall, demanding the Government 'Stand by the Czechs' and 'Chamberlain must go!'[7] Mass-Observation, that unscientific but refreshingly personal means of monitoring opinion, reported a growing dissatisfaction, particularly among men – 67 per cent of whom, in a survey taken on 21–22 September, felt 'indignant' at Chamberlain's treatment of the Czechs, compared to only 22 per cent of women.*[8] The recorded opinions were even more interesting. Responding to the question 'What do you think about Czechoslovakia?' a thrity-year-old bus conductor from Lewisham replied:

> I should think they should reject them. What the hell's he got the right to go over there and do a dirty trick like that? It'll have the whole world against us now. Who'll trust us? It's like throwing your own kid

* The sample was 350 people and revealed a growing disillusionment over the two days.

to the wolves. We helped make it a country and then Chamberlain comes along and wants to buy that swine off. There'll be a war sooner or later, then there'll be nobody to help us. America won't lend us a bloody cent then. It's a cert if they've [the Czechs] any guts they'll not give in.

Or this, from a packer at the *Evening News*:

Why didn't he say straight out six months ago that he wasn't going to do anything about anybody except our own coasts? It seems to me that when Hitler and Mussolini begin to ask for our Empire he'll give it to 'em bit by bit so long as they don't touch us, till we've no Empire left. It's a bit dirty in my opinion when you won't tell the small chap what you're going to do when you've more or less promised that you'll not see him robbed.[9]

Of course, not everyone felt like this and some made an impressive show of carrying on as normal. 'Dear Rab', wrote Michael Beaumont, the Conservative MP for Aylesbury, to the Under-Secretary of State for Foreign Affairs on 21 September, the day of the Czech surrender:

I realise that you are neither in the right time or place to receive shooting invitations, but if we are not all submerged in a holocaust, can you both come and shoot here on the 17th of December, arriving on the 16th and staying the week-end?

Whatever you do, keep us out of the war long enough to shoot with you in October, to which we are much looking forward.

As you know, I am not over ready with praise of His Majesty's Government, but I think Neville and Edward Halifax have been magnificent. You must have had a hell of a time. Damn the Czechs![10]

The most important stiffening of opinion took place within the Foreign Office. Disturbed by the news from Godesberg and detecting the change of mood at home – which included a number of Cabinet Ministers – Halifax now decided to ignore Chamberlain's advice and, at four o'clock on the afternoon of Friday 23 September, authorised Basil Newton in Prague to rescind the Government's advice urging the Czechs not to mobilise. He then sent a 'stiff' telegram to the Prime Minister, strongly endorsed by Sam Hoare:

> Great mass of public opinion seems to be hardening in the sense of feeling that we have gone to limit of concession ... We, of course, can imagine immense difficulties with which you are confronted but from [the] point of view of your own position, that of Government, and of the country, it seems to your colleagues of vital importance that you should not leave without making it plain to [the] Chancellor if possible by special interview, that, after great concessions made by Czechoslovak Government, for him to reject opportunity of peaceful solution in favour of one that must involve war would be an unpardonable crime against humanity.[11]

*

In Godesberg, Chamberlain was unsure what, if anything, he could achieve. Having reached a stalemate on the evening of 22 September, he decided to cancel the meeting with Hitler scheduled for the following morning and instead wrote to him, requesting a written statement of his demands. Reluctantly, Hitler agreed and at 10.30 p.m. on the 23rd the British party returned to the Dreesen. There Hitler read out a memorandum demanding that the Czechs begin the evacuation of the Sudetenland on 26 September – three days' time – and that German troops commence their occupation three days after that. Chamberlain said that this was an ultimatum – a 'diktat', chimed Henderson.[12] Hitler merely pointed out that the document was entitled 'Memorandum'. At this point an aide entered and handed the Führer a note. Having stared at it for some time, he passed it to Schmidt to translate for the Prime Minister. It was the news that the Czechs had mobilised.

For what seemed like an age, nobody spoke. Chamberlain feared Hitler might give the order to retaliate there and then but the Führer surprised him when he said that, owing to the respect he had for the negotiations, he would not respond to this latest provocation. Indeed, he agreed to extend his deadline for the evacuation to 1 October and played on Chamberlain's vanity by telling him that he was one of the few men for whom he had ever made a concession. The atmosphere was transformed. Flattered, Chamberlain said that he would deliver Hitler's terms to the Czechs and the Führer spoke vaguely about the possibility of improved Anglo-German relations. 'There need be no differences between us', Schmidt recalled him saying. 'We shall not get in the way of the exercise of your extra-European interests, while you can leave us a free hand in central and south-eastern Europe without harm.'[13] As the two men said their farewells, Chamberlain declared his belief that 'a relationship of confidence had grown up between himself and the Führer'.[14] In fact, he had been blackmailed.

Back in Downing Street the following afternoon, Sir Alexander Cadogan was 'completely horrified' to hear the Prime Minister recommend acceptance of Hitler's demands.[15] Chamberlain told the Inner Cabinet that he was 'satisfied that Herr Hitler was speaking the truth when he said that he regarded this question as a racial question' and that he would fight if his terms were not accepted. Fortunately, he felt that he had established 'some degree of personal influence' over the Führer – a man who would 'not go back on his word once he had given it' – and that they had the potential to achieve 'a turning point in Anglo-German relations'.[16] It was clear, noted Cadogan, that Hitler had 'hypnotised him to a point': 'He was quite calmly for total surrender.'[17] No less astonishing was the spell the Prime Minister seemed to have cast over his colleagues. The previous day, Halifax, Hoare and Sir John Simon had all opposed the proposals and Simon, in particular, had been 'as bellicose as the Duke of Plaza Toro'.* Now, however, the Chancellor thought that it was only a question of 'modalities' and the Foreign and Home Secretaries joined with him in falling meekly into line behind the Prime Minister.[18]

When the full Cabinet met at 5.30 p.m., however, Chamberlain came up against strong dissent. Despite repeating Hitler's pledge that 'he had no more territorial ambitions in Europe', as well as his own belief that the Führer 'would not deliberately deceive a man whom he respected and with whom he had been in negotiation' and that it would be 'a great tragedy if we lost this opportunity of reaching an understanding with Germany', at least a third of the Cabinet favoured

* The Duke of Plaza Toro was the title character of a poem by W. S. Gilbert. The Duke loves war but always finds a way of allowing others to do the fighting.

resistance.[19] Duff Cooper said that he could not share the Prime Minister's optimistic view of Hitler's assurances and called for immediate general mobilisation. Previously he had thought that there were only two possible outcomes to the crisis: 'peace with dishonour or war'. Now he saw a third possibility: namely 'being kicked into war by the boot of public opinion, when those for whom we were fighting had already been defeated'.[20] He was supported by Leslie Hore-Belisha, Oliver Stanley, Lord Winterton and Lord De La Warr. Chamberlain rejected the call for further defence precautions, though he conceded that the Cabinet could consider the issue again when they reconvened the following morning.

Halifax was not fazed. Having apparently forgotten his defiance of the previous day, he returned to the Foreign Office 'quite happily *défaitiste*-pacifist'. His Permanent Under-Secretary, on the other hand, was in complete despair. 'How can we look any foreigner in the face after this? How can we hold Egypt, India and the rest?' wondered Cadogan. He understood the deficiencies in Britain's defences but had decided it was better to 'be beat than dishonoured' and while driving the Foreign Secretary home, decided to give him a piece of his mind.[21] The next morning, Halifax sent for him. 'Alec, I'm very angry with you', reprimanded the Foreign Secretary. 'You gave me a sleepless night. I woke at 1 and never got to sleep again. But I came to the conclusion you were right.'[22] Accordingly, Halifax told his colleagues, at the resumed Cabinet meeting on 25 September, that he now felt there was some divergence between himself and the Prime Minister. Speaking in 'a low voice and with great emotion', he explained that yesterday he had felt that acceptance of the Godesberg demands did not involve the acceptance of a new principle compared with what the Cabinet had already agreed.[23] Now he was not so sure. There was, he felt, a distinction between an orderly and a disorderly transfer (with all that the latter implied for the minorities in the transferred areas) and 'he could not rid his mind of the fact that Herr Hitler had given us nothing and that he was dictating terms, just as though he had won a war but without having had to fight'. In a staggering volte-face, Halifax then told the Cabinet that the 'ultimate end' he wished to see was the destruction of Nazism:

> So long as Nazi-ism lasted, peace would be uncertain. For this reason he did not feel that it would be right to put pressure on Czechoslovakia

> to accept. We should lay the case before them. If they rejected it he imagined that France would join in and if France went in we should join with them.[24]

Halifax's transformation from appeaser into resister was a massive knock for Chamberlain, who implied in a note he passed across the Cabinet table that he would rather resign than lead his country into war:

> Your complete change of view since I saw you last night is a horrible blow to me, but of course you must form your opinions for yourself.
>
> It remains however to see what the French say.
>
> If they say they will go in, thereby dragging us in, I do not think I could accept responsibility for the decision.

'I feel a brute', Halifax wrote back, 'but I lay awake most of the night, tormenting myself, and did not feel I could reach any other conclusion at this moment, on the point of coercing Cz. E.' 'Night conclusions are seldom taken in the right perspective' was Chamberlain's censorious rejoinder.[25]

Following Halifax's 'fine moral lead', Hore-Belisha and Lord Hailsham came out unambiguously for resistance, along with Stanley, Elliot, De La Warr, Winterton and Cooper.[26] Chamberlain was dismayed. His Cabinet was in open revolt, led by his Foreign Secretary. At first he tried to plaster over the vast crack which had appeared but Cooper stated that he would rather resign than submit to such shoddy masonry. Chamberlain replied that he had been expecting this but begged the First Lord of the Admiralty to do nothing precipitate. Cooper agreed to hold off while the Inner Cabinet met with the French that afternoon. It had been a dramatic meeting – a turning point, which Baffy Dugdale recorded in her diary as the moment when the 'Rubber Stampers' began 'changing back into Men'.[27]

*

Over the preceding week, Sir Eric Phipps had sent a daily (often thrice daily) stream of reports from Paris emphasising both the extreme reluctance and the inability of the French to fight. So defeatist were they, in fact, that the Foreign Office decided that the Ambassador was being deliberately selective with the evidence and ordered all British consuls to send their despatches direct to London. In some ways, this accusation was unfair. Defeatism, particularly among the French right, was certainly in the air and the failure of the Government to prepare for war (there was a serious shortage of gas masks, not to mention air defences) added to a sense of growing panic. On the other hand, the Government continued to call up reservists (753,000 on 24 September) and at a meeting of the Council of Ministers, on the morning of 25 September 1938, Daladier sided with the resisters – Georges Mandel, Paul Reynaud and Auguste Champetier de Ribes – against Bonnet and the *capitulards*. The French Prime Minister then crossed the Channel, where he told Chamberlain that he would rather fight than submit to German dictation.

By this time the Czechs had emphatically rejected the Godesberg demands, declaring that 'the nation of St Wenceslas, John Hus and Thomas Masaryk will not be a nation of slaves'.[28] As in May, the declaration of mobilisation had produced extraordinary scenes. 'Men rushed wildly through the blacked-out streets to get their equipment', recalled the *Daily Express* correspondent, Geoffrey Cox. 'Waiters in restaurants took off their aprons, late-night shop-keepers closed their premises, cars in the streets were halted by the police and asked to take men to their assembly points. Soon the streets were full of men, each with his small suitcase, hurrying towards barracks or the railway stations.'[29]

Chamberlain was in a corner. But he was not prepared to give up. When the Cabinet reconvened after the meeting with the French, at 11.30 on the evening of Sunday 25 September, he announced that he was sending Horace Wilson to Berlin to make a final appeal to Hitler for an international body to arrange the transfer of the territories. If Hitler refused this demand, he continued almost casually, Wilson was to tell him that France would certainly fight for Czechoslovakia and that Britain would certainly follow. 'It was … a complete reversal of what [he] himself had advised us to do the day before. And it was a reversal of the policy which a majority of the Cabinet had supported', noted the pleased but astonished Cooper.[30]

The next morning, the French Commander-in-Chief, General Maurice Gamelin, arrived in London and 'put heart into [the] PM' with his optimistic plans for the start of the war, involving a cautious offensive against the German West Wall – the so-called Siegfried Line – five days after the outbreak.[31] Indeed, the odds were in France's favour, with the Siegfried Line incomplete and only 'eight German divisions facing twenty-three French divisions'.[32]

Meanwhile, the Prime Minister's industrial expert was on his way to Berlin. There he found the city in a state of 'great excitement'.[33] Case Green, the plan for the invasion of Czechoslovakia, was five days away from its launch and anti-Czech propaganda had been brought to the boil. Hitler remained convinced that Britain would not intervene and was preparing a violent denunciation of the Czechs that evening at the Berlin Sportpalast. It was not a propitious moment for Wilson's appeal. Indeed, Hitler hardly had the patience to listen to Chamberlain's letter and at one point jumped out of his chair, saying that it was no use going on, and made for the door. When Wilson did not rise, he returned, only to have the worst fit of violence that Schmidt ever witnessed. The British were so taken aback that Ivone Kirkpatrick, who had accompanied Wilson, stopped taking notes. 'Are you getting everything down? It's frightfully important!' hissed the pen-pushing Wilson. The First Secretary of the British Embassy replied that he was unlikely to forget a word.[34] After Hitler had subsided, Wilson asked if he was prepared to meet with a Czech delegation. Hitler replied that he would only do so on the condition that they had first accepted the Godesberg terms and gave them until 2 p.m. on Wednesday – two days' time – to do so. This would have been the moment for Wilson's warning but the civil servant had been so cowed by Hitler's tirade that he decided not to deliver it. As Kirkpatrick reported to London, 'The epithets applied to Mr Chamberlain and to Sir Horace Wilson could not be repeated in a drawing-room.'[35]

That evening, in the Sportpalast, Hitler trumped his outburst in the Chancellery with what the American journalist William Shirer described as 'the worst paroxysm I had ever seen'.[36] Shouting and shrieking like a banshee, he hurled insults at Beneš and promised the German people that he would have the Sudetenland by 1 October. When Wilson returned to the Chancellery the next morning, he found Hitler no less determined. He was not interested in Chamberlain's overnight statement pledging that Britain would ensure the Czechs handed over the Sudeten territories, and said that if the Godesberg terms were not accepted by 2 p.m. the following day then he would 'smash the Czechs!'[37] With that, Wilson finally delivered his warning, though he was careful to do it 'more in sorrow than in anger'.[38] Hitler replied, blithely, that he was prepared for all eventualities. 'If France and England strike ... let them do so! It's a matter of complete indifference to me ... It is Tuesday today, and by next Monday we shall be at war.'[39]

*

At home the anti-appeasers were doing all they could to prevent the Government from giving in. In a letter to *The Times* on 26 September, Leo Amery declared:

> The issue has become very simple. Are we to surrender to ruthless brutality a free people whose cause we have espoused but are now to throw to the wolves to save our own skins, or are we still able to stand up to a bully? It is not Czechoslovakia but our own soul that is at stake.[40]

In order to deter this 'ruthless brutality', the anti-appeasers were united in their conviction that the Government must belatedly involve Russia in a defensive alliance. Five days earlier, on 21 September, Litvinov had announced, in a speech to the League of Nations' Assembly, the Soviet Union's unequivocal resolve to protect 'one of the oldest, most cultured, most hard-working of European peoples'.[41] Two days later, he told Rab Butler that if the British were serious about opposing a German invasion of Czechoslovakia then they should meet with the French and Russians to co-ordinate a plan of action and show Hitler they meant business.

The failure of the Government to seize on this proposal dismayed Churchill. On the afternoon of 26 September, while Wilson was being shouted at by Hitler, he issued a statement arguing that the only hope of preserving peace lay in telling the Germans that an invasion would lead to war with Britain, France and Russia. That evening, a group of anti-appeasers – including Robert Cecil, Bob Boothby, Archie Sinclair, Harold Macmillan, Amery and Nicolson – met at Churchill's flat in Morpeth Mansions. The Cabinet, they learnt, had been in a 'blue funk' but the younger members had prevailed and resistance appeared to be the new line. They then discussed the Wilson mission, resolving, as Nicolson recorded, that 'if Chamberlain rats again we shall form a united block against him'.[42] Churchill did not think that Chamberlain would 'rat', since he had been assured that the Foreign Office was about to issue a statement warning of French, British and now also Russian involvement if Czechoslovakia was attacked. Chamberlain, he reported, 'was very exhausted and a broken man'. Amery, an old friend, felt very sorry for him:

> The poor fellow, he has done his best valiantly, but he should never have attempted such a task with such slender qualifications for it, and though Germany's folly may cover the traces, history will no doubt say that he made a ghastly muddle of things after his first visit to Hitler, who seems, to some extent, to have deluded him.[43]

At 8 p.m. the Foreign Office released its communiqué, which, as Churchill had been told, warned: 'If, in spite of all efforts made by the British Prime Minister, a German attack is made upon Czechoslovakia, the immediate result must be that France will be bound to come to her assistance, and Great Britain and Russia will certainly stand by France.'[44] This appeared to be the firm stand which the anti-appeasers had been demanding, but any sense that the Prime Minister had abandoned appeasement was an illusion. Chamberlain was furious with Halifax for issuing the statement without consulting him and, even as the sands ran out, continued to do everything he could to bridge the gap between Hitler's demands and his colleagues' defiance.

*

Across the country, queues formed outside town and village halls. It was like the prelude to a department store sale but instead of bargains the British people were being offered gas masks. Mussolini had used gas against the Abyssinians and it seemed likely, as part of the 'knock-out blow' expected from the skies, that Hitler would do the same. Anti-aircraft batteries had been erected on Horse Guards Parade and Westminster Bridge, while a solitary fighter patrolled the clouds above the capital. On Tuesday 27 September, the first evacuees – 3,000 blind children – were taken to safety and the War Office appealed for 25,000 women to volunteer for the Auxiliary Territorial Service. The London Underground closed a number of lines, ostensibly for repairs but really so that stations could be used as air raid shelters, and all police leave was cancelled. At Sissinghurst, Harold Nicolson's wife, the writer Vita Sackville-West, oversaw the digging of a trench in the orchard. This was replicated on a more industrial scale in London, where volunteers transformed the Royal Parks into vast excavation sites. On the financial markets, the pound fell sharply against the dollar but register offices boomed as hundreds of couples rushed to get married.

If there was no jingoistic spirit in the country at large, the country's leaders were actively defeatist. At an extended meeting of the Inner Cabinet on the afternoon of 27 September, the Chiefs of Staff repeated their gloomy prognosis, followed by a depressing account of Czech military morale from the British Military Attaché in Berlin, Colonel Mason-MacFarlane. This annoyed Cadogan, as it was both misleading and based on only the most circumstantial knowledge. After the Godesberg summit, Mason-Mac had been charged with delivering Hitler's memorandum to the Czechs. Accordingly, he drove through the night to the frontier and then walked six miles, climbing over barbed wire and in constant danger of being shot, before he found a Czech border post. It was a courageous mission but it was the sum total of research which now allowed him to tell the Prime Minister that the Czech soldiers were 'scared stiff'.[45] Indeed, in his report earlier in the month, the Military Attaché in Prague, Lieutenant-Colonel Humphrey Stronge, had concluded:

> Everything points to the fact that they [the Czechs] have staying power … The mere fact that they succeeded during those three centuries in maintaining their cultural, linguistic and ethnographical individuality in the face of the assimilating forces brought to bear on them indicates that they possess a certain stubborn quality which cannot be easily suppressed.[46]

As the meeting was breaking up, Chamberlain asked the First Sea Lord, Admiral Sir Roger Backhouse, if he was satisfied that all necessary measures had been taken. Backhouse said he would like to take further steps. Was the Prime Minister prepared to mobilise?

Chamberlain hesitated, then nodded. The First Sea Lord gathered up his papers and rushed back to the Admiralty to give the order. A little while later, Wilson popped his head round the Cabinet door. 'Do you realise that we have not told Duff the Fleet is to be mobilised?'[47]

Throughout the afternoon, a variety of telegrams were brought to the Prime Minister. Roosevelt wrote urging all players not to give up on negotiations, while from Prague Chamberlain learnt that Beneš had agreed to surrender the province of Těšín to the Poles in return for their neutrality. From Berlin, Henderson informed him that the die was cast. German military preparations were complete, the Ambassador stated, and if Czech delegates did not arrive in Berlin by 2 p.m. the following day, Wednesday 28 September, then Hitler would give the order to invade. The British passed this information on to Prague, adding that 'His Majesty's Government cannot take responsibility of advising you what you should do'.[48] The Government had not, however, entirely given up. With Chamberlain's blessing, Halifax and Cadogan had been working on a plan whereby German troops would be allowed to occupy the Asch-Eger territories by 1 October, followed, two days later, by a meeting of German and Czech plenipotentiaries to arrange the evacuation of Czech troops from the remaining areas.

Yet, while Halifax was willing to sell the Czechs in an orderly way, he was not prepared to allow Hitler to march in without any regard for legal or diplomatic due process. Having been ejected from the Cabinet Room at 7.30 p.m. (still Tuesday 27 September) so that electricians could prepare for the Prime Minister to broadcast to the nation at 8 p.m., Chamberlain, Halifax and Cadogan repaired to Wilson's adjoining room. There, Wilson showed the Foreign Secretary a telegram he had drafted urging the Czechs to accept Hitler's demands. It was a 'complete capitulation', noted the aghast Cadogan and both he and Halifax spoke up against it. Chamberlain accepted their reproof without a fight. 'I'm wobbling about all over the place', he mumbled, apologetically.[49] He was, indeed, completely exhausted. By his own admission he had lost 'all sense of time' and only his wife knew the angst he suffered during 'those agonising hours when hope seemed almost extinguished'.[50]

Unfortunately, both his exhaustion and despair were transmitted in his broadcast. Speaking haltingly, with tragedy permeating every sentence, Chamberlain expressed his dream-like bewilderment that 'we should be digging trenches and trying on gas masks here because of a quarrel in a faraway country between people of whom we know nothing'. He spoke of his visits to Germany and, as if trying to persuade his Cabinet colleagues, repeated Hitler's promise that this was his last territorial demand. Then, despite her ostensible pledge to support Czechoslovakia, he went on to say that Britain could not possibly fight purely in defence of Czech sovereignty:

> However much we may sympathise with a small nation confronted by a big and powerful neighbour, we cannot in all circumstances undertake to involve the whole British Empire in war simply on her account. If we have to fight it must be on larger issues than that. I am myself a man of peace to the depths of my soul. Armed conflict between nations is a nightmare to me; but if I were convinced that any nation had made up its mind to dominate the world by fear of its force, I should feel that it must be resisted … war is a fearful thing, and we must be very clear, before we embark on it, that it is really the great issues that are at stake, and that the call to risk everything in their defence, when all the consequences are weighed, is irresistible.[51]

To say that this was not the St Crispin's Day speech would be a massive understatement. Duff Cooper, furious that Chamberlain had failed to mention the mobilisation of the Fleet, thought it 'a most depressing utterance', while Amery believed it would only encourage the Germans. 'If ever there was an essential civilian, a citizen accustomed to deal with fellow citizens on [a] City Council or in Cabinet, and a man quite incapable of thinking in terms of force, or strategy or diplomacy, it is Neville', the former Colonial Secretary noted in his diary.*[52] Indeed, it was a considerable dereliction of Prime Ministerial duty. Britain was on the cusp of war and its democratic leader had failed to give the nation a single positive reason why they should fight.

---

* Not everyone shared this view. Alec Hardinge, the King's Private Secretary, rang up Downing Street to tell Chamberlain that His Majesty thought his broadcast 'marvellous, exactly what was wanted', while Roosevelt noticed tears in the eyes of certain members of his Cabinet who had gathered to listen to it.

On the contrary, he had provided a multitude of reasons why they should not, including the assertion that Czechoslovakia was both too distant and too alien to be worth a drop of British blood. Coming from the son of one of the greatest Victorian imperialists and from a man who currently presided over British political and military interests stretching from the Far East to the Caribbean and from South Africa to India, this was anomalous to say the least.[53]

When the Cabinet met at 9.30 on the evening of 27 September, Chamberlain continued in the same sepulchral vein, repeating the many military difficulties as well as the opposition of the Dominions to war. Wilson then said that the only chance of avoiding a conflagration was to send a telegram to Prague insisting that the Czech Government withdraw its troops and allow the Germans to occupy the Sudeten territories forthwith. This produced a resignation threat from Cooper, who also rounded on Chamberlain for his defeatist broadcast. Halifax said that he was against capitulation but did raise his own 'timetable' for the German occupation. When this too met with angry opposition, Chamberlain distanced himself from the scheme and said, resignedly, that if this was the will of the Cabinet then he would let it be. On the way out, Cooper enquired casually if the Prime Minister thought the mobilisation of the fleet need be kept secret. Chamberlain replied that he supposed not, at which Cooper beetled back to the Admiralty where he told the press section to give it to all the morning papers.[54] The idea was to try, even at this late stage, to deter Hitler with a show of strength. Little did the British Ministers know that the German leader was, of his own accord, having doubts.

*

Following his meeting with Horace Wilson, on the morning of 27 September 1938, Hitler had given the order for the seven divisions which comprised the initial invasion force to move to their 'jumping-off points' near the Czech frontier. He then stood at the balcony of the Reich Chancellery, overlooking Wilhelmstrasse, as a mechanised division of the Wehrmacht rumbled past on its way to the front. The parade was a propaganda exercise, intended to impress foreign diplomats and journalists, but it ended up having quite the reverse effect. Nevile Henderson, who was watching from a window in the British Embassy, noted that 'not a single individual in the street applauded its passage'. 'The picture which it represented was almost that of a hostile army passing through a conquered city.'[55] William Shirer confirmed this, describing the scene as 'the most striking demonstration against war I've ever seen'.[56] Hitler was shaken. Could he wage war with such little enthusiasm from the German people? He began to back off and that evening replied to a telegram from Chamberlain with what appeared to be a modest attempt at conciliation. The German troops, Hitler said, would not move beyond the territories which the Czechs had already agreed to cede and the plebiscite would be a free vote.

The next morning, Wednesday 28 September, Annie Chamberlain came down to breakfast to find her husband busily working on what he would later describe as 'the last desperate snatch at the last tuft of grass on the very verge of the precipice'.[57] Encouraged by Hitler's telegram, he now wrote to the Führer saying that he felt 'certain that you can get all essentials without war and without delay' and offered to fly to Berlin to 'discuss arrangements for transfer with you and representatives of Czech Government, together with representatives of France and Italy if you desire'.[58] At the same time, he appealed to Mussolini to act as intermediary, initiating a four-power conference to settle the dispute. In both Berlin and Rome, diplomats were doing everything they could to save the branch from the fire. To his great alarm, Henderson could not seem to get an appointment with Hitler. He called Göring – still opposed to war at this stage – and explained the problem. 'You need not say a word more', replied the recently promoted Field Marshal. 'I am going immediately to see the Führer.'[59]

Back in London, no one outside the Inner Cabinet and the Foreign Office knew about this last desperate whirl of diplomatic activity and a portentous air hung over the capital. Walking down Whitehall, Harold Nicolson came across a large crowd, 'silent and anxious'. Some were laying fresh flowers at the base of the Cenotaph, the rest 'stare at us with dumb, inquisitive eyes'.[60] Inside the Palace of Westminster, the Commons chamber was filled to bursting. In the peers' gallery sat Lord Baldwin, the Archbishop of Canterbury, the Duke of Kent and even Queen Mary. There were prayers, normally a formality but on this occasion perhaps something more. Then the Prime Minister entered to tumultuous applause. Sadly, Chamberlain, who had been working on his speech until two in the morning, did not match the vitality of his reception. He was tired and did not attempt to disguise his anguish at having to acknowledge the spectre of war. Still, conflict appeared almost inevitable and Chamberlain's few thrusts at Hitler found a warm reception among the anti-appeasers. 'How are your friends the Huns now?' Anthony Crossley gleefully enquired of Chips Channon, who was sitting next to him.[61]

Chamberlain had been speaking for less than an hour when, 500 yards away in the Foreign Office, the telephone rang. It was Henderson, who reported breathlessly that Hitler had invited Mussolini, Daladier and Chamberlain to a conference in Munich the following day. Cadogan quickly scrawled the message down and ran over to the Commons, where he fished Halifax out of the gallery and took him down to behind the Speaker's chair. There they found Wilson, who frantically beckoned to the Prime Minister's Parliamentary Private Secretary, Alec Dunglass (Alec Douglas-Home). 'What on earth has happened? Has he marched in?' the young man asked, viewing their excited faces.[62] Enlightened, he clambered back to his seat behind Chamberlain, and passed the note to John Simon, who, after waiting a few minutes, tugged on the Prime Minister's coat tails. Chamberlain paused as he digested the news. Then, as the lines of anxiety vanished from his face, he cleared his throat and with all the flair of a practised showman announced that he had something further to tell the House:

> I have now been informed by Herr Hitler that he invites me to meet him at Munich tomorrow morning. He has also invited Signor Mussolini and Monsieur Daladier. Signor Mussolini has accepted and I have no doubt Monsieur Daladier will also accept. I need not say what my answer will be.[63]

The Chamber exploded with cheers. When Chamberlain sat down the Conservative benches rose, almost to a man, followed, rather more sheepishly, by the Opposition. Churchill, Eden, Amery and Nicolson were among the few who remained seated and were barracked by their colleagues. 'Stand up, you brute', hissed Walter Liddall, the Conservative MP for Lincoln, at Nicolson.[64] Channon, so lately discomforted, felt 'sick with enthusiasm' and longed to embrace Chamberlain, who was being clapped on the back and shaken by the hand by all and sundry.[65] Finally, as the mêlée began to disperse, Churchill rose and approached the Prime Minister. He shook Chamberlain's hand and wished him 'God speed'.[66]

XVII

A Piece of Paper

> Announced this afternoon that Neville had signed a pact with Hitler – the man is crazy and hypnotized by a loony. Oh dear.
>
> Harry Crookshank MP, 30 September 1938[1]

The drive to Heston was becoming increasingly familiar but the send-off which Chamberlain received early on the morning of 29 September 1938 exceeded those of even his two previous departures. At Sir John Simon's suggestion the entire Cabinet had turned out as a surprise – all 'except that absurd dissenting nanny-goat Eddie Winterton', noted Chips Channon – as had the Australian, Canadian, Irish and South African High Commissioners, the Italian Ambassador, the German Chargé d'Affaires, several members of Parliament and Lord Brocket.[2] The gathering cheered and Chamberlain beamed as he made his way to the aeroplane, shaking hands as he went. Before boarding he turned to the phalanx of newsreel cameras to deliver a carefully prepared sound-bite:

> When I was a little boy I used to repeat: 'If at first you don't succeed, try, try, try again.' That is what I am doing. When I come back I hope I may be able to say, as Hotspur says in *Henry IV*, 'Out of this nettle, danger, we pluck this flower, safety.'[3]

Some wags in the Foreign Office soon satirised this homily as 'If at first you can't concede, fly, fly, fly again.'[4] But such cynicism was alien to most people. Having been ecstatically cheered as he left the Commons the previous afternoon, Chamberlain had set expectations, as well as the front pages, for his third visit to Germany when he called out to reporters waiting for him in Downing Street, 'It's all right this time.'[5] Now the newsreel commentary adjured Britons to listen to the Prime Minister's words and 'take heart', while the *Daily Sketch* celebrated a man whose 'firmness of spirit and gentleness of heart' had stood between two armies and 'raised humanity to a new level'.[6]

Chamberlain himself was not so certain. Despite the smiles and the Shakespeare, he described the forthcoming conference to Alec Dunglass – who, along with Horace Wilson, William Strang, Frank Ashton-Gwatkin, William Malkin (the Foreign Office legal adviser) and Oscar Cleverly (Chamberlain's personal secretary), was accompanying him to Munich* – as 'a last throw' of the dice, although he 'could not see how it could pay Hitler to push things to the point of war'.[7] The previous afternoon, Annie Chamberlain had made a rare political intervention: 'I want you to come back from Germany with peace with honour', she instructed her husband, adding, 'You must speak from the window like Dizzy [Disraeli] did.' But Chamberlain was having none of it. 'I'll do nothing of the sort', he replied tersely. 'I am not the least like Dizzy.'†[8]

It may have been that Chamberlain was already contemplating the extreme difficulty of justifying a conference on the fate of Czechoslovakia from which the Czechs themselves were excluded. Both Beneš and Masaryk had protested at this gross injustice without avail. Hitler would not tolerate the participation of either the Czechs or the Russians, Chamberlain had explained, though Beneš should rest assured that he, Chamberlain, would 'have the interests of Czechoslovakia fully in mind' as he strove for an orderly and equitable cession of territory.[9] Understandably, the overwrought Masaryk was not conciliated. 'If you have sacrificed my nation to preserve the peace

---

* In Munich they were joined by Sir Nevile Henderson, Ivone Kirkpatrick and Geoffrey Harrison from the British Embassy.

† When the British Prime Minister Benjamin Disraeli returned from the Berlin Congress in July 1878, which led to a new territorial settlement in the Balkans following the Russo-Turkish War, he told the jubilant crowd waiting in Downing Street, 'Lord Salisbury and I have brought you back peace – but a peace with honour I hope.'

of the world, I will be the first to applaud you', he told the Prime Minister and Lord Halifax on the evening of 28 September. 'But if not, gentlemen, God help your souls.'*[10]

Whatever Chamberlain's inner anxieties, he and the rest of the British party were heartened by the rapturous reception which awaited them at Munich. Touching down shortly before noon, they descended their aircraft to a cacophony of '*Heils*', followed by a rather more *piano* rendition of 'God Save the King'. They were then driven in open-top cars along a route every inch of which was lined with cheering well-wishers. Chamberlain was clearly pleased and waved his hat at the avenues of raised arms. His cheerfulness was in marked contrast to Daladier, who, forty-five minutes earlier, had arrived looking 'gloomy and preoccupied', his head 'buried deep between his shoulders, his brow deeply furrowed with wrinkles'.[11]

The conference was to take place at the Führerbau, Hitler's Munich headquarters on the south-eastern corner of the nineteenth-century Königplatz. A large plain building of archetypal Nazi-Neoclassical design, its two Doric porticos had been draped with the flags of the four nations.† Red carpet had been placed up the steps, guiding the delegates into a capacious hall of garish marble. François-Poncet thought the interior resembled 'some mammoth modern hotel'.[12] There was a large central staircase, now garlanded with flowers, at the top of which ran a pillared gallery. The meeting itself was to be held in Hitler's private study, a not particularly big room, with a round table surrounded by low armchairs. At one end was a desk and at the other a grand fireplace. Above the mantelpiece hung a portrait of Bismarck – the man who had once declared that 'the master of Bohemia is the master of Europe'.[13]

Despite all the grandeur and flummery, the conference was, as William Strang recalled, 'a hugger-mugger affair'.[14] German efficiency had completely broken down and there were neither pens, pencils nor paper available for the leaders or their officials to use.

* Beneš also sent a telegram to Daladier asking him 'not to forget the twenty years of political collaboration I have had with France'.

† The Führerbau is one of the few pieces of Nazi architecture to survive and is now Munich's University of Music and Performing Arts. The small central room on the first floor overlooking the Arcisstrasse is the room where the conference was held.

For the British civil servants this unbusiness-like way of doing things was shocking. Wilson complained that he was obliged to take notes 'on odd pieces of paper' he happened to have in his pocket, while Ivone Kirkpatrick remembered that the telephone system was so bad that the quickest method of communicating with the outside world was to send a car with a message to the British hotel.[15] Nor was the atmosphere conducive to a friendly and peaceful discussion. As Strang recorded, the Führerbau was crawling with SS officers clicking their heels and asking 'if we required anything', while Dunglass recalled being shepherded about 'as if one was under arrest'.[16]

More shocking than the lack of stationery was that neither the British nor the French had made any effort to co-ordinate or even discuss the line which they intended to take before the conference. Arriving at his hotel shortly before midday, Daladier revealed his strategy to the French delegation in terms which accurately described French foreign policy since the reoccupation of the Rhineland: 'Everything depends on the English ... we can do nothing but follow them.'[17] Yet the British did not know this. As Wilson recorded, 'we were uncertain what line Daladier would take' and it was most unfortunate that the French Prime Minister was 'too far away' from Chamberlain during the opening session to allow them to confer.[18]

By contrast, the Germans had worked out a plan for the cession of the Sudetenland which they had shared with the Italians and even persuaded Mussolini to present as his own. That morning, Thursday 29 September, Hitler had met Mussolini's train at Kufstein, on the former Austrian border. As the two dictators sped towards Munich in Hitler's special train the Führer explained his plans. 'He intends to liquidate Czechoslovakia as it is now', recorded Count Galeazzo Ciano in his diary:

> Because she immobilises forty of his divisions and ties his hands *vis-à-vis* France. When Czechoslovakia has been, as she must be, deflated, ten divisions will be enough to immobilise her. The Duce listens with concentration. The programme is now fixed: either the conference is successful in a short time or the solution will take place by force of arms. 'Besides,' adds the Führer, 'the time will come when we shall have to fight side by side against France and England. All the better

that it should happen while the Duce and I are at the head of our countries, and still young and full of vigour.'[19]

*

The statesmen met each other in a salon on the first floor of the Führerbau shortly after 12.30 p.m. The British were the first to arrive, followed (appropriately) by the French. Neither party, in their dark suits and striped ties, cut much of a dash. François-Poncet described Chamberlain as 'grizzled, bowed, with bushy eyebrows and prominent teeth, his face blotchy, his hands reddened by rheumatism', while Daladier, with his wide pinstripes and comb-over, looked like a stock-broker who had fallen on hard times. The juxtaposition with the resplendent vulgarity of the totalitarians was stark. Göring, who had accompanied Daladier from his hotel, and who was to change his costume three times during the conference, began the day in a tight-fitting dark uniform, covered in decorations and braid. Mussolini, 'laced into his uniform, the features of a Caesar, patronizing, completely at ease as though in his own house', strutted about with his chin in the air.[20] Finally, Hitler, in his simpler uniform of brown jacket and black trousers, the swastika on his arm and iron cross on his chest, made his entrance.

Noticing Hitler's scowl, Chamberlain feared that the 'storm signals' were already up and was relieved when he received the double handshake which the Führer reserved 'for specially friendly demonstrations'.[21] In fact, he need not have worried. Although Hitler was, indeed, in a black temper and made little attempt to disguise his irritation at this 'mini League of Nations' he found himself hosting, the fundamental decision in favour of peace had already been made. Not only had the British and French capitulated to the substance of the German demands on 18 September, they had even coerced the Czechs into accepting them. Now Hitler had been persuaded, against his own preference for a localised war, to accept their capitulation. In this sense, the Munich Conference was just a ceremony – a face-saving exercise for all concerned.

It began with the British and French accepting Mussolini's (in fact Hitler's) demands as the 'basis for discussion'. These stipulated that the occupation of the Sudetenland would begin on 1 October, in two days' time (Clause 1), and be completed by 10 October (Clause 2). Chamberlain immediately agreed to Clause 1 but expressed concern about accepting Clause 2 without the agreement of the Czechs. At this Hitler exploded. If the British and French were not prepared to coerce Czechoslovakia they had better let him resume his way, he shouted, punching his hand into his fist.[22] Chamberlain backed down. He had officially requested a Czech representative but neither he nor Daladier were prepared to push it. On the contrary, the democratic leaders said that they fully appreciated the German insistence on a speedy occupation and Hitler calmed down.

After an adjournment for a late lunch, during which Hitler and Mussolini ate together and the British and French separately, the conference resumed at 4.30 p.m. By this stage the Italian–German demands had been translated into the various languages and the leaders now went through them point by point. Either keen to salvage something for the Czechs or due to British reverence for property rights, Chamberlain kept raising the issue of compensation for the loss of Czech property in the Sudetenland and even asked if livestock might be moved from the zones of occupation. Once again Hitler lost his temper. 'Our time is too valuable to be wasted on such trivialities', he yelled, and the matter was dropped.[23]

The only leader who seemed to be enjoying himself was Mussolini. Although occasionally bored by the 'vaguely parliamentary atmosphere', he relished the role of power-broker and, unlike Hitler, had the linguistic skills to be able to follow the proceedings in real time.[24] François-Poncet, who along with the other Ambassadors had been allowed into the second session, was fascinated to observe the relationship between the two dictators:

> Mussolini was deeply ensconced in his armchair. His extraordinary mobile features were never at rest for a moment; his mouth would part for a wide smile or contract in a pout; his brows rose in surprise or were knit threateningly; his eyes, generally curious and amused in expression, would suddenly dart lightning.
>
> Standing at his side, Hitler gazed intently upon him, subject to his charm and as though fascinated and hypnotized. Did the Duce laugh, the Führer laughed too; did Mussolini scowl, so scowled Hitler. Here

> was a study in mimicry. It was to leave me with the lasting and erroneous impression that Mussolini exercised a firmly established ascendancy over the Führer. At any rate that day he did.[25]

Eventually, late in the evening of 29 September, an agreement was reached and the conference, already disjointed, broke into separate conversations. According to Ciano, Daladier was not only friendly but confessional. 'He says that what is happening today is due solely to the pig-headedness of Beneš' and blames 'warmongers' in France for trying to push the country into an 'absurd and indeed impossible war'.[26] Yet almost everyone else commented on the French Premier's obvious depression. He left the Führer's presence at his earliest chance and was observed, collapsed on a sofa, calling for Munich beer to restore himself.

Chamberlain, by contrast, was using the lull for further diplomacy. He discussed the Spanish situation with Mussolini and then suggested a tête-à-tête with Hitler. According to Chamberlain's account, the Führer 'jumped at the idea' and asked the Prime Minister to visit him next morning at his private flat. Also making the most of the hiatus was Göring. Having embarrassed Daladier by expressing his wish to visit Paris, the Field Marshal – now wearing a white uniform – stationed himself in front of the fire, where, apart from blocking most of the heat, he told loud stories and cracked jokes. Hitler, meanwhile, sat glowering on the sofa.

Finally, just before 2 a.m. on 30 September 1938, the Munich Agreement was signed: a historic moment rendered farcical when Hitler dipped his pen in the ornate inkwell only to discover that it did not contain any ink.[27] For Göring and Mussolini, the conference's chief orchestrators, it was a moment of triumph. The corpulent Field Marshal clapped his hands together and in the newsreel footage the Duce can be seen making jokes with his Nazi hosts. Chamberlain was evidently satisfied. Observing the Prime Minister on his return to his hotel, William Shirer judged him 'particularly pleased with himself' – although he revealed his own thoughts when he likened the Prime Minister to one of those 'black vultures I've seen over the Parsi dead in Bombay'.[28] For the French it was a painful humiliation. Having continually renewed her pledge to defend Czechoslovakia, France was now responsible – along with Britain, Italy and Germany – for guaranteeing that she surrender one-fifth of her territory and 800,000 Czechs. 'See how France treats the only allies who remained faithful to her' was François-Poncet's sarcastic lament as he collated the various documents.[29] Mussolini tried to cheer the French Premier by telling him that he would be applauded on his return to France, but Daladier did not seem to believe him. He declined the British suggestion to personally take the Agreement to Prague for the Czechs to approve and insisted that the British Prime Minister should join him in breaking the news to the Czech 'observers'.

These unfortunate gentlemen – Hubert Masařík, Private Secretary to the Czech Foreign Minister, and Vojtěch Mastný, the Czech Minister to Berlin – had landed earlier in the afternoon at Munich's Oberwiesenfeld airport, where they had been met by the Gestapo and generally treated like police suspects.[30] Deposited at the Regina Hotel (where the British were also staying), they were kept under police guard and forbidden to communicate with Prague or even to leave their rooms. At around 10 p.m., Horace Wilson and Frank Ashton-Gwatkin turned up with a map showing the areas which had been designated for immediate occupation. The Czechs protested but the British were blunt: 'If you do not accept you will have to settle your affairs alone with Germany', explained Ashton-Gwatkin. 'Perhaps the French will say this to you more kindly, but believe me they share our wish … they are disinteresting themselves.'[31]

Now, at 2.15 a.m., the Czech diplomats were invited into Chamberlain's suite, where they found the senior members of the British delegation, as well as Alexis Léger, General Secretary of the Quai d'Orsay, François-Poncet and Daladier. It was an awkward meeting. The Czechs were presented with a copy of the Agreement but were told that they were not expected to make a declaration since the matter was considered to have been settled. Daladier was so morose that he refused to answer the questions that were put to him and left it to Léger to provide the explanations and excuses. Chamberlain, exhausted, yawned repeatedly, while Masařík tried to clarify various points. Mastný broke down in tears. When it was over, the French were caught by the gang of reporters waiting in the hotel lobby. '*Monsieur le Président*, are you satisfied with the agreement?' asked one. The Bull of Vaucluse turned slowly but the words failed to come. Tired and defeated, 'he stumbled out the door in silence'.[32]

The work for the British delegation, however, was not yet over. After only a few hours' sleep, William Strang was woken by a message from the Prime Minister explaining that he had arranged to see Hitler before they left and requesting a short statement on the future of Anglo-German relations which the two leaders could sign. Hauling himself out of bed, Strang managed to compose three short paragraphs – the second of which Chamberlain rewrote – over breakfast. The Prime Minister and Dunglass then drove to Hitler's pied-à-terre on Prinzregentenplatz.

Recounting the subsequent meeting to his sister Hilda, Chamberlain described the conversation as 'very friendly and pleasant'.[33] The interpreter Paul Schmidt, on the other hand, thought Hitler 'moody' and absent-minded.[34] Certainly, it was the Prime Minister who led the Führer through a variety of topics, including Spain, economic relations in south-eastern Europe and aerial disarmament. At the end, he produced the joint statement from his pocket, the crucial passage of which was the declaration that the two leaders regarded the Munich Agreement 'as symbolic of the desire of our two peoples never to go to war with one another again'.[35] According to Chamberlain, Hitler readily agreed to sign it, having exclaimed *'Ja! Ja!'* at several points during the translation.[36] Schmidt's recollection, by contrast, was that Hitler 'agreed to the wording with a certain reluctance'. Whether this was the case or not, Schmidt's second judgement, that Hitler 'appended his signature only to please Chamberlain', was undoubtedly correct.[37] 'The Führer did not think he could refuse', the German intermediary Prince Philip of Hesse explained to Ciano a few days later, while Hitler himself sought to reassure the disgruntled Ribbentrop that afternoon: 'Oh, don't take it all so seriously … That piece of paper is of no significance whatsoever.'[38]

*

While the statesmen deliberated in Bavaria, the people of Britain waited nervously. The war preparations had not been relaxed and the trains from London were packed with fresh evacuees. National Service recruiting stations reported a steady stream of volunteers, and workmen at Canterbury Cathedral began the delicate task of removing the stained glass from the south-east transept. That evening, Thursday

29 September 1938, the Other Club (founded by Churchill and F. E. Smith, later Lord Birkenhead, in 1911) met in the Savoy's Pinafore Room. Churchill was in a fiery temper. He had spent the afternoon trying to gather signatures for a telegram urging Chamberlain not to abandon the Czechs but neither Anthony Eden nor Clement Attlee was prepared to sign. Now, he turned on the two Cabinet Ministers, Duff Cooper and Walter Elliot, who were present. How could 'honourable men with wide experience and fine records in the Great War condone a policy so cowardly?' he demanded. 'It was sordid, squalid, sub-human, and suicidal.' Cooper, who was already deeply depressed, defended himself as best he could. He insulted Professor Lindemann and then, along with Bob Boothby, the pro-appeasement Editor of the *Observer*, J. L. Garvin. Offended, Garvin stormed out of the dining room and refused to return to the club for six years. 'Then everybody insulted everybody else and Winston ended by saying that at the next General Election he would speak on every socialist platform in the country against the Government', recorded Cooper in his diary.[39] At around 1 a.m. someone dashed out to the Strand to buy a first edition of the morning newspapers, already carrying the broad outline of the agreement reached at Munich. Cooper's face coloured as he studied the terms. 'I can't stomach this', he told Boothby. 'I shall resign.'[40] When the dinner finally broke up, Churchill left with the young Conservative MP Richard Law. Outside, they paused in front of a restaurant filled with cheerful patrons. 'Those poor people!' remarked Churchill. 'They little know what they will have to face.'[41]

*

Chamberlain's plane landed shortly after 5.30 p.m. on 30 September 1938.* There had just been a cloudburst but there was no dampening the enthusiasm of the crowds which had gathered not merely at Heston but all along the Great West Road. As the plane door opened and Chamberlain appeared, there was a huge cheer, followed by three cheers, then three more and three more. The jubilation and the relief

---

* He would have arrived sooner but, after his conversation with Hitler, Chamberlain had been taken to see some of Munich's sights, including the Sternecker Bräu – the beer hall in which the Nazi Party had been founded.

had been captured by the *Daily Express*'s headline that morning, which simply read, in huge letters: 'PEACE'.[42] Now the Prime Minister prepared to reveal to the country and the world the extent of the peace he had brought them. In front of a multitude of radio microphones and newsreel cameras, he stated 'that the settlement of the Czechoslovakian problem ... is, in my view, only the prelude to a larger settlement in which all Europe may find peace'. Then, raising the slender sheet of paper so that it flapped in the wind, he read the declaration which bore the signature of the German Chancellor, Herr Hitler, 'as well as mine'.

Chamberlain then drove to Buckingham Palace, where the King invited him and Mrs Chamberlain to join the royal couple on the balcony to acknowledge the applause of a vast crowd. It was a flagrantly unconstitutional act but there was no doubting its popularity. 'Rule Britannia' and 'For He's a Jolly Good Fellow' rang out down the Mall, while the four figures smiled and waved. The King gestured to Chamberlain to step forward and the Prime Minister basked in the adulation, alone, for a full two minutes. The BBC's Tommy Woodroffe tried to convey the excitement to his listeners as the Prime Minister's car then attempted to make its way from the Palace to Downing Street:

> Here he comes, preceded by two policemen, mounted policemen, and the car can hardly turn the corner because the press of people have come out and stopped it for the time being. People here are getting wildly excited and it's one of the most impressive sights I've ever seen: a completely unorganised, spontaneous welcome to a man who has done his best for his country. It's the most wonderful spontaneous effort: nobody has told them to come here, nobody was asked to come here. But somehow people of every walk of life have drifted here to certify their presence.[43]

'You might think that we've won a major victory, instead of just betraying a minor country', commented Orme Sargent, watching from a balcony in the Foreign Office.[44]

Having at last made it inside 10 Downing Street, Dunglass heard someone repeat Annie Chamberlain's suggestion that the Prime Minister should go to the window and reprise Disraeli's famous boast about 'peace with honour'. Once again Chamberlain demurred but then, while ascending the stairs, changed his mind. At 7.27 p.m., the first-floor window opened and the Prime Minister appeared to deliver the words which were to haunt him and his reputation for ever more:

> My good friends, this is the second time in our history that there has come back from Germany to Downing Street peace with honour. I believe it is peace for our time. We thank you from the bottom of our hearts ... Now I recommend you go home and sleep quietly in your beds.[45]

*

The contrast with the scenes taking place in Prague was tragic. At 6.20 on the morning of 30 September, Kamil Krofta, the Czech Foreign Minister, was roused from his bed by the German Chargé d'Affaires to be told that the occupation of his country was to begin at midnight. Beneš was in his bath when he learnt the news. 'It's a betrayal which will be its own punishment', he predicted. 'They [the Western democracies] think that they will save themselves from war and revolution at our expense. They are wrong.' For a flicker, the President contemplated resistance and sent to Moscow for advice. By noon, however, the Government had succumbed. At the Council for the Defence of the Republic, Beneš declared, with tears in his eyes, that history had 'no parallel for dealing with a sovereign state in such a manner ... We are deserted and betrayed.' The leader of the Communist Party, Klement Gottwald, wanted to fight and chastened his colleagues by reminding them that even the 'barefooted Ethiopians' had found the courage to resist the Italians. But the comparison, Beneš insisted, was not correct. 'We were not defeated by Hitler', he explained, 'but by our friends.'[46]

Later that afternoon, the Prime Minister, General Jan Syrový, broadcast to the nation. Loudspeakers had been erected in Wenceslas Square and the crowds listened in teary silence as Syrový declared the blunt truth that the only choice they had been given was between capitulation and 'sacrificing the lives of our wives and children'.[47] As the Czech national anthem died away a wave of anger swept through the crowd, which surged towards the Hradčany Castle shouting 'No, no, no!', 'Down with Beneš!', 'Let Czechoslovakia live!' and 'Long live Czechoslovakia!'[48]

*

This was the reception Daladier had feared. Yet the Parisians welcomed their Prime Minister as if he were a conquering hero. Bonnet, who had not even listened to François-Poncet's description of the Munich terms – 'Peace is assured,' he interrupted, 'that is the main thing' – had ensured that the route along which Daladier's car would pass from Le Bourget airport was broadcast on the radio and the roads were consequently filled with cheering crowds, chanting *'Vive Daladier!'* and *'Vive la paix!'*[49] The Prime Minister thought this elation misguided, yet four days later he defended the Agreement in the Chamber of Deputies, declaring that he regretted 'nothing' and calling it 'a moral victory of peace'.[50] After just six hours of debate, the deputies, with the exception of the Communists and two right-wingers, concurred and when the vote was taken for the adjournment of the session the Government secured a majority of 535 to 75.

In London, the four-day parliamentary debate on the Munich Agreement began with Duff Cooper's resignation statement. 'The Prime Minister has believed in addressing Herr Hitler through the language of sweet reasonableness', he declared from the 'St Helena' bench below the gangway. 'I have believed that he was more open to the language of the mailed fist.'[51] Later he told friends that it was 'peace with honour' that he could not stomach. If Chamberlain had 'come back from Munich saying "peace with terrible, unmitigated, unparalleled dishonour", perhaps I would have stayed. But peace with *honour*!'[52] Other Ministers shared this view but not to the extent that they were prepared to follow Cooper's lead. Harry Crookshank, who thought Chamberlain 'crazy and hypnotized by a loony', sent in his resignation letter but then allowed himself to be talked round. The rest – Stanley, De La Warr, Elliot, Winterton and Bernays – never got as far as letter writing.

The debate which followed Cooper's statement was one of the most passionate and polarising in modern parliamentary history. Opening the bowling for the Opposition, Clement Attlee attacked what he described as 'a victory for brute force', in which a 'gallant, civilised and democratic people' had been betrayed 'to a ruthless despotism'.[53] He was followed by the Liberal leader, Archie Sinclair, who accused Chamberlain of 'wilting' before Nazi threats and throwing 'justice and respect for treaties … to the winds'.[54] At the other end of the spectrum, Victor Raikes, a right-wing, isolationist Tory MP, lavished praise on the Agreement, prophesying that the Prime Minister would 'go down to history as the greatest European statesmen of this or any other time'.[55]

Chamberlain had spoken at the start of the debate and received tributes of gratitude from all corners of the House. Yet it was the criticism from his own side which stood out. Were they really to believe, asked Richard Law, previously a fairly loyal supporter of the Government and son of a Prime Minister, 'that those men who have risen to power through violence and treachery, who have maintained themselves in power by violence and treachery, who have achieved their greatest triumph by violence and treachery, have suddenly been convinced by the magnetic eye of the Prime Minister … that violence and treachery do not pay'?[56] It was true, declared Lord Cranborne, that peace had been temporarily saved but only by 'throwing to the wolves a little country whose courage and dignity in the face of almost intolerable provocation has been a revelation and an inspiration to us all'.[57] For Leo Amery, Munich was simply 'the greatest – and the cheapest – victory ever won by aggressive militarism'.[58]

By the time Churchill spoke on the third day, the House was increasingly fractious. 'We have sustained a total and unmitigated defeat', he declared. 'Nonsense', shouted Nancy Astor. Churchill continued. What, he demanded, had the Prime Minister actually achieved? 'Peace!' cried Tory MPs. But Churchill was not to be shouted down. All that the Munich Agreement had changed, he insisted, was that the German dictator, 'instead of snatching his victuals from the table, has been content to have them served to him course by course'. Now, all was over. 'Silent, mournful, abandoned, broken, Czechoslovakia recedes into the darkness.'[59] Churchill did not begrudge the British people their obvious relief but maintained that they should know the truth:

> They should know that we have sustained a defeat without a war, the consequences of which will travel far with us along our road; they should know that we have passed an awful milestone in our history,

> when the whole equilibrium of Europe has been deranged, and that the terrible words have for the time being been pronounced against the Western democracies: 'Thou art weighed in the balance and found wanting.' And do not suppose that this is the end. This is only the beginning of the reckoning. This is only the first sip, the first foretaste of a bitter cup which will be proffered to us year by year unless by a supreme recovery of moral health and martial vigour, we arise again and take our stand for freedom as in the olden time.[60]

Despite this 'Demosthenic eloquence', the Tory dissenters faced a dilemma: dare they abstain or even vote against the Government?[61] Since the weekend, rumours had been circulating that Chamberlain intended to use the post-Munich euphoria to call a snap general election, in which only those Conservatives who had supported him would get the party 'coupon', while rebels would be marked down for de-selection or have other 'official' candidates run against them. So alarmed was Harold Macmillan by this prospect that he sought out the Labour foreign affairs spokesman, Hugh Dalton, to beg that the motion of censure put down by the Opposition should not be so extreme as to force anti-Munich Tory MPs to rally to the Government. Dalton promised to do his best and even expressed his belief that a deal could be struck, in the event of an election, in which anti-appeasement Conservatives would be given a clear run by the Socialists. Fortunately, such contingency planning proved unnecessary. Angered by the rumours, Sir Sidney Herbert – a highly respected Tory MP, who had been wounded in the Great War and was known to be dying – decided to make a rare intervention and roundly denounced the idea of a 'loyalty' election, calling on the Government to use the time instead for rearmament.

The effect of this speech, delivered from a man who 'represented the Conservative tradition in its most loyal form' and in clear physical difficulty, was tremendous.[62] Talk of a dissolution evaporated and when Chamberlain rose on the fourth day of the debate he made it clear that the general election was off. The Conservative rebels were emboldened. They remained divided, however, on whether to vote against the Government (as Churchill wanted) or merely to abstain (the limit to which Eden and Amery were prepared to go). In the end, it was decided that it was better to present a united front and all abstain rather than to have some in the Opposition lobby while others remained in their seats. Yet even then the anti-Government credentials of some who would profit by their reputation as 'anti-appeasers' and opponents of Munich were not as strong as they later claimed. As Amery admitted to Chamberlain, after the Prime Minister's closing speech – generally acknowledged as a triumph – both he and Eden were tempted to follow him into the Government lobby but felt that they could not disappoint their friends.[63] When the votes were counted, fewer than 30 Tory MPs refused to support the Government, while 366 voted in favour of the Agreement.

*

Munich was – and remains – one of the most controversial agreements ever negotiated. A dishonourable surrender, 'a triumph for all that was best and most enlightened', a vital breathing space: the debate has raged for over eighty years.* That it was a disaster for the Czechoslovak state no one can deny. The Czechs lost 11,000 square miles of territory, comprising 2,800,000 Sudeten Germans and 800,000 Czechs, along with all their fortifications and the vast majority of their natural resources. Their ability to defend themselves disappeared and the future of the reduced state – despite the 'guarantee' conferred by the Munich powers – was rendered precarious at best. For those Sudeten Germans who supported the Nazi regime, this was a cause of celebration. But there was no joy for the 400,000 Social Democrats, the communist refugees or the Jews. The only comfort for the Czechs – and this only evident in retrospect – was that by acquiescing peacefully to the German demands they avoided the war of annihilation and brutal occupation which the Poles, who did resist and were 'supported' by the Western democracies, were to experience. The Czechs suffered under the Nazis but the Poles suffered more.

For Hitler, Munich was ostensibly a triumph. He got everything he had demanded at Godesberg – the only real difference being, as Churchill pointed out, that the occupation was now staggered, over

---

* It was A. J. P. Taylor who said that '[Munich] was a triumph for all that was best and most enlightened in British life', although he later claimed that this was meant ironically (A. J. P. Taylor, *The Origins of the Second World War*, London, 1961, p. 189).

ten days, rather than happening all at once. Of course, as we now know, Hitler wanted a localised war which would have allowed him to annex the whole of Czechoslovakia and almost immediately regretted the deal he had made. 'That fellow [Chamberlain] has spoiled my entry into Prague', he complained shortly afterwards.[64] Yet this does not detract from the fact that he had achieved his stated aim. He had demanded the Sudetenland by 1 October and by the end of September it was his. At the same time, the borders of the Reich had expanded and German power had increased. The weakness of the Western democracies was exposed, while the Führer's own prestige and popularity reached new heights.

Last but not least, though he was not to know this, the Munich Conference destroyed a plot by the German opposition to remove Hitler from office the moment he gave the orders to march. Whether this coup, which was in place by 15 September and was led by the Chief of the General Staff, General Franz Halder, would have succeeded is doubtful. What is beyond doubt is that it was dead the moment the Western Prime Ministers decided to board their aeroplanes. 'We were firmly convinced we would be successful', testified Halder at Nuremberg. 'But now came Mr Chamberlain and with one stroke the danger of war was averted ... The critical hour for force was avoided.'[65]

From the perspective of the Western Powers, the principal defence of the Munich Agreement has rested on the fact that neither Britain nor France were ready for war in 1938 and that Munich granted them an extra year in which to prepare – the so-called 'breathing space'. 'Thank God for Munich', wrote Harold Balfour, Under-Secretary for Air in the Chamberlain Government, who recalled that in the autumn of 1938 Britain only possessed two flying Spitfires and scarcely more Hurricanes.[66] Of course, Balfour was right. The Spitfires, Hurricanes and RADAR – all of which made the difference between victory and defeat in the Battle of Britain – were not ready in 1938 but were in 1939. What this argument ignores, however, is that Germany was in no position to launch the Battle of Britain in 1938. Not only – as the events of 1939 and 1940 were to prove – did she first need to defeat her immediate neighbours and secure airfields along the Channel coast before she could turn her attention to Britain, but in 1938 the Luftwaffe was not equipped for a long-range strategic bombing campaign. Of course, not all of this was known to the Western leaders, many of whom were deceived by German propaganda. The French Air Force would lose 40 per cent of its machines during the first month of war, declared General Joseph Vuillemin, Chief of Staff of the French Air Force, after returning from a six-day tour of the Luftwaffe and its installations in August 1938, during which the Germans flew the same gleaming aeroplanes from airfield to airfield, just ahead of the French party.[67] It is true that the state of the French Air Force was dire. In September 1938, only 700 of its 1,126 aircraft were operational, while fewer than 50 were modern machines. Against this, the Deuxième Bureau estimated that there were 2,760 German aircraft, including 1,368 bombers. What the French failed to appreciate, however – thanks, in part, to the apocalyptic predictions of the American aviator Colonel Charles Lindbergh* – was that a significant proportion of these planes were inoperative. Indeed, of those 2,760 only 1,699 would have been able to take to the skies in September 1938.[68] More importantly, there were only eight German divisions on the Western Front, compared to twenty-three French (something which the Deuxième Bureau was aware of), while the West Wall was little more than a building site. Finally, though they were seldom added to the equation, there were thirty-four well-equipped, highly motivated Czech divisions.

The fact was – as both British and French intelligence were well aware – the Germans were not ready for a major war in 1938 and would have been placed in an extremely difficult, perhaps impossible, position if Britain, France and the Soviet Union had joined forces in defence of Czechoslovakia. 'It was out of the question', testified General Alfred Jodl at Nuremberg, when asked about Germany's chances of success if Britain and France had fought in September 1938,

* Lindbergh, who had leapt to fame after becoming the first man to fly the Atlantic single-handed, was deeply impressed by the Luftwaffe and German air manufacturing capability, both of which he was allowed to inspect on several occasions between 1936 and 1938. He was, however, no expert and, as Hugh Dalton remarked, 'knew no more about military aircraft than our Amy Johnson'. In September 1938, he terrified French Ministers by stating that the Germans possessed 8,000 military aircraft (almost seven times the true number) with an ability to turn out 1,500 a month. 'French and British towns would be wiped out', predicted the 'Lone Eagle', who was also sympathetic to Nazi Germany and later campaigned against American intervention in the war through the America First Committee.

'with five fighting divisions and seven reserve divisions in the western fortifications, which were nothing but a large construction site, to hold out against 100 French divisions. That was militarily impossible.'[69] Nor was the German High Command under any illusions about the strength of the Czech fortifications. 'If a war had broken out,' explained Field Marshal Erich von Manstein in 1946 (unlike Jodl, not on trial for his life), 'neither our western border nor our Polish frontier could really have been effectively defended by us, and there is no doubt whatsoever that had Czechoslovakia defended herself, we would have been held up by her fortifications, for we did not have the means to break through.'[70]

This is not to diminish the serious military deficiencies of the Western Powers, nor to deny that the year gained by Munich allowed for much-needed rearmament. The trouble was that the 'breathing space' was also enjoyed by the Germans, who used it to speed up their own rearmament and complete the West Wall.* Furthermore, the loot gained by the annexation of the Sudetenland was considerable: 1.5 million rifles, 750 aircraft, 600 tanks, 2,000 field guns, not to mention timber and other raw materials.[71] Thus, while the Western Powers made considerable progress in the 'extra year', the Germans made more, considerably outstripping the British and French on land and, to a lesser extent, in the air. Where the defenders of Munich are on stronger ground is when they point out, as was constantly referenced at the time, that war for Czechoslovakia in 1938 would have split public opinion in both Britain and France, while it is unlikely that Britain would have enjoyed the support (at least initially) of the Dominions, all of which had made their opposition to war clear.

Against this, however, must be weighed the effects of losing the opportunity of binding the Soviet Union into a 'Grand Alliance' against Nazi Germany (as advocated by Churchill) which, if it had come to conflict, would have forced the Germans into a protracted two-front war from the very beginning. There were, of course, good reasons for distrusting Stalin (as Churchill was later to discover) but there were even better reasons for distrusting Hitler, whose word Chamberlain was prepared to accept. Time and again, Litvinov had reaffirmed the

---

* Only 517 bunkers had been completed by the end of September 1938 but twelve months later this number had risen to 11,283.

USSR's determination to honour its commitment to Czechoslovakia (provided, as per the terms of the Soviet–Czechoslovak Treaty, that France intervened first), just as he had also made it clear that if this opportunity for checking German aggression was missed then Russia would retreat into isolation. To be sure, there were practical difficulties regarding Soviet aid, principally that the USSR did not share a border with Czechoslovakia and that both Poland and Romania were disinclined to allow the Red Army to cross their territory. As the crisis worsened, however, the Romanians began to hint that Soviet planes would be able to cross their airspace, while Russian material aid alone would have been of significant value. In March, Litvinov had promised Beneš an 'absolute minimum' of 1,000 aeroplanes and between 21 and 24 September Soviet armed forces undertook a partial mobilisation, involving some 330,000 men.[72] But it was to no avail. Throughout the crisis, the British and French repeatedly rejected the Soviet offers to collaborate and when Munich came the Russians, like the Czechs, were excluded. Litvinov's strategy of collective security had failed and minds in the Kremlin began to contemplate the obvious alternative – a deal with Nazi Germany.

Crucially, Munich convinced Hitler that the Western Powers would never fight but continue to accept his demands. 'Chamberlain shook with fear when I uttered the word *war*. Don't tell me *he* is dangerous', the Führer was heard to scoff, shortly after the Agreement.[73] Later, when stiffening his Generals before the Polish campaign he declared, 'Our enemies are small worms. I saw them in Munich.'[74] It was a miscalculation the consequences of which would be felt across the entire world.

XVIII
Peace for Our Time

Peace flapped from the posters, and not upon the wings of angels.
E. M. Forster, 'Two Cheers for Democracy', July 1938

The Munich Agreement took Neville Chamberlain to the summit of popularity. 'Chamberlain dolls', some in suits, some dressed for fishing, flew off the shelves and 90,000 people collected *Daily Sketch* coupons for a photograph of the Prime Minister embossed on a plate. Over 20,000 congratulatory letters were delivered to 10 Downing Street, along with fishing rods, umbrellas, flowers, chocolate, salmon flies, slippers, pipes, kippers, cigars, champagne, cider, pictures, 'beautifully knitted prize winning socks', crates of apples, a saddle of Welsh lamb, grouse, a 'wedding cake', a grand piano, opera glasses, clocks, watches, 'a replica Jersey milk can', a four-leafed shamrock, bulbs, gingerbread, tweed, German hock, clotted cream, 'lucky horse-shoes' and a pair of Dutch clogs.[1]

It was an amazing hoard but some of the more extravagant presents caused a headache for the Foreign Office. On 30 September 1938, the day after the conference, *Paris-soir* announced that it was setting up a public fund to buy the British Prime Minister a house in the French countryside near a trout stream and by 4 October nearly half a million francs had been raised. The Foreign Office was worried. If the Prime Minister rejected the offer he risked offending the French. If, on the other hand, he accepted he would be obliged to visit his property and ensure that it was properly maintained. In the end it was decided that it would be safest to decline. The Prime Minister has 'no territorial ambitions in Europe', declared the Foreign Office, with obvious irony, and sent instructions to embassies telling them to turn down all 'houses, rivers, mountains, and so on'.[2]

Not that this could stem the flood of praise which poured in from across the globe and ranged from a fifteen-year-old Iraqi boy, who realised that 'but for you, the Führer would have plunged Europe into another war, whose terror it is impossible to tell', to the President of the United States.[3] Some of these expressions of gratitude bordered on the sacrilegious. The *New York Daily News* proclaimed that there was something 'Christlike' about the Prime Minister, while the Bombay Buddha Society congratulated the Premier for putting the Buddha's actual 'teachings and his principles' into practice.[4] A few weeks later, on 12 November 1938, Chamberlain learnt of an old Greek peasant woman who had been saving the small hole in the cross she wore round her neck for a relic of the True Cross but now hoped for a 'little bit of Mr Chamberlain's umbrella' instead.[5]

It was not all joy, however, as Duff Cooper's admittedly less voluminous postbag showed. 'As a private soldier in the great war, and one who hates and fears war', wrote A. E. Whitteridge on 2 October 1938 – one of around 4,000 letters which Cooper received – 'I should like to offer you my respectful thanks for the step you have taken on the morrow of the greatest humiliation our country has suffered since the Norman Conquest.'[6] Another correspondent, who ran a small manufacturing business in Ayrshire, declared that Munich brought him 'helpless shame', while ex-seaman John Edward Smith reckoned that the 'whole glorious navy is with you'.[7]

Those who were most certainly not were the royal family. Having offered on more than one occasion during the crisis to write to Hitler as 'one ex-serviceman to another', George VI was full of admiration for the course his Prime Minister had taken and wholeheartedly endorsed the Agreement he had made.[8] Similarly enthused was the Duke of Windsor, who, according to his wife, had been so distressed by the drift to war that he was 'determined to go to Hitler himself if Mr C. had not gone'.[9] Now the Duke sent his heartfelt congratulations to the Prime Minister – adding to those of his younger brother, the Duke of Kent; his sister, the Princess Royal; his sister-in-law, the Queen; and his mother, Queen Mary. The latter was particularly irritated by those, such as Cooper, carping at the Prime

Minister. 'He brought home Peace,' she wrote to her son, the King, 'why can't they be grateful?'[10]

Nor was the delight any less among the majority of the aristocracy. Laudatory letters from peers filled the Prime Minister's in-tray, including one from Cooper's brother-in-law, the Duke of Rutland, apologising for Cooper's behaviour. Another letter, which is particularly revealing, was written by the Duke of Buccleuch to Cooper after the former First Lord's resignation. Having fought for four years during the First World War, Buccleuch – who on his accession to the Dukedom in 1935 had become Britain's largest landowner – possessed an understandable horror of war as well as a profound conviction that Britain and Germany must never fight one another again. After the accession of Hitler, he paid a series of private visits to Germany in order to study the regime and establish friendly contacts. As his diary makes clear, there was much about the Nazis he found distasteful. He was, however, convinced that another war would mean the end of civilisation – certainly the end of the old order in Britain – and that no efforts should, therefore, be spared to reach an understanding with Hitler. His letter, both honest and naïvely optimistic, says much about the mindset of a significant section of the British upper classes at the time:

> Can any of us prove or judge in advance that it is impossible under any circumstances to trust Hitler or Germany? Hitler has perhaps never met a gentleman and statesman before and one able to stand up to him and with whom he could talk and has been more than surprised to find himself giving way quite a lot to our PM … If we have no agreement with Germany our only alternative seems to be war, and preparation for war … will [mean] we have war, to the exclusion of everything else, including the vast expenditure on our social programme … I was hoping so much that the nightmare of European war could be removed, and confidence restored with an impetus to trade recovery which is so needed for all our industries, including the depressed agricultural and Scottish woollen industries with which I am closely associated (not to mention my own agricultural anxieties) and of a revived prosperity which would enable Parliament to carry out all it wants, and [not] to levy even heavier taxes from us … If all our national expenditure is to be on war preparations, deterioration must continue in other directions and discontent will lead to the unpleasant and disastrous effects of some

> socialist party in office ... Don't you think our PM has made a very good start with Hitler? And that Hitler may well profit and learn by further talks. *Please* don't be too bellicose? Mollie [the Duchess] will be very distressed that you are no longer head of the Navy. I am always uncertain about you, though I hope for the best![11]

Despite such civilities it was a fractious time. 'Feeling ran high over the whole country', recalled Barbara Cartland, the popular novelist and sister of the anti-Munich Tory MP Ronald Cartland. 'People who were ordinarily calm and unpolitically-minded lost their tempers, were furious with those who disagreed with them, rude and offensive at the slightest provocation.'[12] 'Husbands and wives stopped speaking to one another, fathers and sons said unforgivable things to one another', wrote Lady Diana Cooper.[13] According to her husband, Duff, it was the husbands who tended to support Munich and the wives who opposed it. To Richard Law and Harold Nicolson the opposite appeared the case. 'English women showed fear, not courage', reprimanded Nicolson, addressing the National Council of Women in early November 1938. 'One can feel a new fear that the cause of pacifism may even have been engendered by general insistence that fear of war is women's prerogative and that naturally to them the fate of peoples is of less importance than the immediate preservation of family skins.'[14] Reflecting on the situation a year later, Law was even more damning:

> If women didn't have the vote there wouldn't be any Women's Conservative Associations. They're the villains of the piece. How foolish our fathers were to suppose that women would ennoble and sanctify politics. The brutes, untouched as they are by any but the most crudely material considerations, they have brought nothing but degradation and dishonour on politics. A phenomenon like Neville Chamberlain would have been inconceivable before 1918.[15]

Mass-Observation tended to support this view. According to an overview of opinions collected during the crisis, men were more in favour of 'standing up to Hitler', while women tended to support Chamberlain and his efforts for peace. Chamberlain certainly believed that this was the case and, over the next year, attempted to bolster support for his policy by appealing to the women of Britain.[16]

Another important, though equally generalised, divide was between young and old. Talking to his Birmingham constituents, Ronald Cartland found that most of the young people were anti-Munich, while their parents, who remembered the Great War, were steadfast in its defence. 'With the possible exception of Our Lord no greater man than Mr Chamberlain has ever trod this earth', declared one elderly resident.[17] Elsewhere, an Oxford undergraduate named Christopher Cadogan returned home to find his father, Commander Francis Cadogan (who had served in the Royal Navy during the First World War), ordering the butler to bring up champagne so that they might toast the Prime Minister's success. When his son declined to raise a glass his father threw him out of the house and refused to speak to him for some time. Christopher later drowned, while on active service, off the coast of Cyprus.[18]

The greatest anger was directed towards those Tory MPs who refused to vote for the Munich Agreement and openly attacked the Prime Minister. 'I should like to crush his head to a jelly', declared Lady Willingdon, a former Vicereine of India, after Duff Cooper's resignation.[19] 'Those traitors – Winston Churchill, your brother, and his like should be shot', Barbara Cartland was told over lunch in London.[20] Not that the 'traitors' gave much quarter. Churchill 'abused me like a Billingsgate fishwife', complained one Tory MP after the Munich debate, while Cooper got so cross during an argument with one pro-appeasement MP that he ended up seizing him by the throat.[21] Harold Macmillan burnt Chamberlain in effigy on Guy Fawkes Night 1938 (to the delight of the village children and the consternation of his wife's ducal relations) and later shocked a cinema audience by shouting 'Ombrello! Ombrello!' when the Prime Minister appeared on screen.[22]

In the weeks following the Munich debate, almost all the anti-Munich MPs faced censure and even the threat of deselection by their local parties, incited by Conservative Central Office. 'All my prominent supporters are furious, my executive have asked to see me, and I get the general impression, that, at one or all of a number of meetings that I have next week, I am likely to be stoned', wrote Lord Cranborne to Anthony Eden, shortly after the Munich debate.[23] A week later, he wrote to his uncle, Viscount Cecil: 'I am in great trouble with my local Blimps, but have extracted from them, after a very long wrangle, a free hand to say what I like about the Government's foreign policy. They think, all the same, that I am (a) a socialist, (b) a war-monger and (c) a poison-pen against the PM. I don't know what has happened to the Conservative Party. They seem to me insanely shortsighted and wrongheaded.'[24]

Other rebellious Tories got off less lightly. Duff Cooper was effectively put on probation by his association of St George's, Westminster, while the Duchess of Atholl responded to the decision of her association of Kinross and Western Perthshire to seek a new candidate at the next election by resigning her seat and standing as an Independent.* In the ensuing by-election, which was positively eighteenth century in the way that smears, dirty tricks and low-level bribery were deployed, the full weight of the Tory Party was brought to bear against the Duchess, who went down to defeat by some 1,300 votes. Shortly afterwards, the National Liberal Secretary of State for War, Leslie Hore-Belisha, commented to *The Times*'s military correspondent, Basil Liddell Hart, that the 'Conservative party machine is even stronger than the Nazi party machine. It may have a different aim, but it is similarly callous and ruthless. It suppressed anyone who does not toe the line.'[25]

Even Churchill – thanks in part to the Government whips – faced trouble in his Epping constituency and was forced to make it known that he would 'appeal to the electors' if he did not receive the backing of his association.[26] When he heard of this, Lord Rothermere (who supported Munich but did not wish to see Churchill ejected from the Commons) wrote to his old friend, urging him to 'go slow'. 'Neville Chamberlain's reputation will be undimmed so long as he is Prime Minister and any member of his Party who challenges that fact may suffer a complete eclipse', the press baron warned. 'The public is so terrified of being bombed that they will support anyone who keeps them out of war … I don't trust the Epping electorate because Epping is on one of the routes by which enemy aeroplanes will approach London.'[27]

In these circumstances, it is scarcely surprising that almost none of the Tory rebels dared to campaign for the anti-Munich Popular Front candidate in the Oxford by-election, scheduled for 27 October 1938.

---

* The 'Red Duchess' – so known for her outspoken support for the Spanish Republicans – had been on a lecture tour in the United States at the time of the Munich debate. On returning to Britain, however, she soon made her opposition felt through both speeches and pamphlets criticising the Agreement.

Indeed, the only sitting Conservative who was brave, or foolhardy, enough to make the journey to Oxford to speak against the Tory candidate was Harold Macmillan, who told a rally of excited anti-Munichos that you 'could always appease lions by throwing Christians to them but the Christians had another word for it'.[28]

At any other time the Oxford by-election would have been an unremarkable contest. The Conservatives had held the seat (with the exception of two years) since 1885 and the Conservative candidate, the thirty-one-year-old Quintin Hogg, was the son of Lord Hailsham, a sitting Cabinet Minister. Coming just four weeks after Munich, however, and with the Labour and Liberal candidates standing aside in favour of a single anti-appeasement candidate, the master of Balliol College, A. D. 'Sandie' Lindsay, the Oxford election was transformed into a referendum on Munich. As elsewhere, the young led the charge against the Agreement. Two weeks before the vote, a Balliol undergraduate and organ scholar named Edward Heath, despite being a leading member of the Oxford University Conservative Association, persuaded members of the Oxford Union to back the motion 'That this House deplores the Government's policy of Peace without Honour'.[29] Other young men – principally on the left – who campaigned for Lindsay and would later go on to have distinguished political careers included Roy Jenkins, Denis Healey, Patrick Gordon Walker, Richard Crossman, Frank Pakenham and Christopher Mayhew.

Sandie Lindsay was an unlikely Popular Front candidate. A professor of moral philosophy and Christian socialist, his way of showing solidarity with the unemployed was to ban the serving of Lobster Newburg in hall. Thanks to his cohort of excited young supporters, however, the Oxford by-election was a thoroughly rowdy affair. 'A vote for Hogg is a vote for Hitler!' chanted the Lindsay supporters. 'Vote for Hogg and save your bacon', retorted Hogg.[30] In the end, Hogg won by over 3,000 votes but the Conservative majority was cut in half. On the eve of the poll, Hogg had described Munich as 'the greatest miracle of modern times performed by a single man'.[31] Now he told his cheering supporters that it was not his victory but Mr Chamberlain's.[32]

*

Chamberlain soon regretted his Disraelian exuberance from the Downing Street window. Winding up the Munich debate on 6 October 1938, he sought to play down his declaration of 'peace for our time' by explaining that these words were spoken 'in a moment of some emotion, after a long and exhausting day, after I had driven through miles of excited, enthusiastic, cheering people'.[33] As his private letters make clear, however, the Prime Minister really did believe that Munich had been a triumph which, if properly nurtured, could lead to the lasting peace for which he had been striving. 'I am sure that some day the Czechs will see that what we did was to save them for a happier future', he wrote, perhaps with a twinge of guilt, to the Archbishop of Canterbury on 2 October. 'And I sincerely believe that we have at last opened the way to that general appeasement which alone can save the world from chaos.'[34] A few weeks later, he confessed to his stepmother that he found it 'difficult to believe that another crisis could arise so acute and dangerous', at least for a considerable period of time, and that what he was seeking was 'a restoration of confidence that would allow us all to stop arming and get back to the task of making the world a better place to live in'.[35]

Few of Chamberlain's colleagues shared this analysis. For many Conservatives, both inside and outside Government, Munich had been a traumatic experience, made unavoidable by the country's unpreparedness for war. They got short Prime Ministerial shrift, however, when they argued – as Munich's supporters would later argue in Chamberlain's defence – that the time purchased by Munich should be used to redouble British rearmament. 'But don't you see, I have brought back peace', expostulated Chamberlain to Lord Swinton, who made just such a demand in return for supporting the Agreement.[36] A few weeks later, on 31 October, he rounded on those Cabinet Ministers – who included Elliot, Winterton, De La Warr, Stanley, Hore-Belisha, Kingsley Wood and, most significantly, Halifax – who were arguing for an expansion or acceleration of rearmament. 'Our foreign policy was one of appeasement', the Prime Minister explained, adding that a 'good deal of false emphasis had been placed … on rearmament, as though one result of the Munich Agreement had been that it will be necessary for us to add to our rearmament programmes. Acceleration of existing programmes was one thing but increases in the scope of our programme which would lead to a new arms race was a different proposition. [He] hoped that it might be possible to take active steps and to follow up the Munich Agreement by other measures, aimed at securing better relations', just as he also hoped that 'some day we should be able to secure a measure of limitation of armaments, but it was too soon to say when this would prove possible'.[37]

Even more annoying to the Prime Minister were those Conservative MPs who continued to attack him and his great achievement. 'It is not one of the characteristics of totalitarian states, at any rate, that they are accustomed to foul their own nests', he snapped in a revealing aside in the Commons on 1 November.[38] In particular, he found it trying to have to keep the 'weaker brethren' (as he was wont to call them) within his own Government onside, while at the same time defending himself against Churchill and his supporters who were 'carrying on a regular conspiracy against me'.[39] In this battle, however, the Prime Minister had a secret advantage. That sinister former MI5 officer Sir Joseph Ball had been far from idle since Eden's resignation and in the intervening period had succeeded in tapping the telephones of a number of leading anti-appeasers, including Churchill's. 'They, of course, are totally unaware of my knowledge of their proceedings', boasted Chamberlain to his sister Ida. But 'I had continual information of their doings and sayings which for the nth time demonstrated how completely Winston can deceive himself.'[40]

More worrying for the Prime Minister was how quickly the adulation of Munich wore off. Although the Conservatives had managed to hang on at Oxford, they lost a by-election at Dartford the following week – also fought largely on the issue of Munich – followed by the sensational victory of Vernon Bartlett, standing as an Independent anti-appeasement candidate, at Bridgwater on 17 November. At around the same time, a poll conducted by the *News Chronicle* found that 86 per cent of Britons questioned did not believe Hitler when he said that he had no further territorial ambitions. This finding was initially suppressed because the paper's Chairman, Sir Walter Layton – who had been heavily sat on by the Government – did not want to 'exacerbate feelings in Germany'.[41] But there were plenty of other signs which suggested that the mood was becoming increasingly disaffected, such as this anonymous letter to the newspapers from mid-October:

> I see that the heart-exporting trade is still very brisk, the Archbishop of Canterbury having announced that our hearts have gone out to the Czechs. I believe that the first large consignment left in 1935, when, as you will remember, our hearts went out to the 'gallant Abyssinians' (our oil, of course, went out to Mussolini). Since then large deliveries have gone to Spain, Austria and China. I hope the consignees have been grateful, although it is rumoured that some of the smaller nations are whispering – maliciously enough – that as well as our hearts we have parted with our guts.[42]

Nor did Hitler make it any easier for Chamberlain. Resentful at the Western Powers for 'cheating' him out of his 'little war' and angry with the German people for showing such enthusiasm for the maintenance of peace, he lashed out in what the German diplomat Ulrich von Hassell described as an 'incomprehensibly rude speech' at Saarbrücken on 9 October, accusing Cooper, Eden and Churchill of warmongering and warning Britain to drop their 'airs from the Versailles epoch' and stay out of Germany's affairs.[43] 'We cannot tolerate any longer the tutelage of governesses!' he declared.[44] A few weeks later, he repeated these attacks at Weimar, while also celebrating the fact that Germany had ceased to be governed by bourgeois leaders of the 'umbrella-carrying type'.[45] Far worse was to come.

*

On the morning of 7 November 1938, the third legation secretary at the German Embassy in Paris was fatally shot by a seventeen-year-old Polish Jew. At Goebbels' urging, Hitler decided that the time had come for the German Jews 'to feel the anger of the people'.[46] The police were pulled back and the SA unleashed. During the night of 9–10 November a wave of anti-Semitic violence and destruction swept through Germany and Austria. Two hundred and sixty-seven synagogues were torched or blown up; over 7,500 Jewish-owned shops were smashed. Jewish homes, broken into by gangs of storm troopers, were vandalised and looted, their occupants beaten or subjected to bestial depravity. Hundreds of Jews were murdered, while others, preferring to take their own lives, cut their wrists or hurled themselves from buildings. In the days that followed the pogrom, around 30,000 Jewish men were arrested and taken to Dachau, Buchenwald and Sachsenhausen.

British and international opinion was appalled by Kristallnacht. The *News Chronicle* spoke of a 'pogrom hardly surpassed in fury since the Dark Ages', while *The Times* declared that 'no foreign propagandist bent upon blackening Germany before the world could outdo the tale of burnings and beatings, of blackguardly assaults upon defenceless and innocent people, which disgraced that country yesterday'.[47] For Wilson Harris, Editor of the Chamberlain-supporting *Spectator*, 'the events of the past week have obliterated the word appeasement' – a sentiment seemingly shared by a majority of the British people, 73 per cent of whom, according to a Gallup opinion poll, agreed with the statement that 'the persecution of the Jews in Germany is an obstacle to good understanding between Britain and Germany'.[48]

Even pro-Germans reacted with revulsion, though for some the chief cause of regret was the damage which had been done to the appeasement cause. 'I must say Hitler never helps, and always makes Chamberlain's task more difficult' was Chips Channon's casual comment in his diary for 15 November 1938. A week later his attitude had stiffened somewhat:

> No-one ever accused me of being anti-German, but really I can no longer cope with the present regime which seems to have lost all sense and reason. Are they mad? The Jewish persecutions carried to such a fiendish degree are short-sighted, cruel and unnecessary and now, so newspapers tell us, we shall have persecutions of Roman Catholics too.[49]

Other Nazi fraternisers who registered disgust and disappointment included Lord Londonderry – who belatedly acknowledged that there could be no talk of colonial appeasement while Germany was indulging in 'a persecution … medieval in its ferocity' – and Lord Mount Temple, who resigned as Chairman of the Anglo-German Fellowship.[50] Lord Brocket, on the other hand, continued with his planned shooting trip with Göring and returned to England to broadcast both his host's and Hitler's insistence that they had neither knowledge of nor involvement in the recent disturbances. He 'must be the most gullible of asses', noted Horace Rumbold, in what can only be regarded as the most charitable judgement.[51]

The country where the protests were loudest and the condemnation of the German Government strongest was the United States. President Roosevelt denounced the violence at a press conference on 15 November and announced that he was recalling the American Ambassador. Further condemnations came from both Houses of Congress as well as from former President Herbert Hoover, who went before the newsreel cameras to deplore a 'brutal intolerance which has no parallel in modern history'.[52] 'Public opinion is without exception incensed against Germany and hostile toward her', reported the German Ambassador, Hans-Heinrich Dieckhoff, on 14 November. Furthermore, the outcry came not 'only from Jews but in equal strength from all camps and classes', including the previously pro-German American camp. 'What particularly strikes me', continued the Ambassador, 'is the fact that, with few exceptions, the respectable patriotic circles, which are thoroughly anti-communist and, for the greater part, anti-Semitic in their outlook also begin to turn away from us.'[53]

The effect of Kristallnacht was to destroy already waning American faith in appeasement. Although Roosevelt had cabled 'Good man' to Chamberlain when he heard about Hitler's invitation for the four-power conference, the President's and most Americans' enthusiasm for Munich was short-lived.[54] Indeed, many Americans had been critical of the British handling of the Czech crisis from the beginning and, as Joseph Kennedy explained to Anthony Eden, the strain of 'anti-British' sentiment in the United States was stronger than ever.[55] In order to counter this, the American Ambassador (who still retained his faith in appeasement even if his compatriots did not) urged Eden to accept an invitation from the National Association of Manufacturers to address their conference in New York on 9 December. Having initially refused the invitation, Eden was persuaded and, on 3 December 1938, boarded the *Aquitania*, armed with a case of the Ambassador's champagne.

Eden's reception was akin to that accorded a Hollywood star. Four thousand people gathered in the Waldorf Astoria to hear his speech, which was also broadcast live on three national radio networks. As he entered the hotel dining room, 'Land of Hope and Glory' struck up and a swarm of photographers buzzed around, photographing his every mouthful. Just before he was about to speak he was handed a note from another table: 'Whatever you do don't mind the photographers – Noël Coward'.[56] There were grave dangers in the world, Eden told his audience, but Great Britain was prepared to meet them just as she had done previously in her history, being 'neither decadent or faint-hearted'. Certainly, she was not hoping to lure others 'to pull our chestnuts out of the fire'.[57]

All this went down extremely well. Congress published the speech in its official record and Eden was clapped and cheered everywhere he went. The American press took hyperbole to new levels. 'He is Prince Charming. He is St George fighting the dragons. He resigned for principle. He isn't a trimmer. He can stand up till the last round and come back after a knockout. He is an Englishman', eulogised the *New York Herald Tribune*.[58] 'You could run for President here and take it in your stride', complimented the former Democratic Presidential candidate Al Smith.[59] Yet, while Eden enjoyed the paeans, he was alarmed by American perceptions of Chamberlain and his Government. 'I was horrified at the atmosphere I found', he wrote to Stanley Baldwin on his return.

> Poor Nancy [Astor] and her Cliveden set has done much damage, and 90 per cent of the US is firmly persuaded that you and I are the only two Tories who are not fascists in disguise ... Most of my time was spent in asserting that Neville was not a fascist, nor John Simon always a 'double crosser' ... I hope that I have not perjured myself too often on J.S.'s behalf ... Kennedy was right to be worried, and I am still. This govt is too far to the right to regain these people, and Nancy should be compelled to shut Cliveden.[60]

Similar attitudes were encountered by the Scottish journalist Robert Bruce Lockhart, a former diplomat and spy, who embarked on a lecture tour of the US in January 1939. 'Nearly everywhere I went, anti-Nazi sentiment was strong. But criticism of the British Government was even more bitter', he noted. Most of the jokes were aimed at the British Prime Minister – exemplified by Dorothy Parker's crack that Chamberlain was 'the first Prime Minister in history to crawl at 250 miles an hour' – while a white umbrella lapel pin was the latest fashion accessory for ladies who thought that Britain should have stood by Czechoslovakia. The prevailing attitude was captured by a pamphlet entitled *England: A Dying Oligarchy,* in which the author, the novelist and journalist Louis Bromfield, set out 'in good Birmingham' style an account of everything which had resulted or would result from Britain's policy of appeasing the dictator states:

1. Immense loss of prestige throughout Europe, Asia and America.
2. Immense damage to the cause of Anglo-American friendship and American respect for England.
3. Immense losses to British investors, as well as foreign investors, both in revenue and capital.
4. Immense comfort and stimulus to the dictators and lawless elements of the world.
5. The loss of British leadership of the democracies.
6. Foreign domination of the Mediterranean, so vital to the life of the British Empire.

Fortunately for the British, the Nazis were even more successful at alienating American opinion. Frustration with the British stemmed from widespread loathing for the Nazis, who managed to compound their crimes by the crassness of their propaganda, exemplified by a pamphlet entitled *George Washington: The First Nazi*. As Bruce Lockhart reflected wryly, 'The best British ambassador we have ever had in the United States was Adolf Hitler.'[61]

*

Like almost everyone else, Chamberlain was shocked by Kristallnacht. 'It is clear that Nazi hatred will stick at nothing to find a pretext for their barbarities', he wrote to Ida, though his principal complaint lay with the fact that 'there does seem to be some fatality about Anglo-German relations which invariably blocks every effort to improve them'.[62] Clearly, further official efforts at appeasement were, for the moment, impossible. Yet Chamberlain was not prepared to abandon his entire policy simply because of domestic German beastliness.

On 23 November 1938, a man wearing a dark grey suit and light tweed coat, around five feet nine inches tall, with blue eyes, a large straight nose and dark hair, slipped into the German Embassy on Carlton House Terrace. George Steward, the Prime Minister's Press Secretary, had come for a secret talk with the German Press Attaché, Fritz Hesse. The relationship between the two men was already established. For some time Steward had acted, probably under the supervision of Sir Joseph Ball, as the Prime Minister's secret channel with the Germans, just as Adrian Dingli had been a conduit to the Italians. On his last visit, twelve days after Munich, Steward had come to beg the Germans to 'emphasise again and again' in their propaganda 'that [they] trusted Chamberlain because he wanted peace' and 'to stress [their] wish to live in lasting friendship with the British people'. The importance of this, Steward explained, was that the Prime Minister was working for an Anglo-German understanding against the wishes of the Foreign Office, who were trying to 'sabotage' his plans, and even some members of his own Cabinet.[63]

Now, two weeks after *Kristallnacht*, the Prime Minister's secret emissary had come to relay Chamberlain's urgent desire that some 'visible step along the line laid down in the Munich agreement' should be taken. In particular, Steward suggested an agreement aimed at 'humanising' aerial warfare, or even 'a joint Anglo-German declaration regarding the recognition of respective principal zones of influence'. For this it would be important for Ribbentrop or some other German Minister to come to London, since it was impossible for Chamberlain to make another visit to Germany without further progress. What the British Government could do, however, was to 'guarantee' that the German Minister would receive a favourable write-up in the British press, since the notoriously anti-Nazi head of press at the Foreign Office, Rex Leeper, had been removed from his role in a post-Munich purge. Hesse's report to Ribbentrop of this extraordinary conversation concluded thus:

> This surprising suggestion is, if I may be allowed to express an opinion, another sign of how great the wish for an understanding with us is, here in England and is also evidence … that Great Britain is ready, during the next year, to accept practically everything from us and to fulfil our every wish. For the rest, it is significant that this representative took the opportunity to give me in detail the measures which the English Government has spontaneously taken to bring to an end the bad feeling resulting from anti-Semitism in order to remove this particular cause for friction in our relations.[64]

Steward's visit did not go unnoticed. MI5 had managed to acquire an agent within the German Embassy and a report of the press officer's visit, together with his description and a copy of Hesse's memorandum, was soon on the desk of the Permanent Under-Secretary of the Foreign Office. Cadogan was appalled by what he read. 'Even if the secret negotiations are successful they can only result in discomforting the moderates in Germany, in comforting the extremists in power, and in some bogus "settlement" which will be the beginning of the end for the British Empire', he minuted.[65] Halifax confronted Chamberlain, who pretended to be 'aghast' at the revelation.[66] Cadogan was not convinced but took comfort from the fact that all such further contacts were now at least impossible. Steward had paid his last visit to Carlton House Terrace.

*

Chamberlain was increasingly demoralised. Although he reported to Hilda that he and Halifax had a 'wonderful reception' during their visit to Paris on 23–26 November 1938 – designed to give the 'French people an opportunity of pouring out their pent up feelings of gratitude and affection', as well as of strengthening Daladier – there had also been boos and cries of *'Vive Eden!'* and *'A bas Munich'*.[67] At the same time, Chamberlain was facing continued and increasing criticism from within his own party. As he continued in a subsequent letter to his sister, that week he had 'actually had a junior Minister [Robert Hudson, the Overseas Trade Secretary] come to me and intimate that unless I got rid of at least two and preferably four of my colleagues', who Hudson and his associates did not believe were pulling their weight on rearmament, then 'he and a number of other younger Ministers would have to reconsider their position'.[68] In the end, the so-called Under-Secretaries' Revolt came to nothing, though it left the Prime Minister feeling both embattled and sorry for himself. 'Sometimes I feel that I wish democracy at the devil and I often wonder what PM ever had to go through such an ordeal as I', he complained to Ida on 17 December.[69]

Far more troubling were the multitude of signs that Hitler, far from settling down to become the satisfied, peaceful statesman Chamberlain had hoped, was preparing for new adventures. On 14 October, just two weeks after the Munich Conference, Göring announced a massive expansion of German rearmament (including a fivefold increase in the size of the Luftwaffe) and, at the beginning of December, the German Government gave formal notice that it intended to exercise a clause in the Anglo-German Naval Treaty which allowed it to build up to 100 per cent of the total of British submarines. Accompanying these public declarations were a series of intelligence reports arguing that Hitler, 'barely sane', was 'consumed by an insensate hatred of this country', while the German press was engaged in a venomous campaign to depict 'Great Britain as "Public Enemy Number One"'.[70]

At first, it was assumed that the next German coup would occur in the east. The intelligence services believed the Ukraine to be Hitler's new objective, a supposition supported by Sir Robert Vansittart's contacts. In mid-December, however, Ivone Kirkpatrick, First Secretary at the British Embassy in Berlin, was told by a retired senior German official with close links to the Wehrmacht that Hitler intended to 'bomb London in March'.[71] As it turned out, this was a false rumour, quite possibly started by the anti-war head of German military intelligence, Admiral Wilhelm Canaris, seeking to frighten the British into a policy of firmness. To a limited extent it worked. Halifax was suitably alarmed and an anti-aircraft battery was placed at Wellington Barracks, in full view of the German Embassy. At around the same time, the Cabinet agreed to the building of a new armaments factory outside Glasgow, intended to produce over 300 anti-aircraft guns a year. For those who had been agitating for increased defence procurement for years this was a crumb of good news. 'On these waves of fear we get propelled a little further forward each time', noted Major-General Henry Pownall, and if 'we have enough of these crises we may even be able to get a properly equipped field force without the Chancellor, Sam Hoare and such like being aware of it!'[72]

In every other respect, however, there was little to celebrate. Writing in his diary on 22 December 1938, the most which Cadogan could say for this 'strenuous and anxious' year was that 'we are all alive and well' at the end of it. Would the same be true for 1939? Cadogan doubted it. 'It seems to me that, unless there is revolution in Germany, we must flounder into war. And the former hope is slender indeed. I can only pray God to help me to do what little I can in my sphere, and to bless us all and bring us safely through.'[73] Surveying the scene from Sissinghurst, the Tudor castle in the Weald of Kent which the Nicolsons had bought in 1930, Harold Nicolson's valediction to 1938, though enlivened by bathos, was similarly gloomy: 'It has been a bad year. Chamberlain has destroyed the Balance of Power, and Niggs [his second son] got a third. A foul year. Next year will be worse.'[74]

XIX

Chamberlain Betrayed

> Nobody in Birmingham had ever broken his promise to the Mayor; surely nobody in Europe would break his promise to the Prime Minister of England.
>
> Duff Cooper, 'Chamberlain: A Candid Portrait'[1]

The special train pulled into Rome's main terminal punctually at 4.20 on the afternoon of 11 January 1939. Two sets of tracks had been covered to create an enlarged platform and the station, like the rest of the city, was bedecked with Union Jacks and Italian Tricolores. Squeezed into a black double-breasted military coat, Mussolini waited on the platform, a 'fine smirk' on his face, along with Ciano, his cap arrogantly askew, and a melange of Fascist bigwigs.[2] Also present was the British Ambassador, Lord Perth, and around a thousand members of the British colony. As the train came to a halt, the bands struck up and Chamberlain emerged smiling from his carriage to receive the fascist salute and the gloved hand of the Duce. According to the newsreel commentator, there was almost a 'moment of relief' when the crowd noticed that the Prime Minister had not forgotten his umbrella, along with a shiny top hat, as he inspected the guard of Sardinian Grenadiers, as well as the Duce's own personal bodyguard.[3] The four men – Chamberlain, Mussolini, Halifax and Ciano – then made their way out of the station where they acknowledged the applause of a large crowd.

Despite the warm welcome, the Chamberlain–Halifax Rome visit was controversial. On 16 November 1938, the British had finally ratified the Anglo-Italian Agreement but only after Mussolini had effectively blackmailed them by threatening to sign a military alliance with

Germany unless the Agreement was brought into immediate effect. This was followed by a rabid propaganda campaign against France, launched on 30 November 1938, when the Fascist Chamber of Deputies erupted in cries of 'Tunis, Corsica, Nice, Savoy'.[4] French public opinion was incensed and Daladier declared that he would not surrender an inch of French territory. British newspapers applauded this defiance – underlined by Daladier's much-publicised New Year tour of French possessions in North Africa and the Mediterranean – and roundly condemned Italian provocation. This did not lessen French perturbation at the idea of an Anglo-Italian summit, however, and, as Sir Alexander Cadogan recorded on 2 December, the French Ambassador was imploring the British to 'give the ice-creamers a crack on the head'.[5]

As it turned out, the French need not have worried. Although Chamberlain was privately in favour of France making territorial concessions in order to achieve rapprochement with Italy, he neither raised the subject nor tried to strike a deal of his own. Indeed, as Ciano reported to Ribbentrop, the visit was 'a big lemonade'.[6] The British were taken to the opera, laid a wreath at the Tomb of the Unknown Warrior, and watched athletic signorinas doing strange exercises with medicine balls. Understandably, they found the *passo romano* – Mussolini's flagrant plagiarism of the German goose-step – ridiculous, though the sight of Italian boys bearing miniature rifles had a sobering effect.

Chamberlain had a whale of a time. Everywhere he was cheered by spontaneous crowds and when he settled down for his first conversation with the Duce the police had to be sent to quieten the tumult outside the Palazzo Venezia. Chamberlain liked Mussolini. Unlike Hitler, he did not seem a 'fanatic' and even had a sense of humour. Writing to the King on his return, the Prime Minister gave a vivid description of the Italian dictator, with his dark skin – 'darker than many Indians' – and muddy brown eyes. In spite of great efforts to keep fit, Chamberlain thought Mussolini had put on weight, though 'he is still extremely alert and vigorous both mentally and physically'.[7] A potential source of this vitality, on which the British speculated, was the gossip that 'Musso' (as Chamberlain always called him) had recently changed mistresses. 'He had an Italian woman who was supposed to be exhausting him', recorded Halifax's Private Secretary, Oliver Harvey, 'and he now has a

German or Czech one who is said to be calmer!' Chamberlain did not pass this information on to the King.[8]

The Prime Minister believed that he had achieved his primary objectives. These were to weaken the German–Italian Axis and persuade Mussolini to restrain Hitler from any 'mad dog' acts.[9] 'I feel confident that the personal contacts we have established will tend to keep Mussolini on the rails', he told the King, while the Cabinet minutes for 18 January 1939 record the Premier's conviction that 'Signor Mussolini and Herr Hitler could not be very sympathetic to each other'.[10] The reality, as almost any ambassador other than the ineffective Perth (Harvey did not think that he could even speak Italian) should have been able to see, was very different. Despite bouts of apprehension over Hitler's ambitions, Mussolini was firmly in the German camp and, only ten days before the British visit, had decided to transform the Anti-Comintern Pact between Germany, Italy and Japan into a full military alliance. In addition to this, and in tragic contrast to Chamberlain's rosy appreciation of him, the Duce was distinctly unimpressed by the British Ministers. Turning to Ciano after the grand dinner at the Palazzo Venezia on the first night of the visit, he passed the withering judgement that Chamberlain and Halifax were not made of the same stuff 'as the Francis Drakes and the other magnificent adventurers who created the Empire' but were 'the tired sons of a long line of rich men and they will lose their Empire'.[11] Worse, he made fun of Chamberlain's umbrella.

*

Meanwhile, rumours of an imminent German attack continued to circulate. Thanks to the work of Admiral Canaris and his Chief of Staff, Hans Oster – still trying to frighten the Western Powers into accelerating their rearmament – the Netherlands now appeared at the forefront of German designs and even Switzerland was talked of as a potential target. At the same time, there were further reports that Hitler was planning a massive aerial attack on Great Britain, since he apparently believed that London 'could be destroyed in a couple of days by unceasing bombing'.[12] 'All the reports are agreed in forecasting that the danger period will begin towards the end of February', explained Halifax in a telegram to President Roosevelt.

> His Majesty's Government have no wish to be alarmist, but today, as in July, August and September of last year, it is remarkable that there is one general tendency running through all the reports, and it is impossible to ignore them ... Moreover, Hitler's mental condition, his insensate rage against Great Britain and his megalomania, which are alarming the moderates around him, are entirely consistent with the execution of a desperate *coup* against the Western Powers.[13]

When the Foreign Policy Committee met on 23 January 1939, it was agreed that an attack on the Netherlands would constitute a *casus belli* and, on 6 February, Chamberlain felt obliged to announce in the Commons that any threat to 'the vital interests of France ... must evoke the immediate co-operation of this country'.[14]

The intelligence reports and the pledge to France presaged the death of limited liability. Having been concerned for some time that the absence of a Continental commitment might make the French so defeatist as to render them incapable of defending even their own borders, or force them into a deal with Germany, Halifax told the Committee of Imperial Defence on 26 January that he was now in favour of a full commitment to the Continent, including tripling the British Expeditionary Force, doubling the Territorials, staff talks and conscription. The Foreign Secretary was speaking in support of Leslie Hore-Belisha, who, in addition to the above, had been pressing for a Ministry of Supply. 'I said that if we were involved in war it would be a struggle for our very existence and not a war in which we could limit our liability', the War Secretary recorded in his diary. Moreover, 'the impact of the next war ... would be so overwhelming that if a Ministry of Supply were not already in being at the outset, there was a danger that the war would be lost before the organisation could be set up'.[15]

Initially, Chamberlain continued to resist these calls. As he told the Cabinet on 2 February, 'an unanswerable case could be made out for increased armaments in every arm, if the financial aspect of the proposals was ignored. But finance could not be ignored since our financial strength was one of our strongest weapons in any war which was not over in a short time.' He was supported by the Chancellor of the Exchequer, Sir John Simon, who baulked at the proposed figure of £81 million for equipping even a modest field force.[16] Within a fortnight, however, the First and Second Lords of the Treasury had capitulated. Four divisions of the regular Army would be equipped for a Continental role (instead of two as previously planned), along with two mobile divisions and four divisions of Territorials. Savings were found by delaying the embarkation of the latter from four to six months after the outbreak of war but neither this nor continued resistance to a Ministry of Supply could lessen the revolutionary nature of the decision. Having struggled to prevent a situation in which British soldiers would have to fight on mainland Europe, as their fathers had done, the Cabinet had now accepted that if war came this would be an unavoidable reality. On 29 January, the Government requested the establishment of detailed staff conversations with the French to plan for a war not only against Germany, but also Italy.[17]

Despite the intelligence warnings, Chamberlain remained remarkably optimistic. He resisted Halifax's attempts to 'put some stiffening' into a speech he was due to deliver in Birmingham on 28 January and appealed instead to Hitler for his 'contribution' to the cause of peace.[18] Two days later, when Hitler addressed the Reichstag on the sixth anniversary of his accession to power and failed to make any fresh territorial demands – although he did prophesy the 'annihilation of the Jewish race in Europe' in the event of another war – Chamberlain believed that his call had been answered.[19] 'I myself begin to feel at last that we are getting on top of the dictators', he boasted to Hilda on 5 February, adding that Hitler had missed the bus the previous September. At any rate, he rejoiced, the Germans 'could not make nearly such a mess of us now as they could have done then, while we could make much more of a mess of them'.[20]

Chamberlain's optimism was fuelled by Sir Nevile Henderson, who, despite a three-month absence from Berlin, owing to an operation for throat cancer, lost no time in contradicting the rumours of impending German aggression. 'My first impression is that the Germans are not contemplating any wild adventure and that their compass is pointing towards peace', communicated the Ambassador on 16 February 1939.[21] The previous evening, Henderson had attended a dinner of the Deutsch-Englische Gesellschaft, at which the President of the association, the Duke of Coburg (a grandson of Queen Victoria and Old Etonian contemporary of the Ambassador), had spoken encouragingly of the future for Anglo-German relations.

According to Henderson, the Duke's speech had been rewritten at the last moment and had probably received the 'personal approval of Herr Hitler himself'.[22] Chamberlain was ecstatic. 'It seems to come closer to that response for which I have been asking than anything I have seen yet', he replied to Henderson, before embarking on a fantasy about imminent disarmament talks and even a fresh attempt at resolving German colonial claims.[23] His enthusiasm was not shared by the Foreign Secretary, however, who wrote to the Ambassador deprecating the Prime Minister's 'rather optimistic' appraisal of the situation: 'I do not myself feel there is any hope of making any sense of colonial discussions ... unless and until your German friends can really show more than smooth words as evidence of friendly hearts.'[24]

As this dig suggests, Halifax's journey from appeaser to resister had only gathered pace since Munich. Oliver Harvey thought him almost 'unrecognisable from the H[alifax] of a year ago', noting that the Foreign Secretary now regarded Hitler as a 'criminal lunatic' who must be confronted.[25] This was a considerable blow for Chamberlain, who was again forced to employ a variety of underhand methods in order to pursue his policy. One of these was to continue to encourage semi-official visits to Germany, such as that undertaken by the pro-appeasement Governor of the Bank of England, Montagu Norman, in January 1939. The Foreign Office was kept entirely in the dark about the trip and found out only by accident via a 'side-wind from Germany itself'. 'We thus see a further use of [the] PM's policy of working behind his Foreign Secretary's back and keeping a side line out to the dictators', recorded the outraged Harvey.[26] Another amateur diplomat of whom the Foreign Office was (and remained) wholly unaware was the former Tory MP and fascist sympathiser Henry Drummond Wolff. According to Drummond Wolff's own account, his visit to Berlin in January 1939 (the first of four which he was to undertake that year) was a purely personal initiative. In fact, as he explained to an official at the German Embassy, he was travelling with the approval of one of the Prime Minister's 'principal advisers', almost certainly Joseph Ball.[27] Doors were opened and Drummond Wolff soon found himself in a meeting with Göring, who succeeded in persuading the entirely uncritical former MP that Hitler was still 'extremely anxious to have a general settlement with the United Kingdom'.[28]

Such reports, along with his appreciation of Germany's increasing economic difficulties, only served to fertilise Chamberlain's already blooming optimism. 'All the information I get seems to point in the direction of peace', he wrote to Hilda on 19 February, 'and I repeat once more that I believe we have at last got on top of the dictators.'[29] A week later, he predicted a 'period of gradually increasing peacefulness' and, on 7 March, told a dinner of Conservative MPs that 'the dangers of a German war [were] less every day, as our rearmament expands'.[30] Two days later, he received the lobby correspondents to express his view that the situation was 'less anxious' than it had been for some time and to float the possibility of a new disarmament conference. This briefing, which was quoted verbatim in much of the press, earned a sharp rebuke from Halifax, who feared that the Germans would be 'encouraged to think that we are feeling the strain'.[31] Chamberlain feigned contrition and wrote to his Foreign Secretary apologising for the 'gaffe'. Privately, however, he was unrepentant. Writing to Ida on 12 March 1939, the Prime Minister explained that he was immune to criticism when he knew he was right and, 'like Chatham, "I know that I can save this country and I do not believe that anyone else can".'[32] Three days later, Hitler invaded the rump of Czechoslovakia.

*

The German takeover of Czechoslovakia should not have come as a surprise. By mid-February 1939, Vansittart's intelligence network was warning of an invasion and, by early March, both SIS and MI5 were echoing these reports. In a memorandum sent to Halifax on 20 February, Vansittart quoted the secretary of the Anglo-German Fellowship, T. P. Conwell-Evans – once an apologist for the regime, now a convinced anti-appeaser – who stated emphatically that Hitler intended to march into Czechoslovakia in the near future. 'The method which Hitler intends to adopt is to stir up a movement for independence among the Slovaks. Czech resistance to these claims will then give Hitler the opportunity to intervene *manu militari*, or in other words to invade the remains of Czechoslovakia.'[33] As the following weeks were to show, this proved an entirely accurate forecast.

On 9 March 1939, in a desperate attempt to keep his reduced country together, Dr Emil Hácha – Beneš's successor as Czecho-Slovak President* – dismissed the subsidiary Slovakian Cabinet, which he believed was on the verge of declaring independence, and imprisoned the deposed Slovak Prime Minister, Father Jozef Tiso. Hitler spotted his chance. The next day he told Goebbels, Ribbentrop and Keitel that he intended to use the situation to occupy the remains of Czechoslovakia and, within a further three days, had instructed the liberated Tiso to proclaim Slovakian independence and formally request the 'protection' of the Reich. By the next morning, 14 March 1939, the Slovak Assembly had, indeed, declared independence and by that afternoon the frail Dr Hácha, along with his Foreign Minister, his secretary and his daughter, was on a train to Berlin to plead for his country's life.

Having kept the nerve-racked President waiting until 1.15 a.m., Hitler listened to Hácha's pathetic speech before launching into a well-practised routine. The German Army would march into Czechoslovakia at six o'clock that morning and, if the President did not wish to see Czech blood spilt and Prague destroyed, he would order the Czech Army to offer no resistance. At one point, Hácha fainted, or had a minor heart attack, and had to be revived with an injection by Hitler's personal physician, Dr Theodor Morell. The thought occurred to Hitler's interpreter, Paul Schmidt, that if anything happened to the Czech President then 'the whole world will say tomorrow that he was murdered at the Chancellery'.[34] Fortunately or not, Hácha recovered and, just before 4 a.m., signed the declaration which placed the future of the Czecho-Slovak nation in the hands of the German Führer. Two hours later, seven German Army corps crossed into Bohemia. They encountered no resistance and by nine o'clock on the morning of 15 March the advance units had reached Prague. Hitler followed by special train, disembarking at Leipa (around sixty miles north of the capital) to continue the journey by car. Despite the falling snow, he stood for much of the drive, his face rigid, his arm outstretched. That

---

* Reflecting the fragmentation of the country, the hyphen was added in the wake of the Munich Agreement.

night he slept in the Hradčany Castle, the ancient residence of the Kings of Bohemia, and on the following morning the citizens of Prague woke to see the swastika fluttering above the balustrade.

*

The invasion of Czechoslovakia – the most flagrant violation of the Munich Agreement – caused outrage in Britain. 'No balder, bolder departure from the written bond has ever been committed in history', noted an indignant Chips Channon. 'The manner of it surpassed comprehension and his [Hitler's] callous desertion of the Prime Minister is stupefying. I can never forgive him.'[35] The *News Chronicle* attacked an act of 'naked and unashamed aggression', while the Editor of the *Observer*, J. L. Garvin (transformed since Munich into an opponent of German, if not Italian, foreign policy), spoke of the 'most shameful and ominous page in the modern annals of Europe'.[36] Every newspaper noted the cynicism or mendacity of Hitler's claims to legitimacy in foreign policy. 'Up till this moment Herr Hitler has repeatedly declared that his aim was the union of the German people, and his military coups have at least had the justification that they brought unification to a great people for whom it had been long withheld', wrote *The Times*, while the *Daily Telegraph* declared that the German leader, by brutally incorporating Czechs into the Reich, had 'dropped the mask'.[37]

The consensus that appeasement was now dead was instantaneous. In one swift stroke, Hitler had broken his word – repudiating the claim that the Sudetenland constituted his last territorial demand – and revealed that 'lust for conquest' with which his critics had always charged him. There could be no further dealings with such a man and, as one Chamberlain loyalist noted in his diary, 'we' should fight him as soon as 'we are strong enough'.[38] In Paris, Daladier captured the mood when he told the French Chamber of Deputies that there was nothing to do except 'prepare for war'. Munich had been 'destroyed', the Franco-German Declaration – France's own 'piece of paper', signed on 6 December 1938 – violated both in 'letter and spirit'.[39] In response, French parliamentarians voted the Prime Minister emergency powers, allowing the Government to order by decree all measures necessary for the nation's defence.

Chamberlain, by contrast, did not immediately grasp the transformative nature of the event. Stunned by Hitler's perfidy, his main concern at the Cabinet meeting on the morning of the invasion was to stress the fact that the guarantee to defend the truncated Czecho-Slovakia – made by both Britain and France following the Munich Agreement – no longer existed since that state 'had now completely broken up'.[40] He then delivered a statement to the Commons of such matter-of-fact frigidity that the *News Chronicle* likened it to 'a company chairman announcing the closure of a branch in foreign parts'.[41] Even more shocking, he declared his intention to continue with his policy of appeasement. This caused an instant backlash. Speaking for the Labour Party, David Grenfell attacked a 'credulity which passes all understanding', while Josiah Wedgwood accused the Prime Minister of being 'blinded by his affection for the dictators'.[42] Though they were largely silent during the debate, Tory critics felt that 'Chamberlain will either have to go or completely reverse his policy' and some senior Ministers worried about the Government's survival.[43]

Chamberlain realised his blunder just in time. Two days after the debate, on the eve of his seventieth birthday, he struck a firmer note during a speech in Birmingham. He condemned the violation of the Munich Agreement and demonstrated a new-found scepticism by raising the inevitable question of Hitler's future ambitions: 'Is this the last attack upon a small state, or is it to be followed by others? Is this, in fact, a step in the direction of an attempt to dominate the world by force?' He then warned, for the first time, that Britain would rather go to war than allow such a situation to develop. There was nothing he was not willing to sacrifice in the interests of peace – nothing, that is, except that 'liberty which we have enjoyed for hundreds of years and which we will never surrender'. 'No greater mistake' could therefore be made than to 'suppose that, because it believes war to be a senseless and cruel thing, this nation has so far lost its fibre that it will not take part to the utmost of its power in resisting such a challenge if it were made'.[44]

*

Initially, Chamberlain was reluctant to enter into 'new unspecified commitments operating under conditions which cannot now be foreseen'.[45] Within hours, however, a new crisis had arisen which was to lead not only to the abandonment of this intention but to a revolution in British foreign policy. On the afternoon of Friday 17 March 1939 – two days after the occupation of Prague – the excitable Romanian Minister in London, Virgil Tilea, called on Halifax and informed him that the Germans were demanding a monopoly of Romanian exports and seemed poised to attack his country. Not only was this information erroneous, it was deliberately misleading. The Foreign Office, rattled by the Prague coup, took it seriously, however, and went into a spin. Cabinet Ministers cancelled their weekend plans and telegrams were soon on their way to Warsaw, Ankara, Athens, Belgrade, Paris and Moscow, asking what the reaction to a German attack would be. Within twenty-four hours the British Ambassador in Bucharest had cabled that there was 'not a word of truth' in Tilea's story, but by then it was too late. The Cabinet had been spooked and rumours of an impending German atrocity had been reported in the press.[46] The search for a diplomatic deterrent was on.

Chamberlain's first thought was for a four-power declaration, whereby Britain, France, Russia and Poland would agree to consult together and offer 'joint resistance' in the event of any threat to the security or independence of another European state.[47] The Russians agreed but the Poles, distrustful of the Soviets and afraid of antagonising Hitler, refused. Chamberlain dropped the scheme. He shared the Poles' 'profound distrust of Russia' and doubted the Soviet Union's ability to wage 'an effective offensive even if she wanted to'.[48] For the Prime Minister, the key to the situation was Poland. As the Chiefs of Staff reminded him, it was vital that the Germans should be forced to fight on two fronts and Poland, with her borders with both Germany and Romania, seemed a better strategic – not to mention ideological – bet than Russia. It was therefore decided at a meeting of the Foreign Policy Committee on 27 March 1939 to abandon any attempt to build a coalition around the Soviet Union and to attempt a system of interlocking defence agreements by which the Poles would be induced to come to the aid of the Romanians, having been assured that Britain and France would join in the struggle once they did so. A number of Cabinet Ministers, most notably Sir Samuel Hoare, objected to the exclusion of the Russians but Chamberlain and Halifax were insistent. It was vital to produce a diplomatic deterrent immediately and the only one available, at the present time, was one which focussed on Poland and Romania but not the Soviet Union.[49]

Propelling Chamberlain towards the Polish guarantee – a liability which even ten days earlier had been anathema to him – were a succession of scare stories. Apart from the 'threat' to Romania, there were the persistent rumours of an aerial attack on Britain and, from 20 March, reports of German plans for an invasion of Poland. On 21 March – the day the French President, Albert Lebrun, arrived in London for a state visit – news came of Hitler's latest ultimatum, this time to Lithuania for the return of the Memelland, the northerly part of East Prussia, taken from Germany by the Versailles Treaty. Arriving at Buckingham Palace for the state banquet that evening, Chamberlain was informed that the Germans had mobilised twenty divisions along their western frontier. This succeeded in ruining the Prime Minister's dinner and, as he complained to Ida, his only moment of light relief was when two bejewelled duchesses complained to him about a senior member of the French delegation who kept making passes at them.[50]

The tipping point came when the recently expelled Berlin correspondent of the *News Chronicle*, the 26-year-old Ian Colvin, arrived at the Foreign Office on 29 March 1939 with 'hair-raising' details of an imminent German strike against Poland.[51] Halifax was impressed and took the young man to repeat his story to the Prime Minister. Chamberlain found much of what he heard – an immediate 'swoop on Poland', followed by the absorption of Lithuania and a Russo-German alliance – so fantastic as to doubt its veracity.[52] There had, however, arrived that day a despatch from the British Military Attaché in Berlin which appeared to corroborate Colvin's story. Halifax pushed for an immediate declaration of support for Poland and Chamberlain acquiesced. At an emergency meeting of the Cabinet the following morning, Ministers agreed to 'cross the stream' and prepared telegrams to Warsaw and Paris were despatched.[53] The slippery Polish Foreign Minister, Colonel Józef Beck – who had been stalling on the British request for a Polish declaration in support of Romania – assented 'between two flicks of the ash of his cigarette' and, at 2.45 p.m. on Friday 31 March 1939, Chamberlain announced, to a packed House of Commons, that in the event of an attack on Poland both His Majesty's Government and the Government of

France would feel 'bound at once to lend the Polish Government all support in their power'.[54]

Reflecting upon the Foreign Secretary's character some months later, Rab Butler decided that the best insight into Halifax was that he was a master of foxhounds. Many of his metaphors came from the chase and a particular favourite was that 'one [should] not jump into a field until one can see a way of jumping out'. In the case of the Polish guarantee, however, 'a jump from a dangerous main road had suddenly to be made over a high hedge in cold blood'.[55] Setting aside the fact that Butler (almost alone among senior figures) would have continued to appease Germany over her claims to Poland, this was not an inaccurate description. The decision to guarantee Poland had been taken without any consideration of Poland's military capabilities or how the Western Powers would implement their pledge should they be called upon to do so. Worse, by simply issuing a unilateral guarantee the British had lost the one lever they possessed for persuading the short-sighted Beck to agree to a series of defensive agreements with Poland's neighbours. The Romanians, despite the 'threat' to their country, formed no part of the declaration and the Soviet Ambassador was only informed of the initiative two hours before Chamberlain announced it. Understandably, the Russians were furious. 'Chamberlain is prompting Hitler to direct his aggression to the north-east', wrote the long-suffering Maxim Litvinov to Ivan Maisky. He 'is counting on us to resist occupation of the Baltic area and expecting that this will lead to the Soviet–German clash he had been hoping for'.[56] Nor were Soviet voices the only ones raised in criticism. Although the guarantee was welcomed in almost every quarter of the House of Commons and in the majority of the press, Lloyd George warned Chamberlain that the exclusion of the Russians was 'damnably dangerous', while Bob Boothby later dubbed it 'one of the most reckless gestures in British history'.[57]

In justice to Chamberlain and Halifax, neither man saw the guarantee to Poland as the final word nor, in isolation, as a practical military proposition. On the contrary, the announcement on 31 March was a temporary solution, designed to deter Hitler from an immediate strike against Poland, which would then be used as the cornerstone of a wider defensive agreement in eastern Europe. Unfortunately, having awarded the prize, the British found it impossible to induce the Poles to play the game. Beck arrived in London on 4 April for talks but, despite the pleas of both Chamberlain and Halifax, refused either to include Russia in the agreement or to pledge Polish assistance for Romania in the event of a German attack. Chamberlain found this attitude, particularly regarding Romania, disappointing. He was, however, able to console himself that his actions had received broad support and that 'Hitler has received a definite check'.[58] No sooner did one crisis seem to be abating, however, than another emerged.

*

Not to be outdone by Hitler, Mussolini invaded the Kingdom of Albania at dawn on 7 April 1939. King Zog exhorted his subjects to fight 'to the last drop of blood' and then fled, along with his Hungarian Queen, their two-day-old son and much of the country's gold reserves. Chamberlain, who was forced, once again, to abandon a fishing holiday, was incandescent. He had staked his reputation on his attempt to win Mussolini over and only the week before had sent word, via Joseph Ball and Adrian Dingli, that he was prepared to act as mediator between Italy and France. Now, like a spurned lover, he cursed the Italian dictator as 'a sneak and a cad' and confessed that 'such faith as I ever had in the assurances of dictators is rapidly being whittled away'. He refused to denounce the Anglo-Italian Agreement but was in no doubt that 'rapprochement with Italy has been blocked by Musso just as Hitler has blocked any German rapprochement'.[59]

As with the Prague coup, the Albanian adventure set off an avalanche of activity. Halifax, emerging from a three-hour church service (it was Good Friday), agreed with Cadogan that Britain must move quickly to set up 'a barrier with Greece and Turkey' to secure the Mediterranean and, on 10 April, the Foreign Policy Committee decided that Greece should be guaranteed.*[60] Rumours of an Italian invasion of Corfu were rife and the Admiralty was jittery about a number of British warships currently 'lolling' outside Italian ports.[61] At the same time, the Romanians were agitating for their own protection. The melodramatic Tilea went into action again but got short

* According to Harold Macmillan, the Foreign Secretary's immediate reaction on hearing of the invasion was: 'And on Good Friday too!'

shrift from the Foreign Office. The British were not yet in the business of issuing unilateral guarantees to all and sundry. Where the British demurred, however, the French bit. Unnerved by stories of a German dash for oil-rich Romania, Daladier demanded an immediate declaration of Western support. The British protested – British strategy was to build a 'dam' of states, not a collection of loose boulders – but gave in when the French proved intransigent. On 13 April 1939, Chamberlain announced guarantees for both Greece and Romania, followed a month later by an Anglo-Turkish declaration of mutual defence.

In tandem with this frenetic diplomacy came a series of major advances in British rearmament. On 29 March, two weeks after the annexation of Czechoslovakia, the Cabinet decided to double the size of the Territorial Army and, on 20 April, Chamberlain finally announced the creation of a Ministry of Supply. On the same day, he was forced to bow to the almost inexorable pressure coming from the French Government, his own party and Hore-Belisha (who threatened to resign as Secretary of State for War over the issue) and agree the introduction of conscription. On 27 April, despite the noteworthy opposition of the Labour Party, the Commons passed the Military Training Bill. It was a limited measure – encompassing only men aged twenty and twenty-one – but it was a momentous signal of intent: the first time that compulsory military service had been introduced in Britain, during peacetime, in nearly 300 years.

*

For many who had supported appeasement, the invasion of Czechoslovakia represented a turning point. 'I have reluctantly become convinced that Nazism is out for nothing short of world domination', wrote the soon-to-be Duke of Hamilton, previously an advocate of Anglo-German friendship and the man whom Hitler's party deputy, Rudolf Hess, was on his way to visit when he parachuted into southern Scotland on 10 May 1941.[62] Lord Lothian admitted that he had been wrong about Hitler – 'in effect a fanatical gangster who will stop at nothing' – while Lord Londonderry complained to a fellow sympathiser that 'the German Chancellor has, I regret to say, overstepped all limits and I see no possibility of any confidence ever again being placed in his statements and undertakings'.[63] Even that apologist for dictators the *Daily Mail*'s George Ward Price experienced a conversion and declared in his new book, *Year of Reckoning*, that the possibility of 'cordial relations' between Britain and Germany had 'passed away'. He also admitted, for the first time, that the Nazis had 'done much evil' within Germany herself.[64]

For a small minority, however, the stakes were too high to abandon the attempt to satisfy Hitler by reasonable concessions. Indeed, some British aristocrats seem to have become so terrified by the prospect of what was now being talked of as an 'inevitable' war that they decided to enter the political fray, just as the original fellow travellers and amateur diplomats were leaving it. Thus, the Duke of Wellington became one of the earliest members of the Right Club – an elite pro-German, pro-peace, anti-Semitic organisation, set up by Captain Archibald Ramsay MP in May 1939; the Duke of Westminster joined 'the Link' – a pro-German, in many cases pro-Nazi and anti-Semitic collection of individuals, bound together by a desire to improve Anglo-German relations; and the Marquess of Tavistock, soon to become the Duke of Bedford, founded the British People's Party – an economically radical, pacifist, pro-German 'movement'.*

Another aristocrat who was to play a small, though increasingly desperate, part in the behind-the-scenes story of appeasement was the Duke of Buccleuch. A keen supporter of the Munich Agreement and implacable opponent of war with Germany, Buccleuch did not believe that the Prague coup should alter the Government's policy. On the contrary, as he wrote to Rab Butler shortly after the event, 'neither Hitler nor Ribbentrop are likely to be quite as inhuman as featured … [and] I think even in these times Britain can guide their general policy into safer channels'. In particular, the Duke was concerned by the self-fulfilling potential of the atmosphere of suspicion which had developed between the two countries. If each side believed that the other was determined on war, then war would surely be the outcome. In these circumstances, he considered it important for 'unofficial visitors'

---

* On 7 December 1941, the Regional Commissioner for Internal Security in Scotland belatedly decided that the then Duke of Bedford was to be detained in the event of a German invasion.

to maintain their contacts with prominent members of the regime, thereby reducing suspicions, and 'even the effect of Miss Mitford's frequent meetings with the Führer should not be underestimated'.[65]

It was in this spirit that Buccleuch, along with Lord Brocket, decided to visit Berlin just ahead of Hitler's fiftieth birthday celebrations, due on 20 April 1939. The Foreign Office, seeking to project an attitude of British firmness, was appalled. 'Ye Gods and little fishes! *Is* the world upside down?' was Sir Alexander Cadogan's response when he learnt the news. The Permanent Under-Secretary did not want the Führer to receive any '"happy returns" (as we don't want any of them!)' and was particularly horrified by a madcap scheme of the rector of St Paul's, Knightsbridge in which Hitler would be induced to use the occasion of his birthday to summon an international peace conference. Both Halifax and Cadogan saw the rector and explained that 'they didn't think anything of his idea', but Buccleuch, to whom the rector had entrusted his scheme, had left for Germany before anyone at the Foreign Office had been able to get hold of him. All Cadogan was left hoping was that 'those two lunatics' (Brocket and Buccleuch) 'make it perfectly clear that they have no *sort* of official approval of any kind'.[66]

Fortunately, the British Embassy was able to act as something of a brake on the peers' activities. Arriving in Berlin on 15 April, the two men lost little time in seeking the advice of the Embassy as to how they should respond if pressed to accept invitations to the Führer's birthday celebrations. The British Counsellor, Sir George Ogilvie-Forbes, was tact itself. He resisted the temptation to tell their Lordships that they could have avoided this dilemma by staying in England and instead stated that while Brocket was a private citizen and must rely on his own judgement (such as it existed), the Duke was Lord Steward of the Household, a 'high official of the King's court'. Given this, Buccleuch must consider the possibility that his presence at the event, which would be 'advertised' and 'made much of', might be considered by some as 'not being all square with the present feeling of the King's Government'. Would it therefore not be prudent to refer the question to Buckingham Palace or, alternatively, 'discover' that there was in fact another engagement, 'outside Germany', which required his urgent attendance?[67] Buccleuch took the advice. The King's Private Secretary was consulted and when the answer came that His Majesty would really rather his Lord Steward did not attend the Führer's birthday celebrations, the Duke caught an early flight back to England.

Despite this, Buccleuch left Germany with a renewed sense of optimism. He had seen a large number of people – mainly members of the German aristocracy – and had a lengthy interview with Ribbentrop. Writing a report of his visit for the Prime Minister and the Foreign Office, he stated that there was 'great confidence and determination' among those with whom he had conversed to avoid war and a widespread 'desire for improvement in Anglo-German relations'. Crucially, he believed that the Polish issue was solvable. Hitler's demands – for the return of Danzig (an almost entirely German city) and freer transit through the Polish Corridor – were, 'in comparison with recent acts of aggression ... very reasonable and natural, and their concession likely to minimise the risk of trouble in a very dangerous zone and of our people being committed to war in a bad cause'. The vital thing was to persuade the Poles to negotiate.[68]

In a covering letter to Butler, Buccleuch gave even freer rein to his optimism, though he feared the effect of warmongers in Westminster:

> The atmosphere and west-end gossip and anti-German bias in London are depressing, and have become more so lately. It seems now so impossible for a few individuals to stand up successfully against the powerful influence of public men of the Churchill, Amery, Eden type, and so many of those who control the press. I feel that they have really scorned all along the possibility of compromise or consideration of any arguments which the other side might advance, and thus bring war much closer. An early success for Mr Chamberlain on a peaceful basis seems most important if we are not to see Winston Churchill and others in the Cabinet, and a complete anti-German bloc leading to a world war to decide, at the expense of many millions, whether Winston or Hitler should take first place.[69]

*

Chamberlain was encouraged by the reports from Buccleuch and Brocket. Unlike the Duke, Brocket had remained for the birthday parade, where he was told that Hitler denied that he had broken the Munich Agreement – Czechoslovakia, he claimed, had simply imploded – and that, only recently, the Führer had been heard to declare that the 'proudest day' of his life would be the day when he could welcome the King and Queen to Berlin.[70] 'So we are all under a complete misunderstanding,' joked Chamberlain, 'Hitler "raly is a good young man" and we have all misjudged him!' He was, nonetheless, heartened. 'Every month that passes without war makes war more unlikely', he wrote to his sisters towards the end of April 1939, and although 'I expect to have more periods of acute anxiety', it is perhaps possible that 'Hitler has realised that he has now touched the limit and has decided to put the best face on it'.[71]

It was a vain hope. Frustrated in his attempts to bully the Poles into ceding the former German port of Danzig and make concessions over the Polish Corridor (which split Germany in two), Hitler had already decided to solve the 'Polish question' by force. He had been infuriated by the British guarantee – 'I'll brew them a devil's potion', he vowed when he heard the news – but not deterred.[72] By 3 April, the directive ordering the planning for 'Case White', the invasion of Poland, was ready and, on 11 April, Hitler issued it. The armed forces, the order stated, must be ready to carry out the operation any time after 1 September 1939. The countdown had begun.

XX

Deterring the Dictators

> I am not prepared to regard Soviet Russia as a freedom-loving nation, but we cannot do without her now ... I know they have shot a lot of people but there are about 170,000,000 of them still left.
>
> Robert Bower MP, House of Commons, 15 March 1939[1]

The British guarantee to Poland contained great risk as well as considerable irony. In one fell swoop, the Government had ceded the decision as to whether the country would be involved in war to a 'faraway country' of which they knew virtually nothing and to a man whom H. G. Wells had recently described as a 'certifiable lunatic'.[2] Austen Chamberlain had previously declared that the Polish Corridor was not worth the bones of a single British grenadier while, only the year before, his half-brother had refused to guarantee Czechoslovakia on the grounds that His Majesty's Government could not possibly yield such a vital decision to the caprice of foreign powers. Of course, the Polish guarantee was not designed to lead to war but to deter Hitler from starting one. In order to make the deterrent effective, however, the Western Powers needed to reach an understanding with Soviet Russia, a nation widely distrusted and against which Nazi Germany had originally been conceived as a bulwark.

Initially, neither the British nor the French considered the USSR particularly important. The Chiefs of Staff cast doubt on her military worth, while the diplomats pointed to the unwillingness of other states to be associated with her. Following the failure of the British to form a system of alliances in eastern Europe and at the noisy insistence of the Opposition in Westminster, however, the issue of the Soviet Union came to the fore. On 14 April 1939, Lord Halifax instructed

Sir William Seeds, the British Ambassador in Moscow, to ask Litvinov whether the Russians would make a declaration pledging support for any neighbour along her western frontier who fell victim to unprovoked aggression. Good-naturedly, Litvinov refused. Instead, he proposed a tripartite mutual assistance pact between Britain, France and Russia, to cover all states between the Baltic and the Black seas. This the British rejected. The Foreign Policy Committee could see no advantages in an alliance with Russia – on the contrary, such a move was likely to perturb Britain's allies in eastern Europe – and, although Chamberlain had assured the Labour leadership that he had 'no ideological objection to an agreement with Russia', he admitted privately of being 'deeply suspicious' of her.[3]

Chamberlain was not unique in his distrust. Chips Channon thought co-operating with the Bolsheviks 'madness', while Britain's former Ambassador to Japan, Sir Francis Lindley, told the Conservative Foreign Policy Committee (just after having hosted the Chamberlains for the Whitsun holiday) that he 'prayed nightly that the Anglo-Russian show might break down as it would mean war and not peace and communist propaganda was the greatest evil of this century'.[4] Within a few weeks, however, Chamberlain was under serious pressure from his own Cabinet to bury his misgivings and accept the Soviet advances.

On 4 May 1939, news broke that Litvinov had been dismissed and Vyacheslav Molotov, Stalin's right-hand man and Chairman of the Council of Ministers, had been appointed as the new People's Commissar for Foreign Affairs. The Foreign Office was confused and apprehensive. Although Maisky insisted that the appointment betokened no change in Soviet policy, Seeds feared that it signalled the abandonment of collective security and a retreat into isolation. Six days later, the Chiefs of Staff performed a startling about-turn and recommended a full military alliance with the Soviet Union. 'The active and whole-hearted assistance of Russia as our ally would be of great value, particularly in containing substantial enemy forces', they wrote, while, conversely, it was important not to 'overlook the danger which would result from a rapprochement between Germany and Russia – an aim which has been in the minds of the German General Staff for many years'.[5]

These developments helped persuade the majority of the Cabinet, including Halifax, that the Russian offer should, in fact, now be accepted. Lord Chatfield, who had replaced Sir Thomas Inskip as Minister for the Co-ordination of Defence, thought that the possibility of war with Russia would be a 'great deterrent' to Germany, while Sir Samuel Hoare argued that 'we should be ... doing everything in our power to bring in Russia on our side' and avoid the nightmare scenario of a Russo-German agreement.[6] The French had already stated their willingness to accept the Soviet proposal and were lobbying for the British to follow suit, while Chamberlain's opponents in Parliament – the Labour Party, Lloyd George and Churchill – had never wavered from what the Prime Minister described as their 'pathetic belief that in Russia is the key to our salvation'.[7]

Chamberlain remained wholeheartedly opposed to the idea of an alliance. He retained his doubts as to Russia's military worth but, more importantly, realised that an alliance would mean the final division of Europe into 'opposing blocs' and thus close the door on any future negotiations or even 'discussion with the totalitarians'.[8] 'I cannot rid myself of the suspicion that they [the Russians] are chiefly concerned to see the "capitalist" powers tear each other to pieces while they stay out themselves', he confessed to Ida on 21 May. The day before, he told Sir Alexander Cadogan that he would rather resign than sign an alliance with the Soviet Union.[9]

Unfortunately for Chamberlain, almost none of his colleagues agreed with him. Halifax had reluctantly concluded that they should go the 'whole-hog' and accept the Soviet proposals and even Sir John Simon now seemed in favour of the alliance.[10] Just when all seemed lost, however, Sir Horace Wilson came up with a diabolically ingenious solution. Rather than simply accept the Russian proposals, the British should insist that their obligations should derive from the Covenant of the League of Nations. Thus, they would 'catch all the mugwumps' (Russophiles, League of Nations cranks, collective security enthusiasts), endow the agreement with a 'temporary character' and, most crucially, not antagonise the Germans.[11] It was a stunningly cynical move. Not only had Chamberlain barely mentioned the League – an institution he held in contempt – since he became Prime Minister, but its failure to resist aggression in Manchuria, Abyssinia, Austria and Czechoslovakia had been one of the most glaring themes of the decade. To resurrect it now would merely arouse Soviet suspicions while doing nothing to frighten the Germans. 'It will only make the

Nazis poke fun at us', rejoiced Channon, who feared that a conventional alliance 'might have been the signal for an immediate war'.[12] Yet while this was, as one historian has written, 'a poisonously stupid and criminally asinine piece of ingenuity', the refusal of Molotov to realise that it was in the interests of the Soviet Union to conclude an alliance with the West, as much as it was in the interests of the West to ally itself with the Soviets, and to compromise accordingly, was equally pig-headed and, from the perspective of 1941–45 and twenty-six million Soviet dead, indictable.[13]

★

One of the reasons Chamberlain was so opposed to the Russian alliance was that he had not fully renounced appeasement. Although he appreciated the danger of German designs on Poland and struggled to see his way towards détente, 'as long as the Jews obstinately go on refusing to shoot Hitler!', he still believed that the situation could be rescued by careful and, if necessary, secret diplomacy.[14] On 3 May 1939, Cadogan saw a telephone intercept which indicated that 'No. 10 were talking "appeasement" again', while Oliver Harvey believed a letter from Lord Rushcliffe in *The Times*, advocating negotiations between Poland and Germany, had been inspired by Horace Wilson. A few weeks later, Chamberlain launched a secret scheme which would see the 'Scandinavians' acting as mediators over Danzig.[15] It came to nothing but is indicative of his continued faith in his policy or, as General Sir Edmund Ironside, Inspector General of British Overseas Forces, put it, his 'firm belief that God has chosen him as an instrument to prevent this threatened war'.[16]

If Chamberlain still hoped that negotiations might yield results, public opinion was both more sceptical and more resolute. 'My old man says now as we can't trust 'Itler any more there's no use arguing with him; now we've got to give 'im a licking', explained Virginia Cowles's landlady shortly after the invasion of Prague.[17] At around the same time the Duke of Devonshire, a junior member of the Government, decided to canvass the views of his chauffeur. 'Well, Gibson, and what do you think about Hitler?' 'Well, your Grace, it seems to me that … he is none too popular in this district', came the understated reply.[18]

The ecstasy and the agony: (*above*) Hitler addresses a delirious crowd in Vienna's Heldenplatz, 15 March 1938, following the declaration of the Anschluss; (*below*) Viennese Jews are forced to scrub the streets.

Left: 'As vain as he is stupid and as stupid as he is vain': former Ambassador, now German Foreign Minister, Joachim von Ribbentrop leaves the German Embassy in London, 13 March 1938.

Below: Two very different conceptions of the German problem: Sir Robert Vansittart (left) and his successor as Permanent Head of the Foreign Office, Sir Alexander Cadogan, in Downing Street, 11 September 1938.

'The flying messenger of peace': Neville Chamberlain prepares to depart Heston airport for his first meeting with Hitler during the Czech crisis, 15 September 1938.

The conversation did not exactly flow: Chamberlain struggles to make small talk at the Berghof, 15 September 1938.

All smiles, but Chamberlain's second meeting with Hitler at Bad Godesberg, 22–24 September 1938, ended in deadlock.

'How horrible … it is that we should be digging trenches and trying on gas masks here because of a quarrel in a faraway country' – Neville Chamberlain, 27 September 1938.

Above: The participants of the Munich Conference, 29 September 1938: Neville Chamberlain, Edouard Daladier, Adolf Hitler, Benito Mussolini and Count Galeazzo Ciano.

Above: 'PEACE!': A London florist expresses her gratitude, 30 September 1938.

Right: 'Peace for our time': Chamberlain makes his infamous boast from the window of 10 Downing Street, 30 September 1938.

Mixed emotions: women in the Sudeten town of Eger react to the entry of German troops, following the Munich Agreement.

Roman holiday: Chamberlain inspects the Duce's personal bodyguard, 11 January 1939.

'Naked and unashamed agression': German troops enter the grounds of the Hradčany Castle in Prague, 15 March 1939.

The Devils' Alliance: Soviet Commissar for Foreign Affairs, Vyacheslav Molotov, signs the Nazi–Soviet Pact, watched by Joachim von Ribbentrop and a clearly pleased Joseph Stalin, 23 August 1939.

Blitzkrieg: German soldiers advance
through Polish countryside,
1 September 1939.

Rivals united in adversity:
Winston Churchill and Neville Chamberlain,
23 February 1940.

Such views appear to have been typical. In July, an opinion poll found that 76 per cent of Britons believed that if Germany and Poland went to war over Danzig then Britain should honour her obligations and declare war, while a French questionnaire suggested that 70 per cent of French citizens were in favour of resisting further German demands. An overwhelming 87 per cent of Britons supported an alliance with the Soviet Union and even that bastion of isolationism the *Daily Express* noted the new spirit of defiance: 'We have forty-nine million foreign secretaries in Britain these days and they all seem to want to make a stand.'[19]

In late April, a spate of articles appeared urging Chamberlain to 'bring back Churchill'. The *Evening News* wanted him as First Lord of the Admiralty or Secretary of State for Air, while the *Sunday Pictorial* suggested he be appointed Lord President of the Council, since the incumbent, Lord Runciman, had had the 'impertinence to embark on a four months' holiday'.[20] Three days later, the editor of the *Pictorial* wrote to Churchill to say that he had received over 2,000 letters, almost all of them supportive: '"No more boot-licking to Hitler" is the general line of comment.'[21] At around the same time, Victor Cazalet recorded his belief that 'Winston' should now be in the Cabinet. 'He has been right about everything for the last five years and his inclusion in the Government would do more to show Germany that we mean business than anything else.'[22]

Many had hoped to see Churchill appointed to lead the newly created Ministry of Supply – an innovation for which he had been campaigning since 1936. But when the Prime Minister rose in the Commons on 20 April, he announced that the post was to be filled by Leslie Burgin, the National Liberal Minister for Transport and a nonentity. Listening to the noise which greeted this announcement, Harold Nicolson could not decide whether it was a 'gasp of horror' or a 'groan of pain'. What was not in doubt was that Chamberlain's decision to overlook Churchill and appoint just another yes-man created a deplorable impression and convinced Nicolson, as well as others, that the Prime Minister was running 'a dual policy – one the overt policy of arming, and the other the *secret de l'Empereur*, namely appeasement plus Horace Wilson'.[23]

This was broadly correct. Writing to Ida on 23 April, Chamberlain explained that the Ministry of Supply was not the right post for

Churchill but, more fundamentally, he was determined to exclude him on the grounds that 'if there is any possibility of easing the tension and getting back to normal relations with the dictators I wouldn't risk it by what would certainly be regarded by them as a challenge'.[24] The following week he revealed that he was contemplating a fresh approach to Mussolini, as a means of 'keeping Master Hitler quiet', and also expressed his relief that Hitler's Reichstag speech of 28 April – in which he had renounced both the Polish Non-Aggression Pact and the Anglo-German Naval Agreement – was 'more conciliatory and less provocative than had been expected'. 'I can't see Hitler starting a world war for Danzig', he stated confidently.[25]

Halifax, on the other hand, had been shorn of his previous illusions and, as Channon noted, 'is weaned away from Neville now on many points'.[26] At the beginning of June he had disturbed anti-appeasers by a speech in the House of Lords in which he had tried to reassure the German people that Britain had not 'abandoned all desire to reach an understanding with Germany' and even spoke of 'rival claims' which might be adjusted to 'secure lasting peace'.[27] Yet this was largely designed as a counter to Nazi propaganda which claimed that Britain was hell-bent on crushing Germany through a policy of encirclement. A few weeks later, his speech to the Royal Institute of International Affairs provided very different meat. The theme, as Cadogan summarised, was 'We don't want to fight, but by Jingo if we do' and Halifax did it full justice, telling his audience that the threat of military force was 'holding the world to ransom' and that the predominant task must be 'to resist aggression'.[28]

Meanwhile, the 'bring back Churchill' campaign was reaching its peak. On 3 July 1939, after lobbying by Nicolson, Anthony Eden and Lord Astor (transformed, since Munich, into the most resolute of resisters), the *Daily Telegraph* came out with a thumping, two-column editorial demanding Churchill's inclusion in the Government. It had been preceded by a similar call from Garvin in the *Observer* and was followed by appeals in the *Yorkshire Post*, the *Manchester Guardian*, the *Daily Mirror*, the *News Chronicle*, the *Star* and the *Evening News*. On 5 July, Lord Rothermere fired the *Daily Mail*'s cannon in support and soon almost the entire press was united, with only the Beaverbrook titles and *The Times* remaining aloof from the campaign. For the Conservative peer Lord Selborne the issue was simple. 'I have never been a follower of Mr Churchill', explained the former Cabinet Minister in a letter to the *Daily Telegraph*, 'but I agree with those who think that [his] inclusion … in the Government at this particular moment would be a gesture which even Dr Goebbels could not fail to understand.'[29]

This point was brought home to the British Government by Lieutenant-Colonel Count Gerhard von Schwerin, an officer on the German General Staff and opponent of war, who travelled to London at the beginning of July to urge the British to make their determination to resist further aggression clear through some ostentatious act. At first, he struggled to find an audience. 'If you want to know what I think of his coming over here, at a time when our country's relations with his are as bad as they are today, I think it is a damned cheek', remarked one officer in military intelligence.[30] Eventually, however, the Count managed to see a number of important people, including the Deputy Chief Whip, James Stuart; the former British Military Attaché to Berlin, General James Marshall-Cornwall; and Gladwyn Jebb from the Foreign Office. To this trio, Schwerin explained that 'Hitler was convinced that British foreign policy was thoroughly flabby'. He did not believe that Britain was prepared to risk her Empire over Poland, and only deeds stood a chance of disabusing him. Schwerin suggested a show of British naval strength in the Baltic and the despatch of an air-striking force to France. By far the most effective means of impressing the Führer, however, would be to recall Churchill. 'Churchill is the only Englishman Hitler is afraid of', the officer explained, and the 'mere fact of giving him a leading ministerial post would convince Hitler that we really mean to stand up to him'.[31]

Chamberlain was not persuaded. He appreciated Churchill's ability but doubted whether his inclusion in Cabinet would make his own task any easier. From his own experience, Churchill tended to dominate proceedings and his constant outpouring of ideas and memoranda had the ability to 'monopolise the time of the whole Ministry'. More fundamentally, however, he was against recalling Churchill because he had 'not yet given up hopes of peace'. The Polish situation was dangerous but 'if Hitler were asking for Danzig in a normal way it might be possible to arrange things'.[32]

*

From wherever Chamberlain derived his optimism, it was not from developments on the international scene. On 22 May 1939, Ciano and Ribbentrop signed a German–Italian military alliance, the so-called Pact of Steel, and in mid-June the Japanese blockaded the British concession of Tientsin in northern China. Chamberlain found it 'maddening to have to hold our hands in face of such humiliations' but recognised that it was too dangerous to put 'such temptations in Hitler's way' by becoming embroiled in conflict with the 'Japs'.[33] Nor could the reports from Germany be said to be providing anything like encouragement. Rumours of a coup in Danzig – apparently teeming with members of the SS – began to spread from the middle of April, while on 5 May Sir Nevile Henderson relayed details of a conversation between General Karl-Heinrich Bodenschatz, liaison officer between Göring and Hitler, and the Polish Military Attaché in which the General had stated that 'war this year was inevitable'.[34]

Equally if not more alarming were the rumours of rapprochement between Berlin and Moscow. Sir Robert Vansittart's intelligence network had begun to report on German–Soviet negotiations at the beginning of May and, on the 8th of that month, Robert Coulondre, the new French Ambassador in Berlin, told Henderson that his sources believed Hitler was aiming at a non-aggression pact with Stalin. The following month, Erich Kordt, Ribbentrop's Chief of Staff and part of the anti-Nazi opposition, arrived in London to warn the British that German–Soviet negotiations were already under way and that if the British wanted an alliance with Russia then they 'had better be quick about it!'[35] According to Kordt, Hitler had not yet decided when he was going to attack the Poles but separate intelligence, provided by Ian Colvin, suggested that 25 August had been earmarked for 'a show-down'.[36]

In this climate, overt or official attempts at appeasement were clearly impossible. Britain was committed to defending Polish independence and the task of the British Government was to convince Hitler that it was in earnest. Behind the scenes, however, a number of semi-official discussions were taking place which undermined this position. On 6 June, Dr Helmut Wohltat, the leading official of the German four-year (economic) plan under Göring, met Sir Horace Wilson, Sir Joseph Ball and Henry Drummond Wolff in the London home of the Duke of Westminster. The Duke was not present and no record of the conversation appears to have been kept. It seems clear from subsequent records, however, that Wohltat presented a scheme for economic appeasement in which Britain would 'recognise Germany's sphere of economic interest in south-eastern and eastern Europe'. The next day, when he repeated his plan to Frank Ashton-Gwatkin, previously an advocate of such ameliorative measures, he got little sympathy. 'If we were looking for a symbol of peace I thought that it would be more effective if Herr Hitler were to remodel his Cabinet and give to certain of his advisers that opportunity for leisure which their services had so amply deserved', commented the Foreign Office official drily.[37] Yet Wohltat had been encouraged by his meeting with the Prime Minister's two closest advisers – sufficient to send a report of the conversation to Göring – and, when he returned to London on 17 July, lost no time in revisiting both Wilson and the topic.

According to his records of the two conversations he had with Wohltat, on 19 and 20 July, Wilson was firm and non-committal. Like any good residents of a street, the Chief Industrial Adviser explained, the British were perfectly willing to be neighbourly but they did not like it 'if one of the householders made lots of nasty noises during the night and the next day went battering in the doors of some of the other residents'. As such, the British Government was prepared to listen to any ideas for the improvement of relations between their two countries but, given the recent history of unneighbourly behaviour, 'the initiative must come from the German side'.[38]

Wohltat's account was very different. According to the German official, Wilson had prepared a memorandum, apparently with Chamberlain's approval, which proposed the establishment of secret negotiations between the two countries, leading to an Anglo-German statement renouncing aggression (this, Wilson explained, would make the British guarantee to Poland 'superfluous'); declarations of 'non-interference' in each other's economic spheres; a disarmament agreement; and a 'colonial condominium' in Africa.[39] It should be stressed that this document has never been found and that Wohltat's objective and that of his ally, the German Ambassador, Herbert von Dirksen, was to avoid war by persuading Hitler to renew negotiations with the British. For these reasons, historians have, probably rightly, dismissed the Wohltat record. There is, however, another source which suggests that more was discussed at the meeting than Wilson admitted in his notes. On 21 July, the day after Wilson's second meeting with Wohltat, Jim Thomas, Eden's former Parliamentary Private Secretary, wrote excitedly to Lord Cranborne to say that he had heard, on the strongest possible authority, that Horace Wilson had a plan to offer Germany 'a huge loan' in return for disarmament and the restoration of Bohemia and Moravia. According to Thomas's source, the Government did not expect this plan to be accepted but believed that it would provide the platform for a General Election in October. 'They will say "we have made a reasonable offer to Germany, she has refused, we must therefore have a united nation behind the Coroner [Chamberlain] to face this irreconcilable Germany"' and then there will be a 'second Hoare–Lavalesque attempt at a deal'.[40] Interestingly, Wohltat also mentioned that Ball told him that a General Election was provisionally scheduled for 14 November and that the Prime Minister had to decide whether he was going to fight it on the issue of peace or preparations for war with Germany.

It is of course more than possible that Thomas's source (who may have been someone within the French Embassy) was wrong, exaggerating, or simply trying to kill off any potential Anglo-German negotiations. Cranborne certainly did not react with undue excitement, commenting that 'with all due deference to Sir H. Wilson, I think that his new plan is the silliest of the many that his puerile brain has produced'.[41] Either way, it was not Wilson who caused a full-scale diplomatic incident but the reckless behaviour of Robert Hudson, the Minister for Overseas Trade.

According to Hudson's account of his conversation with Wohltat – which occurred on the evening of 20 July, almost immediately after Wilson's second meeting – he raised a number of ambitious schemes which might ease international tensions. There were vast areas, such as Russia and China, which offered 'almost unlimited openings for capital development'; Britain, the US and Germany should abolish exchange restrictions and import quotas; and there was Chamberlain's old idea of a new system of colonial administration in Africa. Unfortunately, the unstable state of Europe meant that many people believed that Britain would soon be at war with Germany. If, however, a fundamental change was to take place and Hitler was prepared to agree to some measure of disarmament then there was the possibility of 'establishing Germany on a strong economic basis'.[42] This was the nub. The following evening,

Hudson, who according to a fellow Tory MP 'looks as though he has just inherited a fortune and has been celebrating his luck with a hot bath', boasted about his 'peace-saving' initiative at a dinner attended by the journalists Victor Gordon-Lennox and Vernon Bartlett.[43] And the next morning, 22 July, both the *Daily Telegraph* and the *News Chronicle* announced the sensational news that Britain had offered Germany a £100 million loan in exchange for disarmament.

The uproar was instantaneous. Paris and Warsaw reacted with understandable consternation, while the German and Italian press ridiculed a 'Shylock proposal' which exemplified Britain's 'shark-like mania of buying the world'.[44] British newspapers indulged in a fever of speculative indignation and questions were raised in Parliament. Chamberlain denied that there was or ever had been discussion of a British loan. Hudson had made no such suggestion and had, in any case, been acting on his own initiative. But the damage was done. Although the French and Poles accepted the British denial, the affair was a propaganda gift to the Axis, while the most important effect of this 'piece of super-appeasement' was to increase the already substantial suspicions of the Russians. 'I doubt whether folly could be pushed to a fuller extreme', commented the Foreign Office's Gladwyn Jebb.[45]

*

Chamberlain was annoyed by Hudson's 'gaffe', which had done considerable damage and allowed his enemies to say, 'There, I told you so. He means to sell the Poles.' He was, however, happy to pursue conversations through 'discreeter channels'.[46] On 27 July, Lord Kemsley, the pro-appeasement owner of the *Sunday Times*, had an hour-long interview with Hitler at Bayreuth during which he managed to extract from the Führer the suggestion that Britain and Germany should each put their demands on paper in the hope that 'this might lead to a discussion'.*[47] Downing Street reacted with excitement and a secret reply was despatched.

* Less helpful was Kemsley's assurance to Alfred Rosenberg, the Nazi Party's chief ideologue and self-proclaimed foreign policy expert, that Chamberlain 'would negotiate in Moscow reluctantly and was ready to back out'; while his wife declared that 'only the Jews wanted to bring about a war between Germany and England'.

At the same time, Chamberlain and Halifax were in touch with two Swedish business friends of Göring's, Axel Wenner-Gren and Birger Dahlerus, who had taken it upon themselves to act as intermediaries between the Field Marshal and the British Government. According to Dahlerus, it would be helpful if Göring could meet a group of British businessmen who could explain to him the 'British point of view'.[48] Halifax agreed and, on 7 August, seven leading men from commerce and industry met the Field Marshal at an estate belonging to Dahlerus's wife, in Schleswig-Holstein. There they gave a thorough summary of the British position, emphasising that, while the country did not want war, it had decided that 'the arbitrary use of military power must be limited at some point'.[49] While they spoke Göring scowled and scribbled sarcastic comments, as well as an angry face, on the memorandum he had been handed. When his British interlocutors had finished he launched into a tirade, lambasting the British for their hypocrisy, their interference in other nations' affairs and their warmongering. Britain and Poland must settle the question of Danzig with Germany at once; there must be direct conversations between the British and German Governments; and there must be a four-power conference to settle all outstanding matters, he demanded.[50]

Even less encouraging was the report of that indefatigable seeker of Anglo-German détente Ernest Tennant, who in late July embarked on a final 'peace mission' to Ribbentrop. As Tennant recalled, the previous meeting between the two men, in Berlin in June, had not been a happy one. The German Foreign Minister had been at his most pompous and the merchant banker had been forced to hear of both Ribbentrop's and Hitler's shock at a number of letters he had received from people in England 'asking would he please be good enough to see that war did not break out until after Ascot, or until after the Eton and Harrow match, or until after various other sporting or social engagements'.[51] Despite this and the multitude of evidence to the contrary, Tennant still believed that Ribbentrop was 'anxious' for an Anglo-German understanding. Accordingly, he wrote to Chamberlain asking his permission to try a fresh approach, and on 10 July Horace Wilson conveyed the Prime Minister's conditional blessing. The conditions were that the mission was to be secret and that the banker was to stick to the line that the Government was determined to 'assist any state whose independence is threatened' but was willing to 'reason with reasonable people'.[52]

Unfortunately, as Tennant should have known, there was nothing reasonable about Ribbentrop. Meeting the German Foreign Minister in Salzburg's old castle, he was only allowed to enjoy a brief cup of tea before his host embarked on a four-hour rant on the subject of English stupidity and dastardliness. The Führer had made no fewer than seven offers of friendship but the English, 'too snobby, after centuries of world domination and [the] Oxford and Cambridge tradition, to admit that Germany or anyone else should exist on terms of complete equality', had rejected them. The current state of international tension was entirely down to the British and that 'ridiculous' pact they had made with the Poles. War was now a serious possibility and it would be the most terrible and ruthless war in history:

> It will mean either the end of the German Reich and the destruction of the German race or the end of the British Empire and the destruction of the British race – the Führer has decided that this will be inevitable and necessary, and if Britain wants war (and her war party seems to be growing) she can have it at any time – Germany is ready.

When Tennant pointed to Britain's superiority at sea and (now) equality in the air, the German Foreign Minister gave a display of that bombast for which he was famed: 'My dear Tennant, Britain's strength or weakness never enters into our calculations because Britain could never get at us. For one Maginot Line we have seven or eight impregnable Siegfried Lines, and the stronger you are the more men you will lose.' No, war would spell disaster for Britain and France and if they really wished to avoid it then they would persuade the Poles to yield to the Führer's demands.

The next day, 27 July, Tennant joined Ribbentrop on his eleven-hour train journey back to Berlin. Also on board was Walther Hewel, head of Ribbentrop's personal staff and one of Hitler's few intimate friends. 'Is it going to be a peaceful or a stormy August?' enquired Tennant. Thinking that he had said 'autumn' rather than 'August', Hewel replied that it would be a stormy autumn unless the Poles came to their senses. 'Yes, but what about August?' insisted the banker. 'Oh August, nothing is likely to happen in August. The Führer is prepared to wait – he may even wait a year or more but Danzig will return to the Reich eventually.'[53]

XXI

The Last Season

And so we go on: playing cricket, waiting for the racing specials, planning summer holidays … But are we awake? Worse, have the gods sent us mad before destruction falls?

Ronald Cartland, *Headway*, summer 1939[1]

The Anglo-French interest in Danzig was not intrinsic. A city which had been part of Germany until Versailles, the status of Danzig (or Gdańsk as the Poles called it) as a 'free city' under the auspices of the League of Nations, run internally by the Nazis, externally by the Poles, was regarded in almost every quarter as an unsatisfactory compromise. On 4 May 1939, *The Times* declared that 'Danzig is really not worth a war' and, on the same day, Marcel Déat, a former French Air Minister, stated in *L'Œuvre* that French soldiers should not be expected to 'die for Danzig'.[2] From His Majesty's Ambassador to Berlin – a man who, in the words of his French colleague, had 'failed to learn anything' from the invasion of Czechoslovakia – the advice was consistent.[3] 'I am personally convinced that there can be no permanent peace in Europe until Danzig has reverted to Germany', wrote Sir Nevile Henderson on 24 May. 'The Poles cannot be master of 400,000 Germans in Danzig – ergo Germany must be.'[4] A few weeks earlier he had endorsed the German case against the Polish Corridor – arguing that 'if Scotland were separated from England by an Irish corridor, we would want at least what Hitler now demands' – and stated his view that 'it would be wicked to drift into a world war' for the sake of either of these issues.[5]

This was to miss the point. As Chamberlain himself told the Cabinet on 18 March, the issue was not the rights or wrongs of Danzig or the

Corridor but 'whether or not Germany intended to dominate Europe by force'.[6] In this light, the Polish guarantee was a deliberate challenge: a warning to Germany that if she continued along her present course she would find herself at war with the British Empire. Yet Chamberlain also agreed with Henderson. Although consistent in his public utterances that if Germany tried to take Danzig by force then it would mean war, he nonetheless admitted privately that if Hitler 'would have a modicum of patience I can imagine that a way could be found of meeting German claims while safeguarding Poland's independence and economic security'.[7] On 10 July, he summoned General Edmund Ironside to Downing Street. Nicknamed 'Tiny' (he was over six feet four inches tall), Ironside had recently returned to Britain after a stint as Governor of Gibraltar. Now, as Ironside noted in his diary, Chamberlain was entrusting him with a mission to try to pin down the Poles:

> He told me that they had no idea what the Poles were going to do and wanted me to go there to find out. Beck had always put them off by saying that their action was dependent upon the amount of provocation they got. I told him that our chief card was that we had given a guarantee if Poland felt her independence was menaced and that they must therefore tell us what they intended to do ... Chamberlain said that no undertakings by Hitler would be any use. We must have some definite practical guarantee that with Danzig in the Reich, Poland would have practical rights equal to those she had now. It should not be beyond the brains of the Allies to devise some guarantees that would bind Hitler.[8]

Seven days later – a delay which indicates a striking lack of urgency – Ironside arrived in Warsaw. In many respects, his visit was a terrific success. A swashbuckling and dashing officer (an inspiration for John Buchan's Richard Hannay), Ironside was cheered by the citizens of Warsaw and got on well with Marshal Edward Rydz-Śmigły, the Polish Commander-in-Chief. To the relief of London, he discovered that the Poles had no intention of doing anything rash. Having asked the Marshal what he would do in the event that German troops occupied Danzig, Rydz-Śmigły replied that he would send an officer, under a flag of truce, to ask 'what they were doing there'.[9] Ironside was impressed by Polish military efforts, while the Poles, though embittered by Britain's refusal to provide a substantial loan for rearmament (on financial grounds), were heartened by the General's assurances about the determination of 'His Majesty's Government ... to fulfil the terms of their guarantee to Poland'.[10]

*

Meanwhile, the Russian talks were not going well. As could have been predicted, the mere mention of the League of Nations had inflamed Soviet suspicions. On 27 May, Molotov accused the British of seeking to neuter the proposed alliance by making it conditional on the cumbersome procedures of Geneva. The British Ambassador, Sir William Seeds, protested vigorously. The British had no intention of invoking the *machinery* of the League, only its *principles*. But the Soviet Foreign Minister was having none of it. Sitting behind a vast desk on top of a dais, he refused to accept the Ambassador's assurances and clung obstinately to his suspicions. Seeds despaired. Writing to Lord Halifax after a second frustrating visit to the Kremlin, he lamented that it was his fate to deal with a man 'totally ignorant of foreign affairs and to whom the idea of negotiation – as distinct from imposing the will of his party leader – is utterly alien'. Nevertheless, the Foreign Minister possessed a 'foolish cunning' and Seeds's remark that he had at least managed to clear up some of the Commissar's 'more blatant misunderstandings' suggests that the Ambassador was not entirely convinced by Molotov's obtuseness.[11]

Whatever the intentions of the supple if not subtle Soviet Commissar – with his cannon-ball head, beady eyes and 'smile of Siberian winter' – his colleague in London continued to work unambiguously for an Anglo-Soviet Pact.[12] When the Foreign Office announced that it was sending Sir William Strang to Moscow in order to brief Seeds on the Government's position, Ivan Maisky urged Halifax to go himself. 'If you were to agree immediately, this week or at latest next, to go to Moscow, to carry the negotiations through to the end there and sign the pact, peace in Europe would be preserved.'[13] The same argument was put to Halifax by Anthony Eden, who pointed out that the Prime Minister had flown on no fewer than three occasions to see Hitler, that both Chamberlain and Halifax had visited Mussolini, and that the Soviets would not unreasonably expect the same treatment. If the Foreign Secretary would not go himself then Eden volunteered his own services. Halifax was tempted by this latter suggestion, but Chamberlain refused. 'You would hardly believe that anyone could be so foolish', he exclaimed to Ida. 'To send either a Minister or an ex-Minister would be the worst of tactics with a hard bargainer like Molotoff.' Halifax 'agreed and dropped the proposal' but then 'Lloyd George repeated it to Butler and even suggested that, if we did not approve of Anthony, Winston should go! I have no doubt that the three of them talked it over together, and that they saw in it a means of entry into the Cabinet and perhaps later on the substitution of a more amenable PM!'[14]

The next six weeks consisted of tough, complex and extremely frustrating negotiations. On 2 June, Molotov handed Seeds and the French Ambassador, Paul-Emile Naggiar, the Soviet-amended draft treaty. The principal changes included guarantees for Latvia, Estonia and Finland, in addition to Belgium, Greece, Turkey, Romania and Poland (though not, as the British and French wanted, Switzerland or the Netherlands); the prohibition of a separate peace; and a military agreement to come into operation simultaneously with the political agreement. To each of these points there were objections, the most obvious being that neither the Finns, Estonians nor Latvians wanted to be guaranteed, while the Poles and Romanians were happy to be guaranteed but not by the Russians. The French, who were desperate for an agreement, urged the British to respond quickly. Yet it took two weeks and three meetings of the Foreign Policy Committee before the British were ready with their reply. When they finally produced their redraft of the redraft they had decided to skirt the issue of the Baltic states by not naming any state covered by the treaty and insisting on consultation between the signatories before any intervention in a non-guaranteed state. The Soviet clause prohibiting a separate peace was dropped and the League of Nations made a reappearance in the opening paragraph. Molotov was furious. Giving rare animation to his granite-like face, he accused the British and French of treating the Soviets like 'nitwits and nincompoops'.[15] 'If His Majesty's Government and the French Government treated the Soviet Government as being naïve or foolish people, he himself could afford to smile but he could not guarantee that everyone would take so calm a view' – a clear reference to Stalin.[16]

With the French urging them to accept the Russian demands, the British began to make concessions. Indeed, the entire story of the Russian negotiations consists of the British moving slowly towards the Soviet position, while Molotov remained stationary, perched on his absurd dais. It was not long before the British were showing signs of acute frustration. 'The Russians are impossible', scrawled Sir Alexander Cadogan on 20 June. 'We give them all they want, with both hands, and they merely slap them. Molotov is an ignorant and suspicious peasant.'[17] Three days later, in an interview with Maisky, Halifax accused the Soviets of using the 'German method of negotiation' before asking the Ambassador point-blank if his masters actually wanted an agreement.[18] From Moscow, Strang wrote that he dared say 'we shall arrive at something in the end' but there was a considerable risk that they would all have 'reached the age-limit and gone into retirement' by the time that point was reached.[19]

The frustrations were not all on the British side. On 29 June, Andrei Zhdanov, Deputy Chairman of the Supreme Soviet and advocate of rapprochement with Germany, attacked the Anglo-French negotiating tactics in *Pravda*, accusing the British and French of not wanting a 'real agreement' and using the talks merely as a device to prepare 'their own public opinion for an eventual deal with the aggressors'.[20] That this came after the British had just conceded the issue of the Baltic states, while the Russians were still refusing to include Switzerland or the Netherlands in the agreement, was as unjust as it was alarming. The French, however, were inclined to blame the British for the failure to reach a quick deal. As Georges Bonnet wrote to Charles Corbin, the French Ambassador to London, on 5 July 1939, the latest Russian proposals – which demanded separate yet simultaneous treaties between the USSR, Poland and Turkey as well as a definition of 'indirect aggression' which would allow the Russians to interfere in the Baltic states even if they had not been invaded – were considerably worse than the ones they had started with. 'It appears that we were only too right to insist on the necessity of conducting the negotiations rapidly and, in order to avoid additional difficulties, to accept the Soviet texts each time no question of principle was at stake', wrote the French Foreign Minister. That same day a Quai d'Orsay memorandum lamented 'the extreme slowness' displayed by the British during the negotiations.[21]

The first three weeks of July offered more of the same. The British made incremental concessions but the Russians continued to be difficult. Strang found it a 'humiliating experience'. 'Time after time we have taken up a position and a week later we have abandoned it; and we have had the feeling that Molotov was convinced from the beginning that we should be forced to abandon it', he wrote on 20 July:*

> Their distrust and suspicion of us have not diminished during the negotiations, nor, I think, has their respect for us increased. The fact that we have raised difficulty after difficulty on points which seem to them unessential has created an impression that we may not be seriously seeking an agreement; while the fact that we have yielded in the end would tend to remind them that we are still the same Powers who have (as they see it) capitulated in the past to Japan, Italy and Germany and that we are likely to do so again in the future. We should perhaps have been wiser to pay the Soviet price for this agreement at an earlier stage, since we are not in a good position to bargain and since, as the international situation deteriorates, the Soviet price is likely to rise.[22]

Chamberlain was not worried. Although Henderson had already told Cadogan that he felt 'intuitively that the Germans are getting at Stalin' and that Göring had recently stated that 'Germany and Russia will not always be enemies' – one of nearly twenty warnings the British received over the summer – the Prime Minister, along with the majority of British decision makers, failed to take the possibility of German–Soviet rapprochement seriously.[23] On 10 July, Chamberlain passed on Henderson's contradictory view that 'it would be quite impossible in present circumstances for Germany and Soviet Russia to come together' to the Foreign Policy Committee and, nine days later, told colleagues that he 'could not bring himself to believe that a real alliance between Russia and Germany was possible'.[24] In fact, the Prime Minister was

---

* This diplomatic foresight was not purely due to previous patterns of British behaviour. As was only revealed much later, the Soviets had a spy in the Communications Department of the Foreign Office. This kept them always one step ahead of the British, while also allowing them to respond to the Anglo-French proposals in record time.

more than happy to see the talks collapse. Writing to Hilda on 15 July, he expressed his relief that Halifax was at last getting 'fed up' with the 'maddening' Molotov and, a week later, he confessed that 'we are only spinning out the time before the inevitable break comes, and it is rather hard that I should have to bear the blame for dilatory action when if I wasn't hampered by others I would have closed the discussions one way or another long ago'.[25] Before the break could come, however, both sides made concessions which appeared to augur a new stage of the negotiations and even the prospect of a deal.

On 23 July, Molotov demanded the immediate opening of military talks, assuring the British and French that the remaining political difficulties could be easily cleared up once these were under way. Not unreasonably, the British had always opposed such a move. Military conversations would further delay an agreement, while, as Strang commented, 'it is indeed extraordinary that we should be expected to talk military secrets with the Soviet Government before we are sure that they will be our allies'.[26] In the interests of securing the alliance, however, the British were now prepared to yield this point and, on 25 July, Halifax instructed Seeds to tell Molotov the good news. Unfortunately, an element of farce, or black comedy, now entered the proceedings.

Anticipating the need for military talks (which the Russians had been demanding since the start of the negotiations), the French had selected their military delegation at the beginning of July. Headed by General Aimé Doumenc, a specialist in mechanised warfare, it was now ordered by Bonnet to proceed with all possible haste to Moscow and 'get us an agreement at any price'.[27] The British were less organised. No mission had been selected, let alone prepared, and, as Halifax explained, it would be at least ten days before one could be mustered. Belatedly, the British began to get their act together. As early as 20 July, Strang had advised that the head of the mission must be of at least equivalent rank to General Ironside. Ironside's visit to Warsaw had been widely publicised and the Russians – already offended by the British failure to send a Cabinet Minister to conduct the negotiations – would expect nothing less. The British Government failed to heed this advice. Admiral the Honourable Sir Reginald Aylmer Ranfurly Plunkett-Ernle-Erle-Drax sounded like a character from a Gilbert and Sullivan operetta. In fact, he had one of the best brains in the Royal Navy, had fought with distinction during the First World War, and was one of the earliest pioneers of solar heating. Unfortunately, he was almost entirely unknown outside the service and was not even on the Naval Staff. When Stalin was informed of the composition of the Anglo-French delegations his reaction was exactly as Strang had feared. 'They're not being serious', he remarked to Molotov. 'These people can't have the proper authority. London and Paris are playing poker again.' 'Still the talks should go ahead?' enquired the Foreign Minister. 'Well, if they must, they must', replied the Soviet dictator.[28]

*

The fastest way for the delegations to reach Moscow was either by rail or by air. The French favoured the train but the British pointed out that they would have to go via Berlin and that this was hardly tactful. For different reasons, the air option was similarly discounted. Non-stop flights were impossible and there were concerns that the petrol available at the Russian aerodromes might not be suitable for Western engines. This left the sea. The question of a warship was raised but Halifax thought this 'would have the effect of attaching too much importance to the Mission'. Capturing the absurdities of this discussion, General 'Pug' Ismay, Secretary of the Committee of Imperial Defence, suggested 'they might bicycle'.[29] Eventually, the British settled on the *City of Exeter*, an antiquated merchant ship which could only do thirteen knots and would take the best part of a week to reach Leningrad. When Maisky saw the Labour foreign affairs spokesman, Hugh Dalton, he could not contain his rage: 'Russian irritation with British methods had passed all bounds', recorded the MP.

> We would not send a Minister to Moscow; we sent only a FO clerk. When staff talks were agreed to, we sent only second- and third-rate military representatives, none of whom were fit to speak on equal terms with Voroshilov [the Soviet Minister of War]. And we sent them, he complained, not by air or in a fast warship, but by a slow cargo-boat. 'You have treated us', he said, 'always like poor relations.'[30]

Neither Chamberlain nor Halifax was alarmed by the delay. While Bonnet had impressed on Doumenc the need to reach an agreement 'as quickly as possible', Drax's official instructions stated that he was to 'go very slowly with the conversations, watching the progress of the political negotiations and keeping in very close touch with His Majesty's Ambassador'.[31] On 4 August, he had an interview with the Prime Minister. Drax found Chamberlain 'somewhat worried and uneasy about the Russian situation'. The 'House of Commons had pushed him further than he had wished to go' and, with supreme but apparently unconscious irony, he expressed 'some doubt as to whether "appeasement" was likely to achieve the desired result'.[32]

Eventually, on 5 August 1939, the *City of Exeter* set sail. For the two delegations, unaware that time was running out – as Drax recorded, everyone in London was convinced that the Russians were prepared to make a satisfactory agreement – the next five days were a happy time. Each morning they met in the ship's nursery to discuss tactics, while the evenings were given over to vast curry dinners served by waiters in turbans. When they were not working there was shuffleboard and a deck tennis tournament. In the early hours of the morning of 10 August, they arrived in Leningrad and, after a day of sightseeing (they had missed the train they were meant to catch on 9 August), they caught the midnight train to Moscow. There, they were given a warm welcome by the Russians. A banquet was held in their honour and copious quantities of vodka consumed, the natural accompaniment to an endless succession of toasts. Unfortunately, this proved the high point of Anglo-Franco-Soviet co-operation.

On the following morning, Saturday 12 August 1939, the three delegations met in the Spiridonovka Palace for their first session. It could hardly have got off to a worse start. Voroshilov, the ruthless Soviet War Minister,* began by reading out his credentials, granting him the power to 'negotiate and sign a military convention with the British and French delegations', and asked the others to do the same. The British must have felt like schoolboys who had forgotten their homework. For while Doumenc was able to produce a letter from Daladier, Drax had nothing. 'Though perhaps I ought to have thought of it, it was an astonishing thing that the Government and the Foreign Office should have let us sail without providing us with credentials or any similar document', he later commented.[33]

* He had personally signed 185 execution lists during the purges.

Voroshilov expressed grave disappointment. The Soviet Union had been led to expect that they would be negotiating with people who had been granted plenipotentiary powers. After an awkward moment, however – in which Drax promised to send to London for his credentials – the Marshal agreed to proceed with the discussions. What proposals did the British and French have for how the Soviet Union could best co-operate in the common cause? Drax began to enumerate the 'principles' for co-operation but Voroshilov cut him short. The Soviet Union was not interested in 'principles', only 'concrete plans'.[34] Reluctantly, the British and French began an exaggerated description of their forces and how they planned to use them in the event of war. Voroshilov was unimpressed and interrogated his interlocutors on each of their statements.

It was not until the third meeting on 14 August, however, that the crux of the matter was reached. In order for the Soviet Union to be of assistance in a war against Germany – a country with which she shared no common border – it was necessary for the Red Army to pass through Poland and Romania. Had these two countries, whom Britain and France had guaranteed, agreed to this? Drax dissembled: 'If a man is drowning in a river and another man says he is ready and willing to throw him a lifebelt, will he decline to ask for it?'[35] But Voroshilov pushed on. The Soviet Union must be allowed to send her forces through the Vilno Gap and Polish Galicia (Romania was a secondary consideration). Without assurances that she could do so, further talk was futile and the conversations must be regarded as a failure.

Belatedly, the British and French rushed to persuade the Poles. The French Ambassador saw Beck on 17 August and the British Ambassador the following afternoon. The answer remained the same. Fearing that they would never get them out again, the Poles categorically refused to allow the Soviets to enter their territory. Considering that it was not twenty years since the Russians had been at the gates of Warsaw and that Poland had suffered no fewer than four partitions at the hands of that country in the last 200 years, this was understandable. The Poles feared the Russians as much as, if not more than, the Germans and it would be scant victory indeed if (by some miracle) they were able to repel the German Wolf only to be left in the embrace of the Russian Bear.

On this reef the talks foundered. The delegations met again on 15 and 16 August but on the 17th Voroshilov insisted that they must adjourn until the British and French had received answers from Warsaw and Bucharest. Forced, once again, to go sightseeing, the British visited Lenin's tomb – 'no pleasant addition to the attractions of the City', thought Drax – and strolled through the 'People's Park of Rest and Culture' – an antagonistic concept, considering that the 'culture', along with much propaganda, was indiscriminately conveyed via a series of loudspeakers.[36] Everywhere they went they were followed by the secret police, even discovering a couple of plain-clothes NKVD men hiding in the bushes of the Embassy gardens. On 21 August, they returned to the Spiridonovka Palace but to no avail. The British and French had failed to persuade the Poles, while the Russians were in the advanced stages of courtship with an alternative suitor. The military mission had failed.

*

Despite the gathering war clouds, the rituals of the traditional English summer continued unabated. Half a million people gathered at Epsom to watch Lord Rosebery's colt, Blue Peter, win the Derby and there were other large crowds at Ascot, Henley and Cowes. A great 'display of summer frocks and hats' was noted at the Eton versus Harrow cricket match – which saw Harrow end a thirty-year losing streak – while the elegance of such society figures as the Duchess of Northumberland (printed crêpe dress of buttercup yellow and short-sleeved cape of smoke fur) and the Duchess of Norfolk (pale periwinkle-blue crêpe with tufts of feather plumage on a Breton sailor-hat of blue straw) ensured that Cup Day at Goodwood was well up to 'Ascot standard'.[37]

As for the balls, dinners and parties – the evening fixtures of the London 'season' – they were, if anything, even gayer and more extravagant than in previous years. Over a thousand guests attended the ball at Holland House on 6 July, while the electric, though controversial, presence of a band of black musicians, under the baton of Ken 'Snakehips' Johnson, inspired the guests at Lady Twysden's party to take part in a giant conga down the double staircase at 6 Stanhope Gate. The undisputed highlight, however, was the ball given by the

Duke and Duchess of Marlborough at Blenheim Palace to celebrate the 'coming-out' of their eldest daughter, Lady Sarah Spencer-Churchill. Almost the whole of the socio-political-diplomatic class was there, waited on by an army of footmen in yellow and blue eighteenth-century liveries. Chips Channon had never seen anything like it:

> The palace was floodlit, and its grand baroque beauty could be seen for miles. The lakes were floodlit too and, better still, the famous terraces, they were blue and green and Tyroleans walked about singing; and although there were seven hundred people or even more, it was not in the least crowded. It was gay, young, brilliant, in short, perfection. I was loath to leave, but did so at about 4.30 and took one last look at the baroque terraces with the lake below, and the golden statues and the great palace. Shall we ever see the like again? Is such a function not out of date? Yet it was all of the England that is supposed to be dead and is not. There were literally rivers of champagne.[38]

Ronald Cartland was amazed, even disturbed, that people could go on 'playing cricket, waiting for the racing specials' and 'planning summer holidays'. 'Have the gods sent us mad before our destruction?' he wondered.[39] Yet it would be wrong to suppose that those who enjoyed the summer of 1939 were either ignorant or indifferent to the deteriorating international situation. On the contrary, as one young reveller who had just joined the Territorials recalled: we were 'very well aware that war might be just round the corner' and, so, 'from the male point of view, it was very much an atmosphere of "eat, drink and be merry, for tomorrow we die"'.[40] Peter Studd, the captain of the Cambridge University First XI, exhibited a similar *carpe diem* attitude when he told an interviewer that he 'hoped to God that Hitler wouldn't declare war before the cricket season was over'.[41]

There was, however, legitimate concern about Chamberlain's plan to adjourn Parliament for the full summer recess, from 4 August to 3 October. The Labour and Liberal Opposition, as well as anti-appeasement Conservatives such as Churchill, were appalled by the proposal. German troops were being mobilised, tensions in Danzig were rising, the Russian negotiations were incomplete, and the Prime

Minister was sending MPs off on a two-month holiday. In a speech in which he summoned 'all his powers of oratory, wit, and irony', Churchill attacked the planned adjournment, arguing that it would convey the worst possible signal to Britain's enemies. The Commons represented the most 'formidable expression of the British national will' and it would be 'disastrous', 'pathetic', 'shameful' for the Government to say to the House at this time: 'Begone! Run off and play. Take your gas masks with you.'[42] Speaking for the Labour Party, Arthur Greenwood stated that the Opposition did not trust the Prime Minister not to use Parliament's absence to resurrect his policy of appeasement, a sentiment echoed by the Liberal leader, Archie Sinclair.

To these assaults, as well as solicitations from Leo Amery, Vyvyan Adams and Richard Law, Chamberlain responded with a 'narrow, bitter, partisan speech', in which he declared that the vote on the adjournment would be treated as a vote of confidence in the Government.[43] This ended the matter (Conservative MPs were never going to vote to bring down the Government) but not before Ronald Cartland had attacked the Prime Minister's decision in dramatic terms. To gasps of horror from the Conservative benches, the 32-year-old stated that a 'fantastic and ludicrous impression … exists in this country that the Prime Minister has ideas of dictatorship'. This was of course ridiculous, yet it was an impression which would be strengthened by the Prime Minister's refusal to countenance the early reassembly of Parliament. The fact was, continued Cartland, his emotion rising, 'we are in the situation that within a month we may be going to fight, and we may be going to die'. At this, Sir Patrick Hannon and a number of other Tory MPs laughed. Flushed, Cartland turned on them. It was all very well to mock but there 'are thousands of young men at the moment in training in camps … and the least that we can do here, if we are not going to meet together from time to time and keep Parliament in session, is to show that we have immense faith in this democratic institution'.[44]

The effect of Cartland's speech was 'galvanic'.[45] Within minutes, Hannon was on his feet denouncing the 'poisonous' words of the Honourable Member for King's Norton, while Churchill hurried to offer his congratulations: 'Well done, my boy, well done!'[46] Chamberlain won the division comfortably but nearly forty Conservatives, including

Churchill, Cartland, Harold Macmillan, Anthony Eden and Bob Boothby, abstained. The next day, the front page of the *Evening Standard* blazed: 'Premier calls for list of MPs who did not vote last night. THEY WILL ALL BE BLACKLISTED.'[47] In particular, the knives were out for Cartland. Twenty Tory MPs saw the Government whips to demand his expulsion, while Richard Edwards, the head of the party machine in Birmingham, wrote to Chamberlain to tell him that both he and the Chairman of the King's Norton Conservative Association were of the view that 'another candidate should be sought' to fight the next general election.[48] Chamberlain was pleased. 'As for Master Cartland,' he wrote to Ida, three days after the debate, 'I hope he has effectually blotted his copybook in King's Norton and I am taking steps to stimulate local opposition ... We may lose the seat as a result but I would rather do that (temporarily) than have a traitor in the camp.'[49] Nine months later, while leading his men towards Dunkirk, Major Ronald Cartland was killed by a German bullet.

*

On 6 August, Chamberlain caught the sleeper up to Scotland, where he hoped to spend a fortnight fishing on the Duke of Westminster's Sutherland estate. The news from Germany, where some two million men were reported to be under arms, was disquieting but not, the Prime Minister believed, despairing. 'All my information indicates that Hitler now realises that he can't grab anything else without a major war', he confided to his sister Hilda just before his departure, 'and has decided therefore to put Danzig into cold storage.' He anticipated that they would shortly hear of large movements of troops along the Polish frontier 'and a crop of stories of ominous preparations which will send Winston into hysterics'. But these were merely the necessary ingredients of the 'war of nerves'.[50]

Unfortunately, although the rest of the country was experiencing a downpour, Sutherland was 'bone dry' and the river six inches below fishing level. Incredibly, Chamberlain managed to catch two salmon at the beginning of the week but there his luck stopped. On 14 August, he received an account of an interview between Hitler and Carl Burckhardt, the League of Nations Commissioner in Danzig, in which the Führer had threatened to 'crush the Poles ... in such a way that no trace of Poland can be found afterwards'.[51] Five days later, Halifax wrote to him with intelligence, gleaned from one of Sir Robert Vansittart's sources, stating that the invasion of Poland would commence sometime between 25 and 28 August.[52] Halifax wanted Chamberlain to send Hitler a letter, emphasising the British determination to meet force with force, and asked the Prime Minister to return from Scotland. Chamberlain arrived on the morning of 21 August and began drafting a letter. At the same time, the Foreign Office received a cryptic message from Germany stating that Göring proposed to fly to London for emergency talks with the Prime Minister. Chamberlain accepted this 'curious suggestion' and arrangements were made for the Field Marshal to land at a disused aerodrome, before being driven to Chequers, where the staff would be sent away and the telephone disconnected.[53] The proposed date was Wednesday 23 August 1939. But it never happened. The reason was as simple as it was devastating. Late on the night of 21 August the official German news agency announced that 'the German and Soviet Governments have agreed to conclude a Non-Aggression Pact with each other' and that the 'Minister for Foreign Affairs, Herr von Ribbentrop, will proceed to Moscow on Wednesday August 23 for the purpose of concluding the negotiations'.[54] Stalin had made his choice.

XXII
Final Hours

> We are living through difficult hours, but I hope we may yet be successful in avoiding the worst. If so, I shall still hope for a chance to go after your grouse.
>
> Neville Chamberlain to the Duke of Buccleuch, 30 August 1939[1]

The Nazi–Soviet Pact came as 'a complete bombshell' to the Western Powers.[2] Oliver Harvey found the Foreign Office in a state of shock, while the French Prime Minister, Edouard Daladier, complained that 'he could not understand how the French diplomats and negotiators could have been so deceived'.[3] For those who had always distrusted the Soviets it was a vindication. 'Then I realised that the Russians have double-crossed us, as I always believed they would', recorded Chips Channon, after opening his copy of the *Daily Express* on the morning of 22 August 1939. 'They are the foulest people on earth. Now it looks like war, and the immediate partition of Poland.'[4] Harold Nicolson, who was on board a sailing boat in Plymouth harbour when he heard the news, reached the same conclusion:

> This smashes our peace-front and makes our guarantees to Poland, Rumania [*sic*] and Greece very questionable. How Ribbentrop must chuckle. I feel rather stunned by this news and sit on deck in bewilderment with the fishing smacks around me. I fear that it means that we are humbled to the dust.[5]

Chamberlain was severely downcast. Although he had never wanted a Russian alliance and deserves a large portion of the blame for the Anglo-French failure to secure one, he realised that the path towards a German invasion of Poland was now wide open. 'He looks like a broken man', recorded the American Ambassador, Joseph Kennedy, who visited him on the evening of 23 August. 'He said he could think of nothing further to say or do. He felt that all his work had come to naught. "I can't fly again because that was good only once."'[6] Yet if the Prime Minister felt entitled to self-pity, there was never any question of buckling before this new and most unholy of alliances. On the contrary, within hours of receiving confirmation of the news, the Cabinet had issued a statement declaring that the pact in no way affected Britain's obligations to Poland and, within a few more, the British Ambassador was on his way to Berchtesgaden armed with a letter to Hitler repeating these assurances.

Sir Nevile Henderson found Hitler at his most bellicose. The Führer blamed the British for preventing a peaceful solution to the Polish question and railed against the Poles for their supposed assaults upon the German minority. Henderson's calm defence of British policy had no effect. Hitler accused the English of giving the Poles a 'blank cheque' and warned that he would not shrink from war if Polish provocation continued. Later, when handing the Ambassador his reply to Chamberlain's letter, in which he repeated his determination to resolve the Polish situation by force if necessary, Hitler stated that it was obvious that England was determined to 'annihilate Germany' and that he would prefer war now, when he was fifty, rather than in five or ten years' time. Henderson protested, while still insisting that Britain would most certainly fight for Poland, but Hitler seemed in a mood when 'reason meant nothing to him'.[7] In fact, the Führer thought he was being extremely clever. As soon as Henderson had left, he slapped his thigh and declared in a tone of exultation: 'Chamberlain won't survive this discussion. His Cabinet will fall this evening.'[8]

The next day, Thursday 24 August, the British Cabinet met and decided to call up the remainder of the coastal defence and anti-aircraft units. They had already ordered substantial defence preparations, including the mustering of the Auxiliary Air Force and 5,000 naval reservists, as well as requisitioning some eighty merchant ships and fishing trawlers for war work. The air raid warning scheme was put on stand-by and orders issued for the protection of vulnerable points against sabotage. In France, 900,000 men were in the process of being called to the colours and the Government cancelled what was to have been the first Cannes film festival. The previous day, while Henderson was arguing with Hitler, the entire French defence establishment met in Daladier's chambers to consider the situation. Georges Bonnet wanted to try to wriggle out of France's obligations to Poland but the hawks in the Cabinet, supported by the Chiefs of Staff, prevailed. Preparations for a complete mobilisation of French forces continued and, on the evening of 25 August, Daladier delivered a rousing broadcast to the nation.

Chamberlain's speech to the Commons the previous afternoon was less inspiring. Nicolson likened it to 'a coroner summing up a case of murder'.[9] He did, however, reconfirm Britain's commitment to Poland and, in contrast to his infamous broadcast during the Czech crisis, declared that if war were to break out over Danzig then it would not be 'the political future of a faraway city in a foreign land' for which Britain would be fighting but 'the preservation of those principles … the destruction of which would involve the destruction of all possibility of peace and security for the peoples of the world'.[10] MPs listened in calm silence. There was none of the nervous anticipation of the previous September but resignation and resolution. 'Fear', wrote the anti-appeasement MP General 'Louis' Spears, 'had disappeared.'[11] That evening, Joseph Kennedy visited Downing Street, where he found the Prime Minister depressed but determined. 'Don't worry, Neville, I still believe God is working with you', the Ambassador comforted. Chamberlain could have been forgiven for thinking that He was not working very hard.[12]

*

The invasion of Poland was due to begin at dawn on 26 August, the orders having gone out immediately following the signing of the Nazi–Soviet Pact. Now more than ever, Hitler was confident that the Western powers would not intervene. 'I have met the umbrella men, Chamberlain and Daladier, at Munich and got to know them', he assured his Generals when they expressed doubts on the matter. 'They can never stop me solving the Polish question. The coffee sippers in London and Paris will stay still this time too.'[13] On reading translations of the British newspapers on the morning of 25 August, however – all of which carried strong endorsements of Chamberlain's speech – he began to have doubts and decided that a final effort at detaching Britain (Hitler seems barely to have considered France) should be made. At 1.30 p.m., Henderson arrived at the Reich Chancellery. There, the Führer informed the Ambassador that he had decided to make a final effort towards an understanding with England. The Polish question, he explained, *must* be solved. It was intolerable that Germany should be suffering 'Macedonian conditions' on her frontier.[14] Once this had been achieved, however, he was prepared to make England a broad and generous offer. He would guarantee the British Empire and place the forces of the Reich at its disposal – provided that Britain agreed to meet Germany's 'limited' colonial demands.[15] Henderson should fly immediately to London – he was placing a plane at his disposal – and repeat this to the Cabinet. Hitler's final note was one of self-conscious whimsy. He was by nature an artist and once the Polish issue was resolved he intended to 'end his life as an artist and not as a warmonger'. He did not want 'to turn Germany into nothing but a military barracks'.[16]

The Ambassador dismissed, Hitler gave the order to march at 3.02 p.m. Operations against Poland would begin the following morning, while the British – still debating his offer – would be so surprised and confused that they would stay out of it. Five hours later, however, the order was hastily cancelled. All day, Hitler had been waiting for Mussolini's response to his letter stating that the invasion of Poland was imminent and that he expected his Axis partner to be at his side. The Duce's reply, which arrived at 5.45 p.m. – three hours after German troops had started moving towards their jumping-off points – shook Hitler profoundly. Italy, Mussolini regretted, was in no position to go to war at the present time and would remain neutral in the conflict. Only minutes earlier, Hitler had received the French Ambassador, Robert Coulondre, who had given his word as a French officer that France would fight if Poland was attacked. Even more serious, he learnt, almost simultaneously, that the British had that afternoon signed a formal military alliance with Poland. Hitler was staggered. He had been convinced that the British were bluffing but here they were spurning his 'offer' in the most bellicose manner. (In fact, the British Government had not learnt of the 'offer' when they appended their signature to the Polish alliance.) His expectations were confounded, his confidence shattered. In one hour he had lost the ally he was relying on and gained the two adversaries he had discounted. In a panic, Hitler sent for the head of the Wehrmacht Supreme Command, General Wilhelm Keitel.

'I need time', the Führer stated. 'Can the troops be stopped?'

'I would have to look at the timetable', the General replied.

'Then send for it, man!'

After examining this document Keitel declared that the troops could be stopped but that the order must go out now. Hitler gave the order. The war, for the moment, was off.[17]

*

The British were not tempted by Hitler's proposal. His determination to solve the Polish question in his own way had already been rejected, while his offer to guarantee the British Empire was regarded as impertinence. There was, however, a belief that Hitler was looking for a way out and that the British should help him find it. After Halifax had drafted a 'v. bad reply', late on the evening of 25 August, Horace Wilson and Rab Butler – the only people, along with Henderson, 'working like beavers' for another Munich – produced an even worse one.[18] The Cabinet tore it to shreds. Leslie Hore-Belisha damned it as 'fulsome, obsequious and deferential ... In no circumstances' should we 'give the impression that we would weaken in our undertaking to Poland'.[19] Colleagues agreed and Chamberlain announced that Ministers could send their suggestions to the Chancellor of the Exchequer. That night, Chamberlain, Halifax, Butler, Sir John Simon and Sir Alexander Cadogan worked on a new draft and, the following morning, Halifax and Cadogan, along with Sir William Strang and Sir William Malkin from the Foreign Office, resumed the task. In the afternoon, Sunday 27 August, the Cabinet were asked for their contributions. Sir Thomas Inskip was reminded of school with 'everybody silently bending over their copy, and now and then a low voiced exchange of comments'.[20]

At the same meeting, Chamberlain gave the Cabinet further details of a 'mystery man' who had been acting as intermediary between the Foreign Office and Göring.[21] This was Birger Dahlerus, the naïve but indefatigable Swede who had facilitated the meeting between the British businessmen and the Field Marshal earlier in the month. On

25 August, Dahlerus had visited Halifax at the Foreign Office. Since official negotiations were now under way the Foreign Secretary had declined his services. That evening, however, Dahlerus received a call from Göring in which the Field Marshal stated that the situation was extremely grave and that war might break out at any moment. The following morning, Dahlerus returned to the Foreign Office, where he asked Halifax if he would write Göring a letter emphasising Britain's willingness to work towards a peaceful settlement. After a brief conference with Chamberlain, Halifax obliged and Dahlerus flew to Germany.

Landing at Berlin's Tempelhof airport at 7 p.m., he was taken straight to Göring, who was waiting in his special train, halfway between Berlin and his country retreat. Dahlerus found the Field Marshal grave and nervous. He tore open Halifax's letter, only to remember that his English was not good enough to understand it. 'Herr Dahlerus!' he commanded. 'Translate this letter into German and remember how tremendously important it is that every syllable conveys the correct shade of meaning.'[22] According to Halifax, this missive was simply a 'platitudinous message', repeating Britain's desire for peace.[23] Göring, however, was impressed by what he heard and ordered the train to stop so that he and Dahlerus could return to Berlin. There, Göring woke Hitler and introduced him to Dahlerus. Although it was the middle of the night, Hitler indulged in a twenty-minute monologue, attacking the Poles and bemoaning the British, before either Dahlerus or Göring were allowed to get to the point. He was extremely agitated and at one stage seemed to be cracking up before them. 'I will build U-boats, build U-boats, build U-boats', he shouted in short staccato phrases, forecasting what he would do if war broke out between England and Germany. 'I will build aircraft, build aircraft, build aircraft … If there should be no butter, I shall be the first to stop eating butter, eating butter.'[24]

Eventually, Hitler calmed down enough to give Dahlerus a set of proposals resembling those he had given Henderson the day before. He wanted an alliance with Britain but he also wanted Danzig and the Polish Corridor. Dahlerus was to go to London and repeat this offer to the British. Eagerly, the Swede took his leave. He believed that the peace of the world depended on his mission and was too excited to sleep before his 8 a.m. departure in a German Government plane. That afternoon, Sunday 27 August, he delivered the message to Chamberlain, Halifax and Cadogan.

The three men's reaction was phlegmatic. Although Hitler's latest proposals differed sufficiently from those which had been given to Henderson as to cause confusion, they were essentially the same and, as Cadogan noted, 'didn't add much to what we know'.[25] Chamberlain was unimpressed by Dahlerus, while the Foreign Office revealed its view of the Swedish intermediary by christening him 'the Walrus'.[26] He was, however, a useful conduit to Göring, and the Cabinet agreed with the Prime Minister that they should continue to use him provided he stuck to the line that the British were, indeed, anxious for a peaceful settlement but would not break their obligations to Poland. The British believed that a solution should be negotiated directly between the German and Polish Governments, free from threats and intimidation. If this was achieved, they were prepared to join, with other powers, in guaranteeing that agreement.

This was the substance of the official reply to Hitler's 'offer' which, after three days, at least three separate drafting committees and three Cabinet meetings, was finally finished on the afternoon of Monday 28 August. Nothing could persuade His Majesty's Government to desert the Poles but it was anxious for a peaceful solution and urged the Chancellor to enter into direct negotiations with the Polish Government. Optimism in London and Paris had grown over the weekend as reports arrived of the cancelled German attack. Hitler appeared to be wobbling, while all the indications from Rome suggested that Mussolini was unwilling to support his ally in battle. 'The test of force has turned to our advantage', wrote an exultant Coulondre to Daladier on the afternoon of 30 August:

> I heard from a reliable source that M Hitler has been hesitating for five days, that there is wavering inside the Nazi Party and a growing discontent among the people. The attack was decided for the night between 25 and 26 August. For uncertain reasons, Hitler backed away at the last moment … We must hold, hold, hold.[27]

The Foreign Office shared this view. SIS was reporting divisions within the German High Command and the Counsellor of the German Embassy confirmed to William Strang that there was 'hesitation in Berlin' over what course to follow. 'I take his view to be that with absolute (but unprovocative) firmness on our part and with prudence and moderation on the part of the Poles, a peaceful way out is still just possible', wrote the British official.[28] Hitler, though, had other plans.

Having suffered something approximate to a breakdown following his decision to postpone the invasion of Poland, the German dictator was regaining his nerve. That this would have occurred by his own devices is almost certain, yet it is unfortunate that Dahlerus seems to have played a part in the process with his enthusiastic and exaggerated accounts of British eagerness to reach a settlement. When the Foreign Office later read the Swede's account of these days it was appalled by his simplicity and – as if further proof were needed – the story of Birger Dahlerus, during the last days before the Second World War, exemplifies the overwhelmingly negative effect of amateur diplomacy during this period.

For the moment, however, the official channels were still operating. At 10.30 on the evening of 28 August, Henderson, fortified by half a bottle of champagne, arrived at the Reich Chancellery to present the British reply. Hitler, who had already begun rescheduling the invasion for 1 September, feigned interest. He was calmer than at their last meeting and, although he spoke of 'annihilating Poland', there were none of the usual histrionics. The Führer repeated his demands and the Ambassador reiterated Britain's determination to stand by the Poles. At the end, Hitler asked Henderson – who for once had done most of the talking – whether Britain would be prepared to accept an alliance with Germany. Henderson replied that 'speaking personally' he 'did not exclude such a possibility provided the development of events justified it'.[29] This hostage to fortune given, he then took his leave, Hitler having promised to study the document and give his formal reply in due course.

The next morning, Tuesday 29 August, Dahlerus, primed by Göring, sent word to the Foreign Office that Hitler now believed that a peaceful settlement was a definite possibility. Once again, British optimism rose. Further encouraging communications followed. Although the bulk of the German Army was arrayed along the Polish frontier, the Swede insisted that Hitler 'was so anxious for friendly relations with Great Britain that he was prepared to go a long way to meet the

Poles'.[30] The overwrought Henderson began to relax. Although he resented Dahlerus's intrusion into his sphere, he entertained the intermediary with sherry and took comfort in the attentions of his dachshund. At 7.15 p.m., red carnation in buttonhole, he presented himself once again at the Reich Chancellery to receive Hitler's reply.

Within minutes, his optimism evaporated. Hitler screamed accusations against the Poles and their 'barbaric actions of maltreatment'.[31] The German Government would submit to these provocations no longer. From a sincere desire for friendship with England, however, it would enter negotiations provided that a Polish emissary, with full plenipotentiary powers, arrive in Berlin on Wednesday 30 August 1939 – that is within the next twenty hours. When Henderson read this demand he accused Hitler of issuing an ultimatum and the interview deteriorated further. Hitler began to shout and accused the British of not caring a 'row of pins whether Germans were slaughtered in Poland or not'. Affronted, Henderson proceeded to outshout Hitler. 'I told him that I would not listen to such language from him or anybody.' His slander, in respect to the humanity of the British Government, was intolerable. 'If he wanted a war he would have it.' The German military might be strong but England was no less resolute 'and would hold out a little bit longer than Germany could, and so on, and so forth'.[32] The next day, Henderson wrote to Halifax to say that he hoped he had not gone too far. It was not normally the duty of a British Ambassador to shout but then Hitler was not a normal person, he explained. He had been at pains during his Berchtesgaden interview to contrast Hitler's ravings with his own measured calmness but this had produced no effect and 'I thought for once Hitler must be given a dose of his own medicine'.[33]

Despite this bravura performance, Henderson recommended that the Polish Government agree to Hitler's demand and even urged the French Ambassador to get his Government to convince the Poles. This drew a strong rebuke from Britain's Ambassador in Warsaw, Sir Howard Kennard, who wired that the Poles would 'sooner fight and perish rather than submit to such humiliation especially after [the] examples of Czecho-Slovakia, Lithuania and Austria'.[34] Halifax agreed. The German timetable was completely unreasonable and Henderson was instructed to express this to the German Government, a task he completed by telephoning Ribbentrop at four o'clock in the morning.

*

Throughout the next day, Wednesday 30 August, Henderson continued to urge London to persuade the Poles to 'swallow this eleventh hour effort to establish direct contact with Herr Hitler' and even suggested that Pope Pius XII might be asked to facilitate some 'impartial solution'.[35] The British Government, however, remained firm. There was, Rab Butler later complained, an 'absolute inhibition' on the part of the Foreign Office to press the Poles to negotiate – a result, he believed, of the 'shame engendered in some breasts by Munich'.[36] Chamberlain told the Cabinet that this was another example of Hitler's bullying technique and that it was essential to show that 'we were not going to yield on this point'.[37] Earlier in the day he had replied to a letter from the Duke of Buccleuch with remarkable confidence: 'We are living through difficult hours, but I hope we may yet be successful in avoiding the worst. If so, I shall still hope for a chance to go after your grouse.'[38] Misleading information, conveyed through Dahlerus, claimed that Hitler was willing to consider a plebiscite in the Corridor but this did not alter the issue of the Polish negotiator. At noon, Colonel Józef Beck informed Kennard that the Polish Government had decided to mobilise – a natural response to the sixty German divisions arrayed along their frontier – and, in the afternoon, Henderson forwarded what appeared to be a new German battle plan.

At midnight, just as the German ultimatum for a visit from a Polish emissary expired, Henderson entered the old Foreign Ministry building to see Ribbentrop and deliver the formal British response. Ever since the postponement of the invasion five days earlier, the bellicose Foreign Minister – who had assured Hitler that the British would never fight – had been desperately trying to recover his position and, in the words of one Foreign Ministry official, was positively 'lusting for war'.[39] He had arrived in Bismarck's old office 'almost shivering' with excitement, remembered the interpreter Paul Schmidt, and refused to sit still while the British Ambassador made his communication but kept jumping to his feet, folding his arms, demanding if Henderson had anything more to say. When the Ambassador repeated that it was unreasonable to expect a Polish plenipotentiary to arrive at such short notice, the Foreign Minister cut him off. 'The time is up', he declared with affected coolness. 'Where's the Pole your Government was to provide?' Henderson repeated what he had just said, before stating that the British had asked the Poles to take all possible measures to avoid frontier incidents and now asked the German Government to do the same. Once again, Ribbentrop flared up. It was the Poles who were the aggressors, he spat. Increasingly ruffled, Henderson continued. The British urged the German Government to communicate its proposals to the Polish Government in the normal way, by summoning the Polish Ambassador. Furthermore, they were receiving reports of Germans committing acts of sabotage in Poland. At this, Ribbentrop completely lost his temper. 'That's a damned lie of the Polish Government's', he roared, springing to his feet, his face flushed. 'I can only tell you, Herr Henderson, that the position is damned serious!' Shocked by such undiplomatic language, the prim Ambassador rose and shouted back. 'You have just said "damned" … That is no word for a statesman to use in so grave a situation.' For a moment, Schmidt thought the two men were about to start throwing punches. After some glowering and heavy breathing, however, the tension eased and the diplomats resumed their seats. Ribbentrop then read a series of proposals for the settlement of the 'Polish question'. Henderson asked for a copy but Ribbentrop refused. 'It is out of date anyhow as the Polish envoy has not appeared.'[40] Belatedly, it began to dawn on Henderson that the German Foreign Minister was actively working for war. This did not stop him, however, from asking the Polish Ambassador to call on him at 2 a.m. and urging him, in the 'strongest terms', to telephone Warsaw at once so that Beck could request a copy of the German proposals.[41]

*

Thursday 31 August 1939 was a day of fluctuating emotions, conflicting reports and last-ditch attempts. It began with decision makers in London deciphering and then reading Henderson's account of his conversation with Ribbentrop. 'This did not sound very encouraging', recalled Halifax, with characteristic understatement. There then followed a fresh telegram from the Ambassador (who had only gone to bed at 4 a.m.) stating that, according to information he had just received, unless something happened in the next two or three hours the German Government would declare war on Poland.* Still the Cabinet refused to yield to Hitler's bullying. Instead the Fleet was mobilised and the decision to begin the evacuation of three million women and children from vulnerable areas (mainly London) was taken. To Major-General Henry Pownall's relief, authorisation was finally given to bring the Army Reserve up to full strength and a further batch of RAF ground staff was called up.

In Berlin, General Franz Halder learnt at 6.30 a.m. that Hitler had decided to proceed with the attack, provisionally scheduled for dawn the following morning, Friday 1 September. 'It looks as if the die is finally cast', recorded Goebbels. Even now, though, there were those struggling to save peace. At 11 a.m., Ciano telephoned Halifax to say that if the British could get the Poles to give up Danzig, then Mussolini was prepared to use his influence to try to persuade Hitler to convene a conference. The British refused. While Chamberlain and Halifax were discussing the proposal, however, the Italian Foreign Minister – temporarily transformed into the most devoted of Anglophiles, due to his opposition to war and antipathy for the Germans – telephoned again to convey a new proposal for an international conference to revise the Treaty of Versailles. Chamberlain replied that it would only be possible to consider such a proposal if there was a significant measure of demobilisation first. In France, Daladier was not even prepared to go that far. He would rather resign, he told the British Ambassador, than accept Mussolini's invitation to a second Munich. Bonnet, true to form, was for acceptance but was overruled by the Prime Minister, who read extracts from Coulondre's letter from the previous day. We must 'hold, hold, hold', quoted the 'Bull of Vaucluse', banging his fist on the table.[42]

Meanwhile, the credulous Dahlerus continued to play the role Göring intended. Having furnished the British with a copy of the

---

* The 'informant' was Ernst von Weizsäcker, via the Italian Ambassador, Bernardo Attolico, and represented a final attempt by the State Secretary to preserve peace by getting the British to force the Poles into making concessions. In reality, Hitler never had any intention of doing anything as gentlemanly as formally 'declaring war', while the deadline beyond which the order to invade could not be cancelled was 4 p.m., not mid-morning.

German proposals late on the night of 30–31 August, he visited the Polish Ambassador, Józef Lipski, at eleven o'clock the following morning and advised him to see the Field Marshal, sign whatever he wanted and then 'the whole problem would be settled and we would be able to shoot stags together'.[43] When an outraged Lipski baulked at such a suggestion from a complete stranger with no diplomatic or political authority, the Swede decided that it was the bellicose Poles who were destroying the last opportunity for peace and telephoned London, on an insecure line from the British Embassy, to complain. The German proposals were 'extremely liberal', he told Horace Wilson. He had just been to see Lipski and ... At this point, Wilson heard a German voice repeating Dahlerus's words. Desperately, he tried to get the Swede to stop but Dahlerus continued. It was obvious that the Poles were 'obstructing the possibilities of a negotiation', he said. People around Hitler were 'doing their best to restrain him but ... if the Poles would not come to Berlin—' Wilson put the receiver down.[44]

At almost exactly the same time, Hitler signed the order authorising the invasion of Poland. The proposals (which Ribbentrop had read to Henderson but refused to communicate to the Poles) had merely been his way of creating an alibi: a means by which he could tell the German people that he had offered Warsaw reasonable terms but the Poles had turned them down. When Beck instructed Lipski to communicate the Polish Government's willingness to enter into negotiations, the Ambassador found it initially impossible to get an appointment. Finally, he saw Ribbentrop at 6.30 p.m. but the Foreign Minister ended the interview as soon as Lipski admitted that he had no authority to make concessions on behalf of his country. At 9 p.m., the German proposals were broadcast on German radio, accompanied by the claim that the Poles had had them for two days. In London, Cadogan ordered the Foreign Office Press Department to 'kill this' lie but somewhere the Germans had a transcript of Dahlerus, speaking from within the British Embassy, saying that the proposals were 'extremely liberal' and that it was obvious that the Poles were sabotaging the proposed negotiations.[45] An hour earlier, members of the SS, dressed as Polish nationals, had taken over the Gleiwitz radio station on the Polish frontier, where they had dumped corpses – two taken from a concentration camp, the third murdered by lethal injection – and faked an anti-German broadcast. Other staged acts occurred at the customs house at Hochlinden (more concentration camp victims, shot in the woods nearby) and at a deserted forester's hut at Pitschen. At 4.45 a.m. on Friday 1 September, the guns opened. The war had begun.

*

The ensuing forty-eight hours was a time of high tension and acute frustration. When Churchill saw Chamberlain early on the Friday afternoon, the Prime Minister told him that the die was cast: he could see no hope of avoiding conflict with Germany and invited his rival to become a member of the small War Cabinet he intended to form. Having warned of the Nazi danger for so long and been ignored, it was a moment of personal vindication for the younger man, but the call to arms did not follow this meeting as he expected.

Terrified of being bombed before they had completed their mobilisation and evacuated their women and children, the French Government tried to delay the declaration of war for as long as possible, while Bonnet did everything he could to prevent France from having to honour her obligations. When the British refused to support these endeavours – which centred around Mussolini's proposal for a conference – the French Foreign Minister demanded a forty-eight-hour time lapse between the delivery of an Anglo-French ultimatum and the declaration of war.[46] In this he was supported by Daladier, who had been convinced by General Gamelin of the military advantage of deferral. The British protested, but to no avail. Bonnet 'put forward every wriggle in favour of delay', recorded Oliver Harvey.[47]

By this stage, the afternoon of Saturday 2 September, the patience of even the staunchest Francophiles was being tested. 'If France failed again and ratted on the Poles, as she had ratted on the Czechs', shouted Churchill down the telephone to the French Ambassador, then he, who had always been a friend of France, 'would be utterly indifferent to her fate'. When the unfortunate Charles Corbin, who privately deplored the behaviour of his Government, muttered something about 'technical difficulties', Churchill cut him off. 'Technical difficulties be damned! I suppose you would call it a technical difficulty for a Pole if a German bomb fell on his head.'[48]

The row in the House of Commons later that evening – when Leo Amery urged the Labour Party to 'Speak for England!' and even the Government's firmest supporters seemed on the brink of revolt – settled matters. An ultimatum could be delayed no longer, Chamberlain told Daladier over the telephone at 9.30 p.m.: the Government could not survive it. If France was unable to act in accordance with Britain, then Britain would act alone. Three hours later, Halifax sent Henderson a telegram. The Ambassador was to seek an interview with the German Foreign Minister for nine o'clock that morning and present him with a British ultimatum to expire three hours later – 11 a.m. British Summer Time.

Emotions in the Reich Chancellery had been in a state of flux. Convinced that the British would not intervene, only to have a crisis of confidence on 25 August, Hitler had since been encouraged by Ribbentrop to regard the Anglo-French failure to issue an immediate ultimatum as confirmation of his original assumption. Now, as the British requested an appointment for 9 a.m. on the morning of Sunday 3 September, there could be no doubt that the Foreign Minister had been spectacularly, even wilfully, wrong. Finally confronted with reality, Ribbentrop refused to see Henderson and sent Schmidt to receive the Ambassador in his stead. The British ultimatum demanded the cessation of hostilities and the prompt withdrawal of all German forces – or else war. 'There was complete silence', recalled the interpreter, after he had translated it for Hitler and Ribbentrop in the Führer's study half an hour later: 'Hitler sat immobile, gazing before him.' Then, turning to Ribbentrop 'with a savage look, as though implying that his Foreign Minister had misled him about England's probable reaction', he demanded, 'What now?'[49]

Just over an hour and a half later, millions of listeners in Britain and across the world heard a dry, crackling voice, broadcasting in funereal tones: 'I am speaking to you from the Cabinet Room of 10 Downing Street ...'

XXIII

Ghosts of Appeasement

Onward Neville's soldiers
Marching as to war,
With the Royal Navy
Going on before:
Neville with his brolly
Leads against the foe,
Shuffled into battle
See his darlings go …

Nations small may perish
Leaflets fall like rain,
But the Neville Caucus
Constant will remain.
Czechs and Poles be tortured,
Finland sent to gaol,
We have Neville's promise
And that cannot fail.

Anonymous verses left on the desk of a Chamberlainite MP,
February 1940[1]

For twenty minutes it seemed as if the war had started exactly as the British had feared. No sooner had Chamberlain finished his broadcast announcing the declaration of war than the air raid sirens began to wail. 'That is an air raid warning', the Prime Minister told the assembly, which included Lord Halifax, Sir Alexander Cadogan and Rab Butler in the Cabinet Room. People laughed. 'It would be funny if it were', someone remarked. But Chamberlain persisted. 'That is an air raid warning.' The meeting began to disperse. Annie Chamberlain appeared with a basket of provisions and Butler – who decided that if he was going to die then it ought to be in the Foreign Office – made his way to King Charles Street.[2]

Down the road, a group of anti-appeasement MPs, including Anthony Eden, Duff Cooper, Harold Nicolson and Leo Amery, were leaving a meeting at Ronnie Tree's house in Queen Anne's Gate. 'They ought not to do that after what we have heard on the wireless,' commented Amery, 'people will think it is an air-raid warning.' 'My God!' exclaimed Nicolson. 'It *is* an air-raid warning!' Maintaining their pace and with a valiant attempt at casual conversation, the group headed towards Parliament. They had only gone a few steps, however, when Louis Spears appeared in a car. Everyone piled in – Nicolson on Amery's lap and Eden on top of Nicolson – and the motor lurched off towards the Commons.[3]

In the other direction, Churchill was on the roof of Morpeth Mansions surveying the scene. As the fifteen minutes' warning time expired, he descended, picked up a bottle of brandy and made his way to the shelter.[4] Just before he entered, he imagined the destruction that might ensue: the famous 'cataracts of masonry', which would characterise the much anticipated 'knock-out blow' from the air.[5] But the bombs did not fall.

★

In hindsight, the false alarm of 11.28 a.m. on Sunday 3 September 1939 was an appropriate opening to the war in the West, the first eight months of which were characterised by a notable lack of aggression, except at sea, on both sides. Not only did the 'knock-out blow' fail to materialise but, apart from attacks on British shipping, the Luftwaffe left the British Isles unmolested between September 1939 and July 1940. In return, the RAF dropped leaflets rather than bombs on German cities, while the French made a token advance of five miles into the Saarland before pausing and retreating to the safety of the Maginot Line.

In Poland, it was very different. German bombs rained down on Polish cities, while the Wehrmacht's Panzer divisions moved, with lightning speed, to encircle the brave but underequipped Polish Army.* On 17 September, the date by which the French had promised to launch an offensive along the Western Front, the Poles received a 'stab in the back' as the Red Army crossed their eastern frontier to claim that portion of the country awarded to Stalin as part of the Nazi–Soviet Pact.[6]

By this stage, it was all but over. 'It is like a shooting party', exclaimed the distraught Polish Ambassador to London, Count Edward Raczyński, to Hugh Dalton. 'We are the partridges and they are the guns.'[7] During the final days, Chopin's Military Polonaise and the national anthem were played continually on the radio, but it was not patriotism the Poles lacked. Their inferior Air Force destroyed, Warsaw surrendered on 28 September 1939, after ten days of continual bombing had transformed the city 'into a living inferno'.[8] Seventy thousand Polish soldiers had been killed fighting the Germans; 133,000 had been wounded and 700,000 taken prisoner. Countless civilians had died from the bombing, while thousands, perhaps tens of thousands, were murdered by the SS as well as by the Wehrmacht. In the east, the Soviets reported 50,000 Polish fatalities but no wounded – a statistic implying mass executions such as those which occurred near the Katyn Forest between March and May 1940.[9] Over the next six years an estimated 5.7 million Poles died or were murdered under German and (temporary) Soviet occupation – one-fifth of the pre-war population.[10]

*

With justification, the Poles believed that they had been betrayed by their Western allies. Every day, Raczyński visited the Foreign Office to beg for British assistance but enjoyed no more success than his colleague in Paris. Poland would be saved, British and French leaders had long ago decided, not through direct military assistance but only by the triumph of the Allies after a long war. For those who considered the Anglo-Polish Agreement more than just a paper commitment or exploded deterrent, this was both ignominious and nonsensical. Louis

* It did not help, to put it mildly, that the Poles had given in to Anglo-French pressure and cancelled the order of mobilisation on 29 August, before re-issuing it the following day. The result was widespread confusion and only about a third of the Polish Army was correctly deployed at the time of the invasion.

Spears threatened to raise the issue in Parliament but was dissuaded by Sir Kingsley Wood, the Secretary of State for Air, who insisted that there was nothing the British could do to help the Poles. When Leo Amery urged Wood to destroy the Black Forest (a well-known repository for German munitions) with incendiary bombs, he received an even more ludicrous response: 'Are you aware it is private property? … Why, you will be asking me to bomb Essen next' – referring to the centre of Germany's armaments industry in the Ruhr.[11]

There were in fact sensible reasons behind the Allied decision to defer the air war. As Churchill, who had been appointed First Lord of the Admiralty, explained to Hugh Dalton, it was in Britain's interest to delay the confrontation in the skies, since every month that passed allowed the RAF – now being supplied with Hurricanes and Spitfires at an impressive rate – to close the gap with the Luftwaffe. Furthermore, it was desirable from the point of view of neutral countries, in particular the United States, that it should be the Germans who initiated a bombing campaign which would inevitably result in civilian casualties. Even if you aimed at military objectives 'there is always a splash', Churchill explained, and non-combatants were bound to be killed. 'If we can, let us secure that the first women and children to be hit are British and not German.'[12]

What this strategy ignored was the draining effect on Anglo-French morale as well as the negative conclusions drawn by neutral countries (both friendly and hostile) who assumed that the Allies were not in earnest. 'There has been a general grouse that here we are suffering gross discomfort, black-outs, rising food prices … evacuees in one's spare beds and nothing to show for it – and the Poles bombed to pieces', wrote Jim Thomas to Lord Cranborne on 25 September.[13] The Italian Ambassador to Paris commented that he had seen 'several wars waged without being declared' but this was the first time he had seen one 'declared without being waged', while American journalists began referring to the 'phoney war'.[14]

The action which invited most ridicule was the dropping of millions of propaganda leaflets on German cities, while the Luftwaffe dropped bombs on Polish ones. Branded a 'confetti war', jokes about these grotesque raids were soon circulating. One story, which appeared in the *Daily Telegraph*, told of a pilot returning two hours early from his leaflet-dropping sortie. Questioned by his commanding officer, the young man explained that he had not bothered to cut the cords and had simply thrown the bound bundles out of the plane. 'Good God, man,' the officer spluttered, 'you might have killed somebody!'[15] On another occasion, the American journalist John Gunther called at the newly created Ministry of Information to ask for the text of one of the leaflets only to be told, 'We are not allowed to disclose information which might be of value to the enemy.'[16] Even more extraordinary was the BBC's decision not to allow Sir Horace Rumbold to deliver a broadcast on Germany on the grounds that the former Ambassador was too 'anti-Nazi'.[17]

One argument, made both at the time and since, was that the Allies should have used the opportunity afforded by the Polish campaign to launch a serious offensive against Germany. 'If we did not collapse in 1939, that was due only to the fact that during the Polish campaign' the British and French remained 'completely inactive', testified General Alfred Jodl at his Nuremberg trial.[18] Yet while it is true that the Allies enjoyed a numerical supremacy along the Western Front – eighty-five French and four British divisions compared to thirty-five German – such action was never a realistic possibility. Apart from the factors mitigating the chances of success – deficiencies in Allied materiel, the West Wall, Belgian neutrality – there was simply not the will, either among Anglo-French decision makers (for whom the defensive mentality was deeply ingrained) or the British and French populations, to take the offensive.

As it happened, Chamberlain did not consider offensives necessary. Having previously believed that Germany's economic difficulties would dissuade Hitler from war, he now hoped that these, exacerbated by the blockade of German ports, would precipitate a crisis on the German home front. 'In a waiting war of that kind I believe we could outlast the Germans', he wrote to Ida on 23 September, adding, 'I do not believe that holocausts are required to gain the victory, while they are certainly liable to lose us the peace.' Two weeks later, he was even more confident:

> My policy continues to be the same. Hold on tight. Keep up the economic pressure, push on with munitions production and military preparations with the utmost energy, take no offensive unless Hitler begins it. I reckon that if we are allowed to carry on this policy we shall have won the war by the spring.[19]

Even by Chamberlain's standards, this was fantastically optimistic. It had taken four years for the Royal Navy's blockade to bring Germany to her knees in 1918 and, thanks to the agreement with Stalin, the Germans were now receiving train-loads of grain, oil and other raw materials from the Soviet Union. Furthermore, by deciding to wage a 'waiting war', the Allies ceded the initiative to Hitler, who used it to inflict a series of devastating surprises, while the persistence of the so-called 'Bore War' provoked an understandable political backlash.[20] 'The dead silence from the Front as to British action is very trying to the public nerves', wrote Lord Salisbury, the former Lord Privy Seal, to Lord Halifax on 22 September. 'They are no doubt feeling not only profound compassion for the people we have promised to help, but astonishment that no advantage has been taken of the German difficulties.' Of course, Salisbury acknowledged, there might be good reasons for the lack of British activity. 'But what probably will make the public unduly suspicious is the shadow of "appeasement" which besets them.'[21]

It did not help that Chamberlain showed none of the vitality and resolve expected of a war leader. His weekly statements to Parliament were dull and depressing – like the secretary 'of a firm of undertakers reading the minutes of the last meeting', according to Harold Nicolson – while his retention of former appeasers, such as Sir John Simon and Sir Samuel Hoare, further undermined confidence in the Government's ability to prosecute the war.[22]

When it was announced that the Supreme War Council, which met for the first time at Abbeville on 12 September, was to consist of only Chamberlain, Lord Chatfield, the Minister for the Co-ordination of Defence, Daladier and General Gamelin, the anti-appeasement Richard Law could not contain his despair. 'I'm horrified with the Supreme War Council', he wrote to fellow critic Paul Emrys-Evans.

> Does he [Chamberlain] really imagine that he's a great military leader? ... I was sufficiently alarmed by the War Cabinet, but this is absolutely terrifying. It's all very well to think, as I do think, that this old man won't last very long but he may easily ruin us all while he does last. I comfort myself sometimes by thinking of Anthony [Eden, recalled as Colonial Secretary] and Winston, but they're so outnumbered what can they do, except resign? ... I lie awake at night thinking of how for years I've been telling my constituents that if they voted for a socialist

> it would mean war, and that they must support the govt if they wanted peace. When one thinks of it – all those who were killed last time, all those who are going to be killed now – everything wasted through the stubbornness and lack of imagination of a few old men and the spinelessness of a lot of young men. If ever I engage in politics again I shall leave the Conservative party ... This theory that it's possible to 'educate' the Conservative party won't hold water. But I don't suppose any of us will ever be in politics again.[23]

On the same day that this letter was written, it was announced that Chamberlain had exhumed the former Home Secretary Sir John Gilmour to run the newly created Ministry of Shipping. It almost makes one 'wonder whether he is trying to win the war', commented Violet Bonham Carter, Herbert Asquith's daughter and prominent anti-appeaser.[24]

Churchill's stock, by contrast, was rising. Delighted to return to the Admiralty, the department he had run during the early years of the Great War, he benefited from the fact that the war at sea remained the only active theatre during the eight-month Phoney War. On 26 September, he gave a thrilling account of the Navy's activities over the previous four weeks, in which he sounded every note 'from deep preoccupation to flippancy, from resolution to sheer boyishness'.[25] 'One could feel the spirits of the House rising with every word', recorded Nicolson, who was not alone in contrasting this oratory with Chamberlain's lacklustre performances. 'In those twenty minutes Churchill brought himself nearer the post of Prime Minister than he has ever been before. In the Lobbies afterwards even Chamberlainites were saying, "We have now found our leader."'[26] Jim Thomas thought he had 'never seen the front bench look so furious'.[27]

*

On 12 October 1939, Chamberlain rejected Hitler's much-anticipated 'peace offer', after the Führer, in a speech to the Reichstag, had hinted at the possibility of an international conference provided that the Western Powers accept the partition of Poland. Although the Prime Minister remained optimistic about ending the war within a year, he judged that the Germans were not yet 'sufficiently convinced that they could not win'.[28] Moreover, he regarded the removal of 'that accursed madman', Adolf Hitler, an essential precondition of peace talks.[29] 'He must either die or go to St Helena or become a real public works architect, preferably in a "home"', he wrote to Ida on 5 November.

> His entourage must also go, with the possible exception of Göring, who might have some ornamental position in a transitional government. Having once got rid of the Nazis I don't think we should find any serious difficulty in Germany over Poland, Czecho-Slovakia, Jews, disarmament etc. Our real trouble is much more likely to be with France.[30]

Prior to his speech of 12 October – which effectively passed the buck by demanding the German Government prove its 'desire for peace by definite acts' – Chamberlain had admitted that he was 'more afraid of a peace offer than of an air raid', since it would encourage the 'peace-at-any-price people'.[31] That many such people existed he was in no doubt. Only the previous week 1,860 letters, out of a total of 2,450 received, had urged him to 'Stop the war' by one expedient or another.[32]

More sinister was the meeting which took place at the Duke of Westminster's house on 12 September. Attended by the Duke of Buccleuch, Lord Arnold (a member of the Anglo-German Fellowship), Lord Mottistone (another member and friend of Ribbentrop), Lord Rushcliffe (a former Minister of Labour), Sir Philip Gibbs (journalist and noted appeaser), Henry Drummond Wolff and the vicar of St Alban's Church in London, it began with Westminster reading aloud a manifesto in which he attacked those newspapers, 'controlled by the left and the Jews', which took 'the line that no peace is possible until Nazism is destroyed root and branch'. On the contrary, it was a calamity that the 'two races which are most akin' should be fighting one another and the Government should be prepared to explore peace options at the earliest possible date. Certainly there was no point in continuing the struggle once Poland had been conquered. Germany was 'impregnable on the ground, both in the east and west', while London (of which the Duke owned a considerable portion) constituted 'the best aerial target on the face of the earth'.[33]

Responding to this manifesto, soon circulating in both Downing Street and the Foreign Office, Churchill wrote to the Duke, an old friend with whom he used to go boar hunting in France, cautioning him against such defeatist talk, while Sir Joseph Ball warned

Chamberlain that it 'would be highly dangerous for the Government to give the slightest indication at the present time to listen to any such proposals'.*[34] Having enjoyed Westminster's hospitality in Scotland, Chamberlain seems to have been embarrassed by the manifesto. He was, however, delighted when his old adversary Lloyd George received a drubbing from Duff Cooper on 30 October after calling on the Government to give careful consideration to any peace terms which Hitler might care to offer. 'When he sat down I sprang to my feet', remembered Cooper, who was 'white with anger'. 'I accused him of preaching surrender. I said that his speech would be received with delight in Germany, where it would be said that the man who claimed to have won the last war was already admitting defeat in this one.'[35]

According to the Government whip Charles Waterhouse, the House was 'overwhelmingly against' the former Premier, who left the Chamber 'like a whipped pup'. At a meeting of the Conservative backbench 1922 Committee that evening, however, he heard Cyril Culverwell (MP for Bristol West) demand 'peace at almost any price', Sir Archibald Southby (Epsom) call for 'peace at a very low price', and speeches 'in the same strain' from Sir Arnold Wilson (Hitchin), Sir Charles Cayzer (Chester) and Captain Archibald Ramsay (Peebles and South Midlothian, and founder of the Right Club).[36] A few weeks earlier, he had come across the garrulous Robert Hudson proclaiming the virtues of 'another Munich' and 'a little more appeasement' in the Carlton Club, while on 4 October, the deputy Chief Whip, James Stuart, wrote to the Duke of Buccleuch thus:

> I can't pretend … that I was very sorry to hear Ll. G. say a good deal of what he did yesterday – although some of course regard him as a traitor.
>
> I would welcome anything which would bring this silly war to an end – although it is no good if it produces nothing but a temporary compromise to be followed by further hostilities in a year or so.[37]

---

* Churchill's letter and a subsequent visit from Ball seem to have had an effect. At a second, similarly defeatist, meeting held in Westminster's house on 26 September, the Duke himself was not present. It was, however, a larger meeting, including all previous attendees (with the exception of the vicar of St Alban's) as well as a 'sprinkling' of MPs (including Sir Arnold Wilson), the Labour peer Lord Noel-Buxton, the vicar of St Paul's, Knightsbridge and one of the canons of St Paul's Cathedral.

The truth was that the Government was prepared to consider, or at least listen to, peace offers – which emanated from a variety of sources and at a steady stream during this period – but remained firm in refusing to negotiate with Hitler. 'The central fact is that nobody would dream of putting the smallest trust in any promise that Hitler might make and consequently a method of arriving at a peaceful settlement is extremely difficult to find, short of the overthrow of the German Government, which is only likely to happen at the end of a bloody struggle in which Germany gets the worse of it', recorded Sir John Simon, usually considered foremost among the appeasers, in his diary for 13 October 1939.[38]

One month, later Halifax, who showed great patience in dealing with the multitude of peace feelers, replied to a letter from the Earl of Lytton thus:

> I can suppose it would not be particularly difficult to put down on a sheet of paper the things we wanted about Czechoslovakia, Poland, Austria, disarmament, political and economic co-operation in Europe, etc. But when we had done all this, I certainly could feel no confidence whatever in the security of the position so long as I was dealing with Hitler and the Nazi regime as we know it.[39]

Chamberlain's newly appointed Assistant Private Secretary, Jock Colville, recorded the Prime Minister agreeing, in late October 1939, with 'eight out of the nine points' of a proposed peace deal, which would see the restoration of Polish and Czech independence under a government led by Göring, but was insistent that 'Hitler himself shall play no part in the proposed new order'.[40] Three months later and his attitude was even more resolute. Responding to a missive from the Duke of Buccleuch – which questioned Britain's war aims and enquired about the possibility of negotiations through Göring – Chamberlain was almost Churchillian in tone:

> My dear Walter …
>
> … I have studied carefully all that you say and it seems to me that the differences of opinion between us turn on the question raised in the last typewritten paragraph of your letter. In that paragraph you seem to imply that we are absolved from fighting resolutely against

Germany because her repeated acts of aggression have not been committed directly against the British Empire. If that is your implication [to which Buccleuch scribbled 'NO' in the margin] then indeed our views are widely separated. In my view, the history of the last few years proves beyond all doubt that Germany has set before herself a programme of aggression and expansion and that just as the *Anschluss* was followed by the seizure of Czechoslovakia and the seizure of Czechoslovakia by the invasion of Poland so in due time France would have been assailed and the British Empire attacked.

You know how greatly I desired to halt this tragic sequence by peaceful means. Munich was, I believe, the last chance of a peaceful solution and the final test of German sincerity, but Hitler deliberately rejected that chance and demonstrated his insincerity. When, with abundant warning of the results that must follow, Germany invaded Poland, the last opportunity had come of halting the sequence even by war, and I have no shadow of doubt that when we entered the war in September we did so not merely in defence of Poland but of France and the British Empire. If this is so, it follows, as you yourself recognise, that we must be prepared, if necessary, to fight to the bitter end. Nevertheless, I hope that wiser counsels may yet prevail in Germany and that we may achieve our purpose of halting aggression without suffering and loss on the scale of that endured in the last war …

I am well aware that numerous 'peace feelers' have already been put out from German sources and that these 'feelers' have frequently been associated with the name of Göring, but none of them as yet has contained any satisfactory evidence of the indispensable change of heart …

You fear also that a war begun as a war against Hitler has now become a war against Germany. I would remind you again that what we are in fact fighting is aggression. Aggression has been, and there is certainly no evidence that it has ceased to be, the policy of Hitler. That is why we made war upon Hitler and why, so long as he can persuade or compel Germany to support him in such a policy, we must wage war against Germany …

Let me emphasise again that we shall certainly lose no opportunity of making a just peace provided we can be satisfied that the peace made will be lasting. I shall continue, however, to advise the country

> that nothing could be worse than an inconclusive peace or a reversion to an armed truce and that we and our Allies must be prepared to fight the war resolutely until a true peace can be won.[41]

In fairness to Buccleuch and the many others who felt like him, a precise definition of Britain's war aims proved a considerable difficulty for the Government. Britain had entered the war in defence of Poland but, by the beginning of October, that country had been conquered and Hitler was insisting that he had no quarrel with the Western Powers. 'I wish I knew what we are fighting for', wrote Lord Derby to Lord Beaverbrook, towards the end of the Polish campaign:

> If it is to beat Hitler to a pulp, I understand and strongly sympathise, but if it is to reconstitute Poland, I am not so enthusiastic. If it had not been for the League of Nations, which I abominate – or for Locarno, which I always thought a very much overrated treaty – we should not be fighting now for Poland.[42]

The entry of the Red Army complicated the issue further. If Britain was fighting for Polish independence, then logically she ought to be fighting the Soviet Union as well as Nazi Germany. 'H[alifax] asked me about our "War Aims"', recorded Cadogan on 23 September.

> I told him I saw awful difficulties. We can no longer say 'evacuate Poland' without going to war with Russia, which we don't want to do! I suppose the cry is 'Abolish Hitlerism'. [But] what if Hitler hands over to Göring?! ... What if Germany now sits tight? Gamelin doesn't look to me like flinging himself on the Siegfried line. What do we do? Build up our armaments feverishly? What for? ... Must try and think this out.[43]

It was not long before confusion over Britain's war aims was finding expression in black humour. One limerick, which originated in the Foreign Office, had Chamberlain firmly in its sights:

> An elderly Statesman with gout
> When asked what this War was about

In a Written Reply
Said 'My colleagues and I
Are doing our best to find out.'[44]

This was unfair to Chamberlain, who, despite loathing the war, was in no doubt about what Britain was fighting for. Yet his inability to inspire the country, combined with the continued lack of military action (except at sea), led to growing criticism of his leadership. To this, Chamberlain responded with complaints to his sisters, particularly regarding the Labour Party, which he believed was acting dishonourably. He was, however, far from dissatisfied with the way the war was progressing. Having always doubted Hitler's desire to begin the war in the west – since this would 'entail such frightful losses as to endanger the whole Nazi system' – his optimism that this would not occur increased the longer it did not.[45] On 5 November, he was pleased to report to Ida that the threat of an attack on the Maginot Line, 'prophesied by the soldiers', seemed to be receding. And although 'we are told that *the* testing time will be … in March or in April … I have a "hunch" that the war will be over before the spring'.[46] Later in the month, he received information that Hitler was about to attack the Low Countries but refused to take this seriously, having 'been given definite dates for offensives on so many previous occasions'. Indeed, he saw no reason to change his belief that Hitler would continue to 'abstain from any action which would entail real bad fighting'. He was, however, beginning to 'wonder whether we shall do any good with them [the Germans] unless they first get a real hard punch in the stomach'.[47]

As it turned out, it was the Germans who would do the punching.

XXIV
The Fall of Chamberlain

Onward Neville's soldiers
Prosecute the war,
Clarion call of duty
Calls you as before.
There are now no Parties,
Heed no party hacks,
Only for your country
Use your thinking caps.

Onward Britain's soldiers
Marching straight to war,
With a bold new leader,
Victory as before.

Final verses of an anonymous poem left on the desk of
Captain Charles Waterhouse MP, 1 May 1940.[1]

As 1939 turned into 1940, the majority of the British people could be forgiven for thinking that they were participants in a dress rehearsal for war. Buildings had been sandbagged, uniforms were worn, gas masks were carried, but the sense of danger was missing. Hospital beds – expecting 30,000 casualties a day – remained empty, while the British Expeditionary Force, far from hanging out its washing on the Siegfried Line, as the popular Phoney War song had it, was constructing pillboxes and digging trenches. The only real danger the British faced during this period was from the self-imposed blackout, which claimed over 2,000 lives in motoring accidents during the last four months of 1939, compared to only three British fatalities on the Western Front. Yet if there was little evidence of the war in the West, the same could not be said for other parts of the world.

On 30 November 1939, having failed to achieve his territorial demands by negotiation, Stalin ordered the Red Army to invade neutral Finland. Western opinion was outraged. The Soviet Union was expelled from the League of Nations (a reprisal which caused little anxiety in the Kremlin), while Ivan Maisky noted the 'fury' of the British, who, indeed, displayed greater indignation at this act of aggression than at the German invasion of Poland.[2] Inspired by the heroic resistance of the Finns – who between December 1939 and February 1940 managed to inflict a series of amazing defeats on far larger Soviet forces – there were soon calls to send military aid to Finland. Setting aside the fact that there had been few such demands made on behalf of Poland, to whom the British and French had been contractually obliged, the cataclysmic folly of risking war with the Soviet Union while Nazi Germany remained undefeated seems not to have sufficiently impinged either on popular opinion or some Allied decision makers.

'I regard it as essential to break the back of the Soviet Union in Finland', wrote General Maxime Weygand to General Maurice Gamelin, in a remark typifying the French desire to move the war as far away from French territory as possible.[3] The British were more circumspect. Lord Halifax had no desire to add Russia to Britain's enemies, while Chamberlain did not think that Stalin's adventure required a Western response. By February 1940, however, the idea of helping the Finns had become entangled with another scheme: that of stopping the supply of Swedish iron ore to Germany.

*

The idea of halting the flow of iron ore from Sweden to Germany stemmed naturally from the Allied strategy of economic warfare. The Swedish resource was essential to German arms manufacturing: the Ministry of Economic Warfare in London estimated that the Germans needed to import nine million tons during the first year of the war. Stopping this supply, it was argued, would deal a serious blow to Germany's war-making capacity. It would 'shorten the war and save many thousands of lives', declared Winston Churchill, the leading champion of the scheme, at the War Cabinet of 16 December 1939.[4] Others agreed. 'An attempt to stop [the Germans'] supplies of iron-ore from Sweden ... has many advantages and may be decisive', wrote General Sir Edmund Ironside, Chief of the Imperial General Staff, in a paper submitted to the War Cabinet; while even the naturally cautious Chamberlain conceded that it might prove 'one of the turning points of the war'.[5]

The problem was the neutrality of the Scandinavians. Mined principally in the north of Sweden, near the town of Gällivare, the ore was shipped, during the summer months, through the Gulf of Bothnia and, in the winter (when the gulf froze), from the Norwegian port of Narvik. In order to stop the ore, the British would need to violate Scandinavian neutrality by mining Norwegian territorial waters (thus forcing the German ships onto the open sea, where they could be seized by the Royal Navy) or by occupying the ore fields themselves. This presented a dilemma. Having gone to war in defence of the rights of small nations, how could the Allies justify violating Scandinavian neutrality? More importantly, how would other neutral countries, in particular the United States, react to this flouting of international law? The answer, Halifax assured his colleagues, was 'not well'.

The Finnish war appeared to offer a solution to this quandary. Under the pretext of aiding the Finns, the Allies would send an expeditionary force to seize control of the Swedish ore fields, as well as a number of Norwegian ports. Fortunately (though not for them), the Finns surrendered on 12 March 1940, thus killing this 'hare-brained' plan, which risked war with Norway and Sweden, as well as Russia, before it was launched.[6] But this was not the end of the matter. Determined to stop the ore, Churchill finally succeeded in persuading his colleagues to allow him to mine Norwegian waters and, early on the morning of 8 April, 234 Mark-17 mines were laid in Vestfjord off Narvik. At the same time, an expeditionary force had assembled in the Firth of Forth, ready to react should Hitler respond with an invasion of Norway. Unbeknownst to the British, however, the Germans were already under way.

Anticipating an Allied attempt to block the ore, Hitler had ordered plans for an invasion of Norway to be prepared in mid-December 1939. In the weeks following this decision, the German intent was plain to see. 'Reports that German military and naval preparation in various Baltic ports for possible action against Scandinavia not being kept secret, indeed the contrary', read the Joint Intelligence Committee briefing for 4 January 1940. 'Troops being trained in landing operations at Kiel and other German Baltic ports', stated the report for 7 January. '48 transports said to be preparing in Baltic ports' on 23 January.[7] On 26 March, a high-level Swedish source warned the British Air Attaché in Stockholm that the Germans were 'concentrating aircraft and shipping' for a possible 'seizure of Norwegian aerodromes and ports' and, on 30 March, the French Naval Minister informed his new Premier, Paul Reynaud,* that the Germans had gathered the 'material for an expedition against bases in south Norway'.[8]

The failure to heed this information and prepare for a German assault – or, better still, bomb the ports in which the invasion force was being prepared – is staggering. Equally incomprehensible was Chamberlain's soaring optimism, which led him to declare in a much-publicised speech, on 4 April, that Hitler had 'missed the bus'.[9] Five days later – twenty-four hours after the British mine-laying operation – German air and seaborne forces landed and captured the Norwegian ports of Kristiansand, Stavanger, Bergen, Trondheim, Narvik and Oslo, while also overrunning Denmark. Belatedly, the British realised how badly they had blundered. 'It is a lamentable thing that we went on arglebargling and here we are with the Germans [actually in Norway]', commented General Ironside in his diary.[10] The Chancellor of the Exchequer, Sir John Simon, agreed. The Germans had been 'very clever', he told Jock Colville. And 'we were ninnies, we were ninnies!'[11]

The fiasco that was the British attempt to recapture the ports and expel the Germans from Norway is well chronicled.[12] Lacking maps, vehicles, radios and, most crucially, air support, one French officer remarked that the British seemed to have conceived 'this campaign on the lines of a punitive expedition against the Zulus'.[13] Worse was the constant changing of plans and objectives, resulting in predictable confusion and, ultimately, disaster. The Germans fought with tenacity, while the Allies proved incapable of co-ordinating their mutating operations either with each other or with their respective services. Plans for a naval assault on Trondheim, the ancient capital in the centre of the country, were made, at the cost of the early recapture of Narvik, and then unmade, at the expense of land forces attempting

---

* Daladier had resigned on 20 March, after 300 French deputies abstained on a motion of confidence in his Government, following its failure to aid Finland.

a pincer movement. By 27 April, the War Cabinet had decided to cut its losses. British forces, who had been battling in heavy snow without skis, snow boots or camouflage and under constant air attack, would be evacuated from central Norway, leaving only a small force in the north to focus on the recapture of Narvik. It had been, in the words of an American war correspondent, a 'helluva mess'.[14]

*

The shock engendered by the Norway disaster was considerable. Buoyed by false press reports, the British had been expecting a victory. Instead, the Royal Navy had been outwitted (although a number of German destroyers and U-boats were later sunk), while British land forces had suffered an unambiguous defeat. 'Humiliation and indignation were the key-notes', recorded Robert Bruce Lockhart, after hearing the story from the *Times* journalist Colin Coote.[15] Arriving at a meeting of the Watching Committee – a body of senior Government critics, under the Chairmanship of Lord Salisbury – on the afternoon of 30 April, Harold Nicolson found a 'glum crowd': 'The general impression is that we may lose the war.'[16]

The blame for the defeat fell on Chamberlain. That this was far from fair was clear to those who had been privy to the twists and turns of the previous few weeks. If there was one man responsible for the debacle it was Churchill, who, contrary to the image he painted in his war memoirs, changed his mind repeatedly over whether Narvik or Trondheim should provide the focus for Allied operations. 'We must get the PM to take a hand in this before Winston and Tiny [Ironside] go and bugger up the whole war', declared an exasperated P. J. Grigg, Permanent Under-Secretary of the War Office and friend of Churchill's, on 12 April.[17] A few days later, Chamberlain was forced to resume the Chairmanship of the Military Co-ordination Committee after Churchill had driven the Chiefs of Staff to the point of mutiny. The effect was transformative. Tempers were quelled, business proceeded in an orderly manner and the decision to focus on Trondheim was taken unanimously. Little of this was known outside Whitehall's secret confines, however, and the increasingly established view that Chamberlain lacked the ruthless determination to win the war proved decisive.

There was a 'tide in the House of Commons against the PM', noted Hugh Dalton on 1 May, after news of the decision to evacuate southern Norway began to leak. Even Conservative MPs were saying 'He must go now'.[18] The next day, the Government whip Charles Waterhouse, a firm Chamberlainite, found an anonymous poem on his desk, calling on Conservative MPs to 'heed no party hacks' but use their 'thinking caps' to find a 'bold new leader'.[19] Later, walking the corridors, he observed 'much whispering and cornering' among MPs. Chamberlain's detractors looked 'like boys who have found the key of the jam cupboard', he noted. 'I wonder if they really have?'[20]

Despite all the intrigue, there was nothing inevitable about the events which sprang from the Norway disaster. Chamberlain enjoyed a Commons majority of over 200, while Churchill had also been damaged by the fiasco. Government whips began a whispering campaign, branding the First Lord of the Admiralty as 'the real culprit in the Norwegian catastrophe', while no less strenuous efforts were made to shore up Chamberlain's position.[21] Those hoping that the debate on the debacle would presage the fall of the Prime Minister were pessimistic. The Foreign Office's Orme Sargent felt sure that 'nothing will happen' and that Chamberlain would carry the House. He had always believed that it would take a 'disaster to wake this country up and get rid of this Government' but doubted now whether Norway was sufficiently calamitous to shake Conservative MPs out of their torpor. 'We shall have to wait for more,' he remarked gloomily, 'perhaps an invasion of Scotland.'[22] Others, however, were less sure. Chips Channon feared that Chamberlain's days might be numbered, while the Chief Whip, David Margesson, declared that they were facing the 'greatest political crisis since August 1931'.*[23] Everything hung on the debate on the Government's handling of the war, scheduled for the following week, on 7 and 8 May 1940.

*

The Norway debate has a strong claim to stand as the most important in British history. Certainly it was the most dramatic since the days

---

* In August 1931, the Labour Government of Ramsay MacDonald split over the issue of cuts to unemployment benefits in order to stave off a run on the pound and the National Government was born.

of Cromwell, whose words were to be quoted with devastating effect. Entering the Chamber shortly before 4 p.m., Chamberlain was greeted with cries of 'Missed the bus' from the Labour benches and stage-managed cheers from the Conservative ones.[24] He spoke poorly. Tired and irritated by the Opposition's jeers, he stumbled over his words, looked embarrassed and generally exhibited none of the self-confidence with which MPs had become familiar. His defence of the Norwegian expedition was dull (the Egyptian Ambassador fell asleep) and, to many minds, delusional. Having lauded the success of the evacuation and pointed to the losses the Germans had sustained, he expressed the view that the implications of the reverse had been 'seriously exaggerated'.[25] 'No one listening to his speech would have supposed that Britain had suffered a major defeat', recalled the Liberal MP Dingle Foot and when Chamberlain sat down it was only the Administration's 'yes-men' who applauded.[26]

Nevertheless, the general sense was that the Government was going 'to get away with it'.[27] That this turned out not to be the case owed much to the Conservative MP for Portsmouth North, Admiral Sir Roger Keyes, who, in the full uniform of an Admiral of the Fleet, with six rows of medals across his chest, rose shortly after 7 p.m. to deliver a devastating indictment of the Government's handling of the Norwegian campaign.

A hero of the Great War who had led the 1918 Zeebrugge raid,* Keyes was wearing his uniform, he explained, because he wished to speak on behalf of the many officers and men of the fighting, sea-going Navy, who felt they had been badly let down. It was not their fault, he asserted, in a nervous voice which added weight to his argument, that German warships had managed to enter Norwegian waters and land an invasion force. It was not their fault that vulnerable ports and aerodromes had been left unmolested for nearly a month. It was not their fault that the Germans had been able to resupply their initial force with tanks, heavy artillery and mechanised transport. And it was not their fault that the naval assault on Trondheim, on which British land forces depended, had failed to

* The Zeebrugge raid of 23 April 1918 was an unsuccessful attempt by the Royal Navy to block the Belgian port and thus deny the resident German U-boats and ships access to the English Channel.

materialise. No, the fault lay with pusillanimity in London and the Whitehall committee system of decision-making. It was 'a shocking story of ineptitude', which he assured the House 'ought never to have been allowed to happen'. The Gallipoli tragedy had been repeated 'step by step' and if the Government did not wish to lose the war then they would do well to remember Nelson's dictum that 'the boldest measures are the safest'.[28] It was the most dramatic speech Harold Nicolson had ever heard. But it was not the end.

At 8.03, the deputy Speaker called the leader of the Conservative dissidents, Leo Amery, to speak. Notoriously verbose, Amery's orations usually had a soporific effect on his audience. Not this time. Determined that the Chamberlain Government should be forced from power, he had spent the morning carefully preparing his speech and had even looked up a couple of his favourite quotations from Oliver Cromwell. On rereading the future Lord Protector's dismissal of the Rump Parliament in 1653, he wondered whether this was not 'too strong meat', but decided to keep it by him in case the moment took him.

Having begun with the assertion that it was Parliament itself that was on trial – since 'if we lose this war, it is not this or that ephemeral government but Parliament as an institution that will be condemned for good and all' – Amery launched into a crushing exposition of the whole Scandinavian saga: 'A story of lack of prevision and of preparation, a story of indecision, slowness and fear of taking risks.' If this were an isolated catastrophe that would be one thing, but it was not. The entire conduct of the war, he claimed, was suffering on account of the Government's inertia. 'We cannot go on as we are', he declared to growing applause from all sections of the House. 'There must be a change.' Cheers. 'Somehow or other we must get into the Government men who can match our enemies in fighting spirit, in daring, in resolution and in thirst for victory.' More cheers. 'We are fighting today for our life, for our liberty, for our all; we cannot go on being led as we are.'[29]

Amery paused. He had reached the climax of his peroration: the moment when he had to decide whether or not to read the words he had copied down that morning. Of the dangers of going too far, he was well aware. 'I was not out for a dramatic finish, but for a practical purpose; to bring down the Government', he recalled. But the House was unmistakably with him and, 'swept forward by the surge of feeling which my speech had worked up on the benches round me', he decided to throw caution to the winds.[30]

He had already quoted Cromwell's words to John Hampden, chastising him for employing 'decayed serving men' in the Parliamentary Army (a dig at Chamberlain, Simon and Hoare), now he proposed to quote some more. He did so with reluctance, since he was speaking of 'old friends and associates'* but they were words he considered applicable to the present situation.

> This is what Cromwell said to the Long Parliament when he thought it was no longer fit to conduct the affairs of the nation: 'You have sat too long here for any good you have been doing. Depart, I say, and let us have done with you. In the name of God, go!'[31]

Although there is dispute about whether or not Chamberlain was in the Chamber when this injunction was given, it was, as his Parliamentary Private Secretary, Alec Douglas-Home, recalled, 'a dagger in the heart'.[32]

*

The second day of the debate was no less dramatic. It began with Labour's Herbert Morrison announcing, contrary to expectations, that the Opposition would demand a division at the end of the debate – in effect a vote of confidence in the Government. Immediately, Chamberlain jumped up and, 'showing his teeth like a rat in a corner', accepted the challenge.[33] 'I have friends in the House', he declared – in a phrase as unfortunate and damaging as 'missed the bus' or 'peace for our time', since it appealed to party loyalty at a time of national crisis – 'and I call on my friends to support us in the lobby tonight.'[34]

The next great moment came with David Lloyd George's delivery of what Violet Bonham Carter (whose father, Herbert Asquith, Lloyd George had supplanted during the First World War) described as 'the best and most deadly speech I have ever heard from him'.[35] Castigating

---

* Not only had Chamberlain been responsible for securing Amery his seat, but Amery was godfather to Chamberlain's son, Frank.

the Government for its handling of the Norway expedition, he nevertheless tried to shield Churchill by saying that he did not believe the First Lord was responsible for all of the things that happened there. When Churchill insisted that he took full responsibility for everything that had been done by the Admiralty, his friend and former collaborator enjoined him not to allow himself 'to be converted into an air raid shelter to keep the splinters from hitting his colleagues'.[36] Opposition MPs exploded with laughter, having previously been shouting themselves hoarse in support. Watching from the gallery, Horace Wilson was taken aback by the hatred written on many of their faces: 'It was the pent-up bitterness and personal animosity of years.'[37] Another aerial observer was Annie Chamberlain. Dressed all in black, except for a posy of violets pinned to her chest, she 'looked infinitely sad as she peered down into the mad arena where the lions were out for her husband's blood'. Hoping to surround him with an 'aura of affection', the ever-devoted Chips Channon had found a seat directly behind Chamberlain. But this was no shield against Lloyd George's carefully aimed arrows.[38] The issue was not the Prime Minister's friends, the Welsh Wizard insisted, but the country's one great enemy. The Prime Minister had met Hitler in both peace and war and had 'always been worsted'. Now, he was appealing for sacrifice. 'I say solemnly that the Prime Minister should give an example of sacrifice, because there is nothing which can contribute more to victory in this war than that he should sacrifice the seals of office.'[39]

*

Meanwhile, the whips and Parliamentary Private Secretaries were desperately trying to stem the rebellion. 'Just once more', they pleaded.[40] The Government would be reconstructed; Simon and Hoare would go; the Prime Minister was prepared to accept any demands they cared to make. But it was too late. The rebels were determined and, at a meeting of the various dissident groups, it was decided to go all out against the Government. More alarming for the Prime Minister's supporters was how many former Chamberlainites were saying that they too intended to rebel. 'The fact is that there is no young officer who I know who can wholeheartedly support the Government', explained Quintin Hogg, who as an officer himself in the Tower Hamlets Rifles had been 'training' his men without either Bren guns or ammunition, to an imploring Alec Dunglass.[41] Another loyalist turned rebel was the MP for Smethwick, Roy Wise. A Lieutenant-Colonel in the Queen's Royal Regiment, he had returned from Norway determined to vote against the Government on behalf of his men, who had been consistently 'bombed by German aeroplanes and had nothing with which to reply, not even a machine gun'.[42]

When the division was finally called, following Churchill's creditable defence of the Government, Hugh Dalton was overwhelmed by the number of Tory MPs, many of them in uniform, filing into the Opposition lobby.

> Earlier in the day I had not thought that, at the outside, we should get more than a dozen to fifteen Government supporters in with us ... In fact, we had between forty and fifty. My eyes filled with tears. Many of them giving the last vote they would ever give, for their country and against their Party.[43]

'Quislings!' the Chamberlain supporters shouted at the defectors. 'Rats!' and 'Yes-men!' came the reply.[44] Slowly, David Margesson and three other tellers approached the clerks' desk, below the Speaker's chair. 'The packed benches were so tense that they seemed to be vibrating like taut wire', recalled Louis Spears.[45] They bowed and then, in his clear, commanding voice, Margesson read out the result:

> The Ayes to the right – 281; the Noes to the left – 200.

Pandemonium broke out. The Government's majority of over two hundred had been slashed to a mere eighty-one. Forty-one Government MPs (thirty-three of them Conservatives) had voted against the Government, while another forty-odd had abstained.* It was a crushing moral defeat. Before the result, the consensus among Chamberlain's supporters was that he would have to resign unless

* The exact figure for deliberate abstentions is impossible to ascertain owing to the absence of a number of MPs due to illness or service overseas.

he could get a majority of over a hundred – the minimum support necessary in wartime. The Opposition benches erupted in cheers, soon succeeded by cries of 'Resign!' and 'Go!' Violet Bonham Carter was shocked to see 'prim respectable Conservatives like Harold Macmillan – with his high white collar and tightly fixed pince-nez – yelling "Go! Go! Go!" like inspired baboons'.[46] Josiah Wedgwood began to sing 'Rule Britannia', to which Macmillan, 'like a madly grinning school boy', lent his unmusical voice, before they were both howled down by Tory loyalists.[47]

Chamberlain looked as if he had been punched in the stomach. He rose with dignity, however, and with a brief smile at his supporters – who had been given the signal to cheer by Margesson – began to pick his way over the protruding feet of his Cabinet colleagues. Watching him depart, Spears, who had just voted against the Government, found his anger evaporating:

> He walked out of the House and through the lobby with heavy feet, a truly sad and pathetic figure. His thoughts must have been as black as the clothes he wore. I, who had felt so bitterly opposed to his policy, felt intensely sorry for him as he walked out, solitary, following in the wake of all his dead hopes and fruitless efforts.[48]

*

The next twenty-four hours were spent by Chamberlain trying to persuade the Labour leadership to join a truly national government under his leadership – his only chance of survival – and by everyone else debating his successor. That Halifax, rather than Churchill, was the preference of most Conservative MPs, the Labour and Liberal parties, the Cabinet, the press, Chamberlain and the King, is well documented. Immensely esteemed and devoid of enemies, despite his thirty-year political career, the high priest of respectable Toryism, as opposed to the erratic author of the Dardanelles, appeared to almost everyone as the obvious choice. The problem was that Halifax did not want the job. In May 1939, Victor Cazalet told Lord Tweedsmuir that Halifax 'absolutely refuses to contemplate the idea of being PM'.[49] One year on, little had changed. His peerage was cited as the obvious obstacle: it would be impossible, Halifax argued, to hold the position while being absent from the centre of political action in the Commons. Yet he seems also to have realised his own inadequacies as a potential war leader, particularly when contrasted with Churchill's obvious qualities. Indeed, given that Halifax had displayed even less bellicosity than Chamberlain during the Phoney War and was considerably more languid, it is surprising that this thought did not have wider currency. Either way, it was not to be.

Halifax refused to succumb to multiple entreaties and, when the Labour leadership confirmed at 4.45 p.m. on 10 May (forty hours after the vote) that they were not prepared to serve under Chamberlain, the Prime Minister was left with no alternative. He had hoped that the German invasion of the Low Countries, which had begun at dawn that morning, might offer him a reprieve but was soon disabused. At 6 p.m. he offered his resignation to the King and recommended Churchill as his successor.*

Shortly afterwards, Alec Dunglass and Jock Colville joined Chips Channon and Rab Butler in Butler's room in the Foreign Office. 'I opened a bottle of Champagne', recorded Channon, 'and we four loyal adherents of Mr Chamberlain drank "To the King over the water".'[50] This done, Dunglass and Butler – who twenty-three years later would themselves be rivals for the Premiership – let themselves go. 'Rab said that he thought that the good clean tradition of English politics, that of Pitt as opposed to Fox, had been sold to the greatest adventurer of modern political history', recorded Colville. 'This sudden coup of Winston and his rabble was a serious disaster and an unnecessary one: the "pass had been sold" by Mr C[hamberlain], Lord

---

* 'I accepted his resignation', George VI recorded in his diary that night, 'and told him how grossly unfairly I thought he had been treated, and that I was terribly sorry that all this controversy had happened. We then had an informal talk over his successor. I, of course, suggested Halifax, but he told me that H. was not enthusiastic, as being in the Lords he could only act as a shadow or a ghost in the Commons, where all the real work took place. I was disappointed over this statement, as I thought H. was the obvious man, and that his peerage could be placed in abeyance for the time being. Then I knew that there was only one person whom I could send for to form a Government who had the confidence of the country, and that was Winston. I asked Chamberlain his advice, and he told me Winston was the man to send for.'

Halifax and Oliver Stanley [who had made a notably poor contribution to the Norway debate]. They had weakly surrendered to a half-breed American whose main support was that of inefficient but talkative people of a similar type.'[51]

Meanwhile, Churchill had begun his walk with destiny.

XXV

Appeasement's Last Stand

We shall never surrender.

Winston Churchill, 4 June 1940[1]

Appeasement's last stand occurred just over a fortnight later. Taken by surprise by the German offensive (though it had long been expected), the Allies were soon in disarray and the Wehrmacht deep into Dutch and Belgian territory. On 14 May 1940, General Gerd von Rundstedt's Army Group A broke through the French line at Sedan – the site of Napoleon III's decisive defeat at the hands of the Prussians in 1870 – and by 20 May had reached the Channel, trapping the British and northern French armies. Faced with the collapse of France and the potential loss of the British Expeditionary Force (BEF), the War Cabinet – now consisting of Winston Churchill (Prime Minister), Neville Chamberlain (Lord President), Lord Halifax (Foreign Secretary), Clement Attlee (Lord Privy Seal) and Arthur Greenwood (Minister without Portfolio) – began to discuss the possibility of peace talks.

The man forcing this debate was Halifax. Appalled by the French collapse and defeatist about Britain's prospects, he believed it his duty to see what terms Hitler was prepared to offer. On 25 May, he obtained Churchill's permission to approach the Italian Ambassador, Giuseppe Bastianini, ostensibly to discuss means (bribes) by which Italy would agree to remain neutral but also to judge Mussolini's willingness to act as mediator between the Allies and Hitler. Bastianini was encouraging. Perceiving the Foreign Secretary's real purpose, he asked whether it would be possible to discuss 'not only Great Britain and Italy, but other countries' – in other words, Germany. When Halifax replied that it was hard to visualise such discussions while the war was still proceeding, the Ambassador assured him that once such talks had begun 'war would be pointless'.[2]

The next day, Sunday 26 May, as the British Expeditionary Force began to retreat towards Dunkirk, Halifax raised the possibility of exploring peace terms at three separate meetings of the War Cabinet. 'We had to face the fact that it was not so much now a question of imposing a complete defeat upon Germany but of safeguarding the independence of our own Empire and if possible that of France', he stated. Under these circumstances, was Churchill prepared to enter into discussions, provided that 'matters vital to the independence of this country' were assured?[3] Although Churchill had been bolstered by a report from the Chiefs of Staff, euphemistically entitled 'British Strategy in a Certain Eventuality' (i.e. the collapse of France), which stated that Britain *could* survive on her own, provided that her Navy and Air Force remained intact to repel a German invasion, he did not consider it possible, at this stage, to give an outright refusal. His own position as Prime Minister was far from secure and an open breach with his Foreign Secretary (whom most Conservative MPs had wanted to succeed Chamberlain) had the potential to make it impossible. He, therefore, stated that while he considered it 'incredible that Hitler would consent to any terms that we could accept ... if we could get out of this jam by giving up Malta and Gibraltar [to Italy] and some African colonies [to Germany] he would jump at it'. The only safe course, however, 'was to convince Hitler that he could not beat us'.[4]

The succeeding twenty-four hours brought only the grimmest news. Hitler had lifted his controversial halt order on the morning of 26 May* and by the 27th the German spearheads were less than five miles from Dunkirk. Effective resistance ended in Calais on the afternoon of the 26th but Churchill felt compelled to order the local commander to continue fighting, in order to protect the flank of the main bulk of British forces retreating towards Dunkirk.

---

* Fearful that the terrain would prove too marshy for tanks and reassured by Göring that the Luftwaffe could destroy the trapped BEF on its own, Hitler had ordered the German Panzer divisions to halt on 24 May, just fifteen miles from Dunkirk. This provided the crucial window in which Operation Dynamo was put into action.

At 7 p.m., the order for Operation Dynamo, the evacuation of the BEF from France, was given. Later that evening, the Foreign Office learnt that the King of the Belgians, Leopold III, was preparing to make a separate peace with Germany. At 7.15 the following morning, Monday 27 May, Churchill was woken by a telephone call. It was Vice-Admiral Somerville reporting that the Germans had moved their guns north of Calais and were now shelling ships approaching Dunkirk. The rest of the day saw relentless attacks by the Luftwaffe on the Allied forces stranded at Dunkirk. It was, however, in London that the crucial battle was fought.

At 4.30 p.m., the War Cabinet, plus Sir Archibald Sinclair – the new Secretary of State for Air and, importantly, an ally of Churchill – met, for the second time. The meeting only lasted an hour and a half but was arguably the most important ninety minutes of the war; certainly the closest that Hitler came to winning it.[5] Having been presented with Halifax's memorandum on the 'Suggested Approach to Signor Mussolini', Churchill now stated that he had grave doubts about such a move. Immediately, Sinclair threw his weight behind the Prime Minister. 'He was convinced', the War Cabinet minutes read, 'of the futility of an approach to Italy at this time ... Any weakness on our part would encourage the Germans and the Italians, and would tend to undermine morale both in this country and in the Dominions.' Both Attlee and Greenwood agreed. 'If it got out that we had sued for terms at the cost of ceding British territory, the consequences would be terrible', argued Greenwood. 'It would be heading for disaster to go any further with those approaches.'

Churchill then stated his unambiguous opposition to Halifax's plan. An approach to Mussolini would almost certainly be regarded 'with contempt' and would 'ruin the integrity of our fighting position in this country'.

> At the moment our prestige in Europe was very low. The only way we could get it back was by showing the world that Germany had not beaten us ... Even if we were beaten, we should be no worse off than we should be if we were now to abandon the struggle. Let us therefore avoid being dragged down the slippery slope with France. The whole of this manoeuvre was intended to

> get us so deeply involved in negotiations that we should be unable to turn back.[6]

Having listened to this 'frightful rot', as he described it in his diary, Halifax then made an oblique threat to resign.[7] This led to the famous walk in the Downing Street garden, in which Churchill, if not able to convert his Foreign Secretary to his point of view, evidently succeeded in charming him out of taking a step which, both men knew, had the capacity to destroy the Government.

Nevertheless, Halifax renewed his arguments the next day, Tuesday 28 May, when the War Cabinet met in the House of Commons at four o'clock. Having raised the approach to Mussolini (which the French Government was also urging), the Foreign Secretary asked his colleagues not to 'ignore the fact that we might get better terms before France went out of the war and our aircraft factories were bombed, than we might get in three months' time'. Once again, Churchill disagreed. The chances of Hitler offering terms which did not curtail British independence or integrity were minute and when British negotiators got up to leave the conference table, as they inevitably would, 'we should find that all the forces of resolution which were now at our disposal would have vanished'. At this crucial moment, Chamberlain – who in the previous meetings had tried to maintain a balance between Halifax and Churchill, though inclining towards the latter – came down in support of the Prime Minister. 'The Lord President ... agreed with this general diagnosis', the Cabinet minutes record, and Chamberlain made the point that, while continuing the struggle constituted a serious gamble, 'the alternative to fighting' also 'involved a considerable gamble'. He therefore 'concluded that it was no good making an approach on the lines proposed' at the present time. It was a vital intervention – a role reversal of the situation, eighteen months earlier, when Halifax had opposed Chamberlain over the Godesberg demands – which, if it had gone the other way, had the potential to change the course of history.[8]

Churchill now moved to checkmate Halifax. Having concluded the meeting, he asked that the War Cabinet reconvene at seven o'clock, after he had met with the wider Cabinet, thus far excluded from their deliberations. To these twenty-five Conservative, Labour, Liberal National, Liberal and National Labour Ministers, Churchill gave a summary of the situation at Dunkirk, in no way 'minimising the extent of the disaster or of further disasters which might follow such as a successful German march on Paris and a French surrender'.[9] It was clear, he said, that the Germans would soon begin to turn their attention to the British Isles and that 'attempts to invade us would no doubt be made'. In these circumstances, as the newly appointed Minister of Economic Warfare, Hugh Dalton, recorded, Churchill had wondered whether it was his 'duty to consider entering into negotiations with That Man' but had decided that it was 'idle to think that, if we tried to make peace now, we should get better terms than if we fought it out'.[10]

> The Germans would demand our fleet – that would be called 'disarmament' – our naval bases, and much else. We should become a slave state, though a British Government which would be Hitler's puppet would be set up – 'under [Oswald] Mosley [leader of the British Union of Fascists] or some such person'. And where should we be at the end of all that? On the other side, we had immense reserves and advantages. Therefore, he said, 'We shall go on and we shall fight it out, here or elsewhere and if this long island story of ours is to end at last, let it end only when each one of us lies choking in his own blood upon the ground.'[11]

No one expressed 'even the faintest flicker of dissent' and when Churchill had finished several Ministers hurried to congratulate him. He could not remember 'having ever before heard a gathering of persons occupying high places in political life express themselves so emphatically', he told the War Cabinet when it reconvened at 7 p.m. 'They had not expressed alarm at the position in France, but had expressed the greatest satisfaction when he had told them that there was no chance of our giving up the struggle'.[12]

Confronted with such unanimous resolution, Halifax had no choice but to accept defeat. He raised the French desire for an appeal to President Roosevelt but when Churchill rejected this, arguing that 'a bold stand' would command the respect of the United States 'but a grovelling appeal … would have the worst possible effect', he did not demur. Churchill had won.

Meanwhile, the evacuation from Dunkirk was beginning to improve. Forty-seven thousand men were rescued the next day, Wednesday 29 May, despite continuous air attack. The next day, 53,800 were saved. The day after that, 68,000. By the end of 4 June – nine days after the commencement of Operation Dynamo – 338,226 men had been evacuated, including more than 125,000 French soldiers.[13] Considering that 45,000 was the most the Chiefs of Staff had envisaged possible, it was little short of a miracle and did much to stiffen resolve, within both the War Cabinet and the country, to continue the struggle. Responding to a Foreign Office memorandum in which it was suggested that preparations should be made to evacuate the royal family and the Government to 'some part of the Overseas Empire, whence the war would continue to be waged', Churchill was emphatic: the answer was 'no'. 'I believe we shall make them rue the day they try to invade our island. No such discussion can be permitted', he minuted on 1 June.[14] When the Director of the National Gallery, Kenneth Clark, suggested that the museum's paintings should be sent to Canada for safe keeping, he received a similar response. 'No. Bury them in caves and cellars. None must go. We are going to beat them.'[15]

Three days later, as the last Allied soldiers were being evacuated from Dunkirk, Churchill articulated this spirit in words which have echoed down the generations. He had full confidence, he told the Commons, that they would be able to defend their island home and 'ride out the storm of war ... if necessary for years, if necessary alone'. That, at any rate, was the resolve of His Majesty's Government, 'every man of them':

> We shall fight in France, we shall fight on the seas and oceans, we shall fight with growing confidence and growing strength in the air, we shall defend our island, whatever the cost may be. We shall fight on the beaches, we shall fight on the landing grounds, we shall fight in the fields and in the streets, we shall fight in the hills; we shall never surrender, and even if, which I do not for a moment believe, this island or a large part of it were subjugated and starving, then our Empire beyond the seas, armed and guarded by the British Fleet, would carry on the struggle, until, in God's good time, the new world, with all its power and might, steps forth to the rescue and the liberation of the old.[16]

It was the ultimate signal of Churchill's victory over Halifax and the appeasers: the most dramatic expression of that defiance which would deny Hitler victory in 1940. Just over a fortnight later, France signed an armistice with Germany. Half of Europe was now under Hitler's control. Britain was alone but she would fight on. The age of appeasement was over; the age of war had begun again.

Epilogue

'Guilty Men'

> All those who were killed last time, all those who are going to be killed now – everything wasted through the stubbornness and lack of imagination of a few old men and the spinelessness of a lot of young men.
>
> Richard Law to Paul Emrys-Evans, 13 September 1939[1]

> He was right to make the attempt to save the world from a great catastrophe and history will give this verdict.
>
> Sir Samuel Hoare to Annie Chamberlain, 11 November 1940[2]

One evening during the Phoney War, members of the Foreign Office's Political Intelligence Department discussed which politicians might be considered 'criminally responsible for [the] war and should be hanged on lamp-posts'. As the former journalist and spy Robert Bruce Lockhart recorded, there was consensus as to the leading candidates. Sir John Simon, Foreign Secretary between 1931 and 1935, was first to be placed in the tumbril, followed by Stanley Baldwin and Sir Samuel Hoare. Others to receive capital sentences included 'Labour lunatics who wished to attack everyone and voted against rearmament, Beaverbrook (for isolation and "no war" propaganda), Geoffrey Dawson and *The Times*' and, of course, the Prime Minister, Neville Chamberlain.[3]

Four months later, following the evacuation of the British Expeditionary Force from Dunkirk, a similar conversation took place between three Beaverbrook journalists standing on the roof of the offices of the *Evening Standard*. Appalled by the defeat – the most portentous in British history – as well as by the circumstances that had led to it, Frank Owen, a former Liberal MP, Peter Howard, a Conservative, and Michael Foot, the future leader of the Labour Party, decided to write a book shaming those men they deemed responsible for the debacle. Completed in just four days and displaying a notable talent for invective, *Guilty Men* sold, in the words of one of its authors, 'like a pornographic classic'.[4] By October, it had been reprinted twenty-two times and by the year's end had succeeded in pinning the blame for the catastrophe, not just in the minds of contemporaries but for large swathes of posterity, on the leading members of the National Government in general and on Neville Chamberlain in particular.

Of course, the overwhelming responsibility for the Second World War rests with Adolf Hitler. Only he and his most fanatical henchmen desired it. Only he willed the series of events that led to it. Yet while Hitler was uniquely responsible for the tragedy, the question remains: how was he allowed to inflict such misery? How was it that a country defeated in 1918, reduced in size, restricted in arms and surrounded by potential foes, was allowed to rise in twenty short years to a position where she was able to mount a challenge for global supremacy and almost achieve her objective?

The answer for many contemporaries was a simple failure of European diplomacy. 'With a modicum of statesmanship, this last war could have been quite easily prevented', claimed Bob Boothby in 1947.[5] Churchill dubbed it the 'unnecessary war', while the Anglo-Polish historian Lewis Namier believed that 'at several junctures it could have been stopped without excessive effort or sacrifice'.[6] More intriguing, given his close partnership with Chamberlain for much of the decade, was the damning survey of British foreign policy offered by the former Permanent Secretary of the Treasury, Sir Warren Fisher, three years after the end of the war:

> In 1935 we addressed moral platitudes to the Italians about the integrity of Abyssinia without any advantage to the latter and merely driving Italy into Germany's arms; and in 1936 we addressed questionnaire after questionnaire to the Germans about their military re-occupation of the Rhineland.
>
> When the Spanish Civil War broke out we deceived ourselves with a non-intervention pact which nobody but us observed. And in 1938 we partitioned Czechoslovakia.
>
> This brief sketch omits many things, including our fatuous performance or non-performance about [the Japanese invasion of] Manchuria. But the moral for the future is plain ...

> Had the British Empire, the United States and France squarely faced the facts in unison, the horrors which started up with the rape of Manchuria, followed by the outrage of Abyssinia, the all-out attack on China, the seizure of Austria and Czechoslovakia and culminating in the years from September 1939, could have been prevented; and therefore none of these countries can disclaim or escape a heavy measure of responsibility.[7]

The defence of appeasement has rested on four principal planks: that the parlous state of Anglo-French rearmament meant that neither Britain nor France was ready for war before the autumn of 1939; that the outbreak of war before this date would have split public opinion and, most probably, the British Empire; that it was not until the invasion of Czechoslovakia, in March 1939, that Hitler proved that he could not be trusted; and that the attempt to avoid the horrors of a new world war by making concessions to Nazi Germany was a reasonable policy worth trying.

That there were serious deficiencies in British and French arms in 1938 – the year in which the Western Powers could have taken a stronger line against German expansion and in which war almost broke out – is not in doubt. Only twenty-nine out of the fifty-two British fighter squadrons considered necessary for home defence were ready by the time of Munich (the majority consisting of obsolete Gladiators, Furies, Gauntlets and Demons), while the belated French attempt to close the gap with the Luftwaffe had only begun six months earlier. What is equally true, however, is that the Germans were also in no position to wage a major war in 1938. At the time of the Czech crisis, the Wehrmacht possessed only three lightly armoured tank divisions and just enough ammunition to sustain a mere six weeks of heavy fighting. There were over 2,700 first-line German aircraft in September 1938, but of these only two-thirds were fit to take part in operations and only half of this number were modern machines.[8] Not only was the Luftwaffe incapable of the sort of strategic bombing campaign the British and French feared in the autumn of 1938, but its primary task – as even the French General Staff acknowledged in their calmer moments – was to assist in the destruction of Czechoslovakia.

Of course, the British and French did not enjoy full knowledge of the deficiencies within the Wehrmacht. Having been both dazzled and terrified by Nazi propaganda, their appreciation of German military might was consistently inflationary in the years following the reoccupation of the Rhineland. What they should have realised, however, were their own strategic and military advantages. Aside from her informal alliance with Italy (more of a hindrance than a help, as events were to prove), Germany was diplomatically isolated in September 1938, starved of natural resources and dangerously exposed along her western flank. The Western Powers, by contrast, possessed the resources of the world's largest empire, a mastery of the seas and twenty-three divisions (with a potential for another thirty), facing only eight German divisions and a series of incomplete bunkers along Germany's western border. There was also the Czechoslovak–Soviet Treaty of Alliance.

The role that the Soviet Union would have played in a war over Czechoslovakia will always be a matter for speculation. Aside from the logistical difficulty of reaching her ally, the effectiveness of the Soviet military and the reliability of Stalin were both questionable. What can be stated with confidence, however, is that the Soviet Union would have suffered a considerable loss of face if it had failed to honour its obligations to Czechoslovakia, while having the USSR in even nominal alliance with the West – not retreating into isolation or moving into the German camp – was obviously an Allied interest. The fact was that the strategic advantage lay with the Allies in the autumn of 1938 – certainly to a greater extent than in the following year, after Germany had absorbed Czechoslovakia and concluded a pact with the Soviet Union – but the British and French proved incapable of appreciating or exploiting this reality.

To a large extent this was due to the political and psychological make-up of the two nations. Traumatised by the First World War and terrified of being bombed, the British and French political classes had become imbued with the spirit, if not the doctrine, of pacifism. They were also democrats: convinced, not unreasonably, that something as serious as war required public support and that this would not be forthcoming unless the British and French people felt their security to be directly threatened. To many historians this has been accepted as a fair assumption. The euphoria following the Munich Agreement appeared to reveal considerable support for Chamberlain's policy, while the Dominions had made clear their opposition to war over Czechoslovakia. This was not, however, the whole picture. Asked in an opinion poll, shortly after the *Anschluss*, whether Britain should promise to support the Czechs if they were attacked, less than half responded with a flat 'no' (a third said 'yes', a quarter had no opinion), while a similar exercise conducted at the time of the Godesberg summit revealed only 22 per cent of respondents in favour of appeasement, with 43 per cent opposed.[9] The swiftness with which relief at Munich turned to feelings of shame and distrust seems to support these samples, while the calmness with which the British public prepared for war, in the autumn of 1938, suggests that the politicians underestimated the people. Finally, as the Conservative MP Paul Emrys-Evans observed, following the reoccupation of the Rhineland, the British Government consistently refused to give a lead to public opinion but chose, instead, to shelter behind it. Had Britain's political leaders spelled out the nature of the German threat and the need to resist it – as Churchill did – then public opinion could have appeared very different.[10] This, however, would be to suppose that British decision makers fully appreciated the nature of the German threat themselves.

The failure to perceive the true character of the Nazi regime and Adolf Hitler stands as the single greatest failure of British policy makers during this period, since it was from this that all subsequent failures – the failure to rearm sufficiently, the failure to build alliances (not least with the Soviet Union), the failure to project British power and the failure to educate public opinion – stemmed. For defenders of appeasement, this is an exercise in ahistoricism. It was not until after Hitler tore up the Munich Agreement and marched into Prague, they argue, that he demonstrated his mendacity, while the full horrors of the Nazi regime only became apparent after the end of the war.* This argument, however, is based on a selective reading of the evidence. In 1933, Hitler insisted that all he desired was equality of arms with the other European powers but then rejected the British plan to standardise Continental armies at 200,000 men and pulled Germany out of the Disarmament Conference and the League of Nations. He promised to honour the Treaty of Locarno, guaranteeing the non-military nature of the Rhineland, and

* 'There was always a chance that "appeasement" which reached its climax there [at Munich] would succeed', insisted the then Minister of Health, Malcolm MacDonald, in November 1940, while Keith Feiling, in his authorised *Life of Neville Chamberlain*, argued that 'the man deceives himself who professes that in 1937 he foresaw the decrees of Providence for 1939–41'.

then, after he had violated that agreement, proclaimed that he had no more 'territorial demands to make in Europe'.[11] He disclaimed any intention of planning or desiring an *Anschluss* with Austria and then, following the absorption of that country, repeated the same assurances to the Czechs. Finally, he claimed that all he desired for the Sudeten Germans was equality of status within the Czech state.

The real nature of the Nazi regime was, if anything, more obvious. The suppression of opponents and the persecution of the Jews began within weeks of Hitler coming to power, while the 'Night of the Long Knives' and proliferation of concentration camps made deep impressions on foreign opinion. To those who understood the realities of the regime – whose standard bearers wore skull-and-crossbones on their caps and raised its young to be warriors and racial supremacists – the idea that peace-loving democrats could ever reach a friendly accord with National Socialist Germany was always a delusion. 'You have described your book as "the failure of a mission"', wrote Sir Horace Rumbold to Sir Nevile Henderson, after reading the latter's account of his two and a half years as British Ambassador.

> But for two reasons nobody could have succeeded at Berlin. These reasons are a) the nature of the character of the beast with which any British representative would have to deal and b) the fatuous belief of Chamberlain and, presumably of his Government, that in 1937 it was possible to achieve anything by a policy of appeasement of Germany. Hitler is an evil man and his regime and philosophy are evil. You cannot compromise with evil.[12]

Aside from Rumbold – whose close reading of *Mein Kampf* allowed him to warn the British Government as early as April 1933 of the aggressive and expansionist ideology guiding the new Chancellor – Sir Robert Vansittart, Brigadier A. C. Temperley, Sir Austen Chamberlain, Ralph Wigram and, of course, Churchill stand as examples of men who understood 'the nature of the beast' from the very beginning and argued for remedial action.

*

For all these reasons, it is hard to extenuate the actions of the appeasers and, especially, Neville Chamberlain. Although counterfactual history is, by definition, speculative, it is not hard to imagine how a more robust foreign policy could have produced a better outcome than that which confronted the world in September 1939. Had the British and French enforced the armaments clauses of the Treaty of Versailles; had they called Mussolini's bluff and used the Royal Navy to prevent the conquest of Abyssinia (thus preserving the League of Nations and sending an important message to Hitler); had they called Hitler's bluff and forced the 22,000 German soldiers out of the Rhineland; had they built a coalition aimed at preventing further acts of German aggression, rather than allowing Hitler to pick off his victims one by one; and had they been prepared to face Hitler down or if necessary go to war during the Czech crisis – then it is possible to envisage history taking a different course. There may well still have been a war. With Hitler in power the chances of war were always extremely high. But it did not have to be so vast, so long or so terrible.

Instead, the British tried to reason with Hitler. That the early efforts in this direction were not accompanied by a more urgent rearmament programme remains the primary indictment against Stanley Baldwin;* that they continued in the face of such contradictory evidence and at the expense of alliances aimed at containment that against his successor. It was not that Chamberlain had not seen the evidence. He had read excerpts of *Mein Kampf*, as well as Stephen Roberts' *The House That Hitler Built*. But his faith in his own judgement, coupled with his natural optimism, allowed him to ignore it. 'If I accepted the author's conclusions I should despair', he wrote of Roberts' analysis, 'but I don't and won't.'[13] Reading his private correspondence, it is hard to disagree with those who have accused him of arrogance and vanity. He was 'completely convinced' that the course he was taking was right and refused to change it, despite Hitler's rejection of his colonial scheme, despite the *Anschluss*, despite Godesberg, despite Munich and despite

* As has been pointed out, it was perversely fortunate that Britain did not begin to rearm in earnest until 1936–39, since an earlier effort would have merely saddled the RAF with a mass of obsolescent machines. This irony was, however, only clear in retrospect. Contemporaries did not know that war was not going to break out before September 1939 (indeed, it almost did a year earlier), while the deficiency of Britain's defences – particularly in the air – was one of the many factors inhibiting decision makers from taking a firmer stand against the dictator states.

Kristallnacht.[14] For the anti-appeasement Conservative MP Vyvyan Adams, the Prime Minister's 'inability to appreciate Hitlerism for so long' constituted nothing less than 'an infernal miracle'.[15] But there were more mundane explanations.

Chamberlain detested war as much as any pacifist and although the jokes about his municipal background were often unjust – 'a good Lord Mayor of Birmingham in a lean year', according to David Lloyd George – there is something in the view that both he and his lieutenant, Horace Wilson, approached foreign affairs from the perspective of resolving business or industrial disputes.[16] As Duff Cooper wrote in a brief character sketch of his former chief in early 1939:

> Chamberlain had never met anybody in Birmingham who in the least resembled Adolf Hitler. He had always found that the people he had met, whether in business or in local government, were not very dissimilar to himself – they were reasonable and honest and it had always proved possible, with a certain amount of give and take, to make a deal with them that should prove satisfactory to both sides.
>
> These dictators, so it seemed to him, must also be reasonable men. They wanted certain concessions, and there were certain concessions which Great Britain could afford to make. Therefore, the sooner he could get to grips with them the better. The motive was not dishonourable, the method was not unreasonable. His mistake was only that of the little boy who played with a wolf under the impression that it was a sheep – a pardonable zoological error – but apt to prove fatal to the player who makes it.[17]

For Chamberlain's defenders, the 'extra year' he bought at Munich is central. Although appeasement had failed in its primary aim, the policy had lost 'none of its importance', claimed Malcolm MacDonald in November 1940, since 'by postponing the present war for a whole year it gave Britain time to make military preparations which will turn what would have probably been defeat into what will now … certainly be a victory for European civilisation'.[18] The trouble with this argument is not merely that Germany outarmed Britain in the period between Munich and the outbreak of war – while the strategic situation deteriorated – but that it is, as even its beneficiaries admitted, essentially *ex post facto*. As Alec Dunglass told Jock Colville in February

1940, Britain's unreadiness for war 'weighed very heavily with the PM during the Munich crisis but it was only fair to admit that he and Horace [Wilson] believed that by the sacrifice of Czechoslovakia they could achieve permanent peace and that Hitler would be satisfied'.[19] This truth was later confirmed by Wilson himself, who attested that 'our policy was never designed just to postpone war, or enable us to enter war more united. The aim of appeasement was to avoid war altogether, for all time' – hence Chamberlain's reluctance to increase rearmament after Munich.[20]

In this, Chamberlain, obviously, failed. Given the character and ideology of the man with whom he was dealing, it is inconceivable that he could have done otherwise. What was far from inevitable, however, was that he should also have neglected to build a system of alliances capable of deterring Hitler or, if it came to war, defeating him as swiftly as possible. Unlike his successor, he treated the United States with frigid disdain, while his failure to secure a deal with the Soviet Union stands out as among the greatest blunders in that calamitous decade. His only undisputed achievement was that when Britain finally did decide to stop Hitler by force, she went united and with her Empire behind her. But even this accomplishment was born of the ultimate failure of his policy. Chamberlain's motivation was never in doubt. His efforts were considerable and determined. But his policy critically misunderstood the nature of the man with whom he was treating and neglected those contingencies which might have contained him or defeated him more quickly. It was, in every sense, a tragedy.

Acknowledgements

The first debt I must acknowledge is to those persons and institutions who kindly gave me access and permission to quote from private papers. In this sense I am extremely grateful to Her Majesty the Queen, Viscount Astor, the Countess of Avon, the BBC Archives at Caversham, the British Library, Robert Bell, the Bodleian Library (University of Oxford), the Duke of Buccleuch and Queensberry, the Cadbury Research Library (University of Birmingham), Sir Edward Cazalet, the Churchill Archives (Churchill College, Cambridge), Lord Coleraine, Lord Crathorne, the Earl of Halifax, the Hartley Library (University of Southampton), the Liddell Hart Centre for Military Archives (King's College London), the London School of Economics, the Marquess of Lothian, Julian Metcalfe, Juliet Nicolson, the late Viscount Norwich and Artemis Cooper, Sir Henry Rumbold, the Marquess of Salisbury, Charles Simon, the Wren Library (Trinity College, Cambridge), Michael Waterhouse and the Duchess of Westminster.

Attempts have been made to contact all copyright holders. If, however, I have unintentionally infringed anyone's copyright then both I and the publishers offer our sincere apologies.

For answering various questions, offering advice or pointing me towards materials, I would like to thank Lord Arnold of Ilminster, Dr Catherine Andreyev, Professor Jeremy Black, Denys Blakeway, Professor Sir Richard Evans, Dr Kit Kowol, Lord Lexden, Lord Lisvane, Andrew Riley, Sir Nicholas Soames and Pippa Quarrell.

Dido Connolly, Elizabeth Gausseron, Ingo and Michelle Maerker and Dr Lyuba Vinogradova translated a number of documents and books, while Laura Bailey, Ben Francis and Hilary McClellen assisted by checking various quotations and references. Jeff Hulbert was good enough to share with me several audio and newsreel clips from the period as well as material from the BBC Archives at Caversham.

My friend Robert de Lille kindly arranged for me to visit the former Führerbau – the location of the Munich Conference, now, more happily, the University of Music and Performing Arts – and then accompanied me to Berchtesgaden where, after a trek through the woods and (unintentionally) some private gardens, we found the remains of the Berghof.

My former editor at Channel 4 News, Ben de Pear, was generous in allowing me a period of leave to research and begin this book, and I would like to thank Katherine Davenport and the incomparable Channel 4 News political team for making this possible.

The majority of the manuscript was written in the London Library, where I have been aided by its unfailingly helpful staff as well as the friends I have made on the steps, waiting for the doors to open.

This book would not exist without my superb agent, Bill Hamilton, who took on both me and this project after only a short meeting in November 2015 and who, apart from finding interest among publishers, has offered vital encouragement along the way.

For similar reasons, I am extremely grateful to my publishers, Stuart Williams in the UK and Tim Duggan in the US. Stuart's early enthusiasm for the project was a hugely exciting moment, made all the more so when he introduced me to Tim. Over the last three years I have benefited from Stuart's calm advice, while my editor, the patient and meticulous Jörg Hensgen, has improved the text immeasurably.

A number of friends and colleagues were generous enough to find time in their busy schedules to read the book, or parts of it, in manuscript and offer their thoughts. In this sense, I would like to offer my profound thanks to Michael Crick, Andrew Gilmour and Professor Brian Young. Richard Davenport-Hines read each chapter as it emerged and offered invaluable guidance as well as encouragement. Needless to say, all errors that remain, as well as the judgements, are mine and mine alone.

Finally, I would like to thank my family. My sisters, Lara and Clare, accompanied me to several archives, while my brother, Jamie, read the manuscript and offered wise criticism. My greatest debt, however, is to my parents: to my father, Peter, for reading multiple drafts and mitigating my dyslexia; and to my mother, Jane, for performing the same feat as well as checking my quotations, corroborating my references and typing my virtually illegible pencil notes. The debt I owe them, which naturally extends far beyond these services, I fear I can never repay but this book is dedicated to them as a small token of love and gratitude.

Notes

Preface

1. *New Statesman*, 1944, quoted in Sidney Aster, 'Appeasement: Before and After Revisionism', *Diplomacy & Statecraft*, vol. 19. no. 3 (2008), pp. 443–80; Martin Gilbert, *The Roots of Appeasement* (London, 1966), p. xi.

Prologue

1. John Julius Norwich (ed.), *The Duff Cooper Diaries 1915–1951* (London, 2005), 3 September 1939, p. 274. • 2. Hugh Dalton, *The Fateful Years: Memoirs 1931–1945* (London, 1957), p. 263. • 3. Hansard, HC Deb, 1 September 1939, vol. 351, cols 125–33. • 4. Nigel Nicolson (ed.), *Harold Nicolson Diaries: 1907–1963* (London, 2004), 27 September 1939, p. 203. • 5. Beamish Papers, Diary, 2 September 1939, BEAM 3/3. • 6. Hankey Papers, Hankey to his wife, 3 September 1939, HNKY 3/43. • 7. Beverley Baxter, *Men, Martyrs and Mountebanks: Beverley Baxter's Inner Story of Personalities and Events behind the War* (London, 1940), p. 14. • 8. N. A. Rose (ed.), *Baffy: The Diaries of Blanche Dugdale 1936–1947* (London, 1973), 2 September 1939, p. 149. • 9. Robert Rhodes James (ed.), *'Chips': The Diaries of Sir Henry Channon* (London, 1967), 2 September 1939, p. 212. • 10. Nicolson (ed.), *Harold Nicolson Diaries and Letters*, 2 September 1939, p. 418. • 11. Major-General Sir Edward Spears, *Assignment to Catastrophe, Vol. I: Prelude to Dunkirk July 1939–May 1940* (London, 1954), p. 20. • 12. Hansard, HC Deb, 2 September 1939, vol. 351, col. 281. • 13. Spears, *Assignment to Catastrophe*, p. 20. • 14. John Barnes and David Nicholson (eds), *The Leo Amery Diaries, Vol. II: The Empire at Bay 1929–1945* (London, 1988), 2 September 1939, p. 570. • 15. Hansard, HC Deb, 2 September 1939, vol. 351, cols 282–3. • 16. James (ed.), *'Chips'*, 2 September 1939, p. 213. • 17. Nicolson, *Harold Nicolson Diaries and Letters*, 2 September 1939, p. 419. • 18. Sir Reginald Dorman-Smith, 'Recollections', *Sunday Times*, 6 September 1966. • 19. Ibid.

I: The New Order

1. *DBFP, Second Series, Vol. V* (London, 1956) – Rumbold to Sir John Simon, 30 June 1933, no. 229. • 2. *The Times*, 31 January 1933. • 3. Stuart Ball (ed.), *Parliament and Politics in the Age of Baldwin and MacDonald: The Headlam Diaries 1923–1935* (London, 1992), p. 258. • 4. *Daily Telegraph*, 31 January 1933. • 5. *News Chronicle*, 31 January 1933; *Daily Herald*, 31 January 1933. • 6. *The Times*, 30 January 1933. • 7. *The Times*, 31 January 1933. • 8. *New Statesman*, 4 February 1933. The *New Statesman* was edited by Kingsley Martin, who used the magazine, throughout this period, to champion pacifism and, later, appeasement. • 9. *Morning Post*, 30 January 1933. • 10. Quoted in *Scotsman*, 31 January 1933. • 11. *L'Ami du peuple*, 31 January

1933; Coty in *L'Ami du peuple*, 7 February 1933. • 12. Quoted in Martin Gilbert, *Sir Horace Rumbold: Portrait of a Diplomat 1869–1941* (London, 1973), p. 367. • 13. *DDF, First Series, Vol. II*, François-Poncet to Paul-Boncour, 1 February 1933, no. 253. • 14. *Scotsman*, 4 April 1933. • 15. Kenneth Young (ed.), *The Diaries of Sir Robert Bruce Lockhart, Vol. I: 1915–1938* (London, 1973), 6 March 1933, pp. 248–9. • 16. Hamilton Papers, Heyne to Hamilton, 1 April 1933, Hamilton 14/2/3. • 17. Hamilton Papers, Hamilton to Heyne, 23 October 1933. • 18. Hamilton Papers, Hamilton to Frau von Flesch-Brunningen, 30 November 1933. • 19. Hamilton Papers, Hamilton to Rebecca West, 15 March 1933. • 20. John Lee, *A Soldier's Life: General Sir Ian Hamilton, 1853–1947* (London, 2000), p. 263. • 21. Quoted in Richard Griffiths, *Fellow Travellers of the Right: British Enthusiasts for Nazi Germany 1933–9* (Oxford, 1980), p. 76. • 22. *DBFP, Second Series, Vol. V*, Simon to Rumbold, 10 May 1933, no. 126. • 23. *The Scarlet Pimpernel* (London Films/United Artists, 1934). • 24. Martin Gilbert, *The Roots of Appeasement* (London, 1966), Appendix I, 'The "Fontainebleau Memorandum"', p. 189. • 25. United States Department of State, *Peace and War: United States Foreign Policy 1931–1941* (Washington, 1943), pp. 179–81. • 26. Robert Graves, *Goodbye to All That*, rev. ed. (Harmondsworth, 1960), p. 240. • 27. MacDonald Diary, 2 February 1930, MS MacDonald, PRO 30/69/1753; Gilbert, *The Roots of Appeasement*, pp. 127, 131. • 28. Thomas C. H. Jones, *A Diary with Letters 1931–1950* (London, 1954), 29 April 1933, p. 108. • 29. Harold Nicolson, quoted in Gilbert, *Sir Horace Rumbold*, p. 318. • 30. Robert Vansittart, *The Mist Procession: The Autobiography of Lord Vansittart* (London, 1958), p. 476. • 31. *DBFP, Second Series, Vol. V*, Rumbold to Simon, 26 April 1933, no. 36. • 32. Ibid., enclosure no. 127. • 33. Vansittart Papers, Minutes, 6 May 1933, VNST 2/3. • 34. Cabinet Minutes, 17 May 1933, CAB 23/76/7/88. • 35. Jeremy Noakes and Geoffrey Pridham (eds), *Documents on Nazism 1919–1945* (London, 1974), pp. 509–10. • 36. Quoted in Peter Jackson, *France and the Nazi Menace: Intelligence and Policy Making 1933–1939* (Oxford, 2000), p. 64. • 37. Joseph Goebbels, confidential speech to members of the German press, 5 April 1940, quoted in Volker Ullrich, *Hitler: Ascent 1889–1939* (London, 2016), p. 478. • 38. Adolf Hitler, *Mein Kampf* (New York, 1939), pp. 978–9. • 39. *DDF, First Series, Vol. III*, no. 259. • 40. Sir Ivone Kirkpatrick, *The Inner Circle: Memoirs* (London, 1959), p. 90. • 41. Gaynor Johnson (ed.), *Our Man in Berlin: The Diary of Sir Eric Phipps 1933–1937* (Basingstoke, 2007), pp. 30–31. • 42. Vernon Bartlett, *Nazi Germany Explained* (London, 1933), p. 199. • 43. Brian Bond (ed.), *Chief of Staff: The Diaries of Lieutenant-General Sir Henry Pownall, Vol. I – 1933–1940* (London, 1972), 7 July 1933, p. 20. • 44. Phipps Papers, Hankey to Phipps, September 1933, PHPP I 3/3. • 45. Robert Rhodes James, *Bob Boothby: A Portrait* (London, 1991), p. 60. • 46. Ibid., p. 138. • 47. Robert Boothby, *Boothby: Recollections of a Rebel* (London, 1978), pp. 110–11. • 48. Robert Boothby, *I Fight to Live* (London, 1947), p. 124.

II: 'I Sing of Arms and the Man'

1. Winston Churchill, speech at Winchester House, Epping, 23 February 1931. • 2. Hansard, HC Deb, 23 November 1932, vol. 272, col. 81. • 3. Hansard, HC Deb, 23 March 1933, vol. 276, col. 542. • 4. Hansard, HC Deb, 13 April 1933, vol. 276, col. 2792. • 5. David Lloyd George, *War Memoirs, Vol. I* (London, 1933), p. 52. • 6. *Daily Express*, 13 February 1933. • 7. Martin Gilbert, *Winston Churchill, Vol. V, 1922–1939; Daily Telegraph*, 11 February 1933. • 8. Hansard, HC Deb, 30 July 1934, vol. 292, col. 2401. • 9. Denis Mack Smith, *Mussolini* (London, 1981), pp. 194–5. • 10. Quoted in *Nottingham Evening Post*, 9 March 1933. • 11. Keith Middlemas and John Barnes, *Baldwin: A Biography* (London, 1969), p. 745. • 12. Hansard, HC Deb, 12 November 1936, vol. 317, col. 1144. • 13. Winston S. Churchill, *The Second World War, Vol. I: The Gathering Storm* (London, 1948), pp. 169, 615. • 14. Nick Smart (ed.), *The Diaries and Letters of Robert Bernays 1932–1939: An Insider's Account of the House of Commons* (Lewiston, NY, 1996), 9 July 1936, p. 271. • 15. Robert Boothby, *I Fight to Live* (London, 1947), pp. 35–6. • 16. Quoted in Middlemas and Barnes, *Baldwin*, p. 722. • 17. Hansard, HC Deb, 10 November 1932, vol. 270, col. 632. • 18. J. F. C. Fuller, *The Reformation of War* (London, 1923), p. 150. • 19. Hansard, HC Deb, 30 July 1934, vol. 292, col. 2368. • 20. *Leeds Mercury*, 29 June 1933.

• 21. War Cabinet Minutes, 15 August 1939, CAB 23/15/270. • 22. Simon Papers, Naval Staff Memorandum, 31 January 1932. • 23. Chiefs of Staff Annual Review of Defence Policy, February 1932, CAB 53/22/10. • 24. *DBFP, Second Series, Vol. V* (London, 1956), Rumbold to Simon, 27 June 1933, no. 223. • 25. S. W. Roskill, *Hankey: Man of Secrets, Vol. III 1931–1963* (London, 1974), p. 86. • 26. Hansard, HC Deb, 7 November 1933, vol. 281, col. 138. • 27. Hansard, HC Deb, 7 February 1934, vol. 285, col. 1197. • 28. *DBFP, Second Series, Vol. V*, Rumbold to Simon, 27 June 1933, no. 223. • 29. Ibid., Memorandum by Vansittart on German rearmament, 14 July 1933, no. 253. • 30. N. H. Gibbs, *History of the Second World War: Grand Strategy, Vol. I – Rearmament Policy* (London, 1976), p. 135. • 31. Cabinet Minutes, 28 February 1934, CAB 23/78/7. • 32. Hansard, HC Deb, 8 March 1934, vol. 286, col. 2027. • 33. Ibid., col. 2048. • 34. Ibid., col. 2057. • 35. Ibid., col. 2072. • 36. Ibid., col. 2078. • 37. Committee of Defence Requirements Sub-Committee Report, 28 February 1934, PREM 1/175/79. • 38. 52nd Conclusions, 2 July 1934, CAB 27/504; Michael Howard, *The Continental Commitment: The Dilemma of British Defence Policy in the Era of the Two World Wars* (London, 1972), p. 108. • 39. Gibbs, *History of the Second World War: Grand Strategy*, p. 106. • 40. DC(M)(32) Paper 120, 'Note by the Chancellor of the Exchequer on the Report of the DRC', 20 June 1934, CAB 16/111. • 41. Hansard, HC Deb, 10 November 1932, vol. 270, col. 632. • 42. Brian Bond (ed.), *Chief of Staff: The Diaries of Lieutenant-General Sir Henry Pownall, Vol. I – 1933–1940* (London, 1972) – 3 May and 21 June 1934 pp. 42, 46. • 43. Ibid. • 44. Ibid., p. 48. • 45. For an in-depth study of the relationship between French intelligence and French policy making see Peter Jackson, *France and the Nazi Menace: Intelligence and Policy Making 1933–1939* (Oxford, 2000), pp. 53–76. • 46. Quoted in Piers Brendon, *The Dark Valley: A Panorama of the 1930s* (London, 2000), p. 139. • 47. Quoted in Martin Gilbert, *Winston S. Churchill, Vol V: 1922–1939* (London, 1976), p. 552. • 48. Ibid., p. 552. • 49. Hansard, HC Deb, 30 July 1934, vol. 292, col. 2349. • 50. Ibid., cols 2373–4. • 51. Hansard, HC Deb, 13 July 1934, vol. 292, col. 675. • 52. Cabinet Minutes, 26 November 1934, CAB 23/80/10. • 53. *DBFP, Second Series, Vol. XII* (London, 1972), Memoranda by Phipps on German rearmament, 23 November 1934, no. 208. • 54. *DBFP, Second Series, Vol. XII*, Minute by Simon, 28 November 1934, no. 231. • 55. Cabinet Minutes, 21 November 1934, CAB 23/80/214. • 56. Quoted in Gilbert, *Winston S. Churchill, Vol. V*, pp. 571–2. • 57. Harold Macmillan, *Winds of Change 1914–1939* (London, 1966), p. 575. • 58. Hansard, HC Deb, 28 November 1934, vol. 295, col. 863. • 59. *Daily Telegraph*, 29 November 1934. • 60. *Daily Mail*, 29 November 1934. • 61. Hansard, HC Deb, 28 November 1934, vol. 295, col. 883. • 62. Ibid., col. 917.

III: Tea with Hitler

1. Thomas C. H. Jones, *A Diary with Letters 1931–1950* (London, 1954), p. 125. • 2. Earl of Avon, *Facing the Dictators* (London, 1962), p. 61. • 3. Ibid., p. 69. • 4. Avon Papers, Diary, 20 February 1934, AP 20/1/14. • 5. Baldwin Papers, Eden to Baldwin, 21 February 1934, vol. 122, ff. 31–3. • 6. Avon Papers, Eden to MacDonald, 22 February 1934, AP 14/1/338/4. • 7. Robert Vansittart, *The Mist Procession: The Autobiography of Lord Vansittart* (London, 1958), p. 346. • 8. *DBFP, Second Series, Vol. VI* (London, 1957), Simon to Phipps, 23 February 1934, No. 308. • 9. Avon Papers, Diary, 24 February 1934, AP 20/1/14. • 10. *DBFP, Second Series, Vol. VI*, Phipps to Simon, 21 March 1934, no. 360. • 11. Reported in *The Times*, 12 March 1934. • 12. Robert Rhodes James, *Anthony Eden* (London, 1986), p. 135; D. R. Thorpe, *Eden: The Life and Times of Anthony Eden* (London, 2003), p. 130 • 13. Nicolson Papers, Diary, 2 February 1934. • 14. Hansard, HC Deb, 13 April 1933, vol. 276, col. 2759. • 15. John Hallett (E. H. Carr), 'The Prussian Complex', *Fortnightly Review*, 1 January 1933, pp. 37–45. • 16. John Maynard Keynes, *The Economic Consequences of the Peace* (London, 1919), p. 209. • 17. Quoted in Martin Gilbert, *The Roots of Appeasement* (London, 1966), p. 52. • 18. Reported in *The Times*, 13 March 1933. • 19. Ben Pimlott (ed.), *The Political Diary of Hugh Dalton 1918–40, 1945–60* (London, 1986), 18 August 1933, p. 179. • 20. *The Times*, 10 April 1933. • 21. Hansard, HC Deb, 23 March 1933, vol. 276, col. 617. • 22. Quoted in Michael Bloch, *Ribbentrop*

(London, 1992), p. 52. • 23. *Manchester Guardian*, 12 May 1933. • 24. *DGFP, Series C, Vol. II* (London, 1959), Ambassador in Great Britain to Foreign Ministry, 10 November 1933, no. 57. • 25. Jones, *A Diary with Letters*, 3 July 1932, p. 44; J. R. M. Butler, *Lord Lothian (Philip Kerr) 1882–1940* (London, 1960), p. 237. • 26. Letter to *Manchester Guardian*, 10 May 1935. • 27. Butler, *Lord Lothian*, p. 197. • 28. Vernon Bartlett, *Nazi Germany Explained* (London, 1933), p. 267. • 29. *DGFP, Series C, Vol. III* (London, 1959), Ambassador in Great Britain to Foreign Ministry, no. 445. • 30. *DBFP, Second Series, Vol. XII* (London, 1972), no. 391; Lothian Papers, Lothian to Simon, 30 January 1935. • 31. *The Times*, 1 February 1935. • 32. Pimlott (ed.), *The Political Diary of Hugh Dalton*, p. 164. • 33. Allen to Ellen Wilkinson, 30 April 1934, quoted in Martin Gilbert, *Plough My Own Furrow: The Story of Lord Allen of Hurtwood as Told through His Writings and Correspondence* (London, 1965), pp. 354–5. • 34. Allen notes, quoted ibid., p. 358. • 35. *Daily Telegraph*, 28 January 1935, quoted ibid., p. 358. • 36. Butler Papers, Dorothy Bonareies to R. A. Butler, 9 November 1932, RAB G4-73; Nick Smart (ed.), *The Diaries and Letters of Robert Bernays 1932–1939: An Insider's Account of the House of Commons* (Lewiston, NY, 1996), 9 May 1933, p. 75. • 37. Eric Hobsbawm, *The Age of Extremes: The Short Twentieth Century 1914–1991* (London, 1994). • 38. Quoted in Martin Gilbert, *Winston S. Churchill, Vol V: 1922–1939* (London, 1976), p. 226; quoted in Andrew Gilmour, 'The Changing Reactions of the British Press towards Mussolini's Italy' (unpublished thesis, Oxford University, 1986), p. 3; quoted in Alexander Anievas, 'The International Political Economy of Appeasement: The Social Sources of British Foreign Policy During the 1930s', *Review of International Studies*, vol. 37, no. 2 (2011), p. 617. • 39. S. J. Taylor, *The Great Outsiders: Northcliffe, Rothermere and the Daily Mail* (London, 1996), p. 191. • 40. Gavin Bowd, *Fascist Scotland: Caledonia and the Far Right* (Edinburgh, 2013), pp. 19–20. • 41. *Daily Mail*, 10 July 1933. • 42. *Daily Mail*, 28 November 1933. • 43. *Daily Mail*, 28 December 1934. • 44. Letter from Rothermere to Churchill, 13 May 1935, quoted in Martin Gilbert, *Winston S. Churchill, Vol. V: Companion, Part 3: The Coming of War 1936–1939* (London, 1982), p. 1171. • 45. *Daily Mail*, 7 November 1933; ibid., 13 November 1934. • 46. Quoted in Taylor, *The Great Outsiders*, p. 290. • 47. Quoted in Griffiths, *Fellow Travellers of the Right*, p. 157; Arnold Wilson, 'Germany in May', *English Review*, June 1934. • 48. Quoted in Karina Urbach, *Go-Betweens for Hitler* (Oxford, 2015), p. 246. • 49. *DBFP, Second Series, Vol. XII*, Phipps to Simon, 16 December 1934, no. 294. • 50. Gaynor Johnson (ed.), *Our Man in Berlin: The Diary of Sir Eric Phipps 1933–1937* (Basingstoke, 2007), p. 85. • 51. *DBFP, Second Series, Vol. XII*, Vansittart to Phipps, 2 February 1935, No. 453, footnote 5. • 52. Phipps Papers, Hankey to Phipps, 3 September 1933, PHPP I 3/3. • 53. *Manchester Guardian*, 24 May 1934. • 54. Phipps Papers, Hankey to Phipps, 3 September 1933, PHPP I 3/3. • 55. Adam Sisman, *Hugh Trevor-Roper: The Biography* (London, 2010), p. 39. • 56. *DBFP, Second Series, Vol. XII*, Phipps to Simon, 26 September 1934, no. 120. • 57. Ibid., Drummond to Simon, 18 February 1935, no. 466. • 58. Ian Kershaw, *Making Friends with Hitler: Lord Londonderry and Britain's Road to War* (London, 2004), p. 33. • 59. L. S. Amery, *My Political Life, Vol. III: The Unforgiving Years 1929–1940* (London, 1955), p. 380. • 60. Hamilton Papers, Hamilton to T. J. Schwartz, 24 July 1934, 14/2/3. • 61. Gordon Martel (ed.), *The Times and Appeasement: The Journals of A. L. Kennedy 1932–1939* (Cambridge, 2000), 19 September 1934, p. 146. • 62. *Manchester Guardian*, 2 July 1934. • 63. Smart (ed.), *The Diaries and Letters of Robert Bernays*, 2 July 1934, pp. 145–6. • 64. *Daily Telegraph*, 7 July 1934. • 65. Robert Self (ed.), *The Neville Chamberlain Diary Letters, Vol. IV: The Downing Street Years 1934–1940* (Aldershot, 2005), 7 July 1934, p. 78. • 66. Ibid., 28 July 1934, p. 81. • 67. Avon Papers, Astor to Eden, 2 October 1933, AP 14/1/139. • 68. Kenneth Young (ed.), *The Diaries of Sir Robert Bruce Lockhart, Vol. I: 1915–1938* (London, 1973), 7 July 1933, p. 260. • 69. Richard Davenport-Hines, *Universal Man: The Seven Lives of John Maynard Keynes* (London, 2015), p. 308; Stuart Ball (ed.), *Parliament and Politics in the Age of Baldwin and MacDonald: The Headlam Diaries 1923–1935* (London, 1992), 23 June 1933, p. 273. • 70. Martin Gilbert, *Sir Horace Rumbold: Portrait of a Diplomat 1869–1941* (London, 1973), p. 319. • 71. Hamilton Papers, Londonderry to Hamilton, 9 August 1938, 14/2/10. • 72. Robert Bernays, *Special Correspondent* (London, 1934), pp. 234. • 73. Ibid., pp. 239, 228, 239. • 74. Ibid., p. 210. • 75. Ibid., p. 213–14. • 76. Ibid. • 77. Ian Kershaw, *Hitler 1889–1936: Hubris* (London, 1998), p. 547. • 78. *DBFP, Second Series,*

Vol. XII, Phipps to Simon, 4 February 1935, no. 412. • 79. Lloyd Papers, Lloyd to Blanche Lloyd, February/March 1935, GLLD 4/3. • 80. *DBFP, Second Series, Vol. XII*, Memorandum by Vansittart, 21 February 1935, no. 484. • 81. N. J. Crowson (ed.), *Fleet Street, Press Barons and Politics: The Journals of Collin Brooks 1932–1940* (Cambridge, 1998), 25 January 1934, p. 56. • 82. Martel (ed.), *The Times and Appeasement*, 11 July 1934, p. 143; Vansittart, *The Mist Procession*, pp. 427–8; Colin R. Coote, *Editorial: The Memoirs of Colin R. Coote* (London, 1965), p. 175. • 83. Roy Jenkins, *The Chancellors* (London, 1998), p. 367. • 84. Coote, *Editorial*, p. 175. • 85. David Dutton, *Simon: A Political Biography of Sir John Simon* (London, 1992), p. 337. • 86. Simon Papers, Diary, 11 March 1935, MS. Simon 7. • 87. Hansard, HC Deb, 11 March 1935, vol. 299, col. 35. • 88. Ibid., col. 77. • 89. *DBFP, Second Series, Vol. XII*, Campbell to Simon, 17 March 1935, no. 587. • 90. Ibid., Campbell to Simon, 18 March 1935, no. 590. • 91. Paul Schmidt, *Hitler's Interpreter* (London, 1951), p. 16. • 92. Salisbury Papers, Cranborne to Ormsby-Gore, March 1935, box 63. • 93. Ball (ed.), *Parliament and Politics in the Age of Baldwin and MacDonald*, 18 March 1935, p. 327; Gilbert, *Sir Horace Rumbold*, p. 393. • 94. Martel (ed.), *The Times and Appeasement*, 14 May 1936, p. 225. • 95. Salisbury Papers, Cranborne to Ormsby-Gore, March 1935, box 63. • 96. Schmidt, *Hitler's Interpreter*, pp. 17–18. • 97. *DGFP, Series C, Vol. III, 1934–5*, no. 555. • 98. Avon, *Facing the Dictators*, p. 135. • 99. *DBFP, Second Series, Vol. XII*, no. 651. • 100. Avon Papers, Diary, 25 March 1935, AP 20/1. • 101. Salisbury Papers, Cranborne Diary, 23 March 1935, box 63. • 102. Avon, *Facing the Dictators*, p. 139. • 103. Salisbury Papers, Cranborne to William Ormsby-Gore, March 1935, box 63. • 104. Salisbury Papers, Cranborne Diary, 23 March 1935, box 63. • 105. Simon Papers, 27 March 1935, MS Simon 7. • 106. Avon Papers, Diary, 26 March 1935, AP 20/1. • 107. Schmidt, *Hitler's Interpreter*, p. 34. • 108. *DBFP, Second Series, Vol. XII*, 'Notes of Anglo-French-Italian Conversations', 18 April 1935, no. 722 (footnote 43). • 109. Hansard, HC Deb, 11 July 1935, vol. 304, col. 543. • 110. Joachim von Ribbentrop, *The Ribbentrop Memoirs* (London, 1954), p. 41. • 111. Fred Kupferman, *Laval* (Paris, 1987), p. 150.

IV: The Abyssinian Imbroglio

1. *DDF, Second Series, Vol. I*, no. 288; cited in Zara Steiner, *The Triumph of the Dark: European International History 1933–1939* (Oxford, 2011), p. 31. • 2. *Daily Telegraph*, 17 July 1935; *The Times*, 17 July 1935. • 3. Nick Smart (ed.), *The Diaries and Letters of Robert Bernays 1932–1939: An Insider's Account of the House of Commons* (Lewiston, NY, 1996), Bernays to Lucy Brereton, 19 July 1935, p. 214. • 4. *DBFP, Second Series, Vol. XIV* (London, 1976), Barton to Simon, 11 April 1935, no. 229. • 5. Nicholas Farrell, *Mussolini: A New Life* (London, 2003), p. 261. • 6. Kenneth Rose, *The Later Cecils* (London, 1975), p. 130. • 7. Helen McCarthy, 'Democratizing British Foreign Policy: Rethinking the Peace Ballot 1934–1935', *Journal of British Studies*, vol. 49, no. 2 (2010), pp. 358–87. • 8. *Daily Express*, 25 October 1934. • 9. Robert C. Self (ed.), *The Austen Chamberlain Diary Letters* (Cambridge, 1995), p. 487. • 10. Smart (ed.), *The Diaries and Letters of Robert Bernays*, 5 May 1934, p. 134. • 11. Quoted in John Charmley, *Churchill: The End of Glory* (London, 1993), p. 202. • 12. *The Times*, 24 July 1935. • 13. *DBFP, Second Series, Vol. XIV*, Minute by Vansittart, no. 301. • 14. Earl of Avon, *Facing the Dictators* (London, 1962), p. 224. • 15. William E. Dodd and Martha Dodd (eds), *Ambassador Dodd's Diary 1933–1938* (London, 1941), 22 May 1935, p. 255. • 16. *Daily Mail*, 15 July 1935. • 17. *Evening Standard*, 13 February 1935; Robert Rhodes James (ed.), *'Chips': The Diaries of Sir Henry Channon* (London, 1967), 30 July 1935, p. 40. • 18. Kenneth Rose, *King George V* (London, 1983), p. 387. • 19. Victor Cazalet Papers, MS 917 02 05. • 20. *The Times*, 30 August 1935; *Daily Herald*, 10 July 1935. • 21. J. A. Cross, *Sir Samuel Hoare: A Political Biography* (London, 1977), pp. 219–20. • 22. Salisbury Papers, Cranborne to Ormsby-Gore, 24 September 1935, box 63. • 23. Philip Williamson and Edward Baldwin (eds), *Baldwin Papers: A Conservative Statesman 1908–1947* (Cambridge, 2004), p. 352. • 24. Chamberlain Papers, Hoare to Chamberlain 18 August 1935, NC 7/11/28/24–5. • 25. *DBFP, Second Series, Vol. XV* (London, 1976), Phipps to Hoare, 13 November 1935, no. 213. • 26. Cross, *Sir Samuel Hoare*, p. 235. • 27. Avon, *Facing*

the Dictators, p. 298. • 28. *The Times*, 16 December 1935. • 29. Quoted in *DBFP, Second Series, Vol. XV*, Lindsay to Hoare, 17 December 1935, no. 387. • 30. Robert Self (ed.), *The Neville Chamberlain Diary Letters, Vol. IV: The Downing Street Years 1934–1940* (Aldershot, 2005), 15 December 1935, p. 166. • 31. Nigel Nicolson (ed.), *Harold Nicolson: Diaries and Letters 1930–1939* (London, 1966), 10 December 1935, p. 230. • 32. Victor Cazalet Papers, Diary, December 1935. • 33. Avon, *Facing the Dictators*, p. 317. • 34. David Gilmour, *The Pursuit of Italy: A History of a Land, Its Regions and Their Peoples* (London, 2011), p. 322. • 35. *Selected Speeches of His Imperial Majesty Haile Selassie I, 1918 to 1967* (Addis Ababa, 1967) p.313–14.

V: Across the Rhine

1. Liddell Hart Papers, 11/1938/98. • 2. Ian Kershaw, *Hitler 1888–1936: Hubris* (London, 1998), p. 587. • 3. William L. Shirer, *Berlin Diary: The Journal of a Foreign Correspondent 1934–1941* (London, 1941), 7 March 1936, pp. 50–51. • 4. Gaynor Johnson (ed.), *Our Man in Berlin: The Diary of Sir Eric Phipps 1933–1937* (Basingstoke, 2007), 14 December 1935, p. 140. • 5. Jonathan Haslam, *The Vices of Integrity: E. H. Carr 1892–1982* (London, 1999), p. 59. • 6. Norman Rose, *Vansittart: Study of a Diplomat* (London, 1978), p. 190. • 7. Hankey Papers, Hankey to Phipps, 2 January 1936, HNKY 5/5. • 8. *DBFP, Second Series, Vol. XV* (London, 1976), 'The German Danger', Memorandum by Eden, 17 January 1936, no. 460. • 9. Martin S. Alexander, *The Republic in Danger: General Maurice Gamelin and the Politics of French Defence 1933–1940* (Cambridge, 1992), p. 258. • 10. Ibid., p. 259. • 11. *The Times*, 9 March 1936. • 12. Quoted in Zara Steiner, *The Triumph of the Dark: European International History 1933–1939* (Oxford, 2011), p. 144. • 13. Nigel Nicolson (ed.), *Harold Nicolson: Diaries and Letters 1930–1939* (London, 1966), 9 March 1936, p. 248. • 14. *DBFP, Second Series, Vol. XVI* (London, 1977), Law to Sargent, 9 March 1936, no. 55; *The Times*, 9 March 1936. • 15. Thomas C. H. Jones, *A Diary with Letters 1931–1950* (London, 1954), 8 March 1936, pp. 180–81. • 16. *DBFP, Second Series, Vol. XVI*, 'Eden, Memorandum for the Cabinet', 8 March 1936, no. 48. • 17. Ibid., 'Account of a Meeting of the Locarno Powers', 10 March 1936, no. 61. • 18. Avon Papers, 'Points to Be Made to M. Flandin', undated, 13/1/33 B. • 19. Victor Cazalet Papers, Diary, March 1936. • 20. N. A. Rose (ed.), *Baffy: The Diaries of Blanche Dugdale 1936–1947* (London, 1973), p. 8. • 21. *DGFP, Series C, Vol. V* (London, 1961), Ambassador in Great Britain to Foreign Ministry, 9 March 1936, no. 33. • 22. Earl of Avon, *Facing the Dictators* (London, 1962), p. 346. • 23. N. J. Crowson, *Facing Fascism: The Conservative Party and the European Dictators 1935–1940* (London, 1997), p. 41. • 24. Nicolson (ed.), *Harold Nicolson: Diaries and Letters*, 12 March 1936, pp. 249–50. • 25. Cabinet Minutes, 11 March 1936, CAB 23/83/18. • 26. Ben Pimlott (ed.), *The Political Diary of Hugh Dalton 1918–40, 1945–60* (London, 1986), 11 March 1936, p. 196. • 27. Nicolson (ed.), *Harold Nicolson: Diaries and Letters*, 17 March 1936, p. 251. • 28. Keith Feiling, *The Life of Neville Chamberlain* (London, 1946), p. 279. • 29. Jones, *A Diary with Letters*, 22 March 1936, pp. 183–4. • 30. Avon Papers, Simon to Baldwin, 26 March 1936, 14/1/621. • 31. Nicolson (ed.), *Harold Nicolson: Diary and Letters*, 23 March 1936, p. 254. • 32. Ian Colvin, *None So Blind: A British Diplomatic View of the Origins of World War II* (New York, 1965), p. 99. • 33. Hansard, HC Deb, 26 March 1936, vol. 310, col. 1439. • 34. Brian Bond (ed.), *Chief of Staff: The Diaries of Lieutenant-General Sir Henry Pownall, Vol. I – 1933–1940* (London, 1972), 15 April 1936, p. 109. • 35. Steiner, *The Triumph of the Dark*, p. 151. • 36. Quoted in William Shirer, *The Rise and Fall of the Third Reich: A History of Nazi Germany* (London, 1962), p. 293. • 37. Emrys-Evans Papers, Emrys-Evans to Margesson, 13 July 1936, MS 58248.

VI: The Defence of the Realm

1. *Morning Post*, 16 January 1936. • 2. Robert C. Self (ed.), *The Austen Chamberlain Diary Letters* (Cambridge, 1995), AC to Hilda, 15 February 1936, p. 499. • 3. Victor Cazalet Papers, Diary, 13 February 1936. • 4. Martin Gilbert, *Winston S. Churchill, Vol. V: 1922–1939* (London,

1976), p. 687. • 5. Martin Gilbert, *Winston S. Churchill, Vol. V, Companion, Part 3: The Coming of War 1936–1939* (London, 1982), p. 18. • 6. Ibid., p. 7. • 7. Gilbert, *Winston S. Churchill, Vol. V*, p. 703. • 8. N. J. Crowson (ed.), *Fleet Street, Press Barons and Politics: The Journals of Collin Brooks 1932–1940* (Cambridge, 1998), 14 March 1936, p. 160. • 9. Lloyd Papers, GL to George Lloyd, March 1936, GLDD 5/5. • 10. 'Cato', *Guilty Men* (London, 1940), p. 75; *The Times*, 16 March 1936. • 11. Victor Cazalet Papers, Diary, 4 March 1936. • 12. Thomas C. H. Jones, *A Diary with Letters 1931–1950* (London, 1954), 22 May 1936, p. 204. • 13. Gilbert, *Winston S. Churchill, Vol. V*, p. 686. • 14. Chamberlain Papers, Hoare to Chamberlain, 23 February 1936, NC 7/11/29/29. • 15. *Evening Standard*, 1 May 1936. • 16. Brian Bond (ed.), *Chief of Staff: The Diaries of Lieutenant-General Sir Henry Pownall, Vol. I – 1933–1940* (London, 1972), 27 January 1936, p. 99. • 17. Hansard, HC Deb, 10 March 1936, vol. 309, col. 1973. • 18. Gilbert, *Winston S. Churchill, Vol. V, Companion, Part 3*, p. 164. • 19. Quoted in B. H. Liddell Hart, *The Memoirs of Captain Liddell Hart, Vol. I* (London, 1965), p. 261. • 20. Philip Williamson and Edward Baldwin (eds), *Baldwin Papers: A Conservative Statesman 1908–1947* (Cambridge, 2004), p. 379. • 21. Nigel Nicolson (ed.), *Harold Nicolson: Diaries and Letters 1930–1939* (London, 1966), 12 November 1938, p. 278. • 22. Hansard, HC Deb, 10 November 1936, vol. 317, col. 742. • 23. Hansard, HC Deb, 12 November 1936, vol. 317, col. 1107. • 24. Ibid., col. 1145. • 25. Michael Fry, *Hitler's Wonderland* (London, 1934).

VII: Hitler's Wonderland

1. Dawson Papers, Horace Rumbold to Dawson, 10 June 1936, MS.Dawson 78. • 2. Mount Temple Papers, 'Tennant Report on Nuremberg Rally 1935', BR 81/10. • 3. Ernest W. D. Tennant, *True Account* (London, 1957), p. 169. • 4. Quoted in Kenneth Rose, *The Later Cecils* (London, 1975), p. 179. • 5. Douglas Reed, *Insanity Fair* (London, 1938), pp. 420 21, 362; Nigel Nicolson (ed.), *Harold Nicolson Diaries and Letters 1907–1964* (London, 2004), 18 May 1938, p. 166. • 6. Nicolson (ed.), *Harold Nicolson Diaries and Letters*, 6 June 1938, p. 346. • 7. Kenneth Young (ed.), *The Diaries of Sir Robert Bruce Lockhart, Vol. I: 1915–1938* (London, 1973), 14 September 1934, p. 305; ibid., 8 August 1933, p. 267; Jessica Mitford, *Hons and Rebels* (London, 1960), p. 62. • 8. Young (ed.), *The Diaries of Sir Robert Bruce Lockhart, Vol. I*, 13 July 1933, p. 263. • 9. Philip Ziegler, *King Edward VIII: The Official Biography* (London, 1990), p. 206; Robert Rhodes James (ed.), *'Chips': The Diaries of Sir Henry Channon* (London, 1967), Whitsuntide 1935, p. 35. • 10. Graham Wootton, *The Official History of the British Legion* (London, 1956), p. 185, cited in Richard Griffiths, *Fellow Travellers of the Right: British Enthusiasts for Nazi Germany 1933–9* (Oxford, 1980), p. 130. • 11. James Murphy, *Who Sent Rudolf Hess?* (London, 1941), p. 11, cited in Griffiths, *Fellow Travellers of the Right*, p. 130. • 12. Stuart Ball (ed.), *Parliament and Politics in the Age of Churchill and Attlee: The Headlam Diaries 1935–1951* (Cambridge, 1999), 21 November 1938, p. 145; Stuart Ball (ed.), *Parliament and Politics in the Age of Baldwin and MacDonald: The Headlam Diaries 1923–1935* (London, 1992), 1 November 1926, p. 103. • 13. A. J. P. Taylor (ed.), *Lloyd George: A Diary by Frances Stevenson* (London, 1971), 22 November 1934, p. 292; Robert Rhodes James (ed.), *Memoirs of a Conservative: J. C. C. Davidson's Memoirs and Papers 1910–1937* (London, 1969), p. 405. • 14. Ian Kershaw, *Making Friends with Hitler: Lord Londonderry and Britain's Road to War* (London, 2004), p. 130. • 15. Ibid., pp. 139–41. • 16. Nicolson (ed.), *Harold Nicolson Diaries and Letters*, 20 February 1936, p. 245. • 17. Marquess of Londonderry, *Ourselves and Germany* (London, 1938), pp. 13–14. • 18. Thomas C. H. Jones, *A Diary with Letters 1931–1950* (London, 1954), March 1936, p. 179. • 19. Quoted in Martin Gilbert, *The Roots of Appeasement* (London, 1966), p. 165. • 20. Neville Thompson, *The Anti-Appeasers: Conservative Opposition to Appeasement in the 1930s* (Oxford, 1971), pp. 156–7. • 21. A. L. Rowse, *A Man of the Thirties* (London, 1979), p. 4. • 22. Gaynor Johnson (ed.), *Our Man in Berlin: The Diary of Sir Eric Phipps 1933–1937* (Basingstoke, 2007), 10 November 1936, p. 188. • 23. Quoted in Gilbert, *The Roots of Appeasement*, pp. 166–7. • 24. Dawson Papers, Horace Rumbold to Dawson, 10 June 1936, MS.Dawson 78. • 25. KV 5/3, 'Anglo-German Fellowship Annual Report 1935–

1936'. • 26. Michael Bloch, *Ribbentrop* (London, 1992), p. 110. • 27. Ibid., p. 117. • 28. The American novelist Thomas Wolfe, a spectator, quoted in Duff Hart-Davis, *Hitler's Olympics* (London, 1986), p. 151. • 29. Joachim von Ribbentrop, *The Ribbentrop Memoirs* (London, 1954), p. 62. • 30. Ibid.; André François-Poncet, *The Fateful Years: Memoirs of a French Ambassador in Berlin 1931–1938* (London, 1949), p. 206. • 31. James (ed.), *'Chips'*, 6, 11 & 13 August 1936, p. 106; Nicolson (ed.), *Harold Nicolson Diaries and Letters*, 20 September 1936, p. 273. • 32. François-Poncet, *The Fateful Years*, p. 206. • 33. T. P. Conwell-Evans, 'Notes of a Conversation between Lloyd George and Hitler at Berchtesgaden, 4 September 1936', quoted in Gilbert, *The Roots of Appeasement*, Appendix 2, p. 209. • 34. *Daily Express*, 17 September 1936. • 35. KV 5/6, 'Security Service Report on the 1937 Nuremberg Rally'. • 36. Avon Papers, Diary, 20 May 1936, AP 20/1/16. • 37. James (ed.), *'Chips'*, 22 November 1936, p. 84. • 38. Fritz Hesse, *Hitler and the English* (London, 1954), pp. 31–2. • 39. Ibid., p. 33.

VIII: The New Man

1. Robert Self (ed.), *The Neville Chamberlain Diary Letters, Vol. IV: The Downing Street Years 1934–1940* (Aldershot, 2005), 8 August 1937, p. 265. • 2. Quoted in *The Times*, 1 February 1937. • 3. The first line of John Cornford's poem, written shortly before he was killed on the Cordoba front, December 1936, aged twenty-one. • 4. This figure includes both executions and those who died of maltreatment in Soviet camps – see Robert Conquest, *The Great Terror: A Reassessment*, 40th anniversary ed. (London, 2008), pp. 485–6. • 5. Martin Gilbert, *Winston S. Churchill, Vol. V, Companion, Part 3: The Coming of War 1936–1939* (London, 1982), p. 2. • 6. Ibid., p. 143. • 7. Thomas C. H. Jones, *A Diary with Letters 1931–1950* (London, 1954), 19 February 1937, p. 316. • 8. *The Times*, 31 May 1937; *Sunday Times*, 30 May 1937. • 9. *Daily Telegraph*, 29 May 1937. • 10. Winston. S. Churchill, *Great Contemporaries* (London, 1937), p. 52. • 11. Quoted in Robert Self, *Neville Chamberlain: A Political Life* (Aldershot, 2006), p. 19. • 12. Ibid., p. 20. • 13. Douglas-Home Papers, Neville Chamberlain character sketch. • 14. Self, *Neville Chamberlain*, p. 25. • 15. Ibid., p. 27. • 16. Robert Self (ed.), *The Neville Chamberlain Diary Letters, Vol. I: The Making of a Politician 1915–1920* (Aldershot, 2000), NC to Hilda, 1 July 1917, p. 208. • 17. Self (ed.), *The Neville Chamberlain Diary Letters, Vol. IV*, 30 May 1937, p. 253. • 18. Roger Middleton, 'British Monetary and Fiscal Policy in the 1930s', *Oxford Review of Economic Policy*, vol. 26, no. 3 (2010), pp. 414–41. • 19. Self (ed.), *The Neville Chamberlain Diary Letters, Vol. IV*, 12 May 1934, p. 70. • 20. Ibid., 23 March 1935, p. 125. • 21. Douglas-Home Papers, '20th Century Remembered', BBC interview, 11 May 1983. • 22. Robert Self (ed.), *The Neville Chamberlain Diary Letters, Vol. II: The Reform Years 1921–1927* (Aldershot, 2000), NC to Ida 19 June 1927, p. 412. • 23. Douglas-Home Papers, Notes, 'Neville Chamberlain 1940'. • 24. Quoted in Self, *Neville Chamberlain*, p. 13; Earl of Swinton, *Sixty Years of Power: Some Memories of the Men Who Wielded It* (London, 1966), p. 111. • 25. This was Churchill's phrase uttered to Lloyd George at lunch on 21 February 1938 (Colin Cross (ed.), *Life with Lloyd George: The Diary of A. J. Sylvester 1931–1945* (London, 1975), p. 196) though Robert Self points out that it was also used by Aneurin Bevan in June 1937 (Michael Foot, *Aneurin Bevan: A Biography, Vol. I – 1897–1945* (London, 1962), p. 257). • 26. Swinton, *Sixty Years of Power*, p. 110; Harold Macmillan, *The Past Masters: Politics and Politicians 1906–1939* (London, 1975), p. 134; Alistair Horne, *Macmillan 1894–1956: Vol. I of the Official Biography* (London, 1988), p. 80. • 27. Lord Salter, *Memoirs of a Public Servant* (London, 1961), p. 251. • 28. Douglas-Home Papers, '20th Century Remembered', BBC interview, 11 May 1983. • 29. Self (ed.), *The Neville Chamberlain Diary Letters, Vol. IV*, NC to Ida, 29 February 1936, p. 178. • 30. Malcolm Muggeridge, *The Thirties: 1930–1940 in Great Britain* (London, 1940), p. 77. • 31. Self, *Neville Chamberlain*, p. 4; Self (ed.), *The Neville Chamberlain Diary Letters, Vol. IV*, NC to Ida, 16 October 1937, p. 275. • 32. Earl of Avon, *Facing the Dictators* (London, 1962), p. 445. • 33. Self (ed.), *The Neville Chamberlain Diary Letters, Vol. IV*, NC to Hilda, 28 July 1934, pp. 82–3. • 34. Chamberlain Papers, NC to Hilda, 4 February 1933, NC 18/1/815. • 35. *The Times*, 11 June 1936. • 36. Self (ed.), *The Neville*

Chamberlain Diary Letters, Vol. IV, NC to Hilda, 14 June 1936, pp. 194–5. • 37. Hansard, HC Deb, 26 March 1936, vol. 310, col. 1446. • 38. Keith Feiling, *The Life of Neville Chamberlain* (London, 1946), p. 324. • 39. Self (ed.), *The Neville Chamberlain Diary Letters, Vol. IV*, 18 March 1935, p. 123. • 40. Ibid., 14 November 1936, p. 219. • 41. Gabriel Gorodetsky (ed.), *The Maisky Diaries: Red Ambassador to the Court of St James's 1932–1943* (New Haven, 2015), 29 July 1937, p. 84. • 42. Cadogan Papers, Diary, 24 September 1936, ACAD 1/5. • 43. Lothian Papers, 'German Memo', 11 May 1937, 250–60. • 44. Avon Papers, Ormsby-Gore to Eden, 19 October 1936, AE 13/1/50 L. • 45. Avon Papers, Vansittart to Eden, 21 September 1936, AE 13/1/50 F. • 46. Self, *Neville Chamberlain*, p. 280. • 47. Chamberlain Papers, Chamberlain to Leo Amery, 15 November 1937, NC7/11/30/6–7. • 48. Avon Papers, Churchill to Eden, 3 September 1937, AE 13/1/58 F. • 49. Avon Papers, Churchill to Eden, 3 September 1937, AE 13/1/58 I. • 50. Malcolm Muggeridge (ed.), *Ciano's Diary 1937–1938* (London, 1952), 21 September 1937, p. 15. • 51. Cabinet Minutes, 6 October 1937, CAB 23/89/7. • 52. Self (ed.), *The Neville Chamberlain Diary Letters, Vol. IV*, NC to Ida, 30 October 1937, p. 280. • 53. Ibid., NC to Ida, 4 July 1937, p. 259.

IX: Hunting for Peace

1. Helen P. Kirkpatrick, *Under the British Umbrella: What the English Are and How They Go to War* (New York, 1939), p. 260. • 2. Robert Bernays, *Naked Fakir* (London, 1931), p. 52. • 3. Quoted in Robert Self, *Neville Chamberlain: A Political Life* (Aldershot, 2006), p. 291. • 4. Thomas C. H. Jones, *A Diary with Letters 1931–1950* (London, 1954), 2 June 1936, p. 215. • 5. Andrew Roberts, *The Holy Fox: A Biography of Lord Halifax* (London, 1991), p. 64. • 6. Earl of Avon, *Facing the Dictators* (London, 1962), p. 503. • 7. Nevile Henderson, *Water under the Bridges* (London, 1945), p. 100. • 8. Nevile Henderson, *Failure of a Mission: Berlin 1937–1939* (London, 1940), p. 13. • 9. John Harvey (ed.), *The Diplomatic Diaries of Oliver Harvey 1937–1940* (London, 1970), p. 41; *DBFP, Second Series, Vol. XIX* (London, 1982), no. 53. • 10. *The Times*, 2 June 1937. • 11. Avon, *Facing the Dictators*, p. 504. • 12. Henderson, *Failure of a Mission*, p. 17. • 13. *DBFP, Second Series, Vol. XIX*, no. 273. • 14. Hickleton Papers, Henderson to Halifax, 29 October 1937, A4/410/3/2/ii. • 15. Hickleton Papers, Henderson to Halifax, 4 November 1937, A4/410/3/2/ii. • 16. Halifax to Chamberlain, 8 November 1938, PREM 1/330/175. • 17. R. A. C. Parker, *Chamberlain and Appeasement: British Policy and the Coming of the Second World War* (Basingstoke, 1993), p. 98. • 18. Quoted in Roberts, *The Holy Fox*, p. 67. • 19. Hickleton Papers, Diary, 17 November 1937, A4/410/3/3/vi. • 20. Hickleton Papers, Lord Halifax's Diary: 'Visit of Lord President to Germany, 17–21 November 1937', A4/410/3/3/vi. • 21. Sir Ivone Kirkpatrick, *The Inner Circle: Memoirs* (London, 1959), p. 94. • 22. Lord Halifax, *Fullness of Days* (London, 1957), pp. 184–5. • 23. The substance of these talks is attested to by Halifax's diary of the trip (which he sent to the Foreign Office as well as Chamberlain), the official German record and the memoirs of Paul Schmidt (Hitler's interpreter) and Kirkpatrick. • 24. Kirkpatrick, *The Inner Circle*, p. 95. • 25. *DGFP, Series D, Vol. I* (London, 1949), Memorandum, 10 November 1937, no. 19. • 26. *DGFP, Series C, Vol. I* (London, 1949), German Embassy in Great Britain to German Foreign Ministry, 18 November 1937, no. 29. • 27. Hickleton Papers, Diary, 19 November 1937, A4/410/3/3/vi. • 28. Paul Schmidt, *Hitler's Interpreter* (London, 1951), p. 77. • 29. Kirkpatrick, *The Inner Circle*, pp. 95–7. • 30. Hickleton Papers, Diary, 19 November 1937, A4/410/3/3/vi. • 31. Schmidt, *Hitler's Interpreter*, p. 77. • 32. Gaynor Johnson (ed.), *Our Man in Berlin: The Diary of Sir Eric Phipps 1933–1937* (Basingstoke, 2007), p. 58. • 33. Hickleton Papers, Diary, 20 November 1937, A4/410/3/3/vi. • 34. Ibid. • 35. Ibid. • 36. *DBFP, Second Series, Vol. XIX*, Henderson to Eden, 23 November 1937, no. 343, enclosure. • 37. Hickleton Papers, Diary, 21 November 1937, A4/410/3/3/vi. • 38. Ibid. • 39. Cabinet Minutes, 24 November 1937, CAB 23/90A/5. • 40. Robert Self (ed.), *The Neville Chamberlain Diary Letters, Vol. IV: The Downing Street Years 1934–1940* (Aldershot, 2005), 26 November 1937, pp. 286–7. • 41. Lothian Papers, Dawson to Lothian, 23 May 1937, CD 40/17/337/340.

• 42. *Daily Herald*, 1 December 1937. • 43. Hickleton Papers, Halifax to Southwood, 1 December 1937, A4/410/3/2. • 44. Ibid. • 45. Quoted in Timothy S. Benson, *Low and the Dictators* (London, 2008) • 46. Henderson, *Failure of a Mission*, p. 65. • 47. *DBFP, Second Series, Vol. XIX*, Henderson to Eden, 29 November 1937, no. 353. • 48. Hickleton Papers, A4/410/3/2/ii. • 49. Hickleton Papers, Halifax to Ormsby-Gore, 12 November 1937. • 50. *DGFP, Series D. Vol. I*, no. 93.

X: 'Bowlers Are Back!'

1. Earl of Avon, *Facing the Dictators* (London, 1962), p. 559. • 2. Sumner Welles, *Seven Major Decisions* (London, 1951), p. 41. • 3. *DBFP, Second Series, Vol. XIX* (London, 1982), Lindsay to Foreign Office, 12 January 1938, no. 422. • 4. Ibid., Lindsay to Foreign Office, 12 January 1938, no. 423. • 5. Ibid., Lindsay to Foreign Office, 12 January 1938, no. 425. • 6. Hansard, HC Deb, 3 November 1937, vol. 328, col. 583. • 7. David Dilks (ed.), *The Diaries of Sir Alexander Cadogan, OM, 1938–1945* (London, 1971), 13 January 1938, p. 36. • 8. *DBFP, Second Series, Vol. XIX*, Foreign Office to Lindsay, 13 January 1938, enclosure no. 431. • 9. Sumner Welles, *The Time for Decision* (New York and London, 1944), p. 66. • 10. Robert Self, *Neville Chamberlain: A Political Life* (Aldershot, 2006), p. 281. • 11. *DBFP, Second Series, Vol. XIX*, Foreign Office to Lindsay, 13 January 1938, enclosure no. 431. • 12. Richard Lamb, *Mussolini and the British* (London, 1997), p. 180. • 13. *DBFP, Second Series, Vol. XIX*, 'Record by Chamberlain of a Conversation with Grandi', 27 July 1937, no. 64. • 14. Chamberlain Papers, Diary, 19 February 1938, NC 2/24 A; PREM 1/276/340. • 15. Robert Self (ed.), *The Neville Chamberlain Diary Letters, Vol. IV: The Downing Street Years 1934–1940* (Aldershot, 2005), 8 August 1937, p. 265. • 16. John Harvey (ed.), *The Diplomatic Diaries of Oliver Harvey 1937–1940* (London, 1970), 19–23 December 1937, p. 65. • 17. Avon, *Facing the Dictators*, p. 455. • 18. Self (ed.), *The Neville Chamberlain Diary Letters*, 12 September 1937, p. 270. • 19. Harvey (ed.), *The Diplomatic Diaries of Oliver Harvey*, 17 November 1937, p. 61. • 20. Ibid. • 21. Avon Papers, Eden to Chamberlain, 3 November 1937, AE 13/1/49 I. • 22. Avon Papers, Diary, 8 November 1937, AP 20/1/18. • 23. *DBFP, Second Series, Vol. XIX*, Memorandum by Chiefs of Staff Sub-Committee of Committee of Imperial Defence, 4 February 1938, no. 491. • 24. Self (ed.), *The Neville Chamberlain Diary Letters*, 12 December 1937, p. 292. • 25. Ibid. • 26. Avon Papers, Diary, 16 January 1938, AP 20/1/18. • 27. Harvey (ed.), *The Diplomatic Diaries of Oliver Harvey*, 16 January 1938, p. 71. • 28. *DBFP, Second Series, Vol. XIX*, Lindsay to Eden, 18 January 1938, no. 446. • 29. Harvey (ed.), *The Diplomatic Diaries of Oliver Harvey*, 18 January 1938, p. 73. • 30. Avon Papers, Diary, 18 January 1938, AP 20/1/18. • 31. Avon, *Facing the Dictators*, p. 560. • 32. Ibid., p. 563. • 33. *DBFP, Second Series, Vol. XIX*, Eden to Lindsay, 21 January 1938, no. 456. • 34. Ibid., Lindsay to Halifax, 25 February 1938, no. 588. • 35. Robert Rhodes James (ed.), *Memoirs of a Conservative: J. C. C. Davidson's Memoirs and Papers, 1910–1937* (London, 1969), p. 272. • 36. William C. Mills, 'Sir Joseph Ball, Adrian Dingli, and Neville Chamberlain's "Secret Channel" to Italy 1937–1940', *International History Review*, vol. 24, no. 2 (2002), pp. 278–317, at pp. 284–6. • 37. Dingli Diary, 10 January 1938, quoted ibid., p. 292. • 38. Ibid., p. 294. • 39. Chamberlain Papers, Diary, 19 February 1938, NC 2/24 A. • 40. *DBFP, Second Series, Vol. XIX*, Earl of Perth to Eden, 6 February 1938, no. 497. • 41. Eden to Chamberlain, 8 February 1938, PREM 1/276/99–100. • 42. Chamberlain to Eden, 8 February 1938, PREM 1/276/96. • 43. *DBFP, Second Series, Vol. XIX*, Perth to Eden, 17 February 1938, no. 538. • 44. Ibid., no. 543. • 45. Chamberlain Papers, Diary, 19 February 1938, NC 2/24 A. • 46. Malcom Muggeridge (ed.), *Ciano's Diary 1937–1938* (London, 1952), 16 February 1938, p. 76. • 47. Ibid., 7 February 1938, p. 71. • 48. Mills, 'Sir Joseph Ball, Adrian Dingli, and Neville Chamberlain's "Secret Channel" to Italy', p. 297. • 49. Chamberlain Papers, Diary, 19 February 1938, NC 2/24 A. • 50. Avon, *Facing the Dictators*, p. 582. • 51. Malcolm Muggeridge (ed.), *Ciano's Diplomatic Papers* (London, 1948), p. 183. • 52. Chamberlain Papers, Diary, 19 February 1938, NC 2/24 A. • 53. Muggeridge (ed.), *Ciano's Diplomatic Papers*, p. 171. • 54. Avon, *Facing the Dictators*, p. 582. • 55. Muggeridge

(ed.), *Ciano's Diplomatic Papers*, p. 183. • 56. Hickleton Papers, 'A Record of Events Connected with Anthony Eden's Resignation February 19–20 1938', A4/410/4/11. • 57. Cabinet Minutes, 19 February 1938, CAB 23/92/6/187. • 58. John Julius Norwich (ed.), *The Duff Cooper Diaries 1915–1951* (London, 2005), p. 242. • 59. Chamberlain Papers, Diary, 19 February 1938, NC 2/24 A. • 60. Muggeridge (ed.), *Ciano's Diary*, 20 February 1938, p. 78. • 61. Winston S. Churchill, *The Second World War, Vol. I: The Gathering Storm* (London, 1948), p. 201. • 62. Robert Rhodes James (ed.), *'Chips': The Diaries of Sir Henry Channon* (London, 1967), 21 February 1938, p. 145. • 63. Astor Papers, newspaper cutting hand-dated 12 March 1938. • 64. 'Public Opinion Survey 1: British Institute of Public Opinion', *Public Opinion Quarterly*, vol. 4, no. 1 (1940), pp. 77–82, at p. 78. • 65. Avon Papers, Lord Auckland to Eden, AP 8/2/11; quoted in Martin Gilbert, *Sir Horace Rumbold: Portrait of a Diplomat 1869–1941* (London, 1973), p. 432. • 66. Harvey (ed.), *The Diplomatic Diaries of Oliver Harvey*, 27 February 1938, p. 103. • 67. Hansard, HC Deb, 21 February 1938, vol. 332, col. 51. • 68. Martin Gilbert, *Winston S. Churchill, Vol. V, Companion, Part 3* (London, 1982), p. 914, footnote 4. • 69. Hansard, HC Deb, 22 February 1938, vol. 332, cols 243, 247. • 70. Chamberlain Papers, NC to Ivy Chamberlain, 3 March 1938, NC1/15/5. • 71. James (ed.), *'Chips'*, 5 March 1938, pp. 148–9. • 72. Ibid., 4 March 1938, p. 148. • 73. Harvey (ed.), *The Diplomatic Diaries of Oliver Harvey*, 23 February 1938, p. 100. • 74. James (ed.), *'Chips'*, 7 March 1938, p. 149.

XI: The Rape of Austria

1. Quoted in Robert C. Self (ed.), *The Austen Chamberlain Diary Letters* (Cambridge, 1995), p. 505. • 2. Stuart Ball (ed.), *Parliament and Politics in the Age of Churchill and Attlee: The Headlam Diaries 1935–1951* (Cambridge, 1999), 10 March 1938, p. 125. • 3. *DBFP, Second Series, Vol. XVII* (London, 1979), Phipps to Eden, 10 November 1936, no. 365. • 4. Proposed invitation to General Göring to visit England for the Grand National, FO 954/10A/3594/70 • 5. Hansard, HC Deb, 10 February 1938, vol. 331, col. 1239. • 6. Hugh Dalton, *The Fateful Years: Memoirs 1931–1945* (London, 1957), p. 108. • 7. Nigel Nicolson (ed.), *Harold Nicolson Diaries and Letters 1907–1964* (London, 2004), 26 May 1938, p. 344. • 8. Stephen H. Roberts, *The House That Hitler Built* (London, 1937), p. 363. • 9. Robert Self (ed.), *The Neville Chamberlain Diary Letters, Vol. IV: The Downing Street Years 1934–1940* (Aldershot, 2005), 30 January 1938, p. 300. • 10. Foreign Policy Committee Minutes, 24 January 1938, CAB 27/623/4–30. • 11. Ian Kershaw, *Hitler 1936–45: Nemesis* (London, 2000), p. 53. • 12. Ibid., p. 59. • 13. John Julius Norwich (ed.), *The Duff Cooper Diaries 1915–1951* (London, 2005), 13 February 1938, p. 240. • 14. Henderson to Halifax, 24 May 1938, FO 800/269/153. • 15. Henderson to Halifax, 27 February 1938, FO 800/313/1. • 16. Henderson to Halifax, 9 March 1938, FO 800/313/20. • 17. Reinhard Spitzy, *How We Squandered the Reich*, tr. G. T. Waddington (Wilby, Norfolk, 1997), p. 68. • 18. *DBFP, Second Series, Vol XIX* (London, 1982), Henderson to Halifax, 5 March 1938, no. 615. • 19. Ibid., Henderson to Halifax, 4 March 1938, no. 609; *DGFP, Series D, Vol. I* (London, 1949), Ribbentrop to Henderson, 4 March 1938, no. 138; Paul Schmidt, *Hitler's Interpreter* (London, 1951), pp. 86–7; Nevile Henderson, *Failure of a Mission: Berlin 1937–1939* (London, 1940), pp. 114–18. • 20. *DBFP, Second Series, Vol. XIX*, Henderson to Halifax, 5 March 1938, no. 615. • 21. *DGFP, Series D, Vol. I*, 'Record of Conversation between Halifax and Ribbentrop', 10 March 1938, no. 145. • 22. Ibid., Ribbentrop to Hitler, 10 March 1938, no. 146. • 23. Spitzy, *How We Squandered the Reich*, p. 187. • 24. Michael Bloch, *Ribbentrop* (London, 1992), p. 171. • 25. A. J. P. Taylor (ed.), *Lloyd George: A Diary by Frances Stevenson* (London, 1971), 21 May 1934, p. 262. • 26. Charles Stuart (ed.), *The Reith Diaries* (London, 1975), 10 March 1938, p. 219. • 27. *DBFP, Third Series, Vol. I* (London, 1949), Palairet to Halifax, 11 March 1938, no. 10. • 28. Ibid., Henderson to Halifax, 11 March 1938, no. 13. • 29. Ibid., no. 37. • 30. *DGFP, Series D, Vol. I*, 'Memorandum by the Foreign Minister', 11 March 1938, no. 150. • 31. Self (ed.), *The Neville Chamberlain Diary Letters*, 13 May 1938, p. 304. • 32. John Harvey (ed.), *The Diplomatic Diaries of Oliver Harvey 1937–1940* (London, 1970), 11 March 1938, p. 113. • 33. *DBFP, Third Series. Vol. I*, Halifax

to Henderson, 11 March 1938, no. 44. • 34. David Dilks (ed.), *The Diaries of Sir Alexander Cadogan, OM, 1938–1945* (London, 1971), 11 March 1938, p. 60. • 35. Spitzy, *How We Squandered the Reich*, p. 190. • 36. Volker Ullrich, *Hitler: Ascent 1889–1939* (London, 2016), p. 717. • 37. Spitzy, *How We Squandered the Reich*, p. 191. • 38. Ibid., p. 194. • 39. George Ward Price, *Extra-Special Correspondent* (London, 1957), p. 229. • 40. *The Times*, 15 March 1938; Ullrich, *Hitler: Ascent*, p. 718. • 41. *DBFP, Third Series, Vol. I*, Palairet to Halifax, 14 March 1938, no. 76. • 42. *The Times*, 17 February 1938. • 43. *The Times*, 14 March 1938. • 44. Victor Cazalet Papers, Diary, 12 & 11 March 1938. • 45. Letter to *The Times*, 14 March 1938. • 46. *History of The Times, Vol. IV: The 150th Anniversary and Beyond, 1912–1948* (London, 1952), Part II, p. 917. • 47. Martin Gilbert, *Sir Horace Rumbold: Portrait of a Diplomat 1869–1941* (London, 1973), p. 432. • 48. Letters to *The Times*, 14 & 17 March 1938. • 49. Gilbert, *Sir Horace Rumbold*, pp. 433–4. • 50. Mount Temple Papers, 'Memorandum by Tennant after the Austrian Plebiscite', BR 81/10. • 51. Buccleuch Papers, Halifax to Buccleuch, 16 February 1938. • 52. Dilks (ed.), *The Diaries of Sir Alexander Cadogan*, 15 February 1938, p. 47. • 53. Harvey (ed.), *The Diplomatic Diaries of Oliver Harvey*, 15 February 1938, p. 90. • 54. Dilks (ed.), *The Diaries of Sir Alexander Cadogan*, 21 February 1938, p. 55. • 55. Self (ed.), *The Neville Chamberlain Diary Letters*, NC to Hilda, 13 March 1938, pp. 304–5. • 56. Ibid., p. 305. • 57. Earl of Woolton, *The Memoirs of the Rt Hon. the Earl of Woolton* (London, 1959), p. 132. • 58. William Shirer, *The Rise and Fall of the Third Reich: A History of Nazi Germany* (London, 1962), p. 351. • 59. George Glenton and William Pattinson, *The Last Chronicle of Bouverie Street* (London, 1963), pp. 73–4; Will Wainewright, *Reporting on Hitler: Rothay Reynolds and the British Press in Nazi Germany* (London, 2017), pp. 206–7. • 60. G. E. R. Gedye, *Fallen Bastions: The Central European Tragedy* (London, 1939), pp. 305–7. • 61. Hansard, HL Deb, 29 March 1938, vol. 108, cols 448–9, 452, 465. • 62. Gabriel Gorodetsky (ed.), *The Maisky Diaries: Red Ambassador to the Court of St James's 1932–1943* (New Haven, 2015), 29 March 1938, p. 111. • 63. Hansard, HC Deb, 24 March 1938, vol. 333, col. 1454. • 64. Nick Smart (ed.), *The Diaries and Letters of Robert Bernays 1932–1939: An Insider's Account of the House of Commons* (Lewiston, NY, 1996), 28 March 1938, p. 348.

XII: Last Train from Berlin

1. Quoted in John Julius Norwich (ed.), *The Duff Cooper Diaries 1915–1951* (London, 2005), 27 March 1938, p. 245. • 2. David Dilks (ed.), *The Diaries of Sir Alexander Cadogan, OM, 1938–1945* (London, 1971), 12 March 1938, p. 62. • 3. G. E. R. Gedye, *Fallen Bastions: The Central European Tragedy* (London, 1939), p. 396. • 4. *DBFP, Third Series, Vol. II* (London, 1949), 'Notes by Chamberlain of His Conversation with Hitler', 15 September 1938, no. 340. • 5. John Barnes and David Nicholson (eds), *The Leo Amery Diaries, Vol. II: The Empire at Bay 1929–1945* (London, 1988), 12 March 1938, p. 496. • 6. *The Times*, 19 March 1938. • 7. Martin Gilbert, *Winston S. Churchill, Vol V: 1922–1939* (London, 1976), p. 922. • 8. Butler Papers, Beaumont to Butler, 16 March 1938, RAB G9/5. • 9. Memorandum by the Secretary of State for Foreign Affairs, 'Possible Measures to Avert German Action in Czechoslovakia', PREM 1/265/290. • 10. Foreign Policy Committee Minutes, 18 March 1938, CAB 27/623/161. • 11. *DBFP, Third Series, Vol. I* (London, 1949), Newton to Halifax, 15 March 1938, no. 86. • 12. Foreign Policy Committee, 18 March 1938, CAB 27/623/159–65. • 13. Dilks (ed.), *The Diaries of Sir Alexander Cadogan*, 18 March 1938, p. 63. • 14. Robert Self (ed.), *The Neville Chamberlain Diary Letters, Vol. IV: The Downing Street Years 1934–1940* (Aldershot, 2005), NC to Ida, 20 March 1938, p. 307. • 15. Roderick Macleod and Denis Kelly (eds), *The Ironside Diaries 1937–1940* (London, 1962), 24 May 1938, p. 57; Dilks (ed.), *The Diaries of Sir Alexander Cadogan*, 16 March 1938, p. 63. • 16. Foreign Policy Committee, 18 March 1938, CAB 27/623/164. • 17. Halifax to Henderson, 19 March 1938, FO/800/269/56. • 18. Self (ed.), *The Neville Chamberlain Diary Letters*, NC to Ida, 20 March 1938, p. 307. • 19. Cabinet Minutes, 22 March 1938, CAB 23/93/2. • 20. Hansard, HC Deb, 24 March 1938, vol. 333, cols 1405–6. • 21. J. L. Garvin, *Observer*, 27 March 1938. Garvin, editor of the *Observer*, was a Czechophobe

and a leading supporter of appeasement. • 22. *DBFP, Third Series Vol. I*, Soviet Ambassador to Halifax, 17 March 1938, no. 90. • 23. Self (ed.), *The Neville Chamberlain Diary Letters*, NC to Ida, 20 March 1938, p. 307. • 24. *DBFP, Third Series, Vol. I*, Chilston to Halifax, 19 April 1938, no. 148. • 25. Ibid., Phipps to Halifax, 15 March 1938, no. 81. • 26. Phipps to Halifax, 11 April 1938, FO 800/311/27. • 27. Joseph Paul-Boncour, *Entre deux guerres: souvenirs sur la IIIe République* (Paris, 1946), pp. 97–101. • 28. Self (ed.), *The Neville Chamberlain Diary Letters*, NC to Hilda, 27 March 1938, p. 309; NC to Ida, 3 April 1938, p. 313. • 29. Ibid., NC to Hilda, 9 April 1938, p. 314. • 30. Hansard, HC Deb, 5 May 1938, vol. 335, col. 583. • 31. Self (ed.), *The Neville Chamberlain Diary Letters*, NC to Hilda, 13 March 1938, p. 306. • 32. Ibid., NC to Ida, 16 April 1938, p. 316. • 33. *DGFP, Series D, Vol. I* (London, 1949), Woermann to Ribbentrop, 22 April 1938, no. 750. • 34. *DBFP, Third Series, Vol. I*, 'Record of Anglo-French Conversations', 28 April 1938, no. 164. • 35. Dilks (ed.), *The Diaries of Sir Alexander Cadogan*, 29 April 1938, p. 73. • 36. *DGFP, Series D, Vol. II* (London, 1950), Dirksen to Ribbentrop, 6 May 1938, no. 147. • 37. *DBFP, Third Series, Vol. I*, Henderson to Halifax, 6 May 1938, no. 184. • 38. *DGFP, Series D, Vol. II*, unsigned report with enclosures, 28 March 1938, no. 107. • 39 *DBFP, Third Series, Vol. I* – Henderson to Halifax, 20 May 1938, no. 240. • 40. Self (ed.), *The Neville Chamberlain Diary Letters*, NC to Hilda, 22 May 1938, p. 323. • 41. Shiela Grant Duff, *Europe and the Czechs* (Harmondsworth, 1938), p. 175. • 42. Virginia Cowles, *Looking for Trouble* (London, 1941), p. 123. • 43. Ibid., p. 125. • 44. Robert Rhodes James (ed.), *'Chips': The Diaries of Sir Henry Channon* (London, 1967), 22 May 1938, p. 196. • 45. *DBFP, Third Series, Vol. I*, Henderson to Halifax, 21 May 1938, no. 249; Nevile Henderson, *Failure of a Mission: Berlin 1937–1939* (London, 1940), p. 136. • 46. Dilks (ed.), *The Diaries of Sir Alexander Cadogan*, 21 May 1938, p. 79. • 47. *DBFP, Third Series, Vol. I*, Halifax to Henderson, 21 May 1938, no. 250. • 48. *DGFP, Series D, Vol. II*, Memorandum by Foreign Minister, 21 May 1938, no. 186. • 49. Henderson, *Failure of a Mission*, pp. 137–8. • 50. David Faber, *Munich: The 1938 Appeasement Crisis* (London, 2008), p. 178. • 51. Henderson, *Failure of a Mission*, p. 140. • 52. Volker Ullrich, *Hitler: Ascent 1889–1939* (London, 2016), p. 727. • 53. *DGFP, Series D, Vol. II*, 'Directive for Operation "Green"', 30 May 1938, no. 221. • 54. Jeremy Noakes and Geoffrey Pridham (eds), *Documents on Nazism 1919–1945* (London, 1974), p. 542. • 55. Brian Bond (ed.), *Chief of Staff: The Diaries of Lieutenant-General Sir Henry Pownall, Vol. I – 1933–1940* (London, 1972), 23 May 1938, p. 147. • 56. Self (ed.), *The Neville Chamberlain Diary Letters*, NC to Ida, 28 May 1938, p. 325. • 57. Norwich (ed.), *The Duff Cooper Diaries*, 29 May 1938, pp. 249–50. • 58. *DBFP, Third Series, Vol. I*, Halifax to Newton, 25 May 1938, no. 315. • 59. Ibid., Phipps to Halifax, 23 May 1938, no. 286.

XIII: Hons and Rebels

1. Avon Papers, 14/1/731. • 2. Nigel Nicolson (ed.), *Harold Nicolson Diaries and Letters 1907–1964* (London, 2004), 16 March 1938, p. 332. • 3. Ben Pimlott (ed.), *The Political Diary of Hugh Dalton 1918–40, 1945–60* (London, 1986), 7 April 1938, p. 225; Hugh Dalton, *The Fateful Years: Memoirs 1931–1945* (London, 1957), p. 162. • 4. Avon Papers, Sir Timothy Eden to AE, 16 March 1938, 14/1/731. • 5. Avon Papers, Sir Timothy Eden to AE, 26 March 1938, 14/1/732. • 6. Avon Papers, Sandys to Eden, 28 April 1938, 14/1/803. • 7. Avon Papers, Cranborne to Eden, 8 June 1938, 14/1/174. • 8. Robert Rhodes James, *Anthony Eden* (London, 1986), p. 203. • 9. Nicolson (ed.), *Harold Nicolson Diaries and Letters*, 18 July 1939, p. 406. • 10. Quoted in Kenneth Rose, *The Later Cecils* (London, 1975), p. 103. • 11. Thomas C. H. Jones, *A Diary with Letters 1931–1950* (London, 1954), Abraham Flexner to Jones, 8 March 1938, p. 392. • 12. Ibid., Lord Astor to Jones, March 1938, pp. 389–90. • 13. Quoted in *The Times*, 6 October 1937. • 14. Quoted in C. A. MacDonald, *The United States, Britain and Appeasement 1936–1939* (London, 1981), p. 73–4. • 15. *The Times*, 18 March 1938. • 16. Ted Schwarz, *Joseph P. Kennedy: The Mogul, the Mob, the Statesman, and the Making of an American Myth* (Hoboken, NJ, 2003), p. 236. • 17. *The Times*, 19 March 1938. • 18. Amanda Smith (ed.), *Hostage to Fortune: The Letters of Joseph P. Kennedy* (New York, 2001), p. 227. • 19. Margesson

Papers, Lord Bruntisfield to Margesson, 1 December 1938, MRGN 2/1; G. S. Harvie-Watt, *Most of My Life* (London, 1980), p. 133; J. L. P. Thomas, quoted in Andrew Roberts, *Eminent Churchillians* (London, 1994), p. 153. • 20. Margesson Papers, 'Harold Macmillan's Reflections on David Margesson', MRGN 2/1. • 21. 'Cato', *Guilty Men* (London, 1940), p. 91. • 22. Quoted in Piers Brendon, *The Dark Valley: A Panorama of the 1930s* (London, 2000), p. 50. • 23. Chamberlain Papers, Ball to Chamberlain, 21 February 1938, NC 7/11/31/10. • 24. Robert Self (ed.), *The Neville Chamberlain Diary Letters, Vol. IV: The Downing Street Years 1934–1940* (Aldershot, 2005), 23 July 1939, p. 432. • 25. Kenneth Clark, *Another Part of the Wood: A Self-Portrait* (London, 1974), p. 271. • 26. Robert Vansittart, *The Mist Procession: The Autobiography of Lord Vansittart* (London, 1958), pp. 442–3; W. J. Brown, *So Far ...* (London, 1943), pp. 220–21. • 27. *DGFP Series D, Vol. I* (London, 1949), Memorandum, London, 25 February 1938, no. 223. • 28. Emrys-Evans Papers, Emrys-Evans to Julian Amery, 22 May 1956, MS 58247. • 29. Rose, *The Later Cecils*, p. 171. • 30. Alistair Horne, *Macmillan 1894–1956: Vol. I of the Official Biography* (London, 1988), p. 115; Norman Rose, *Harold Nicolson* (London, 2005), p. 213. • 31. *Reynold's News*, 27 February 1938. • 32. Claud Cockburn, *I, Claud* (Harmondsworth, 1967), p. 180. • 33. Roberts, *Eminent Churchillians*, p. 12. • 34. See Richard Carr, 'Veterans of the First World War and Conservative Anti-Appeasement', *Twentieth Century British History*, vol. 22, no. 1 (2011), pp. 28–51. • 35. Quoted in Andrew Boyle, *'Poor, Dear Brendan': The Quest for Brendan Bracken* (London, 1974), p. 218. • 36. Quoted in Rose, *The Later Cecils*, p. 280.

XIV: A Faraway Country

1. Henderson to Halifax, 20 March 1938, FO 800/309/127. • 2. Lord Ponsonby, Hansard, HL Deb, 29 March 1938, vol. 108, col. 461. • 3. Robert Bruce Lockhart, *Jan Masaryk: A Personal Memoir* (London, 1951), p. 18. • 4. Henderson to Halifax, 7 April 1938, FO 800/269/90–91. • 5. Ibid. • 6. *DBFP, Third Series, Vol. I* (London, 1949), Henderson to Halifax, 1 April 1938, no. 121; Mount Temple Papers, Henderson to Mount Temple, 7 March 1938, BR 76/2. • 7. Mount Temple Papers, Henderson to Mount Temple, 14 March 1938, BR 76/2. • 8. Nigel Nicolson (ed.), *Harold Nicolson Diaries and Letters 1907–1964* (London, 2004), 11 April 1938, p. 334. • 9. Henderson to Cadogan, 2 June 1938, FO 800/269/158; David Dilks (ed.), *The Diaries of Sir Alexander Cadogan, OM, 1938–1945* (London, 1971), 31 May 1938, p. 81. • 10. *DBFP, Third Series, Vol. I*, Halifax to Phipps, 31 May 1938, no. 354. • 11. *The Times*, 3 June 1938. • 12. *DBFP, Third Series, Vol. I*, Halifax to Newton, 4 June 1938, no. 374. • 13. Ibid., Halifax to Newton, 4 June 1938, no. 374; *The History of The Times, Vol. IV: The 150th Anniversary and Beyond, 1912–1948* (London, 1952), Part II, p. 921. • 14. Gordon Martel (ed.), *The Times and Appeasement: The Journals of A. L. Kennedy 1932–1939* (Cambridge, 2000), Kennedy to Dawson, 18 March 1938, p. 263. • 15. Robert Self (ed.), *The Neville Chamberlain Diary Letters, Vol. IV: The Downing Street Years 1934–1940* (Aldershot, 2005), NC to Ida, 18 June 1938, p. 328. • 16. David Gilmour, Obituary of Mary, Duchess of Buccleuch, *Scotsman*, 13 February 1993. • 17. *The Times*, 4 July 1938. • 18. Robert Rhodes James (ed.), *'Chips': The Diaries of Sir Henry Channon* (London, 1967), 22 June 1938, p. 160. • 19. Dilks (ed.), *The Diaries of Sir Alexander Cadogan*, 18 July 1938, p. 87. • 20. Zetland Papers, Zetland to Brabourne, 8 August 1938, Mss Eur D609/10/35; Lord Halifax, 'Note on His Conversations with Captain Wiedemann', 18 July 1938, FO 371/217/185. • 21. Zetland Papers, Zetland to Brabourne, 2 August 1938, Mss Eur D609/10/31. • 22. *DGFP, Series D, Vol. VII* (London, 1956), Appendix III, 'Report to v. Ribbentrop'. • 23. Hansard, HC Deb, 26 July 1938, vol. 338, col. 2963. • 24. Ibid., col. 2959. • 25. Ibid., col. 2994. • 26. John Barnes and David Nicholson (eds), *The Leo Amery Diaries, Vol. II: The Empire at Bay 1929–1945* (London, 1988), 26 July 1938, p. 508. • 27. *The Times*, 27 July 1938; *Observer*, 31 July 1938. • 28. Robert Coulondre, French Ambassador to Berlin 1938–39, quoted in Paul Vyšný, *The Runciman Mission to Czechoslovakia 1938: Prelude to Munich* (Basingstoke, 2003), p. 81; Horace Wilson to Halifax, 22 June 1938, FO 800/309/194. • 29. Quoted in Piers Brendon, *The Dark Valley:*

A Panorama of the 1930s (London, 2000), p. 450. • 30. Hansard, HL Deb, 27 July 1938, vol. 110, col. 1282. • 31. *DBFP, Third Series, Vol. II* (London, 1949), Ashton-Gwatkin to Strang, 9 August 1938, no. 598; ibid., Runciman to Halifax, 10 August 1938, no. 602. • 32. Ibid., Halifax to Runciman, 18 August 1938, no. 643. • 33. *DBFP, Third Series, Vol. I*, Strang to Henderson, 21 July 1938, no. 538. • 34. Memorandum by Vansittart, 25 July 1938, FO 371/21729/198. • 35. *DBFP, Third Series, Vol. II*, Mason-MacFarlane to Henderson, 25 July 1938, no. 533, enclosure 2. • 36. Henderson to Halifax, 3 August 1938, FO 800/269/219. • 37. Henderson to Halifax, 26 July 1938, FO 800/269/205–8. • 38. *DBFP, Third Series, Vol. II*, Henderson to Halifax, 6 August 1938, no. 590. • 39. Halifax to Henderson, 5 August 1938, FO 800/314/25–31. • 40. Self (ed.), *The Neville Chamberlain Diary Letters*, NC to Hilda, 13 August 1938, p. 340. • 41. Henderson to Halifax, 8 August 1938, FO 800/269/222. • 42. *DBFP, Third Series, Vol. II*, Mason-MacFarlane to Henderson, 7 August 1938, no. 595, enclosure. • 43. Ibid., 'Memorandum Communicated to His Majesty's Ambassador, Berlin, for Transmission to Herr Hitler', 11 August 1938, no. 608, enclosure. • 44. Quoted in Ian Kershaw, *Hitler 1936–45: Nemesis* (London, 2000), p. 106.

XV: The Crisis Breaks

1 *DBFP, Third Series, Vol. II* (London, 1949), Henderson to Halifax, 21 August 1938, no. 658. • 2. Vansittart Papers, Vansittart to Halifax, 18 August 1938, VNST, 1/2/37. • 3. Chamberlain to Halifax, 19 August 1938, FO 800/314/60. • 4. Sir John Simon, Speech, PREM 1/265/186, reported in *The Times*, 29 August 1938. • 5. Cabinet Minutes, 30 August 1938, CAB 23/94/10. • 6. Ibid. • 7. Vansittart Papers, Vansittart to Halifax, 18 August 1938, VNST 1/2/37. • 8. Gabriel Gorodetsky (ed.), *The Maisky Diaries: Red Ambassador to the Court of St James's 1932–1943* (New Haven, 2015), 30 August 1938, p. 119. • 9. Churchill to Halifax, 31 August 1938, PREM 1/265/120. • 10. Martin Gilbert, *Winston S. Churchill, Vol. V, Companion, Part 3: The Coming of War 1936–1939* (London, 1982), pp. 1123, 1139. • 11. Gorodetsky (ed.), *The Maisky Diaries*, 4 September 1938, p. 124. • 12. Viscount Templewood, *Nine Troubled Years* (London, 1954), p. 299. • 13. Ian Kershaw, *Hitler 1936–45: Nemesis* (London, 2000), p. 88. • 14. Henderson to Halifax, 13 September 1938, FO 800/269/285. • 15. *DBFP, Third Series, Vol. II*, Newton to Halifax, 4 September 1938, no. 758. • 16. John W. Wheeler-Bennett, *Munich: Prologue to Tragedy* (London, 1948), p. 92. • 17. David Dilks (ed.), *The Diaries of Sir Alexander Cadogan, OM, 1938–1945* (London, 1971), 6–7 September 1938, pp. 94–5. • 18. Dawson Papers, Diary, 7 September 1938, MS.Dawson 42. • 19. Vansittart to Halifax, 7 September 1938, PREM 1/265/40. • 20. Gorodetsky (ed.), *The Maisky Diaries*, 7 September 1938, p. 126; John Harvey (ed.), *The Diplomatic Diaries of Oliver Harvey 1937–1940* (London, 1970), 8 September 1938, p. 171; Gordon Martel (ed.), *The Times and Appeasement: The Journals of A. L. Kennedy 1932–1939* (Cambridge, 2000), 7 September 1938, pp. 276–7. • 21. Dawson Papers, Diary, 7 September 1938, MS.Dawson 42; Dawson Papers, Dawson to Barrington-Ward, 7 September 1938, 80/24. • 22. Nick Smart (ed.), *The Diaries and Letters of Robert Bernays 1932–1939: An Insider's Account of the House of Commons* (Lewiston, NY, 1996), Bernays to Lucy Brereton, 9 September 1938, p. 370. • 23. Nigel Nicolson (ed.), *Harold Nicolson Diaries and Letters 1907–1964* (London, 2004), 11 September 1938, p. 359. • 24. Ibid., 6 June 1938, p. 345. • 25. Chamberlain Papers, NC to Annie Chamberlain, 2 September 1938, NC 1/26/530. • 26. *DBFP, Third Series, Vol. II*, Halifax to Kirkpatrick, 9 September 1938, no. 815. • 27. Ibid., Henderson to Halifax, via Ogilvie-Forbes, 10 September 1938, no. 819. • 28. Templewood, *Nine Troubled Years*, pp. 301–2. • 29. Cabinet Minutes, 12 September 1938, CAB 23/95/1/8. • 30. *DBFP, Third Series, Vol. II*, 7 September 1938, no. 798. • 31. Gilbert, *Winston S. Churchill, Vol. V, Companion, Part 3*, p. 1155. • 32. Robert Self (ed.), *The Neville Chamberlain Diary Letters, Vol. IV: The Downing Street Years 1934–1940* (Aldershot, 2005), NC to Ida, 11 September 1938, p. 344. • 33. Caldecote Papers, Diary, 'August 26th–September 19th 1938 – Munich', 7 September 1938, INKP 1. • 34. Self (ed.), *The Neville Chamberlain Diary Letters*, NC to Ida, 11 September 1938, p. 345. • 35. Cabinet Minutes, 12 September

1938, CAB 23/95/1/4–11. • 36. John Julius Norwich (ed.), *The Duff Cooper Diaries 1915–1951* (London, 2005), 12 September 1938, p. 258. • 37. Virginia Cowles, *Looking for Trouble* (London, 1941), pp. 154–5. • 38. Thelma Cazalet Papers, 'Nuremberg 1938 and 1946'. • 39. Cowles, *Looking for Trouble*, pp. 155–6. • 40. Lord Brocket, 'Notes on Conversations with Hitler and Ribbentrop', 10 September 1938, PREM 1/249/70. • 41. Norman H. Baynes (ed.), *The Speeches of Adolf Hitler, April 1922–August 1939* (Oxford, 1942), pp. 1489–91. • 42. Harvey (ed.), *The Diplomatic Diaries of Oliver Harvey*, 12 September 1938, p. 176; John Barnes and David Nicholson (eds), *The Leo Amery Diaries, Vol. II: The Empire at Bay 1929–1945* (London, 1988), 11 September, 1938, p. 508. • 43. Nicolson (ed.), *Harold Nicolson Diaries and Letters*, 11 September 1938, p. 171. • 44. Smart (ed.), *The Diaries and Letters of Robert Bernays*, Bernays to Lucy Brereton, 28 September 1938, p. 371. • 45. Gilbert, *Winston S. Churchill, Vol. V, Companion, Part 3*, p. 1154. • 46. Ibid., pp. 1158–9. • 47. Self (ed.), *The Neville Chamberlain Diary Letters*, NC to Ida, 19 September 1938, p. 345. • 48. Phipps to Halifax, 13 September 1938, FO 371/21737/39–44. • 49. *DBFP, Third Series, Vol. II*, Halifax to Henderson, 13 September 1938, no. 862. • 50. L. B. Namier, *Diplomatic Prelude 1938–1939* (London, 1948), p. 35. • 51. Self (ed.), *The Neville Chamberlain Diary Letters*, NC to Ida, 19 September 1938, p. 346. • 52. Zetland Papers, Zetland to Brabourne, 16/20 September 1938, Mss Eur D609/10/57. • 53. Robert Rhodes James (ed.), *'Chips': The Diaries of Sir Henry Channon* (London, 1967), 14 September 1938, p. 166. • 54. David Faber, *Munich: The 1938 Appeasement Crisis* (London, 2008), p. 284. • 55. *Daily Express*, 16 September 1938; *The Times*, 16 September 1938. • 56. Barnes and Nicholson (eds), *The Leo Amery Diaries*, 14 September 1938, p. 509. • 57. Harvey (ed.), *The Diplomatic Diaries of Oliver Harvey*, 15 September 1938, p. 180. • 58. *DBFP, Third Series, Vol. II*, Phipps to Halifax, 14 September 1938, no. 874. • 59. Ibid., Lindsay to Halifax, 12 September 1938, no. 841. • 60. Galeazzo Ciano, *Diary 1937–1943: The Complete, Unabridged Diaries of Count Galeazzo Ciano*, tr. Robert L. Miller (London, 2002), 14 September 1938, p. 126. • 61. *The Times*, 16 September 1938. • 62. Robert Self, *Neville Chamberlain: A Political Life* (Aldershot, 2006), p. 312. • 63. Margesson Papers, Duff Cooper, 'Chamberlain: A Candid Portrait', MRGN 1/5. • 64. 'Appreciation of the Situation in the Event of War against Germany', 14 September 1938, FO 371/21737/142–4. • 65. Tom Harrisson and Charles Madge, *Britain by Mass-Observation*, 2nd ed. (London, 1986), p. 64. • 66. Self (ed.), *The Neville Chamberlain Diary Letters*, NC to Ida, 19 September 1938, p. 346. • 67. *Manchester Guardian*, 16 September 1938; Geoffrey Harrison interviewed in *God Bless You, Mr Chamberlain*, BBC 2, 23 September 1988. • 68. Self (ed.), *The Neville Chamberlain Diary Letters*, NC to Ida, 19 September 1938, p. 346. • 69. Horace Wilson, 'Notes on Munich', CAB 127/158. • 70. Self (ed.), *The Neville Chamberlain Diary Letters*, NC to Ida, 19 September 1938, p. 346. • 71. Paul Schmidt, *Hitler's Interpreter* (London, 1951), p. 91. • 72. Self (ed.), *The Neville Chamberlain Diary Letters*, NC to Ida, 19 September 1938, p. 346. • 73. Caldecote Papers, Diary, 'August 26th–September 19th 1938 – Munich', 17 September 1938, INKP 1; Cabinet Minutes, 17 September 1938, CAB 23/95/3/72. • 74. Self (ed.), *The Neville Chamberlain Diary Letters*, NC to Ida, 19 September 1938, p. 347. • 75. *DBFP, Third Series, Vol. II*, 'Notes by Mr Chamberlain on His Conversation with Herr Hitler at Berchtesgaden on September 15, 1938', no. 895; ibid., 'Translation of Notes Made by Herr Schmidt of Mr Chamberlain's Conversation with Herr Hitler at Berchtesgaden, September 15, 1938', no. 896. • 76. Self (ed.), *The Neville Chamberlain Diary Letters*, NC to Ida, 19 September 1938, p. 347. • 77. *DBFP, Third Series, Vol. II*, 'Notes by Mr Chamberlain on His Conversation with Herr Hitler at Berchtesgaden on September 15, 1938', no. 895. • 78. Self (ed.), *The Neville Chamberlain Diary Letters*, NC to Ida, 19 September 1938, p. 348. • 79. Ibid. • 80. Chamberlain Papers, 'Notes by Sir Horace Wilson on Conversations During Mr Chamberlain's Visit to Berchtesgaden', 16 September 1938, NC 8/26/2. • 81. Volker Ullrich, *Hitler: Ascent 1889–1939* (London, 2016), pp. 735–6. • 82. Dilks (ed.), *The Diaries of Sir Alexander Cadogan*, 16 September 1938, p. 99. • 83. 'The Czechoslovakian Crisis 1938 – Notes of Informal Meetings of Ministers', 16 September 1938, CAB 27/646/36. • 84. Cabinet Minutes, 17 September 1938, CAB 23/95/3/72–86. • 85. Cabinet Minutes, 17 September 1938, CAB 23/95/86–7; Norwich (ed.), *The Duff Cooper Diaries*, 17 September 1938, p. 261; Cabinet Minutes, 17 September

1938, CAB 23/95/88–9. • 86. Cabinet Minutes, 17 September 1938, CAB 23/95/3/92. • 87. Caldecote Papers, Diary, 'August 26th–September 19th 1938 – Munich', 17 September 1938, INKP 1. • 88. Dilks (ed.), *The Diaries of Sir Alexander Cadogan*, 18 September 1938, p. 100; *DBFP, Third Series, Vol. II*, 'Record of Anglo-French Conversations Held at No 10 Downing Street on September 18, 1938', no. 928. • 89. Caldecote Papers, Diary, 'August 26th–September 19th 1938 – Munich', 19 September 1938, INKP 1. • 90. N. A. Rose (ed.), *Baffy: The Diaries of Blanche Dugdale 1936–1947* (London, 1973), 18 September 1938, p. 98. • 91. Self (ed.), *The Neville Chamberlain Diary Letters*, NC to Ida, 9 October 1938, p. 351; Harvey (ed.), *The Diplomatic Diaries of Oliver Harvey*, 10 September 1938, p. 175. • 92. Dilks (ed.), *The Diaries of Sir Alexander Cadogan*, 20 September 1938, p. 102. • 93. *DBFP, Third Series, Vol. II*, Newton to Halifax, 21 September 1938, no. 1002.

XVI: To the Brink

1. David Dilks (ed.), *The Diaries of Sir Alexander Cadogan, OM, 1938–1945* (London, 1971), 21 September 1938, p. 102. • 2. Ibid. • 3. Martin Gilbert, *Winston S. Churchill, Vol. V, Companion, Part 3: The Coming of War 1936–1939* (London, 1982), pp. 1171–2. • 4. John Julius Norwich (ed.), *The Duff Cooper Diaries 1915–1951* (London, 2005), 21 September 1938, pp. 262–3. • 5. Sir Ivone Kirkpatrick, *The Inner Circle: Memoirs* (London, 1959), p. 113. • 6. Nigel Nicolson (ed.), *Harold Nicolson Diaries and Letters 1907–1964* (London, 2004), 22 September 1938, pp. 363–4. • 7. David Faber, *Munich: The 1938 Appeasement Crisis* (London, 2008), p. 333. • 8. Tom Harrisson and Charles Madge, *Britain by Mass-Observation*, 2nd ed. (London, 1986), p. 75. • 9. Ibid., pp. 72–3. • 10. Butler Papers, Beaumont to Butler, 21 September 1938, RAB G9/8. • 11. John Harvey (ed.), *The Diplomatic Diaries of Oliver Harvey 1937–1940* (London, 1970), 23 September 1938, p. 194; *DBFP, Third Series, Vol. II* (London, 1949), Halifax to British Delegation (Godesberg), 23 September 1938, no. 1058. • 12. Paul Schmidt, *Hitler's Interpreter* (London, 1951), p. 100; Nevile Henderson, *Failure of a Mission: Berlin 1937–1939* (London, 1940), p. 157; Kirkpatrick, *The Inner Circle*, p. 120. • 13. Schmidt, *Hitler's Interpreter*, p. 102. • 14. *DGFP, Series D, Vol. II* (London, 1950), 'Memorandum on the Conversation between the Führer and Reich Chancellor and Neville Chamberlain, the British Prime Minister, at Godesberg on the Evening of September 23, 1938', no. 583. • 15. Dilks (ed.), *The Diaries of Sir Alexander Cadogan*, 24 September 1938, p. 103. • 16. 'The Czechoslovakian Crisis – Notes of Informal Meeting of Ministers', 24 September 1938, CAB 27/646/91–2. • 17. Dilks (ed.), *The Diaries of Sir Alexander Cadogan*, 24 September 1938, p. 103. • 18. Ibid. • 19. Cabinet Minutes, 24 September 1938, CAB 23/95/6/178–80. • 20. Norwich (ed.), *The Duff Cooper Diaries*, 24 September 1938, p. 264. • 21. Dilks (ed.), *The Diaries of Sir Alexander Cadogan*, 24 September 1938, pp. 103–4. • 22. Ibid., 25 September 1938, p. 105. • 23. Norwich (ed.), *The Duff Cooper Diaries*, 25 September 1938, p. 265. • 24. Cabinet Minutes, 25 September 1938, CAB 23/95/7/197–9. • 25. Hickleton Papers, 'Pencil Notes Exchanged between NC and Halifax', 25 September 1938, A4/410/3/7. • 26. R. J. Minney, *The Private Papers of Hore-Belisha* (London, 1960), 25 September 1938, p. 146. • 27. N. A. Rose (ed.), *Baffy: The Diaries of Blanche Dugdale 1936–1947* (London, 1973), 25 September 1938, p. 105. • 28. Masaryk to Halifax, 23 September 1938, PREM 1/266a/122. • 29. Geoffrey Cox, *Countdown to War: A Personal Memoir of Europe 1938–1940* (London, 1988), p. 71. • 30. Norwich (ed.), *The Duff Cooper Diaries*, 25 September 1938, p. 267. • 31. Dilks (ed.), *The Diaries of Sir Alexander Cadogan*, 27 September 1938, p. 106. • 32. Cabinet Minutes, 26 September 1938, CAB 23/95/7/258. • 33. Horace Wilson, 'Notes on Munich', CAB 127/158. • 34. Kirkpatrick, *The Inner Circle*, p. 123. • 35. *DBFP, Third Series, Vol. II*, 'Notes of a Conversation between Sir Horace Wilson and Herr Hitler at Berlin on September 26, 1938, 5.0 p.m.', no. 1118. • 36. William Shirer, *The Rise and Fall of the Third Reich: A History of Nazi Germany* (London, 1962), p. 397. • 37. Kirkpatrick, *The Inner Circle*, p. 125; Henderson, *Failure of a Mission*, p. 160. • 38. PREM 1/266A. • 39. Henderson, *Failure of a Mission*, p. 160. • 40. *The Times*, 26 September 1938. • 41. *League of Nations Official Journal*, Special Supplement No. 183 (1938),

p. 74. • 42. Nicolson (ed.), *Harold Nicolson Diaries and Letters*, 26 September 1938, p. 367. • 43. John Barnes and David Nicholson (eds), *The Leo Amery Diaries, Vol. II: The Empire at Bay 1929–1945* (London, 1988), 26 September, 1938, p. 517. • 44. *DBFP, Third Series, Vol. II*, Halifax to Henderson, 26 September 1938, no. 1111. • 45. 'The Czechoslovakian Crisis – Notes of Informal Meeting of Ministers', 27 September 1938, CAB 27/646/101. • 46. *DBFP, Third Series, Vol. II*, Newton to Halifax, 6 September 1938, no. 794, enclosure. • 47. Dilks (ed.), *The Diaries of Sir Alexander Cadogan*, 27 September 1938, p. 108. • 48. *DBFP, Third Series, Vol. II*, Halifax to Newton, 27 September 1938, no. 1136. • 49. Dilks (ed.), *The Diaries of Sir Alexander Cadogan*, 27 September 1938, p. 107. • 50. Robert Self (ed.), *The Neville Chamberlain Diary Letters, Vol. IV: The Downing Street Years 1934–1940* (Aldershot, 2005), NC to Hilda, 2 October 1938, p. 349. • 51. BBC National Programme radio broadcast, 27 September 1938, recording available at http://www.bbc.co.uk/archive/ww2outbreak/7904.shtml (accessed 20 September 2018). • 52. Barnes and Nicholson (eds), *The Leo Amery Diaries*, 27 September, 1938, p. 519. • 53. This point has been elegantly made by Andrew Roberts in *The Holy Fox: A Biography of Lord Halifax* (London, 1991), p. 120. • 54. Cabinet Minutes, 27 September 1938, CAB 23/95/10; Norwich (ed.), *The Duff Cooper Diaries*, 27 September 1938, pp. 267–9. • 55. Henderson, *Failure of a Mission*, p. 161. • 56. Shirer, *The Rise and Fall of the Third Reich*, p. 399. • 57. Self (ed.), *The Neville Chamberlain Diary Letters*, NC to Hilda, 2 October 1938, p. 349. • 58. *DBFP, Third Series, Vol. II*, Halifax to Henderson, 28 September 1938, no. 1158. • 59. Henderson, *Failure of a Mission*, p. 163. • 60. Nicolson (ed.), *Harold Nicolson Diaries and Letters*, 28 September 1938, p. 369. • 61. Robert Rhodes James (ed.), *'Chips': The Diaries of Sir Henry Channon* (London, 1967), 28 September 1938, p. 171. • 62. Douglas-Home Papers, 'Notes on Munich'. • 63. *The Times*, 29 September 1938. • 64. Nicolson (ed.), *Harold Nicolson Diaries and Letters*, 28 September 1938, p. 371; Nigel Nicolson (ed.), *The Harold Nicolson Diaries 1907–1963* (London, 2005), 28 September 1938, p. 177. • 65. James (ed.), *'Chips'*, 28 September 1938, p. 171. • 66. Gilbert, *Winston S. Churchill, Vol. V, Companion, Part 3*, p. 1184.

XVII: A Piece of Paper

1. Crookshank Papers, Diary, 30 September 1938, MS. Eng. Hist. d. 359. • 2. Robert Rhodes James (ed.), *'Chips': The Diaries of Sir Henry Channon* (London, 1967), 29 September 1938, p. 172. • 3. 'The Crisis: Four Power Conference', British Pathé, 3 October 1938. • 4. R. H. Bruce Lockhart, *Comes the Reckoning* (London, 1947), p. 9. • 5. *The Times*, 29 September 1938. • 6. 'The Crisis: Four Power Conference'; *Daily Sketch*, 29 September 1938. • 7. Lord Home, *The Way the Wind Blows: An Autobiography* (London, 1976), p. 65. • 8. Douglas-Home Papers, 'Notes on Munich'. • 9. *DBFP, Third Series, Vol. II* (London, 1949), Halifax to Newton, 28 September 1938, no. 1184, enclosure. • 10. Quoted in John W. Wheeler-Bennett, *Munich: Prologue to Tragedy* (London, 1948), p. 171. • 11. André François-Poncet, *The Fateful Years: Memoirs of a French Ambassador in Berlin 1931–1938* (London, 1949), p. 269. • 12. Ibid. • 13. J. E. Kaufmann and H. W. Kaufmann, *The Forts and Fortifications of Europe 1815–1914: The Central States – Germany, Austria-Hungary and Czechoslovakia* (Barnsley, 2014), p. 173. • 14. Lord Strang, *Home and Abroad* (London, 1956), p. 144. • 15. Horace Wilson, 'Notes on Munich', CAB 127/158; Sir Ivone Kirkpatrick, *The Inner Circle: Memoirs* (London, 1959), p. 127. • 16. Strang, *Home and Abroad*, p. 145; Douglas-Home Papers, 'Notes on Munich'. • 17. These remarks were recalled by Paul Stehlin, the French assistant air attaché. Quoted in Telford Taylor, *Munich: The Price of Peace* (Sevenoaks, 1979), p. 18. • 18. Horace Wilson, 'Notes on Munich', CAB 127/158. • 19. Galeazzo Ciano, *Diary 1937–1943: The Complete, Unabridged Diaries of Count Galeazzo Ciano*, tr. Robert L. Miller (London, 2002), 29 September 1938, pp. 134–5. • 20. François-Poncet, *The Fateful Years*, p. 269. • 21. Robert Self (ed.), *The Neville Chamberlain Diary Letters, Vol. IV: The Downing Street Years 1934–1940* (Aldershot, 2005), NC to Hilda, 2 October 1938, p. 350. • 22. Horace Wilson, 'Contemporary Notes on Munich', T 273/407/4. • 23. Paul Schmidt, *Hitler's Interpreter*

(London, 1951), p. 110. • 24. Ciano, *Diary 1937–1943*, 29–30 September 1938, p. 136. • 25. François-Poncet, *The Fateful Years*, p. 271. • 26. Ciano, *Diary 1937–1943*, 29–30 September 1938, pp. 135–6. • 27. Horace Wilson, 'Notes on Munich', CAB 127/158. • 28. William L. Shirer, *Berlin Diary: The Journal of a Foreign Correspondent 1934–1941* (London, 1941), 30 September 1938, p. 121. • 29. Ciano, *Diary 1937–1943*, 29–30 September 1938, p. 136. • 30. 'Account by Dr Hubert Masařík of the Munich Conference Completed at 4 a.m. on the Morning of 30 September 1938', T 273/408. • 31. Ibid. • 32. Shirer, *Berlin Diary*, 30 September 1938, p. 121. • 33. Self (ed.), *The Neville Chamberlain Diary Letters*, NC to Hilda, 2 October 1938, p. 350. • 34. Schmidt, *Hitler's Interpreter*, p. 112. • 35. *DBFP, Third Series, Vol. II*, Halifax to Newton, 28 September 1938, no. 1228, appendix. • 36. Self (ed.), *The Neville Chamberlain Diary Letters*, NC to Hilda, 2 October 1938, p. 350. • 37. Schmidt, *Hitler's Interpreter*, pp. 112–13. • 38. Ciano, *Diary 1937–1943*, 2 October 1938, p. 137; Reinhard Spitzy, *How We Squandered the Reich*, tr. G. T. Waddington (Wilby, Norfolk, 1997), p. 254. • 39. John Julius Norwich (ed.), *The Duff Cooper Diaries 1915–1951* (London, 2005), 29 September 1938, p. 270. • 40. Robert Boothby, *I Fight to Live* (London, 1947), p. 165. • 41. Quoted in Colin R. Coote, *The Other Club* (London, 1971), p. 91. • 42. *Daily Express*, 30 September 1938. • 43. Tommy Woodroffe at Downing Street, 30 September 1938, BBC recording LP, 1955. • 44. 'Munich', Sir John Colville interview, LSE Archive, 1/1/5/26. • 45. *The Times*, 1 October 1938. • 46. Zbyněk Zeman and Antonín Klimek, *The Life of Edvard Beneš 1884–1948: Czechoslovakia in Peace and War* (Oxford, 1997), pp. 134–7. • 47. *Manchester Guardian*, 1 October 1938. • 48. Virginia Cowles, *Looking for Trouble* (London, 1941), p. 178. • 49. François-Poncet, *The Fateful Years*, p. 273; *The Times*, 1 October 1938. • 50. Taylor, *Munich*, p. 59; Alexander Werth, *France and Munich: Before and After the Surrender* (London, 1939), pp. 328–9. • 51. Hansard, HC Deb, 3 October 1938, vol. 339, col. 34. • 52. Cowles, *Looking for Trouble*, p. 188. • 53. Hansard, HC Deb, 3 October 1938, vol. 339, col. 51. • 54. Ibid., col. 70. • 55. Ibid., col. 97. • 56. Ibid., cols 112–13. • 57. Hansard, HC Deb, 4 October 1938, vol. 339, col. 233. • 58. Ibid., col. 203. • 59. Hansard, HC Deb, 5 October 1938, vol. 339, cols 361, 365. • 60. Ibid., col. 373. • 61. John Barnes and David Nicholson (eds), *The Leo Amery Diaries, Vol. II: The Empire at Bay 1929–1945* (London, 1988), 5 October 1938, p. 527. • 62. Harold Macmillan, *Winds of Change 1914–1939* (London, 1966), p. 570. • 63. Amery Papers, Amery to Chamberlain, 6 October 1938. • 64. William Shirer, *The Rise and Fall of the Third Reich: A History of Nazi Germany* (London, 1962), p. 427. • 65. Quoted in Patricia Meehan, *The Unnecessary War: Whitehall and the German Resistance to Hitler* (London, 1992), p. 180. • 66. Harold Balfour, *Wings over Westminster* (London, 1973), p. 111. • 67. Anthony Adamthwaite, *France and the Coming of the Second World War 1936–1939* (London, 1977), p. 240. • 68. Peter Jackson, *France and the Nazi Menace: Intelligence and Policy Making 1933–1939* (Oxford, 2000), pp. 270–71. • 69. Quoted in Shirer, *The Rise and Fall of the Third Reich*, p. 424. • 70. Ibid. • 71. Niall Ferguson, *The War of the World: History's Age of Hatred* (London, 2006), p. 367. • 72. Hugh D. Phillips, *Between the Revolution and the West: A Political Biography of Maxim M. Litvinov* (Boulder, CO, 1992), p. 164; Zara Steiner, *The Triumph of the Dark: European International History 1933–1939* (Oxford, 2011), p. 619. • 73. Fritz Hesse, *Hitler and the English* (London, 1954), p. 62. • 74. Quoted in Ian Kershaw, *Hitler 1936–45: Nemesis* (London, 2000), p. 123.

XVIII: Peace for Our Time

1. Chamberlain Papers, NC 13/7/183, 13/7/195. • 2. Chamberlain Papers, Memorandum from Foreign Office to Prime Minister, NC 7/914; Chamberlain Papers, Letter from Foreign Office to Sir Nevile Bland (British Ambassador in The Hague), 7 October 1938, NC 13/7/639. • 3. Chamberlain Papers, Alex. O. Kouyoumdjian to Chamberlain, 9 October 1938, NC 13/7/720. • 4. Chamberlain Papers, *New York Daily News*, NC 13/7/844; Chamberlain Papers, Buddha Society of Bombay to Chamberlain, NC 13/10/109. • 5. Robert Self (ed.), *The Neville Chamberlain Diary Letters, Vol. IV: The Downing Street Years*

1934–1940 (Aldershot, 2005), NC to Ida, 13 November 1938, p. 363. • 6. Cooper Papers, DUFC 2/25. • 7. Cooper Papers, DUFC 2/26, DUFC 2/25. • 8. Royal Archives, Letter from King's Private Secretary, Alec Hardinge, to George VI, 15 September 1938, GVI/235/04. • 9. Victor Cazalet Papers, Diary, 24–28 February 1939. • 10. Quoted in John W. Wheeler-Bennett, *King George VI: His Life and Reign* (London, 1958), p. 356. • 11. Duff Cooper Papers, Duke of Buccleuch to Cooper, 2 October 1938, DUFC 2/19. • 12. Barbara Cartland, *Ronald Cartland* (London, 1942), p. 185. • 13. Quoted in William Manchester, *The Caged Lion: Winston Spencer Churchill 1932–1940* (London, 1988), p. 372. • 14. Julie V. Gottlieb, *'Guilty Women', Foreign Policy, and Appeasement in Inter-War Britain* (Basingstoke, 2015), p. 173. • 15. Emrys-Evans Papers, Law to Emrys-Evans, 30 December 1939, MSS.58239. • 16. Quoted in Gottlieb, *'Guilty Women'*, p. 187. • 17. Cartland, *Ronald Cartland*, p. 185. • 18. Robert Shephard, *Appeasement and the Road to War* (London, 1988), p. 230–1 • 19. Kenneth Clark, *Another Part of the Wood: A Self-Portrait* (London, 1974), p. 274. • 20. Cartland, *Ronald Cartland*, p. 185. • 21. Robert Shepherd, *A Class Divided: Appeasement and the Road to Munich 1938* (London, 1988), p. 247; Victor Cazalet Papers, Diary, 'Munich'. • 22. Harold Macmillan, *Winds of Change 1914–1939* (London, 1966), p. 573; Lynne Olson, *Troublesome Young Men: The Rebels Who Brought Churchill to Power and Helped Save England* (New York, 2007), p. 174. • 23. Avon Papers, Cranborne to Eden, 9 September 1938, AE 14/1/718. • 24. Quoted in Neville Thompson, *The Anti-Appeasers: Conservative Opposition to Appeasement in the 1930s* (Oxford, 1971), p. 193. • 25. B. H. Liddell Hart, *The Memoirs of Captain Liddell Hart, Vol. II* (London, 1965), p. 228. • 26. Martin Gilbert, *Winston S. Churchill, Vol. V, Companion, Part 3: The Coming of War 1936–1939* (London, 1982), p. 1229. • 27. Ibid., p. 1216. • 28. Quoted in Geoffrey Lewis, *Lord Hailsham: A Life* (London, 1997). p. 56. • 29. Edward Heath, *The Course of My Life* (London, 1998), p. 58. • 30. Lord Hailsham, *A Sparrow's Flight: The Memoirs of Lord Hailsham of St Marylebone* (London, 1990), p. 123. • 31. Lewis, *Lord Hailsham*. p. 56. • 32. *The Times*, 28 October 1938. • 33. Hansard, HC Deb, 6 October 1938, vol. 339, col. 551. • 34. Quoted in Keith Feiling, *The Life of Neville Chamberlain* (London, 1946), p. 375. • 35. Chamberlain Papers, NC to Mary Endicott Chamberlain, 5 November 1938, 1/20/180–202. • 36. Ian Colvin, *The Chamberlain Cabinet* (London, 1971), p. 168. • 37. Cabinet Minutes, 31 October 1938, CAB 23/96/3. • 38. Hansard, HC Deb, 1 November 1938, vol. 340, col. 73. • 39. Self (ed.), *The Neville Chamberlain Diary Letters*, NC to Ida, 9 October 1938, p. 351. • 40. Ibid., p. 352. • 41. Quoted in Richard Cockett, *Twilight of Truth: Chamberlain, Appeasement and the Manipulation of the Press* (London, 1989), p. 101. • 42. Avon Papers, Cutting sent by Timothy Eden to Anthony Eden, c. 20 October 1938, 14/1/736B. • 43. Ulrich von Hassell, *The von Hassell Diaries 1938–1944* (London, 1948), 15 October 1938, p. 7. • 44. Norman H. Baynes (ed.), *The Speeches of Adolf Hitler, April 1922–August 1939* (Oxford, 1942), vol. 2, pp. 1533–6. • 45. Ibid., p. 1544. • 46. Quoted in Ian Kershaw, *Hitler 1936–45: Nemesis* (London, 2000), p. 138. • 47. *News Chronicle*, 11 November 1938; *The Times*, 11 November 1938. • 48. *Spectator*, 18 November 1938; *News Chronicle*, 28 November 1938. • 49. Robert Rhodes James (ed.), *'Chips': The Diaries of Sir Henry Channon* (London, 1967), 15 November 1938, p. 177; 21 November 1938, p. 178. • 50. Lord Londonderry, speech to the Over-Seas League, reported in *The Times*, 14 December 1938. • 51. Martin Gilbert, *Sir Horace Rumbold: Portrait of a Diplomat 1869–1941* (London, 1973), p. 440. • 52. Fox Movietone News: 'America Condemns Nazi Terrorism'. • 53. *DGFP, Series D, Vol. IV* (London, 1951), Dieckhoff to German Foreign Ministry, 14 November 1938, no. 501. • 54. Quoted in Robert Dallek, *Franklin D. Roosevelt and American Foreign Policy 1932–1945* (Oxford, 1979), p. 166. • 55. Earl of Avon, *The Memoirs of the Rt Hon. Sir Anthony Eden, KG, PC, MC, Vol. III: The Reckoning* (London, 1965), p. 39. • 56. Ibid., p. 40. • 57. Ibid., p. 41. • 58. Quoted in D. R. Thorpe, *Eden: The Life and Times of Anthony Eden, First Earl of Avon, 1897–1977* (London, 2003), p. 230. • 59. Ibid., pp. 230–31. • 60. Baldwin Papers, Eden to Baldwin, 19 December 1938, Foreign Affairs Series B, vol. 124, fol. 155. • 61. R. H. Bruce Lockhart, *Comes the Reckoning* (London, 1947), pp. 23–9. • 62. Self (ed.), *The Neville Chamberlain Diary Letters*, NC to Ida, 13 November 1938, p. 363. • 63. *DGFP, Series D, Vol. IV*, 'Fritz Hesse Memorandum', 11 October 1938, no. 251, enclosure 2. • 64. 'Clandestine Negotiations between

George Steward and Dr Fritz Hesse', 25 November 1938, FO 1093/107. • 65. Ibid. • 66. David Dilks (ed.), *The Diaries of Sir Alexander Cadogan, OM, 1938–1945* (London, 1971), 24 November 1938, p. 127. • 67. Self (ed.), *The Neville Chamberlain Diary Letters*, NC to Hilda, 27 November 1938, p. 364; John Harvey (ed.), *The Diplomatic Diaries of Oliver Harvey 1937–1940* (London, 1970), 23 November 1938, p. 223. • 68. Self (ed.), *The Neville Chamberlain Diary Letters*, NC to Hilda, 11 December 1938, p. 368. 69. Ibid., NC to Ida, 17 December 1938, p. 369–70. • 70. 'Memorandum Summarising Intelligence Reports on Germany by Gladwyn Jebb', 19 January 1939, CAB 27/627/177–9; Zetland Papers, Zetland to Lord Linlithgow, 22 November 1938, Mss Eur D609/9/140. • 71. Dilks (ed.), *The Diaries of Sir Alexander Cadogan*, 15 December 1938, p. 130. • 72. Brian Bond (ed.), *Chief of Staff: The Diaries of Lieutenant-General Sir Henry Pownall, Vol. I – 1933–1940* (London, 1972), pp. 174–5. • 73. Dilks (ed.), *The Diaries of Sir Alexander Cadogan*, 31 December 1938, pp. 131–2. • 74. Nigel Nicolson (ed.), *Harold Nicolson Diaries and Letters 1907–1964* (London, 2004), 31 December 1938, p. 384.

XIX: Chamberlain Betrayed

1. Margesson Papers, Duff Cooper, 'Chamberlain: A Candid Portrait', MRGN 1/5 • MRGN 1/5. • 2. William L. Shirer, *Berlin Diary: The Journal of a Foreign Correspondent 1934–1941* (London, 1941), 11 January 1939, p. 128. • 3. 'The Prime Minister in Rome', Pathé News, 16 January 1939. • 4. Malcolm Muggeridge (ed.), *Ciano's Diary 1939–1943* (London, 1947), 2 December 1938, p. 200. • 5. David Dilks (ed.), *The Diaries of Sir Alexander Cadogan, OM, 1938–1945* (London, 1971), 2 December 1938, p. 127. • 6. Muggeridge (ed.), *Ciano's Diary*, 12 January 1939, p. 10. • 7. Royal Archives, Chamberlain to HM the King, 17 January 1939, PS/PSO/GVI/C/47/14. • 8. John Harvey (ed.), *The Diplomatic Diaries of Oliver Harvey 1937–1940* (London, 1970), 14 January 1939, p. 242. • 9. Cabinet Minutes, 21 December 1938, CAB 23/96/12/430. • 10. Cabinet Minutes, 18 January 1939, CAB 23/97/1/6. • 11. Muggeridge (ed.), *Ciano's Diary*, 11 January 1939, p. 10. • 12. Quoted in Keith Jeffery, *MI6: The History of the Secret Intelligence Service 1909–1949* (London, 2010), p. 310. • 13. *DBFP, Third Series, Vol. IV* (London, 1951), Halifax to Mallet, 24 January 1939, no. 5. • 14. Hansard, HC Deb, 6 February 1939, vol. 343, col. 623. • 15. R. J. Minney, *The Private Papers of Hore-Belisha* (London, 1960), Diary, 26 January 1939, p. 171. • 16. Cabinet Minutes, 2 February 1939, CAB 23/97/5/176–8. • 17. *DDF, Second Series, Vol. XIII*, 29 January 1939, no. 454. • 18. *The Times*, 30 January 1939. • 19. 'Herr Hitler's Speech in the Reichstag', *Bulletin of International News*, vol. 16, no. 3 (1939), p. 6. • 20. Robert Self (ed.), *The Neville Chamberlain Diary Letters, Vol. IV: The Downing Street Years 1934–1940* (Aldershot, 2005), NC to Hilda, 5 February 1939, p. 377. • 21. Henderson to Cadogan, 16 February 1939, FO 800/270/5. • 22. *DBFP, Third Series, Vol. IV*, Henderson to Foreign Office, 16 February 1939, Appendix I, part III, footnote 1. • 23. Chamberlain to Henderson to Cadogan, 19 February 1939, FO 800/270/12. • 24. Halifax to Henderson, 20 February 1939, FO 800/270/13. • 25. Harvey (ed.), *The Diplomatic Diaries of Oliver Harvey*, 17 February 1939, p. 255; 29 September 1938, p. 202. • 26. Ibid., 4 January 1939, p. 235. • 27. Quoted in Martin Gilbert and Richard Gott, *The Appeasers* (London, 1963), p. 201. • 28. Drummond Wolff Papers, 'Report on a visit to Berlin', January 1939, MS 709/875. • 29. Self (ed.), *The Neville Chamberlain Diary Letters*, NC to Hilda, 19 February 1939, p. 382. • 30. Ibid., NC to Ida, 26 February 1939, p. 387; Robert Rhodes James (ed.), *'Chips': The Diaries of Sir Henry Channon* (London, 1967), 7 March 1939, p. 185. • 31. Chamberlain Papers, Halifax to NC, 10 March 1939, NC7/11/32/111. • 32. Self (ed.), *The Neville Chamberlain Diary Letters*, NC to Hilda, 12 March 1939, pp. 391–2. • 33. Vansittart to Halifax, 20 February 1939, FO 371/22965/199. • 34. Paul Schmidt, *Hitler's Interpreter* (London, 1951), p. 125. • 35. James (ed.), *'Chips'*, 15 March 1939, pp. 185–6. • 36. *News Chronicle*, 16 March 1939; *Observer*, 19 March 1939 • 37. *The Times*, 15 March 1939; *Daily Telegraph*, 16 March 1939. • 38. Stuart Ball (ed.), *Parliament and Politics in the Age of Churchill and Attlee: The Headlam Diaries 1935–1951* (Cambridge, 1999), 15 March 1939, p. 151. • 39. Daladier to

Chamber of Deputies, 17 March 1939, and Daladier to Senate, 19 March 1939, quoted in Daniel Hucker, *Public Opinion and the End of Appeasement in Britain and France* (Farnham, Surrey, 2011), p. 136. • 40. Cabinet Minutes, 15 March 1939, CAB 23/98/1/3. • 41. *News Chronicle*, 17 March 1939. • 42. Hansard, HC Deb, 15 March 1939, vol. 345, cols 446, 462. • 43. Nigel Nicolson (ed.), *Harold Nicolson Diaries and Letters 1907–1964* (London, 2004), 17 March 1939, p. 393. • 44. Reported in *The Times*, 18 March 1939. • 45. Quoted in Robert Self, *Neville Chamberlain: A Political Life* (Aldershot, 2006), p. 353. • 46. *DBFP, Third Series, Vol. IV*, Hoare to Halifax, 19 March 1939, no. 399, enclosure. • 47. Ibid., Halifax to Phipps, Seeds and Kennard, 20 March 1939, no. 446 • 48. Self (ed.), *The Neville Chamberlain Diary Letters*, NC to Ida, 26 March 1939, p. 396. • 49. Ibid. • 50. Ibid., NC to Ida, 26 March 1939, p. 398. • 51. Dilks (ed.), *The Diaries of Sir Alexander Cadogan*, 29 March 1939, p. 164. • 52. Self (ed.), *The Neville Chamberlain Diary Letters*, NC to Hilda, 1 April 1939, p. 400. • 53. Cabinet Minutes, 30 March 1939, CAB 23/98/6/161. • 54. L. B. Namier, *Diplomatic Prelude 1938–1939* (London, 1948), p. 107; Hansard, HC Deb, 31 March 1939, vol. 345, col. 2415. • 55. Butler Papers, Notes, June 1939, RAB G110/28. • 56. Quoted in Zara Steiner, *The Triumph of the Dark: European International History 1933–1939* (Oxford, 2011), p. 739. • 57. Robert Boothby, *I Fight to Live* (London, 1947), p. 187. • 58. Self (ed.), *The Neville Chamberlain Diary Letters*, NC to Hilda, 1 April 1939, p. 402. • 59. Ibid., NC to Hilda, 15 April 1939, p. 405; NC to Ida, 9 April 1939, p. 403; NC to Hilda, 15 April 1939, p. 405. • 60. Dilks (ed.), *The Diaries of Sir Alexander Cadogan*, 7 April 1939, p. 170. • 61. Hansard, HC Deb, 13 April 1939, vol. 346, col. 31. • 62. Quoted in Martin Pugh, *'Hurrah for the Blackshirts!' Fascists and Fascism in Britain between the Wars* (London, 2005), p. 284. • 63. J. R. M. Butler, *Lord Lothian (Philip Kerr) 1882–1940* (London, 1960), p. 227; Ian Kershaw, *Making Friends with Hitler: Lord Londonderry and Britain's Road to War* (London, 2004), p. 278. • 64. Richard Griffiths, *Fellow Travellers of the Right: British Enthusiasts for Nazi Germany 1933–9* (Oxford, 1980), p. 349. • 65. Buccleuch Papers, Buccleuch to Butler, 24 April 1939. • 66. Cadogan Papers, Diary, 15 & 20 April 1939, ACAD 1/8. • 67. Ogilvie-Forbes to Foreign Office, 17 April 1939, FO/800/315/94. • 68. Buccleuch Papers, 'Berlin, 15–18 April 1939: Some Notes and Impressions Following Conversations with the Foreign Minister and Others'. • 69. Buccleuch Papers, Buccleuch to Butler, 24 April 1939. • 70. Lord Brocket, 'Memorandum on Visit to Berlin, April 16–22nd, 1939', FO 800/315/103–15. • 71. Self (ed.), *The Neville Chamberlain Diary Letters*, NC to Hilda, 29 April 1939, pp. 412–13; NC to Ida, 23 April 1939, p. 409. • 72. Quoted in Ian Kershaw, *Hitler 1936–45: Nemesis* (London, 2000), p. 178.

XX: Deterring the Dictators

1. Hansard, HC Deb, 15 March 1939, vol. 345, col. 488. • 2. Cited in Franklin Reid Gannon, *The British Press and Germany 1936–1939* (Oxford, 1971), p. 46. • 3. Ian Colvin, *The Chamberlain Cabinet* (London, 1971), p. 201; Robert Self (ed.), *The Neville Chamberlain Diary Letters, Vol. IV: The Downing Street Years 1934–1940* (Aldershot, 2005), NC to Hilda, 29 April 1939, p. 412. • 4. Robert Rhodes James (ed.), *'Chips': The Diaries of Sir Henry Channon* (London, 1967), 23 April 1939, p. 194; Salisbury Papers, Jim Thomas to Lord Cranborne, 15 June 1939, box 63. • 5. Report by the Chiefs of Staff Sub-Committee, 'Balance of Strategical Value in War as between Spain as an Enemy and Russia as an Ally', FO 371/22972/265–6. • 6. Colvin, *The Chamberlain Cabinet*, p. 213. • 7. Self (ed.), *The Neville Chamberlain Diary Letters*, NC to Ida, 9 April 1939, p. 404. • 8. Ibid., NC to Hilda, 28 May 1939, p. 418. • 9. Ibid., NC to Ida, 21 May 1939, p. 417; David Dilks (ed.), *The Diaries of Sir Alexander Cadogan, OM, 1938–1945* (London, 1971), 20 May 1939, p. 182. • 10. John Harvey (ed.), *The Diplomatic Diaries of Oliver Harvey 1937–1940* (London, 1970), 20 May 1938, p. 290. • 11. Self (ed.), *The Neville Chamberlain Diary Letters*, NC to Hilda, 28 May 1939, p. 418. • 12. James (ed.), *'Chips'*, 24 May 1939, p. 201. • 13. Donald Cameron Watt, *How War Came: The Immediate Origins of the Second World War 1938–1939* (London, 1989), p. 247. • 14. Self (ed.), *The Neville Chamberlain Diary Letters*, NC to Hilda, 29 April 1939, p. 411; NC to Hilda, 28 May 1939, p. 419. • 15.

Dilks (ed.), *The Diaries of Sir Alexander Cadogan*, 3 May 1939, p. 178; 22 May 1939, p. 182. • 16. Roderick Macleod and Denis Kelly (eds), *The Ironside Diaries 1937–1940* (London, 1962), 25 July 1939, p. 83. • 17. Virginia Cowles, *Looking for Trouble* (London, 1941), p. 245. • 18. Nigel Nicolson (ed.), *Harold Nicolson Diaries and Letters 1907–1964* (London, 2004), 3 April 1939, p. 394. • 19. Quoted in Geoffrey Cox, *Countdown to War: A Personal Memoir of Europe 1938–1940* (London, 1988), p. 109. • 20. Quoted in Martin Gilbert, *Winston S. Churchill, Vol. V: 1922–1939* (London, 1976), p. 1064. • 21. Martin Gilbert, *Winston S. Churchill, Vol. V, Companion, Part 3: The Coming of War 1936–1939* (London, 1982), Hugh Cudlipp to Churchill, 26 April 1939, p. 1475. • 22. Victor Cazalet Papers, Diary, April 1939. • 23. Nicolson (ed.), *Harold Nicolson Diaries and Letters*, 20 April 1939, p. 399. • 24. Self (ed.), *The Neville Chamberlain Diary Letters*, NC to Ida, 23 April 1939, p. 410. • 25. Ibid., NC to Hilda, 29 April 1939, pp. 411–13. • 26. James (ed.), *'Chips'*, 13 April 1939, p. 193. • 27. Hansard, HL Deb, 8 June 1939, vol. 113, cols 358–61. • 28. Dilks (ed.), *The Diaries of Sir Alexander Cadogan*, 29 June 1939, p. 190. • 29. *Daily Telegraph*, 8 July 1939. • 30. Quoted in Watt, *How War Came*, p. 391. • 31. Gilbert, *Winston S. Churchill, Vol. V, Companion, Part 3*, Major-General James Marshall-Cornwall to Halifax, 'Conversation with Count Schwerin', 6 July 1939, pp. 1553–4. • 32. Ibid., 'Lord Camrose: notes of a conversation with Neville Chamberlain', p. 1544. • 33. Self (ed.), *The Neville Chamberlain Diary Letters*, NC to Ida, 25 June 1939, p. 424; NC to Hilda, 17 June 1939, p. 421. • 34. *DBFP, Third Series, Vol. V* (London, 1952), Henderson to Halifax, 5 May 1939, no. 377. • 35. 'Conversation with Dr Kordt', 16 June 1939, FO 371/22973/31226. • 36. Ian Colvin, Memorandum, 17 July 1939, FO 371/22975/3. • 37. *DBFP, Third Series, Vol. V*, Minute by Ashton-Gwatkin, 7 June 1939, no. 741. • 38. Horace Wilson, 'Notes on a Conversation with Herr Wohltat', 19 July 1939, PREM 1/330/32–3. • 39. *DGFP, Series D, Vol. VI* (London, 1956), 'Memorandum by an Official on the Staff of the Four Year Plan', 24 July 1939, no. 716. • 40. Salisbury Papers, Thomas to Cranborne, 21 July 1939, box 63. • 41. Ibid., Cranborne to Thomas, July 1939. • 42. 'Record of a Conversation between R. S. Hudson and Dr Wohltat', 20 July 1939, PREM 8/1130. • 43. Watchman, *What of the Night?* (London, 1940), pp. 154. • 44. *DBFP, Third Series, Vol. VI* (London, 1953), Loraine to Halifax, 24 July 1939, no. 425. • 45. Lord Gladwyn, *The Memoirs of Lord Gladwyn* (London, 1972), p. 93. • 46. Self (ed.), *The Neville Chamberlain Diary Letters*, NC to Ida, 23 July 1939, pp. 430–31; NC to Hilda, 30 July 1939, p. 435. • 47. Lord Kemsley, 'Notes of the Conversation with Herr Hitler, Bayreuth', 27 July 1939, FO 800/316/157. • 48. 'Halifax Notes on Meeting with Dahlerus', 25 July 1939, FO 800/316/135. • 49. *DGFP, Series D, Vol. VI*, Unsigned Memorandum, no. 783. • 50. *DBFP, Third Series, Vol. VI*, 'Record of Conversations with Field-Marshal Göring', 10 August 1939, Appendix IV(iii); *DGFP, Series D, Vol. VI*, Unsigned Memorandum, no. 783; Watt, *How War Came*, p. 404. • 51. Ernest W. D. Tennant, *True Account* (London, 1957), pp. 214–17. • 52. 'Horace Wilson Notes on a Meeting with Ernest Tennant', 10 July 1939, PREM 1/335/53–5. • 53. 'Record by E. W. D. Tennant', 31 July 1939, PREM 1/335/15–28.

XXI: The Last Season

1. Quoted in Barbara Cartland, *Ronald Cartland* (London, 1942), p. 218. • 2. *The Times*, 4 May 1939; *The Times*, 5 May 1939. • 3. Quoted in Jean-Baptiste Duroselle, *France and the Nazi Threat: The Collapse of French Diplomacy 1932–1939* (New York, 2004), p. 337. • 4. Henderson to Wilson, 24 May 1939, PREM 1/331A. • 5. Henderson to Halifax, 26 April 1939, FO 800/270/40–41. • 6. Cabinet Minutes, 18 March 1939, CAB 23/98/2. • 7. Robert Self (ed.), *The Neville Chamberlain Diary Letters, Vol. IV: The Downing Street Years 1934–1940* (Aldershot, 2005), NC to Hilda, 15 July 1939, p. 428. • 8. Roderick Macleod and Denis Kelly (eds), *The Ironside Diaries 1937–1940* (London, 1962), 10 July 1939, p. 77. • 9. *DBFP, Third Series, Vol. VI* (London, 1953), Norton to Halifax, 20 July 1939, no. 374. • 10. Macleod and Kelly (eds), *The Ironside Diaries*, 18 July 1939, p. 81; *DBFP, Third Series, Vol. VI*, Norton to Halifax, 20 July 1939, no. 374. • 11. *DBFP, Third Series, Vol. V* (London, 1952), Seeds to Halifax, 30 May 1939,

no. 665. • 12. Winston S. Churchill, *The Second World War, Vol. I: The Gathering Storm* (London, 1948), p. 288. • 13. Gabriel Gorodetsky (ed.), *The Maisky Diaries: Red Ambassador to the Court of St James's 1932–1943* (New Haven, 2015), 12 June 1939, p. 200. • 14. Self (ed.), *The Neville Chamberlain Diary Letters*, NC to Ida, 10 June 1939, pp. 420–21. • 15. Lord Strang, *Home and Abroad* (London, 1956), p. 176. • 16. *DBFP, Third Series, Vol. VI*, Seeds to Halifax, 17 June 1939, no. 73. • 17. David Dilks (ed.), *The Diaries of Sir Alexander Cadogan, OM, 1938–1945* (London, 1971), 20 June 1939, p. 189. • 18. Gorodetsky (ed.), *The Maisky Diaries*, 23 June 1939, p. 201. • 19. *DBFP, Third Series, Vol. VI*, Strang to Sargent, 21 June 1939, no. 122. • 20. Ibid., no. 193, enclosure. • 21. *DDF, Second Series, Vol. XVII* (Paris, 1984), Bonnet to Corbin, 5 July 1939, no. 100; 'Négociations franco-anglo-russes, 12 mai 1939–5 juillet 1939', 5 July 1939, no. 107. • 22. *DBFP, Third Series, Vol. VI*, Strang to Sargent, 20 July 1939, no. 376. • 23. Henderson to Cadogan, June 1939, FO 800/294/68. • 24. CAB 27/625/269; Cabinet Minutes, 19 July 1939, CAB 23/100/6/187. • 25. Self (ed.), *The Neville Chamberlain Diary Letters*, NC to Hilda, 15 July 1939, p. 428; NC to Ida, 23 July 1939, p. 432. • 26. *DBFP, Third Series, Vol. VI*, Strang to Sargent, 20 July 1939, no. 376. • 27. Quoted in Duroselle, *France and the Nazi Threat*, p. 357. • 28. Simon Sebag Montefiore, *Stalin: The Court of the Red Tsar* (London, 2003), p. 272. • 29. Drax Papers, 'Mission to Moscow, August 1939', DRAX 6/14. • 30. Hugh Dalton, *The Fateful Years: Memoirs 1931–1945* (London, 1957), p. 257. • 31. *DBFP, Third Series, Vol. VI*, 'Instructions to the British Military Mission to Moscow', August 1939, Appendix V. • 32. Drax Papers, 'Mission to Moscow, August 1939', DRAX 6/14. • 33. Ibid. • 34. Ibid. • 35. Ibid. • 36. Ibid. • 37. *The Times*, 17 July 1939; *The Times*, 28 July 1939. • 38. Robert Rhodes James (ed.), *'Chips': The Diaries of Sir Henry Channon* (London, 1967), 7 July 1939, p. 205. • 39. Cartland, *Ronald Cartland*, p. 218. • 40. Angela Lambert, *1939: The Last Season of Peace* (London, 1989), p. 97. • 41. T. E. B. Howarth, *Cambridge between Two Wars* (London, 1978), p. 236. • 42. Hansard, HC Deb, 2 August 1939, vol. 350, cols 2438, 2440, 2441. • 43. Geoffrey Mander, ibid., col. 2490. • 44. Ibid., cols 2494, 2495; Cartland, *Ronald Cartland*, p. 225. • 45. Nigel Nicolson (ed.), *Harold Nicolson Diaries and Letters 1907–1964* (London, 2004), 2 August 1939, p. 407. • 46. Hansard, HC Deb, 2 August 1939, vol. 350, col. 2503. • 47. Cartland, *Ronald Cartland*, p. 225. • 48. Chamberlain Papers, Richard Edwards to Chamberlain, 4 August 1939, NC 7/11/32/38. • 49. Self (ed.), *The Neville Chamberlain Diary Letters*, NC to Ida, 5 August 1939, p. 438. • 50. Ibid., NC to Hilda, 30 July 1939, p. 435. • 51. *DBFP, Third Series, Vol. VI*, 'Record of Interview between Burckhardt and Hitler', 14 August 1939, no. 659, enclosure 2. • 52. Halifax to Chamberlain, 19 August 1939, FO 800/316/204–6. • 53. Butler Papers, 'A Record of Events before the War by Lord Halifax', G10/01. • 54. *DBFP, Third Series, Vol. VII* (London, 1954), Henderson to Halifax, 22 August 1939, no. 153.

XXII: Final Hours

1. Buccleuch Papers, Chamberlain to Buccleuch, 30 August 1939. • 2. Hore-Belisha Papers, Diary, 21 August 1939, HOBE 1/7. • 3. *FRUS, 1939, Vol. I* (Washington, 1956), Bullitt to Hull, 22 August 1939, p. 302. • 4. Robert Rhodes James (ed.), *'Chips': The Diaries of Sir Henry Channon* (London, 1967), 22 August 1939, p. 208. • 5. Nigel Nicolson (ed.), *Harold Nicolson Diaries and Letters 1907–1964* (London, 2004), 22 August 1939, p. 411. • 6. Amanda Smith (ed.), *Hostage to Fortune: The Letters of Joseph P. Kennedy* (New York, 2001), Diary, 25 August 1939, p. 362. • 7. Henderson to Halifax, 24 August 1939, FO 800/316/221. • 8. Ian Kershaw, *Hitler 1936–45: Nemesis* (London, 2000), p. 213. • 9. Nicolson (ed.), *Harold Nicolson Diaries and Letters*. 24 August 1939, p. 413. • 10. Hansard, HC Deb, 24 August 1939, vol. 351, col. 10. • 11. James (ed.), *'Chips'*, 24 August 1939, p. 209; Major-General Sir Edward Spears, *Assignment to Catastrophe, Vol. I: Prelude to Dunkirk July 1939–May 1940* (London, 1954), p. 13. • 12. Smith (ed.), *Hostage to Fortune*, Diary, 24 August 1939, p. 360. • 13. Quoted in Donald Cameron Watt, *How War Came: The Immediate Origins of the Second World War 1938–1939* (London, 1989), p. 480. • 14. Paul Schmidt, *Hitler's Interpreter* (London, 1951), p. 143. • 15. *DBFP, Third Series, Vol. VII* (London, 1954), Henderson to Halifax, 25 August 1939, no. 283.

• 16. Ibid., Henderson to Halifax, 25 August 1939, no. 284. • 17. Keitel quoted in Leonard Mosley, *On Borrowed Time: How World War II Began* (London, 1969), p. 398. • 18. David Dilks (ed.), *The Diaries of Sir Alexander Cadogan, OM, 1938–1945* (London, 1971), 25 August 1939, p. 201; John Harvey (ed.), *The Diplomatic Diaries of Oliver Harvey 1937–1940* (London, 1970), 27 August 1939, p. 307. • 19. Hore-Belisha Papers, Diary, 26 August & 2 September 1939, HOBE 1/7. • 20. Caldecote Papers, Diary, 27 August 1939, INKP 2. • 21. Dilks (ed.), *The Diaries of Sir Alexander Cadogan*, 27 August 1939, p. 202. • 22. Birger Dahlerus, *The Last Attempt* (London, 1948), p. 56. The accounts of Dahlerus' activities are also taken from his 'Report on Negotiations between Great Britain and Germany from Thursday August 24th, until September 3rd, 1939', Hickleton Papers, A4/410/3/10/i. • 23. Butler Papers, Lord Halifax, 'A Record of Events before the War', 1939, RAB G10/101. • 24. Dahlerus, *The Last Attempt*, pp. 62–3. • 25. Dilks (ed.), *The Diaries of Sir Alexander Cadogan*, 27 August 1939, p. 202. • 26. James (ed.), *'Chips'*, 28 August 1939, p. 210. • 27. *DDF, Second Series, Vol. XIX* (Paris, 1986), Coulondre to Daladier, 30 August 1939, no. 235. • 28. Strang to Cadogan, 26 August 1939, PREM 1/331a. • 29. *DBFP, Third Series, Vol. VII*, Henderson to Halifax, 29 August 1939, no. 455. • 30. Ibid., Henderson to Halifax, 29 August 1939, no. 467. • 31. Ibid., Henderson to Halifax, 30 August 1939, no. 502. • 32. Ibid., Henderson to Halifax, 30 August 1939, no. 508. • 33. Henderson to Halifax, 30 August 1939, FO 800/316/237–8. • 34. *DBFP, Third Series, Vol. VII*, Kennard to Halifax, 30 August 1939, no. 512. • 35. Ibid., Henderson to Halifax, 30 August 1939, no. 520. • 36. Butler Papers, 'September 1939', RAB G10/110. • 37. Cabinet Minutes, 30 August 1939, CAB 23/100/14/425. • 38. Buccleuch Papers, Chamberlain to Buccleuch, 30 August 1939. • 39. Ulrich von Hassell, *The von Hassell Diaries 1938–1944* (London, 1948), 30 August 1939, p. 44. • 40. The account of this famous confrontation is taken from Schmidt, *Hitler's Interpreter*, pp. 150–54; Nevile Henderson, *Failure of a Mission: Berlin 1937–1939* (London, 1940), pp. 269–73; *DBFP, Third Series, Vol. VII*, nos 571 & 574; and *DGFP, Series D, Vol. VII* (London, 1956), Memorandum by an Official of the Foreign Minister's Secretariat, 31 August 1939, no. 461. • 41. *DBFP, Third Series, Vol. VII*, Henderson to Halifax, 31 August 1939, no. 575. • 42. Anthony Adamthwaite, *France and the Coming of the Second World War 1936–1939* (London, 1977), p. 346. • 43. Wacław Jędrzejewicz (ed.), *Diplomat in Berlin 1933–1939: Papers and Memoirs of Józef Lipski, Ambassador of Poland* (New York and London, 1968), p. 608. • 44. Horace Wilson Minute, 31 August 1939, PREM 1/331a/82; *DBFP, Third Series, Vol. VII*, Minute by Cadogan, 31 August 1939, no. 589. • 45. Dilks (ed.), *The Diaries of Sir Alexander Cadogan*, 31 August 1939, p. 206. • 46. Jean-Baptiste Duroselle, *France and the Nazi Threat: The Collapse of French Diplomacy 1932–1939* (New York, 2004), p. 408. • 47. Harvey (ed.), *The Diplomatic Diaries of Oliver Harvey*, 2 September 1939, p. 314. • 48. Hugh Dalton, *The Fateful Years: Memoirs 1931–1945* (London, 1957), p. 271. • 49. Schmidt, *Hitler's Interpreter*, p. 158.

XXIII: Ghosts of Appeasement

1. Waterhouse Papers, Diary, 21 February 1940. • 2. Butler Papers, 'Recollections on the Outbreak of War, September 1939', RAB G10/110. • 3. Nigel Nicolson (ed.), *Harold Nicolson: Diaries and Letters 1930–1939* (London, 1966), 3 September 1939, p. 421. • 4. Winston S. Churchill, *The Second World War, Vol. I: The Gathering Storm* (London, 1948), p. 319. • 5. Hansard, HC Deb, 7 February 1934, vol. 285, col. 1197; Hansard, HC Deb, 15 November 1937, vol. 329, col. 55. • 6. Halifax to Salisbury, 31 October 1939, FO 800/325/14731. • 7. Ben Pimlott (ed.), *The Political Diary of Hugh Dalton 1918–40, 1945–60* (London, 1986), 11 September 1939, p. 299. • 8. Official Polish broadcast, reported in *Manchester Guardian*, 28 September 1939. • 9. Antony Beevor, *The Second World War* (London, 2012), p. 35. • 10. Wojciech Materski and Tomasz Szarota (eds), *Polska 1939–1945: Straty osobowe i ofiary represji pod dwiema okupacjami* ('Poland 1939–1945: Human Casualties and Victims of Repression under Two Occupations') (Warsaw, 2009), p. 9. • 11. Major-General Sir Edward Spears, *Assignment to Catastrophe, Vol. I: Prelude to Dunkirk July 1939–May 1940* (London, 1954), p. 32. • 12. Hugh Dalton, *The Fateful Years:*

Memoirs 1931–1945 (London, 1957), pp. 277–8. • 13. Salisbury Papers, Thomas to Cranborne, 25 September 1939, box 63. • 14. John Colville, *The Fringes of Power: Downing Street Diaries 1939–1955, Vol. I – September 1939–September 1941* (London, 1985), 27 September 1939, p. 28. • 15. Lynne Olson, *Troublesome Young Men: The Rebels Who Brought Churchill to Power and Helped Save England* (New York, 2007), p. 221. • 16. Nicolson (ed.), *Harold Nicolson: Diaries and Letters 1930–1939*, Nicolson to Vita Sackville-West, 14 September 1939, p. 200. • 17. Salisbury Papers, Thomas to Cranborne, 29 October 1939, box 63. • 18. Martin Gilbert and Richard Gott, *The Appeasers* (London, 1963), p. 342. • 19. Robert Self (ed.), *The Neville Chamberlain Diary Letters, Vol. IV: The Downing Street Years 1934–1940* (Aldershot, 2005), NC to Ida, 8 October 1939, p. 456. • 20. Ibid., NC to Ida, 23 September 1939, p. 451. • 21. Salisbury to Halifax, 22 September 1939, FO 800/317/30–34. • 22. Nigel Nicolson (ed.), *Harold Nicolson: Diaries and Letters 1939–1945* (London, 1967), 20 September 1939, p. 35. • 23. Emrys-Evans Papers, Law to Emrys-Evans, 13 September 1939, MS 58239. • 24. Avon Papers, Violet Bonham Carter to Eden, 13 September 1939, AP 20/7/67. • 25. Nicolson (ed.), *Harold Nicolson: Diaries and Letters 1939–1945*, 26 September 1939, p. 37. • 26. Ibid. • 27. Salisbury Papers, Thomas to Cranborne, 28 September 1939, box 63. • 28. Hansard, HC Deb, 12 October 1939, vol. 352, cols 563–5; Self (ed.), *The Neville Chamberlain Diary Letters*, NC to Ida, 8 October 1939, p. 454. • 29. Self (ed.), *The Neville Chamberlain Diary Letters*, NC to Hilda, 15 October 1939, p. 458. • 30. Ibid., NC to Ida, 5 November 1939, p. 467. • 31. Hansard, HC Deb, 12 October 1939, vol. 352, col. 568. • 32. Self (ed.), *The Neville Chamberlain Diary Letters*, NC to Ida, 8 October 1939, p. 454. • 33. Hankey to Halifax, 12 September 1939, FO 800/317/7–14. • 34. PREM 1/443. • 35. Duff Cooper, *Old Men Forget: The Autobiography of Duff Cooper, Viscount Norwich* (London, 1953), p. 267. • 36. Waterhouse Papers, Diary, 4 October 1939, 6 September 1939. • 37. Buccleuch Papers, Stuart to Buccleuch, 4 October 1939. • 38. Simon Papers, Diary, 13 October 1939, MS Simon 11. • 39. Halifax to Lytton, 11 November 1939, FO 800/317/196–7. • 40. Colville, *The Fringes of Power*, 29 October 1939, p. 45. • 41. Buccleuch Papers, Chamberlain to Buccleuch, 12 February 1940. • 42. Quoted in Gilbert and Gott, *The Appeasers*, p. 344. • 43. David Dilks (ed.), *The Diaries of Sir Alexander Cadogan, OM, 1938–1945* (London, 1971), 23 September 1939, p. 219. • 44. Lord Gladwyn, *The Memoirs of Lord Gladwyn* (London, 1972), p. 96. • 45. Self (ed.), *The Neville Chamberlain Diary Letters*, NC to Ida, 22 October 1939, p. 460. • 46. Ibid., NC to Ida, 5 November 1939, p. 467. • 47. Ibid., NC to Ida, 3 December 1939, p. 475.

XXIV: The Fall of Chamberlain

1. Waterhouse Papers, Diary, 1 May 1940. • 2. Gabriel Gorodetsky (ed.), *The Maisky Diaries: Red Ambassador to the Court of St James's 1932–1943* (New Haven, 2015), 1 December 1939, p. 243. • 3. Quoted in Max Hastings, *All Hell Let Loose: The World at War 1939–1945* (London, 2011), p. 35. • 4. War Cabinet Minutes, 16 December 1939, CAB 65/2/51. • 5. Roderick Macleod and Denis Kelly (eds), *The Ironside Diaries 1937–1940* (London, 1962), p. 176; War Cabinet Minutes, 22 December 1939, CAB 65/2/165. • 6. Air Chief Marshal Cyril Newall, quoted in Nicholas Shakespeare, *Six Minutes in May: How Churchill Unexpectedly Became Prime Minister* (London, 2017), p. 56. • 7. Chamberlain Papers, 'JIC Intelligence Briefings in Lead Up to Invasion of Norway', NC 8/35/64. • 8. Martin Gilbert, *Winston S. Churchill, Vol. VI: 1939–1941* (London, 1983), p. 197; Paul Reynaud, *In the Thick of the Fight 1930–1945* (London, 1955), p. 270. • 9. Reported in *The Times*, 5 April 1940. • 10. Macleod and Kelly (eds), *The Ironside Diaries*, 9 April 1940, p. 249. • 11. John Colville, *The Fringes of Power: Downing Street Diaries 1939–1955, Vol. I – September 1939–September 1941* (London, 1985), 9 April 1940, p. 100. • 12. For the most vivid account, see Shakespeare, *Six Minutes in May*. • 13. Colville, *The Fringes of Power*, 3 May 1940, p. 116. • 14. Leland Stowe, *No Other Road to Freedom* (London, 1942), p. 110. • 15. Kenneth Young (ed.), *The Diaries of Sir Robert Bruce Lockhart, Vol. II: 1939–1965* (London, 1980), 2 May 1940, p. 52. • 16. Nigel Nicolson (ed.), *Harold Nicolson: Diaries and Letters 1939–1945* (London, 1967), 30 April 1940, p. 74. • 17. Colville, *The Fringes of Power*, 12 April 1940, p. 102. • 18. Ben Pimlott (ed.), *The Political Diary*

of Hugh Dalton 1918–40, 1945–60 (London, 1986), 1 May 1940, p. 332. • 19. Waterhouse Papers, Diary, 1 & 2 May 1940. • 20. Ibid. • 21. Emanuel Shinwell, *I've Lived through It All* (London, 1973), p. 157. • 22. Young (ed.), *The Diaries of Sir Robert Bruce Lockhart*, 3 May 1940, p. 53. • 23. Robert Rhodes James (ed.), *'Chips': The Diaries of Sir Henry Channon* (London, 1967), 2 & 3 May 1940, p. 244. • 24. Nigel Nicolson (ed.), *The Harold Nicolson Diaries 1907–1963* (London, 2004), 7 May 1940, p. 215. • 25. Hansard, HC Deb, 7 May 1940, vol. 360, cols 1073–86. • 26. Sir Dingle Foot, *British Political Crises* (London, 1976), p. 178. • 27. Colville, *The Fringes of Power*, 7 May 1940, p. 92. • 28. Hansard, HC Deb, 7 May 1940, vol. 360, cols 1125–30. • 29. Ibid., cols 1140–50. • 30. L. S. Amery, *My Political Life, Vol. III: The Unforgiving Years 1929–1940* (London, 1955), p. 365. • 31. Hansard, HC Deb, 7 May 1940, vol. 360, col. 1150. • 32. Lord Home, *The Way the Wind Blows: An Autobiography* (London, 1976), p. 74. • 33. Pimlott (ed.), *The Political Diary of Hugh Dalton*, 8 May 1940, p. 341. • 34. Hansard, HC Deb, 8 May 1940, vol. 360, col. 1266. • 35. Mark Pottle (ed.), *Champion Redoubtable: The Diaries and Letters of Violet Bonham Carter 1914–1945* (London, 1998), 2–14 May 1940, p. 210. • 36. Hansard, HC Deb, 8 May 1940, vol. 360, col. 1283. • 37. Colville, *The Fringes of Power*, 8 May 1940, p. 119. • 38. James (ed.), *'Chips'*, 8 May 1940, p. 245. • 39. Hansard, HC Deb, 8 May 1940, vol. 360, col. 1283. • 40. John Barnes and David Nicholson (eds), *The Leo Amery Diaries, Vol. II: The Empire at Bay 1929–1945* (London, 1988), 8 May 1940, p. 610. • 41. Shakespeare, *Six Minutes in May*, p. 297. • 42. Pimlott (ed.), *The Political Diary of Hugh Dalton*, 9 May 1940, p. 343. • 43. Ibid., 8 May 1940, p. 342. • 44. James (ed.), *'Chips'*, 8 May 1940, pp. 246–7. • 45. Major-General Sir Edward Spears, *Assignment to Catastrophe, Vol. I: Prelude to Dunkirk July 1939–May 1940*, p. 129. • 46. Pottle (ed.), *Champion Redoubtable*, 2–14 May 1940, p. 211. • 47. Waterhouse Papers, Diary, 11 May 1940. • 48. Spears, *Assignment to Catastrophe*, p. 130. • 49. Victor Cazalet Papers, Cazalet to Tweedsmuir, 9 May 1939. • 50. James (ed.), *'Chips'*, 10 May 1940, p. 250. • 51. Colville, *The Fringes of Power*, 10 May 1940, p. 122.

XXV: Appeasement's Last Stand

1. Hansard, HC Deb, 4 June 1940, vol. 361, col. 796. • 2. Annexe to War Cabinet Minutes, Halifax to Sir Percy Loraine, 25 May 1940, CAB 65/13/159. • 3. War Cabinet Minutes, 26 May 1940, CAB 65/13/20/138–45; John Lukacs, *Five Days in London: May 1940* (New Haven, 1999), p. 113. • 4. Chamberlain Papers, Diary, 26 May 1940, NC 2/24 A. • 5. Professor John Lukacs has argued persuasively that the days 24–28 May 1940 were the real 'hinge of fate' of the Second World War. See Lukacs, *Five Days in London*. • 6. War Cabinet Minutes, 4.30 p.m., 27 May 1940, CAB 65/13/23/175–81. • 7. Hickleton Papers, Halifax Diary, 27 May 1940, A7/8/4. • 8. War Cabinet Minutes, 4 p.m., 28 May 1940, CAB 65/13/24/184–90. • 9. John Barnes and David Nicholson (eds), *The Leo Amery Diaries, Vol. II: The Empire at Bay 1929–1945* (London, 1988), 28 May 1940, p. 619. • 10. Hugh Dalton, *The Fateful Years: Memoirs 1931–1945* (London, 1957), pp. 335–6. • 11. The quotation in Hugh Dalton's original diary entry reads: '… and if at last the long story is to end, it were better it should end, not through surrender, but only when we are rolling senseless on the ground.' Later, however, he corrected it to those words as quoted in the main text. (Ben Pilmott (ed.), *The Second World War Diary of Hugh Dalton 1940–45* (London, 1986), 28 May 1940, p. 28; Dalton, *The Fateful Years*, pp. 335–6.) • 12. War Cabinet Minutes, 7 p.m., 28 May 1940, CAB 65/13/24/189. • 13. Lukacs, *Five Days in London*, p. 191. • 14. Martin Gilbert (ed.), *The Churchill War Papers, Vol. II: Never Surrender, May 1940–December 1940* (London, 1994), Churchill to Desmond Morton, 1 June 1940, p. 221. • 15. Ibid., Churchill Note, 1 June 1940, p. 221. • 16. Hansard, HC Deb, 4 June 1940, vol. 361, cols 795–6.

Epilogue

1. Emrys-Evans Papers, Law to Emrys-Evans, 13 September 1939, MS 58239. • 2. Quoted in Keith Feiling, *The Life of Neville Chamberlain* (London, 1946), p. 464. • 3. Kenneth Young

(ed.), *The Diaries of Sir Robert Bruce Lockhart, Vol. II: 1939–1965* (London, 1980), p. 42. • 4. Michael Foot, Preface, in 'Cato', *Guilty Men* (London, [1940] 1998), p. v. • 5. Robert Boothby, *I Fight to Live* (London, 1947), p. 9. • 6. Winston S. Churchill, *The Second World War, Vol. I: The Gathering Storm* (London, 1948), p. viii; L. B. Namier, *Diplomatic Prelude 1938–1939* (London, 1948), p. ix. • 7. Quoted in D. C. Watt, *Personalities and Policies: Studies in the Formulation of British Foreign Policy in the Twentieth Century* (London, 1965), p. 105. • 8. Richard Overy, 'German Air Strength 1933 to 1939: A Note', *Historical Journal*, vol. 27, no. 2 (1984), pp. 465–71, at pp. 468–70. • 9. Quoted in Niall Ferguson, *The War of the World: History's Age of Hatred* (London, 2006), p. 336 and David Dutton, *Neville Chamberlain* (London, 2001), p. 50. • 10. BBC radio broadcast, 27 September 1938. • 11. Ian Kershaw, *Hitler, 1936–1945: Nemesis* (London, 2000), p. xxxv. • 12. Quoted in Peter Neville, *Appeasing Hitler: The Diplomacy of Sir Nevile Henderson 1937–1939* (Basingstoke, 2000), p. 60. • 13. Robert Self (ed.), *The Neville Chamberlain Diary Letters, Vol. IV: The Downing Street Years 1934–1940* (Aldershot, 2005), NC to Hilda, 30 January 1938, p. 300. • 14. Chamberlain Papers, NC to Hilda, NC/18/1/1057. • 15. Watchman, *What of the Night?* (London, 1940), p. 99. • 16. Robert Self, *Neville Chamberlain: A Political Life* (Aldershot, 2006), p. 4. • 17. Margesson Papers, Duff Cooper, 'Chamberlain: A Candid Portrait', MRGB 1/5. • 18. Quoted in Feiling, *The Life of Neville Chamberlain*, p. 465. • 19. John Colville, *The Fringes of Power: Downing Street Diaries 1939–1955, Vol. I – September 1939–September 1941* (London, 1985), 15 February 1940, p. 83. • 20. Quoted in Martin Gilbert, 'Horace Wilson: Man of Munich?', *History Today*, October 1982, p. 6.

Sources and Bibliography

Archives

Vyvyan Adams Papers, London School of Economics and Political Science
Leopold Amery Papers, Churchill College, Cambridge
Frank Ashton-Gwatkin Papers, National Archives
Lady Astor Papers, Reading University
Earl of Avon Papers, Birmingham University Library
Stanley Baldwin Papers, Cambridge University Library
Harold Balfour Papers, Churchill College, Cambridge
Sir Joseph Ball Papers, Bodleian Library, Oxford
BBC Papers, BBC Written Archives, Caversham
Rear Admiral Tufton Beamish Papers, Churchill College, Cambridge
Commander Robert Bower Papers, Churchill College, Cambridge
Brendan Bracken Papers, Churchill College, Cambridge
Arthur Bryant Papers, Liddell Hart Military Archives, Kings College London
Duke of Buccleuch and Queensberry Papers, private collection
Patrick Buchan-Hepburn Papers, Churchill College, Cambridge
R. A. Butler Papers, Trinity College, Cambridge
Cabinet Papers, National Archives
Sir Alexander Cadogan Papers, Churchill College, Cambridge
Lord Caldecote Papers, Churchill College, Cambridge
Thelma Cazalet Papers, Eton College
Victor Cazalet Papers, Eton College
Neville Chamberlain Papers, Birmingham University Library
Lady Diana Cooper Papers, Churchill College, Cambridge
Duff Cooper Papers, Churchill College, Cambridge
Lord Crathorne Papers, private collection
Harry Crookshank Papers, Bodleian Library, Oxford
Geoffrey Dawson Papers, Bodleian Library, Oxford
Alec Douglas-Home Papers, private collection
Admiral Sir Reginald Drax Papers, Churchill College, Cambridge
Henry Drummond Wolff Papers, Leeds University Library
Paul Emrys-Evans Papers, British Library
His Majesty's Government Papers, National Archives
General Sir Ian Hamilton Papers, Liddell Hart Military Archives, Kings College London
Sir Maurice Hankey Papers – Churchill College Cambridge
Hickleton Papers, Borthwick Institute, University of York
Leslie Hore-Belisha Papers, Churchill College, Cambridge

Sir Roger Keyes Papers, Churchill College, Cambridge
Basil Liddell Hart Papers, Liddell Hart Archives, Kings College London
Lord Lloyd Papers, Churchill College, Cambridge
Marquess of Lothian Papers, Scottish Records Office
Ramsay MacDonald Papers, National Archives
David Margesson Papers, Churchill College, Cambridge
Lady Alexandra Metcalfe Papers, private collection
Lord Mount Temple Papers, Hartley Library, Southampton University
Harold Nicolson Papers, Balliol College, Oxford
Philip Noel-Baker Papers, Churchill College, Cambridge
Sir Henry Page Croft Papers, Churchill College, Cambridge
Sir Eric Phipps Papers, Churchill College, Cambridge
Sir John Reith Papers, BBC Archives, Caversham
Royal Archives, Windsor Castle
Lord Runciman Papers, National Archives
Marquess of Salisbury Papers, private collection
Duncan Sandys Papers, Churchill College, Cambridge
Sir Orme Sargent Papers, National Archives
Sir John Simon Papers, Bodleian Library, Oxford
Sir Archibald Sinclair Papers, Churchill College, Cambridge
Edward Spears Papers, Churchill College, Cambridge
William Strang Papers, Churchill College, Cambridge
Lord Swinton Papers, Churchill College, Cambridge
Lord Templewood Papers, Cambridge University Library
Sir Robert Vansittart Papers, Churchill College, Cambridge
Charles Waterhouse Papers, private collection
Sir Horace Wilson Papers, National Archives
Marquess of Zetland Papers, British Library

Newspapers, magazines and journals

Contemporary Review
Daily Express
Daily Herald
Daily Mail
Daily Telegraph
English Review
Evening Standard
Fortnightly Review
Leeds Mercury
Manchester Guardian
Morning Post
New Statesman
News Chronicle
Nineteenth Century and After
Nottingham Evening Post
Observer
Reynold's News
Scotsman
Spectator
Sunday Times
The Times
Yorkshire Post

Official document collections

Documents diplomatiques français 1932–1939, Series I and II
Documents on British Foreign Policy 1919–1939, Second and Third Series (London, 1946–84)
Documents on German Foreign Policy 1918–1945, Series C and Series D (London, 1949–66)
Foreign Relations of the United States: Diplomatic Papers, 1938 and 1939 (Washington, 1954–7)
Parliamentary Debates, House of Commons, Official Report, Fifth Series
Parliamentary Debates, House of Lords, Official Report, Fifth Series
Peace and War: United States Foreign Policy 1931–1941 (Washington, 1943)

Published primary sources

Allen of Hurtwood, Lord, *Britain's Political Future: A Plea for Liberty and Leadership* (London, 1934)
Amery, L. S., *My Political Life, Vol. III: The Unforgiving Years 1929–40* (London, 1955)
Annan, Noel, *Our Age: Portrait of a Generation* (London, 1990)
Ashton-Gwatkin, F. T. A., *The British Foreign Service* (Syracuse, NY, 1950)
Atholl, Duchess of, *Working Partnership: Being the Lives of John George, 8th Duke of Atholl, and His Wife Katharine Marjory Ramsay* (London, 1958)
Attlee, Clement, *As It Happened* (London, 1954)
Avon, Earl of, *Facing the Dictators* (London, 1962); *The Memoirs of the Rt Hon. Sir Anthony Eden, KG, PC, MC, Vol. III: The Reckoning* (London, 1965)
Balfour, Harold, *Wings over Westminster* (London, 1973)
Ball, Stuart (ed.), *Parliament and Politics in the Age of Baldwin and MacDonald: The Headlam Diaries 1923–1935* (London, 1992); *Parliament and Politics in the Age of Churchill and Attlee: The Headlam Diaries 1935–1951* (Cambridge, 1999)
Barnes, John and David Nicholson (eds), *The Leo Amery Diaries, Vol. II: The Empire at Bay 1929–1945* (London, 1988)
Bartlett, Vernon, *Nazi Germany Explained* (London, 1933); *This is My Life* (London, 1937); *And Now, Tomorrow* (London, 1960); *I Know What I Liked* (London, 1974)
Baxter, Beverley, *Men, Martyrs and Mountebanks: Beverley Baxter's Inner Story of Personalities and Events behind the War* (London, 1940)
Baynes, Norman H. (ed.), *The Speeches of Adolf Hitler, April 1922–August 1939* (Oxford, 1942)
Bedford, John, Duke of, *A Silver-Plated Spoon* (London, 1959)
Bernays, Robert, *Naked Fakir* (London, 1931); *Special Correspondent* (London, 1934)
Bond, Brian (ed.), *Chief of Staff: The Diaries of Lieutenant-General Sir Henry Pownall, Vol. I – 1933–1940* (London, 1972)
Boothby, Lord, *My Yesterday, Your Tomorrow* (London, 1962)
Boothby, Robert, *I Fight to Live* (London, 1947); *Boothby: Recollections of a Rebel* (London, 1978)
Brooks, Collin, *Can Chamberlain Save Britain? The Lesson of Munich* (London, 1938)
Brown Book of the Hitler Terror and the Burning of the Reichstag (London, 1933)
Brown, W. J., *So Far …* (London, 1943)
Bruce Lockhart, R. H., *Guns or Butter: War Countries and Peace Countries of Europe Revisited* (London, 1938); *Comes the Reckoning* (London, 1947); *Jan Masaryk: A Personal Memoir* (London, 1951); *Your England* (London, 1955)
Bruce Lockhart, Sir Robert, *Friends, Foes and Foreigners* (London, 1957); *Giants Cast Long Shadows* (London, 1960)
Bryant, Arthur, *The Man and the Hour: Studies of Six Great Men of Our Time* (London, 1934)
Burckhardt, Carl Jacob, *Meine Danziger Mission 1937–1939* (Munich, 1960)
Butler, Lord, *The Art of the Possible: The Memoirs of Lord Butler, KG, CH* (London, 1971)
'Cato', *Guilty Men* (London, 1940)
Cazalet-Keir, Thelma, *From the Wings* (London, 1967)
Chair, Somerset de, *Die? I Thought I'd Laugh* (Braunton, Devon, 1993)

Churchill, Randolph S., *Twenty-One Years* (London, 1964)
Churchill, Winston S., *Great Contemporaries* (London, 1937); *The Second World War, Vol. I: The Gathering Storm* (London, 1948); *The Second World War, Vol. II: Their Finest Hour* (London, 1949); *Great Contemporaries* (London, 1937)
Ciano, Galeazzo, *Diary 1937–1943: The Complete, Unabridged Diaries of Count Galeazzo Ciano* (London, 2002)
Citrine, Lord, *Men and Work: An Autobiography* (London, 1964); *Two Careers* (London, 1967)
Clark, Kenneth, *Another Part of the Wood: A Self-Portrait* (London, 1974)
Cockburn, Claud, *In Time of Trouble: An Autobiography* (London, 1956); *I, Claud* (Harmondsworth, 1967)
Colville, John, *The Fringes of Power: Downing Street Diaries 1939–1955, Vol. I – September 1939–September 1941* (London, 1985)
Colvin, Ian, *None So Blind: A British Diplomatic View of the Origins of World War II* (New York, 1965); *The Chamberlain Cabinet* (London, 1971)
Cooper, Diana, *The Light of Common Day* (London, 1959)
Cooper, Duff, *Old Men Forget: The Autobiography of Duff Cooper, Viscount Norwich* (London, 1953)
Coote, Colin, *Editorial: The Memoirs of Colin R. Coote* (London, 1965)
Cowles, Virginia, *Looking for Trouble* (London, 1941)
Cox, Geoffrey, *Countdown to War: A Personal Memoir of Europe 1938–1940* (London, 1988)
Cross, Colin (ed.), *Life with Lloyd George: The Diary of A. J. Sylvester 1931–1945* (London, 1975)
Crowson, N. J. (ed.), *Fleet Street, Press Barons and Politics: The Journals of Collin Brooks 1932–1940* (Cambridge, 1998)
Dahlerus, Birger, *The Last Attempt* (London, 1948)
Dalton, Hugh, *The Fateful Years: Memoirs 1931–1945* (London, 1957)
Dietrich, Otto, *The Hitler I Knew: Memoirs of the Third Reich's Press Chief* (London, 1957)
Dilks, David (ed.), *The Diaries of Sir Alexander Cadogan, OM, 1938–45* (London, 1971)
Dodd, William E. and Martha Dodd, *Ambassador Dodd's Diary 1933–1938* (London, 1941)
Donner, Patrick, *Crusade: A Life against the Calamitous Twentieth Century* (London, 1984)
Eberle, Henrik and Matthias Uhl (eds), *The Hitler Book: The Secret Dossier Prepared for Stalin* (London, 2005)
François-Poncet, André, *The Fateful Years: Memoirs of a French Ambassador in Berlin 1931–1938* (London, 1949)
Fry, Michael, *Hitler's Wonderland* (London, 1934)
Fuller, J. F. C., *The Reformation of War* (London, 1923)
Gafencu, Grigore, *The Last Days of Europe: A Diplomatic Journey in 1939* (London, 1947)
Gedye, G. E. R., *Fallen Bastions: The Central European Tragedy* (London, 1939)
Germains, Victor Wallace, *The Tragedy of Winston Churchill* (London, 1931)
Gilbert, Martin, *Plough My Own Furrow: The Story of Lord Allen of Hurtwood as Told through His Writings and Correspondence* (London, 1965); *Winston S. Churchill, Vol. V, Companion, Part 2: The Wilderness Years 1929–1935* (London, 1981); *Winston S. Churchill, Vol. V, Companion, Part 3: The Coming of War 1936–1939* (London, 1982)
Gladwyn, Lord, *The Memoirs of Lord Gladwyn* (London, 1972)
Gorodetsky, Gabriel (ed.), *The Maisky Diaries: Red Ambassador to the Court of St James's 1932–1943* (New Haven, 2015)
Grant Duff, Shiela, *Europe and the Czechs* (Harmondsworth, 1938); *The Parting of Ways: A Personal Account of the Thirties* (London, 1982)
Graves, Robert, *Goodbye to All That*, rev. ed. (Harmondsworth, 1960)
Grigg, Sir Edward, *Britain Looks at Germany* (London, 1938)
Grimond, Jo, *Memoirs* (London, 1979)
Gunther, John, *Inside Europe*, rev. ed. (New York and London, 1938)
Hadley, W. W., *Munich Before and After* (London, 1944)

Hailsham, Lord, *A Sparrow's Flight: The Memoirs of Lord Hailsham of St Marylebone* (London, 1990)
Halifax, Lord, *Fullness of Days* (London, 1957)
Harvey, John (ed.), *The Diplomatic Diaries of Oliver Harvey 1937–1940* (London, 1970)
Harvie-Watt, G. S., *Most of My Life* (London, 1980)
Hassell, Ulrich von, *The Ulrich von Hassell Diaries 1938–1944* (London, 1948)
Healey, Denis, *The Time of My Life* (London, 1989)
Heath, Edward, *The Course of My Life* (London, 1998)
Henderson, Nevile, *Failure of a Mission: Berlin 1937–1939* (London, 1940); *Water under the Bridges* (London, 1945)
Hesse, Fritz, *Hitler and the English* (London, 1954)
Hill, Leonidas E. (ed.), *Die Weizsäcker-Papiere 1933–1950* (Frankfurt-am-Main, 1974)
Hitler, Adolf, *Mein Kampf* (New York, 1939)
Hogg, Quintin, *The Left was Never Right* (London, 1945)
Home, Lord, *The Way the Wind Blows: An Autobiography* (London, 1976); *Letters to a Grandson* (London, 1983)
James, Robert Rhodes (ed.), *'Chips': The Diaries of Sir Henry Channon* (London, 1967); *Memoirs of a Conservative: J. C. C. Davidson's Memoirs and Papers 1910–1937* (London, 1969); *Winston S. Churchill: His Complete Speeches, Vol. V 1928–1935* (New York, 1974); *Winston S. Churchill: His Complete Speeches, Vol. VI 1935–1942* (New York, 1974)
Jay, Douglas, *Change and Fortune: A Political Record* (London, 1980)
Jędrzejewicz, Wacław (ed.), *Diplomat in Berlin 1933–1939: Papers and Memoirs of Józef Lipski, Ambassador of Poland* (New York and London, 1968)
Johnson, Gaynor (ed.), *Our Man in Berlin: The Diary of Sir Eric Phipps 1933–1937* (Basingstoke, 2007)
Jones, F. Elwyn, *Hitler's Drive to the East* (London, 1937)
Jones, Thomas C. H., *A Diary with Letters 1931–1950* (London, 1954)
Jovanovich, William (ed.), *The Wartime Journals of Charles A. Lindbergh* (New York, 1970)
Kennedy, A. L., *Britain Faces Germany* (London, 1937)
Kennedy, John F., *Why England Slept* (London, 1940)
Keynes, John Maynard, *The Economic Consequences of the Peace* (London, 1919)
King, Cecil H., *Strictly Personal: Some Memoirs of Cecil H. King* (London, 1969); *With Malice toward None: A War Diary* (London, 1970)
Kirkpatrick, Helen, *This Terrible Peace* (London, 1939); *Under the British Umbrella: What the English Are and How They Go to War* (New York, 1939)
Kirkpatrick, Sir Ivone, *The Inner Circle: Memoirs* (London, 1959)
Kordt, Erich, *Wahn und Wirklichkeit* (Stuttgart, 1947); *Nicht aus den Akten* (Stuttgart, 1950)
Liddell Hart, B. H., *The Memoirs of Captain Liddell Hart, Vols I & II* (London, 1965)
Lloyd George, David, *War Memoirs, Vol. I* (London, 1938)
Londonderry, Marquess of, *Ourselves and Germany* (London, 1938)
Low, David, *Low's Autobiography* (London, 1956)
Macleod, Roderick and Denis Kelly (eds), *The Ironside Diaries 1937–1940* (London, 1962)
Macmillan, Harold, *Winds of Change 1914–1939* (London, 1966); *The Past Masters: Politics and Politicians 1906–1939* (London, 1975)
Macnamara, J. R. J., *The Whistle Blows* (London, 1938)
Martel, Gordon (ed.), *The Times and Appeasement: The Journals of A. L. Kennedy 1932–1939* (Cambridge, 2000)
Maugham, Viscount, *The Truth about the Munich Crisis* (London, 1944); *At the End of the Day* (London, 1954)
Minney, R. J., *The Private Papers of Hore-Belisha* (London, 1960)
Mitford, Jessica, *Hons and Rebels* (London, 1960)
Mosley, Charlotte (ed.), *Love from Nancy: The Letters of Nancy Mitford* (London, 1993)
Muggeridge, Malcolm, *The Thirties: 1930–1940 in Great Britain* (London, 1940)

Muggeridge, Malcolm (ed.), *Ciano's Diplomatic Papers* (London, 1948); *Ciano's Diary 1937–1938* (London, 1952)
Namier, L. B., *In the Margin of History* (London, 1939)
Nicolson, Harold, *Peacemaking 1919* (London, 1933); *Why Britain is at War* (Harmondsworth, 1939)
Nicolson, Nigel (ed.), *Harold Nicolson Diaries and Letters 1930–1939* (London, 1966); *Harold Nicolson Diaries and Letters 1939–1945* (London, 1967); *The Harold Nicolson Diaries 1907–1963* (London, 2004)
Noakes, Jeremy and Geoffrey Pridham (eds), *Documents on Nazism 1919–1945* (London, 1974)
Norwich, John Julius (ed.) *The Duff Cooper Diaries 1915–1951* (London, 2005)
Paul-Boncour, Joseph, *Entre deux guerres: souvenirs sur la IIIe République* (Paris, 1946)
Pertinax, *The Gravediggers of France: Gamelin, Daladier, Reynaud, Pétain, and Laval* (Garden City, NY, 1944)
Pimlott, Ben (ed.), *The Political Diary of Hugh Dalton 1918–40, 1945–60* (London, 1986); *The Second World War Diary of Hugh Dalton 1940–45* (London, 1986)
Pottle, Mark, *Champion Redoubtable: The Diaries and Letters of Violet Bonham Carter 1914–1945* (London, 1998)
Price, George Ward, *I Know These Dictators* (London, 1937); *Extra-Special Correspondent* (London, 1957)
'Public Opinion Survey 1: British Institute of Public Opinion', *Public Opinion Quarterly*, vol. 4, no. 1 (1940)
Raczynski, Count Edward, *In Allied London* (London, 1962)
Ravensdale, Baroness, *In Many Rhythms: An Autobiography* (London, 1953)
Reed, Douglas, *Insanity Fair* (London, 1938); *Disgrace Abounding* (London, 1939); *A Prophet at Home* (London, 1941)
Reith, J. C. W., *Into the Wind* (London, 1949)
Reynaud, Paul, *In the Thick of the Fight 1930–1945* (London, 1955)
Reynolds, Rothay, *When Freedom Shrieked* (London, 1939)
Ribbentrop, Joachim von, *The Ribbentrop Memoirs* (London, 1954)
Roberts, Stephen H., *The House That Hitler Built* (London, 1937)
Rose, Norman (ed.), *Baffy: The Diaries of Blanche Dugdale 1936–1947* (London, 1973)
Rothermere, Viscount, *My Fight to Rearm Britain* (London, 1939); *Warnings and Predictions* (London, 1939)
Rowse, A. L., *All Souls and Appeasement: A Contribution to Contemporary History* (London, 1961); *A Man of the Thirties* (London, 1979)
Salter, Arthur, *Slave of the Lamp: A Public Servant's Notebook* (London, 1967)
Salter, Lord, *Memoirs of a Public Servant* (London, 1961)
Schmidt, Paul, *Hitler's Interpreter* (London, 1951)
Selected Speeches of His Imperial Majesty Haile Selassie First, 1918 to 1967 (Addis Ababa, 1967)
Self, Robert (ed.), *The Austen Chamberlain Diary Letters* (Cambridge, 1995); *The Neville Chamberlain Diary Letters, Vol. I: The Making of a Politician 1915–1920* (Aldershot, 2000); *The Neville Chamberlain Diary Letters, Vol. II: The Reform Years 1921–1927* (Aldershot, 2000); *The Neville Chamberlain Diary Letters, Vol. III: The Heir Apparent 1928–1933* (Aldershot, 2002); *The Neville Chamberlain Diary Letters, Vol. IV: The Downing Street Years 1934–1940* (Aldershot, 2005)
Shinwell, Emanuel, *I've Lived through It All* (London, 1973)
Shirer, William L., *Berlin Diary: The Journal of a Foreign Correspondent 1934–1941* (London, 1941)
Simon, Viscount, *Retrospect: The Memoirs of the Rt Hon. Viscount Simon* (London, 1952)
Smart, Nick (ed.), *The Diaries and Letters of Robert Bernays 1932–1939: An Insider's Account of the House of Commons* (Lewiston, NY, 1996)
Smith, Amanda (ed.), *Hostage to Fortune: The Letters of Joseph P. Kennedy* (New York, 2001)
Smith, Howard K., *Last Train from Berlin* (London, 1942)

Spears, Major-General Sir Edward, *Assignment to Catastrophe, Vol. I: Prelude to Dunkirk July 1939–May 1940* (London, 1954)
Spier, Eugen, *Focus: A Footnote to the History of the Thirties* (London, 1963)
Spitzy, Reinhard, *How We Squandered the Reich* (Wilby, Norfolk, 1997)
Steed, Henry Wickham, *The Press* (Harmondsworth, 1938)
Stowe, Leland, *No Other Road to Freedom* (London, 1942)
Strang, Lord, *Home and Abroad* (London, 1956)
Stuart, Charles (ed.), *The Reith Diaries* (London, 1975)
Stuart, James, *Within the Fringe: An Autobiography* (London, 1967)
Swinton, Earl of, *Sixty Years of Power: Some Memories of the Men Who Wielded It* (London, 1966)
Swinton, Viscount, *I Remember* (London, 1948)
Sylvester, A. J., *The Real Lloyd George* (London, 1947)
Taylor, A. J. P. (ed.), *Lloyd George: A Diary by Frances Stevenson* (London, 1971)
Templewood, Viscount, *Nine Troubled Years* (London, 1954)
Tennant, Ernest W. D., *True Account* (London, 1957)
Toynbee, Arnold J., *Acquaintances* (London, 1967)
Tree, Ronald, *When the Moon Was High: Memoirs of Peace and War 1897–1942* (London, 1975)
Urquhart, Brian, *A Life in Peace and War* (London, 1987)
Vansittart, Robert, *The Mist Procession: The Autobiography of Lord Vansittart* (London, 1958)
Watchman, *Right Honourable Gentlemen* (London, 1939); *What of the Night?* (London, 1940)
Wedgwood, Josiah C., *Memoirs of a Fighting Life* (London, 1940)
Weizsäcker, Ernst von, *Memoirs of Ernst von Weizsäcker* (London, 1951)
Welles, Sumner, *The Time for Decision* (New York and London, 1944); *Seven Major Decisions* (London, 1951)
Wells, H. G., *The Shape of Things to Come* (London, 1933)
Werth, Alexander, *France and Munich: Before and After the Surrender* (London 1939)
Westminster, Loelia, Duchess of, *Grace and Favour: The Memoirs of Loelia, Duchess of Westminster* (London, 1961)
Wheeler-Bennett, John W., *Munich: Prologue to Tragedy* (London, 1948); *Knaves, Fools and Heroes* (London, 1974)
Williams, Francis, *Press, Parliament and People* (London, 1946)
Williamson, Philip and Edward Baldwin (eds), *Baldwin Papers: A Conservative Statesman 1908–1947* (Cambridge, 2004)
Wilson, Sir Arnold, *Walks and Talks Abroad: The Diary of a Member of Parliament in 1934–6* (London, 1936); *More Thoughts and Talks: The Diary and Scrap-Book of a Member of Parliament from September 1937 to August 1939* (London, 1939)
Winterton, Earl, *Orders of the Day* (London, 1953)
Woolton, Earl of, *The Memoirs of the Rt Hon. the Earl of Woolton* (London, 1959)
Wrench, Evelyn, *I Loved Germany* (London, 1940)
Young, Kenneth (ed.), *The Diaries of Sir Robert Bruce Lockhart, Vol. I: 1915–1938* (London, 1973); *The Diaries of Sir Robert Bruce Lockhart, Vol. II: 1939–1965* (London, 1980)

Secondary sources

Adamthwaite, Anthony, *France and the Coming of the Second World War 1936–1939* (London, 1977)
Aldrich, Richard J. and Rory Cormac, *The Black Door: Spies, Secret Intelligence and British Prime Ministers* (London, 2016)
Alexander, Martin S., *The Republic in Danger: General Maurice Gamelin and the Politics of French Defence 1933–1940* (Cambridge, 1992)
Andrew, Christopher, *Secret Service: The Making of the British Intelligence Community* (London, 1985)

Aster, Sidney, *1939: The Making of the Second World War* (London, 1973)
Aster, Sidney (ed.), *Appeasement and All Souls: A Portrait with Documents 1937–1939* (Cambridge, 2004)
Ball, Simon, *The Guardsmen: Harold Macmillan, Three Friends, and the World They Made* (London, 2004)
Barnes, James J. and Patience P. Barnes, *Hitler's Mein Kampf in Britain and America: A Publishing History 1930–39* (Cambridge, 1980)
Beevor, Antony, *The Second World War* (London, 2012)
Bell, P. M. H., *France and Britain 1900–1940: Entente and Estrangement* (London, 1996)
Benson, Timothy S., *Low and the Dictators* (London, 2008)
Berg, A. Scott, *Lindbergh* (London, 1998)
Bethell, Nicholas, *The War Hitler Won: September 1939* (London, 1972)
Bew, John, *Citizen Clem: A Biography of Attlee* (London, 2016)
Birkenhead, Earl of, *Halifax: The Life of Lord Halifax* (London, 1965)
Blake, Robert, *The Conservative Party: From Peel to Major* (London, 1997)
Blakeway, Denys, *The Last Dance: 1936, The Year of Change* (London, 2010)
Bloch, Michael, *Ribbentrop* (London, 1992)
Bowd, Gavin, *Fascist Scotland: Caledonia and the Far Right* (Edinburgh, 2013)
Boyce, Robert and Esmonde M. Robertson (eds), *Paths to War: New Essays on the Origins of the Second World War* (Basingstoke, 1989)
Boyd, Julia, *Travellers in the Third Reich: The Rise of Fascism through the Eyes of Everyday People* (London, 2017)
Boyle, Andrew, *'Poor, Dear Brendan': The Quest for Brendan Bracken* (London, 1974)
Brendon, Piers, *The Dark Valley: A Panorama of the 1930s* (London, 2000)
Brodrick, Alan Houghton, *Near to Greatness: A Life of the Sixth Earl Winterton* (London, 1965)
Butler, Ewan, *Mason-Mac: The Life of Lieutenant-General Sir Noel Mason-Macfarlane* (London, 1972)
Butler, J. R. M., *History of the Second World War: Grand Strategy, Vol. II September 1939–June 1941* (London, 1957); *Lord Lothian (Philip Kerr) 1882–1940* (London, 1960)
Cannadine, David, *Class in Britain* (New Haven, 1998); *The Decline and Fall of the British Aristocracy* (New Haven and London, 1990)
Cartland, Barbara, *Ronald Cartland* (London, 1942)
Charmley, John, *Chamberlain and the Lost Peace* (London, 1991); *Churchill: The End of Glory* (London, 1993); *A History of Conservative Politics 1900–1996* (Basingstoke, 1996)
Chisholm, Anne and Michael Davie, *Beaverbrook: A Life* (London, 1992)
Clarke, Peter, *Hope and Glory: Britain 1900–1990* (London, 1996)
Cockett, Richard, *Twilight of Truth: Chamberlain, Appeasement and the Manipulation of the Press* (London, 1989)
Conquest, Robert, *The Great Terror: A Reassessment*, 40th anniversary ed. (Oxford, 2008)
Cooke, Alistair (ed.), *Tory Policy-Making: The Conservative Research Department 1929–2009* (London, 2010)
Coote, Colin R., *The Other Club* (London, 1971)
Courcy, Anne de, *The Viceroy's Daughters: The Lives of the Curzon Sisters* (London, 2000)
Cowling, Maurice, *The Impact of Hitler: British Politics and British Policy 1933–1940* (Cambridge, 1975)
Cross, J. A., *Sir Samuel Hoare: A Political Biography* (London, 1977)
Crowson, N. J., *Facing Fascism: The Conservative Party and the European Dictators 1935–40* (London, 1997)
Dallek, Robert, *Franklin D. Roosevelt and American Foreign Policy 1932–1945* (Oxford, 1979)
Davenport-Hines, Richard, *Universal Man: The Seven Lives of John Maynard Keynes* (London, 2015)
Deist, Wilhelm, Manfred Messerschmidt, Hans-Erich Volkmann and Wolfram Wette (eds), *Germany and the Second World War, Vol. I: The Build-up of German Aggression* (Oxford, 1990)

Dinshaw, Minoo, *Outlandish Knight: The Byzantine Life of Steven Runciman* (London, 2016)

Dullin, Sabine, *Men of Influence: Stalin's Diplomats in Europe 1930–1939* (Edinburgh, 2008)

Duroselle, Jean-Baptiste, *France and the Nazi Threat: The Collapse of French Diplomacy 1932–1939* (New York, 2004)

Dutton, David, *Simon: A Political Biography of Sir John Simon* (London, 1992); *Anthony Eden: A Life and Reputation* (London, 1997); *Neville Chamberlain* (London, 2001)

Edgerton, David, *Britain's War Machine: Weapons, Resources, and Experts in the Second World War* (London, 2011)

Egremont, Max, *Under Two Flags: The Life of Major-General Sir Edward Spears* (London, 1997)

Emmerson, James Thomas, *The Rhineland Crisis 7 March 1936: A Study in Multilateral Diplomacy* (London, 1977)

Evans, Richard J., *The Third Reich in Power* (London, 2005)

Faber, David, *Munich: The 1938 Appeasement Crisis* (London, 2008)

Farrell, Nicholas, *Mussolini: A New Life* (London, 2003)

Feiling, Keith, *The Life of Neville Chamberlain* (London, 1946)

Ferguson, Niall, *The War of the World: History's Age of Hatred* (London, 2006)

Fest, Joachim C., *Hitler* (London, 1974)

Foot, Sir Dingle, *British Political Crises* (London, 1976)

Gannon, Franklin Reid, *The British Press and Germany 1936–1939* (Oxford, 1971)

Gibbs, N. H., *History of the Second World War: Grand Strategy, Vol. I – Rearmament Policy* (London, 1976)

Gilbert, Martin, *The Roots of Appeasement* (London, 1966); *Sir Horace Rumbold: Portrait of a Diplomat 1869–1941* (London, 1973); *Winston S. Churchill, Vol. V: 1922–1939* (London, 1976); *Winston Churchill: The Wilderness Years* (London, 1982); *Winston S. Churchill, Vol. VI, 1939–1941* (London, 1983); *Churchill: A Life* (London, 1991)

Gilbert, Martin and Richard Gott, *The Appeasers* (London, 1963)

Gilmour, David, *The Pursuit of Italy: A History of a Land, Its Regions and Their Peoples* (London, 2011)

Glenton, George and William Pattinson, *The Last Chronicle of Bouverie Street* (London, 1963)

Gottlieb, Julie V., *'Guilty Women', Foreign Policy, and Appeasement in Inter-War Britain* (Basingstoke, 2015)

Granzow, Brigitte, *A Mirror of Nazism: British Opinion and the Emergence of Hitler 1929–1933* (London, 1964)

Grayzel, Susan R., *At Home and under Fire: Air Raids and Culture in Britain from the Great War to the Blitz* (Cambridge, 2012)

Greene, Nathanael, *From Versailles to Vichy: The Third French Republic 1919–1940* (New York, 1970)

Griffiths, Richard, *Fellow Travellers of the Right: British Enthusiasts for Nazi Germany 1933–9* (Oxford, 1980)

Harrisson, Tom and Charles Madge, *Britain by Mass-Observation*, 2nd ed. (London, 1986)

Hart-Davis, Duff, *Hitler's Olympics: The 1936 Games* (Sevenoaks, 1988)

Haslam, Jonathan, *The Soviet Union and the Struggle for Collective Security in Europe 1933–39* (Basingstoke, 1984); *The Vices of Integrity: E. H. Carr 1892–1982* (London, 1999)

Hastings, Max, *All Hell Let Loose: The World at War 1939–1945* (London, 2011)

Heimann, Mary, *Czechoslovakia: The State That Failed* (New Haven and London, 2009)

Hermiston, Roger, *All Behind You, Winston: Churchill's Great Coalition 1940–45* (London, 2016)

History of The Times, Vol. IV: The 150th Anniversary and Beyond, 1912–1948 (London, 1952)

Hobsbawm, Eric, *The Age of Extremes: The Short Twentieth Century 1914–1991* (London, 1994)

Horne, Alistair, *Macmillan 1894–1956: Vol. I of the Official Biography* (London, 1988)

Howard, Michael, *The Continental Commitment: The Dilemma of British Defence Policy in the Era of the Two World Wars* (London, 1972)
Howarth, T. E. B., *Cambridge between Two Wars* (London, 1978)
Hucker, Daniel, *Public Opinion and the End of Appeasement in Britain and France* (Farnham, Surrey, 2011)
Jackson, Peter, *France and the Nazi Menace: Intelligence and Policy Making 1933–1939* (Oxford, 2000)
Jago, Michael, *Rab Butler: The Best Prime Minister We Never Had?* (London, 2015)
James, Robert Rhodes, *Churchill: A Study in Failure 1900–1939* (London, 1970); *Victor Cazalet: A Portrait* (London, 1976); *Anthony Eden* (London, 1986); *Bob Boothby: A Portrait* (London, 1991)
Jeffery, Keith, *MI6: The History of the Secret Intelligence Service 1909–1949* (London, 2010)
Jenkins, Roy, *Baldwin* (London, 1987); *The Chancellors* (London, 1998); *Churchill* (London, 2001)
Kaufmann, J. E. and H. W. Kaufmann, *The Forts and Fortifications of Europe 1815–1914: The Central States – Germany, Austria-Hungary and Czechoslovakia* (Barnsley, 2014)
Kemp, Anthony, *The Maginot Line: Myth and Reality* (London, 1981)
Kennedy, Paul, *The Realities behind Diplomacy: Background Influences on British External Policy 1865–1980* (London, 1981)
Kershaw, Ian, *Hitler 1889–1936: Hubris* (London, 1998); *Hitler 1936–1945: Nemesis* (London, 2000); *Making Friends with Hitler: Lord Londonderry and Britain's Road to War* (London, 2004); *To Hell and Back: Europe 1914–1949* (London, 2015)
Klemperer, Klemens von, *German Resistance against Hitler: The Search for Allies Abroad 1938–1945* (Oxford, 1992)
Kocho-Williams, Alastair, *Russian and Soviet Diplomacy 1900–1939* (Basingstoke, 2012)
Kupferman, Fred, *Laval* (Paris, 1987)
Lamb, Richard, *Mussolini and the British* (London, 1997)
Lambert, Angela, *1939: The Last Season of Peace* (London, 1989)
Lee, John, *A Soldier's Life: General Sir Ian Hamilton, 1853–1947* (London, 2000)
Leitz, Christian, *Nazi Foreign Policy 1933–1941: The Road to Global War* (London, 2004)
Lewis, Geoffrey, *Lord Hailsham: A Life* (London, 1997)
Longerich, Peter, *Goebbels: A Biography* (London, 2015)
Lukacs, John, *Five Days in London: May 1940* (New Haven, 1999)
Lukes, Igor, *Czechoslovakia between Stalin and Hitler: The Diplomacy of Edvard Beneš in the 1930s* (New York, 1996)
Lysaght, Charles, *Brendan Bracken* (London, 1979)
MacDonald, C. A., *The United States, Britain and Appeasement 1936–1939* (London, 1981)
Mack Smith, Denis, *Mussolini* (London, 1981)
Macleod, Iain, *Neville Chamberlain* (London, 1961)
MacMillan, Margaret, *Peacemakers: The Paris Peace Conference of 1919 and its Attempt to End War* (London, 2001)
Maier, Klaus A., Horst Rohde, Bernd Stegemann and Hans Umbreit, *Germany and the Second World War, Vol. II: Germany's Initial Conquests in Europe* (Oxford, 1991)
Maiolo, Joseph A., *The Royal Navy and Nazi Germany 1933–39: A Study in Appeasement and the Origins of the Second World War* (Basingstoke, 1998)
Manchester, William, *The Caged Lion: Winston Spencer Churchill 1932–1940* (London, 1988)
Materski, Wojciech and Tomasz Szarota, (eds), *Polska 1939–1945: Straty osobowe i ofiary represji pod dwiema okupacjami* ('Poland 1939–1945: Human Casualties and Victims of Repression under Two Occupations') (Warsaw, 2009)
Meehan, Patricia, *The Unnecessary War: Whitehall and the German Resistance to Hitler* (London, 1992)
Middlemas, Keith and John Barnes, *Baldwin: A Biography* (London, 1969)
Morris, Benny, *The Roots of Appeasement: The British Weekly Press and Nazi Germany during the 1930s* (London, 1991)

Mosley, Leonard, *On Borrowed Time: How World War II Began* (London, 1969)
Mulvey, Paul, *The Political Life of Josiah C. Wedgwood: Land, Liberty and Empire 1872–1943* (Woodbridge, Suffolk, 2010)
Murray, Williamson, *The Change in the European Balance of Power 1938–1939: The Path to Ruin* (Princeton, 1984)
Namier, L. B., *Diplomatic Prelude 1938–1939* (London, 1948)
Neville, Peter, *Appeasing Hitler: The Diplomacy of Sir Nevile Henderson 1937–1939* (Basingstoke, 2000)
Olson, Lynne, *Troublesome Young Men: The Rebels Who Brought Churchill to Power and Helped Save England* (New York, 2007)
Overy, Richard, *1939: Countdown to War* (London, 2009)
Owen, Frank, *Tempestuous Journey: Lloyd George, His Life and Times* (London, 1954)
Parker, R. A. C., *Chamberlain and Appeasement: British Policy and the Coming of the Second World War* (London, 1993); *Churchill and Appeasement* (London, 2000)
Peden, G. C., *British Rearmament and the Treasury 1932–1939* (Edinburgh, 1979)
Phillips, Hugh D., *Between the Revolution and the West: A Political Biography of Maxim M. Litvinov* (Boulder, CO, 1992)
Pimlott, Ben, *Hugh Dalton* (London, 1985)
Preston, Adrian (ed.), *General Staffs and Diplomacy before the Second World War* (London, 1978)
Pugh, Martin, *'Hurrah for the Blackshirts!' Fascists and Fascism in Britain between the Wars* (London, 2005)
Reynolds, David, *The Long Shadow: The Great War and the Twentieth Century* (London, 2013)
Roberts, Andrew, *The Holy Fox: A Biography of Lord Halifax* (London, 1991); *Eminent Churchillians* (London, 1994)
Rose, Kenneth, *The Later Cecils* (London, 1975); *King George V* (1983)
Rose, Norman, *Vansittart: Study of a Diplomat* (London, 1978); *The Cliveden Set: Portrait of an Exclusive Fraternity* (London, 2000); *Harold Nicolson* (London, 2005)
Roskill, S. W., *Hankey: Man of Secrets, Vol. III 1931–1963* (London, 1974)
Rostow, Nicholas, *Anglo-French Relations 1934–1936* (London, 1984)
Schwarz, Ted, *Joseph P. Kennedy: The Mogul, the Mob, the Statesman, and the Making of an American Myth* (Hoboken, NJ, 2003)
Sebag Montefiore, Simon, *Stalin: The Court of the Red Tsar* (London, 2003)
Self, Robert, *Neville Chamberlain: A Political Life* (Aldershot, 2006)
Shakespeare, Nicholas, *Six Minutes in May: How Churchill Unexpectedly Became Prime Minister* (London, 2017)
Shay, Robert Paul, Jr, *British Rearmament in the Thirties: Politics and Profits* (Princeton, 1977)
Shepherd, Robert, *A Class Divided: Appeasement and the Road to Munich 1938* (London, 1988)
Shirer, William, *The Rise and Fall of the Third Reich: A History of Nazi Germany* (London, 1962)
Sisman, Adam, *Hugh Trevor-Roper: The Biography* (London, 2010)
Sked, Alan and Chris Cook (eds), *Crisis and Controversy: Essays in Honour of A. J. P. Taylor* (London, 1976)
Skidelsky, Robert, *Oswald Mosley* (London, 1975); *Britain since 1900: A Success Story?* (London, 2014)
Steiner, Zara, *The Triumph of the Dark: European International History 1933–1939* (Oxford, 2011)
Stone, Dan, *Responses to Nazism in Britain 1933–1939: Before War and Holocaust* (Basingstoke, 2003)
Strobl, Gerwin, *The Germanic Isle: Nazi Perceptions of Britain* (Cambridge, 2000)
Symons, Julian, *The Thirties: A Dream Revolved* (London, 1975)
Taylor, A. J. P., *The Origins of the Second World War* (London, 1961)
Taylor, S. J., *The Great Outsiders: Northcliffe, Rothermere and the Daily Mail* (London, 1996)

Taylor, Telford, *Sword and Swastika: The Wehrmacht in the Third Reich* (London, 1953); *Munich: The Price of Peace* (Sevenoaks, 1979)
Thompson, Neville, *The Anti-Appeasers: Conservative Opposition to Appeasement in the 1930s* (Oxford, 1971)
Thorpe, D. R., *Eden: The Life and Times of Anthony Eden, First Earl of Avon, 1897–1977* (London, 2003); *Supermac: The Life of Harold Macmillan* (London, 2010)
Tooze, Adam, *The Deluge: The Great War and the Remaking of Global Order 1916–1931* (London, 2014)
Ullrich, Volker, *Hitler: Ascent 1889–1939* (London, 2016)
Urbach, Karina, *Go-Betweens for Hitler* (Oxford, 2015)
Vyšný, Paul, *The Runciman Mission to Czechoslovakia 1938: Prelude to Munich*
Wainewright, Will, *Reporting on Hitler: Rothay Reynolds and the British Press in Nazi Germany* (London, 2017)
Waley, Daniel, *British Public Opinion and the Abyssinian War 1935–6* (London, 1975)
Wapshott, Nicholas, *The Sphinx: Franklin Roosevelt, the Isolationists, and the Road to World War II* (New York, 2015)
Wark, Wesley K., *The Ultimate Enemy: British Intelligence and Nazi Germany 1933–1939* (London, 1985)
Watt, D. C., *Personalities & Policies: Studies in the Formulation of British Foreign Policy in the Twentieth Century* (London, 1965)
Watt, Donald Cameron, *How War Came: The Immediate Origins of the Second World War 1938–1939* (London, 1989)
Weber, Eugen, *The Hollow Years: France in the 1930s* (London, 1995)
Wedgwood, C. V., *The Last of the Radicals: Josiah Wedgwood, MP* (London, 1951)
Weinberg, Gerhard L., *The Foreign Policy of Hitler's Germany: Diplomatic Revolution in Europe 1933–36* (Chicago and London, 1970)
West, Nigel, *MI6: British Secret Intelligence Service Operations 1909–1945* (London, 1983)
Wheeler-Bennett, John W., *King George VI: His Life and Reign* (London, 1958)
Wilson, Jim, *Nazi Princess: Hitler, Lord Rothermere and Princess Stephanie von Hohenlohe* (Stroud, 2011)
Wrench, Evelyn, *Geoffrey Dawson and Our Times* (London, 1955)
Zeman, Zbyněk and Antonín Klimek, *The Life of Edvard Beneš 1884–1948: Czechoslovakia in Peace and War* (Oxford, 1997)
Ziegler, Philip, *King Edward VIII: The Official Biography* (London, 1990)

Articles

Adamthwaite, Anthony, 'French Military Intelligence and the Coming of War 1935–1939', in Christopher Andrew and Jeremy Noakes (eds), *Intelligence and International Relations 1900–1945* (Exeter, 1987)
Anievas, Alexander, 'The International Political Economy of Appeasement: The Social Sources of British Foreign Policy During the 1930s', *Review of International Studies*, vol. 37, no. 2 (2011)
Aster, Sidney, 'Appeasement: Before and After Revisionism', *Diplomacy and Statecraft*, vol. 19, no. 3 (2008), pp. 443–80
Bell, Phillip M. H., 'Great Britain and the Rise of Germany 1932–4', *International Relations*, vol. 2, no. 9 (1964), pp. 609–18
Carr, Richard, 'Veterans of the First World War and Conservative Anti-Appeasement', *Twentieth Century British History*, vol. 22, no. 1 (2011), pp. 28–51
Ceadel, Martin, 'The "King and Country" Debate, 1933: Student Politics, Pacifism and the Dictators', *Historical Journal*, vol. 22, no. 2 (1979), pp. 397–422
Gilbert, Martin, 'Horace Wilson: Man of Munich?', *History Today*, October 1982, pp. 3–9

Holt, Andrew, '"No More Hoares to Paris": British Foreign Policymaking and the Abyssinian Crisis, 1935', *Review of International Studies*, vol. 37, no. 3 (2011), pp. 1383–401

Hucker, Daniel, 'Public Opinion between Munich and Prague: The View from the French Embassy', *Contemporary British History*, vol. 25, no. 3 (2011), pp. 407–27

Johnson, Gaynor, 'Sir Eric Phipps, the British Government, and the Appeasement of Germany 1933–1937', *Diplomacy and Statecraft*, vol. 16, no. 4 (2005), pp. 651–69

Jukes, G., 'The Red Army and the Munich Crisis', *Journal of Contemporary History*, vol. 26, no. 2 (1991), pp. 195–214

Kelly, Bernard, 'Drifting towards War: The British Chiefs of Staff, the USSR and the Winter War, November 1939–March 1940', *Contemporary British History*, vol. 23, no. 3 (2009), pp. 267–91

Kennedy, Paul M., '"Appeasement" and British Defence Policy in the Inter-War Years', *British Journal of University Studies*, vol. 4, no. 2 (1978), pp. 161–77

Kersten, Lee, '*The Times* and the Concentration Camp at Dachau, December 1933–February 1934: An Unpublished Report', *Shofar*, vol. 18, no. 2 (2000), pp. 101–9

Luckhurst, Tim, 'When Yorkshire Ruled the World', *British Journalism Review*, vol. 27, no. 3 (2016), pp. 59–65

McCarthy, Helen, 'Democratizing British Foreign Policy: Rethinking the Peace Ballot 1934–1935', *Journal of British Studies*, vol. 49, no. 2 (2010), pp. 358–87

Marder, Arthur, 'The Royal Navy and the Ethiopian Crisis of 1935–36', *American Historical Review*, vol. 75, no. 5 (1970), pp. 1327–56

Middleton, Roger, 'British Monetary and Fiscal Policy in the 1930s', *Oxford Review of Economic Policy*, vol. 26, no. 3 (2010), pp. 414–41

Mills, William C., 'Sir Joseph Ball, Adrian Dingli, and Neville Chamberlain's "Secret Channel" to Italy 1937–1940', *International History Review*, vol. 24, no. 2 (2002), pp. 278–317

Neilson, Keith, 'Stalin's Moustache: The Soviet Union and the Coming of War', *Diplomacy and Statecraft*, vol. 12, no. 2 (2001), pp. 197–208

Peden, G. C., 'Sir Horace Wilson and Appeasement', *Historical Journal*, vol. 53, no. 4 (2010), pp. 983–1014

Reynolds, David, 'Churchill's Writing of History: Appeasement, Autobiography and *The Gathering Storm*', *Transactions of the Royal Historical Society*, Sixth Series, vol. 11 (2001), pp. 221–47

Robbins, Keith G., 'VI. Konrad Henlein, the Sudeten Question and British Foreign Policy', *Historical Journal*, vol. 12, no. 4 (1969), pp. 674–97

Soucy, Robert J., 'French Press Reactions to Hitler's First Two Years in Power', *Contemporary European History*, vol. 7, no. 1 (1998), pp. 21–38

Stannage, C. T., 'VIII. The East Fulham By-Election', *Historical Journal*, vol. 14, no. 1 (1971), pp. 165–200

Steiner, Zara, 'The Soviet Commissariat of Foreign Affairs and the Czechoslovakian Crisis in 1938: New Material from the Soviet Archives', *Historical Journal*, vol. 42, no. 3 (1999), pp. 751–79

Dissertations

Gilmour, Andrew, 'The Changing Reactions of the British Press towards Mussolini's Italy from 1935–1940' (Oxford, 1986)

Grimwood, Ian, 'Aftermath of Munich: Strategic Priorities in British Rearmament October 1938–August 1939' (LSE, 1996)

Picture Credits

Hitler at Nuremberg, May 1933 (Hulton Archive/Getty Images).

Nazi boycott of Jewish shops, 1 April 1933 (Hulton Archive/Getty Images).

Sir Horace Rumbold (Alamy Stock Photo).

Winston Churchill, September 1938 (Picture Press/Alamy Stock Photo).

Stanley Baldwin crosses Parliament Square, 7 June 1935 (Popperfoto/Getty Images).

Anthony Eden at a reception at the Polish Embassy, November 1936 (Keystone-France/Gamma-Rapho/Getty Images).

Lord Halifax (Margaret Bourke-White/The LIFE Picture Collection/Getty Images).

Lord Lothian reading *Mein Kampf*, *c.*1935 (Keystone/Hulton Archive/Getty Images).

Hitler with Sir John Simon and Anthony Eden, 25 March 1935 (ullstein bild/Getty Images).

Viscount Cecil presents three million signatures in support of the International Disarmament Conference, January 1932 (Keystone-France/Gamma-Rapho/Getty Images).

Haile Selassie appeals to the League of Nations, 30 June 1936 (Bettmann/Getty Images).

German troops enter the demilitarised Rhineland, 7 March 1936 (Fox Photos/Getty Images).

Crowds in the Berlin Olympic Stadium, August 1936 (Heinrich Hoffmann/ullstein bild/Getty Images).

David Lloyd George visits Hitler at the Berghof, 4 September 1936 (World History Archive/Alamy Stock Photo).

Sir Neville Henderson with Hermann Göring at the Nuremberg Rally (Heinrich Hoffmann/ullstein bild/Getty Images).

Lord Halifax with Hitler and Neurath at the Berghof, 19 November 1937 (Heinrich Hoffmann/ullstein bild/Getty Images).

Neville Chamberlain fishing, 8 June 1938 (Keystone/Hulton Archive/Getty Images).

Chamberlain with Mussolini, September 1938 (Keystone-France/Gamma-Rapho/Getty Images).

Hitler addresses a crowd in Vienna's Heldenplatz, 15 March 1938 (ullstein bild/Getty Images).

Viennese Jews are forced to scrub the streets after the *Anschluss* (Hulton Deutsch Collection/Corbis/Getty Images).

Joachim von Ribbentrop leaves the German Embassy in London, 13 March 1938 (Harry Todd/Fox Photos/Getty Images).

Sir Robert Vansittart and Sir Alexander Cadogan leave Downing Street, 11 September 1938 (H. F. Davis/Topical Press Agency/Hulton Archive/Getty Images).

Chamberlain prepares to depart Heston airport for his first meeting with Hitler, 15 September 1938 (Imagno/Getty Images).

Chamberlain with Hitler at the Berghof, 15 September 1938 (Heinrich Hoffmann/Getty Images).

Hitler welcomes Chamberlain at the Hotel Dreesen in Bad Godesberg, 22 September 1938 (Corbis/Getty Images).

Trying on gas masks, September 1938 (Keystone-France/Gamma-Rapho/Getty Images).

The participants of the Munich Conference, 29 September 1938 (PhotoQuest/Getty Images).

Tribute to Chamberlain at a London florist's, 30 September 1938 (Harry Todd/Getty Images).

Chamberlain at the window of 10 Downing Street, 30 September 1938 (TopFoto).

Women in the Sudeten town of Eger react to the arrival of German troops, 3 October 1938 (Bettmann/Getty Images).

Chamberlain inspects the Duce's personal bodyguard, 11 January 1939 (ullstein bild/Getty Images).

German troops enter the grounds of the Hradčany Castle in Prague, 15 March 1939 (Universal History Archive/UIG/Getty Images).

Molotov signs the Nazi–Soviet Pact, watched by Ribbentrop and Stalin, 23 August 1939 (Corbis/Getty Images).

German soldiers advance through Polish countryside, 1 September 1939 (Ann Ronan Pictures/Print Collector/Getty Images).

Winston Churchill and Neville Chamberlain, 23 February 1940 (Print Collector/Getty Images).

Index